ORGANIZATIONAL Behavior and Theory in Healthcare

HAP/AUPHA Editorial Board for Graduate Studies

Olena Mazurenko, MD, PhD, Chairman
Indiana University

Julie Agris, PhD, FACHE
SUNY at Stony Brook

Ellen Averett, PhD
University of Kansas School of Medicine

Robert I. Bonar, DHA
George Washington University

Lynn T. Downs, PhD, FACHE
University of the Incarnate Word

Laura Erskine, PhD
UCLA Fielding School of Public Health

Cheryl J. Holden, DHS
University of Arkansas

Diane M. Howard, PhD, FACHE
Rush University

Ning Lu, PhD
Governors State University

Kourtney Nieves, PhD, MSHS
University of Central Florida

Martha C. Riddell, DrPH
University of Kentucky

Gwyndolan L. Swain, DHA
Belmont Abbey College

Mary Ellen Wells, FACHE
C-Suite Resources

Asa B. Wilson, PhD
Southeast Missouri State University

ORGANIZATIONAL Behavior and Theory in Healthcare

Leadership Perspectives and Management Applications

STEPHEN L. WALSTON
KENNETH L. JOHNSON

SECOND EDITION

AUPHA

Health Administration Press, Chicago, Illinois
Association of University Programs in Health Administration, Washington, DC

Your board, staff, or clients may also benefit from this book's insight. For information on quantity discounts, contact the Health Administration Press Marketing Manager at (312) 424-9450.

This publication is intended to provide accurate and authoritative information in regard to the subject matter covered. It is sold, or otherwise provided, with the understanding that the publisher is not engaged in rendering professional services. If professional advice or other expert assistance is required, the services of a competent professional should be sought.

The statements and opinions contained in this book are strictly those of the authors and do not represent the official positions of the American College of Healthcare Executives or the Foundation of the American College of Healthcare Executives.

Copyright © 2022 by the Foundation of the American College of Healthcare Executives. Printed in the United States of America. All rights reserved. This book or parts thereof may not be reproduced in any form without written permission of the publisher.

26 25 24 23 22   5 4 3 2 1

Library of Congress Cataloging-in-Publication Data

Names: Walston, Stephen Lee, author. | Johnson, Kenneth L., 1957– author. | Association of University Programs in Health Administration, issuing body.
Title: Organizational behavior and theory in healthcare : leadership perspectives and management applications / Stephen L. Walston and Kenneth L. Johnson.
Description: Second edition. | Chicago, Illinois : Health Administration Press ; Washington, DC : Association of University Programs in Health Administration, [2022] | Includes bibliographical references and index. | Summary: "This book examines the theories of organizational design, leadership, management, and social psychology as they apply to health services"—Provided by publisher.
Identifiers: LCCN 2021027583 (print) | LCCN 2021027584 (ebook) | ISBN 9781640553026 (hardcover : alk. paper) | ISBN 9781640552999 (epub) | ISBN 9781640553002 (mobi)
Subjects: MESH: Public Health Administration | Health Care Sector—organization & administration | Organizational Culture | Personnel Management
Classification: LCC R729.5.H4 (print) | LCC R729.5.H4 (ebook) | NLM WA 525 | DDC 326.1068—dc23
LC record available at https://lccn.loc.gov/2021027583
LC ebook record available at https://lccn.loc.gov/2021027584

The paper used in this publication meets the minimum requirements of American National Standard for Information Sciences—Permanence of Paper for Printed Library Materials, ANSI Z39.48-1984. ∞™

Acquisitions editor: Jennette McClain; Manuscript editor: DeAnna Burghart; Project manager: Andrew Baumann; Cover designer: James Slate; Layout: Integra

Found an error or a typo? We want to know! Please e-mail it to hapbooks@ache.org, mentioning the book's title and putting "Book Error" in the subject line.

For photocopying and copyright information, please contact Copyright Clearance Center at www.copyright.com or at (978) 750-8400.

Health Administration Press
A division of the Foundation of the American
  College of Healthcare Executives
300 S. Riverside Plaza, Suite 1900
Chicago, IL 60606-6698
(312) 424-2800

Association of University Programs
  in Health Administration
1730 M Street, NW
Suite 407
Washington, DC 20036
(202) 763-7283

BRIEF CONTENTS

Preface xix

Chapter 1	Organizational Behavior, Organizational Theory, and Their Importance in Healthcare 1
Chapter 2	Theories of Managing People 19
Chapter 3	Supporting Diversity, Equity, and Inclusion 39
Chapter 4	Individual and Organizational Learning 67
Chapter 5	Attitudes and Satisfaction 85
Chapter 6	Individual and Organizational Values and Ethics 107
Chapter 7	Individual and Organizational Motivation 129
Chapter 8	Emotions, Moods, and Stress on the Job 151
Chapter 9	Paradigms and Perceptions 177
Chapter 10	Decision-Making 199
Chapter 11	Creativity and Innovation 221
Chapter 12	Group Behavior 243
Chapter 13	Work Teams 263
Chapter 14	Communication 283
Chapter 15	Leadership Theories and Styles 305
Chapter 16	Power, Politics, and Influence 335
Chapter 17	Conflict Management and Negotiation 357
Chapter 18	Organizational Design and Structure 381

Chapter 19	Performance Management	417
Chapter 20	Developing Employees Through Mentoring, Coaching, and Delegation	441
Chapter 21	Organizational Culture	461
Chapter 22	Human Resources Policies and Practices	481
Chapter 23	Strategy and Change Management	503
Case 1	A Dilemma of Loyalties	523
Case 2	Theranos and Elizabeth Holmes	525
Case 3	The Injured Migrant Worker	533
Case 4	The Overutilizing Orthopedist	535
Case 5	The Busy Regional Vice President	537
Case 6	Thalidomide and Grünenthal	541
Case 7	Prospect Medical: Imperfect Incentives Drive Actions Not Consistent with Mission	545
Case 8	Pegasus Health's Integration of Care	551
Case 9	Purduc's Dilemma to Increase Sales	555
Case 10	OrthoIndy	559
Case 11	The New CEO	563
Case 12	Liver Allocation	565
Case 13	Letter from a Bereaved Mother	567
Case 14	HealthT Seeks Healthier Employees	569
Case 15	HealthSouth	573
Case 16	FHP—Utah	581
Case 17	Starting as CEO at Skyview Hospital	587
Case 18	Director of Marketing Versus Operations	591
Case 19	The Ogre and the Playroom	593
Case 20	A Saudi Bid and I	595
Case 21	A Proposed Merger Gone Bad: A Lack of Confidence in Leadership	597
Case 22	Night Staffing and Job Commitment	601
Case 23	Mike and the Walk-Around	603
Case 24	Sakal's Dilemma	605
Case 25	Sam's Deposit Recovery	607
Case 26	Shannon's Extreme Uninsured Healthcare Costs	611
Case 27	The Ethical Challenge of Treating Hepatitis C	615

Case 28 Governance and Decision-Making in Hospital-Based
Surgical Services 617
Case 29 Mentoring, Coaching, and Delegating: Combating
High Turnover and Poor Culture 623

Appendix: Case Matrix 625
Glossary 629
Index 643
About the Authors 697

DETAILED CONTENTS

Preface xix

Chapter 1 Organizational Behavior, Organizational Theory,
and Their Importance in Healthcare 1
Learning Objectives 2
Key Terms 2
Organizational Behavior 3
Organizational Theory 4
History and Development 5
Relevance to the Healthcare Industry 8
Chapter Summary 12
Chapter Questions 12
Chapter Cases 13
Chapter Activity 14
References 15

Chapter 2 Theories of Managing People 19
Learning Objectives 19
Key Terms 19
Weber's Efficient Bureaucracy 21
Administrative Theory 23
Maslow's Hierarchy of Needs 25
Human Relations 27
Decision-Making Theory 30
Institutional Theory 31
Chapter Summary 31
Chapter Questions 32
Chapter Cases 33
Chapter Activity 35
References 36

Chapter 3	Supporting Diversity, Equity, and Inclusion	39
	Learning Objectives	39
	Key Terms	40
	Cultural, Racial, and Ethnic Diversity	43
	Gender and Age Diversity	45
	Racial and Ethnic Disparities in Healthcare	49
	Affirmative Action and Diversity Management	51
	Federal, State, and Private Resources to Improve Diversity	55
	Chapter Summary	56
	Chapter Resources	58
	Chapter Questions	58
	Chapter Cases	59
	Chapter Activities	61
	References	62
Chapter 4	Individual and Organizational Learning	67
	Learning Objectives	67
	Key Terms	68
	Role of Motivation in Learning	72
	Challenges of Learning in Healthcare	73
	Chapter Summary	76
	Chapter Questions	77
	Chapter Case	78
	Chapter Activities	80
	References	80
Chapter 5	Attitudes and Satisfaction	85
	Learning Objectives	85
	Key Terms	86
	Attitudes	87
	Engagement	90
	Satisfaction	92
	Job Satisfaction Outcomes and Measurement	95
	Chapter Summary	99
	Chapter Questions	99
	Chapter Cases	100
	Chapter Activities	101
	References	102

Chapter 6	Individual and Organizational Values and Ethics	107
	Learning Objectives	107
	Key Terms	108
	Business Ethics and Corporate Social Responsibility	108
	Ethical Models	110
	Ethical Challenges in Business and Healthcare	114
	Professional Ethics	117
	A Rule of Thumb for Ethical Behavior: The Newspaper Test	119
	Chapter Summary	120
	Chapter Questions	121
	Chapter Cases	121
	Chapter Activities	123
	References	124
Chapter 7	Individual and Organizational Motivation	129
	Learning Objectives	129
	Key Terms	130
	External Stimuli	131
	Intrinsic Stimuli	132
	Job Crafting	139
	Myths About Motivation	140
	Chapter Summary	142
	Chapter Questions	144
	Chapter Cases	144
	Chapter Activity	146
	References	146
Chapter 8	Emotions, Moods, and Stress on the Job	151
	Learning Objectives	151
	Key Terms	152
	Emotions	152
	Stress	156
	Locus of Control	159
	Chapter Summary	164
	Chapter Questions	166
	Chapter Cases	166
	Chapter Activities	171
	References	171

Chapter 9 Paradigms and Perceptions 177
Learning Objectives 177
Key Terms 178
Paradigms 178
Perceptions 180
Perceptual Biases 183
Effects on Job Commitment 189
Chapter Summary 189
Chapter Questions 190
Chapter Cases 191
Chapter Activities 193
References 195

Chapter 10 Decision-Making 199
Learning Objectives 199
Key Terms 200
Models of Decision-Making 201
Biases in Decision-Making 204
Groupthink 206
Decision-Making in Healthcare 207
Improving Decision-Making 208
Chapter Summary 211
Chapter Resources 212
Chapter Questions 212
Chapter Cases 213
Chapter Activities 215
References 216

Chapter 11 Creativity and Innovation 221
Learning Objectives 221
Key Terms 221
The Link Between Creativity and Innovation 222
Types of Healthcare Innovations 224
Strategies for Increasing Creativity and Innovation 226
Diffusion of Healthcare Creativity and Innovation 228
Disruptive Innovation and Sustaining Innovation 232
Chapter Summary 233
Chapter Questions 234
Chapter Cases 235

	Chapter Activities	238
	References	238
Chapter 12	Group Behavior	243
	Learning Objectives	243
	Key Terms	243
	Groups Versus Teams	245
	Interdependence	245
	Conformity and Norms	246
	Cohorts and Reference Groups	248
	Groupthink and Group Shift	249
	Group Polarization	250
	Obedience	251
	Social Facilitation and Social Loafing	252
	Advantages and Disadvantages of Group Decision-Making	253
	Chapter Summary	254
	Chapter Questions	255
	Chapter Cases	256
	Chapter Activities	258
	References	258
Chapter 13	Work Teams	263
	Learning Objectives	263
	Key Terms	263
	The Nature of Teams	264
	Team Composition	265
	Multidisciplinary and Interdisciplinary Teams	265
	Diversity	266
	Team Formation	267
	Team Building	269
	Signs of an Effective Team	272
	Conflict	274
	Team Viability	275
	Chapter Summary	276
	Chapter Questions	277
	Chapter Cases	278
	Chapter Activities	280
	References	281

Detailed Contents

Chapter 14 Communication 283
Learning Objectives 283
Key Terms 283
Communication Process... 284
Nonverbal Communication 290
Barriers to Effective Communication..................................... 292
Impact of Culture on Communication 293
Virtual Communication 294
Successful Communication 295
Chapter Summary 296
Chapter Questions 297
Chapter Cases 298
Chapter Activity 300
References... 301

Chapter 15 Leadership Theories and Styles....................................... 305
Learning Objectives 305
Key Terms 306
Defining Leadership 307
Trait Theory 308
Behavior Theory 308
Contingency Theory 310
Transactional Leadership and Situational Leadership 311
Transformational Leadership 313
Emerging Theories.. 321
Chapter Summary 323
Chapter Questions 325
Chapter Cases 326
Chapter Activities... 329
References... 330

Chapter 16 Power, Politics, and Influence 335
Learning Objectives 335
Key Terms 335
Power and Influence Defined 336
Influence Tactics 339
Organizational Politics 342
Chapter Summary 347
Chapter Questions 348
Chapter Cases 348

	Chapter Activities 353
	References 353
Chapter 17	Conflict Management and Negotiation 357
	Learning Objectives 357
	Key Terms 357
	Conflict Basics 358
	Types of Work-Related Conflict 360
	Dealing with Conflict 361
	Contributing Factors to Conflicts in Healthcare 362
	Zero-Sum Games and Competition 364
	Conflict and COVID-19 365
	Managing Conflict 366
	Negotiation Skills 368
	Chapter Summary 371
	Chapter Questions 373
	Chapter Cases 374
	Chapter Activities 377
	References 378
Chapter 18	Organizational Design and Structure 381
	Learning Objectives 381
	Key Terms 382
	Corporations 382
	Organizational Structure and Organizational Design 384
	Structure Types 391
	Advantages and Disadvantages of Different Structures 398
	Possible Future Structures in Healthcare 400
	Organizational Structure and the Environment 402
	Governing Boards 402
	Chapter Summary 403
	Chapter Questions 406
	Chapter Cases 406
	Chapter Activities 411
	References 412
Chapter 19	Performance Management 417
	Learning Objectives 417
	Key Terms 418

	Performance Management Tools	420
	Individual Performance Management	423
	360-Degree Feedback Appraisal Systems	428
	Competency-Based Performance Systems	430
	Chapter Summary	432
	Chapter Questions	433
	Chapter Cases	433
	Chapter Activities	438
	References	438
Chapter 20	Developing Employees Through Mentoring, Coaching, and Delegation	441
	Learning Objectives	441
	Key Terms	442
	Mentoring and Coaching	442
	Delegation	446
	Beware of Micromanaging	451
	Communicate Clearly When Delegating	451
	Eight Steps to Effective Delegation	452
	Chapter Summary	453
	Chapter Questions	454
	Chapter Cases	454
	Chapter Activities	457
	References	457
Chapter 21	Organizational Culture	461
	Learning Objectives	461
	Key Terms	462
	Components of Organizational Culture	463
	Cultural Differences	466
	Changing a Culture	470
	Chapter Summary	472
	Chapter Questions	473
	Chapter Cases	474
	Chapter Activities	476
	References	476
Chapter 22	Human Resources Policies and Practices	481
	Learning Objectives	481
	Key Terms	481
	Job Descriptions and Specifications	482

	Performance Simulation	483
	Additional Testing Techniques	484
	Interviews	486
	Training	488
	The Leadership Role of HR	492
	Chapter Summary	493
	Chapter Questions	494
	Chapter Cases	494
	Chapter Activities	496
	References	497
Chapter 23	Strategy and Change Management	503
	Learning Objectives	503
	Key Terms	504
	Values, Mission, and Vision	504
	Gap Analysis and Organizational Change	510
	Chapter Summary	515
	Chapter Resource	516
	Chapter Questions	516
	Chapter Cases	516
	Chapter Activities	519
	References	520
Case 1	A Dilemma of Loyalties	523
Case 2	Theranos and Elizabeth Holmes	525
Case 3	The Injured Migrant Worker	533
Case 4	The Overutilizing Orthopedist	535
Case 5	The Busy Regional Vice President	537
Case 6	Thalidomide and Grünenthal	541
Case 7	Prospect Medical: Imperfect Incentives Drive Actions Not Consistent with Mission	545
Case 8	Pegasus Health's Integration of Care	551
Case 9	Purdue's Dilemma to Increase Sales	555
Case 10	OrthoIndy	559
Case 11	The New CEO	563
Case 12	Liver Allocation	565
Case 13	Letter from a Bereaved Mother	567
Case 14	HealthT Seeks Healthier Employees	569
Case 15	HealthSouth	573
Case 16	FHP—Utah	581

Case 17	Starting as CEO at Skyview Hospital	587
Case 18	Director of Marketing Versus Operations	591
Case 19	The Ogre and the Playroom	593
Case 20	A Saudi Bid and I	595
Case 21	A Proposed Merger Gone Bad: A Lack of Confidence in Leadership	597
Case 22	Night Staffing and Job Commitment	601
Case 23	Mike and the Walk-Around	603
Case 24	Sakal's Dilemma	605
Case 25	Sam's Deposit Recovery	607
Case 26	Shannon's Extreme Uninsured Healthcare Costs	611
Case 27	The Ethical Challenge of Treating Hepatitis C	615
Case 28	Governance and Decision-Making in Hospital-Based Surgical Services	617
Case 29	Mentoring, Coaching, and Delegating: Combating High Turnover and Poor Culture	623

Appendix: Case Matrix 625
Glossary 629
Index 643
About the Authors 697

PREFACE

Healthcare is a dynamic and demanding field that involves continuous human interaction. Successful leaders in this field are characterized by their ability to work well with others. The success or failure of leaders is primarily tied to how they interact with and motivate their employees. This book is designed to prepare and instruct existing and future healthcare leaders to understand and apply the principles of organizational behavior and theory to improve their management abilities and skills. Ultimately, honing these abilities and skills will lead to greater success and satisfaction with one's accomplishments.

This text examines theories of organizational design, leadership, and management and the social psychology of organizations as they apply to health services organizations. It provides the tools and framework needed to understand, structure, and change organizational behavior in our dynamic healthcare environment.

Specifically, this book approaches these concepts from a practical, applied perspective. Through the chapters and cases, the book provides an understanding of not only theory but also the way the interactions and interrelationships of people, organizations, and structures affect the extent to which companies succeed or fail. Having spent many years as healthcare administrators, we have sought to demonstrate real-world experiences in useful and direct ways.

This second edition offers more in-depth, focused chapters on diversity, attitudes and satisfaction, work teams, and human resources policies and practices. All chapters have been rewritten, and each includes activities and questions designed to prompt deeper reflection on the complexity and challenge of working with individuals in organizations. Thought-provoking cases are provided at the end of each chapter, most based on actual occurrences that either we or one of our associates experienced. Furthermore, 29 new cases have been added to the end of the book, which can be used to enrich learning and improve understanding of the book's concepts. A matrix in the appendix shows how each case can be used in conjunction with specific chapters. We believe the second edition gives instructors many more options to enrich their classes and provides more material on critical healthcare topics.

Text Competencies

Our educational and professional environment, along with accrediting bodies, now strongly encourages—indeed, mandates—the use of competency-based learning models that seek to identify performance needs and demonstrate the value of learning. From an educational perspective, course curricula should provide students with the knowledge and skills required for future careers. Recognizing the wide variation of healthcare administration roles and professional settings, accrediting bodies such as the Commission on Accreditation of Healthcare Management Education allow individual programs to develop their own unique competencies.

Likewise, several professional organizations propose different sets of competencies for healthcare leaders. The Healthcare Leadership Alliance (HLA)—a consortium of professional healthcare administration associations composed of the American College of Healthcare Executives (ACHE), the American Organization for Nursing Leadership, the Healthcare Financial Management Association, the Healthcare Information and Management Systems Society, and the Medical Group Management Association—has identified five domains of competencies as being valuable to healthcare executives, administrators, and managers: (1) communication and relationship management, (2) leadership, (3) professionalism, (4) knowledge of the healthcare environment, and (5) business skills and knowledge (see the Competency Directory page on the HLA website for additional information and resources). ACHE, in conjunction with the Global Consortium for Healthcare Management Professionalization, adapted the same HLA competencies and published a document titled "Leadership Competencies for Healthcare Services Managers" (available from www.ache.org/about-ache/resources-and-links/healthcare-leadership-competencies/ at "See the full list of competencies"). ACHE also offers its members the *Healthcare Executive Competencies Assessment Tool* (available from www.ache.org/career-resource-center/ at "Competency Assessment"), which helps healthcare administrators self-assess their strengths and priorities for skill development. ACHE deems the identification and improvement of members' competencies so important that it updates this tool annually.

Given the wide variation of possible competencies, we have chosen the ACHE *Healthcare Executive Competencies Assessment Tool* to identify competencies in this book. Using the following list, instructors can quickly ascertain which competencies are covered in each chapter to appropriately develop their course and syllabus according to their competency-based curricula.

Competencies by Chapter

Chapter 1. Organizational Behavior, Organizational Theory, and Their Importance in Healthcare

Competencies:
- Knowledge of the healthcare environment
  - The community and the environment
    - Socioeconomic environment in which the organization functions
    - Healthcare trends
- Business skills and knowledge
  - Organizational dynamics and governance
    - Organization systems theories and structures
    - Governance structure
    - Principles and practices of management and organizational behavior

Chapter 2. Theories of Managing People

Competencies:
- Business skills and knowledge
  - Organizational dynamics and governance
    - Organization systems theories and structures
    - Governance theory
    - Principles and practices of management and organizational behavior
  - Strategic planning and marketing
    - Organizational mission, vision, objectives, and priorities

Chapter 3. Supporting Diversity, Equity, and Inclusion

Competencies:
- Communication and relationship management
  - Relationship management
    - Build collaborative relationships
    - Demonstrate effective interpersonal relationships
- Leadership
  - Organizational climate and culture
    - Create an organizational culture that values and supports diversity
- Professionalism
  - Personal and professional accountability

- Cultural and spiritual diversity for patients and staff as they relate to healthcare needs

Chapter 4. Individual and Organizational Learning

Competencies:
- Leadership
  - Managing change
    - Explore opportunities for the growth and development of the organization on a continuous basis
    - Promote continuous organizational learning/improvement
- Professionalism
  - Professional development and lifelong learning
    - Acquire and stay current with the professional body of knowledge

Chapter 5. Attitudes and Satisfaction

Competencies:
- Business skills and knowledge
  - Human resource management
    - Employee satisfaction measurement and improvement techniques
    - Employee motivational techniques
    - Labor relations practices and strategies

Chapter 6. Individual and Organizational Values and Ethics

Competencies:
- Professionalism
  - Personal and professional accountability
    - Consequences of unethical actions
    - Organizational business and personal ethics
    - Professional standards and codes of ethical behavior
    - Uphold and act upon ethical and professional standards
    - Adhere to ethical business principles

Chapter 7. Individual and Organizational Motivation

Competencies:
- Leadership
  - Communicating vision
    - Create an organizational climate that facilitates individual motivation

- Business skills and knowledge
  - Human resource management
    - Employee satisfaction measurement and improvement techniques
    - Employee motivational techniques

Chapter 8. Emotions, Moods, and Stress on the Job

Competencies:
- Professionalism
  - Professional development and lifelong learning
    - Time and stress management techniques
- Business skills and knowledge
  - Human resource management
    - Conflict resolution and grievance procedures

Chapter 9. Paradigms and Perceptions

Competencies:
- Knowledge of the healthcare environment
  - Healthcare personnel
    - Staff perspective in organizational settings
- Business skills and knowledge
  - Human resource management
    - Employee motivational techniques

Chapter 10. Decision-Making

Competencies:
- Leadership
  - Leadership skills and behavior
    - Potential impacts and consequences of decision-making in situations both internal and external
- Business skills and knowledge
  - General management
    - Ability to analyze and evaluate information to support a decision or recommendation
    - Ability to integrate information from various sources to make decisions or recommendations
    - Distinguish between important and unimportant aspects of business and clinical situations as a basis for sound decision-making

- Human resource management
    - Decision-making on operations, finances, healthcare, and quality of care

Chapter 11. Creativity and Innovation

Competencies:
- Leadership
    - Managing change
        - Promote and manage change
        - Explore opportunities for the growth and development of the organization on a continuous basis

Chapter 12. Group Behavior

Competencies:
- Communication and relationship management
    - Facilitation and negotiation
        - Team building techniques
        - Build effective physician and administrator leadership teams
        - Create, participate in, and lead teams
        - Facilitate group dynamics, process, meetings, and discussions
- Leadership
    - Organizational climate and culture
        - Create an organizational climate that encourages teamwork

Chapter 13. Work Teams

Competencies:
- Communication and relationship management
    - Facilitation and negotiation
        - Team building techniques
        - Create, participate in, and lead teams

Chapter 14. Communication

Competencies:
- Communication and relationship management
    - Communication skills
        - Principles of communication and their specific applications
        - Sensitivity to what is correct behavior when communicating with diverse cultures, internal and external
        - Identify and use human and technical resources to develop and deliver communications

Chapter 15. Leadership Theories and Styles

Competencies:
- Leadership
  - Leadership skills and behavior
    - Leadership styles/techniques
    - Leadership theory and situational applications
    - Incorporate and apply management techniques and theories into leadership activities
  - Managing change
    - Promote and manage change

Chapter 16. Power, Politics, and Influence

Competencies:
- Leadership
  - Leadership skills and behavior
    - Incorporate and apply management techniques and theories into leadership activities
- Business skills and knowledge
  - Organizational dynamics and governance
    - Organizational dynamics, political realities, and culture

Chapter 17. Conflict Management and Negotiation

Competencies:
- Communication and relationship management
  - Facilitation and negotiation
    - Mediation, negotiation, and dispute resolution techniques
    - Facilitate conflict and alternative dispute resolution
- Business skills and knowledge
  - Human resource management
    - Conflict resolution and grievance procedures

Chapter 18. Organizational Design and Structure

Competencies:
- Communication and relationship management
  - Relationship management
    - Organizational structure and relationships
- Knowledge of the healthcare environment
  - Healthcare systems and organizations
    - The interdependency, integration, and competition among healthcare sectors

- Business skills and knowledge
  - General management
    - Organize and manage the human and physical resources of the organization to achieve input, buy-in, and optimal performance
  - Organizational dynamics and governance
    - Organization systems theories and structures
    - Governance structure
    - Construct and maintain governance systems

Chapter 19. Performance Management

Competencies:
- Business skills and knowledge
  - General management
    - Collect and analyze data from internal and external sources relevant to each situation
    - Analyze the current way of doing business and clinical processes
    - Perform audits of systems and operations
    - Measure quantitative dimensions of systems and departmental effectiveness
  - Financial management
    - Outcomes measures and management
    - Fundamental productivity measures
    - Develop and use performance monitoring metrics
  - Human resource management
    - Performance management systems
    - Develop and manage employee performance management systems
  - Strategic planning and marketing
    - Develop and monitor departmental strategic and tactical objectives
    - Develop a benefits realization model that measures product or service performance to ensure that strategic goals are met

Chapter 20. Developing Employees Through Mentoring, Coaching, and Delegation

Competencies:
- Communication and relationship management
  - Relationship management
    - Practice and value shared decision-making

- Leadership
  - Leadership skills and behavior
    - Support and mentor high-potential talent within the organization
- Professionalism
  - Contributions to the community and profession
    - Mentor, advise, and coach

Chapter 21. Organizational Culture

Competencies:
- Communication and relationship management
  - Communication skills
    - Sensitivity to what is correct behavior when communicating with diverse cultures, internal and external
- Leadership
  - Organizational climate and culture
    - Create an organizational culture that values and supports diversity
    - Knowledge of own and others' cultural norms
    - Assess the organization, including corporate values and culture, business processes, and impact of systems on operations
- Professionalism
  - Personal and professional accountability
    - Cultural and spiritual diversity for patients and staff as they relate to healthcare needs
- Business skills and knowledge
  - Organizational dynamics and governance
    - How an organization's culture impacts its effectiveness

Chapter 22. Human Resources Policies and Practices

Competencies:
- Business skills and knowledge
  - Human resource management
    - Human resources laws and regulations
    - Performance management systems
    - Compensation and benefits practices
    - Organizational policies and procedures and their functions

Chapter 23. Strategy and Change Management

Competencies:
- Communication and relationship management
  - Communication skills
    - Communicate organizational mission, vision, objectives, and priorities
- Leadership
  - Communicating vision
    - Establish a compelling organizational vision and goals
  - Managing change
    - Promote and manage change
    - Anticipate and plan strategies for overcoming obstacles
- Business skills and knowledge
  - Strategic planning and marketing
    - Strategic planning processes development and implementation
    - Develop and monitor departmental strategic and tactical objectives

Acknowledgments

We would like to thank Britt Berrett, Benjamin Whisenant, Steven Bateman, Brian Cottle, Rand Kerr, Tiffany Vickers, and Joseph Horton for their contribution of materials and writing of cases. All have extraordinary experience in business and academics. We appreciate their influence and friendship.

—*Stephen L. Walston and Kenneth L. Johnson*

INSTRUCTOR RESOURCES

This book's instructor resources include PowerPoint slides, case study guidelines, answer guides to the chapter discussion questions, and a test bank.

For the most up-to-date information about this book and its instructor resources, go to ache.org/HAP and browse for the book's order number: 2446I.

This book's instructor resources are available to instructors who adopt this book for use in their course. For access information, please e-mail hap-books@ache.org.

CHAPTER 1

ORGANIZATIONAL BEHAVIOR, ORGANIZATIONAL THEORY, AND THEIR IMPORTANCE IN HEALTHCARE

> Healthcare is complex and involves the interaction of many people and systems. Daily, people receive care from highly educated professionals who must communicate and make joint decisions. For instance, Mary entered a hospital to have a minor procedure. Her parents, Bill and Beth, came with her. Toward the end of the procedure, the nurse sees that Mary has turned blue, has stopped breathing, and has a heart rate of less than 30. The nurse halts the procedure and tells the doctor, who calls for a code blue, which activates a team that includes physicians, nurses, a pharmacist, a respiratory therapist, and lab personnel.
>
> The code blue team arrives quickly and begins to administer CPR. However, appropriate care is delayed while three physicians argue about the proper course of treatment. After five minutes of intense debate, the team moves forward and reestablishes Mary's normal heart rate, blood pressure, and blood oxygen level.
>
> The devices monitoring Mary's condition report a period of almost seven minutes during which she was not breathing adequately, which could have been the result of receiving too much sedation medication during her procedure. The nurse charged with overseeing the monitoring appears visibly shaken and says that getting equipment for the procedure distracted attention from the monitors.
>
> In the waiting room, Mary's parents are clearly worried. The procedure has gone on much longer than they were told. They heard the call for code blue and saw many people running into the procedure area. A hospital chaplain has now entered the room to speak with them.
>
> *Source*: Agency for Healthcare Research and Quality (2017).

Learning Objectives

After studying this chapter, readers should be able to

- provide a brief history of the study of organizational behavior and organizational theory,
- list some of the challenges making healthcare management more complex than management in many other industries,
- discuss social and technological changes that create greater needs for better management,
- explain why the differentiating factor for any healthcare organization is the engagement and value of its employees, and
- describe how the transformation of healthcare services will require greater interaction and cooperation among healthcare workers and organizations.

Key Terms

- Henri Fayol
- Max Weber
- organizational behavior
- organizational theory
- organizations
- scientific management

organizations
Socially constructed entities created for specific purposes that are goal directed; composed of people tied together in formal and informal relationships; and linked to their external environment through their customers, suppliers, competitors, and government regulators.

We live in a world full of organizations, and nearly everyone is associated with multiple organizations at any one time—as an employee, a boss, a volunteer, or a recipient of service. No matter the role or roles we play in organizations, those affiliations are a constant presence in our lives.

Organizations are socially constructed entities created for specific purposes. They are goal directed, composed of people tied together in formal and informal relationships, and linked to their external environment through their customers, suppliers, competitors, and government regulatory bodies. The central aspect of an organization is the coordination of people and resources to produce a product or provide a service (Daft 2012).

Organizational behavior and organizational theory are made up of numerous theories that seek to explain the factors that influence the behaviors, successes, and failures of individuals and organizations—large corporations, small entrepreneurial ventures, governmental agencies, military groups, social groups, family and religious organizations, and so on. This book explores organizational behavior and organizational theory in the context of healthcare organizations—doctors' offices, pharmaceutical companies, public health agencies, hospitals, nursing homes, home health agencies, outpatient surgery centers, medical device manufacturers, volunteer groups, insurance companies, and many others. As Mary's story shows in the introduction, these organizations are complex and deal with life-or-death decisions.

Most organizations are similar in that they typically have rules and policies, decision-making lines of authority with formal and informal relationships, and divisions of labor, but their performance and effectiveness vary radically. Some organizations are highly organized, have nurturing cultures, and seem to accomplish astonishing results; others languish and appear to stumble from one crisis to another. As discussed in this chapter, organizational behavior and organizational theory were developed to help academics and managers understand the way businesses work and the dynamics of organizations' internal and external environments.

Both fields evolved in the early to mid-1900s, when management theorists suggested a variety of ways to improve management practices and explain the human factor in organizational success and failure. Over time, theorists began to consider guidance relating to the behavior of people and of organizations as separate fields.

Organizational Behavior

Organizational behavior broadly explores the behavior and influence of individuals, groups, and structures in an organization and their impact on the function and effectiveness of that organization. These three levels of organizations are highly interactive, such that changes in one area affect the other areas (exhibit 1.1). Individual behavior is linked to the broader

organizational behavior
The study of the behavior and influence of individuals, groups, and structures in an organization and their impact on the function and effectiveness of that organization.

EXHIBIT 1.1
Interactive Nature of the Three Levels of Organizational Behavior

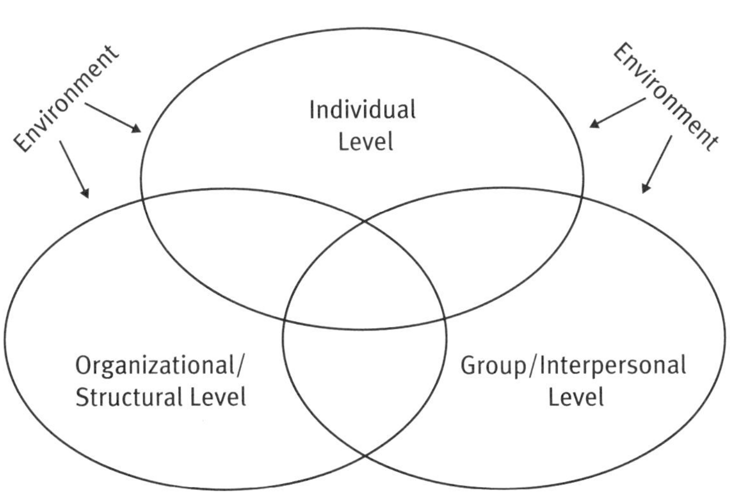

context of the organization, and group behavior influences and is influenced by individual and organizational (structural) factors. Each individual brings unique characteristics, personal background, perspectives, and experiences to the organization. Furthermore, each person acts and reacts uniquely to the organization's rules and processes and to interactions with teams and groups.

Understanding the dynamics of organizational behavior gives us insight into the organization's processes and activities and the consequences of behavior. It also provides the means to study and understand leadership, power, communication, teamwork, satisfaction, commitment, decision-making, conflict, learning, and other important management issues. In short, organizational behavior allows managers to appreciate why employees act as they do and to help them improve their behavior. Long-term, organizations will only perform as desired when employees are engaged in their work, and employees become engaged only when their leaders provide a work context that promotes positive group and organizational interactions.

Organizational behavior encapsulates many of the theories explored in this book, which come from disparate disciplines such as economics, psychology, social psychology, sociology, political science, and anthropology and consider the interactions of people, structure, technology, and the external environment (Investopedia 2021). The book's chapters address topics, practical applications, and definitions commonly considered under the umbrella of the field of organizational behavior.

Organizational Theory

organizational theory
The study of organizations as a whole or populations of organizations that seeks to explain the processes and factors that influence the structure and outcomes of organizations.

In some settings, organizational behavior and organizational theory are taught jointly, as presented in this book. However, at many schools, each is considered a separate management specialization. Their differentiation can be seen in exhibit 1.2.

Organizational theory focuses on the organization as a whole or on populations of organizations. It seeks to explain the processes and factors that influence the structure and outcomes of organizations, including how

EXHIBIT 1.2
Relationship of Organizational Behavior to Organizational Theory

Level	Individual	Group/Team	Organizational	Industry
Theory	Organizational Behavior			Organizational Theory

//// Denotes overlap

organizations interact in and across industries and societies. Jeffrey Pfeffer (1997) wrote that organizational theory focuses on how the characteristics and actions of social organizations and individuals can affect behaviors, attitudes, and the performance, success, and survival of organizations, as well as the organizations' political, cultural, and resource and task environments. Chapters 2 and 10 discuss in detail the concepts, applications, and subtheories of organizational theory.

History and Development

Both organizational behavior and organizational theory are rooted in the Second Industrial Revolution, which began in the late 1800s. The new technology of the nineteenth century ushered in factories, which created novel organizational and managerial problems. This environment required the management of immense flows of material, people, and information across large distances and the creation of new methods for dealing with these management challenges.

One early theorist was sociologist **Max Weber**. Born in Germany in 1864, he lived in a rapidly changing Europe that had experienced centuries of feudal control, primarily under small principalities. Promotions and authority had been most often tied to familial relationships. Weber, writing primarily about the Prussian civil service, postulated that the ideal organization was a formalized, somewhat rigid bureaucracy that had rules everyone in the company obeyed; positions awarded on the basis of competence; clear, formal hierarchies that established chains of command for decision-making; and a division of labor that allowed employees to align their skills with work needs (Anter 2014). His bureaucracy theory was widely perceived as an improvement over the nepotism, irrational behaviors, and lack of professionalism that existed in firms during that time.

Max Weber
A German sociologist and political economist who postulated that the ideal organization had rules every worker obeyed, competency-based positions, chains of command for decision-making, and division of labor.

Although the term *bureaucracy* has a negative connotation today, Weber's writings had a profound influence on the way managers and leaders organized and ran companies. Today, bureaucracies can be seen in almost all organizations and can be seen clearly in healthcare. Some now believe that bureaucracies in healthcare are expanding, destroying value, and preventing timely

> **Fighting Healthcare's Bureaucracy**
>
> To escape the negative aspects of bureaucracy, leaders must create learning mechanisms outside of the traditional chains of command. For instance, the CEO of the University of Virginia Health System leads a daily "huddle" where leaders and representatives from each part of their organization examine the previous day's unexpected patient deaths and injuries from incidents such as medication errors and falls. The huddle also seeks to strengthen the system's problem-solving and improve how warnings and lessons are shared across the system (Segel 2017).

Henri Fayol
A French mining engineer, considered to be one of the founders of modern management, who distilled management practices into 14 principles to frame a general management perspective.

decision-making. As the example in the box shows, avoiding the negative aspects of bureaucracy, as it was defined by Weber, requires constant leadership effort.

Another early, influential contributor to management theory, a contemporary of Weber, was Frenchman **Henri Fayol**, who developed a general theory of business and is recognized as one of the founders of modern management. As a mining engineer and director of mines, he observed a variety of management practices, which he distilled into 14 principles of management to frame a general management perspective (exhibit 1.3). As can be seen, many of these principles are widely accepted today and form the foundation of current management practice.

EXHIBIT 1.3
Fayol's 14 Principles of Management

Principle	Definition
Division of work	Employees are assigned to different tasks or parts of a work process and become specialized in those tasks. Also known as *division of labor*.
Authority and responsibility	Management has the authority to give orders but also the responsibility to be accountable for actions and outcomes.
Discipline	Management must instill obedience among employees. Penalties and sanctions will encourage discipline.
Unity of command	Each employee should receive orders from only one manager.
Unity of direction	Activities should have common objectives and the organization should be moving toward a common goal.
Subordination	Individual interests should not take priority over the interests of the organization.
Remuneration	Cost of living should be considered to ensure that workers are paid a fair wage.
Centralization	Centralization addresses the degree to which subordinates are involved in organizational decision-making. The level of centralization should depend on the needs of the organization.
Scalar chain	The line of authority from top management to the lowest ranks forms a scalar chain. Employees should communicate by following this path.
Order	All resources, including people and materials, should be treated systematically and have a specific place in the organization.

(continued)

EXHIBIT 1.3
Fayol's 14 Principles of Management *(Continued)*

Principle	Definition
(continued from previous page)	
Equity	Managers should treat their subordinates fairly and without bias.
Stability of tenure of personnel	Managers should seek to retain productive employees, because high turnover is wasteful. Organizations should have orderly personnel planning to ensure that replacements are available to fill vacancies that arise.
Initiative	Managers should encourage employees to be self-directed.
Esprit de corps	Managers need to promote team spirit to build harmony and unity.

Fayol's principles are often further condensed to five core management functions of

1. planning,
2. organizing,
3. coordinating,
4. commanding, and
5. controlling.

He is also credited with identifying strategic planning and employee recruitment and motivation as critical management functions and was one of the first to promote management as a separate discipline (Pugh and Hickson 1993).

Weber's and Fayol's writings complemented the concurrent work and theories of American mechanical engineer Frederick W. Taylor, who advanced the concept of management control in the late 1800s and early 1900s. To create greater efficiency and address the new management challenges created by the Industrial Revolution, Taylor promoted systematic use of time and motion studies to analyze human behavior at work. He developed the theory of **scientific management**, which proposes that human input is among the cheap, interchangeable components that can be "engineered" to maximize efficiency. In the scientific management approach, production processes are broken into small units, and employee and material movements are studied to find the most efficient way to perform each job. Management was encouraged to control work processes, closely supervise employees, and dictate how labor was to be accomplished. Workers were left with little discretion in their jobs, as processes were standardized and decisions to maximize efficiency were made by managers (Kanigel 2005; Taylor 2017).

scientific management
A theory, developed by American mechanical engineer Frederick W. Taylor, that human input is among the cheap, interchangeable components that can be "engineered" to maximize efficiency.

At the time, Taylor's work was groundbreaking, and many businesses adopted his advice and processes; the human influence on work outcomes was largely ignored. Advances in fields such as psychology, threats of unionization, growing urbanization, and world events such as the Great Depression and the two world wars called attention to the discrepancy between scientific management theory and actual human behavior in organizations. Research conducted in the 1920s—the most famous being the Hawthorne experiments at Western Electric Company in Chicago (discussed in chapter 2)—suggested that human behaviors were significantly affected by social and other nonwork factors (Parsons 1974). As the twentieth century progressed, managers began to see their organizations not only as a formal arrangement of structures and functions but also as work embedded in and highly influenced by an organizational social system. Taylor focused on individual motives and job structures, but managers realized that teams, groups, culture, and informal networks heavily influenced productivity. The Human Relations Movement evolved from these studies and efforts, which helped produce the theories that make up organizational behavior and which are discussed in detail in this book.

Organizational theory owes its existence to the same social and technological changes that influenced organizational behavior. Initially, the term *organizational theory* encompassed scientific management and prior management theories. However, by 1960 organizational theory diverged from organizational behavior's intraorganizational focus and concentrated on interorganizational theories (Starbuck 2003). The rapid increase in the number of large, formalized, organized businesses made the study and theories of organizations relevant and meaningful to many more people.

Relevance to the Healthcare Industry

For managers in the healthcare industry, the study of organizational behavior and organizational theories can be exceptionally helpful. Healthcare organizations consist of complex, changing relationships and reporting structures. They involve multiple specialties with different professional cultures providing a wide variety of services, making healthcare one of the most challenging industries to manage. As Marcus (1995, 3) stated, in healthcare

> work is accomplished via an intricately structured set of relationships. Formal and informal rules determine who speaks to whom, who makes what decisions, and who has what information. People are organized and decisions are aligned in a cautiously defined order.

Service providers in this industry are highly professionalized, with their own distinct ethics and cultures. Healthcare professionals (e.g., doctors, nurses, radiology technicians) are differentiated by their training, licensure, and skills and often interact under "pecking orders" of importance. The implications of this structure are heightened in acute care settings, where conflicts in priorities often arise because "doctors and nurses are trained differently" (Brown 2013). These differences are often identified as factors that damage communication and teamwork, and that lead to medical errors and adverse patient safety events (Samuriwo et al. 2020).

Delivering patient care and services is no longer an individual effort driven by a single physician. Instead, it has shifted to a team-based approach that often finds physicians, nurses, pharmacists, respiratory therapists, dietitians, and other providers with advanced degrees working side by side. As they work, these complex, cross-disciplinary teams must coordinate their efforts and constantly adapt to rapid knowledge expansion (Dinh et al. 2020; Nembhard and Edmondson 2006). Healthcare is complicated, and getting more so.

Another factor increasing provider interdependence and interaction is the emergence of accountable care organizations (ACOs)—networks of primary care and specialist doctors, home health agencies, and hospitals that share the coordination of patient care to create more efficient, effective outcomes. As of January 2021, according to the website for the National Association of ACOs, hundreds of these organizations served 10.7 million Medicare recipients in the United States. This unprecedented reliance on other medical professionals for joint decision-making and to provide services complicates the human factor in healthcare and distinguishes hospitals and health systems from many other organizational types.

In addition, the critical nature of healthcare requires precise actions to ensure specific positive outcomes. Unlike many other industries, healthcare has limited room for error in the provision of its services. Yet errors continue to plague the industry, being the third leading cause of death in the United States, with hundreds of thousands of patients dying annually in the United States alone from errors, injuries, accidents, and infections (Makary and Daniel 2016). Many of these events are caused by a failure to adequately communicate critical information and coordinate efforts. Approximately 80 percent of serious medical errors may involve miscommunication among caregivers, a situation being addressed by the Joint Commission Center for Transforming Healthcare (2012) and participating health systems.

Organizational behavior and organizational theory are similarly relevant to the healthcare industry's rapid reorganization and transformation. Economic forces, government regulations, technology, consumers, and employers are all driving change (PwC 2021), with governments and

> **The Impact of COVID-19 on Healthcare Services**
> The COVID-19 pandemic dramatically changed healthcare delivery. Concerned about the risk of transmitting or contracting the coronavirus, both healthcare providers and patients put off elective services and deferred preventive care such as vaccines and annual physicals. Telemedicine, previously only a tiny part of most physician practices, jumped to 13 percent of all claims by April 2020 (Gelburd 2020). In addition, 577,600 US healthcare workers lost their jobs between February 2020 and February 2021, with the greatest losses occurring in nursing homes (182,400), ambulatory services (165,100), and hospitals (102,400) (Hut 2021).

businesses worldwide altering their existing healthcare systems to improve quality, increase access, and control costs. In 2020, the rapid spread of COVID-19 forced additional major changes. As described in the box, this pandemic altered existing healthcare relationships, resulting in major disruptions to healthcare services and seriously stressing leaders, patients, and workers. Public health screenings were postponed and organizations implemented new strategies to care for the sickest patients (World Health Organization 2020).

To cope with these disruptions, many healthcare organizations are altering strained relationships, reordering hierarchical power bases, upending long-standing incentives, and demanding greater leadership and direction from executives than ever before. Healthcare leaders helping their organizations navigate these changes must ask themselves questions such as those posed by Marcus (1995, xiii):

- Who will be responsible for the new service delivery systems?
- How will the new responsibilities change the jobs of the people involved, and can their work become more meaningful and interesting?
- How will reporting relationships change?
- Who among the healthcare organizations will be seen as, or will see themselves as, winners or losers?

Organizational behavior can help inform the answers to these questions and direct actions across the many relational and structural changes.

Furthermore, healthcare is a service industry, with patient satisfaction driven by the provision of services by employees, many of whom provide direct care to patients. Thus, employees are not only the key component in but also the main cost of healthcare. The manner in which they interact affects patient and staff satisfaction, the degree to which the organization is in compliance with regulations, and the extent to which the patient achieves clinical benefit. Likewise, the level of positive interaction among employees, their managers, and others in the organization influences the organization's ability to achieve its mission and objectives. As a result, some observers have long suggested that healthcare managers' most important asset remains their employees, and that success is dictated by the presence of collegial relationships and employee engagement rather than by the implementation of patient- or customer-focused efforts (Spiegelman and Berrett 2013). Yet, a 2020 Gallup survey found that employees often have tenuous relationships with management (Ratanjee and Foy 2020):

- Only 47 percent of healthcare workers felt their employer communicated a clear action plan during the COVID-19 pandemic.
- Just 36 percent were confident that they would be safe if they followed their organization's policies.

Lasting strategic advantage and differentiation evolve from and are sustained by positive relationships, culture, and communication—all factors in organizational behavior and organizational theory—rather than purchased assets, documents, and directives (Walston 2018).

The skills learned from organizational behavior and organizational theory are needed now more than ever, to energize the rapid transformation of the healthcare system now occurring in many countries. Many nations are experimenting with models that will alter employee incentives, worker behaviors, and organizational structures—and thus interactions and relationships—all of which will make the understanding of organizational behavior and organizational theories much more important in the future.

This book divides organizational behavior and theory into three general levels—individual, group, and organizational—and presents 22 additional chapters that will help you gain competencies in these areas. Exhibit 1.4 shows the concepts associated with the three levels of organizational behavior

EXHIBIT 1.4 Chapter Topics as They Relate to Levels of Organizational Behavior

Individual Chapters	Group Chapters	Organizational Chapters
• 2 – Theories of Managing People • 3 – Diversity, Equity, and Inclusion • 4 – Learning • 5 – Attitudes and Satisfaction • 6 – Values and Ethics • 7 – Motivation • 8 – Emotions, Moods, and Stress • 9 – Paradigms and Perceptions • 10 – Decision-Making	• 11 – Creativity and Innovation • 12 – Group Behavior • 13 – Work Teams • 14 – Communication • 15 – Leadership • 16 – Power, Politics, and Influence	• 17 – Conflict Management and Negotiation • 18 – Organizational Design and Structure • 19 – Performance Management • 20 – Mentoring, Coaching, and Delegation • 21 – Culture • 22 – HR Polices and Practices • 23 – Strategy and Change Management

and the chapters in which these concepts are discussed. Although slotted into one area, the concepts are interactive and may affect more than one level. For example, values and ethics appear at the individual level yet greatly affect the group and organizational levels as well. Learning and understanding these concepts will prepare managers to work in an organization and to lead others.

Chapter Summary

This book gives the reader a thorough overview of organizational behavior and organizational theory as it applies directly to the healthcare field. Organizational behavior broadly explores the behaviors of individuals, groups, and structures in an organization and their effect on the organization's outcomes and functioning. Organizational theory examines how organizations interact in and across industries and societies. Both concepts originated in the late 1800s, triggered by the Second Industrial Revolution. Early theorists included Max Weber, Henri Fayol, and Frederick W. Taylor.

The concepts and application of organizational behavior and organizational theory are extremely important in healthcare, given its heavy reliance on services provided by numerous personnel (who come from distinct cultures and professions) and the team-based nature of healthcare delivery (which involves complicated relationships that, if not managed correctly, can be prone to tragic errors). Successful healthcare executives master these concepts and know how to apply them in their organization.

Chapter Questions

1. What are some of the challenges that make organizational management in healthcare more complex than in many other industries?
2. Why are organizations important in our lives?
3. What were the precursors to the development of organizational theory and organizational behavior?
4. What did Max Weber and Fredrick W. Taylor mostly miss in their theories?
5. What is the difference between organizational behavior and organizational theory?
6. Why did the Industrial Revolution in the late 1800s affect work relationships so greatly?
7. What events encouraged managers to seek means to address the human influence on work?

Chapter Cases

The Frustrated New Employee
During orientation, the new hospital employee was impressed with the time leaders took to speak with her about the company's values, especially teamwork. A recent college graduate, she is just beginning work as a medical technician and dreams of working with a team of physicians, scientists, and other researchers to help in the discovery of new treatments.

After two days of invigorating orientation, she was ready to exemplify the values she had been taught. But she has quickly learned that *teamwork* often means doing what she is told and not speaking up. She has tried to engage with the physicians and has listened in on their conversations, but they tend to ignore her, and most of the time she only understands about half of what they are saying. She is frequently frustrated, and has found that the only people who listen to her are the other new medical technicians she sees during breaks.

Case Questions
1. What should the new employee do?
2. How does the professionalization of healthcare personnel influence this situation?

The CEO's Salary Dilemma
Mark is the CEO of a midsize hospital in the Intermountain West region of the United States. He has worked at the facility for more than five years and has a close relationship with the medical staff and his employees. He has a habit of going into different departments and getting to know the employees personally. He is generally liked by most of the employees and empathetic when he hears stories about their family problems and financial struggles. Mark prides himself on his honesty and integrity.

On the other hand, Mark represents a for-profit company that sets very high goals and financial standards. It has been a trying year, and the hospital is barely meeting its financial targets.

As the hospital was preparing its budget, Mark proposed that all his employees receive a 3.5 percent cost-of-living increase. This request seemed reasonable, considering that employment surveys have found that many of his employees are on the low side of market wages. When it appeared that this increase had been approved, Mark told his employees that they should expect the indicated raise.

The following week, Mark's regional vice president calls. She informs Mark that his facility is not profitable enough and demands that he rescind the cost-of-living wage increase and allow the budgeted amount (about $1.5 million) to be posted as net profits for the organization. Mark explains that he has already announced the increase and says rescinding it now would damage both employee morale and his credibility. The regional vice president bluntly replies that if Mark will not do it, she will fire him and find someone who will.

Case Questions
1. Given the circumstances, what would you do?
2. What are some of the group and individual consequences of following the regional vice president's directive? Of not following the directive?
3. What individual, group, and organizational issues are involved in this case?

Chapter Activity

Teamwork and Architecture
This activity introduces general concepts found throughout this book and demonstrates how individual, group, and organizational factors can interact to influence outcomes. The class will divide into teams, and each team's builders will attempt to build the required structure within the time allowed. Once time is up, the class will reconvene as a group and each team's observers will report on what they saw during the activity.

Materials
Each team will need these items before beginning:

- Enough LEGO or similar toy building bricks (all the same size and shape) to build the required structure—about 200 bricks per team
- An unopened 10-ounce can of food (e.g., a standard can of soup, fruit, vegetables)
- Notetaking supplies for the observers (whatever form is most convenient)

Preparation
Before beginning, make sure that the bricks are evenly divided between teams and that each team has enough bricks to create the required structure. (An easy way to ensure roughly equal brick allotments is to stack the bricks and compare the length of the stacks.)

Activity

Your instructor will determine the time limit for this activity (30–45 minutes is recommended).

1. Choose about one-third of your group to be observers—ideally at least two people. The rest will be builders.
2. Builders: Work as a group to connect all the available bricks to create a single structure that (1) holds the weight of the unopened can and (2) allows the unopened can to pass through the structure. For example, if you build a simple tunnel, the unopened can must be able to fit through the tunnel and the tunnel must stay intact if the unopened can is placed on top. You must not have any loose bricks when the structure is complete.
3. Observers: Watch the builders as they work and take notes. You may not help the builders in any way—not even with suggestions or nonverbal cues. Concentrate instead on taking notes so you can report on the builders' activity. Consider the organizational behavior concepts discussed in this chapter, including things such as communication, leadership, motivation, group dynamics, and decision-making.
4. When your team's builders have completed their structure, your team can rejoin the larger group. Once all teams are finished (or time has run out), each team's observers should report to the class on what they saw while the builders were working.

Source: Adapted from a similar activity with permission of Ray W. Coye, PhD, associate professor emeritus, Department of Management, DePaul University.

References

Agency for Healthcare Research and Quality. 2017. "Case Scenarios: Handling Challenging Communications." Reviewed February. www.ahrq.gov/patient-safety/capacity/candor/modules/guide5/scenarios.html.

Anter, A. 2014. *Max Weber's Theory of the Modern State*. Basingstoke, UK: Palgrave Macmillan.

Brown, T. 2013. "Healing the Hospital Hierarchy." *New York Times*. Published March 16. http://opinionator.blogs.nytimes.com/2013/03/16/healing-the-hospital-hierarchy/.

Daft, R. 2012. *Organizational Theory and Design*, 11th ed. Boston, MA: Cengage Learning.

Dinh, J. V., A. M. Traylor, M. P. Kilcullen, J. A. Perez, E. J. Schweissing, A. Venkatesh, and E. Salas. 2020. "Cross-Disciplinary Care: A Systematic Review on Teamwork Processes in Health Care." *Small Group Research* 51 (1): 125–66.

Gelburd, R. 2020. "Telehealth Continues Rapid Growth Tied to COVID-19." *U.S. News & World Report.* Published July 13. www.usnews.com/news/healthiest-communities/articles/2020-07-13/telehealth-continues-rapid-growth-amid-coronavirus-pandemic.

Hut, N. 2021. "Hospital Job Losses Continued in February and Were Greater in January Than Previously Reported." Healthcare Financial Management Association (blog). Published March 8. www.hfma.org/topics/finance-and-business-strategy/article/hospital-job-losses-continued-in-february-and-were-greater-in-ja.html.

Investopedia. 2021. "Organizational Behavior." Accessed March 15. www.investopedia.com/terms/o/organizational-behavior.asp.

Joint Commission Center for Transforming Healthcare. 2012. "TST for Hand-off Communications." Published June 21. www.centerfortransforminghealthcare.org/why-work-with-us/video-resources/tst-for-hand-off-communications/.

Kanigel, R. 2005. *The One Best Way: Frederick Winslow Taylor and the Enigma of Efficiency.* New York: Penguin Random House.

Makary, M., and M. Daniel. 2016. "Medical Error—the Third Leading Cause of Death in the US." *British Medical Journal* 353 (8056): i2139. https://doi.org/10.1136/bmj.i2139.

Marcus, L. J. 1995. *Renegotiating Health Care.* San Francisco: Jossey-Bass.

Nembhard, I., and A. Edmondson. 2006. "Making It Safe: The Effects of Leader Inclusiveness and Professional Status on Psychological Safety and Improvement Efforts in Health Care Teams." *Journal of Organizational Behavior* 27 (7): 941–66.

Parsons, H. M. 1974. "What Happened at Hawthorne?" *Science* 183 (4128): 922–32.

Pfeffer, J. 1997. *New Directions for Organization Theory: Problems and Prospects.* Oxford, UK: Oxford University Press.

Pugh, D. S., and D. J. Hickson. 1993. *Great Writers on Organizations,* Omnibus edition. Aldershot, UK: Ashgate Publishing Limited.

PwC. 2021. "Top Health Industry Issues of 2021: Will a Shocked System Emerge Stronger?" www.pwc.com/us/en/industries/health-industries/top-health-industry-issues.html.

Ratanjee, V., and D. Foy. 2020. "What Healthcare Workers Need from Leaders in COVID-19 Crisis." Gallup *Workplace* (blog). Published April 22. www.gallup.com/workplace/308957/healthcare-workers-need-leaders-covid-crisis.aspx.

Samuriwo, R., E. Laws, K. Webb, and A. Bullock. 2020. "'I Didn't Realise They Had Such a Key Role.' Impact of Medical Education Curriculum Change on Medical Student Interactions with Nurses." *Advances in Health Sciences Education* 25 (1): 75–93. https://doi.org/10.1007/s10459-019-09906-4.

Segel, K. 2017. "Bureaucracy Is Keeping Health Care from Getting Better." *Harvard Business Review.* Published October 13. https://hbr.org/2017/10/bureaucracy-is-keeping-health-care-from-getting-better.

Spiegelman, P., and B. Berrett. 2013. *Patients Come Second: Leading Change by Changing the Way You Lead.* New York: An Inc. Original.

Starbuck, W. H. 2003. "The Origins of Organization Theory." In *The Oxford Handbook of Organization Theory: Meta-theoretical Perspectives*, edited by H. Tsoukas and C. Knudsen, 143–82. Oxford, UK: Oxford University Press.

Taylor, F. 2017 (1911). *The Principles of Scientific Management.* New York: Productivity Press.

Walston, S. L. 2018. *Strategic Healthcare Management: Planning and Execution*, 2nd edition. Chicago: Health Administration Press.

World Health Organization. 2020. "COVID-19 Significantly Impacts Health Services for Noncommunicable Diseases." June 1. www.who.int/news/item/01-06-2020-covid-19-significantly-impacts-health-services-for-noncommunicable-diseases.

CHAPTER 2

THEORIES OF MANAGING PEOPLE

> Why do people in healthcare treat each other so poorly? Nurses report doctors yelling at them. Operating personnel fail to tell the surgeon when an instrument has fallen on the floor. People who have to rely on each other say things such as, "I can't ask questions, or the older nurses look at me like I am stupid." One intensive care nurse ran into the hall to ask a coworker for help with a crashing patient and was told, "Going on a smoke break now." What explains such disruptive behaviors, which about 30 percent of healthcare workers experience?
>
> *Source*: Hospital News (2015).

Learning Objectives

After studying this chapter, readers should be able to

- explain the historical progression of prominent early management theories;
- compare and contrast the principal management theories; and
- summarize scientific management theory, administrative theory, human relations theory, theory X and theory Y, the contingency approach, open systems theory, resource dependence theory, decision-making theory, and institutional theory.

Key Terms

- administrative theory
- bounded rationality
- contingency approach
- human relations theory
- Maslow's hierarchy of needs
- mimetic isomorphism
- open systems theory
- satisfice
- theory X and theory Y

Conflicts occur frequently in healthcare organizations. As anyone who has held a managerial position knows, dealing with people is the biggest challenge in making a business work well, especially in employee-intensive healthcare companies. Although it is important to understand money, strategy, economics, and statistics, most managers' time is spent handling employees. Being a boss can be lonely. Managing often requires making unpopular decisions, allocating resources to one group over another, and balancing personal and business priorities.

Healthcare managers confront these types of issues as well. While it is important to be transparent about most activities, managers must also be able to withhold confidential information. Healthcare leaders constantly face quality-versus-cost trade-offs, and have to meet budgets and financial targets while delivering high-quality services. They must properly and consistently apply policies—a duty that can quickly become a headache. Policies are only a means to an end and some can be appropriately ignored, but some policies are critical, and it can be difficult to apply them to an organizational superstar. Resolving conflicts between employees—who often tell contradictory stories—requires an inordinate amount of time spent uncovering and addressing the issues. Furthermore, healthcare leaders must constantly challenge themselves to learn, serve, and place their patients first. Boxer (2019) proposes three qualities of successful healthcare leaders:

1. Stay curious and continue learning. Healthcare continues to evolve. The best leaders relentlessly pursue knowledge, both formally and informally.
2. Maintain empathy and serve your employees. Model the behaviors you want your employees to embrace. Show that you care by your words and actions.
3. Place the patient first. Seek to meet patients' evolving demands and preferences.

At issue is that many managers do not handle these challenges well and fail to arrive at positive resolutions. The fact that about half of American workers are not engaged and are psychologically detached from their work bears out the poor management skills of many bosses. It is estimated that disengaged employees have higher absenteeism and lower productivity (Harter 2020). Employee disengagement costs the United States as much as $600 billion annually in lost productivity (Jouany and Mäkipää 2021). Specific to healthcare, research suggests that disengaged healthcare workers exhibit negative behaviors that can diminish quality of care and damage their organization, and provider burnout and disengagement have been identified as potentially disruptive forces (AMN Healthcare 2021).

Yet people are often more involved in relationships at work than in any other aspect of their lives. Most employees spend far more time working than with family and friends, and the majority of employees' organizing and coordinating activities, disagreements, and conflicts occur in work environments and involve coworker relationships (Ortiz-Ospina 2020). Clearly, human relationships matter a great deal in management.

As mentioned in chapter 1 and discussed in the adjacent box, the Hawthorne studies demonstrated that relationships and social context, along with organizational design and structure, affect employee performance. This finding led to the creation of many management theories that centered the influence of interpersonal relationships and human dimensions. In this chapter, the more prominent of these management theories are explored.

> **The Hawthorne Studies**
>
> One of the early major advances in organizational behavior resulted from research conducted by Elton Mayo and Fritz Roethlisberger in the 1920s, often called the Hawthorne studies because they were conducted on workers at Western Electric Company's Hawthorne factory, near Chicago. The Hawthorne findings were influential in refocusing management strategy from scientific management to include the social and psychological aspects of human behavior in organizations.
>
> Mayo and Roethlisberger hypothesized that worker productivity would improve if employees chose their own coworkers, worked as a group, were treated distinctively, and had sympathetic supervisors. After numerous experiments, they concluded that monetary incentives and working conditions were generally less important to productivity than employees' need and desire to be part of a group and their inclusion in decision-making. Employees were motivated by more than money, and productivity was affected by factors other than just pay and optimizing workflow.
>
> *Source*: Adapted from Boundless (2021).

Weber's Efficient Bureaucracy

As discussed in chapter 1, the early theorists developed administrative theories about the optimal structures and operations of businesses. Max Weber, a prominent scholar in the late nineteenth and early twentieth centuries, believed that work structures and processes should be rationally organized to increase the economic efficiency of a company. Weber's writings, juxtaposed at that time with Marxism's theories of class struggle, promoted modern capitalism as a means for rational efficiency through bureaucratic management. One of his most influential works was *Wirtschaft und Gesellschaft* (*Economy and Society*), the first volume of which was published in English as *The Theory of Social and Economic Organization* after his death. He proposed that as organizations mature, bureaucracy—with its structures, processes, and routines—is the best way to achieve efficiency and is even required by modern society's move to larger, more mature organizations driven by capitalism, rather than the management approaches based on lineage, patronage, and kinship of previous eras. "Precision, speed, unambiguity, knowledge of files, continuity, discretion, unity, strict subordination, reduction of friction and of material and personal costs—these are raised to the optimum point in the strictly bureaucratic administration," he wrote (Weber 1958, 214).

Weber's ideal bureaucracy was defined by the following six characteristics:

1. Hierarchy of command. Each office has a clearly defined chain of command, and each person reports to a specific leader. Planning and decision-making are exercised along the chain of command.
2. Impersonality. Officeholders are selected on the basis of their technical qualifications, and rules are systematically applied. All employees are treated equally.
3. Written rules of conduct. Rules are clearly defined and understood by all employees, allowing higher-level decisions to be executed at lower levels.
4. Advancement on the basis of achievement. The best-qualified people, as determined by their work performance and skills, are promoted.
5. Specialized division of labor. Each job has clear duties that are broken down into component parts and performed by specialists. The organization is divided into units according to worker specialties.
6. Efficiency. The overall goal of the organization is to structure itself to maximize its efficiency.

Although bureaucracies today have gained a reputation for being complex, inefficient, inflexible, and dehumanizing, in the late 1800s and early 1900s Weber's work found many adherents who were seeking ways to improve organization and management. His work did have significant benefit and became the foundation for most large companies and public employment (Reeves, Wesselink, and Whitaker 2020).

Yet, as previously mentioned, bureaucracy is now associated with endless red tape and administrative procedures. Costs attributed to bureaucracy in the US healthcare system are extremely high. Over one-third of all US healthcare costs are spent

---

The Costs of Medical Bureaucracy

Tufts Medical Center is a prominent teaching hospital located in Boston, Massachusetts, and during his tenure as its CEO, Dr. Mike Apkon frequently commented on the problem of too much bureaucracy in his medical center. The business office employs more than 200 workers that spend their time handling billing and insurance functions. Dr. Apkon feels there is far too much administrative complexity between the patient, the payer, and the provider. Just for authorizations, billings, and collections, Tufts spent about $54 million per year in 2019 and 2020. (Goldberg 2020)

on overhead, billing, and administration (Himmelstein, Campbell, and Woolhandler 2020). As one physician commented, "The average American is paying more than $2,000 a year for useless bureaucracy" (Carroll 2020). Medical centers in the United States have many of the characteristics that Weber espoused, but somehow they seem to have forgotten efficiency.

Administrative Theory

Building on Weber's propositions, in the early 1900s a number of individuals sought rational ways to design and structure an organization. Their theories aimed to describe best management practices for all firms. The best organizations were thought to have a formal administrative structure, a clear division of labor, and delegation of power and authority. The formal administrative structure recommends clear lines of authority from the top to the bottom of a company, forming the organization's hierarchical framework. The division of labor provides an obvious demarcation, organizing work and employees by function and purpose (the most enduring of Fayol's principles). Furthermore, managers were to be given both the power and authority for their specific areas of responsibility (Burns, Bradley, and Weiner 2020).

As mentioned in chapter 1, Henri Fayol was one of the primary contributors to **administrative theory** and proposed 14 general management principles (distilled into five managerial functions). Others, such as Luther Gulick, James Mooney, and Alan Reiley, using historical precedents, formulated systematic guidelines for organizations, including the scalar principle, functional principle, coordinative principle, and staff principle (Longest 1996; Mooney and Reiley 1939).

administrative theory
A principle of bureaucracy and management that seeks a rational way to design an organization.

Scalar Principle

According to the scalar principle, subordinates at each level communicate only through a chain of command to their immediate supervisor or subordinate (exhibit 2.1).

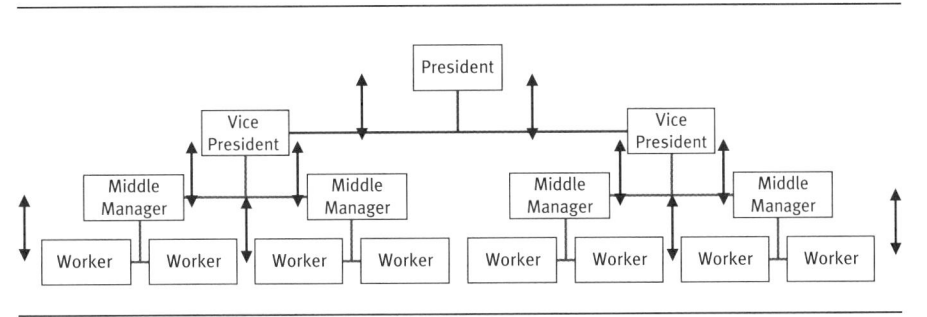

EXHIBIT 2.1
The Scalar Principle

Functional Principle

Under the functional principle, the function of each job and activity is defined by objectives, implementation, and control to clearly denote the nature of the job. Job descriptions, such as the following key responsibilities from a nursing job description, follow the functional principle:

Staff Nurse
KEY RESPONSIBILITIES

The Registered Nurse (RN) delivers nursing care for patients and adheres to institutional policies, procedures, and standards.

Duties may include any or all of the following:

- Collects and documents assessment data.
- Develops a Plan of Care (POC) per standard.
- Implements POC including medical order and interdisciplinary approach.
- Evaluates the progress of patient toward attainment of desired outcomes.
- Provides effective patient/family education/discharge planning.
- Administers medication per standard including drug information to patients/families.
- Contributes to a positive work environment that is conducive to clinical education while serving as a resource for student nurses and staff.

Source: Adapted from UAMS (2019).

Coordinative Principle

The coordinative principle describes an orderly arrangement of a group's effort, creating unity of action to seek a common objective. This principle can be institutionalized by emphasizing the organizational mission and vision statements. Strong Memorial Hospital's mission and vision as of 2021 provide an example of the coordinative principle:

Our Mission
We improve the well-being of patients and communities by delivering innovative, compassionate, patient- and family-centered health care, enriched by education, science, and technology.

Our Vision
We will define and deliver "Medicine of the Highest Order" and set the standard for compassion and innovation, always placing patients and their families first.

Staff Principle

In the staff principle, sometimes called the line-staff principle, staff members provide advice and ideas while line management makes sure tasks are accomplished (Archibald 2017). The following description of the duties of rehabilitation counselors demonstrates their line duties:

Rehabilitation Counselor Duties

Rehabilitation counselors help people with disabilities at various stages in their lives. Some work with students, to develop strategies to live with their disability and transition from school to work. Others help veterans cope with the mental or physical effects of their military service. Still others help elderly people adapt to disabilities developed later in life from illness or injury. Some may provide expert testimony or assessments during personal-injury or workers' compensation cases.

- Provide individual and group counseling to help clients adjust to their disability.
- Evaluate clients' abilities, interests, experiences, skills, health, and education.
- Develop a treatment plan for clients, in consultation with other professionals, such as doctors, therapists, and psychologists.
- Arrange for clients to obtain services, such as medical care or career training.
- Help employers understand the needs and abilities of people with disabilities, as well as laws and resources that affect people with disabilities.
- Help clients develop their strengths and adjust to their limitations.
- Locate resources, such as wheelchairs or computer programs, that help clients live and work more independently.
- Maintain client records and monitor clients' progress, adjusting the rehabilitation or treatment plan as necessary.
- Advocate for the rights of people with disabilities to live in a community and work in the job of their choice.

Source: US Bureau of Labor Statistics (2021).

Maslow's Hierarchy of Needs

By the 1940s, management theorists were attempting to understand what factors motivated humans to work. In 1943, Abraham Maslow published his first book, which sought to explain the stages of human motivation and needs. What became known as **Maslow's hierarchy of needs** is often portrayed as a pyramid with five levels, representing categories of needs (exhibit 2.2). Maslow categorized these needs by complexity, with the least complex (most basic) need—physiological requirements for survival—at the base of the pyramid, and increasingly complex (less basic) needs building upward. Maslow theorized that each type of need has to be met before an

Maslow's hierarchy of needs
A theory that human needs fall into five categories, from less to more complex, and that less complex needs must be fulfilled before more complex needs will be pursued.

EXHIBIT 2.2 Maslow's Hierarchy of Needs

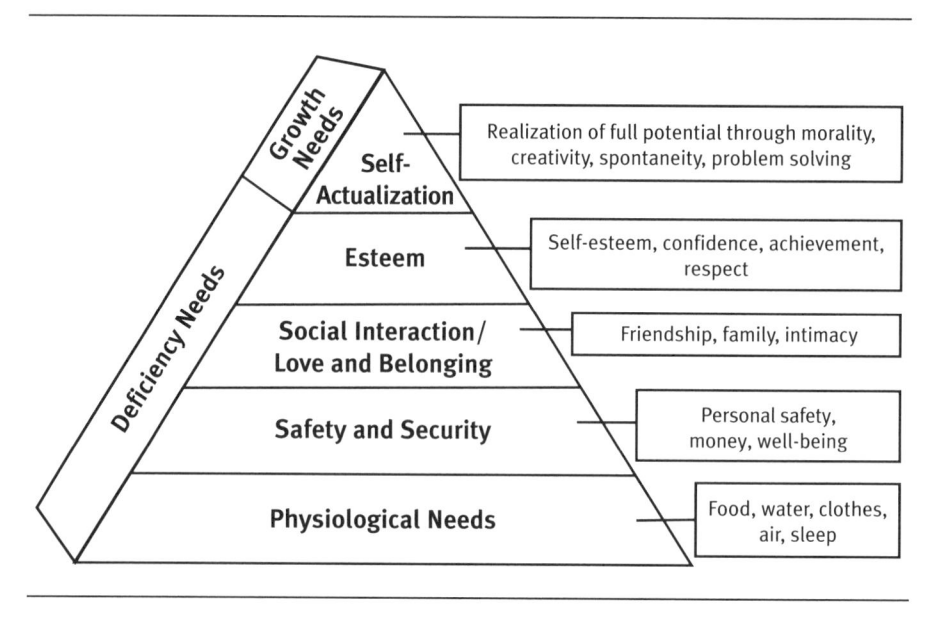

- **Growth Needs**
  - **Self-Actualization**: Realization of full potential through morality, creativity, spontaneity, problem solving
- **Deficiency Needs**
  - **Esteem**: Self-esteem, confidence, achievement, respect
  - **Social Interaction/Love and Belonging**: Friendship, family, intimacy
  - **Safety and Security**: Personal safety, money, well-being
  - **Physiological Needs**: Food, water, clothes, air, sleep

individual can move to fulfilling the next level of need. For example, a person who is starving seeks to satisfy the need for food before addressing the needs for safety and social interaction.

Maslow saw the uppermost level of need as different from the rest. He believed the highest set of needs were *growth needs* that came from a person's desire to grow, while the lower needs were triggered by the absence of something and thus were *deficiency needs*. From a work perspective, Maslow's hierarchy calls for managers to first help workers meet basic needs before helping them achieve their full individual potential. If workers lack basic physiological, security, social, or esteem needs, they cannot self-actualize.

Although the theory makes intuitive sense, most research has not supported Maslow's hierarchy.

Debate Time: Jean's Irritation

A huge open house is planned this week at the medical clinic where Jean works, and she is not pleased with the response of her employee, Sue. Jean had been unable to plan for the open house until a couple of weeks ago, and she has stressed to Sue that Sue will have to devote herself to preparing for the event. But Sue was at her sister's wedding on Saturday, and did not even answer her phone or return e-mails until late Sunday. By Monday morning, Jean is fuming. The open house is in just a few days, she has worked all weekend, and she wants to motivate Sue to get going. Jean calls Sue into her office and threatens to fire her if she ever again fails to answer her phone and e-mails when they have a critical function to coordinate. After the meeting, Jean feels she has motivated Sue and is sure she will not fail to respond in the future.

According to Maslow's hierarchy of needs, would this behavior help a person to become self-actualized? How does Jean's behavior affect Sue's lower deficiency needs, as described by Maslow? If you were Jean, what would you do to motivate Sue?

However, despite this lack of empirical support, Maslow's theory helped make managers aware of categories of needs that should be addressed, and it still has relevance today. Many managers now understand that the greatest level of productivity generally occurs when employees are fully engaged and self-actualized (Jouany and Mäkipää 2021). Yet, as illustrated by Jean's story (see box), supervisors too often seek to motivate using threats and fear. This strategy may change employees' immediate behaviors, but it impedes their growth and ultimately their positive outputs.

Human Relations

As discussed earlier, the Hawthorne studies in the 1920s were the first significant empirical examination of the effect of the human element on organizational outcomes. These and other early studies suggested that workers' needs for achievement, recognition, and social interaction could affect their productivity. Researchers in the 1950s established the importance of group influence and of managers addressing social interaction and other group factors, as well as monetary incentives. Employees were perceived as less rational than Taylor suggested and driven more by human sentiments (Burns, Bradley, and Weiner 2020). Theories evolved that accepted these human relations principles, perhaps most notably McGregor's theory X and theory Y.

human relations theory
A theory that focuses on organizational development and the influence of people. It originated in the 1930s with the advent of the Hawthorne studies.

Theory X and Theory Y

One of the founders of modern **human relations theory** was Douglas McGregor, who became known for his theory X and theory Y paradigm (Cooley 2016). Developed in the 1960s, his seminal work at the Massachusetts Institute of Technology Sloan School of Management has been applied to many management perspectives.

Theory X and theory Y seek to describe how managers perceive their employees and how these perceptions affect motivation and behavior. McGregor suggested that individuals have differing opinions and expectations regarding human nature (Cooley 2016). As shown in exhibit 2.3, managers with a theory X perception supervise their workers closely and adopt strict control systems involving incentives and threats; managers with a theory Y perspective allow their employees more freedom to make decisions, focus on developing workers' skills, and encourage participation.

McGregor's theory X and theory Y describe fundamental distinctions in management style and contrast the extremes of scientific management with the underlying assumptions of the human relations movement. This has become a foundation for much of current management philosophy.

theory X and theory Y
Developed by Douglas McGregor, these contrasting theories describe how managers perceive their employees and how these perceptions affect employee motivation and behavior. In McGregor's view, theory X managers focus on controlling workers and theory Y managers focus on engaging and empowering workers.

EXHIBIT 2.3
A Comparison of Theory X and Theory Y Beliefs About Employees

Theory X Managers Believe Employees	Theory Y Managers Believe Employees
Are inherently lazy	May be ambitious and self-motivated
Avoid and dislike work	Enjoy mental and physical work
Need incentive programs for motivation	Have abilities to problem solve
Require a narrow span of control	Seek out and accept responsibility
Avoid responsibility and work	Exercise self-control and self-direction
Respond to threats and coercion	Want to do well at work
Need to identify person at fault to solve problems	Find satisfaction in doing a good job—a strong motivation
Need managers to structure the work and provide motivation	Need to be challenged to discover and innovate
Need restrictive controls and constant pressure to perform well	Should be involved in decision-making
Prefer security at work	
Resist change at work	
May be gullible and easy to manipulate	

McGregor claimed that both the X and Y perspectives have value in different contexts; however, theory Y has been widely adopted as the preferred model in business and management literature. Nevertheless, as many workers can attest, theory X persists across many industries and work settings, and companies with a theory X perspective that workers would rather be lazy tend to implement micromanagement oversight that often deteriorates into hostile work environments (Lutgen-Sandvik and McDermott 2008).

Contingency Approach

In the 1950s, several researchers and management writers explored the effects of the internal and external situational environment on management actions. Those proposing the **contingency approach** suggested that Weber's bureaucracy and Frederick Taylor's scientific management theories had failed because they ignored the effects of the environment on management style and organizational structure. It has long been believed that there is no one best way to lead and organize, they contended; instead, how an organization is led depends on which of a variety of management structures is in place (Mintzberg 1979). The critical issue is the fit of the organizational structure with the contingent environmental factors. Firms that fit into, or match up

contingency approach
The view that personal, situational, and organizational factors dictate different management styles and the effective use of a management style is contingent on internal and external conditions.

with, the environment are more likely to succeed than are firms that are not well matched to the environment.

Different management theories proposed different factors. Joan Woodward (1958) believed that key contingencies included the following:

- Technology
- Suppliers and distributors
- Consumer interest groups
- Customers and competitors
- Government
- Unions

She suggested that the degree of span of control, centralization of authority, and formulation of rules and procedures should vary according to the existence, strength, and power of these factors.

Later management theorists named the theory the structural contingency theory (Pfeffer 1982) and expanded the methods and processes that organizations use to adapt to environmental influences.

Open Systems and Resource Dependence Theories

Concurrent with the contingency approach, other theorists developed the concept of open systems. Earlier management theories typically were based on the assumption that organizations are largely self-contained entities that can be relatively closed off from their environments. **Open systems theory** proposes that firms are highly influenced by their environments, from which they obtain resources, support, and legitimacy (exhibit 2.4). The environmental context in which an organization exists affects how a firm is structured and operates. Almost all management theories are founded on the open systems concept (Scott 2016).

open systems theory
A theory that firms are highly influenced by their environments.

Resource dependency theory built on the open system concepts, characterizing organizations as open systems dependent on their external environment. Managers act to reduce their dependency and environmental uncertainty, but organizations are constrained by their interdependencies with other organizations and by their need for external resources. Resource dependency also exists within organizations, where units jockey for power and resources and affect the behaviors of an organization. Resource dependence theory has been used to explain mergers, joint ventures, actions of boards, political action, and executive succession (Scott 2016). Firms buy and sell raw goods and finished products with other firms in their environments. These beneficial exchanges of goods create dependencies. A firm can gain power over another when they control a strategic resource that is all of the following (Barney and Hesterly 2018):

EXHIBIT 2.4
Closed Systems vs. Open Systems

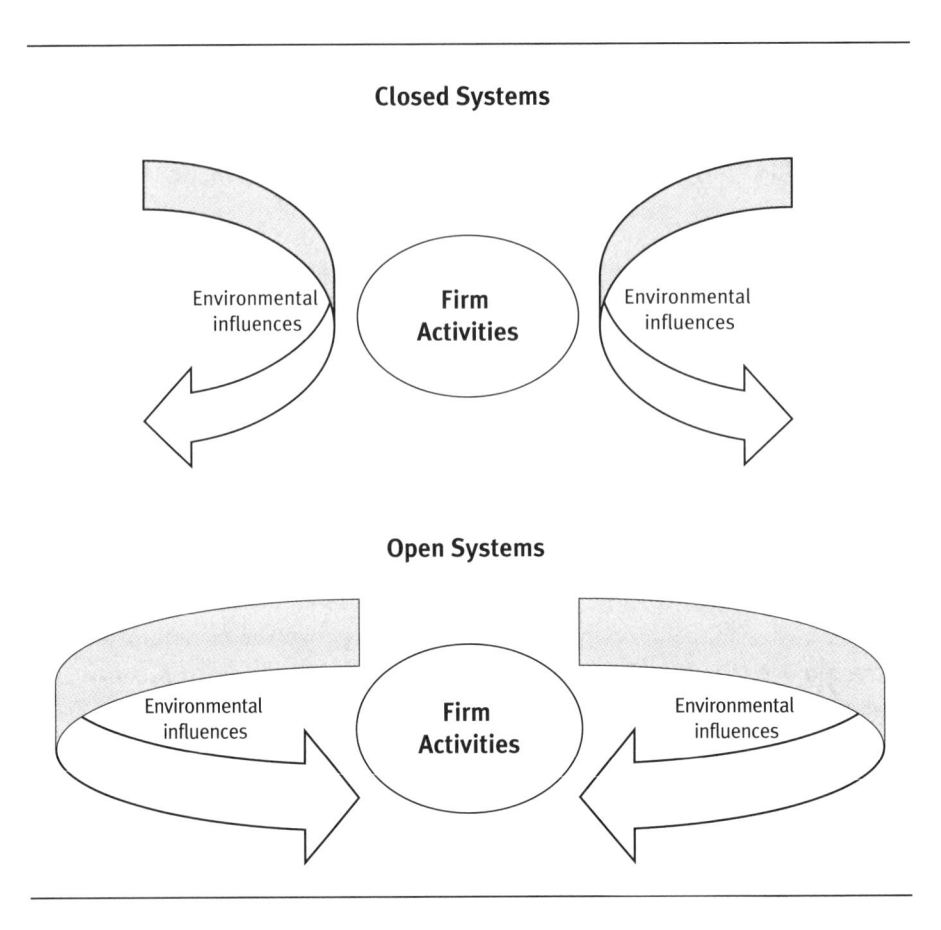

Closed Systems

Environmental influences → Firm Activities ← Environmental influences

Open Systems

Environmental influences → Firm Activities ← Environmental influences

- valuable
- rare
- difficult to imitate
- nonsubstitutable

Valuable resources allow organizations to gain advantages and minimize threats. Rare resources are difficult to create, obtain, or sustain. Resources that are difficult to imitate, such as brands and reputation, may be protected by patents and evolve over time. Nonsubstitutable resources are those with no available alternatives. All four of these factors contribute to a company's capabilities and are needed to secure a sustained advantage (Barney and Hesterly 2018).

Decision-Making Theory

In the 1950s and 1960s, management theorists at the Carnegie Mellon University in Pittsburgh, Pennsylvania, developed a decision-making theory of management. Contrary to the scientific management theory that managers were motivated by financial incentives and made rational, optimal decisions, decision-making theory proposed that managers were constrained by limited information, time, resources, pressures, and mental capabilities. These constraints mean that decision makers adopt a **bounded rationality** perspective and choose to **satisfice** (derived from *satisfy* and *suffice*)—to make satisfactory decisions rather than optimal ones. Bounded rationality theory holds that managers only know some of the possible decision alternatives and will settle for adequate solutions. This theory has been extended to the use of standard operating procedures, goal setting, and professionalization (Burns, Bradley, and Weiner 2020).

Institutional Theory

Institutional theory arose from applying a sociological view of adaptation to organizational behavior and reactions to internal and external factors. This theory proposes that organizations survive by gaining and sustaining legitimacy within the social, political, and economic systems that form their environmental context. Three key factors drive institutional conformity (Scott 2016):

- *Regulative pressures.* These are the formal and legally codified laws and regulations and the use of coercive force for compliance (e.g., nursing licensure laws—things that must be done).
- *Normative pressures.* These are the expectations and attitudes within the social context and use social pressures to indicate what is accepted and appropriate (e.g., certification of physicians—things that should be done).
- *Cognitive pressures.* These are conceptual beliefs and perceptions of reality that are valued (e.g., that the merger of health systems will achieve efficiency).

As a result of these pressures, firms' processes and structures often become similar as companies seek greater legitimacy—a phenomenon called **mimetic isomorphism** (Burns, Bradley, and Weiner 2020).

Chapter Summary

Organizations frequently struggle with their employee relationships. Human relationships matter a great deal to organizations, as they are a key factor in productivity. Early management theorists often ignored the human relations aspect of business while seeking to explain how organizations could best be

bounded rationality
The idea that individuals' decision-making is constrained by available information, their cognitive limits, and the time they have to make decisions.

satisfice
To make a decision that is acceptable or adequate, rather than optimal. A portmanteau of *satisfy* and *suffice*.

mimetic isomorphism
In institutional theory, the tendency of an organization to imitate other organizations in its environment in an effort to gain legitimacy.

structured and operated. Weber crafted rules for an ideal bureaucracy, which became the foundation for most public administration and civil service systems. Others formulated principles of management to derive efficient and effective business practices.

In the 1940s, Maslow and others began to explore what motivates employees. Maslow's hierarchy of needs grouped workers' needs into five levels, with the highest—self-actualization—said to be unachievable until lower-level deficiency needs are met.

Other theories evolved to address the human relations aspect of work, including theory X and theory Y, which are contrasting manager perspectives of employees. The contingency approach informs managers that effective management style and organizational structure change depending on the firm's internal and external conditions. Companies with a greater fit with these conditions have a greater likelihood of success. Along with this, the open systems theory, resource dependency theory, and institutional theory suggested that organizations are subject to pressures in and influences by their environments. Decision-making theory suggests that managers do not necessarily optimize decisions but—because of constraints on information, capabilities, and time—will make decisions that satisfice.

All these theories have contributed greatly to the modern theories of organizational behavior and are the foundation of the leadership and management perspectives discussed in the remainder of this book. Later chapters will explore the application and practice of these theories and behaviors in healthcare at the individual, group, and organizational levels.

Chapter Questions

1. How might the components and application of the principles of bureaucracy in a public health agency benefit the community?
2. What is a hierarchical structure?
3. How does the coordinative principle differ from the scalar principle? How could they conflict?
4. Maslow divided human needs into five categories and contended that lower-level needs have to be met before someone can achieve the highest need of self-actualization. Describe a situation in which this hierarchy holds. Describe one in which it might not hold.
5. Would a manager with a theory X perception of workers give more or less responsibility to employees? Why?
6. The contingency approach suggests that a firm will be more successful when what occurs?

7. Open systems theory suggests that the external environment affects a company's ability to function. Identify any similarities between the contingency approach and open systems theory.
8. Why would all four resource factors (valuable, rare, difficult to imitate, and nonsubstitutable) have to exist to maintain a strategic advantage from a resource?
9. What is the difference between making an optimal decision and one that satisfices?
10. Describe an example of mimetic isomorphism in healthcare.

Chapter Cases

Nepotism at Central Illinois Community Hospital

Central Illinois Community Hospital is a new 67-bed acute care hospital in semirural Redmon, Illinois. The hospital—the first in the county—was planned and financed by a community board. The first executive the community board hired was Syd Baker, as CEO. Syd had been a successful pharmacist in town and is respected by many. Because his family has lived in the area for generations, he is also related to a large portion of the county's small population.

Immediately on accepting the role, Syd was swamped by requests for positions. One board member joked that Syd probably had enough relatives to staff the entire hospital. Other prominent community members are also lobbying to hold positions of responsibility in the new hospital because of their status and political connections in the county. Syd has concerns about showing favoritism to any group, especially his relatives.

At the first board meeting (at which his second cousin presided as board chair), Syd proposes a set of hiring policies for the new hospital. He suggests creating job descriptions for each position, which would establish minimum degree and experience requirements. The hiring process for each department head will involve a panel composed of the human resources director, one board member, and Syd. In addition, he proposes the following nepotism policy, which will apply to all new hires:

Nepotism Policy

It is the goal of this policy to avoid creating or maintaining circumstances in which the appearance or possibility of favoritism, conflicts, or management disruptions exist. The hospital will not allow related* persons to be hired into or to work in the following conditions:

1. Related individuals may not work under the supervision of the same manager.

2. Assignments may not create a supervisor/subordinate relationship with a related individual.
3. Individuals may not supervise or evaluate a relation.
4. Work relationships will not create an adverse impact on work productivity or performance.
5. Work relationships may not create an actual or perceived conflict of interest.
6. Employees may not audit or review in any manner a related individual's work.
7. No individual may be employed at the hospital if anyone related to the individual serves on the hospital's Board or on any Committee or Council which has authority to review or order personnel actions or wage and salary adjustments which could affect the individual's job.

*For purposes of this policy, "related" persons shall include relationships established by blood, marriage, or legal action. Examples include the employee's spouse, parent, grandparent, child, grandchild, or sibling, including in-law or step-relations, as well as the employee's niece, nephew, uncle, aunt, and similar relations.

After Syd proposes the policy, one board member says that the new hospital should be an innovative, adaptive organization and this kind of policy will turn it into a bureaucracy. The board member then launches into a story about how the hospital in the neighboring county refused to take responsibility for billing errors and how its policies had prohibited the hospital from helping his family members receive the care and respectful treatment they deserved.

The rest of the board seems to agree with the member's comments, but no action is taken and the meeting adjourns. Syd is now left wondering what he should do.

Source: Nepotism policy adapted from Northeast Institute for Quality Community Action (2015).

Case Questions
1. Would establishing a nepotism policy create a bureaucracy?
2. Is a bureaucracy necessarily bad?
3. How could Syd convince the board that a nepotism policy would protect the hospital and promote general goodwill and productivity?
4. If a nepotism policy were necessary, how could Syd make certain that it would not have negative effects on the organization?

Believing Theory Y but Living Theory X
When Elizabeth was interviewed for the manager position at Stonybrook Medical Clinic, she was asked what management style she used. She had

recently graduated with a master's in business administration from Stonybrook College, and in her organizational behavior class she had learned about theory X and theory Y. She told the interviewer that she believed people should be trusted and engaged and that she was a theory Y manager. She was hired and started work a month ago.

Elizabeth's boss, James, is now asking for improved productivity from her staff. He says times are tough and if Elizabeth wants to receive a good year-end review she must quickly increase productivity by 20 percent. Elizabeth and James discussed the reasons for the staff's low productivity and have concluded that many of the workers were just lazy. They seem to call in sick more often on Fridays and Mondays than on other days. They also seem to be surfing the internet and using social media on their smartphones more often than doing their work. Elizabeth and James have concluded that the best way to get productivity up is to institute a series of controls: All employees must begin documenting their activities and must ask permission to go anywhere outside their work area.

Case Questions
1. How are Elizabeth and James living theory X?
2. What could they have done from a theory Y perspective?
3. Why do managers often implement controls that are based on a theory X perspective?

Chapter Activity

Applying Management Theories

1. Break into evenly sized teams, with each team representing one of the theories outlined in this chapter. You might have, for example, teams representing Maslow's hierarchy of needs, Fayol's administrative theory, the contingency approach, the Hawthorne studies, Weber's bureaucracy theory, and the decision-making theory. Any of the theories will work.
2. Next, read the following scenario and consider it in terms of the theory your team represents:

Conrad manages a dermatology clinic—part of a much larger group of outpatient clinics—in southern Florida. It seems as though he constantly needs the help of the information technology (IT) team to update and maintain their old, outdated computers. Physicians and other staff members regularly complain that their equipment is too slow or does not work the way they expect. To get IT's help,

Conrad has to complete a work request via an online system. The request makes its way to the IT department and a technician is assigned. It often takes hours, sometimes days, before someone shows up.

Conrad, however, is clever. He has found a technician or two whom he really likes, and he has learned that if he offers them a small token of appreciation when they show up—say, a couple of movie tickets—they come much quicker the next time he needs their help. Conrad has learned how to best work within the system he was given to get the job done.

3. As a team, discuss the story using the theoretical frame your team represents.
4. Return to the full class group and share the theory your team represents, along with some of the points your team considered.

References

AMN Healthcare. 2021. "Survey: Provider Burnout and Disengagement Seen as Most Potentially Disruptive Forces in Healthcare." Published March 16. https://ir.amnhealthcare.com/press-releases/press-releases-details/2021/Survey-Provider-Burnout-and-Disengagement-Seen-as-Most-Potentially-Disruptive-Forces-in-Healthcare/default.aspx.

Archibald, M. E. 2017. "Line-Staff Organization." *Britannica*. Published November 20. www.britannica.com/topic/line-staff-management.

Barney, J. B., and W. S. Hesterly. 2018. *Strategic Management and Competitive Advantage: Concepts and Cases*, 6th ed. Upper Saddle River, NJ: Pearson Education.

Boundless. 2021. "The Human Side: Hawthorne." *Boundless Management*, version 10. http://oer2go.org/mods/en-boundless/www.boundless.com/management/textbooks/boundless-management-textbook/organizational-theory-3/behavioral-perspectives-30/the-human-side-hawthorne-170-8381/index.html.

Boxer, M. 2019. "Three Emerging Leader Qualities That Guarantee Success." *Managed Healthcare Executive* 29 (5): 3. www.managedhealthcareexecutive.com/view/three-emerging-leader-qualities-guarantee-success.

Burns, L. R., E. H. Bradley, and B. J. Weiner. 2020. *Shortell and Kaluzny's Health Care Management: Organization Design and Behavior*, 7th ed. Boston, MA: Cengage Learning.

Carroll, L. 2020. "More Than a Third of U.S. Healthcare Costs Go to Bureaucracy." *Reuters*. Published January 6. www.reuters.com/article/us-health-costs-administration/more-than-a-third-of-u-s-healthcare-costs-go-to-bureaucracy-idUSKBN1Z5261.

Cooley, S. 2016. "Human Relations Theory of Organizations." In *Global Encyclopedia of Public Administration, Public Policy, and Governance*, edited by A. Farazmand. Cham, Switzerland: Springer. https://doi.org/10.1007/978-3-319-31816-5_2998-1.

Goldberg, C. 2020. "Boston Hospital Leader: U.S. Health Care Has a Bureaucracy Problem." *WBUR* (Boston), January 17. www.wbur.org/commonhealth/2020/01/17/tufts-hospital-administrative-complexity.

Harter, J. 2020. "U.S. Employee Engagement Reverts Back to Pre-COVID-19 Levels." Gallup *Workplace* (blog). Published October 16. www.gallup.com/workplace/321965/employee-engagement-reverts-back-pre-covid-levels.aspx.

Himmelstein, D. U., T. Campbell, and S. Woolhandler. 2020. "Healthcare Administrative Costs in the United States and Canada, 2017." *Annals of Internal Medicine* 172 (2): 134–42. https://doi.org/10.7326/m19-2818.

Hospital News. 2015. "A Hidden Truth: Hostility in Healthcare." Updated August 25. https://hospitalnews.com/a-hidden-truth-hostility-in-healthcare/.

Jouany, V., and M. Mäkipää. 2021. "8 Employee Engagement Statistics You Need to Know in 2021." Smarp. Published January 4. https://blog.smarp.com/employee-engagement-8-statistics-you-need-to-know.

Longest, B. B. 1996. *Health Professionals in Management*. Stamford, CT: Appleton & Lange.

Lutgen-Sandvik, P., and V. McDermott. 2008. "The Constitution of Employee-Abusive Organizations: A Communication Flows Theory." *Communication Theory* 18 (2): 304–33. https://doi.org/10.1111/j.1468-2885.2008.00324.x.

Mintzberg, H. 1979. *The Structuring of Organizations*. Englewood Cliffs, NJ: Prentice-Hall.

Mooney, J., and A. Reiley. 1939. *The Principles of Organization*. New York: Harper & Brothers.

Northeast Institute for Quality Community Action. 2015. "Draft Nepotism Policy." Accessed May 27, 2021. http://niqca.org/documents/Draft_Nepotism_Policy.pdf.

Ortiz-Ospina, E. 2020. "How Do People Across the World Spend Their Time and What Does This Tell Us About Living Conditions?" Our World in Data. Published December 8. https://ourworldindata.org/time-use-living-conditions.

Pfeffer, J. 1982. *Organizations and Organization Theory*. Marshfield, MA: Pitman.

Reeves, M., E. Wesselink, and K. Whitaker. 2020. "The End of Bureaucracy, Again?" Boston Consulting Group. Published July 27. www.bcg.com/publications/2020/changing-business-environment-pushing-end-to-bureaucracy.

Scott, W. R. (ed.). 2016. *Organizational Sociology*. London: Taylor & Francis.

University of Arkansas for Medical Sciences (UAMS). 2019. "Nursing Position Description Form." Revised April. https://nurses.uams.edu/wp-content/uploads/sites/76/2019/06/RN-I-PCQ-new-form.pdf.

US Bureau of Labor Statistics. 2021. "What Rehabilitation Counselors Do." *Occupational Outlook Handbook.* Modified April 9. www.bls.gov/ooh/community-and-social-service/rehabilitation-counselors.htm#tab-2.

Weber, M. 1958. *From Max Weber: Essays in Sociology,* translated and edited by H. Gerth and C. Mills. New York: Oxford University Press.

Woodward, J. 1958. *Management and Technology.* London: Her Majesty's Stationary Office.

CHAPTER 3

SUPPORTING DIVERSITY, EQUITY, AND INCLUSION

> The COVID-19 pandemic that swept across the globe in 2020 highlighted and exacerbated the long-standing ethnic and cultural inequities in the United States, as Blacks, Latinos, and Native Americans died at disproportionately high rates. These populations were three times more likely to be infected with the coronavirus and almost twice as likely to die of COVID-19. In some states the differences were even more startling: In Illinois, Latinos were seven times more likely to be infected than white people. In California, the death rate for Pacific Islanders was 2.6 times that of other groups. (Asian Americans, who have the lowest age-related death rate from COVID-19 in the United States, are not part of that group.) In New Mexico, Native Americans, only 11 percent of the state's population, accounted for more than half of COVID-19 cases. These alarming differences reflect disparities in poverty rates, greater likelihood of working low-paid "essential" jobs, lower rates of health insurance, and higher incidences of chronic medical conditions (Wen and Sadeghi 2020).

Learning Objectives

After studying this chapter, readers should be able to

- analyze the concepts of diversity, equity, and inclusion and their importance to organizations;
- identify the problems created by ethnocentrism and suggest ways to address them;
- differentiate among the generations and their cultures and values;
- define affirmative action and summarize why an organization may engage in affirmative action; and
- formulate ideas for increasing diversity, equity, and inclusion in the workplace.

Key Terms

- affirmative action
- baby boomers
- collective cultures
- cultural competence
- diversity
- diversity management
- ethnocentrism
- Generation X
- Generation Z (post-millennials)
- individualistic cultures
- intersectionality
- millennials

cultural competence
"A set of congruent behaviors, attitudes and policies that come together in a system, agency, or amongst professionals and enables that system, agency or those professionals to work effectively in cross-cultural situations" (Cross et al. 1989).

Cultural competence has been defined by Cross and colleagues (1989, 13) as "a set of congruent behaviors, attitudes and policies that come together in a system, agency, or amongst professionals and enables that system, agency or those professionals to work effectively in cross-cultural situations." Cultural competence enables healthcare workers to effectively care for patients from diverse backgrounds in ways that incorporate the patient's personal values, beliefs, and social circumstances. The continued significant inequities and health disparities in the United States are evidence of the need to develop greater cultural competence in the healthcare workforce.

A systematic approach to achieving diversity, equity, and inclusion goals involves using organizational leadership and diversity management to create high-functioning teams that work to achieve those goals. When considering a systematic approach, we must consider how the parts within the system can be integrated to solve problems and reach a strategic diversity goal—in healthcare, that goal is the health of all the people in all our communities. Healthcare in the United States is transactional, moving a huge volume of people from varied backgrounds through the system, and a major source of employment; so healthcare organizations must consider both patient and workforce diversity.

Healthcare workers must adopt attitudes, skills, and beliefs that allow them to work effectively in multidisciplinary teams, which is most achievable when leadership teams adopt cultural diversity as an organizational imperative. Patients and employees alike must understand their role, and the promotion of diversity, equity, and inclusion must become a core tenet of the organization for this to be most successful (Dreachslin, Gilbert, and Malone 2012).

diversity
An employee population characterized by a wide array of differences and similarities.

Diversity has become almost a buzzword in most industries, but this does not diminish the value and benefits it can bring to an organization. **Diversity** in the workplace means an employee population characterized by a wide array of differences and similarities. Workforce diversity is typically considered in terms of seven characteristics. All of these dimensions overlap and intersect in healthcare (Dreachslin, Gilbert, and Malone 2012).

Diversity is about having and valuing differences. Because each person is a unique individual with a distinct culture, background, and identity, diversity is relative to the degree of similarity and difference between the people involved. Cultural and ethnic diversity influence how people see themselves and how they interact with others in work settings (Patrick and Kumar 2012). Inclusion is a partner to diversity, recognizing individuals' strengths and differences and using those strengths and differences as a group or organization. The attitudes and beliefs of a healthcare workforce influence how patient care is structured and delivered, and if not managed properly, may increase health disparities for certain patient populations.

Several industry observers produce lists of the most diverse organizations as a way to promote diversity and to provide benchmarks for other organizations. For example, Exhibit 3.1 shows the 2019 workforce diversity statistics for Stryker Corporation, a medical supply company employing a number of talented, diverse individuals at all levels. The study found Stryker the "#1 Best Workplace for Diversity." One employee commented in the survey, "Diversity is great. Seeing women in higher roles is encouraging. A lot of opportunities for individuals that are eager to grow. They also care about you personally, not just as a worker, but as a human being" (*Fortune* 2020). What is evident in the illustration, however, is that Stryker's diversity percentages are still low relative to the makeup of the general

The Diversity Pipeline Program at Cleveland Clinic

In 2019, Dr. Tomislav Mihaljevic, CEO and president of Cleveland Clinic, pledged that within five years the organization would "have leadership that fully reflects the diversity of those they lead" (Mihaljevic 2019). The clinic also joined the Time's Up Healthcare movement, which is dedicated to fighting sexual harassment and gender discrimination, as part of an overall drive toward "the goal of a safe, respectful, and equitable workplace."

According to the Cleveland Clinic website, an Office of Diversity and Inclusion promotes an inclusive culture in the organization, with particular attention to employee resources that support language enrichment programs and cultural competence training. A supplier diversity initiative provides opportunities to businesses owned by minorities, women, and members of the LGBTQ community, to name a few. Of significant note are the resources provided to underrepresented students interested in healthcare careers.

Cleveland Clinic's diversity pipeline program offers students from historically Black colleges and universities and the Hispanic Association of Colleges and Universities opportunities to participate in STEMM (science, technology, engineering, math and medicine) programs that provide team-based experiential learning and career coaching. This enables Cleveland Clinic to manage their talent pipeline, recruit from a more diverse pool of candidates, and better meet the needs of their patient populations. The organization has also implemented culturally specific service lines that connect LGBTQ and Latino community members with health providers.

EXHIBIT 3.1
Workforce Diversity at Stryker in 2019

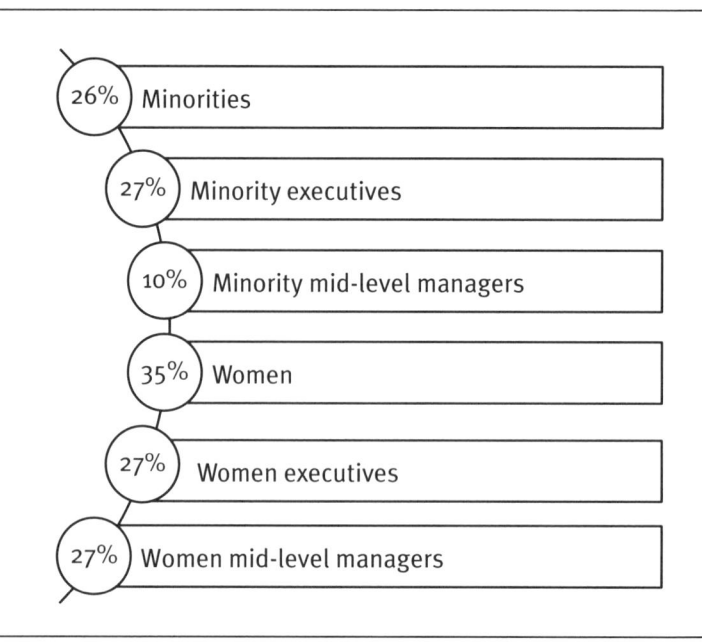

- 26% Minorities
- 27% Minority executives
- 10% Minority mid-level managers
- 35% Women
- 27% Women executives
- 27% Women mid-level managers

Source: Data from *Fortune* (2020).

population. This disparity underlines the challenges associated with recruiting and retaining a diverse workforce.

A similar evaluation by DiversityInc that scored organizations in four areas—talent pipeline, talent development, leadership commitment, and supplier diversity—ranked the following hospitals and health systems among the most diverse (Paavola 2019):

- Cleveland Clinic (Cleveland, Ohio)
- Northwell Health (New Hyde Park, New York)
- Moffitt Cancer Center (Tampa, Florida)
- Henry Ford Health System (Detroit)
- NYU Langone Health (New York City)

Attention to diversity, equity, and inclusion has increased in recent years. Because of globalization, many large organizations have a diverse workforce. Changes in the racial and ethnic makeup of many countries' populations, due to increases in immigration and rising numbers of expatriate workers, are directly reflected in the healthcare organizations that operate in those countries. For example, in the Middle East, more than three-quarters of healthcare professionals are nonnationals (expatriates) and large healthcare organizations often employ staff from as many as 50 countries (Whitman 2015). Likewise, the United States has become a more diverse nation. US Census

Bureau population estimates as of July 2019 show that 40 percent of the US population describes their origin as something other than "White alone, not Hispanic or Latino"; by 2060, that figure is projected to grow to more than 55 percent (US Census Bureau 2020).

Cultural, Racial, and Ethnic Diversity

Culture, race, and ethnicity are overlapping aspects of diversity. Race is associated with appearance or physical traits; however, no biological basis exists for racial classification. Instead, race is a socially defined concept—an attempt to segregate humans based on skin color or other physical differences (Goodman 2020; Nittle 2021). Race and ethnicity overlap. Ethnicity is a term used to identify group characteristics such as a common language, behavioral norms, worldview, nationality, cultural heritage, ancestry, religion, dress, and customs (Nittle 2021).

Culture is associated with behaviors and practices. Art, music, dance, customs, and habits are part of culture. It passes from generation to generation in a nonbiological way. Culture includes material objects and artifacts such as tools and jewelry. All of these manifestations of culture—material, spiritual, customs, and processes—link together (Mironenko and Sorokin 2018).

People frequently try to distill race and ethnicity into smaller categories. For example, the US government has established the following six categories for its collection of data on race and ethnicity (Pew Research Center 2020b):

- *American Indian or Alaska Native.* A person with origins in any of the original peoples of North and South America (including Central America) and who maintains tribal affiliation or community attachment.

> **The Racial Justice Movement in 2020**
>
> In the shadow of the surging COVID-19 pandemic in 2020, the prominently reported deaths of Black men and women at the hands of US police, and the subsequent public protests, raised awareness of the Black Lives Matter campaign. The deaths of civil rights activists John Lewis and C. T. Vivian, who both began their crusades for equality in the 1960s, further amplified the public dialogue. Most Americans expressed support for the Black Lives Matter movement in 2020. The Pew Research Center (2020a) reported that 67 percent of all adults strongly or somewhat supported the movement. That included 60 percent of white, 86 percent of Black, 77 percent of Hispanic, and 75 percent of Asian adults.
>
> Just a few years earlier, White Coats for Black Lives (2015), a medical student–run organization, suggested four ways for physicians and other health professionals to support racial justice: recruiting, supporting, and promoting Black, Latino, and Native American people in medicine; eliminating implicit racial biases in the care of patients of color; advocating for a single-payer healthcare system to eliminate cost barriers to accessing care; and working to "alter socioeconomic and environment factors, including structural racism, that directly affect our patients' health."
>
> The events of 2020 brought with them a focus on racial diversity. Many organizations—including those in the healthcare industry—began to look more closely at their diversity, equity, and inclusion policies.

- *Asian.* A person with origins in any of the original peoples of the Far East, Southeast Asia, or the Indian subcontinent.
- *Black or African American.* A person with origins in any of the Black racial groups of Africa.
- *Hispanic or Latino.* A person of Cuban, Mexican, Puerto Rican, South or Central American, or other Spanish culture origin, regardless of race.
- *Native Hawaiian or Pacific Islander.* A person with origins in any of the original peoples of Hawaii, Guam, or other Pacific Islands.
- *White.* A person with origins in any of the original peoples of Europe, the Middle East, or North Africa.

The generality of these categories points to the problem of classifying individuals in a work setting. People who fall into one of these groups may have cultures, backgrounds, and perspectives that are dramatically different from those of other members in the group. Lumping individuals into such broad categories allows stereotyping, which, as described in chapter 9, can lead to serious misconceptions and even prejudice. Organizations need to understand diverse cultural orientations within singular-appearing categories and welcome the differences.

ethnocentrism
The "exaggerated tendency to think the characteristics of one's own group or race are superior to those of other groups or races" (Hofstede 1984, 25).

individualistic cultures
Cultures that value loose social relationships that encourage individuals to take responsibility for themselves and their relatives.

collective cultures
Cultures that emphasize group responsibility to protect and care for their communities.

Ethnocentrism

People commonly cluster into groups and distinguish between their "in" groups and outsiders. Although more cohesive cultures can contain both "in" and "out" populations, the danger of ethnocentrism results. **Ethnocentrism** is the "exaggerated tendency to think the characteristics of one's own group or race are superior to those of other groups or races" (Hofstede 1984, 25). If not addressed appropriately, ethnocentrism can lead to implicit or explicit segregation, racism, and discrimination.

Ethnocentrism includes the idea that the culture of using a fork or spoon to eat is better or worse than chopsticks. Families who suggest their neighbors are "different" in a demeaning way exhibit ethnocentrism. A discussion of "Western medicine" versus "traditional Chinese medicine" may lead to an argument that one is better than the other. Ethnocentrism among coworkers contributes to conflict and poor productivity.

Individualistic and Collective Cultures

Exhibit 3.2 shows the major cultural differences among the three most populous countries in the world. One major difference stems from the relative value placed on individualism versus collectivism. **Individualistic cultures** value loose social relationships that encourage individuals to take responsibility for themselves and their relatives. **Collective cultures** emphasize group responsibility to protect and care for their communities. The United States

China:	Respect, obedience, humility, group loyalty, importance of personal connections, and ordered hierarchy	
India:	Collectivism, fatalism, hierarchy, and duty	
USA:	Individualism, freedom and equality, pragmatism, and achievement and material gain	

EXHIBIT 3.2 Major Cultural Values of Select Countries

Source: Osland et al. (2007).

has a relatively individualistic culture, whereas countries in Asia and the Middle East have highly collective cultures. Individualism in the United States can be seen in workers who promote their self-interests and organizations through active office politics. In contrast, collectivism encourages workers to seek the good of the group and self-sacrifice.

Misperceptions can occur when a person from an individualistic culture encounters someone from a collectivist culture. For example, some people may perceive those from Asian cultures as quiet, passive, and nonconfrontational when they act on their culture of maintaining harmony, valuing the opinions of others, and doing what is best for the group. Rather than being unengaged, their behavior may reflect their backgrounds and be appropriate from their perspective.

Gender and Age Diversity

Diversity is also often expressed in terms of gender and age. A fundamental and pervasive workplace diversity issue involves gender. Although women participate in most professions and workplace settings, significant barriers in corporate cultures remain, impeding women from entering leadership positions. These barriers have been static for decades because of men's failure to recognize and remove these impediments. In a McKinsey & Company (2014) survey, three-fourths of men thought having diverse leadership teams with significant numbers of women improved company outcomes, but a strong majority of men failed to recognize the challenges women face in reaching leadership positions.

Globally, even in traditionally conservative countries, increasing gender diversity is seen as positive and desired. A survey of 3,000 women and men across the United Arab Emirates (UAE), the Kingdom of Saudi Arabia (KSA), and Egypt points out the following (PwC Middle East 2019):

- 56 percent of women felt they were treated equally to men when it came to promotions.

- 64 percent of those from UAE and 60 percent from KSA suggested national programs were in place to support women through their careers; a smaller percentage (48 percent) from Egypt agreed with this statement.
- The Saudi government has a target to increase women's participation in the workforce to 30 percent by 2030. That number was 14.2 percent in 1900 and 22.3 percent in 2018.

The Foundation of the American College of Healthcare Executives (2019) surveyed 647 people in 2018 to evaluate the impact of 28 pro-diversity initiatives on women executives' views about their workplace. Participants were asked to share "(1) their feelings about whether their organizations had gender equity, (2) their satisfaction with their current positions and (3) their plans to remain with their organizations in the coming year." The study authors found that women executives viewed their workplace more positively when a zero-tolerance policy for sexual harassment was in place, opportunities existed to develop senior executives, and short lists for senior executive positions were required to include women candidates. The survey results also indicated significant disparities in how men and women perceived and experienced diversity in their workplace:

- Eighty-eight percent of men, but only 64 percent of women, agreed with the statement: "All in all I think there is gender equity in my organization."
- Eighty-six percent of women, but only 62 percent of men, felt that an effort should be made to increase the percentage of women in senior healthcare management positions.
- Sixty-nine percent of men, but only 38 percent of women felt that, based on their own experiences, healthcare workplaces are better at providing fair opportunities to women executives than they were five years ago.

The study authors further pointed out the large work pool represented by women—three-quarters of the current healthcare workforce—and the need for talented leaders in the coming years, as a generation of senior leaders will soon retire. They also argued that organizations with women in senior leadership roles outperformed their peers financially. In addition, studies suggest the current generation of future healthcare executives expect a greater degree of gender equity (Rau and Williams 2017). According to the Foundation of the American College of Healthcare Executives (2019), suggestions for recruiting and retaining women include

- setting target goals for hiring and promoting women,
- having succession plans in place,

- including women on key committees,
- offering formal career development programs,
- developing mentoring programs that pair women with senior executives, and
- seeking to have more women on boards.

Studies in the United States point to the advantages of having women in leadership positions, particularly as CEOs. Firms with women in top leadership positions tend to employ more women, be more productive, and support higher pay for women in top positions (Flabbi et al. 2016). However, a study of firms of all sectors and sizes throughout California found that women are less likely to lead large and higher performing firms, and more likely to be in charge of firms that are less stable, supporting the idea of a "glass cliff"—where women who achieve leadership roles are more likely to do so in risky situations where the chance of failure is higher (Sanchez and Frey 2019).

Age differences are also important to address in today's multigenerational workforce. Economic factors in most of the industrialized world are encouraging older employees to remain in the workforce longer and, as a result, will increase the number of generations working together. A generation is defined as roughly the first two decades of a person's life, when core values and attitudes are formed (Delcampo et al. 2011). Generational values influence how employees are motivated. Without an understanding of those values, these motivations can create conflict between workers from different generations.

Generational Differences

The Pew Research Center (Fry 2020) describes four generations that currently make up the workforce:

- **Baby boomers.** Born between 1946 and 1964, members of this generation are products of post–World War II optimism and are known for challenging traditions and conventions. Boomers tend to remain employed or pursue new careers late in life. They may appear highly eccentric and less competent to younger generations.
    - Positive attributes: accountability, adaptability, clear communication, initiative, organizational management, problem-solving, service orientation, collaborative skills
    - Weaknesses: desire for instant gratification, ignorance of new technology, lack of appreciation for diversity
- **Generation X.** Born between 1965 and 1980, this generation lived their adolescence during a time of failing schools and marriages.

baby boomers
The generation born between 1946 and 1964. Adaptable and unconventional, boomers tend to maintain active careers longer than previous generations.

Generation X
The generation born between 1965 and 1980. Gen Xers tend to seek job security and push for efficiency and innovation.

They learned to distrust institutions, prefer entrepreneurship, and lack corporate loyalty. Gen Xers seek job security, but their risky behaviors clash with younger people. They also push for efficiency and innovation by negotiating their own deals. They tend to switch employers frequently.
- Positive attributes: adaptability, initiative, resource management and problem-solving skills, knowledge of technology, appreciation for diversity
- Weaknesses: lack of organizational management skills, service orientation, collaborative skills, and corporate loyalty

- **Millennials.** Born between 1981 and about 1996 (definitions vary), members of this generation are more aligned with teamwork and less risk-seeking than Gen Xers, and they value work–life balance. Many have become more traditional than the preceding generations. Millennials adhere to community norms; favor rituals; demonstrate loyalty to friends, family, and community; and seek community building. They tend to be confident, trusting, and teachable at work. Conversely, they may be seen as pampered, risk-averse, and dependent and thus may require more consistent feedback and direction.
  - Positive attributes: accountability, organizational management skills, service orientation, knowledge of technology, appreciation for diversity, collaborative skills
  - Weaknesses: lack of communication skills, problem-solving ability, and corporate loyalty; excessive dependence on technology

> **millennials**
> The generation born between 1981 and about 1996. Millennials tend to be risk-averse and value teamwork and work–life balance.

- **Generation Z (post-millennials).** Members of this generation, born after about 1996, are the most recent generation to enter the workforce. This generation is the first to grow up with the internet; as a result, they tend to be comfortable with technology. Post-millennial households are significantly nontraditional, with many members of this generation coming from multiracial and single-parent families. They represent the country's changing ethnic and racial background. Most post-millennials place a high value on education. They will likely be the best-educated generation yet (Dimock 2019; Parker and Igielnik 2020).
  - Positive attributes: technology savvy, ambitious, entrepreneurial, able to multitask, racially diverse and accepting of diversity
  - Weaknesses: possibly more cynical than earlier generations, little concept of a time before social media, too reliant on technology to solve problems

> **Generation Z**
> The generation born after about 1996. Gen Zers tend to be tech savvy, and place a high value on diversity and education.

Understanding backgrounds that are different from ours allows us to interpret others' behavior based on their—instead of our—cultural norms.

Racial and Ethnic Disparities in Healthcare

The World Health Organization (WHO) argues "it is not sufficient to protect or improve the average health of the population, if—at the same time—inequality worsens or remains high because the gain accrues disproportionately to those already enjoying better health." Good health, according to the WHO, is the "best attainable average level" and the "smallest feasible differences among individuals and groups" (WHO 2000). The differences among individuals or groups are, in many cases, health disparities. Disparities occur as a result of discrimination and bias based on race, ethnicity, socioeconomic status, age, location, gender, disability status, and sexual orientation (Orgera and Artiga 2020).

The healthcare industry and the United States as a whole are affected by health disparities, which limit the quality of care for all and create a huge financial burden on society. A 2018 analysis estimated that health disparities resulted in $93 billion in excess medical care costs and $42 billion in lost productivity each year. The economy also suffers due to premature deaths (Turner 2018).

The Agency for Healthcare Research and Quality ([AHRQ] 2020)

This helps us perceive actual motives and rationale while avoiding stereotyping, misperceptions, and false attributions of behavior. Healthcare managers may need to redesign work and roles to accommodate generational differences and expectations to avoid a future shortage of healthcare professionals (Dreachslin, Gilbert, and Malone 2012).

COVID-19 Heightens Disparities

The Centers for Disease Control and Prevention (CDC) (2020) reported that the COVID-19 pandemic heightened the disparities of racial and ethnic minority groups and increased their risk of getting sick and dying in several ways.

- *Discrimination.* Systems meant to protect health are not always available to the poor and individuals of color. These systems include healthcare, housing, education, criminal justice, and finance.
- *Healthcare access.* Underinsured or uninsured groups have limited access to care because of difficulties with childcare, transportation, and being able to take time off work. Some distrust government and healthcare systems.
- *Occupation.* Individuals from some racial and ethnic minorities are more likely to have jobs that put them at higher risk of contracting COVID-19. Jobs at farms, factories, grocery stores, and even healthcare facilities put them at higher risk.
- *Income and education.* Lower-paying jobs that do not allow individuals to miss work, even when they are sick, put them at higher risk. Lack of income also affects access to high-quality education, limiting the potential for better jobs in the future.
- *Housing.* Some individuals from racial and ethnic minorities face crowded living conditions. Some face homelessness or live in shared housing. All of these scenarios put these individuals at higher risk.

reports that minorities consistently receive worse quality and access to healthcare than whites do. Barriers to proper healthcare arise when physicians and other health professionals lack cultural awareness, as patients' cultural values may conflict with traditional Western medicine and those conflicts can damage communication. Also, when even subtle racism exists among healthcare providers, the healthcare of minorities is marginalized (Marrone 2007).

Several models and frameworks are used to build cultural competency in healthcare providers. Campinha-Bacote (2002) offered one such model, called the Process of Cultural Competence in the Delivery of Healthcare Services. This model views cultural competence as "the ongoing process that encourages healthcare providers to continuously strive to achieve the ability to effectively work within the cultural context of the client," (181) and integrates cultural awareness, cultural knowledge, skills, encounters, and desires. Given the organic nature of setting organizations' strategic goals around cultural competence, it seems prudent to adopt physician training models that adapt to a changing workforce and allow for personal development and growth.

Evidence would suggest the key is integration of what LaVeist and Pierre (2014) called *the 3Ds*: social determinants, health disparities, and healthcare workforce diversity. Exhibit 3.3 illustrates the six public health benefits associated with a more racially and ethnically diverse workforce (LaVeist and Pierre 2014).

As reported by the Institute of Medicine (2002, 5):

> Patients' and providers' behavior and attitudes may therefore influence each other reciprocally, but reflect the attitudes, expectations, and perceptions that each has developed in a context where race and ethnicity are often more salient

EXHIBIT 3.3
Benefits of a Diverse Healthcare Workforce

- Improved quality of care by increasing patient satisfaction and trust
- Enhanced cultural competency in healthcare
- Increased healthcare access for minority patients
- Increased healthcare for geographically underserved communities
- Enhanced breadth and scope of health and healthcare research
- More minority-owned practices

Source: Adapted from LaVeist and Pierre (2014).

than these participants are even aware of. . . . Bias, stereotyping, prejudice, and clinical uncertainty on the part of healthcare providers may contribute to racial and ethnic disparities in healthcare. . . . Prejudice may stem from conscious bias, while stereotyping and biases may be conscious or unconscious, even among the well intentioned.

Intersectionality

Some groups and individuals experience the overlapping and interdependent systems of discrimination or disadvantage because of their combined characteristics of race, class, and gender. Kimberlé Crenshaw (1989) described this in her theory of **intersectionality**, which proposes that a Black woman, for example, will experience discrimination different from that experienced by a white woman or a Black man. Intersectionality is not limited to race and gender; consider how a gay white man who uses a wheelchair may be treated differently than either a gay white man with no visible disabilities or a straight white man who uses a wheelchair. While political opponents debate the significance of this concept, Crenshaw's teachings focus on the deep structural and systemic issues surrounding discrimination (Coaston 2019).

Healthcare managers employ the idea of intersectionality by viewing employee and patient experiences through an intersectional lens. They consider the combination of multiple social dynamics and power relations—the differences described by race, ethnicity, gender, age, and a variety of other characteristics. The managers then build trust and design corporate culture with an understanding of how diversity leads to the success of their organization.

Affirmative Action and Diversity Management

Many of the regulatory guidelines and laws regarding diversity evolved from legislation addressing equal employment and affirmative action. In the 1960s and 1970s, the US government created laws to help minorities receive "equal pay for equal work" and prevent race and gender discrimination. In the 1980s, affirmative action programs made discrimination illegal and set up quotas for employing members of disadvantaged groups (Woodward and Saini 2006). Affirmative action is not diversity management, however. **Affirmative action** is the development of policies or procedures that seek to improve opportunities given to groups who have experienced discrimination, especially as it relates to employment. Affirmative action is legally driven, quantitative, problem-focused, and reactive. In contrast, **diversity management** is voluntary, opportunity and benefit focused, and proactive (Digh 1998). Diversity management promotes the unique differences of people and highlights the economic benefits organizations can gain from a diverse

> **intersectionality**
> "A frame that prompts us to ask what falls between movements and what happens when . . . different systems of power and oppression overlap" (Equal Rights Trust 2016).
>
> **affirmative action**
> The development of policies or procedures that seek to improve opportunities given to groups who have experienced discrimination, especially as it relates to employment.
>
> **diversity management**
> The practice of acknowledging employees' differences and allowing employees to use these traits to achieve organizational goals.

workforce. In other words, it seeks to form a culture that acknowledges employees' differences and allows employees to use these traits to achieve organizational goals (Woodward and Saini 2006).

Fulfilling the promise of diversity requires overcoming many obstacles. Organizations simultaneously must recognize differences, address the difficulties of working together, and perhaps change long-standing practices to promote equity and inclusiveness. Diversity's benefits can be immense (Clapp 2010):

- Support for diversity, equity, and inclusion provides a strong ethical foundation for the organization.
- A diverse workforce improves organizational decision-making.
- An organizational culture that welcomes diversity can reduce conflict and improve employee communication.
- Employees in a diverse workforce may feel more connected and relevant, resulting in improved performance.
- Diverse organizations may enjoy a better relationship between the institution and its community.
- Because diversity attracts diversity, diverse organizations are better able to recruit and retain an even more diverse workforce.

Diversity problems in organizations will not be eliminated by legal and regulatory initiatives but by the active participation of healthcare leaders (Institute of Medicine 2002). The likelihood of instituting a well-functioning, diverse workforce dramatically increases with the involvement and commitment of the organization's top management. If the leaders can model behaviors and create processes that promote diversity, the rest of the organization will generally follow. A 2013 study found the most significant predictors of diversity in an organization were the characteristics of the leaders (Guerrero 2013). To fulfill this role, the Joint Commission recommends that leaders adopt the following practices (Wilson-Stronks et al. 2008):

1. Create policies and procedures that build cultural competence to meet the needs of diverse populations.
2. Collect and use data to identify and monitor health disparities in an effort to provide quality healthcare to culturally and linguistically diverse patients.
3. Develop services and activities tailored to meet the needs of diverse populations.
4. Establish collaborative practices that bring together multiple departments, organizations, providers, and individuals to devise initiatives that meet diverse patient needs.

Chapter 3: Supporting Diversity, Equity, and Inclusion

In addition, the US Department of Health and Human Services Office of Minority Health (2018) has issued guidelines in three areas—(1) governance, leadership, and workforce; (2) communication and language assistance; and (3) engagement, continuous improvement, and accountability (see exhibit 3.4).

EXHIBIT 3.4
National CLAS Standards

The National Standards for Culturally and Linguistically Appropriate Services in Health and Health Care (The National CLAS Standards) aim to improve health care quality and advance health equity by establishing a framework for organizations to serve the nation's increasingly diverse communities.

Principal Standard

1. Provide effective, equitable, understandable, and respectful quality care and services that are responsive to diverse cultural health beliefs and practices, preferred languages, health literacy and other communication needs.

Governance, Leadership and Workforce

2. Advance and sustain organizational governance and leadership that promotes CLAS and health equity through policy, practices and allocated resources.
3. Recruit, promote and support a culturally and linguistically diverse governance, leadership and workforce that are responsive to the population in the service area.
4. Educate and train governance, leadership and workforce in culturally and linguistically appropriate policies and practices on an ongoing basis.

Communication and Language Assistance

5. Offer language assistance to individuals who have limited English proficiency and/or other communication needs, at no cost to them, to facilitate timely access to all health care and services.
6. Inform all individuals of the availability of language assistance services clearly and in their preferred language, verbally and in writing.
7. Ensure the competence of individuals providing language assistance, recognizing that the use of untrained individuals and/or minors as interpreters should be avoided.
8. Provide easy-to-understand print and multimedia materials and signage in the languages commonly used by the populations in the service area.

Engagement, Continuous Improvement and Accountability

9. Establish culturally and linguistically appropriate goals, policies and management accountability, and infuse them throughout the organization's planning and operations.
10. Conduct ongoing assessments of the organization's CLAS-related activities and integrate CLAS-related measures into assessment measurement and continuous quality improvement activities.

(continued)

EXHIBIT 3.4
National CLAS Standards (Continued)

(continued from previous page)

11. Collect and maintain accurate and reliable demographic data to monitor and evaluate the impact of CLAS on health equity and outcomes and to inform service delivery.
12. Conduct regular assessments of community health assets and needs and use the results to plan and implement services that respond to the cultural and linguistic diversity of populations in the service area.
13. Partner with the community to design, implement and evaluate policies, practices and services to ensure cultural and linguistic appropriateness.
14. Create conflict- and grievance-resolution processes that are culturally and linguistically appropriate to identify, prevent and resolve conflicts or complaints.
15. Communicate the organization's progress in implementing and sustaining CLAS to all stakeholders, constituents and the general public.

Source: Reprinted from US Department of Health and Human Services Office of Minority Health (2018).

One way to stress the importance of diversity and inclusion is to create an organizational diversity statement and then take specific action toward equity. These statements often fall within or appear near a company's values statement and express how diverse employee characteristics benefit the organization. Intermountain Healthcare, a large US healthcare system in Utah, Idaho, and Nevada, reaffirmed their commitment to equity and diversity in September 2020 (exhibit 3.5). This statement came with a video and press release from the organization's CEO.

Organizations also need to align their human resources (HR) systems to promote diversity. Often, HR systems are structured to promote conformity and similarities, which help the organization apply common evaluations. As discussed in chapter 9, managers can unknowingly introduce bias into their hiring and promotion processes, as they are more likely to give positive evaluations to employees who resemble them. Such processes can seemingly

EXHIBIT 3.5
Intermountain's Push for Equity and Diversity

In September 2020, Intermountain Healthcare announced five actions the organization would take "to move equity forward in significant ways" within the organization and in the surrounding community:

1. Add equity "as both a Fundamental and a Value" of the organization.
2. Hire a chief equity officer.
3. Hire an equity advocate.
4. Dedicate funding to "support equity opportunities for current and future caregivers and to support community organizations" by allocating charitable funds to "scholarships, tuition reimbursement, fellowship stipends, and impact investments."
5. Work with other organizations to "address racism as a public health crisis."

Source: Intermountain Healthcare (2020).

benefit the organization by employing similar workers—those who "fit" the firm's culture, are expected to cause minimal conflict, and relate well to its managers. As Barnard (1938, 224) noted long ago,

> the general method of maintaining an informal executive organization is so to operate and to select and promote executives that a general condition of compatibility of personnel is maintained. . . . Men cannot be promoted or selected, or even must be relieved . . . because they "do not fit." . . . This question of "fitness" involves such matters as education, experience, age, sex, personal distinctions, prestige, race, nationality, faith, politics, sectional antecedents, and very specific personal traits as manners, speech, personal appearance, etc.

Thus, unintentionally, many organizations have created barriers to diversity. The result of many HR processes is to ensure employees fit the organization, which can create a highly homogeneous work environment where conformity is valued. But some would argue that "misfit" is more beneficial to the success of an organization (Mickos 2020). HR managers must understand how policies might negatively affect diversity and seek to change those that do. These changes are frequently difficult, as "diversity is not a problem to be solved, but an ongoing and lengthy process" that comes into existence with "small, everyday actions taken by people at all levels of the organization" (Kreitz 2008, 104). No single best way exists to create an inclusive culture that values diversity; suffice it to say here that the full organization must be involved.

Federal, State, and Private Resources to Improve Diversity

Diversity may have been driven initially by state and federal laws, but the positive

---

Diversity, Equity, and Inclusion at Work

Here are a few examples of organizations that promote diversity, equity, and inclusion in their workforce.

- As of June 2020, Chevron states on its website that it is committed to its own diversity program and the diversity programs of its suppliers. The company also states that it will continue to fund contributions, grants, and scholarships focused on diversity. It has created videos in which Chevron employees are interviewed and tell their story about what diversity means to them.
- As of June 2020, Pinterest had created resources on its website to help parents talk to their children about diversity, equity, and inclusion issues, and provided educational information about systemic racism in the United States. It also invested resources for growing the diversity of content on its platform.
- Rather than going to more schools such as Stanford and the Massachusetts Institute of Technology, Slack recruited programmers from all-women coding camps and groups that focus on training Black and Latino programmers (Nordell 2018).
- Twitter and Square declared Juneteenth a corporate holiday to commemorate the end of slavery and show support for the Black Lives Matter movement (Givens 2020).

benefits come when it is integrated throughout the organization. This integration occurs through the strong support of management and is institutionalized by organizational policies and processes. Diversity, equity, and inclusion should become part of the organizational strategic plan, and measures should be established to hold managers accountable for meeting related goals. Recruiting, succession planning, and training should be key elements of these goals.

The following resources may help an organization meet its diversity, equity, and inclusion goals:

- *Office of Minority Health.* This office of the US Department of Health and Human Services is dedicated to improving the health of racial and ethnic minority populations through the development of health policies and programs to eliminate health disparities (https://minorityhealth.hhs.gov).
- *US Government Accountability Office.* The GAO created a helpful document entitled "State Department: Additional Steps Are Needed to Identify Potential Barriers to Diversity" (www.gao.gov/products/GAO-20-237).
- *National Academy of Medicine.* The Culture of Health Program is designed to create equitable good health across the United States (https://nam.edu/programs/culture-of-health/). The institute also published (under its previous name, the Institute of Medicine) a relevant book called *Unequal Treatment: Confronting Racial and Ethnic Disparities in Health Care* (www.nap.edu/openbook.php?record_id=12875).
- *Institute for Diversity and Health Equity.* This organization works to advance health equity, diversity, and inclusion in healthcare organizations (https://ifdhe.aha.org).

Chapter Summary

Diversity is an important concept in today's business environment. Across the globe, nations have experienced an influx of expatriate workers and immigrants, radically shifting the demographics of employees and customers. Companies have responded by identifying barriers and setting goals to increase the diversity of their workforce and meet the needs of diverse customers.

Culture and race are aspects of diversity that overlap with ethnicity. Ethnic groups have common languages, behavioral norms, worldviews, backgrounds, and ancestry. The US government has established six categories for tracking and reporting on race and ethnicity, although many variations and subdivisions are included. People should be careful when lumping others into racial and ethnic categories, as stereotyping and ethnocentrism can result.

National culture differences are expressed in what is valued by that culture. One major way national cultures differ is in the importance placed on individualism versus collectivism. Collective cultures, as seen in many Asian countries, emphasize group responsibility and accountability, while individualistic cultures, as often seen in the United States, focus on self-interest. When individuals from different cultures work together, their approaches and motivations can be misunderstood, perhaps resulting in distrust.

Gender and age are also significant diversity issues in the workplace. Although great progress has been made, significant barriers remain for women at work. These barriers tend to remain because men often do not recognize them, although most men do see the value in having more women in leadership roles.

Different generations work together but tend to have different values and motivations. Each generation has different positive attributes and weaknesses. For example, baby boomers tend to be accountable and adaptable, while Generation X values diversity and problem-solving. Understanding differences allows one to correctly interpret behaviors.

Diversity in healthcare is important, as racial and ethnic disparities continue to occur in healthcare access and outcomes. Barriers arise when providers lack cultural awareness or harbor conscious or unconscious biases.

Diversity became a more prominent issue in the workplace beginning in the 1960s because of legislation that promoted equal pay and affirmative action. But diversity management goes beyond these legal mandates; it seeks to develop a culture that promotes the unique differences of people to gain economic benefits for the firm. The benefits for a company include developing a strong ethical foundation, improving decision-making, reducing conflict, connecting employees with the organization and the community, and enhancing recruitment and retention of a diverse workforce.

To leverage diversity, organizations need the support and commitment of top management, who must model proper behaviors and create policies and processes to promote diversity. Healthcare CEOs should become their organization's chief cultural officer and work to eliminate diversity barriers that limit employee and customer satisfaction. The Joint Commission and the US Department of Health and Human Services have suggested comprehensive steps for healthcare organizations to take toward this end.

Organizations should also closely examine their HR systems and policies to be certain they promote, not restrict, diversity. Often, traditional HR practices have introduced bias in evaluations and promotions. HR managers must understand how their policies and processes affect the level of organizational diversity and adjust accordingly.

Developing a happy, productive, diverse organization is not a problem to solve; it requires deep engagement in a long process. There is no single way to undertake this journey, but ultimately everyone in the company needs to be involved and efforts must be integrated throughout the organization. Diversity, equity, and inclusion should become part of the organizational strategic plan, with measures in place to hold managers and executives accountable for meeting related goals through recruiting, succession planning, and training.

Chapter Resources

For an expanded discussion of international culture and diversity, see the following two sources:

1. *Hofstede model* (http://geert-hofstede.com/). The Hofstede model uses six dimensions to distinguish among different cultures: power distance, individualism, masculinity, uncertainty avoidance, long-term orientation, and indulgence. The website allows comparisons of countries along these dimensions.
2. *GLOBE model* (www.nnli.org/uploads/2/9/4/1/29412281/globesummary-by-michael-h-hoppe.pdf). GLOBE consists of nine dimensions that encompass societal practices and values: uncertainty avoidance, power distance, institutional collectivism, in-group collectivism, gender egalitarianism, assertiveness, future orientation, performance orientation, and humane orientation.

Chapter Questions

1. What advantages accrue with a diverse employee population?
2. What is an ethnic group?
3. How does nationality differ from ethnicity?
4. How might ethnocentrism create problems for an organization?
5. How do cultural differences influence the choices an organization may make?
6. What are the differences between generations?
7. How does affirmative action differ from diversity management?
8. How can organizations better align their HR systems to promote diversity?

Chapter Cases

Diversity Efforts at Novant Health

Novant Health—consisting of 14 medical centers, 24,000 employees, and more than 1,100 physicians across Virginia and South Carolina—seeks to become more inclusive, which would further its efforts to become a world-class healthcare system. To accomplish this goal, Novant established six diversity action committees:

1. Workforce
2. Care/Operations
3. Service Line Planning
4. Community Involvement
5. Supplier
6. Marketing and Government Relations

The manager of each area was asked to lead the relevant committee. Each committee has 8 to 12 members, who report to the manager and are considered influential. The system's chief diversity officer is also a member of each committee. Moreover, the system has eight business resource groups, chaired by management-level employees, which focus on different diversity issues: women's, generational, Asian, Black, Hispanic/Latino, LGBTQ, veterans, and people with disabilities. To integrate all of these committees, Novant created a diversity council.

Each diversity action committee has established specific goals, some of which have been used to determine bonuses. These goals include the following:

- Maintain parity in majority and minority groups.
- Reduce low-acuity emergency department visits by improving access and education regarding alternatives for low-income populations.
- Increase market share among Hispanics and Blacks by offering screening and preventive care.
- Raise the percentage of supplies purchased from diverse suppliers to above 11 percent.

Novant believes its committee structure and diversity efforts have allowed it to better fulfill its mission and serve its patients. Its leadership suggests that diversity has become an integral part of Novant's operations and is no longer confined to isolated initiatives or projects. However, Novant leadership recognizes that much could still be done to continually improve services and meet the growing needs of diverse populations.

Source: Adapted from Institute for Diversity in Health Management (2015).

Case Questions
1. What are the positive and negative aspects of creating multiple committee structures to address diversity across a large system?
2. What else could Novant do to promote diversity?

Problems in a Diverse Culture

MediHealth, a healthcare support firm in India, has experienced great growth in its business of providing coding, billing, and accounts receivable management for international firms. From a small group of 25 employees, it grew in three years to employ more than 250 people. Department cultures across the company vary widely. For example, the accounts receivable group works mostly at night and dresses casually. Workers from the billing and coding group wear more traditional dress and often use their local languages during meetings.

MediHealth's HR director, Neel, is proud of his ability to recruit qualified, productive employees and expand the workforce in an organized, constructive manner. His plan was to employ loyal workers who would stay with the firm for many years. In addition, he recruited nationally across India for diverse employees. Employees hired early on are still with the company, but the turnover rate among those hired in the past two years now exceeds the industry average, and Neel is concerned because the bulk of those leaving are hires he made specifically to increase the company's diversity. Managing MediHealth's diversity to retain these valued employees and increase their unity and productivity now seems even more important. Neel conducted an employee survey to try to understand why people are leaving, and received several comments such as these:

> I feel like a complete outsider in the company. I am from north India and do not understand the language spoken by the employees in my team. I have taken repeated initiatives to bond with the team, but I always feel like the odd one out.

> The CEO's talk about the organizational commitment to quality is a farce. (This employee also indicated that she had been passed over for a promotion and was told that because she was a woman, she would not able to complete the travel required for the new position.)

> My children's day care closes at 6:00 p.m., but if there is work, I am supposed to complete it before I go. Sometimes I also work on holidays and there is no

compensatory time off. There are all men in the top management, and no one seems to understand the issues and concerns of a woman here.

Neel is depressed and frustrated. It feels like his efforts to diversify the company are coming apart. He brought in workers with varied backgrounds from across the country, but his success at creating a diverse workforce appears short-lived.

Source: Adapted from Pant and Vijaya (2015).

Case Questions
1. What issues of diversity may be affecting turnover?
2. What could Neel do to address the concerns of his employees?

Chapter Activities

Debating Diversity
Read the summary and at least the first paragraph of the 2010 Massachusetts Institute of Technology study "Cognitive Intelligence: Number of Women in Group Linked to Effectiveness in Solving Difficult Problems" (www.sciencedaily.com/releases/2010/09/100930143339.htm).

Split into two groups and debate the issue of diversity in the workplace. Each group should defend its assigned topic in good faith. (Note: The authors suggest this exercise only as a way to debate the value of diversity.)

- Group 1: Support the idea that a diverse workforce will help organizations solve problems and be more successful. You might use a healthcare setting such as an outpatient clinic or hospital department as an example.
- Group 2: Support the idea that sometimes the best candidate for a job might not be the most diverse candidate. For example, a hospital unit where the majority of the staff are women (regardless of race or ethnicity) might ask whether a white man (the diverse candidate) would be the best fit.

Experiencing Ethnocentrism
This exercise illustrates how easily people create "in" and "out" groups and how quickly they can affect our interactions.

Preparation
This activity works best with 12 to 40 participants—enough for three to five teams.

You will need some sort of colored sticker or other quick visual identifier for each participant, in different colors for each group.

Activity
1. Randomly assign each participant to a team; for example, if you have colored dots in blue, green, yellow, and red, you might count off to break into four teams randomly assigned to each color. Do not form teams on the basis of race, ethnicity, or another obvious marginalized identity.
2. Within your teams, discuss team members' similarities and strengths (e.g., previous healthcare experience, education, age, background, talents). Choose a team name and decide how you will wear your team identifier.
3. Once each team has chosen their name and identifier, gather as a large group again so each group can explain how they identify themselves.
4. Break into teams again and discuss your team's advantages. What makes your team stand out in this group? What are the other teams' weaknesses?
5. Return to the larger group again and share your conversations about your team's special advantages compared to others. Then, as a group, examine those conversations while considering the concept of ethnocentrism. How have teams started to consider themselves exceptional or superior? Did you find yourself thinking of your team's background as "normal" and others' as "different"? Did your team make any assumptions about how other teams would behave or perform based on their self-described identity? How does this apply to bias in healthcare and in society at large?

References

Agency for Healthcare Research and Quality (AHRQ). 2020. "2018 National Healthcare Quality and Disparities Report." Updated April. www.ahrq.gov/research/findings/nhqrdr/nhqdr18/index.html.

Barnard, C. 1938. *The Functions of the Executive*. Cambridge, MA: Harvard University Press.

Campinha-Bacote, J. 2002. "The Process of Cultural Competence in the Delivery of Healthcare Services: A Model of Care." *Journal of Transcultural Nursing* 13 (3): 181–84. https://doi.org/10.1177/10459602013003003.

Centers for Disease Control and Prevention (CDC). 2020. "Health Equity Considerations and Racial and Ethnic Minority Groups." Published July 24. www.cdc.gov/coronavirus/2019-ncov/community/health-equity/race-ethnicity.html.

Clapp, J. 2010. "Diversity Leadership: The Rush University Medical Center Experience." *Hospital Topics* 88 (2): 61–66.

Coaston, J. 2019. "The Intersectionality Wars." *Vox*. Published May 29. www.vox.com/the-highlight/2019/5/20/18542843/intersectionality-conservatism-law-race-gender-discrimination.

Crenshaw, K. 1989. "Demarginalizing the Intersection of Race and Sex: A Black Feminist Critique of Antidiscrimination Doctrine, Feminist Theory and Antiracist Politics." University of Chicago Legal Forum 1989 (Article 8): 139–67. https://chicagounbound.uchicago.edu/uclf/vol1989/iss1/8.

Cross, T., B. Bazron, K. Dennis, and M. Isaacs. 1989. *Towards a Culturally Competent System of Care*, Vol. 1. Washington, DC: CASSP Technical Assistance Center. Center for Child Health and Mental Health Policy, Georgetown University Child Development Center.

Delcampo, R., L. Haggerty, M. Haney, and L. Knippel. 2011. *Managing the Multigenerational Workforce*. Farnham, UK: Grower.

Digh, P. 1998. "Coming to Terms with Diversity." *HR Magazine* 43 (12): 117–21.

Dimock, M. 2019. "Defining Generations: Where Millennials End and Generation Z Begins." Pew Research Center. Published January 17. www.pewresearch.org/fact-tank/2019/01/17/where-millennials-end-and-generation-z-begins/.

Dreachslin, J. L., M. J. Gilbert, and B. Malone. 2012. *Diversity and Cultural Competence in Health Care: A Systems Approach*. San Francisco: Jossey-Bass.

Equal Rights Trust. 2016. "Intersectionality in Promoting Equality." *Equal Rights Review* 16: 205–19. www.equalrightstrust.org/equal-rights-review-volume-sixteen-2016.

Flabbi, L., M. Macis, A. Moro, and F. Schivardi. 2016. "Do Female Executives Make a Difference? The Impact of Female Leadership on Gender Gaps and Firm Performance." NBER Working Paper Series No. 22877. Published November 30. https://doi.org/10.3386/w22877.

Fortune. 2020. "The 100 Best Workplaces for Diversity." https://fortune.com/best-workplaces-for-diversity/2019/stryker/.

Foundation of the American College of Healthcare Executives. 2019. *Addressing Gender Equity in Healthcare Organizations*. CEO Circle White Paper. Published Summer. www.ache.org/-/media/ache/learning-center/research/2019-ceo-circle-white-paper.pdf.

Fry, R. 2020. "Millennials Overtake Baby Boomers as America's Largest Generation." Pew Research Center. Published April 28. www.pewresearch.org/fact-tank/2020/04/28/millennials-overtake-baby-boomers-as-americas-largest-generation/.

Givens, D. 2020. "Twitter CEO Jack Dorsey Has Made Juneteenth an Official Corporate Holiday." *Black Enterprise*. Published June 11. www.blackenterprise.com/twitter-ceo-jack-dorsey-has-made-juneteenth-an-official-corporate-holiday/.

Goodman, A. 2020. "Race Is Real, but It's Not Genetic." *Discover*. Published June 25. www.discovermagazine.com/planet-earth/race-is-real-but-its-not-genetic.

Guerrero, E. 2013. "Workforce Diversity in Outpatient Substance Abuse Treatment: The Role of Leaders' Characteristics." *Journal of Substance Abuse* 44 (2): 208–15. https://doi.org/10.1016/j.jsat.2012.05.004.

Hofstede, G. 1984. *Culture's Consequences: International Differences in Work-Related Values.* Thousand Oaks, CA: Sage.

Institute for Diversity in Health Management (IFD). 2015. "Learning Moments Case Study Template."

Institute of Medicine. 2002. *Unequal Treatment: Confronting Racial and Ethnic Disparities in Health Care.* Published March. www.nap.edu/openbook.php?record_id=12875.

Intermountain Healthcare. 2020. "Moving Equity and Diversity Forward at Intermountain Healthcare." Published September 8. https://intermountainhealthcare.org/news/2020/09/moving-equity-and-diversity-forward-at-intermountain-healthcare/.

Kreitz, P. A. 2008. "Best Practices for Managing Organizational Diversity." *Journal of Academic Librarianship* 34 (2): 101–20.

LaVeist, T., and G. Pierre. 2014. "Integrating the 3Ds—Social Determinants, Health Disparities, and Health-Care Workforce Diversity." *Public Health Reports* 129 (1, Suppl. 2): 9–14. https://doi.org/10.1177/00333549141291S204.

Marrone, S. 2007. "Understanding Barriers to Healthcare: A Review of Disparities in Health Care Services Among Indigenous Populations." *International Journal of Circumpolar Health* 66 (3): 188–98.

McKinsey & Company. 2014. "Moving Mind-Sets on Gender Diversity." Published January 1. www.mckinsey.com/business-functions/organization/our-insights/moving-mind-sets-on-gender-diversity-mckinsey-global-survey-results.

Mickos, M. 2020. "On Diversity and Inclusion: Why the Misfit May Be the Best Fit." *Human Resources Director.* Published February 2. www.hcamag.com/us/specialization/diversity-inclusion/on-diversity-and-inclusion-why-the-misfit-may-be-the-best-fit/212223.

Mihaljevic, T. 2019. "Breaking Bias: Diversity and Inclusion in Healthcare Cannot Be Left to Chance." *Modern Healthcare.* Published May 18. www.modernhealthcare.com/opinion-editorial/breaking-bias-diversity-and-inclusion-healthcare-cannot-be-left-chance.

Mironenko, I., and P. Sorokin. 2018. "Seeking for the Definition of 'Culture': Current Concerns and Their Implications." *Nursing and Allied Health* 52 (2): 331–40. https://doi.org/10.1007/s12124-018-9425-y.

Nittle, N. 2021. "Understanding the Difference Between Race and Ethnicity." ThoughtCo. Published March 13. www.thoughtco.com/difference-between-race-and-ethnicity-2834950.

Nordell, J. 2018. "How Slack Got Ahead in Diversity." *The Atlantic.* Published April 26. www.theatlantic.com/technology/archive/2018/04/how-slack-got-ahead-in-diversity/558806/.

Orgera, K., and S. Artiga. 2020. "Disparities in Health and Health Care—Five Key Questions and Answers." We Care Healthcare. Published January 12. https://wecare-healthcare.com/index.php/2020/01/12/disparities-in-health-and-health-care-five-key-questions-and-answers/.

Osland, J., D. Kolb, I. Rubin, and M. Turner. 2007. *Organizational Behavior: An Experiential Approach*. Upper Saddle River, NJ: Prentice-Hall.

Paavola, A. 2019. "6 Most Diverse Hospitals, Health Systems." *Becker's Hospital Review*. Published May 9. www.beckershospitalreview.com/rankings-and-ratings/6-most-diverse-hospitals-health-systems.html.

Pant, J., and V. Vijaya. 2015. "Challenges in Diversity Management: A Case Study of MediHealth Systems." *South Asian Journal of Management* 22 (1): 159–86.

Parker, K., and R. Igielnik. 2020. "On the Cusp of Adulthood and Facing an Uncertain Future: What We Know About Gen Z So Far." Pew Research Center. Published May 14. www.pewsocialtrends.org/essay/on-the-cusp-of-adulthood-and-facing-an-uncertain-future-what-we-know-about-gen-z-so-far/.

Patrick, H., and Kumar, V. 2012. "Managing Workplace Diversity: Issues and Challenges." *SAGE Open*. Published April 25. https://doi.org/10.1177/2158244012444615.

Pew Research Center. 2020a. "Most Americans Express Support for the Black Lives Matter Movement." Published June 12. www.pewsocialtrends.org/2020/06/12/amid-protests-majorities-across-racial-and-ethnic-groups-express-support-for-the-black-lives-matter-movement/psdt_06-12-20_protests-00-1/.

———. 2020b. "What Census Calls Us." www.pewresearch.org/interactives/what-census-calls-us/.

PwC Middle East. 2019. "Women in Work: Insights from Middle East and North Africa." www.pwc.com/m1/en/publications/women-in-work-index.html.

Rau, H., and J. Williams. 2017. "A Winning Parental Leave Policy Can Be Surprisingly Simple." *Harvard Business Review*. Published July 28. https://hbr.org/2017/07/a-winning-parental-leave-policy-can-be-surprisingly-simple.

Sanchez, D. V., and E. F. Frey. 2019. "Where Do Females Rise to Leadership Positions? A Cross-Sector Analysis." *Applied Economics Letters* 27 (15): 1252–55. https://doi.org/10.1080/13504851.2019.1676385.

Turner, A. 2018. *The Business Case for Racial Equity: A Strategy for Growth*. W. K. Kellogg Foundation. Published July 24. https://wkkf.org/resource-directory/resources/2018/07/business-case-for-racial-equity.

US Census Bureau. 2020. "Demographic Turning Points for the United States: Population Projections for 2020 to 2060." Revised February. www.census.gov/content/dam/Census/library/publications/2020/demo/p25-1144.pdf.

US Department of Health and Human Services Office of Minority Health. 2018. "The National CLAS Standards." Modified October 2. https://minorityhealth.hhs.gov/omh/browse.aspx?lvl=2&lvlid=53.

Wen, L., and N. Sadeghi. 2020. "Addressing Racial Health Disparities in the COVID-19 Pandemic: Immediate and Long-Term Policy Solutions." *Health Affairs*. Published July 20. https://www.healthaffairs.org/do/10.1377/hblog20200716.620294/full/.

White Coats For Black Lives. 2015. "About WC4BL." Accessed May 27, 2021. https://whitecoats4blacklives.org/about/.

Whitman, E. 2015. "Gulf Countries' Migrant Workers: Health Care Providers Are Mostly Foreigners in Saudi Arabia and Neighboring Countries." *International Business Times*. Published February 12. www.ibtimes.com/gulf-countries-migrant-workers-health-care-providers-are-mostly-foreigners-saudi-1814550.

Wilson-Stronks, A., K. K. Lee, C. L. Cordero, A. L. Kopp, and E. Galvez. 2008. *One Size Does Not Fit All: Meeting the Health Care Needs of Diverse Populations*. Oakbrook Terrace, IL: Joint Commission.

Woodward, N., and D. Saini. 2006. "Diversity Management Issues in the USA and India: Some Emerging Perspectives." In *Future of Work: Mastering Change*, edited by P. Singh, J. Bhatnagar, and A. Bhandarker, 149–64. New Delhi, India: Excel Books.

World Health Organization (WHO). 2000. "World Health Organization Assesses the World's Health Systems." Published February 7. www.who.int/news/item/07-02-2000-world-health-organization-assesses-the-world's-health-systems.

CHAPTER 4

INDIVIDUAL AND ORGANIZATIONAL LEARNING

> Seattle's Virginia Mason Medical Center was able to respond quickly and effectively to the COVID-19 pandemic because of their past two decades focusing on learning and improvements. "We are a learning organization," explained their chairman and CEO, Dr. Gary Kaplan. "You have rapid-cycle improvements, rapid-cycle change management where some things work and some things don't. Then you leverage the learning and do it again." Virginia Mason's long-term preparation allowed them to be nimble and make changes rapidly to meet the changing needs.
>
> When COVID-19 erupted in Washington State, Virginia Mason was ready. A command center and a dedicated COVID-19 unit were quickly created. Special workflows were designed, and the nascent telemedicine program quickly scaled up to provide thousands of visits a week. COVID-19 had a dramatic impact on the healthcare industry, but Dr. Kaplan cautioned that unless healthcare leaders choose to leverage the learning from the pandemic, the opportunities for positive change will be lost (Robeznieks 2020).

Learning Objectives

After studying this chapter, readers should be able to

- evaluate the mechanisms and processes that allow individuals and organizations to learn,
- compare and contrast models of learning,
- state the definition and purpose of organizational learning,
- identify the components and processes of organizational learning,
- describe the learning cycle and how it repeats,

- explain the barriers to individual and organizational learning, and
- explain the differences and similarities between organizational learning and a learning organization.

Key Terms

- double-loop learning
- learning communities
- learning management systems
- learning organization
- organizational learning
- single-loop learning

organizational learning
An "organizationally regulated collective learning process in which individual and group-based learning experiences concerning the improvement of organizational performance and/or goals are transferred into organizational routines, processes, and structures" (Schilling and Kluge 2009, 338).

Learning has been defined as a change in knowledge that occurs as the result of experiences (Argote and Levine 2020). **Organizational learning**, then, is "an organizationally regulated collective learning process in which individual and group-based learning experiences concerning the improvement of organizational performance and/or goals are transferred into organizational routines, processes and structures" (Schilling and Kluge 2009, 338). In essence, an organization gains experience that produces knowledge used to improve itself through changes in how it operates and functions. However, learning does not necessarily improve an organization. The introduction describes how Virginia Mason's decades of organizational learning positioned the firm to rapidly adapt to new circumstances. But as Dr. Kaplan warned, if leaders do not capitalize on what the organization learns, opportunities for improvement will be lost.

Learning can be achieved by gaining new facts and information; acquiring new procedures, processes, or skills; or establishing new routines and knowledge of action-outcome relationships (Smerek 2018). Learning can result from direct or indirect experiences and from actual participation or observation. For instance, a doctor may learn a new procedure by observing it first and then performing it under supervision.

Learning is critical in healthcare, which is constantly evolving and continues to be challenged with patient safety issues. Change drives the need for learning, and learning allows the implementation of new knowledge and practices to initiate change. Learning in healthcare must be a continuous function that occurs by both formal and informal means to produce the best possible outcomes for the organization and those it serves (Lyman 2018).

The following four processes constitute the act of learning in an organization (Schilling and Kluge 2009):

1. *Understanding*—gaining new insights and ideas based on personal experience

2. *Interpreting*—deducing relationships among insights, including the ability to explain the relationship to self and others
3. *Integrating*—assimilating new insights into groups to allow for collective action
4. *Institutionalizing*—implementing the shared understanding through organizational rules, procedures, and strategies

As this list implies, organizational learning also occurs at different levels in an organization: individual, group, and institutional (Argote and Levine 2020).

Because organizational learning processes are ongoing, learning can be seen as a cycle, as shown in exhibit 4.1. In step 1, people or organizations observe or experience an activity and gain understanding. The new understanding can be vicarious or personal, depending on whether it comes from training, news, interactions, or other means. The information is processed, interpreted, and reflected on in step 2, leading to generalizations and judgments in step 3 that allow integration of new insights. In step 4, actions occur that apply and test the generalizations and judgments made in the previous step to institutionalize the learning, which leads back to step 1, where the individual or organization again makes observations and gains experiences from its actions.

Argyris and Schon (1978) proposed that organizational learning can be either single- or double-loop learning. **Single-loop learning** occurs when employees search for solutions within the confines of given goals, values, plans, and rules. **Double-loop learning** takes place when the "governing

single-loop learning
Learning that occurs when employees search for solutions within the confines of given goals, values, plans, and rules.

double-loop learning
Learning that occurs when the governing variable is questioned, causing shifts in strategies, values, or mission.

EXHIBIT 4.1
The Cycle of Learning

Step 1: Observe/experience/understand

Step 2: Reflect/interpret

Step 3: Generalize/judge/integrate

Step 4: Apply/test/act/institutionalize

Source: Adapted from Beard and Wilson (2006).

variable" is questioned, causing shifts in strategies, values, or mission. Argyris and Schon (1978, 2–3) explained the difference this way:

> When the error detected and corrected permits the organization to carry on its present policies or achieve its present objectives, then that error and correction process is a single-loop learning. . . . Double-loop learning occurs when error is detected and corrected in ways that involve the modifications of an organization's underlying norms, policies, and objectives.

Of course, organizations are only a composite of individuals, and the type and degree of learning that transpire in an organization are only a reflection of the aggregation of all its employees and stakeholders. As a result, the term **learning organization**, which has gained popularity in recent decades, is viewed differently from organizational learning. Organizational learning is a process, whereas a learning organization is a place in which ingrained structures and culture constantly facilitate and encourage learning (Green 2020).

A learning organization purposely creates appropriate strategies and structures to enhance education and training. As a reflection of this concept's level of popularity, some firms employ a chief learning officer, who typically reports directly to the CEO and is responsible for corporate training, development, and knowledge management. (The growth of this role is demonstrated by the creation of *Chief Learning Officer* magazine [www.chieflearningofficer.com].) Efforts to transform into learning organizations help companies transcend single-loop learning and produce creative solutions to position themselves for success today and in the future.

One of the early proponents of the learning organization concept, Peter Senge (2006), noted the presence of five main characteristics of learning organizations:

1. *System thinking*—understanding and analyzing how all the components of an organization influence each other within the whole to find and eliminate obstacles to learning
2. *Personal mastery*—individual commitment to self-improvement and the process of learning
3. *Mental models*—assumptions held by individuals and the organization that promote learning through their culture and mindsets
4. *Shared vision*—a common vision that stimulates learning
5. *Team learning*—group cohesiveness and dialogue that motivate common team learning

Hoe (2019, 19) further defined learning organizations as those that "harness the power of groups and individuals to solve complex problems using system thinking."

---

learning organization
An entity in which ingrained structures and culture are in place that constantly facilitate and encourage learning.

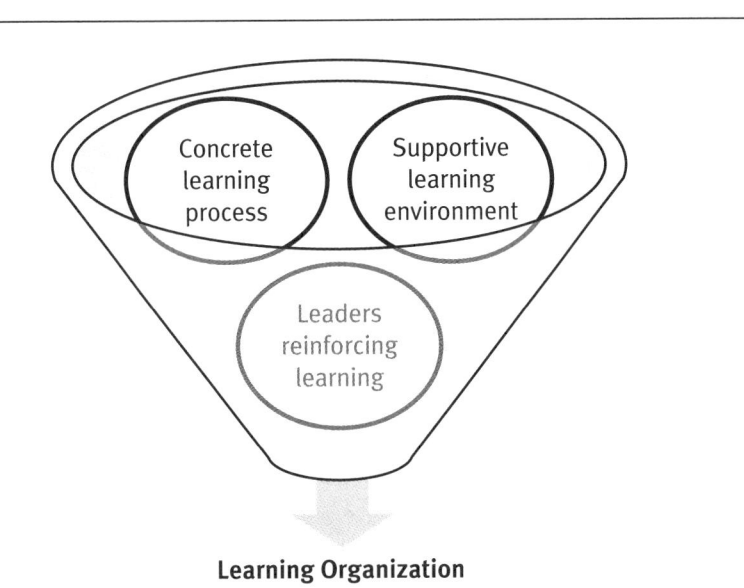

EXHIBIT 4.2
Components of a Learning Organization

```
        ┌─────────────┬─────────────┐
        │  Concrete   │ Supportive  │
        │  learning   │  learning   │
        │  process    │ environment │
        └─────────────┴─────────────┘
              │   Leaders     │
              │  reinforcing  │
              │   learning    │
               ╲             ╱
                ╲           ╱
                 ▼
         Learning Organization
```

Source: Adapted from Garvin, Edmondson, and Gino (2008).

For learning to be sustained, an organization needs a supportive environment that allows employees to disagree, ask questions, and take risks by providing a sense of psychological safety that eliminates fear of disagreement and failure, an appreciation of the differences among employees, openness to new ideas, and adequate time for thought and reflection (exhibit 4.2). Learning organizations also structure learning in a concrete way that identifies, collects, interprets, and allocates data for decision-making and problem-solving. Finally, such organizations hire and retain leaders who reinforce learning: Bosses encourage employees to question things and voice alternative viewpoints, and listen when employees share ideas (Anderson and Escher 2010; Argote and Levine 2020).

Although these concepts may seem simple and logical, many organizations struggle to learn and often fail as a result. Many factors—personal, group, or organizational—can impede learning in organizations:

Personal barriers:
- Personal biases
- Lack of motivation
- High degree of stress
- Lack of skills
- Deficit of trust
- Fear of punishment

> **The High Costs of a Failure to Learn**
>
> Sadly, the leadership of the United States federal government demonstrated a failure to learn when the pandemic started in early 2020, often ignoring and rejecting its key scientists' advice regarding precautions to reduce the spread of COVID-19.
>
> The Centers for Disease Control and Prevention (CDC) recommended for almost all of 2020 that all people aged 3 and older "wear masks in public settings and when around people... especially when social distancing measures are difficult to maintain" (CDC 2020). Other researchers and scientific journals also supported the wearing of masks during the pandemic. Yet, only about 50 percent of the public used masks by late summer (Peeples 2020). Fifteen states individually did implement mask mandates that some suggested may have prevented up to 450,000 COVID-19 cases, while many Republican governors barred city leaders in their states from mandating masks (North 2020).
>
> By October 2020, Peeples could report in *Nature* that "the science supports that face coverings are saving lives during the coronavirus pandemic." In addition, other countries were able to dramatically reduce their incidence of hospitalizations and deaths due to COVID-19 by implementing countrywide mandates, which was found to be the most important factor in controlling COVID-19 (Marino 2020). But in the United States the question had become political, and many individuals and jurisdictions refused to recognize the science and protested mask use well into the pandemic's third wave. Clearly, many did not integrate and institutionalize the knowledge that was available and, as a result, hundreds of thousands of people perished from COVID-19.

Group and organizational barriers:
- Lack of clear goals
- Minimal feedback
- Strict work rules
- Excessive competition
- Blaming culture

Barriers to learning can have a profound impact on an organization's outcomes. As shown in the adjacent box, the leader's behavior can dramatically influence the actions and learning behaviors of even very senior, highly trained individuals. One of the most destructive impediments to individuals' learning is being publicly embarrassed and shamed for mistakes. The old adage to praise publicly and punish privately remains an essential management strategy to allow organizational learning to take place.

Role of Motivation in Learning

People can be motivated to learn. Furthermore, certain motivation techniques have been shown to affect the amount of time individuals devote to learning (Argote and Levine 2020).

Motivation can come from both extrinsic and intrinsic sources. Extrinsic rewards are external incentives offered to encourage a certain behavior. As discussed in chapter 7, extrinsic rewards can be monetary, social, or organizational. Most changes in work activities and behavior require some amount of extrinsic motivation, as the work itself may not be inherently interesting. Companies often seek to motivate learning by giving external monetary and nonmonetary rewards to their employees. However, the primary reason people perform a behavior or an activity is that they feel valued by their social and work group (Carr et al. 2019), which constitutes intrinsic motivation.

Because much of the learning in organizations occurs in and through groups and not in a classroom setting, effective organizations structure learning opportunities in social contexts to take advantage of intrinsic motivational factors. They create a sense of community by developing norms for behavior and creating an emotionally safe environment to allow employees and supervisors to teach one another (Carr et al. 2019; Darling-Hammond et al. 2001).

Exploration and Exploitation

All organizations struggle with balancing the amount of effort and time they spend to advance their learning while efficiently using existing assets. In the learning literature this is called the tension between exploration and exploitation. Exploration includes experimentation, exploration, discovery, and innovation. Exploitation involves refinement, implementation, and the proverbial "putting one's nose to the grindstone."

Strategic firms can choose to exploit their resources by producing existing products and services cheaper and faster. This might involve adding a new shift, implementing time and motion controls, reducing staff, or just working harder and faster. For instance, for-profit nursing homes have been found to have lower levels of nurse staffing (Harrington et al. 2016). These companies may spend little on education and innovation.

Other companies focus much more on learning and exploration. These firms will seek to develop new products and services and expand their capabilities and competencies. A strategic focus on exploration drives building skills for long-term results. It should generate new ways of thinking and novel processes (Smerek 2018). As shown in the box, one healthcare company that has emphasized learning and exploration is Kaiser Permanente. Kaiser's internal training institute has helped create a company focus on learning and long-term success.

Challenges of Learning in Healthcare

Organizational learning in healthcare is tremendously important today. Healthcare technology and complexity have grown and continue to rapidly evolve, as new

> **Kaiser Permanente's Learning Organization**
> Recognizing the dynamism of healthcare, Kaiser Permanente places an increasing emphasis on learning and exploration. Their Health Plan Institute supports the learning and development of their sales, marketing, and business development. Each year the institute analyzes the company's learning needs and priorities to further their learning culture and create novel approaches to business. Their learning efforts are coordinated by a chief learning officer, who has been instrumental in working to develop new technologies such as career development platforms, online coaching, personalized learning, virtual reality, and augmented learning. The learning efforts have also helped to dramatically increase their membership and to succeed in times of uncertainty and upheaval (Burjek 2018).

scientific knowledge has accumulated at incredible rates in the areas of genetics, proteomics, telemedicine, robotic medicine, and molecular biology. All medical professionals are struggling to keep up with knowledge that is often "fragmented and uncoordinated," while the amount of new knowledge doubles roughly every two and a half months (Corish 2018). At the same time, healthcare professionals must remain focused on those they serve.

Creating a learning healthcare organization can be a complex endeavor because it demands instantaneous access to rapidly evolving knowledge (exhibit 4.3). Healthcare systems must also be able to digitally capture experiences of patient care, engage their patients in the learning opportunity, provide proper incentives to staff, allow full transparency, develop a culture directed by enlightened leaders, and offer training and system analysis that allow competency development.

Healthcare demands high quality and no failures to ensure the safety and well-being of patients on a daily basis. However, process failures in healthcare occur and recur far too frequently when learning does not take place. Nurses have been found to effect short-term fixes to processes that solve the immediate issue but fail to resolve the problem, which then recurs. For example, a lack of clean linen may motivate a nurse to walk to another unit to borrow linen. This action may provide the needed linen but does not solve the lack of adequate linen in the original location and may create secondary problems for other departments (Tucker and Edmondson 2003).

In some respects, learning in healthcare is more complicated than in other industries. The professionalism, functional organizational structures, and tight interdependencies that exist in healthcare create situations ripe for disaster unless diligence is practiced and learning takes place. For example, doctors and nurses are taught to make independent decisions and address individual patient problems. Their time is also very costly, so their organizations design their jobs to provide limited nonstructured time. Moreover, the

EXHIBIT 4.3
Characteristics of a Continuously Learning Healthcare System

- Real-time access to knowledge
- Digital capture of the care experience for care improvement
- Engaged, empowered patients
- Incentives aligned to reward high-value care
- Full transparency
- Leadership-instilled culture of learning
- Supportive system competencies developed through training, system analysis, and feedback loops

Source: Adapted from Institute of Medicine (2013).

work design often does not provide for an on-site manager to facilitate communication and activity across departmental boundaries, hindering problem resolution (Coughlan et al. 2020; Tucker and Edmondson 2003).

In addition, medical professional training programs have been designed to focus almost exclusively on clinical knowledge and to minimize nonclinical learning. These formal clinical training programs often take place in settings that lack "self-reflection, dialogue, inquiry, and reciprocal communication" and leave little room for new learning and exploration of improved routines for healthcare providers (Hoff, Pohl, and Bartfield 2006).

Some healthcare systems have developed **learning management systems** to formalize their learning processes. Southwestern Vermont Health Care, a small, not-for-profit health system located in Bennington, Vermont, uses a learning management system to "provide on-the-job support and resources . . . which reinforce the patient-centric culture." (Healthcare Source 2014). The system allows ready access for employees and permits managers to rapidly communicate changes in policy and archive meeting results in a consistent manner.

A key component of transitioning to a learning organization is strong leadership. Learning as a strategic priority has to start with senior leaders. If the top executives are not supportive, efforts to create a culture of learning will dissipate quickly. The leader needs to communicate the vision and rally employees to a common cause. A focus on learning does not happen in the short-term; it takes the personal involvement of leaders for perhaps years to imbue learning into their organizations (Morain, Kass, and Grossman 2017).

learning management systems Software used to plan, track, and record the outcomes of learning processes. LMS software may include applications to help organizations create and deliver instruction, monitor participation, assess performance, and provide student interaction.

Others, such as Bon Secours Health System, in Marriottsville, Maryland (see the box), have crafted learning communities to redesign and improve their patient care. **Learning communities** have been defined as "a select group of potential adopters and stakeholders who engage in a shared learning process to facilitate adaptation and implementation of innovations. . . . Learning Community participants work together in an interactive group setting and

---

Learning Communities Spread Best Practices Across a System

Bon Secours Health System's implementation of learning communities has helped the organization decrease infection rates by half and aggressive use of open heart surgery by 45 percent. In 2007, Bon Secours, comprising 19 acute care hospitals in six Eastern states, began creating learning communities, each focused on a specific topic, to redesign its patient care. The learning communities establish best practices that then become part of Bon Secours leadership's performance expectations. Staying focused on what is important to patients, achieving measurable outcomes, persisting across several years, spreading what is learned, and institutionalizing accountability from the C-suite to the bedside have been key factors in the success of Bon Secours.

Source: Information from Butcher (2012).

learning communities
A "select group of potential adopters and stakeholders who engage in a shared learning process to facilitate adaptation and implementation of innovations" (Agency for Healthcare Research and Quality 2016).

leverage . . . resources to address a defined problem" (Agency for Healthcare Research and Quality 2016).

An organization can more easily embed learning if it adheres to the following tenets:

- Reinforce key concepts (e.g., key ideas introduced at meetings) through complementary online learning modules.
- Tailor education to specific needs, such as by customizing training for individual units.
- Give employees firsthand experience by using tools that allow hands-on training.
- Develop a safe environment in which learners may ask challenging questions.

A defining component of many organizational improvement movements is embedding learning as a primary work function. To be successful, many quality improvement approaches now extensively used in healthcare require an organizational culture that promotes learning. For example, Lean, which originated in the Toyota Production System, seeks to drive out waste and make all work add value. The approach is focused on a strategy of improving organizational processes by identifying the value desired by the user, examining each step in a process, and eliminating steps that do not add value. Like most quality improvement programs, Lean requires difficult changes throughout an organization, as well as strong leadership and a culture that motivates learning and adaptation (Institute for Healthcare Improvement 2005; York 2020).

Chapter Summary

Organizational learning has emerged as a critical operational element for businesses across the globe, especially for healthcare firms. It involves the collective application of individual and group experiences to improve company routines, processes, and structures. Such learning is critical in healthcare, with its rapidly growing knowledge base and persistent concerns for patient safety. The learning process has four separate, cyclical processes that include (1) understanding, (2) interpreting, (3) integrating, and (4) institutionalizing. Learning can be either single-loop (where employees search for solutions within given goals, values, plans, and rules) or double-loop (where shifts in strategies, values, and mission may occur).

The concept of learning organizations has become popular, with some firms now employing chief learning officers. Learning organizations are characterized by their systems thinking, personal mastery, positive mental models, a shared vision, and team learning. Learning can be sustained only if a supportive environment exists, including a safe space in which workers are free to ask difficult questions, take risks, and disagree; leaders who reinforce learning are in place; concrete/structured processes are available for exploring new ideas; and adequate time is provided for thought and reflection.

Learning can be impeded by personal, group, or organizational barriers. If left unaddressed, barriers can greatly damage an organization's ability to adapt and learn. However, leaders can identify and reduce barriers and can motivate learning, in particular through social and group motivators.

Healthcare organizations must invest heavily in learning today, as clinical and managerial knowledge continues to rapidly expand. Successful healthcare firms have processes and systems for knowledge dissemination and training, and engage their employees and patients in an atmosphere of transparency. This balance can be difficult to achieve in healthcare, which is complicated by professional training, interdependencies, and structures that make novel learning a challenge. Some healthcare systems have developed or purchased learning management systems to formalize their learning processes.

Organizational learning is also a key component of most quality improvement programs that have proliferated in healthcare in recent decades. Lean is an example of an improvement approach that heavily uses learning concepts.

Chapter Questions

1. What is the difference between individual and organizational learning?
2. How does the learning process of integrating differ from institutionalizing?
3. How does the apply/test/act/institutionalize cycle lead to the observe/experience/understand cycle?
4. How could double-loop learning be disruptive to an organization?
5. Why are leaders' behaviors so important to organizational learning?
6. Of the three components of a learning organization, which do you think is the most important?
7. How do barriers to learning come to exist in organizations?
8. How does public punishment damage organizational learning?
9. Why is learning more difficult in healthcare than in other industries?
10. How is Lean quality improvement related to organizational learning?

Chapter Case

The Role of Information Technology in Healthcare Learning

St. James Medical System's CEO, Stephanie, knows her organization faces many current and future challenges. Diminishing reimbursement, potential restructuring as an accountable care organization, increased regional competition, and greater difficulty in recruiting and retaining skilled professional staff, among other factors, will make the next decade a transition period requiring many innovative changes. She is not certain her organization is prepared to learn new ways to meet these challenges.

Stephanie recently read the Institute of Medicine's nearly 400-page report *Best Care at Lower Cost: The Path to Continuously Learning Health Care in America*, which indicated that the US healthcare system has squandered billions of dollars per year on unnecessary care, unnecessary administrative costs, and preventable health conditions while failing to deliver high-quality care. She was impressed by the Institute's ten recommendations:

1. *Digital infrastructure.* Increase the capability to capture clinical, care delivery process, and financial data to improve care and performance, and generate new knowledge.
2. *Data utility.* Simplify and revise research regulations to improve care, promote the capture of clinical data, and generate knowledge.
3. *Clinical decision support.* Accelerate integration of the best clinical knowledge into care decisions.
4. *Patient-centered care.* Involve patients and families in decisions regarding health and healthcare, tailored to fit their preferences.
5. *Community links.* Promote community–clinical partnerships and services aimed at managing and improving health at the community level.
6. *Care continuity.* Improve coordination and communication within and across organizations.
7. *Optimized operations.* Continuously improve healthcare operations to reduce waste, streamline care delivery, and focus on activities that improve patient health.
8. *Financial incentives.* Structure payment to reward continuous learning and improvement in the provision of higher-quality care at lower cost.
9. *Performance transparency.* Increase transparency on healthcare system performance.
10. *Broad leadership.* Expand commitment to the goals of a continuously learning healthcare system (Institute of Medicine 2013).

St. James has been working on many of these steps for years. The organization is constantly upgrading its information technology (IT) system, has developed clinical support decision systems, spent the past five years trying to shift to a patient-centered focus, and at the same time worked hard to lower its costs. Moving to a patient-centered care focus required a great deal of information gathering and learning, encapsulated in St. James's four core concepts:

1. *Respect and dignity.* Healthcare practitioners listen to and honor patient and family perspectives and choices. Patient and family knowledge, values, beliefs, and cultural backgrounds are incorporated into the planning and delivery of care.
2. *Information sharing.* Healthcare practitioners communicate and share complete and unbiased information with patients and families in ways that are affirming and useful. Patients and families receive timely, complete, and accurate information in order to effectively participate in care and decision-making.
3. *Participation.* Patients and families are encouraged and supported in participating in care and decision-making at the level they choose.
4. *Collaboration.* Patients and families are also included on an institution-wide basis. Healthcare leaders collaborate with patients and families in policy and program development, implementation, and evaluation; in healthcare facility design; and in professional education, as well as in the delivery of care (adapted from MHA Keystone Center 2015).

Operating under these core concepts has been challenging, and Stephanie is worried about the organization's ability to truly become patient-centered without adopting many major changes. Just improving the speed and data capacity of the health system's IT infrastructure and electronic health record had been difficult; linking providers to streamline care continuity and providing financial incentives to reward continuous learning while running a transparent performance system seems especially challenging. She decides to make a few notes and discuss the difficulties with St. James's executive team.

Case Questions
1. If St. James truly wants to become a learning organization and be prepared for the future, what does it need to do?
2. How can the organization increase transparency and implement an IT system that facilitates and improves decision-making?

Chapter Activities

Learning Organizations, More or Less

Choose an organization you have worked in and score it on each of the following six statements, from 1 (not at all) to 10 (consistently):

1. My organization makes time for sharing and reflection.
2. My organization engages key stakeholders in the learning process.
3. My organization uses a method of evaluation as part of the learning process.
4. My organization handles setbacks and failures well.
5. My organization adapts well to challenges.
6. My organization has good communication between organizational levels.

Total your score and consider what it means about the organization: Would you classify it as a learning organization based on these experiences? What actions did the company take that influenced the scores on each item and on the overall learning processes?

If you are doing this activity with others, compare your experiences in different organizations. What makes a company more or less likely to be a learning organization?

Organizational Learning and Growth

First, watch Peter Senge's short introduction to organizational learning (https://youtu.be/OpiqnCAQ6S8; 3 minutes). Answer the following questions:

- According to Peter Senge, what is organizational learning?
- How do mental models affect learning?
- How do systems influence learning and intelligence?

Next, watch Yves Givel's TEDxSHMS Talk "Growing Through Change: A How-To for Leaders of Learning Organizations" (https://youtu.be/D1iO2QwJYAI; 18 minutes). Answer the following questions:

- How do organizations adapt using learning?
- What skills do leaders need today for learning in an organization?

References

Agency for Healthcare Research and Quality. 2016. "Innovations Exchange Learning Communities." Accessed March 22. https://innovations.ahrq.gov/learning-communities (site discontinued).

Anderson, M., and P. Escher. 2010. *The MBA Oath: Setting a Higher Standard for Business Leaders.* New York: Penguin.

Argote, L., and J. M. Levine (eds.). 2020. *The Oxford Handbook of Group and Organizational Learning.* New York: Oxford University Press.

Argyris, C., and D. A. Schon. 1978. *Organizational Learning: A Theory of Action Perspective.* Reading, MA: Addison-Wesley.

Beard, C., and J. Wilson. 2006. *Experiential Learning,* 2nd ed. Bodmin, Cornwall, UK: MPG Books.

Burjek, A. 2018. "HPI, Kaiser Permanente Flourishes in Face of Uncertainty." *Chief Learning Officer* 17 (5): 34–35.

Butcher, L. 2012. "'Learning Communities' Spread Best Practices Across a System." *Hospitals & Health Networks.* Published December 2012. www.hhnmag.com/articles/6063-learning-communities-spread-best-practices-across-a-system.

Carr, E. W., A. Reece, G. R. Kellerman, and A. Robichaux. 2019. "The Value of Belonging at Work." *Harvard Business Review.* Published December 16. https://hbr.org/2019/12/the-value-of-belonging-at-work.

Centers for Disease Control and Prevention (CDC). 2020. "Considerations for Wearing Masks." Accessed August 7. www.cdc.gov/coronavirus/2019-ncov/prevent-getting-sick/cloth-face-cover-guidance.html (content routinely updated).

Corish, B. 2018. "Medical Knowledge Doubles Every Few Months; How Can Clinicians Keep Up?" *Elsevier Connect* (blog). Published April 23. www.elsevier.com/connect/medical-knowledge-doubles-every-few-months-how-can-clinicians-keep-up.

Coughlan, C., N. Manek, Y. Razak, and R. E. Klaber. 2020. "How to Improve Care Across Boundaries." *British Medical Journal* 369 (8242): m1045. https://doi.org/10.1136/bmj.m1045.

Darling-Hammond, L., K. Austin, S. Orcutt, and J. Rosso. 2001. "How People Learn: Introduction to Learning Theory" (session 1 introduction for "The Learning Classroom" telecourse, Stanford University School of Education). Posted online December 27. web.stanford.edu/class/ed269/hplintrochapter.pdf.

Garvin, D. A., A. C. Edmondson, and F. Gino. 2008. "Is Yours a Learning Organization?" *Harvard Business Review.* Published March. https://hbr.org/2008/03/is-yours-a-learning-organization.

Green, S. 2020. "How to Build a Learning Organization for the Coming Decade." Forbes *Coaches Council* (blog). Published February 28. www.forbes.com/sites/forbescoachescouncil/2020/02/28/how-to-build-a-learning-organization-for-the-coming-decade/.

Harrington, C., J. F. Schnelle, M. McGregor, and S. F. Simmons. 2016. "The Need for Higher Minimum Staffing Standards in U.S. Nursing Homes." *Health Service Insights* 9: 13–19. https://doi.org/10.4137/hsi.s38994.

Healthcare Source. 2014. "HCAHPS and the Bottom Line: 5 Ways to Improve Scores Through Talent and Learning Management." Accessed May 27, 2021. http://solutions.healthcaresource.com/2253-hcahps-whitepaper.html.

Hoe, S. L. 2019. "The Topicality of the Learning Organization: Is the Concept Still Relevant Today?" In *The Oxford Handbook of the Learning Organization*, edited by A. Örtenblad, 19–31. New York: Oxford University Press.

Hoff, T., H. Pohl, and J. Bartfield. 2006. "Teaching but Not Learning: How Medical Residency Programs Handle Errors." *Journal of Organizational Behavior* 27 (7): 869–96.

Institute for Healthcare Improvement. 2005. *Going Lean in Health Care*. IHI Innovation Series white paper. Accessed May 27, 2021. www.ihi.org/resources/Pages/IHIWhitePapers/GoingLeaninHealthCare.aspx.

Institute of Medicine. 2013. *Best Care at Lower Cost: The Path to Continuously Learning Health Care in America*. Washington, DC: National Academies Press. https://doi.org/10.17226/13444.

Lyman, B. 2018. "Organizational Learning in Hospitals: A Concept Analysis." *Journal of Nursing Management* 27 (3): 633–46. https://doi.org/10.1111/jonm.12722.

Marino, K. 2020. "Early Face Mask Policies Curbed COVID-19's Spread, According to a 198-Country Analysis." *VCU News*. Published July 6. https://news.vcu.edu/article/Early_face_mask_policies_curbed_COVID19s_spread_according_to.

MHA Keystone Center. 2015. "A Road Map to Patient and Family Engagement: Recommended Policies & Practices for Hospitals." Revised August. www.mha.org/keystone_center/docs/pfe_roadmap.pdf.

Morain, S. R., N. E. Kass, and C. Grossman. 2017. "What Allows a Healthcare System to Become a Learning Health Care System: Results from Interviews with Health System Leaders." *Learning Health Systems* 1 (1): e10015. https://doi.org/10.1002/lrh2.10015.

North, A. 2020. "Why Masks Are (Still) Politized in America." *Vox*. Published July 22. www.vox.com/2020/7/21/21331310/mask-masks-trump-covid19-rule-georgia-alabama.

Peeples, L. 2020. "Face Masks: What the Data Say." *Nature* 586 (7828): 186–89. https://doi.org/10.1038/d41586-020-02801-8.

Robeznieks, A. 2020. "Virginia Mason's Rapid COVID-19 Response Had 18 Years of Preparation." American Medical Association. Published June 5. www.ama-assn.org/practice-management/sustainability/virginia-mason-s-rapid-covid-19-response-had-18-years.

Schilling, J., and A. Kluge. 2009. "Barriers to Organizational Learning: An Integration of Theory and Research." *International Journal of Management Reviews* 11 (3): 337–60.

Senge, P. 2006. *The Fifth Discipline: The Art and Practice of the Learning Organization*. New York: Doubleday.

Smerek, R. 2018. *Organizational Learning and Performance*. New York: Oxford University Press.

Tucker, A., and A. Edmondson. 2003. "Why Hospitals Don't Learn from Failures: Organizational and Psychological Dynamics That Inhibit System Change." *California Management Review* 45 (2): 55–72.

York, J. M. 2020. "Organizational Learning and Its Influence on the Lean Startup: A Unique Lens from Which to View This Popular Entrepreneurship Methodology." *Entrepreneurship & Organization Management* 9 (5). www.hilarispublisher.com/open-access/organizational-learning-and-its-influence-on-the-lean-startup-a-unique-lens-from-which-to-view-this-popular-entrepreneurship-metho-52452.html.

CHAPTER 5

ATTITUDES AND SATISFACTION

> The COVID-19 pandemic put great pressures on healthcare organizations to maintain positive employee attitudes and satisfaction. According to Brian Crawford, chief administration officer of Willis-Knighton Health System in Shreveport, Louisiana, the organization "boosted employee satisfaction during the pandemic" because providers and staff were valued and appreciated "every day, long before COVID-19 ever darkened our doors." Crawford maintains that "employee satisfaction, like trust, is something that is built over time and not something that can or should be expected to emerge, if not already there, during times of crisis." Because Willis-Knighton built this long-standing relationship with workers, their workforce responded during the pandemic with effort that was "truly remarkable." Crawford attributes this to the health system's philosophy of teamwork, a family-oriented environment, and dedication to its employees,
>
>> that in turn compelled our physicians, nurses, and other clinical and support staff to rise to the overwhelming challenges when faced with this monster. Not because they had to, but because they wanted to. This is what happens when an employer combines the intangibles of gratitude, respect and appreciation with the tangibles of fair and honest pay and benefits, respectful work areas and open offers for advancement opportunities to all (Gooch 2020).

Learning Objectives

After studying this chapter, readers should be able to

- explain how attitudes influence employee satisfaction,
- describe the relationship between attitudes and behaviors,
- define and differentiate between an employee's job satisfaction and organizational commitment,
- list the factors related to job satisfaction and organizational commitment,

- describe the consequences of job satisfaction and organizational commitment, and
- identify the ways in which companies can track employees' work attitudes in the workplace.

Key Terms

- affective commitment
- affective component
- attitudes
- behavioral component
- cognitive component
- cognitive dissonance
- continuance commitment
- dispositional approach
- engagement
- hygiene factors
- motivators
- normative commitment
- organizational citizenship behaviors
- two-factor theory
- value theory

Attitudes and job satisfaction are extremely important to how we interact in organizations and to organizational outcomes. As mentioned in the introduction, employee attitudes and satisfaction are built over time by a multitude of actions and efforts. Positive and negative attitudes grow from different inputs. For instance, Americans' positive attitudes toward and confidence in medical scientists grew in 2020. The COVID-19 pandemic outbreak placed national medical research doctors in the public arena, educating and advising leaders across the nation. Two prominent physicians, Anthony Fauci and Deborah Birx, appeared frequently with national governmental officials. Thanks in part to their visible work, the share of Americans who strongly felt that medical scientists acted in the best interests of the public increased from only 24 percent in 2016 to 43 percent in 2020. On the other hand, the public's attitudes toward elected officials did not improve, despite elected officials also having greater visibility during the pandemic. In 2016 and 2020, only 3 percent of Americans had a great deal of confidence that their elected officials would act in their best interests (Funk, Kennedy, and Johnson 2020).

Poor work attitudes and lack of engagement and commitment are costly for employers. Some studies indicate that low employee engagement costs companies in the United States as much as $500 billion annually and that over 80 percent of employees are considering leaving their jobs (Stevenson 2020).

Attitudes

Individual attitudes influence work outcomes and are directly tied to job satisfaction. **Attitudes** are the ways we evaluate things, people, information, or experiences based on our individual opinions, beliefs, feelings, and values. Attitudes may be influenced by our personality, motivation, and even behavior, and in turn help define how we evaluate or behave toward a situation, person, or thing. For instance, a physician who has poor handwriting may have the attitude that handwriting is difficult, unpleasant, or unimportant. But if that physician is then sued because poor handwriting resulted in a severe patient error, handwriting may seem much more important—the physician's attitude has changed. After this experience, the physician may write very clear notes. Although we cannot visibly see the feelings and beliefs that make up the doctor's attitudes, we can observe the behaviors resulting from the attitudes.

> **attitude**
> A relatively enduring set of beliefs and feelings used to evaluate something either favorably or unfavorably and typically reflected in one's behavior.

Our attitudes are formed from our life experiences. The attitudes of those with whom we associate—especially our family members and close friends—influence our own attitudes. Social norms and expected roles also influence our attitudes and behaviors. Attitudes are not fixed across our lives; they may change as we gain more experience, learn new things, and interact with different people. These changes can occur at an individual or societal level. For instance, attitudes of healthcare professionals toward mental illness have changed significantly since the 1960s, reducing the stigma attached to a diagnosis (Lien et al. 2019). In another example, the number of men working as registered nurses has increased about 50 percent since 1980, driven partially by changing gender role attitudes in the United States (Munnich and Wozniak 2020).

Some observers predict that the COVID-19 pandemic will permanently alter work attitudes and behaviors. Major societal events in the past have shifted attitudes, as shown in the box on the following page. During the pandemic, American work habits changed dramatically. Before the pandemic, about 25 percent of employees worked from home. By April 2020, over 60 percent were home working (Boland et al. 2020). Cerutti and Grodoski (2020) predicted that the following work-related behaviors and attitudes would change because of the pandemic:

- *Heightened concern about cleanliness and crowding.* In 2020, 30 percent of people avoided touching public surfaces. Work traffic patterns, cleaning protocols, and the use of touchless technology may change.
- *Greater concern about personal safety.* Work design may involve more personal control of the workspace.

> **Societal Attitude Shifts**
>
> Past traumatic events have changed societies' attitudes and way of life. For instance, the Black Death in the 1300s killed up to one-third of Europe's population and was a major driver in ending feudalism and serfdom. Likewise, World War II increased labor participation by women in America and the 9/11 terrorist attacks changed transportation and security policies (Reeves et al. 2020).

- *Increased attention to mental health and well-being.* Employers may add work-free zones, private space, and mental health support and counseling.
- *Innovative ways to connect to a work-based community.* Activities to bridge the distance the pandemic created among people will be important.
- *Increased permanent use of remote working.* Flexible hours and distance work arrangements will probably continue.

Components of Attitudes

Most people feel that attitudes are an important or the most important cause of behaviors. For example, if a manager complains that an employee has a "bad attitude" and someone asks for an explanation, the manager may point to a specific behavior of the employee. Perhaps the worker simply questioned something their supervisor said or consistently reported to work late. However, attitudes consist of more than behaviors and have long been seen as composed of three interrelated concepts: affective, behavioral, and cognitive components (Eiser 1987).

The **affective component** comprises a person's feelings and emotions about something. For instance, a person might dislike injections or shots. The **behavioral component** involves the influence of attitudes on how one acts and behaves; for example, avoiding an annual flu shot. The **cognitive component** consists of a person's beliefs and knowledge about something. Cognitive beliefs do not have to be based on facts and people's cognitive beliefs can be contradictory. For instance, people say "I know vaccines are important" and simultaneously "I read that vaccines cause autism and vaccines are harmful."

What we know, feel, and do are intricately woven together. As shown in exhibit 5.1, knowledge and new information (the cognitive component) influence feelings (the affective component), which affect actions (the behavioral component). Behaviors then affect what we learn and feel, which continues a feedback loop. Media messages such as advertising and political campaigns are all based on the idea that behaviors follow what people know and feel. Furthermore, we often learn when we do something, and what we do frequently becomes comfortable and pleasing to do, which further encourages the behavior.

affective component
A person's feelings and emotions about something.

behavioral component
The influence of attitudes on how one acts and behaves.

cognitive component
A person's beliefs and knowledge about something.

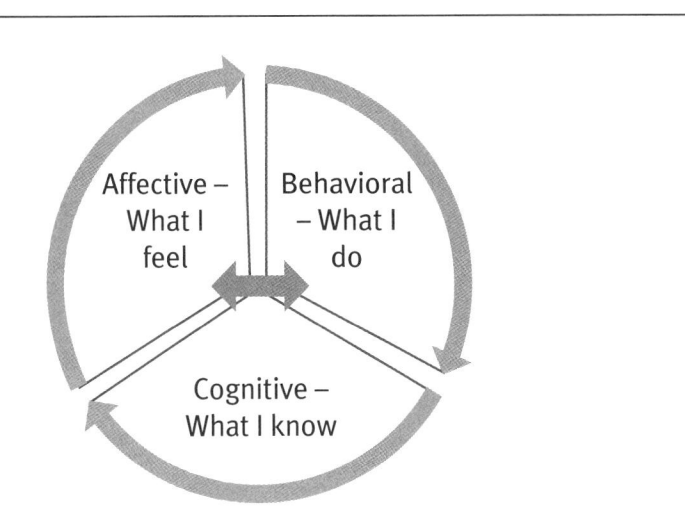

EXHIBIT 5.1
Interrelationship Between the Components of Attitudes

Affective – What I feel
Behavioral – What I do
Cognitive – What I know

Behaviors do not always mirror attitudes, though. We may have a positive attitude toward something but not behave consistently with our attitude. For example, someone may have a very positive attitude toward medicine and know it is important but rarely, if ever, go to the doctor for annual examinations and preventive tests. Behaviors that are inconsistent with our beliefs and attitudes may lead to internal conflict, which is called **cognitive dissonance**. The inconsistency between knowledge and behavior may make a person uncomfortable; significant discomfort may prompt someone to make their attitudes and actions consistent by changing one or the other. For example, someone might preach to their children not to smoke, but continue smoking themselves. Over time, guilt and cognitive dissonance may prompt behavior changes (seeking to quit smoking).

cognitive dissonance
Having inconsistent thoughts, beliefs, or attitudes, especially as relating to behavioral decisions and attitude change.

Measurement of Attitudes

For decades, businesses have routinely used surveys to ascertain employee and customer attitudes. Such surveys can provide valuable information to help managers understand employees' feelings about their jobs. Surveys of healthcare workers have shown that those scoring higher on attitude surveys have higher job satisfaction, greater organizational commitment, and lower absenteeism (Ahmad and Farzeen 2017). Different surveys can be used to measure different audiences' attitudes to set goals and action plans. For instance, one Midwest hospital uses their annual employee engagement survey to create action plans to improve their workplace (Siwicki 2019).

Although employers have traditionally conducted employee attitude surveys once a year, many recognize that more frequent surveys across

EXHIBIT 5.2
Example Employee Survey Questions

	Disagree	Mostly Disagree	Neutral	Mostly Agree	Agree
The people I work with cooperate to get our work done.	1	2	3	4	5
I receive the information I need to effectively do my job.	1	2	3	4	5
There is open and honest communication in my department.	1	2	3	4	5
Our senior managers behave consistently with our company's values.	1	2	3	4	5
I am empowered to make decisions to meet my goals.	1	2	3	4	5
I am proud to work for this company.	1	2	3	4	5

organizational changes and employee tenures are needed to accurately capture employees' work experiences, engagement, and perceptions. Employee surveys can be focused on specific groups that can be segmented to understand those involved in a process change, who were hired at similar times, or who share other important work-related characteristics. Employee surveys should be considered diagnostic tools to assist management in identifying issues and improving employees' work lives.

Many employee surveys ask questions that solicit responses on some type of Likert scale (exhibit 5.2).

Engagement

engagement
The mutual commitment between employees and employers.

Employee engagement drives the success of organizations. **Engagement** refers to the mutual commitment between employees and employers. Engaged employees are motivated and tend to remain with their employers. Measurements of engagement include (Greenberg and Baron 2008)

- the degree of pride employees have in their organization and its products and services,

- the belief that the organization helps its employees improve and be their best,
- employees' willingness to help others with their jobs and work beyond their job descriptions, and
- how well employees understand and buy into the mission and vision of the organization.

The twenty-first century has been a time of increasing employee engagement in the United States, with the percent of those "actively disengaged"—those who have a miserable work experience and spread their unhappiness to fellow workers—declining from 18 percent to 14 percent (exhibit 5.3). However, a Gallup survey showed that 78 percent of healthcare workers felt that COVID-19 will have a detrimental impact on their workplace. Further, only 44 percent of healthcare workers believed during the pandemic that their organization cared about their overall well-being—a measurement that is crucial to healthcare employees' work commitment (Ratanjee and Foy 2020).

The COVID-19 pandemic strained many work relationships by overworking providers and in some cases forcing physicians to ration equipment and care. Restrictions on visitors also isolated patients, which meant more pressure and stress for providers (Senior 2020). Preliminary reports show that the fear and uncertainty created by COVID-19 may have led to decreased job satisfaction, psychological distress, and greater turnover (Labrague and De los Santos 2020).

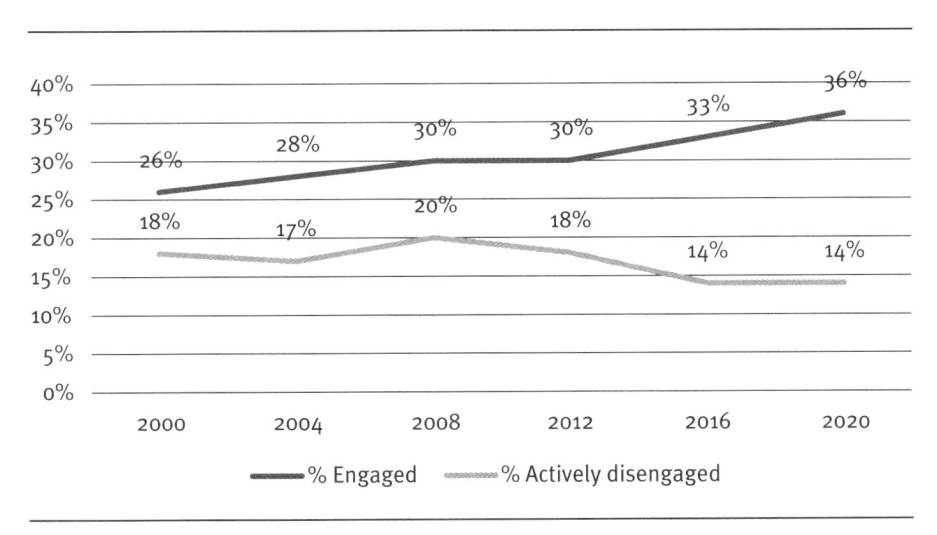

EXHIBIT 5.3
US Employee Engagement (Annual Averages)

Year	% Engaged	% Actively disengaged
2000	26%	18%
2004	28%	17%
2008	30%	20%
2012	30%	18%
2016	33%	14%
2020	36%	14%

Source: Adapted from Harter (2020).

Physician engagement in healthcare organizations is critical for better patient care, improved efficiency, lower costs, and better quality and patient safety (Perreira et al. 2019). Improving employee engagement, with physicians as all other workers, must involve addressing things that matter to the workers. Nursing and other staff have indicated that they would value reductions in school debt, assurance of appropriate time off, promotion of wellness, and amenities that save employees time outside of work (Green 2019). Engagement can also be facilitated through strong communication and worker involvement in decision-making. The Institute for Healthcare Improvement suggests that to engage physicians one must discover what they are passionate about and provide them opportunities to participate (Peden 2018).

Exhibit 5.4 lists some questions managers can use to better engage their employees. These questions could be used in surveys, focus groups, public forums, or one-on-one interviews.

Higher nurse engagement also results in better organizational outcomes and improved patient care. More engaged nurses can mean higher patient satisfaction scores, decreased patient mortality, and fewer patient falls (Heath 2020). Nurses that are more engaged also enjoy greater job satisfaction, have more energy, and put more effort into their work. And greater physician engagement results in improved clinical and financial performance (Redmond 2020).

Satisfaction

Healthcare organizations must be focused on both worker and patient satisfaction. Healthcare remains a labor-intensive industry and personnel costs

EXHIBIT 5.4
Employee Engagement Questions

- Are you happy at work?
- What matters to you?
- How can we improve?
- How is our culture getting in the way of our success?
- What is getting in the way of loving what you do?
- Is this what you want to do?
- How do you want to contribute?
- How can I help you?
- What can I do to make your job easier?
- How is this role helping you reach your dreams?

Source: Adapted from Forbes Coaches Council (2018).

account for more than 55 percent of hospital expenses (Michas 2019), making employee job satisfaction an important metric. Simply put, employee satisfaction concerns how workers feel about their jobs. On the other side of the healthcare experience, patient satisfaction scores are now commonly used for payment penalties or bonuses, and may be integral in transitioning to value-based care (Bickmore and Merkley 2019).

Different theories have suggested from where satisfaction comes. Three common theories include the two-factor theory, the dispositional approach, and the value theory of job satisfaction.

Herzberg's Two-Factor Theory

Popularized in the 1960s, the **two-factor theory** suggests that job satisfaction stems from two primary aspects of a job: hygiene factors and motivators (exhibit 5.5). **Hygiene factors** are related to the conditions of employment—supervision, pay, policies, working environments, good personal relationships, job security, and so on. Hygiene factors are expected to exist; their absence leads to worker dissatisfaction, but their existence does not necessarily create satisfaction. Therefore, hygiene factors are not considered things that motivate people. **Motivators**, items related to the work itself rather than its structure, include things such as promotional opportunities, personal growth, recognition, responsibility, autonomy, and achievement. The presence of motivators can make workers more satisfied, but the absence of motivators will not necessarily lead to dissatisfaction—merely to less satisfaction (see the box "Job Motivators Lend Meaning").

Research has supported the two-factor theory that money and compensation are not the most influential factors in worker satisfaction. The strongest predictions of employee job satisfaction come from the fit of an organization's culture and values with the employee's, how the organization's senior management leads and treats employees, and career opportunities (exhibit 5.6). Of the six most important contributing factors, compensation and benefits rank lowest.

Other studies have supported these findings and suggest that, more than higher compensation, employees want meaningful work, an ability to contribute, and the opportunity to

> **two-factor theory**
> A theory developed by Frederick Herzberg that factors in the workplace called motivators cause job satisfaction, while a separate set of hygiene factors, if absent, causes dissatisfaction.
>
> **hygiene factors**
> Work conditions that do not increase satisfaction or lead to motivation, although their absence can lead to dissatisfaction.
>
> **motivators**
> Work conditions that increase satisfaction from intrinsic conditions of the job.

Job Motivators Lend Meaning

Paige works as a certified nursing assistant at a major academic medical center—one of the best healthcare employers in the area. She is paid well, has good supervision, decent working conditions, and great job security. But Paige is not enthused about her job. When asked about how she likes her work, she most likely will say "it's a job." Although there are many hygiene factors present, there are few motivators. She would like to become a registered nurse and get promoted but cannot see that happening. She has little responsibility and recognition, and frequently feels her work has limited meaning. No wonder Paige is not enthusiastic about her job!

EXHIBIT 5.5
Hygiene Factors and Motivators

Hygiene Factors (absence drives dissatisfaction)	Motivators (presence drives satisfaction)
Supervision quality	Promotional opportunities
Compensation	Personal growth opportunities
Company policies	Recognition
Working conditions	Responsibility
Interpersonal relations	Autonomy
Job security	Achievement
Status	Meaningful work

EXHIBIT 5.6
Primary Contributors to US Job Satisfaction

	Relative Importance (%)
Culture and values	22
Senior leadership	21
Career opportunities	19
Business outlook	14
Work–life balance	13
Compensation and benefits	12

Source: Data from Stansell (2019).

advance. Employees who understand and buy into their organization's purpose tend to be happier and more committed. Companies who provide perks such as free lunches, fitness rooms, and on-site daycare often find that these benefits are appreciated, but do not improve job satisfaction. On the other hand, dead-end jobs have been shown to destroy workers' happiness (Carucci 2019), and almost 40 percent of workers are dissatisfied with their options for advancement at their current job (Spiegel 2019). Clearly, there is much room for improvement for employers to create jobs that intrinsically motivate their employees.

dispositional approach
A theory that job satisfaction is a result of individual traits—behaviors, thoughts, actions, and emotions. Also known as *trait theory*.

The Dispositional Approach

Another way of explaining job satisfaction is the **dispositional approach**. Basically, this theory suggests that some individuals enjoy their work more because they are inherently happier than others. Most people intuitively accept that an individual's nature contributes somewhat to job satisfaction. Some people tend to experience more positive feelings and to be more enthusiastic, confident, and cheerful; while others may be more likely to be fearful, hostile, or grumpy (Houmanfar and Mattaini 2018). Some employers have recognized that this dispositional factor has predictive value for hiring new employees (see the adjacent box for one example).

Value Theory
A third popular theory to explain job satisfaction is the **value theory**, which predicts that anything the employee values can produce satisfaction. The bigger the gap between what a person has and what they want in the job, the greater their job dissatisfaction. The path to worker satisfaction lies in finding out what employees want and, as far as possible, providing those things (Castejon et al. 2021; Greenberg and Baron 2008). Value theory has motivated frequent employee surveying in an attempt to discover what employees value.

> **Using Past Job Happiness for Hiring**
> One of the authors used to ask candidates who applied for administrative positions if they had been happy in their last job. This appeared to be a predictive question, as those who stated that they had been happy in their past job also seemed to be happy if they were hired. Conversely, if a person complained about how bad their last job had been, they tended to be unhappy in the new position. Therefore, those who answered negatively were rarely hired.

value theory A theory suggesting that anything the individual values or desires can produce job satisfaction.

Factors Affecting Satisfaction
Overall, job satisfaction has been found to be affected by the work environment, individual factors, and psychological factors. The work environment includes the physical and relational aspects of a job. It consists of communication within and across work groups and up and down the organizational structure. Probably the most important relationship for job satisfaction lies with the supervisor. Employee recognition that connects the employee to their organizational core values and goals is also important.

In addition, individual factors such as the employee's own moods and emotions influence job satisfaction. Personality and past experiences can strongly influence the employee's attitudes and thus job satisfaction. Psychological factors such as personal and family issues frequently intrude on work feelings and can affect job satisfaction. Employees who endure stressful family conflict and illness will generally have lower work satisfaction. In addition, community pressures may directly affect job satisfaction (Dugguh and Ayaga 2014).

Job Satisfaction Outcomes and Measurement

Generally, most believe that a happy worker is a more productive worker. This productivity manifests in cooperative behavior and better organizational outputs. Greater job satisfaction leads to **organizational citizenship behaviors**—discretionary employee behavior, outside the formal organizational reward system, that overall promotes the effective and efficient

organizational citizenship behaviors Discretionary employee behavior, outside the formal organizational reward system, that overall promotes the effective and efficient functioning of a company.

> **Using Employee Surveys to Improve Satisfaction**
>
> Unity Health Care has found it hard, almost impossible, to get job satisfaction information from conversations, so they use customized employee surveys to better understand their employees' morale, job satisfaction, and engagement. These surveys tell Unity what they are doing well and help them identify and act on employee concerns.
>
> These surveys have consistently shown that their benefits package is one of the top three factors for job satisfaction, but rising deductibles were causing employees to avoid needed care. So Unity moved to a partially self-insured health plan that reduced deductibles, which increased job satisfaction (Ledford 2019).

functioning of a company. Organizational citizenship behaviors extend beyond formal job descriptions to actions that might be considered "going the extra mile." Employees may do small things such as escorting a lost visitor to their destination instead of giving directions. Employees displaying organizational citizenship behaviors may find new ways to improve their jobs or serve on voluntary committees (Ocampo et al. 2018; Organ, Podsakoff, and MacKenzie 2005).

Healthcare job satisfaction is important and affects patient care. For instance, as mentioned before, worker satisfaction is strongly correlated with improved patient care. Hospitals with higher job satisfaction also provided higher quality of care and generate high patient satisfaction scores (Kang et al. 2019).

Healthcare companies commonly use surveys to identify and address employee concerns as part of managing job satisfaction. For example, Unity Health Care increased job satisfaction by changing health insurance plans in response to feedback from a periodic employee survey (see the adjacent box).

Patient Satisfaction

Patient satisfaction is highly correlated to employee job satisfaction. Sadly, a large percent of patients reports experiences that leave them unsatisfied and frustrated with their care (Park 2020). Patients today have greater choices for care, and if they are not satisfied with their experience, they often can change providers. About 7 percent of healthcare customers annually switch their healthcare providers, which "could add up to more than $100 million in lost annual revenue per hospital" (Wynne 2018).

Many healthcare organizations do invest significant resources in service training to improve customer relations. However, Green (2019) advises that patient satisfaction will only result if organizations understand the link between leadership and patient experiences:

- A patient's experience and satisfaction are defined by what they remember.
- What a patient remembers almost always comes from their interactions with employees.

- Great patient experiences come from great employee experiences.
- Leadership is the biggest single factor in great employee experiences.

Generally, what a patient remembers about their healthcare experience revolves around a few interactions that may only last a few minutes. A healthcare company may invest millions of dollars in state-of-the-art equipment and beautiful facilities, only to find that the attitude of a single nurse, doctor, or greeter makes or breaks a patient's experience. Similarly, one employee with a "bad attitude" can affect the job satisfaction and performance of the remaining employees.

Organizational Commitment

Job satisfaction leads to organizational commitment. In addition to affecting the safety and quality of patient experiences, nursing engagement has been tied to organizational commitment and individual work satisfaction (Dempsey and Reilly 2016).

Three types of organizational commitment are generally recognized: what we need to do, ought to do, and want to do. The first is **continuance commitment**, the degree to which a person stays with an organization because they believe they must remain. Continuance commitment is recognition of the costs of leaving a job. For instance, pension vesting and bonuses are often scheduled across multiple years, and employees who leave their organization before these deadlines may lose access to these awards. During periods of high unemployment, workers may have few choices of jobs and thus feel a high degree of continuance commitment.

Normative commitment, in contrast, reflects feelings of obligation to continue a job because it is the right thing to do. Normative commitment is often driven by culture and socialization—what employees believe their families, cultures, and organizations expect of them. Employees with high normative commitment may stay because they would feel guilty about quitting and leaving their colleagues with more work or disappointing their family.

The third component, **affective commitment**, relates to what we want to do. Affective commitment involves employees' emotional attachment to their organization. These employees continue employment because of the positive feelings that bind them to their company. Workers with high affective commitment may identify with and strongly support an organization's goals and values. As with satisfaction, affective commitment results from the fulfillment of individual needs in a work setting (Mercurio 2015; Meyer and Allen 1991).

Although organizational commitment has been shown to be important in many businesses, over the past decades many workers remain unengaged in their work. As mentioned earlier in this chapter, only 14 percent

continuance commitment
The desire felt by employees to remain at their organization.

normative commitment
The feelings of obligation to continue a job because it is the right thing to do.

affective commitment
Employees' emotional attachment to and identification with their organization.

of employees are actively disengaged (those who feel miserable at work and spread this to others), but about 50 percent of all workers report that they are not fully engaged—they show up to work but are psychologically detached (Harter 2020). A survey of 29,000 healthcare workers found that engaged employees were far more positive toward their work than unengaged workers. Engaged employees are also far more likely to display caring attitudes toward patients, see their employers as dedicated to patient care, and want to use their organization for their own healthcare (exhibit 5.7).

Healthcare leaders understand that positive patient experiences are connected to their workforce's engagement. The greater the engagement and commitment of nurses, physicians, and other healthcare personnel, the better the patient outcomes (Lee 2017). When healthcare organizations improve both employee engagement and patient satisfaction, overall hospital ratings and profits increase (Buhlman and Lee 2019).

Employers can take actions to increase their workers' satisfaction, engagement, and commitment, starting with putting their employees first—even above customers. Give employees a voice. Better communication and listening are critical. In addition, employees should be acknowledged and appreciated through awards and recognition programs. Helping employees to find a work–life balance through flexible work, allowing work from home and giving employees control over when work takes place, also improves satisfaction. Embracing diversity, equity, and inclusion is expected and appreciated, especially by younger workers, and makes it more likely that innovative ideas and solutions will surface. Create an environment that fosters professional growth and opens opportunities for employees. Finally, wellness and mental health are essential for a company's employees. A healthy workforce will be more satisfied, engaged, and committed (Achievers 2021).

Attention to employees' needs increases employee work satisfaction, engagement, and commitment. Given the importance of individual worker input in the delivery of healthcare, these factors are critical to the organization's success.

EXHIBIT 5.7
Effect of Employee Engagement on Attitudes

	Engaged (%)	Unengaged (%)
Display a caring attitude toward patients	85	38
Recognize workplace as dedicated to patient care	91	42
Desire to use facility for their own healthcare	82	22

Source: Data from HealthcareSource (2021).

Chapter Summary

Understanding employees' attitudes and satisfaction remains critical in healthcare organizations. Attitudes reflect one's opinions, beliefs, and feelings, and affect how a person responds and behaves. Attitudes are formed from experiences, including the interactions among friends, family, and work colleagues. Attitudes may change as a person gains different experiences and learns new things.

Attitudes are formed and changed through the interaction of three components: affective (what I feel), behavioral (what I do), and cognitive (what I know). Behaviors do not have to mirror attitudes. When people act against their attitudes and knowledge they may experience cognitive dissonance, which may encourage a change in attitudes or actions to bring them back into alignment. Businesses commonly measure employee and customer attitudes through the use of surveys. Although annual surveys are popular, more frequent surveys may be needed to fully understand employee and customer feedback.

Employee engagement—the mutual commitment between employers and employees—drives organizational success. More engaged healthcare providers obtain better patient satisfaction and outcomes. More engaged employees also remain with their employers longer. Many healthcare workers feel that the COVID-19 pandemic will have a detrimental impact on employee engagement, as it has strained many work relationships.

The two-factor theory, the dispositional approach, and the value theory are three popular theories about the origins of job satisfaction. The two-factor theory proposes that hygiene factors related to working conditions affect job dissatisfaction, while motivators related to the work itself, such as the possibility for advancement, affect job satisfaction. The dispositional approach suggests that a person's inherent nature is a primary source of their job satisfaction. The value theory holds that satisfaction only comes from things that employees value, and that gaps between what a person wants and has in a job cause dissatisfaction; managers need to determine what employees value and seek to meet those needs.

Satisfied, engaged workers manifest organizational citizenship behaviors. Employee job satisfaction also leads to greater patient satisfaction—both directly, because of the impact of positive patient–employee interactions, and indirectly, through the effects of increased organizational commitment.

Chapter Questions

1. How is an attitude different from an emotion?
2. What are the three components of attitudes?
3. What causes cognitive dissonance?

4. What are four measures of employee engagement?
5. Why is job satisfaction so important in healthcare?
6. What are hygiene factors? Give three examples.
7. The suggestion that some people are just never happy could be explained by which theory?
8. Going the extra mile could be considered what kind of behavior in a job satisfaction context?
9. What are the three components of organizational commitment?

Chapter Cases

Paula's Commitment Dilemma

Paula worked almost full-time during college, taking six years to finish her degree and become a laboratory technologist. It was hard, but she loves the work, and she was excited to finally finish and take a position at a regional laboratory. She has health insurance for the first time in four years, and a good salary so she can start paying off her student loans. Her new employer also offers matching contributions (up to 5 percent of her salary) to a 401(k), which will vest in five years.

The first few months went very well. She was given a mentor, who showed her how to best accomplish her work and explained which policies were actually used and which could be safely ignored. She made friends with other technologists and started seeing a few of them outside of work. Things seemed to be great.

Now, about six months into her new career, the lab has hit a busy time. Paula has discovered that her supervisor, rushing to hit deadlines and meet quotas, is not following all proper procedures, which could lead to errors in their tests. Paula mentioned this to her colleagues and work friends, and they all told her to ignore it. A few of them have tried to bring it up before, but their supervisor threatened their jobs if they pursued it. One person actually did report it to their boss's boss; they were fired the next day.

Paula now faces a dilemma. She thinks of herself as an ethical person and feels she should report this violation. But she needs the job, enjoys her work, and does not want to cause problems for her friends and colleagues, who could be seen as complicit. She isn't sure what to do.

Case Questions:
1. What continuance, normative, and affective commitment factors may influence Paula's next actions?
2. What do you think Paula will do, and why?

Fred's Approach to Building a Great Business

Fred, an ambitious entrepreneur, is a long-time admirer of Amazon.com, and particularly of the company's consistent efficiency. A couple of years ago he took advantage of some strong financial backing to buy a pharmaceutical compounding company. Fred plans to make his company the most efficient compounder in the market, but he also wants to treat his employees well and develop a highly motivated workforce. To accomplish this, he created a nice work facility, pays at the top of the range for comparable firms, and provides clear policies and generous vacation time.

After two years, Fred decided to survey his employees. The results were disappointing. His employees rank their benefits highly, but the other survey responses indicate that they are not very motivated in their jobs. Fred needs to do something if he is going to meet his goal of best-in-class efficiency.

Case Questions

1. Using the two-factor theory, explain why Fred's employees may be pleased with their benefits but not motivated in their work?
2. What could Fred do from the perspective of the value theory of job satisfaction to better meet his employees' needs?

Chapter Activities

Exploring Employee Engagement

1. Watch the TEDxNormal Talk "Why Aren't More of Us Engaged at Work?" by Jeff Havens (https://youtu.be/xR7Z_3aE5cE) and answer the following questions:
   - Why are there satisfied employees who are not engaged?
   - What leadership does Havens suggest is needed to better engage employees?
   - Which theories described in this chapter match the "Top 6 Motivators of Engaged Employees" that Haven describes in the video?
2. Watch the TEDxWilmingtonSalon Talk "Improving Patient Experience Means Reducing Suffering" by Deirdre Mylod, PhD (https://youtu.be/nDgKGo7B-lE) and answer the following questions:
   - How does patient satisfaction influence patient outcomes?
   - How are surveys used to understand patient opinions and patient satisfaction?

Understanding Cognitive Dissonance Activity

Your instructor will lead you in an exercise that induces cognitive dissonance to help you understand the concept. You will complete two short surveys (part of this book's instructor resources) and discuss the anxiety and discomfort that arise when dissonance is operating. You will then consider the strategies people use to minimize these feelings, such as rationalization, denial, or minimization, and will learn to recognize these feelings and work through this discomfort.

Source: Adapted from Breaking the Prejudice Habit (www.breakingprejudice.org) with the permission of Awareness Harmony Acceptance Advocates.

References

Achievers. 2021. "8 Actionable Employee Engagement Strategies." *Human Resources Today*. Published February 4. www.humanresourcestoday.com/2021/employee-engagement/productivity/?open-article-id=15405084.

Ahmad, A., and M. Farzeen. 2017. "Relationship Among Job Satisfaction, Attitude Towards Work and Organizational Commitment." *Journal of Management Information* 4 (3): 1–4.

Bickmore, A., and K. Merkley. 2019. "The Top Five Recommendations for Improving the Patient Experience." Health Catalyst. Published October 16. www.healthcatalyst.com/insights/patient-satisfaction-and-outcomes-five-recommendations.

Boland, B., A. De Smet, R. Palter, and A. Sanghvi. 2020. "Reimagining the Office and Work Life After COVID-19." McKinsey & Company. Published June 8. www.mckinsey.com/business-functions/organization/our-insights/reimagining-the-office-and-work-life-after-covid-19.

Buhlman, N. W., and T. H. Lee. 2019. "When Patient Experience and Employee Engagement Both Improve, Hospitals' Ratings and Profits Climb." *Harvard Business Review*. Published May 8. https://hbr.org/2019/05/when-patient-experience-and-employee-engagement-both-improve-hospitals-ratings-and-profits-climb.

Carucci, R. 2019. "Balancing the Company's Needs and Employee Satisfaction." *Harvard Business Review*. Published November 1. https://hbr.org/2019/11/balancing-the-companys-needs-and-employee-satisfaction.

Castejon, J. L., J. C. Núñez, R. Gilar-Corbi, and I. M. J. Abellán (eds.). 2021. *New Challenges in the Research of Academic Achievement: Measures, Methods, and Results*. Lausanne: Frontiers Media SA. https://doi.org/10.3389/978-2-88966-507-5.

Cerutti, K., and L. Grodoski. 2020. "Five Post-COVID Behaviors and Attitudes That Will Reshape the Workplace." *WorkDesign Magazine*.

Published June. www.workdesign.com/2020/06/five-post-covid-behaviors-and-attitudes-that-will-reshape-the-workplace/.

Dempsey, C., and B. A. Reilly. 2016. "Nursing Engagement: What Are the Contributing Factors for Success?" *Online Journal of Issues in Nursing* 21 (1): 2. https://pubmed.ncbi.nlm.nih.gov/27853182/.

Dugguh, S. I., and D. Ayaga. 2014. "Job Satisfaction Theories: Traceability to Employee Performance in Organizations." *Journal of Business and Management* 16 (5): 11–18. http://doi.org/10.9790/487X-16511118.

Eiser, J. 1987. "Attitude-Relevant Behavior and the 'Three-Component' View." In *The Expression of Attitude*, 10–17. New York: Springer.

Forbes Coaches Council. 2018. "15 Questions to Ask Employees If You Want Them to Be More Engaged." *Forbes*. Published July 19. www.forbes.com/sites/forbescoachescouncil/2018/07/19/15-questions-to-ask-employees-if-you-want-them-to-be-more-engaged/.

Funk, C., B. Kennedy, and C. Johnson. 2020. "Trust in Medical Scientists Has Grown in U.S., but Mainly Among Democrats." Pew Research Center. Published May 21. www.pewresearch.org/science/2020/05/21/trust-in-medical-scientists-has-grown-in-u-s-but-mainly-among-democrats/.

Gooch, K. 2020. "How Forbes' Best Employers Are Improving Employee Satisfaction." *Becker's Hospital Review*. Published September 18. www.beckershospitalreview.com/workforce/how-forbes-best-employers-are-improving-employee-satisfaction.html.

Green, S. 2019. "The Hospitality Truths That Will Deliver Better Patient Experiences in Health Care." *Forbes Coaches Council* (blog). Published September 10. www.forbes.com/sites/forbescoachescouncil/2019/09/10/the-hospitality-truths-that-will-deliver-better-patient-experiences-in-health-care/.

Greenberg, J., and R. A. Baron. 2008. *Behavior in Organizations: Understanding and Managing the Human Side of Work*. Upper Saddle River, NJ: Prentice Hall.

Harter, J. 2020. "Historic Drop in Employee Engagement Follows Record Rise." *Workplace* (blog). *Gallup*. Published July 2. www.gallup.com/workplace/313313/historic-drop-employee-engagement-follows-record-rise.aspx.

HealthcareSource. 2021. "Employee Engagement Drives Quality Patient Care." Accessed May 21. http://education.healthcaresource.com/employee-engagement-drives-quality-patient-care/.

Heath, S. 2020. "Pushing for Nurse Engagement to Drive Better Patient Experience." *Patient Engagement HIT*. Published February 25. https://patientengagementhit.com/news/pushing-for-nurse-engagement-to-drive-better-patient-experience.

Houmanfar, R., and M. Mattaini (eds.). 2018. *Leadership and Cultural Change: Managing Future Well-Being*. New York: Routledge.

Kang, R., S. T. Kunkel, J. A. Columbo, P. P. Goodney, and S. L. Wong. 2019. "Association of Hospital Employee Satisfaction with Patient Safety and Satisfaction

Within Veterans Affairs Medical Centers." *American Journal of Medicine* 132 (4): 530–34. https://doi.org/10.1016/j.amjmed.2018.11.031.

Labrague, L. J., and J. De los Santos. 2020. "Fear of COVID-19, Psychological Distress, Work Satisfaction and Turnover Intention Among Front Line Nurses" (preprint). Published June 16. Research Square. https://doi.org/10.21203/rs.3.rs-35366/v1.

Ledford, D. 2019. "Measuring Employee Satisfaction with Healthcare Benefits." Northwest Regional Primary Care Association. Published February 14. www.nwrpca.org/news/438437/Measuring-Employee-Satisfaction-with-Healthcare-Benefits.htm.

Lee, T. H. 2017. "How U.S. Health Care Got Safer by Focusing on the Patient Experience." *Harvard Business Review*. Published May 31. https://hbr.org/2017/05/how-u-s-health-care-got-safer-by-focusing-on-the-patient-experience.

Lien, Y., H. Lin, C. Tsai, Y. Lien, and T. Wu. 2019. "Changes in Attitudes Toward Mental Illness in Healthcare Professionals and Students." *International Journal of Environmental Research and Public Health* 16 (23): 4655. https://doi.org/10.3390/ijerph16234655.

Mercurio, Z. 2015. "Affective Commitment as a Core Essence of Organizational Commitment." *Human Resource Development* 14 (4): 389–414.

Meyer, J., and N. Allen. 1991. "A Three-Component Conceptualization of Organizational Commitment." *Human Resource Management Review* 1 (1): 61–89.

Michas, F. 2019. "Percentage of US Hospital Costs in 2016, by Type of Expense." Statista. Published December 4. www.statista.com/statistics/204985/percent-of-hospital-costs-by-type-of-expense/.

Munnich, E., and A. Wozniak. 2020. "What Explains the Rising Share of US Men in Registered Nursing?" *ILR Review* 73 (1): 91–123. https://doi.org/10.1177/0019793919838775.

Ocampo, L., V. Acedillo, A. M. Bacunador, C. C. Balo, Y. J. Lagdameo, and N. S. Tupa. 2018. "A Historical Review of the Development of Organizational Citizenship Behavior (OCB) and Its Implications for the Twenty-First Century." *Personnel Review* 47 (4): 821–62. https://doi.org/10.1108/PR-04-2017-0136.

Organ, D. W., P. M. Podsakoff, and S. B. MacKenzie. 2005. *Organizational Citizenship Behavior: Its Nature, Antecedents, and Consequences*. London, UK: SAGE.

Park, A. 2020. "71% of Patients Are 'Frustrated' with Healthcare Experience: Report." *Health IT* (blog), *Becker's Hospital Review*. Published February 21. www.beckershospitalreview.com/consumerism/71-of-patients-are-frustrated-with-healthcare-experience-report.html.

Peden, C. 2018. "A New Way to Engage Physicians." Institute for Healthcare Improvement (blog). Published April 25. www.ihi.org/communities/blogs/a-new-way-to-engage-physicians.

Perreira, T. A., L. Perrier, M. Prokopy, L. Neves-Mera, and D. Persaud. 2019. "Physician Engagement: A Concept Analysis." *Journal of Healthcare Leadership* 2019 (11): 101–13. https://doi.org/10.2147/JHL.S214765.

Ratanjee, V., and D. Foy. 2020. "What Healthcare Workers Need from Leaders in COVID-19 Crisis." *Workplace* (blog), *Gallup*. Published April 22. www.gallup.com/workplace/308957/healthcare-workers-need-leaders-covid-crisis.aspx.

Redmond, K. 2020. "Steps to Improve Physician Engagement." Physicians Practice. Published March 24. www.physicianspractice.com/view/steps-improve-physician-engagement.

Reeves, M., P. Carlsson-Szlezak, K. Whitaker, and M. Abraham. 2020. "Sensing and Shaping the Post-COVID Era." BCG Henderson Institute (blog). Published April 3. www.bcg.com/publications/2020/8-ways-companies-can-shape-reality-post-covid-19.

Senior, J. 2020. "The Psychological Trauma That Awaits Our Doctors and Nurses." *New York Times*, March 29. www.nytimes.com/2020/03/29/opinion/coronavirus-ventilators-rationing-triage.html.

Siwicki, B. 2019. "How One Hospital's Staff Engagement Survey Boosts Workforce Development—and Patient Care." *Healthcare IT News*, July 30. www.healthcareitnews.com/news/how-one-hospital-s-staff-engagement-survey-boosts-workforce-development-and-patient-care.

Spiegel, D. 2019. "Beyond a Raise, This Is What the Majority of American Workers Want to Be Happier at Work." *CNBC*. Updated June 3. www.cnbc.com/2019/04/01/to-be-happier-at-work-this-is-what-the-majority-of-us-workers-want.html.

Stansell, A. 2019. "Which Workplace Factors Drive Employee Satisfaction Around the World?" Glassdoor Economic Research. Published July 11. www.glassdoor.com/research/employee-satisfaction-drivers/.

Stevenson, M. 2020. "Employee Engagement in 2020." *HR Exchange Network*, February 3. www.hrexchangenetwork.com/employee-engagement/articles/employee-engagement-in-2020.

Wynne, B. 2018. "The Real Reason Loyalty Lacks in Healthcare." *Becker's Hospital Review*, May 2. www.beckershospitalreview.com/care-coordination/the-real-reason-loyalty-lacks-in-healthcare.html.

CHAPTER 6

INDIVIDUAL AND ORGANIZATIONAL VALUES AND ETHICS

> Some places seem to ignore values and ethical behavior and become known for a culture of corruption. A *Modern Healthcare* article suggested that a culture of corruption has become normalized in some parts of Florida. In such an environment "it's easy to rationalize lying, stealing, and cheating." Hundreds of people in Florida have been charged by the US Justice Department with fraudulently billing Medicare. Southern Florida has been identified as "ground zero for Medicare fraud." However, more vigorous enforcement has not seemed to reduce the incidence of fraud and those committing fraud are getting better at hiding their illegal actions. Even with greater enforcement, a representative of the US Justice Department believes that for each indicted case, there may be 100 others (Schencker 2016). In just 2019, the United States Government filed charges against 673 defendants across the United States, who were accused of illegally billing $5.1 billion (US Department of Justice 2021). Clearly, enforcement and prosecution are not enough; values must drive change.

Learning Objectives

After studying this chapter, readers should be able to

- appraise the means for creating environments that foster both ethical and unethical behavior,
- describe the relationship of ethics to individual and organizational values and culture,
- summarize the influence of professionalization on ethics in healthcare,
- identify the conflicts between ethics and values,
- state their own values,
- differentiate among the ethical models,
- compare cultural and personal factors that create variations in ethics, and
- discuss factors that promote organizational justice and ethics.

Key Terms

- autonomy
- beneficence
- corporate social responsibility
- distributive justice
- egoist model
- ethical relativism
- ethics
- justice model (fairness model)
- interactional justice
- justice
- nonmaleficence
- procedural justice
- rights model
- utilitarianism

ethics
The often unwritten codes that constrain and guide actions. Context, facts, cultures, beliefs, values, and attitudes influence ethics and how they are practiced.

The expectation of ethical behavior exists in every nation, culture, company, and organizational position. **Ethics** are the often unwritten codes that constrain and guide actions. As discussed in this chapter, ethics are not homogeneous around the world; context, facts, cultures, beliefs, values, and attitudes influence how ethics are defined and practiced. Too frequently, individuals violate ethical codes to pursue self-interest, which can have embarrassing or tragic consequences.

Business Ethics and Corporate Social Responsibility

Businesses across all industries recognize the importance of ethics and proper ethical behavior for sustained success. To codify this understanding, an organization should integrate ethical principles with its mission.

corporate social responsibility
The self-regulated ethical behavior that goes beyond legal requirements to promote positive social and environmental improvements; sometimes called *corporate citizenship*.

Corporate social responsibility, sometimes called corporate citizenship, is often a major component of the mission of most organizations. **Corporate social responsibility** is self-regulated ethical behavior of doing more than what is legally required to make and promote social and environmental improvements. Many large companies have established ethics-based programs to improve the environment, promote clean energy, and sponsor social welfare initiatives to benefit their stakeholders. In a significant expansion of this effort, the Business Roundtable, an association of CEOs of leading US companies, updated its "Statement on the Purpose of a Corporation" in 2019 to reframe the ethics of corporate governance in terms of responsibility to all stakeholders, not just their financial shareholders:

> While each of our individual companies serves its own corporate purpose, we share a fundamental commitment to all of our stakeholders. We commit to:
>
> - Delivering value to our customers. We will further the tradition of American companies leading the way in meeting or exceeding customer expectations.

- Investing in our employees. This starts with compensating them fairly and providing important benefits. It also includes supporting them through training and education that help develop new skills for a rapidly changing world. We foster diversity and inclusion, dignity and respect.
- Dealing fairly and ethically with our suppliers. We are dedicated to serving as good partners to the other companies, large and small, that help us meet our missions.
- Supporting the communities in which we work. We respect the people in our communities and protect the environment by embracing sustainable practices across our businesses.
- Generating long-term value for shareholders, who provide the capital that allows companies to invest, grow and innovate. We are committed to transparency and effective engagement with shareholders.

Each of our stakeholders is essential. We commit to deliver value to all of them, for the future success of our companies, our communities and our country.

Signatories of this statement included the CEOs from market-defining companies such as Amazon, Exxon Mobil, and Ford Motor Company, as well as major healthcare organizations including Abbott, Anthem, Bristol-Myers Squibb, Cigna, CVS Health, Eli Lilly and Company, Humana, Johnson & Johnson, Mallinckrodt Pharmaceuticals, McKesson, Medtronic, Siemens, and Stryker. In all, more than 200 major firms signed the statement.

Ethics are especially important in the healthcare industry. Decisions are made daily in healthcare that present difficult moral choices. In both clinical and organizational situations, workers encounter many opportunities to make challenging ethical decisions, some affecting issues of life and death and of patient and employee rights. An understanding of ethics and their application is essential for any healthcare manager.

Ethics in Healthcare

An organization's core values should lay the foundation for its mission, vision, and code of ethics (exhibit 6.1). The mission describes what an organization is, and the vision describes what it wants to become. Ethics set the parameters for acceptable actions and behaviors in accomplishing the mission and vision. In essence, ethics describe how a firm should act in accomplishing its mission and achieving its vision.

In contrast to many other industries, healthcare introduces clinical issues that can complicate ethical decisions. Some ethical decisions are straightforward, with a clear right and wrong. But conflicting values—especially in medical practices and clinical decisions—can make the choices more challenging. For instance, the American Medical Association (AMA

EXHIBIT 6.1
The Interactions Between Core Values, Ethics, and Mission and Vision

Core values → Ethics: How a firm should act in accomplishing its mission and vision

Core values → Mission and vision: What a firm is and what it wants to become

Ethics → Mission and vision

---

utilitarianism
An ethical model that defines the moral value of actions based on a valuation of their consequences. Actions are right when they produce positive consequences or the greatest happiness for the greatest number of people.

rights model
An ethical model that distinguishes right from wrong based on the underlying intentions. Individual moral or legal rights are paramount in this model.

justice model (fairness model)
An ethical model that relates to the perceived fairness of actions. Just actions involve consistent, fair treatment on the basis of ethical, religious, or legal standards.

2020) identified key ethical issues that medical students should be taught to prepare them for their careers:

- Using social media professionally
- Deciding whether to receive gifts from patients
- Deciding whether to report an impaired colleague
- Determining when a surrogate decision maker is needed when a patient lacks the capacity to make their own decisions
- Providing equitable quality of and access to care for all patients
- Always placing the welfare of patients above personal interests
- Making decisions when professional and personal values diverge.

Ethical Models

Numerous ethical models have been developed to explain human actions in the face of behavioral dilemmas. Each model makes different assumptions and focuses on different outcomes. Four are discussed here: (1) the utilitarian model, or utilitarianism; (2) the rights model; (3) the justice model, or fairness model; and (4) ethical egoism, or the egoist model.

Utilitarianism defines the moral value of actions based on a valuation of their consequences. Actions are right when they produce positive consequences, or the greatest happiness for the greatest number of people. For example, during times of disaster, patients are triaged on the principle of utilitarianism: The care and resources available are provided to those most likely to survive, rather than to a single critically ill person unlikely to live. This approach is deemed ethical under a utilitarian view of ethics.

The **rights model** distinguishes right from wrong based on the underlying intentions. Individual moral or legal rights are paramount. Many rights are either explicitly or implicitly understood by certain groups: civil rights, women's rights, religious rights, consumer rights, nonsmoker rights, fetal rights, and animal rights. The rights that are accepted and promoted will differ by group. However, respect for others is woven throughout this model, highlighted by the importance of autonomous decision-making.

An example of this model is informed consent, which gives patients the right to a full understanding of the risks and potential outcomes of treatments, allowing them to choose whether to accept or reject medical alternatives.

Deciding whether something is a right can be difficult and controversial. For example, the debate over whether access to healthcare is a right or a privilege continues in the United States. Is it "a contract between the nation and its inhabitants at birth" or an entitlement "that must be earned as opposed to universally provided" (Maruthappu, Ologunde, and Gunarajasingam 2013, 15)? Opinions vary widely among political persuasions and across states (Jacobs and Mettler, 2020).

The **justice model**, or **fairness model**, is concerned with the perceived fairness of actions. Just actions involve consistent, fair treatment based on ethical, religious, or legal standards. Everyone, and every group, is treated equitably; no group is favored over another.

The justice model recognizes three subcategories of justice (described in terms of organizational ethics):

1. **Distributive justice**—the perceived fair distribution of resources, evaluated by the benefits derived and equity in awards
2. **Procedural justice**—the perceived fairness of the process by which a decision is made, evaluated by compliance with decision-making processes, level of access, openness, and participation by employees
3. **Interactional justice**—the perceived fairness of actions, decisions, and treatment of individuals, evaluated by the accuracy of information and the respect and courtesy shown throughout the decision-making process.

Research suggests that employees perceiving greater organizational justice exhibit greater innovation and knowledge sharing (Akram et al. 2020). Likewise, employees experience greater job satisfaction and are more motivated when they perceive greater organizational justice (Pan et al. 2018).

The **egoist model** defines the moral value of action based on whether the foreseeable impacts of the action are favorable for the actor. Simply stated, this model holds that self-interested behavior is ethical. Like utilitarianism, ethical egoism is a consequential theory; that is, the ethical value of a decision depends not on the action taken but on the resulting outcome.

In one view of egoism, an individual or organization is justified in any action taken to advance its own long-term interests. While this self-interested

distributive justice
The perceived fair distribution of resources, evaluated by the benefits derived and equity in awards.

procedural justice
The perceived fairness of the process by which a decision is made, evaluated by compliance with decision-making processes, level of access, openness, and participation by employees.

interactional justice
The perceived fairness of actions, decisions, and treatment of individuals, evaluated by the accuracy of information and the respect and courtesy shown throughout the decision-making process.

egoist model
An ethical model that defines the moral value of action on the basis of whether the foreseeable effects of the action are favorable for the actor—in other words, that self-interested behavior is ethical.

approach to ethics remains unsettling in individual behavior, some might argue that the egoist approach to ethics is an organization's fiduciary obligation. Organizations can, by their actions, direct and strengthen egoistic behavior through their norms and leadership behaviors. Such behaviors may benefit the organization but may be considered unethical from an external perspective (Graham et al. 2020).

Perhaps the most objectionable part of the egoist model is the intent that accompanies it. Although actions and outcomes may mirror those of other ethical approaches, the purpose behind the behavior seems fundamentally Machiavellian.

Four General Ethical Principles

Four general principles are commonly accepted across most ethical models and are particularly applicable in healthcare: autonomy, beneficence, nonmaleficence, and justice (Varkey 2021).

Autonomy—the ability of a person to make meaningful choices free of interference from others—is a fundamental principle in medical ethics. Medical professionals should create conditions that allow patients to make meaningful, informed choices and should not inappropriately interfere with those patient choices. Autonomy necessitates that providers present treatment options, explain risks in understandable terms, and ensure patients understand and consent to selected treatments.

This principle of medical ethics is also directly applicable to any healthcare leader or manager who supervises the work of subordinates. To ensure the autonomy of a patient or subordinate, providers and leaders must

- teach people to make their own decisions,
- support people in the choices they make, and
- not force or coerce people to do things.

Beneficence means taking action that benefits others. Beneficence includes the acts of mercy, charity, and kindness and requires active effort to improve the well-being and status of another.

Nonmaleficence is defined as "doing no harm." Especially for healthcare practitioners, this principle can be challenging, as almost every treatment carries potential risks. Therefore, the risks and burdens must be weighed against the benefits.

Justice, as with the justice model of ethics, requires the fair distribution of benefits, risks, and costs and the equitable treatment of all people.

Promoting Ethical Behavior

Ethics can be boiled down to behaviors that promote honesty and truth-telling: keeping promises; being loyal, fair, accountable, and committed to excellence;

---

autonomy
A person's ability to make meaningful choices free of interference from others.

beneficence
Taking action that benefits others. Beneficence includes the acts of mercy, charity, and kindness and requires active efforts to improve the well-being and status of another.

nonmaleficence
The ethical principle of doing no harm. For healthcare practitioners, this principle often involves weighing the risks and burdens inherent to almost every treatment against the potential benefits to the patient.

justice
The ethical principle of fairly distributing benefits, risks, and costs and treating all people equitably.

obeying laws; and showing concern and respect for others (Varkey 2021). Rather than treating the concept as a mystical and nontangible ideal, ethics should be taught primarily by example. Leaders must display their ethics in their words and deeds. Employees scrutinize even the smallest actions of organizational leaders, and often replicate the leaders' behaviors and attitudes. During the COVID-19 pandemic, for example, CEOs who shared their employees' pain by taking salary cuts were perceived as good leaders. Those who continued to take their normal salaries and bonuses were vilified by their workers. (See the adjacent box.) Leaders who try to cut corners or take advantage of a situation for personal benefit foster an unethical culture and encourage similar actions by employees. On the other hand, leaders whose actions emphasize ethical behavior engender similar employee conduct.

> **CEOs Respond to COVID-19 Cost Reductions**
>
> COVID-19 decimated the revenues of many healthcare systems, especially in early 2020 when most elective surgeries and many physician visits were canceled and deferred. By April 2020, industrywide, hospitals and health providers saw a 40–45 percent decrease in their operating revenues. Hospitals across the United States were losing $1.4 billion per month. Large layoffs and staff cutbacks followed; the Mayo Clinic cut $1.6 billion in employee pay, and Quest Diagnostics furloughed more than 4,000 employees (Thompson 2020).
>
> As their employees were losing their livelihoods, many CEOs and executives cut their own salaries by up to 50 percent for 2020 (Haefner 2020). Other CEOs—including some in Colorado, Utah, Michigan, and Kentucky—continued to take large bonuses and six- or seven-figure salaries while slashing employee paychecks. At the University of Kentucky, the university president furloughed 1,500 workers and halved retirement contributions for the year, but did not agree to cut his own salary (Shugerman 2020). These actions and the perception of a lack of shared sacrifice led many workers, whether or not they were laid off, to question the fairness and ethics of their leaders.

Leaders, and indeed all employees, must do more than comply with legal obligations; they must choose values-based behaviors to become an ethical organization. Everyone in the organization must work to sustain an ethical culture and let a recognized code of conduct govern their actions. In the words of Deloitte's global chief ethics officer, Debbie Rheder, "we aim to do the right thing even—and especially—when it is difficult to do so" (Deloitte 2020). All companies have challenging decisions to make. However, companies living ethical principles will consistently choose the ethical, right thing, even when it is very difficult and not immediately beneficial to the finances of the firm.

Cultural Effects

Ethics and ethical behavior are derived from and take place in the context of the society's culture or cultures. The moral and ethical behavior of one culture may be considered immoral and unethical behavior in another. Ethical decisions are based on content-rich and concrete norms, ideals, and attitudes that emanate from culture. Some cultures find infanticide, genocide, racism,

> **The Ethics of Surprise Billing**
>
> Surprise billing—unexpected medical bills sent by unfamiliar out-of-network providers—has been a major problem for those needing healthcare services. Two-thirds of adults list surprise billing as a major concern. Thousands of patients a year received unexpected charges for emergency care, usually for more than $600, sometimes for thousands or even tens of thousands of dollars. Surprise billing happens when groups of physicians (often emergency doctors and anesthesiologists), ambulance companies, and air transport companies refuse to join health insurance networks and accept the lower payments generally paid under those contracts. Because patients typically will not and cannot choose these providers, even if they do everything right and choose a hospital and physician who are part of their health network, the providers can then bill these patients their usual private-pay rates; in other words, out-of-network billing is part of their business model. The resulting bills are usually unexpected and almost always much higher than normal deductibles and copays, and patients often struggle to pay these legal debts (Kaiser Family Foundation 2021; Kellett, Spratt, and Miller 2019).
>
> Providers who engage in surprise billing frequently take patients to collection, which can ruin credit ratings. For instance, Southeastern Emergency Physicians, owned by the private equity firm Blackstone Group, filed over 5,000 collection lawsuits in just one county in Tennessee, mostly against low-income patients (Thomas 2019). Fortunately, a federal law goes into effect in 2022 that will ban most of the negative impacts of surprise billing (Kaiser Family Foundation 2021).

and torture morally acceptable, while others condemn such behaviors. Differences in ethics across cultures are referred to as **ethical relativism**, which is the concept that an action is considered right or wrong depending on the context and environment in which the action takes place. As the controversy around surprise billing illustrates (see the box), what is ethical often depends on perspective. Surprise billing is considered a legitimate part of many providers' business models and an acceptable way to increase earnings. Yet, from a patient's perspective, receiving a large bill that is not covered by your insurance company from a provider you did not choose seems very wrong.

Many observers argue that not all values are relative but that a core, universally moral standard exists across most cultures (Gowans 2021). Values such as honesty, loyalty, trust, and compassion tend to transcend cultures and nationalities. Even though groups and individuals may frequently violate them, these values translate to common ethical standards for most people around the world (Lampton and Razack 2020; Sanderson and Pugliese 2012).

ethical relativism The concept that an action is considered right or wrong depending on the context and environment in which the action takes place.

Ethical Challenges in Business and Healthcare

Adhering to ethical values can be a significant challenge to all businesses, including those in healthcare. Research has shown that although almost all large companies have written codes of ethics, rampant unethical behavior may exist in their business culture and the actual behaviors often do not support the desired behaviors espoused by their ethical code (Babri, Davidson, and Helin, 2019; Webley and Werner 2008). Following are some of the more egregious healthcare ethical violations since 2000:

- *Tenet Healthcare.* Tenet was accused of not just healthcare fraud but also "rank patient abuse." The for-profit health system agreed in 2003 to pay $54 million to the government to resolve accusations that heart physicians at its Redding, California, hospital conducted unnecessary heart procedures and operations on hundreds of patients (Eichenwald 2003).
- *Columbia/HCA.* In 2003, the US Department of Justice settled the second of two complaints against for-profit health system Columbia/HCA. The company was fined $1.7 billion for improperly billing Medicare and Medicaid, falsifying diagnostic codes, illegally claiming nonreimbursable expenses, and billing for services for patients who did not qualify to receive them (US Department of Justice 2003).
- *HealthSouth.* One of the largest companies in the United States at one time, HealthSouth's problems surfaced soon after then-CEO Richard Scrushy sold $100 million in stock a few days prior to the company reporting a loss. Investigation by authorities revealed that the firm had falsely inflated its earnings by $1.4 billion. Many of the company's officers served jail time (Beam 2009). For more details on the HealthSouth case, see case 15 in the back of this book.
- *Theranos.* This privately held health technology company claimed to be able to perform a wide variety of laboratory tests with tiny amounts of blood, such as from fingersticks. Founded in 2003, it had a market capitalization of $10 billion and its founder, Elizabeth Holmes, was listed by Forbes as the youngest self-made female billionaire in 2015. In 2016 the company was charged with fraud by multiple federal agencies: the promised technology did not exist, and Theranos executives were accused of falsifying claims about test efficacy. Holmes and former company president Ramesh Balwani have been indicted for their actions (Carreyrou 2020). Case 2 in the back of this book discusses Theranos in more detail.

As a result of prior ethics violations, the federal government passed a number of laws to regulate ethical behavior and encourage compliance, including the Sarbanes-Oxley Act of 2002. The Office of Inspector General (OIG) of the US Department of Health and Human Services, which has enforcement responsibility for Sarbanes-Oxley, operates a website to "help healthcare providers such as hospitals and physicians comply with relevant Federal health care laws and regulations, OIG creates compliance resources"

(OIG 2021). It provides guidance on establishing a compliance program (along with materials for boards and physicians) to encourage ethical behavior and to help them follow applicable laws.

Healthcare Ethics Issues

Even though most healthcare managers and professionals never violate the law, ethical challenges are still common in the healthcare industry. Exhibit 6.2 shows the top ethical dilemmas in 2019 for chief financial officers (CFOs) in the healthcare industry. These challenges include balancing patient rights, societal benefits, and access to care.

Moreover, nearly every day, ethical healthcare challenges arise for clinicians and other staff who interact with patients. Providers represent multiple stakeholders and must balance the needs and demands of each. The box on this page illustrates how the healthcare worker must occasionally weigh the costs to the organization against the risks and benefits to the patient.

Many situations do not have obvious resolutions, which can make the decision stressful for the provider or staff member. Providers frequently differ on whether or not an action is ethical. For instance, 34 percent of physicians in one survey indicated they would prescribe a placebo to a patient, while 47 percent would not. Plus, 50 percent believe that those engaging in unhealthy behavior should pay more for their medical insurance, but 29 percent disagreed (Gallegos 2020).

Healthcare organizations have reacted to ethical violations and challenges by creating their own ethical codes of conduct. Most large healthcare companies now have firm, specific regulations governing ethics. Hospital Corporation of America (HCA) instituted a strict ethics and compliance program after they were found guilty of ethical violations in the early 1990s. HCA has now been named one of the world's most ethical companies by Ethisphere 11 times (HCA Healthcare 2021). According to the "Ethics and Compliance" section of the company's website, the HCA code of conduct includes direction for patients, physicians, third-party payers, subcontractors, vendors, and

EXHIBIT 6.2
Top Ethical Concerns Facing Healthcare CFOs in 2019

1. How long should care be delayed to obtain prior authorization and ensure services are covered?
2. What level of nonemergent care should be provided to undocumented patients?
3. How can organizations be more transparent about pricing?
4. How can organizations improve access to care?

Source: Hegwer (2019).

consultants to ensure ethical standards, laws, and regulations are followed, and the company provides an extensive set of compliance policies and procedures covering every aspect of their business. HCA also maintains a 24-hour ethics hotline to receive reports. The company implemented mandatory ethics training and communications and audits the program for effectiveness. In addition, they have ethics and compliance officers at the corporate, division, and facilities levels throughout the organization.

> **Ethical Challenge at Redmond District Hospital**
>
> It is 10:00 a.m., and Gary, a lead nurse at Redmond District Hospital, has received a discharge order for a homeless patient with pneumonia who has been in the hospital for more than a month. Gary knows that his patient requires further treatment that is normally received at home. The hospital has already spent a huge sum treating this man, and the Medicaid reimbursement covered only the first week of his care.
>
> Gary is struggling with the thought of discharging this patient, knowing that he will probably not recover, but he feels that admission and discharge authority lies only with the physician. If he wants to change the discharge order, he will have to call the patient's doctor, Dr. Granis, who can be rather unpleasant. Gary called Dr. Granis earlier that morning about an IV antibiotic. He was told that the prescription was correct and not to bother the physician unless it was a life-or-death issue. Gary needs to decide what to do before noon.
>
> What should Gary do? What ethical principles are present in this case?

Professional Ethics

Many professional organizations have developed and published codes of ethics for their members. With these codes, they seek to reinforce desirable behaviors and ethical conduct, which signal their commitment to specific values and moral standards. For example, the American College of Healthcare Executives (ACHE), the largest professional association for healthcare leaders in the world, has established a code of ethics for its members, which "incorporates standards of ethical behavior governing individual behavior, particularly when that conduct directly relates to the role and identity of the healthcare executive" (ACHE 2017).

> **Ascension Health's Healthcare Ethics**
>
> As of March 2021, the "Our Mission" section of Ascension Health's website features the following ethics statement (Ascension 2021):
>
> Healthcare ethics focuses on supporting personalized care that is consistent with each patient's individual values and promotes the good of the human person.
>
> Our Mission, Vision, Values, and identity as a healing ministry of the Catholic Church guide our practices, with our Ethics Department serving a critical role by:
>
> - Fostering disciplined decision-making processes that promote our Mission, Vision, Values and Catholic identity in clinical and organizational realms
> - Sharing research and counsel to Ascension leaders working through organizational and clinical ethical issues
>
> *(continued)*

(continued from previous page)
- Educating and providing resources for leaders and work teams that help them carry out their ethics responsibilities Ascension-wide
- Supporting and promoting dialogue between Ascension ministry leaders and local Ordinaries (diocesan bishops) to strengthen our relationship with the Church and our identity as one of its healing ministries
- Leading our palliative care program

Ascension Health, the largest Catholic and not-for-profit health system in the United States, has established two primary ethics goals as part of its code of conduct (see the box).

Similarly, the American Physical Therapy Association (APTA), which has more than 100,000 practitioner members, provides ethical guidance for its affiliates through its code of ethics, which is based on the association's established core values. Each of the eight principles included in the code is tied to the related core values (APTA 2020):

1. Physical therapists shall respect the inherent dignity and rights of all individuals. (Core Values: Compassion and Caring, Integrity)
2. Physical therapists shall be trustworthy and compassionate in addressing the rights and needs of patients and clients. (Core Values: Altruism, Collaboration, Compassion and Caring, Duty)
3. Physical therapists shall be accountable for making sound professional judgments. (Core Values: Collaboration, Duty, Excellence, Integrity)
4. Physical therapists shall demonstrate integrity in their relationships with patients and clients, families, colleagues, students, research participants, other health care providers, employers, payers, and the public. (Core Value: Integrity)
5. Physical therapists shall fulfill their legal and professional obligations. (Core Values: Accountability, Duty, Social Responsibility)
6. Physical therapists shall enhance their expertise through the lifelong acquisition and refinement of knowledge, skills, abilities, and professional behaviors. (Core Value: Excellence)
7. Physical therapists shall promote organizational behaviors and business practices that benefit patients and clients and society. (Core Values: Integrity, Accountability)
8. Physical therapists shall participate in efforts to meet the health needs of people locally, nationally, or globally. (Core Value: Social Responsibility)

Links to other professional healthcare associations' ethical codes can be found in exhibit 6.3. Each code delineates the organization's expectations for professional behavior.

EXHIBIT 6.3
Codes of Ethics and Behavior for Select Healthcare Associations

Academy of Nutrition and Dietetics
www.eatright.org/codeofethics/

American Academy of Ophthalmology
www.aao.org/ethics-detail/code-of-ethics

American Cancer Society
www.cancer.org/aboutus/acspolicies/code-of-ethics-and-conflict-of-interest-policy

American College of Nurse-Midwives
www.midwife.org/ACNM-Documents

American Dental Association
www.ada.org/en/about-the-ada/principles-of-ethics-code-of-professional-conduct/

American Occupational Therapy Association
www.aota.org/about-occupational-therapy/ethics.aspx

American Public Health Association
www.apha.org/apha-communities/member-sections/ethics

Medical Group Management Association
www.mgma.com/about/organization/organizational-documents

A Rule of Thumb for Ethical Behavior: The Newspaper Test

Would you like to have a quick test to see if your behavior is ethical? Try the newspaper test. Imagine that your decision or action has been described in detail on the front page of a major newspaper such as the *Washington Post*. Would you be proud to have your family and community know what you are doing? If publishing it on the front page of a major newspaper would embarrass you or your family, you might want to reconsider the decision. If you would be proud to have your behavior reported for all to see, you should probably do it.

Transparency is the key here: If you are comfortable that others have general knowledge of your behavior, you may be confident that you are proceeding ethically. However, if you do not want your actions to be known by a wide audience, you should reconsider your decision because unethical behavior may be taking place.

Other Methods to Determine Whether Decisions Are Ethical

Every day, individuals confront situations and decisions requiring ethical judgments that may not necessarily be resolved by consulting a formal code of ethics. Several methods are available to test whether a decision is ethical or unethical. Velasquez and colleagues (2015), for example, suggest asking the following questions:

- What benefits and what harms will each course of action produce, and which alternative will lead to the best overall consequences?
- What moral rights do the affected parties have, and which course of action best respects those rights?
- Which course of action treats everyone the same, except where there is a morally justifiable reason not to, and does not show favoritism or discrimination?
- Which course of action advances the common good?
- Which course of action develops moral virtues?

Chapter Summary

Ethics delineate proper actions and behaviors for individuals and organizations. They may be written as codes of conduct, or they may be unwritten societal norms. Ideally, a set of ethics is a tool used to determine whether behaviors are acceptable in accomplishing an organization's mission and vision. Healthcare managers and workers must demonstrate highly ethical conduct that reflects their core values.

The utilitarian, rights, justice (or fairness), and egoist ethical models make different assumptions as the basis of ethical decisions. Utilitarianism defines ethical behavior as an action that produces the greatest value to the greatest number of people; the rights model focuses on a party's underlying moral or legal rights; the justice model relates to the perceived fairness of actions; and the egoist model values the outcomes that are most favorable to the actor. Four general principles are commonly accepted across most ethical models: autonomy, beneficence, nonmaleficence, and justice.

Leaders' behaviors dictate the ethical or unethical practices in an organization, as their actions, good and bad, are typically emulated by employees. In addition, whether an action is considered ethical may depend on the values and culture of the society in which the conduct takes place. Although ethical relativism holds that standards of ethics may vary in different cultures, the core values of honesty, loyalty, trust, and compassion are common to most ethical standards around the world.

Although most firms have established written codes of ethics for their staff or members, unethical conduct persists. To discourage and punish these ethical violations, the US government has passed laws such as the 2002 Sarbanes-Oxley Act, and healthcare companies and professional organizations have adopted ethical codes of conduct. Still, many companies struggle to behave ethically. To guide ethical decisions, companies and organizational leaders should become knowledgeable of applicable ethical codes, the newspaper test, and other simple metrics that may help them assess transparency and determine whether an action could be unethical.

Chapter Questions

1. How are ethics and values related?
2. How do ethics and organizational mission and vision interrelate?
3. What is the difference between the rights model and the justice model?
4. What are some challenges to using utilitarianism when considering ethical issues?
5. How do laws relate to the rights model?
6. Explain how more than one of the subcategories of the justice model could occur at the same time. Provide an example.
7. What role does autonomy have in patient care?
8. When does ethical relativism not apply?
9. Why do some businesses routinely violate their written code of ethics?
10. What role do professional organizations have in establishing guidelines for ethical conduct?
11. How does transparency promote ethical behavior?

Chapter Cases

Brain Death in the ICU

You are the chief operating officer of Mt. Pleasant Hospital, a 150-bed regional hospital. You are on call one night, the Thursday before Labor Day, when paramedics bring Jared, a 17-year-old boy, to the emergency department. Jared was riding a motorcycle without a helmet when he became distracted and crashed. Although he was not driving more than 35 miles per hour, he struck his head in the crash, causing severe brain damage. Jared was brought by helicopter to your hospital and arrived unconscious. The emergency department physicians were able to stabilize him and he was admitted to the intensive care unit (ICU).

After three days, the intensivists have determined that Jared is brain dead. They met with his parents to explain that there is no hope of recovery, and recommended that the boy be taken off the respirator and that all treatment be discontinued. Jared's parents responded that they belong to a Christian church, that the boy's father has faith that their son will recover, and that they now have many people in their congregation praying for his recovery. They are convinced that their son will be healed by a miracle, and they are adamant that they do not want him removed from life support.

After several conversations produced no change in the parents' position, the attending intensivist brought the case to the hospital bioethics committee for review. The committee includes ethicists, a pastor, a social worker, a pediatric intensivist, a neonatologist, a community pediatrician, a member of the hospital board, the medical director, and you. The committee reviewed the situation in detail and, after considerable discussion, agreed that the boy should be taken off life support. The arguments in favor of this action are that because the boy is brain dead, he is beyond any hope of recovery, and continued treatment by definition is futile. In addition, Labor Day weekend will begin in 24 hours and all ten ICU beds are now occupied. Based on past experience it is a virtual certainty that the boy will remain in ICU for at least several days, so the hospital currently has no ICU capacity if something happens over the holiday weekend. The committee also believes it is unethical to continue billing the family's health insurer (Medicaid) for continuing to provide expensive and futile treatment. While the committee's opinion is based on compelling reasons, many members of the committee are uneasy about taking the boy off life support over his parents' adamant objection.

After the bioethics committee meeting, you go upstairs to see the boy. He is surrounded by family members, and his father is kneeling at his bedside, his hand on his brow, fervently praying for his recovery. You are concerned about showing respect for the family's religious beliefs. This hospital has a respectful and family-friendly culture, and you want to honor that. You meet with Jared's attending physician to review bioethics committee's recommendation, and you ask him to meet with the chair of the committee to jointly inform the family of the recommendation, and to try to get their support for discontinuing life support.

Several hours later, you are contacted by the attending physician. The parents were not persuaded by the committee's recommendation, and they remain adamant that their son should remain on life support indefinitely until he is healed.

Case Questions
1. What would you do? Defend your decision.
2. Would your choice be different if the issue of organ harvesting had been discussed and the boy was available to donate almost all of his organs?
3. What are the ethical issues at play in this case?

Possible CEO Misuse of Company Funds

You are the head actuary in a large health insurance company headquartered just north of Indianapolis. The company has a written code of ethics in place that promotes the values of teamwork and equal treatment. The CEO and company founder feels strongly that his employees should treat each other equally.

However, it is apparent that the CEO does not feel the code applies to him. He lives only three miles from corporate headquarters in a $12 million mansion, and commutes to work by helicopter. Everyone is certain that the company is paying for these excesses, and many employees are disturbed by it.

You also find it difficult to get an appointment with the CEO—a common complaint for most top executives in the company. As a result of his unavailability, most employees get news about their company and their CEO primarily from the press or from social media.

Employee morale is already suffering, and the turnover rate has begun climbing. Now, fraud charges have been filed against members of the company's top management team.

Case Questions
1. What ethical issues does this case raise?
2. How would you handle these ethical issues differently under different ethical models?
3. If you were to replace this CEO, what actions would you take?

Chapter Activities

Compare and Contrast Ethical Statements

Pick two professional codes of ethics (you may use those in this chapter) and answer the following questions:

1. What differences do you see between the two ethical statements? What similarities, if any?
2. Do you think the differences influence the behavior of the respective association's members, or does the behavior of the organization's members influence the written code of ethics?

Ethical Breakdowns in Healthcare Organizations

Read the 2011 article "Ethical Breakdowns" by Max Bazerman and Ann Tenbrunsel (*Harvard Business Review* 89 (4): 58–65; https://hbr.

org/2011/04/ethical-breakdowns). Give an example of each of the following in healthcare:

1. Goals that have rewarded unethical behavior.
2. Conflicts of interest that motivated people to ignore bad behavior.
3. Unethical decisions that were overlooked because the outcome was good.

A Deeper Dive into Complex Healthcare Ethics

Watch the video of the one-hour panelist session "A Conversation About Challenging Cases in Clinical Ethics" (Seattle Children's Hospital [2013]; https://youtu.be/3QoxMX2kIn8; 57 minutes) in which seven bioethicists discuss complex cases in pediatric clinical ethics. Answer the following questions:

1. What are the main issues in clinical ethics in this video?
2. What are some of the ways the panelists seek to find better solutions to the ethical issues?

Watch Ferdinand Waldenberger's 2015 TEDx Talk "The Ethical Dilemma of a Heart Surgeon" (https://youtu.be/ZScCiXNyD6M; 19 minutes). Answer the following questions:

1. What are the ethical dilemmas of a heart surgeon, as presented in this video?
2. How would you address these, given your own values and perspectives?

References

Akram, T., S. Lei, M. Haider, and S. Hussain. 2020. "The Impact of Organizational Justice on Employee Innovative Work Behavior." *Journal of Innovation & Knowledge* 5 (2): 117–29.

American College of Healthcare Executives (ACHE). 2017. "ACHE Code of Ethics." Amended November 13. www.ache.org/about-ache/our-story/our-commitments/ethics/ache-code-of-ethics.

American Medical Association (AMA). 2020. "The Top 10 Ethical Issues Medical Students Should Be Taught." February 14. www.ama-assn.org/education/accelerating-change-medical-education/top-10-ethical-issues-medical-students-should-be.

American Physical Therapy Association (APTA). 2020. "Code of Ethics for the Physical Therapist." www.apta.org/apta-and-you/leadership-and-governance/policies/code-of-ethics-for-the-physical-therapist.

Ascension. 2021. "Healthcare Ethics." Accessed March 31. https://ascension.org/our-mission/healthcare-ethics.

Babri, M., B. Davidson, and S. Helin. 2019. "An Updated Inquiry into the Study of Corporate Codes of Ethics: 2005–2016." *Journal of Business Ethics* 168 (1): 71–108. https://doi.org/10.1007/s10551-019-04192-x.

Beam, A. 2009. *HealthSouth: The Wagon to Disaster*. Fairhope, AL: Wagon Publishing.

Business Roundtable. 2019. Our Commitment. https://opportunity.businessroundtable.org/ourcommitment/.

Carreyrou, J. 2020. *Bad Blood: Secrets and Lies in a Silicon Valley Startup*. New York: Vintage Books.

Deloitte. 2020. "Ethics at Deloitte." www2.deloitte.com/global/en/pages/about-deloitte/articles/ethics-at-deloitte.html.

Eichenwald, K. 2003. "Tenet Healthcare Paying $54 Million in Fraud Settlement." *New York Times*, August 7. www.nytimes.com/2003/08/07/business/tenet-healthcare-paying-54-million-in-fraud-settlement.html.

Gallegos, A. 2020. "Money, Patients, Romance: Physician Ethics 2020." Medscape. www.medscape.com/slideshow/2020-ethics-report-money-romance-6013380#1.

Gowans, C. 2021. "Moral Relativism." *Stanford Encyclopedia of Philosophy*. Published March 10. https://plato.stanford.edu/entries/moral-relativism/.

Graham, K. A., C. J. Resick, J. A. Margolis, P. Shao, M. B. Hargis, and J. D. Kiker. 2020. "Egoistic Norms, Organizational Identification, and the Perceived Ethicality of Unethical Pro-Organizational Behavior: A Moral Maturation Perspective." *Human Relations* 73 (9): 1249–77. https://doi.org/10.1177/0018726719862851.

Haefner, M. 2020. "Hospital CEOs, Execs Forgo Pay Amid COVID-19." *Becker's Hospital Review*, June 9. www.beckershospitalreview.com/hospital-management-administration/hospital-ceos-execs-forgo-pay-amid-covid-19-7-updates.html.

HCA Healthcare. 2021. "HCA Healthcare Named a 2021 World's Most Ethical Company." *HCA Today* (blog). Published February 23. https://hcatodayblog.com/2021/02/23/hca-healthcare-named-a-2021-worlds-most-ethical-company/.

Hegwer, L. 2019. "The Most Pressing Ethical Issues in Healthcare." Healthcare Financial Management Association. Published November 26. www.hfma.org/topics/hfm/2019/december/the-most-pressing-ethical-issues-in-healthcare.html.

Jacobs, L. R., and S. Mettler. 2020. "What Health Reform Tells Us About American Politics." *Journal of Health Politics, Policy and Law* 45 (4): 581–93. https://doi.org/10.1215/03616878-8255505.

Kaiser Family Foundation. 2021. "Surprise Medical Bills: New Protections for Consumers Take Effect in 2022." *Private Insurance* (blog). *KFF*. Published February 4. www.kff.org/private-insurance/fact-sheet/surprise-medical-bills-new-protections-for-consumers-take-effect-in-2022/.

Kellett, H., A. Spratt, and M. E. Miller. 2019. "Surprise Billing: Choose Patients Over Profits." *Health Affairs* (blog). Published August 12. www.healthaffairs.org/do/10.1377/hblog20190808.585050/full/.

Lampton, J. A., and B. I. Razack. 2020. "Ethics Must Be Global." *Strategic Finance*, February 1. https://sfmagazine.com/post-entry/february-2020-ethics-must-be-global/.

Maruthappu, M., R. Ologunde, and A. Gunarajasingam. 2013. "Is Health Care a Right? Health Reforms in the USA and Their Impact upon the Concept of Care." *Annals of Medicine and Surgery* 2 (1): 15–17. https://doi.org/10.1016/S2049-0801(13)70021-9.

Office of the Inspector General (OIG). 2021. Compliance. https://oig.hhs.gov/compliance/index.asp.

Pan, X., M. Chen, Z. Hao, and W. Bi. 2018. "The Effects of Organizational Justice on Positive Organizational Behavior: Evidence from a Large-Sample Survey and a Situational Experiment." *Frontiers in Psychology* 8 (2315). https://doi.org/10.3389/fpsyg.2017.02315.

Sanderson, R. B., and M. A. Pugliese. 2012. *Beyond Naïveté: Ethics, Economics and Values*. Lanham, MD: University Press of America.

Schencker, L. 2016. "What's the Matter with Florida? Healthcare Fraud Flourishes Despite Enforcement Efforts." *Modern Healthcare*, May 7. www.modernhealthcare.com/article/20160507/MAGAZINE/305079988/.

Shugerman, E. 2020. "The Hospital CEOs Keeping Seven-Figure Salaries as Frontline Workers Go Without Pay." *Daily Beast*, May 2. www.thedailybeast.com/frontline-workers-are-going-without-pay-as-hospital-ceos-keep-their-seven-figure-salaries.

Thomas, W. 2019. "This Doctors Group Is Owned by a Private Equity Firm and Repeatedly Sued the Poor Until We Called Them." *ProPublica*, November 27. www.propublica.org/article/this-doctors-group-is-owned-by-a-private-equity-firm-and-repeatedly-sued-the-poor-until-we-called-them.

Thompson, D. 2020. "Layoffs and Losses: COVID-19 Leaves U.S. Hospitals in Financial Crisis." *U.S. News and World Report*, May 6. www.usnews.com/news/health-news/articles/2020-05-06/layoffs-and-losses-covid-19-leaves-us-hospitals-in-financial-crisis.

US Department of Justice. 2021. "Facts & Statistics." www.justice.gov/criminal-fraud/facts-statistics.

———. 2003. "Largest Health Care Fraud Case in U.S. History Settled: HCA Investigation Nets Record Total of $1.7 Billion" (press release). Published June 26, 2003. www.justice.gov/archive/opa/pr/2003/June/03_civ_386.htm.

Varkey, B. 2021. "Principles of Clinical Ethics and Their Application to Practice." *Medical Principles and Practice* 30 (1): 17–28. https://doi.org/10.1159/000509119.

Velasquez, M., C. Andre, T. Shanks, and M. J. Meyer. 2015. "Thinking Ethically." Markkula Center for Applied Ethics, Santa Clara University. Published August 1. www.scu.edu/ethics/ethics-resources/ethical-decision-making/thinking-ethically/.

Webley, S., and A. Werner. 2008. "Corporate Codes of Ethics: Necessary but Not Sufficient." *Business Ethics: A European Review* 17 (4): 405–15. https://doi.org/10.1111/j.1467-8608.2008.00543.x.

CHAPTER 7

INDIVIDUAL AND ORGANIZATIONAL MOTIVATION

> A physician and former medical group CEO noted (Pearl 2019):
>
> For decades, elite business schools have touted the benefits of financial incentives to motivate sales teams, factory workers and rising executives. Results are mixed.
>
> In medicine, financial incentives rarely achieve their intended goals. It's not because they don't work. . . . It's because they work too well. Monetary rewards always change doctor behavior, but rarely achieve the outcomes desired.
>
> The physician referenced a *JAMA* study that suggested that using money to motivate improvements in clinical quality could lead to fatal consequences. Doctors were paid to prevent readmissions to hospitals. Readmission rates went down, but deaths after discharge from hospitals increased.

Learning Objectives

After studying this chapter, readers should be able to

- compare and contrast the theories presented, including Maslow's hierarchy of needs, Herzberg's two-factor theory, equity theory, reinforcement theory, and expectancy theory;
- discuss the methods of setting goals and the effects of goals on motivation;
- describe the benefits and challenges of job enrichment and job expansion; and
- distinguish between the advantages of intrinsic stimuli and those of external stimuli.

Key Terms

- dissatisfiers
- equity theory
- ERG theory of motivation
- expectancy
- expectancy theory
- external stimuli
- frustration-regression
- goal-setting theory
- instrumentality
- intrinsic stimuli
- job characteristics model
- satisfiers
- two-factor theory
- valence

One of the critical challenges for any leader is motivating employees. Motivation is defined as "the willingness to work at a certain level of effort," and motivation theories "explain the causes of workplace effort and direction of effort" (Sullivan 1989, 346).

Motivation takes a central position in any performance theory and has been cited as essential to the success of healthcare systems (Cerasoli, Nicklin, and Ford 2014). Scholars and managers have sought for many decades to identify methods to motivate and inspire employees. As mentioned in chapters 1 and 2, early ideas about motivation included Frederick W. Taylor's scientific management theory, Abraham Maslow's hierarchy of needs, and Douglas McGregor's theory X and theory Y. This chapter continues the examination of theories and practices of motivation.

Evidence suggests that many managers struggle to motivate their employees. Most agree that strategies promoting positive employee commitment and motivation strengthen a firm's competitive position (Snyder et al. 2021). Yet surveys reveal that almost two-thirds of US employees are not engaged in and motivated by their work; as a result, perhaps 20 percent act out negatively to damage their organization (Harter 2018; Seidman 2012). Exhibit 7.1 lists troubling statistics from 2018 and 2019 related to motivation. Motivating and engaging employees remain important skills needed by managers.

The failure of many organizations to motivate their employees has been attributed to an overreliance on external motivators (Herzberg 2003). Most theories explaining motivation divide motivational efforts into external and internal stimuli (Cerasoli, Nicklin, and Ford 2014). Motivation by external stimuli was promoted in the 1930s by behavioralists such as B. F. Skinner, who systematically changed animal behaviors by providing rewards and punishments. The concept of external stimuli as sources of motivation (also called *operant conditioning*) became deeply rooted in business practices. Managers continue the behaviorist strategy of seeking to motivate employees with rewards and punishments. However, most studies show that external

EXHIBIT 7.1
Employee Engagement Statistics

- 65% of US employees are not engaged.
- 17% of employees worldwide are actively disengaged.
- Organizations with engaged employees are 21% more profitable.
- 93% of employees in not-for-profit work feel engaged.
- 33% of employees are so bored they want to leave their jobs.

Source: Data from Harter (2018), Mackey (2019).

stimuli from rewards and punishments deliver only short-term results, and long-term, heavy reliance on these types of stimuli may damage work relationships (Chamorro-Premuzic 2013; Strickler 2006). Kohn (1993) characterized it this way:

> Research suggests that, by and large, rewards succeed at securing one thing only: temporary compliance. When it comes to producing lasting change in attitudes and behavior, however, rewards, like punishment, are strikingly ineffective. Once the rewards run out, people revert to their old behaviors.

Managers too often use external factors such as threats and adjustments to salary and benefits to enforce work performance standards.

External Stimuli

Managers frequently use **external stimuli**—means of instigation that originate outside of a person—because they are the quickest way to obtain the desired results. Herzberg (2003) suggested that although kicking is the most rapid way to move and stimulate a person, kicking does not create lasting motivation and may even inspire negative behaviors, because the person might kick back or sabotage the work being done. Furthermore, to sustain the person's momentum and performance, the kicking or threat of kicking must continue.

Certainly, kicking is not the primary external stimulus used for motivation in businesses today. However, other types of threats and punishments—such as forced performance rankings, letters of reprimand, and verbal chastisement—are often used. Negative forms of external stimuli are, in fact, used regularly by managers because movement of some sort does occur as

external stimuli Means of instigation that originate from outside an individual; the use of external stimuli for motivation is also called *operant conditioning*.

a result; the problem is that these managers often confuse movement with desired outcomes (Gardner 2012).

Other, less intrusive types of external incentives include promotions, performance-based bonuses, grades, awards, and employee recognition programs. External incentives have been shown to increase output. However, motivation is multifaceted, and organizations often use multiple means—both external and intrinsic (described in detail in the next section)—to encourage desired outcomes. The support of supervisors, for example, showed an increase in motivation among healthcare workers in one study. The same study found a high correlation between low levels of support and a lack of motivation (Ullah, Khan, and Siddique 2017).

Good leaders must learn to merge external methods appropriately with intrinsic methods to achieve sustainable motivation. The type and mix of stimuli should be carefully selected to achieve the behaviors sought (Volini et al. 2020).

Intrinsic Stimuli

intrinsic stimuli
Stimuli that originate from within an individual.

Internal or **intrinsic stimuli** originate from within the individual. Workers find meaning in their labor rather than in performance for some external gain. Herzberg (2003, 88) stated that internal stimuli are the only mechanisms that induce motivation, as "only when one has a generator of one's own [can we] talk about motivation." The degree to which an individual or a group experiences internal motivation determines their level of satisfaction and commitment (Kihlstrom 2020).

Work that is found more intrinsically satisfying motivates greater effort. For example, managers have been found to be motivated by intrinsic factors of support, relationships, and greater autonomy (Breed, Downing, and Ally 2020). As illustrated in exhibit 7.2, the more internal stimuli are present, the greater the resulting employee satisfaction and commitment to the work. Conversely, greater use of external controls and external stimuli decreases employee satisfaction and commitment. The level of satisfaction and commitment drops rapidly as external controls are introduced and can quickly overshadow internal stimuli.

ERG theory of motivation
The theory (a refinement of Maslow's hierarchy of needs) that motivation results from three factors: existence, relatedness, and growth.

Alderfer's ERG Theory

As a refinement of Maslow's hierarchy of needs, Clayton Alderfer proposed the **ERG theory of motivation**, which posits that motivation results from three factors: existence, relatedness, and growth. This theory collapses Maslow's five categories into three simpler and broader classes: (1) existence needs, ensuring physiological and physical safety; (2) relatedness needs,

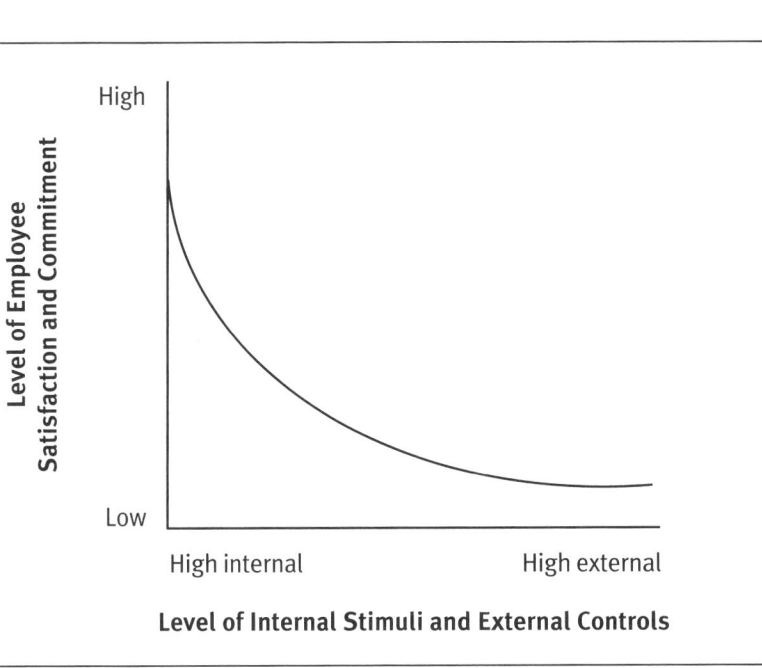

EXHIBIT 7.2
Effect of Internal and External Controls on Employee Satisfaction and Commitment

Level of Employee Satisfaction and Commitment (High to Low) vs. *Level of Internal Stimuli and External Controls* (High internal to High external)

addressing interpersonal relationships with family, peers, or superiors and public recognition; and (3) growth needs, covering self-actualization, personal growth, and advancement (exhibit 7.3).

Alderfer's theory suggests that at any time, more than one need may be active. Therefore, lower needs do not have to be met before higher needs are attained, as Maslow proposed. Alderfer also suggested that individuals' needs may change over time, as circumstances and situations change. The stage of life and career may dictate which need predominates. Early-career

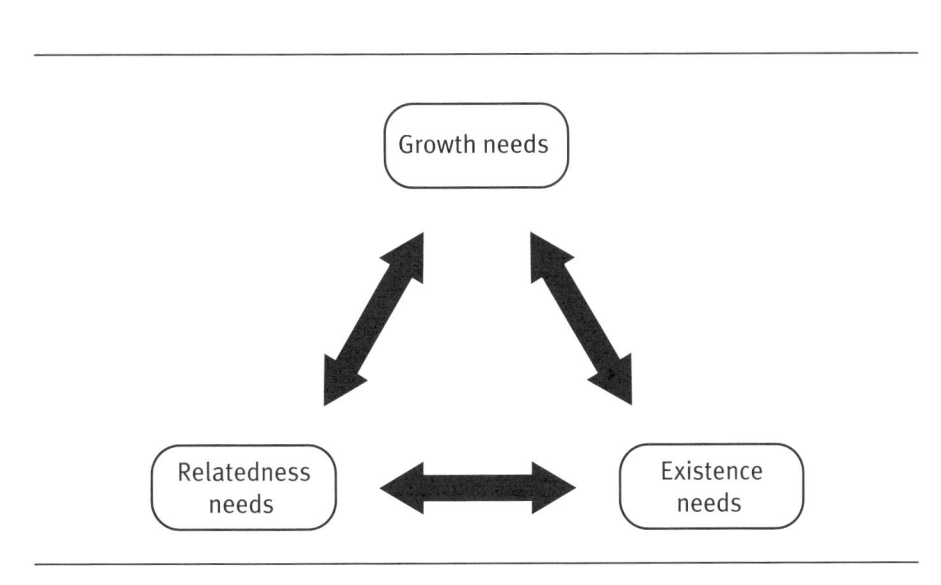

EXHIBIT 7.3
Alderfer's ERG Theory of Motivation

Growth needs ↔ Relatedness needs ↔ Existence needs

frustration-regression
The concept that people who unsuccessfully seek a higher need become frustrated and regress to pursue a lower need.

workers may focus more on existence or relatedness needs, while mid-career employees may find growth needs much more important.

Alderfer also proposed a **frustration-regression** element, which suggests that people who unsuccessfully seek a higher need become frustrated and regress to pursue a lower need. For example, an employee who desires personal growth and advancement but feels blocked and unable to attain it may revert to relatedness or existence needs either by further developing friendships with family or fellow workers or by becoming more financially independent.

Herzberg's Two-Factor Theory

A further extension of Maslow's hierarchy of needs is the two-factor theory developed by Frederick Herzberg, introduced in chapter 5, who postulated that job satisfaction and dissatisfaction are not opposites but simply reflect different employee needs (see exhibit 7.4). Herzberg categorized work factors as dissatisfiers, which match Maslow's lower needs, and satisfiers, which relate to Maslow's higher needs. **Dissatisfiers**, also called *maintenance* or *hygiene factors*, do not motivate because they do not produce satisfaction. Dissatisfiers may include working conditions, interpersonal relations, job security, and salary. A fundamental suggestion from Herzberg's work is that the presence of these factors does not motivate personnel, but their absence can create negative consequences and diminish employee satisfaction. For example, while operating policies are motivators, organizations without clear policies may produce unhappiness and frustration in employees.

Satisfiers, on the other hand, do motivate employees and have longer-lasting effects than dissatisfiers. These factors relate to job content and may

EXHIBIT 7.4
Herzberg's Two-Factor Theory as an Extension of Maslow's Hierarchy of Needs

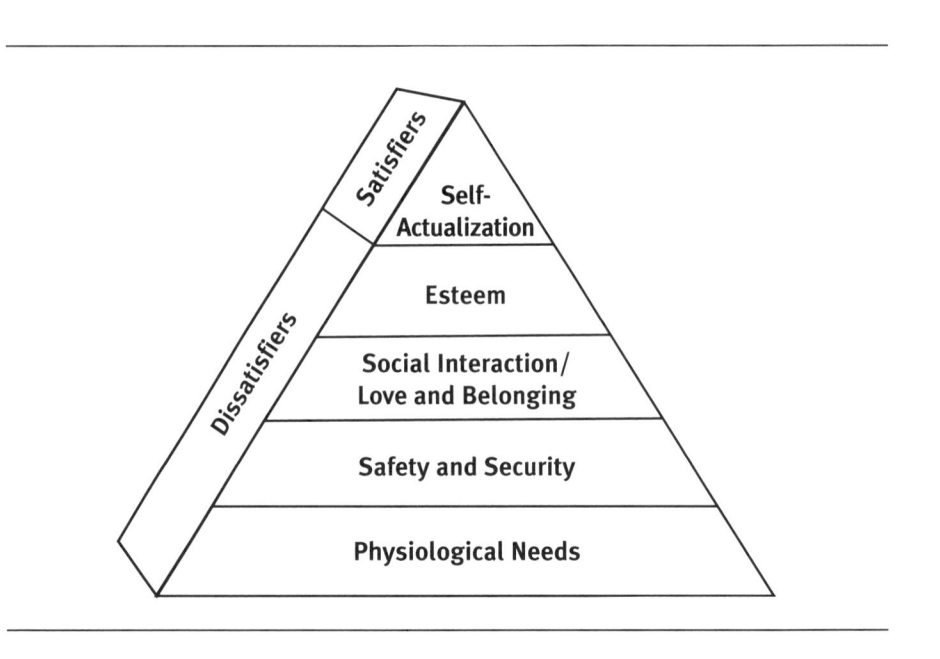

include achievement, recognition, advancement, and growth. They help employees achieve psychological growth and self-realization, which leads to satisfaction. However, the absence of satisfiers does not lead to dissatisfaction, only to a lack of positive satisfaction (Sapru 2010).

Evidence to support the two-factor theory shows that employers should not expect significant motivation from the addition of work policies, enhancements to the work environment, or salary increases and bonuses. However, the lack of improvements can cause workers to become dissatisfied, which can lead to higher absenteeism and turnover. In healthcare, the work satisfaction of employees, who constantly deal directly with patients, affects every aspect of care. Recognition and achievement have been shown to motivate employees to be more productive, creative, and committed (Afolabi, Fernando, and Bottiglieri 2018).

Herzberg (2003) suggested that the most positive attempts to instill motivation involve removing controls while retaining accountability. Such actions should include the following:

- Increase employees' accountability for their own work.
- Give employees a complete, natural unit of work they can accomplish.
- Grant additional authority to employees in their activity.
- Make periodic reports directly available to the workers rather than just to supervisors.
- Introduce new and more difficult tasks not previously attempted by workers.
- Assign employees specific or specialized tasks to enable them to become experts in those tasks.

Job Design

Job design is the outgrowth of intrinsic motivation theories that point to self-actualization and job content as the main methods of motivating workers. Considerable research has demonstrated that the structure and content of job design can have significant consequences for employees' attitudes, satisfaction, work motivation, learning, and sense of well-being (Parker 2014; Volini et al. 2020). Creating meaningful, fulfilling jobs has become a priority for many on an international scale, as shown in the box on page 136.

A central theme of job design has long been the **job characteristics model** developed by Hackman and Oldham (1976). According to their perspective, jobs should be designed to have five core characteristics:

1. *Variety*—use of varied activities and different skills
2. *Autonomy*—discretion over daily work decisions

---

dissatisfiers
A set of factors—one of two in Herzberg's two-factor theory—that do not motivate because they do not produce satisfaction. Dissatisfiers may include working conditions, interpersonal relations, job security, and salary; also called *maintenance* or *hygiene factors*.

satisfiers
A set of factors—one of two in Herzberg's two-factor theory—that relate to job content and which may include achievement, recognition, advancement, and growth. Satisfiers, also called *motivators*, have longer-lasting effects than dissatisfiers have.

job characteristics model
A model that posits job enrichment should be designed with five core characteristics: work variety, work autonomy, work feedback, work significance, and work identity.

> **Decent Work**
>
> The content and function of jobs have become topics of importance across the globe. The concept of decent work—which according to the International Labour Organization (ILO) (2016) "involves opportunities for work that is productive and delivers a fair income, security in the workplace and social protection for families, better prospects for personal development and social development and social integration"—suggests that the job design model is ideal. The ILO has created an index to compare countries against its decent-work measurement.

3. *Feedback*—clarity of information regarding the worker's job performance and effectiveness
4. *Significance*—impact on the lives or work of others
5. *Identity*—responsibility for completing an identifiable segment of work from beginning to end

Job Enrichment

Enriching work by increasing the degree of these characteristics contrasts with Taylor's scientific management theory (discussed in chapter 1), which includes dividing jobs into small, repetitive components. Job enrichment expands the scope of jobs to decrease repetitive work, making them more challenging to employees. Expanding workers' jobs serves to "enrich" employment and may result in high internal work motivation, higher-quality work outcomes, higher work satisfaction, and lower absenteeism and turnover (Hackman and Oldham 1980).

The optimal job enrichment may vary according to the individual characteristics of the employee. Skill level, desire for growth, and satisfaction with contextual job factors affect the appropriate level of job enrichment and its effectiveness. Employees who have little need or desire for growth, who have limited skills, or who are unhappy about aspects of their work may not be prepared for job enrichment.

However, for employees prepared to expand their work, companies often approach job enhancement in the following three ways:

1. *Job rotation*—moving employees from one job to another periodically, which decreases boredom, improves work variety, and permits learning new skills
2. *Job enlargement*—increasing the number of tasks assigned to employees to strengthen work identity
3. *Job enrichment*—broadening responsibilities, giving more decision-making autonomy, and increasing feedback.

Enrichment of workers' jobs is contrary to the high degree of micromanaging that occurs at many firms. Many managers believe that leading requires a detailed knowledge of a company's operations, so they respond by delving too deeply into minutiae and seeking to correct and direct insignificant decisions. Prominent leaders such as former US president Jimmy Carter and Walt Disney CEO Michael Eisner demonstrated micromanagement. President Carter personally reviewed requests to schedule the White House tennis courts, while Eisner chose the types of light bulbs to be used in Disney hotels (Tuna 2008).

Employees generally hate being micromanaged, whereas bosses frequently find micromanagement validating and engaging.

Equity Theory

The equity that workers perceive in their jobs also can influence motivation. People want to feel that they are treated fairly, and the perception of being treated fairly or unfairly can influence motivation. **Equity theory**, first proposed by J. Stacy Adams in 1965, sought to explain how perceptions of equity affect work performance. The theory suggests that employees seek to balance their work inputs and the outcomes or benefits they receive as compared with those of others. Inputs may include a wide variety of activities and efforts, such as time, loyalty, commitment, dedication, enthusiasm, personal sacrifice, and skill development. Outputs, although often focused on salary and compensation, also include job security, benefits, recognition, and reputation. Individuals look at the ratio of what they receive from a job to what they contribute and then compare it with others' or with their past experiences (Adams 1965).

equity theory
The theory that employees seek to balance their work inputs and the outcomes or benefits they receive as compared with those of others.

Equity equilibrium exists when inputs equal outputs (exhibit 7.5). However, when an inequity exists, people seek to equalize their ratios by increasing or decreasing their inputs or outputs to bring them back to an equity equilibrium.

Equity issues often arise when salary increases are given. Managers may attempt to reward perceived excellent work by giving high performers larger increases. However, as discussed in chapter 19, performance evaluations that

---

Equity in Athletics

In 2015, Jim Harbaugh, former head coach of the National Football League's San Francisco 49ers, was hired by the University of Michigan at a base salary of $5 million (Feinstein 2015). At the time, the average base salary of an NCAA Football Bowl Subdivision head coach was $1.75 million—an average that was 75 percent higher than seven years previously (Baumbach 2014). On top of this, under NCAA rules enacted around the same time, student athletes in selected Power Five conferences received greater compensation, perhaps up to $10,000 each (Trahan 2014). This seems to have led to a diminished focus among college athletes on gaining an education; as one former quarterback tweeted shortly after arriving at Ohio State, "Why should we go to class if we came here to play FOOTBALL, we ain't come to play SCHOOL, classes are POINTLESS." (CBS Cleveland 2012). How might equity theory explain the relentless increases in compensation and diminished focus on education?

EXHIBIT 7.5
Equity Equilibrium

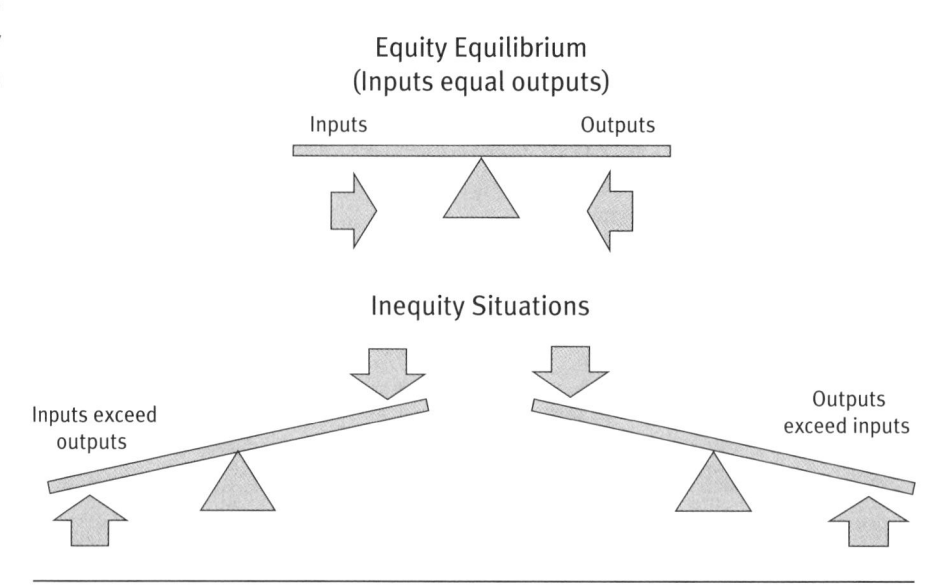

Equity Equilibrium
(Inputs equal outputs)

Inputs — Outputs

Inequity Situations

Inputs exceed outputs | Outputs exceed inputs

---

expectancy theory
The theory that motivation is a function of three linked factors: expectancy, instrumentality, and valence.

expectancy
The belief that one's efforts will result in the desired outcomes.

instrumentality
The belief that one will receive a reward if expected performance is achieved.

valence
The value a person places on expected rewards.

reward individual effort with comparably higher salary increases can have detrimental consequences: Those who receive lower increases may feel under-rewarded and may try to restore the equity by asking for additional compensation or by decreasing their outputs through diminished production, quality, or time on the job.

Expectancy Theory

First proposed in the 1960s by Victor Vroom, **expectancy theory** hypothesizes (as illustrated in exhibit 7.6) that motivation is a function of three linked factors: (1) **expectancy**, the belief that one's efforts will result in the desired outcomes; (2) **instrumentality**, the belief that one will receive a reward if expected performance is achieved; and (3) **valence**, the value a person places on the expected rewards. All of these factors are important to employee motivation; if any one is lacking, the worker's efforts decrease to zero (DuBrin 2008; Fisher College of Business 2018).

EXHIBIT 7.6
Expectancy Theory

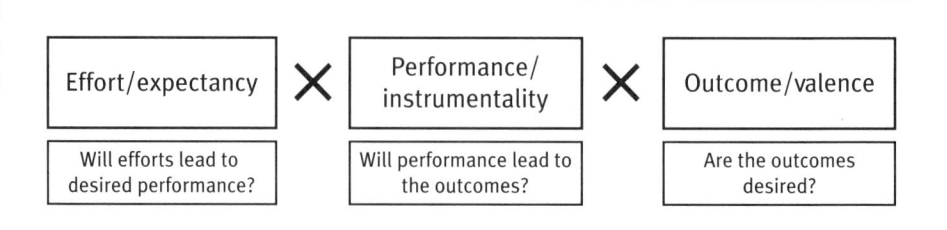

Effort/expectancy	×	Performance/instrumentality	×	Outcome/valence
Will efforts lead to desired performance?		Will performance lead to the outcomes?		Are the outcomes desired?

Employees must believe that their efforts will affect the results they seek and that the reward will be given if the output is met. In addition, employees must want the rewards and assign value to them. Managers should judiciously examine reward systems to tie rewards closely to performance and make sure the incentives provided are deserved and desired by employees. Goals and standards should be clearly communicated, and workers should have the skills and abilities to accomplish them. Employees' efforts will diminish if they feel that hard work does not lead to recognition and reward. Likewise, if the rewards are not desired, workers will be less inclined to work diligently.

Goal-Setting Theory

Also originated in the 1960s, **goal-setting theory** proposes that goal-directed work and quantified and clearly defined goals lead to higher performance (Locke 1968). Managers are encouraged to set clear goals that ensure each worker is aware of performance expectations. Groups that set goals achieve higher performance than those that lack goals.

Goal-setting theory evolved into management by objectives (MBO), which involves participative goal setting and was used at one time by many companies (Koontz and Weihrich 2010; "Motivating Employees" 2021). In addition, it became popular to follow the advice of Doran (1981) and craft goals that are SMART:

- S—write *specific* areas for improvement
- M—make the goal *measurable,* and quantify the indicators for progress
- A—*assign* someone to be responsible for the goal
- R—make the goal *realistic* given the available resources
- T—specify the *time* in which the results will be achieved

goal-setting theory
The theory that goal-directed work and quantified and clearly defined goals lead to higher performance.

Other management writers have extended goal setting to organization-wide efforts. Collins and Porras (1994) promoted the concept of big hairy audacious goals (BHAGs), which establishes difficult, vision-related goals that assist in attaining strategic results. As they state, "A true BHAG is clear and compelling, serves as a unifying focal point of effort and acts as a clear catalyst for team spirit. It has a clear finish line, so the organization can know when it has achieved the goal" (Collins and Porras 1994, 113).

Job Crafting

Another idea that has been explored in the past decade is job crafting, where individuals work with their employers to create jobs aligned with their needs and abilities. This might involve both formal and informal aspects of work. Employees take advantage of opportunities to customize their tasks and interactions with others. Data would suggest that job crafting and intrinsic motivation are positively related (Lee and Song 2019).

Job crafting includes changing up employees' responsibilities (task crafting), changing their interactions (relationship crafting), or changing their mindset (cognitive crafting). An employee working on a hospital's custodial crew, for example, might learn how important cleaning duties are to maintaining the sterile environment of a surgical suite and improving patient outcomes, and so come to see that work in a new light.

Job crafting seems to be especially viable with employees who have more proactive personalities. They work to better align job resources, job demands, their personal needs, and their own skills. Researchers have shown that these individuals are noticed by their peers. For example, when employees work to make positive changes for themselves—job crafting—those changes may also affect their colleagues. Peers offered high performance ratings of their proactive coworkers (Moore 2020; Tims et al. 2012).

Myths About Motivation

Motivation remains a critical determining factor in organizational success. Yet managers often do not appear to understand its underlying concepts and frequently misapply methods, which leads to lack of motivation and employee discouragement. Following are some of the myths managers believe (Grenny, Maxfield, and Shimberg 2008; Nohria, Groysberg, and Lee 2008):

- *Money is a motivator.* Providing monetary compensation to motivate employees has limited long-term effects. Money may, in the short term, galvanize attention, but its effects quickly wear off and will not motivate employees across time.
- *Motivated employees can accomplish anything.* Motivation is important but needs to be coupled with the appropriate skills, ability, and training for employees to achieve objectives.
- *More time off motivates employees.* Employees who are motivated tend to work longer hours and do not seek more time off.
- *Motivation can be accomplished through singular efforts.* Motivation involves many facets, and different employees can gain encouragement through different means. Successful motivators use multiple sources of influence, including individual, social, and organizational resources and processes.

Motivating Millennials and Generation Z

More than 35 percent of the American workforce—56 million individuals—are millennials (those born between 1981 and 1996). As of 2019, they outnumbered baby boomers as the nation's largest living adult population (Fry 2018, 2020). Exhibit 7.7 represents population estimates of the US Census Bureau by defined generations. Members of Generation Z, born after 1996, are less likely to be working as teens and young adults; however, they will likely be the most educated of all these generations and have grown up using the internet. In a March 2020 Pew survey, "half of the oldest Gen Zers (ages 18 to 23) reported that they or someone in their household had lost a job or taken a cut in pay" due to the COVID-19 pandemic (Parker and Igielnik 2020). That percentage is much higher than for millennials and Gen Xers. Gen Zers remain optimistic, however, and in many ways are motivated by the same issues and desires as are millennials.

The COVID-19 pandemic changed millennial attitudes about job loyalty. In a 2020 Deloitte Global Millennial Survey, respondents who said they would like to stay with their current employers for at least five years outnumbered those who want to leave within two years. This was a much stronger show of loyalty than seen in previous Deloitte surveys (Parker and Igielnik 2020). According to this study, when choosing a job, the highest priority for millennials is a good work–life balance. They look for flexible schedules and job crafting (described earlier in this chapter).

Half of the millennials and Gen Zers questioned in the Deloitte survey recognize stress as a reason to take time off from work. They seem to place

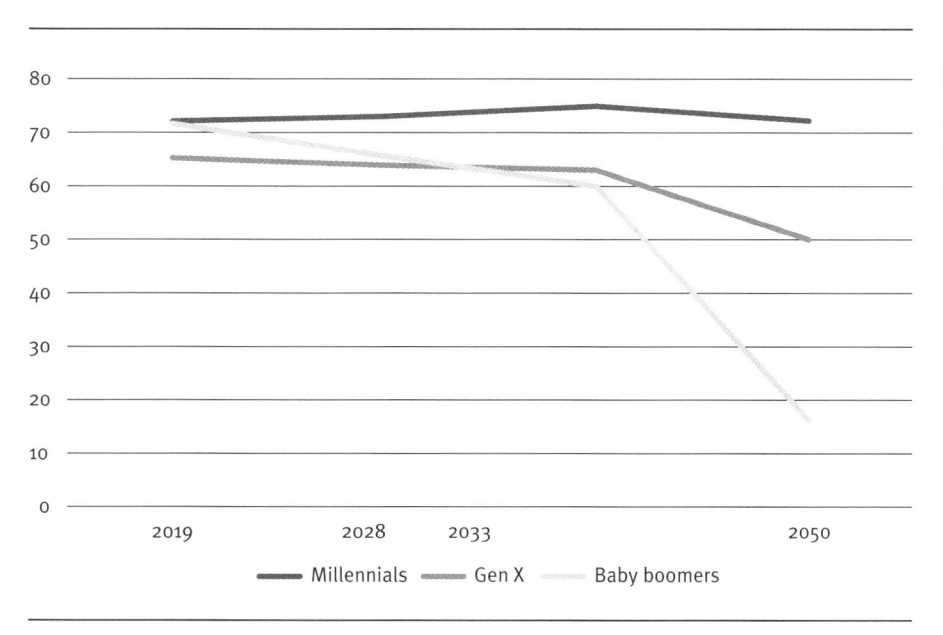

EXHIBIT 7.7
Projected US Population by Generation (in millions)

Source: Data from Fry (2020).

greater importance on mental health, compared with previous generations. Stigmas of mental health remain, however, and employers would be wise to know their millennial and Gen Z employees may not admit that is why they are taking time off (Deloitte 2020).

Another idea reinforced by the COVID-19 pandemic is that most millennials and Gen Zers employees enjoy the option of working from home, and say that working remotely gives them a better work–life balance. As of May 2020, almost two-thirds of millennials (64 percent) and Gen Zers (60 percent) said they want to work from a remote location after the COVID-19 disruption is over (Deloitte 2020).

Studies would suggest a few other ideas for motivating millennials. High performers in this group seek feedback in the workplace and tend to motivate themselves rather than being pushed by some sort of external motivation (De Jong et al. 2017). They like new tasks, changing tasks, and not being stagnant at work. Other factors important to millennials include a pleasant and open atmosphere, enthusiastic and encouraging colleagues, and equality among employees. Flexibility in working hours, working methods, and work arrangements are a motivator, but millennials also indicated they might sacrifice some free time outside of a normal workday if needed for specific projects (Kultalahti and Viitala 2015).

Finally, while all the motivational theories and motivators discussed in this chapter are important to millennials—and to all generations—financial well-being still matters, too. A 2020 Gallup poll indicated that a smaller percentage of Americans described their financial situation as "excellent" or "good" when compared with earlier surveys, and half of all Americans said their situation is getting worse. Of those surveyed, younger adults (aged 18–29) had about twice the decline in rating their current finances positively as compared with those aged 50 and older (Jones 2020).

Chapter Summary

Many theories and explanations exist for the rationale for and methods of motivation. What all agree on is that there is a need for motivated employees and that most businesses struggle to find the right mix of activities to motivate their employees. Many observers feel that the failure to motivate has been the result of using external factors to stimulate and motivate. Internal, or intrinsic, stimuli seem to better instill motivation than external stimuli do.

Several common motivational theories are covered in this chapter. Alderfer's ERG theory recasts Maslow's hierarchy of needs from five categories into three simpler and broader classes. It suggests that individuals can experience any category of need without having lower needs fulfilled and that needs may change across a person's life and career.

Herzberg's two-factor theory groups work factors into two categories: dissatisfiers (maintenance or hygiene factors) and satisfiers. Dissatisfiers do not motivate, because they do not produce satisfaction. Not having them, however, causes dissatisfaction. Dissatisfiers may be working conditions, interpersonal relations, job security, or salary. Satisfiers relate to job content and motivate employees. These factors include achievement, recognition, advancement, and growth.

Job design proposes that job content significantly affects the ability to motivate workers. The structure and content of jobs influence the attitudes, satisfaction, work motivation, learning, and sense of well-being of employees. Jobs that motivate employees should involve work variety, autonomy, feedback, significance, and identity to enrich tasks and the labor of workers.

Equity theory focuses on how perceived fairness affects work behavior. It suggests that employees seek to balance the ratio of their work efforts (inputs) with their outputs and then compare it with that of others. If their ratio compares unfavorably, they will alter their inputs or outputs to correct the imbalance.

Expectancy theory defines motivation as the multiple of three factors: expectancy, or the belief that one's efforts lead to the desired outcome; instrumentality, or the belief that the desired reward can be obtained through a given performance level; and valence, the value a person places on the expected rewards.

Goal-setting theory suggests that setting challenging and clear goals results in higher performance. Advances from goal-setting theory include MBO (management by objectives), SMART (specific, measurable, assigned, realistic, and time-bound) goals, and BHAGs (big hairy audacious goals).

Millennials make up most of the US workforce and Gen Zers are adding to that group. Mental health is important to this group and they are seeking a positive work–life balance. They want feedback and are motivated by an open atmosphere, enthusiastic colleagues, and equality. Flexibility is also important to them.

The actions of managers greatly contribute to the creation of motivated employees. Managers frequently appear not to appreciate the basics of motivation; they misunderstand the effects of money, which acts poorly as a long-term stimulus, and may not realize that linked skills and training must be coupled with motivational efforts to achieve the desired outcomes. Managers may erroneously equate short-term actions and movement caused by external stimuli (e.g., money, threats, benefits, time off) with motivation. Motivation requires a multifaceted, complex approach that ultimately leads to mutual respect and loyalty. Only through improved understanding of the principles and applications of motivation can companies stimulate employees to proper long-term actions.

Chapter Questions

1. Why do managers often use external stimuli to motivate their employees?
2. What are the major differences between Maslow's hierarchy of needs and Alderfer's ERG theory of motivation?
3. Why do dissatisfiers or hygiene factors in Herzberg's two-factor theory not motivate?
4. Why are satisfiers difficult to implement in a workplace?
5. What is an argument against work variety?
6. An employee thinks she is working as hard as everyone else in her department and her results are better than theirs. However, at her annual evaluation, she is given a 1 percent lower raise than most of her colleagues. Given equity theory, what might be a predicted change in this employee's behavior?
7. Under expectancy theory, if any of the three factors are missing, what is the result?
8. Should money ever be used as a motivator?

Chapter Cases

Micromanaging Leads to Motivation: Illusion or Reality?

Greg knew that he was getting results at the large home health company that he founded and manages. Activity is a given when he is around. He sees people jump when he yells during his staff meetings. He is great at getting people back on track by interrupting conversations, identifying people's mistakes, and telling subordinates which decisions to make.

Greg considers himself the quarterback of the company: He has the football and decides who will receive the pass. Greg also enjoys being the center of attention. He knows he is indispensable and he is constantly busy. He starts meetings by stating his opinion of what should be done and receives almost unanimous agreement. However, his staff has grown from a few people to more than 200. Now he is spread thin trying to remain involved in most decisions, and his employees have stopped showing initiative and simply wait for his direction.

Encouraged by his top executives, Greg has come to realize that his micromanaging is damaging his firm. His actions have expressed unwillingness to trust his employees and are leading to turnover and decreased innovation. He recognizes that he has difficulty understanding when to personally engage and when to delegate. An executive coach he hired asked him, "Who wants to be in a company where you are not allowed to think?" To shift his management approach, Greg has to learn to act differently toward his employees. He has even considered having his employees rewrite his job description.

Source: Adapted from Tuna (2008).

Case Questions
1. Using two theories from this chapter, describe six changes in Greg's job description that would lead to better motivation for his employees.
2. What other changes would you make?

Korean Air Executive Motivates Change with Nuts

Heather Cho, a top executive for Korean Air, was in charge of the company's international in-flight service and had set the standards for flight attendants. She had been actively involved in establishing a new corporate identity for Korean Air during her 15-year tenure at the company. She had made her father, the company chairman, proud by her direct involvement and constant efforts.

Imagine her surprise and concern when, aboard a Korean Air plane waiting to fly out of New York, she was served a bag of nuts in first class when the standards explicitly required the nuts to be served on a plate. Cho was enraged. She yelled at the flight attendant and demanded that the plane return to the gate to "get rid" of the lazy employee. After she got the captain involved and identified her position in the company, the plane turned around and returned to the gate. The errant flight attendant was sent back into the terminal, and the plane departed.

The story made headlines across the globe, but especially in Korea, where Cho's father apologized and, when asked how the incident could have happened, blamed himself for failing to raise his daughter properly. The airline also issued an apology on Cho's behalf, and she requested forgiveness and promised to take full responsibility for her actions. Ultimately, she resigned her position at Korean Air. The airline stated publicly that this was an "excessive act" and that it would seek to reeducate employees to make certain that service met the airline's high standards.

Source: Adapted from Mullen (2014).

Case Questions

1. What went wrong with Cho's efforts at direct motivation?
2. How could she have used principles of motivation discussed in this chapter to ensure the implementation of Korean Air's high standards for employees?

Chapter Activity

Describe the best and worst job you have had. For each, describe the level of (1) skill variety, (2) task significance, (3) autonomy, (4) feedback, and (5) work identity. If you contrast the best and worst job by these factors, what patterns do you see?

References

Adams, J. 1965. "Inequality in Social Exchange." In *Advances in Experimental Psychology,* edited by L. Berkowitz, 267–99. New York: Academic Press.

Afolabi, A., S. Fernando, and T. Bottiglieri. 2018. "The Effect of Organisational Factors in Motivating Healthcare Employees: A Systematic Review." *British Journal of Healthcare Management* 24 (12): 603–10. https://doi.org/10.12968/bjhc.2018.24.12.603.

Baumbach, J. 2014. "College Football Coaches' Salaries and Perks Are Soaring." *Newsday,* October 4. www.newsday.com/sports/college/college-football/fbs-college-football-coaches-salaries-are-perks-are-soaring-newsday-special-report-1.9461669.

Breed, M., C. Downing, and H. Ally. 2020. "Factors Influencing Motivation of Nurse Leaders in a Private Hospital Group in Gauteng, South Africa: A Quantitative Study." *Curationis* 43 (1): 2011. https://doi.org/10.4102/curationis.v43i1.2011.

CBS Cleveland. 2012. "Ohio State QB: 'Why Should We Go to Class If We Came Here to Play Football.'" Published October 5. https://cleveland.cbslocal.com/2012/10/05/ohio-state-qb-why-should-we-go-to-class-if-we-came-here-to-play-football/.

Cerasoli, C. P., J. M. Nicklin, and M. T. Ford. 2014. "Intrinsic Motivation and Extrinsic Incentives Jointly Predict Performance: A 40-Year Meta-Analysis." *Psychological Bulletin* 140 (4): 980–1008. https://doi.org/10.1037/a0035661.

Chamorro-Premuzic, T. 2013. "Does Money Really Affect Motivation? A Review of the Research." *Harvard Business Review* digital article, April 10. https://hbr.org/2013/04/does-money-really-affect-motiv.

Collins, J. C., and J. I. Porras. 1994. *Built to Last: Successful Habits of Visionary Companies*. New York: HarperBusiness.

De Jong, L., R. Favier, C. Vleuten, and H. Bok. 2017. "Students' Motivation Toward Feedback-Seeking in the Clinical Workplace." *Medical Teacher* 39 (9): 954–58.

Deloitte. 2020. The Deloitte Global Millennial Survey 2020. Published June 2020. www2.deloitte.com/global/en/pages/about-deloitte/articles/millennialsurvey.html.

Doran, G. 1981. "There's a S.M.A.R.T. Way to Write Management's Goals and Objectives." *Management Review* 70 (11): 35–36.

DuBrin, A. J. 2008. *Essentials of Management*, 8th ed. Mason, OH: South-Western Cengage Learning.

Feinstein, J. 2015. "Why Jim Harbaugh Is Worth $40 Million to the University of Michigan's Football Team." *Washington Post*. Published January 2. www.washingtonpost.com/opinions/why-jim-harbaugh-is-worth-40-million-to-the-university-of-michigan/2015/01/02/ad591542-9292-11e4-a900-9960214d4cd7_story.html.

Fisher College of Business. 2018. "Leadership in Athletics: Expectancy Theory." *Lead Read Today* (blog). Ohio State University. Published October 23. https://fisher.osu.edu/blogs/leadreadtoday/blog/leadership-in-athletics-expectancy-theory.

Fry, R. 2020. "Millennials Overtake Baby Boomers as America's Largest Generation." Pew Research Center, April 28. www.pewresearch.org/fact-tank/2020/04/28/millennials-overtake-baby-boomers-as-americas-largest-generation/.

———. 2018. "Millennials Are the Largest Generation in the U.S. Labor Force." Pew Research Center, April 11. www.pewresearch.org/fact-tank/2018/04/11/millennials-largest-generation-us-labor-force/.

Gardner, H. 2012. "Performance Pressure as a Double-Edge Sword: Enhancing Team Motivation but Undermining the Use of Team Knowledge." *Administrative Science Quarterly* 57 (1): 1–46.

Grenny, J., D. Maxfield, and A. Shimberg. 2008. "How to Have Influence." *MIT Sloan Management Review* 50 (1): 47–52.

Hackman, J. R., and G. R. Oldham. 1980. *Work Redesign*. Upper Saddle River, NJ: Pearson.

———. 1976. "Motivation Through the Design of Work: Test of a Theory." *Organizational Behavior and Human Performance* 16 (2): 250–79. https://doi.org/10.1016/0030-5073(76)90016-7.

Harter, J. 2018. "Employee Engagement on the Rise in the US." *News* (blog). *Gallup*. Published August 26. https://news.gallup.com/poll/241649/employee-engagement-rise.aspx.

Herzberg, H. 2003. "Motivating People." *Harvard Business Review* 81 (1): 87–96.

International Labour Organization (ILO). 2016. "Decent Work." Accessed May 13. www.ilo.org/global/topics/decent-work/lang--en/index.htm.

Jones, J. 2020. "U.S. Personal Finances: Future More Concerning than Present." *News* (blog). *Gallup.* Published April 21. https://news.gallup.com/poll/308936/personal-finances-future-concerning-present.aspx.

Kihlstrom, G. 2020. "The Relationship Between Employee Motivation, Engagement, and Revenue." *Leadership* (blog). *Forbes.* Published March 13. https://www.forbes.com/sites/forbesagencycouncil/2020/03/13/the-relationship-between-employee-motivation-engagement-and-revenue/.

Kohn, A. 1993. "Why Incentives Plans Cannot Work." *Harvard Business Review* 71 (5). https://hbr.org/1993/09/why-incentive-plans-cannot-work.

Koontz, H., and H. Weihrich. 2010. *Essentials of Management,* 8th ed. New York: McGraw-Hill.

Kultalahti, S., and R. Viitala. 2015. "Generation Y: Challenging Clients for HRM?" *Journal of Managerial Psychology* 30 (1): 101–14.

Lee, J. W., and Song, Y. 2019. "Promoting Employee Job Crafting at Work: The Roles of Motivation and Team Context." *Personnel Review* 49 (3): 689–708. https://doi.org/10.1108/PR-07-2018-0261.

Locke, E. 1968. "Toward a Theory of Task Motivation and Incentives." *Organizational Behavior and Human Performance* 3 (2): 157–89.

Mackey, Z. 2019. "10 Startling Employee Engagement Statistics." Berrett-Koehler Publishers (blog). Published January 11. https://ideas.bkconnection.com/10-startling-employee-engagement-and-statistics.

Moore, C. 2020. "What Is Job Crafting?" PositivePsychology.com. Published January 9. https://positivepsychology.com/job-crafting/.

"Motivating Employees Through Goal Setting." 2021. LibreTexts. Published March 2. https://biz.libretexts.org/@go/page/34494.

Mullen, J. 2014. "Korean Air Executive to Quit Remaining Posts After Nuts Scandal." CNN. Published December 12. http://edition.cnn.com/2014/12/12/world/asia/korean-air-nuts-scandal/.

Nohria, N., B. Groysberg, and L. Lee. 2008. "Employee Motivation: A Powerful New Model." *Harvard Business Review* 86 (4). https://hbr.org/2008/07/employee-motivation-a-powerful-new-model.

Parker, K., and R. Igielnik. 2020. "On the Cusp of Adulthood and Facing an Uncertain Future: What We Know About Gen Z So Far." Pew Research Center. Published May 14. www.pewsocialtrends.org/essay/on-the-cusp-of-adulthood-and-facing-an-uncertain-future-what-we-know-about-gen-z-so-far/.

Parker, S. 2014. "Beyond Motivation: Job and Work Design for Development, Health, Ambidexterity, and More." *Annual Review of Psychology* 65 (1): 661–91.

Pearl, R. 2019. "The Deadly Consequences of Financial Incentives in Healthcare." *Forbes* (blog). Published January 28. https://www.forbes.com/sites/robertpearl/2019/01/28/financial-incentives/.

Sapru, R. 2010. *Administrative Theories and Management Thought.* New Delhi, India: PHI Learning.

Seidman, D. 2012. "(Almost) Everything We Think About Employee Engagement Is Wrong." *Forbes* (blog). Published September 20. www.forbes.com/sites/dovseidman/2012/09/20/everything-we-think-about-employee-engagement-is-wrong/.

Snyder, C. R., S. J. Lopez, L. M. Edwards, and S. C. Marques. 2021. *The Oxford Handbook of Positive Psychology*, 3rd ed. New York: Oxford University Press.

Strickler, J. 2006. "What Really Motivates People?" *Journal for Quality and Participation* 29 (1): 26–28.

Sullivan, J. J. 1989. "Self Theories and Employee Motivation." *Journal of Management* 15 (2): 345–63.

Tims, M., A. B. Bakker, and D. Derks. 2012. "Development and Validation of the Job Crafting Scale." *Journal of Vocational Behavior* 80 (1): 173–86. https://doi.org/10.1016/j.jvb.2011.05.009.

Trahan, K. 2014. "Texas Is Not Special for Planning to Pay Athletes $10,000." *SB Nation*, October 22. www.sbnation.com/college-football/2014/10/22/7041515/texas-college-athletes-paid-10000-dollars.

Tuna, C. 2008. "Micromanagers Miss Bull's-Eye: Dealing with Every Detail Robs Subordinates of the Freedom to Solve Problems." *Wall Street Journal*, November 3. www.wsj.com/articles/SB122566866580091589.

Ullah, Z., M. Z. Khan, and M. Siddique. 2017. "Analysis of Employees' Perception of Workplace Support and Level of Motivation in Public Sector Healthcare Organization." *Business & Economic Review* 9 (3): 240–57. https://doi.org/10.22547/BER/9.3.10.

Volini, E., B. Denny, J. Schwartz, D. Mallon, Y. Van Durme, M. Hauptmann, R. Yan, and S. Poynton. 2020. "The Compensation Conundrum: Principles for a More Human Approach." *Deloitte Insights* (blog). Deloitte. Published May 15. www2.deloitte.com/us/en/insights/focus/human-capital-trends/2020/new-compensation-trends-for-the-future-of-work.html.

CHAPTER 8

EMOTIONS, MOODS, AND STRESS ON THE JOB

> Heightened emotions are often displayed in healthcare settings. At times, work and personal factors can escalate to hostile acts that may include verbal confrontations and incivility. A meta-analysis of more than 50 studies over the past decade showed that a significant percentage of nurses experience incivility, discrimination, verbal abuse, sexual harassment, and even physical abuse on the job. Such conflicts lower productivity, morale, and the quality of patient care. They also have been shown to increase employee turnover and dampen employee efficiency (Wei et al. 2018). If existing problems were not enough, evidence points to COVID-19 as the cause of a number of emotional experiences and psychological disorders among healthcare professionals (Raudenská et al. 2020).

Learning Objectives

After studying this chapter, readers should be able to

- differentiate between emotions and moods;
- explain the composition and impact of individual and organizational emotions and stress;
- distinguish between primary and secondary emotions;
- describe the methods discussed for managing emotions and stress;
- compare the interrelationships and conflicts among individuals, groups, and organizations that result in emotions and stress;
- discuss burnout and ways to avoid it; and
- contrast role- and job-related causes of stress.

Key Terms

- burnout
- distress
- emotional intelligence
- emotions
- employee assistance programs
- eustress
- hardiness
- moods
- primary emotions
- qualitative overload
- qualitative underload
- quantitative overload
- quantitative underload
- role ambiguity
- role conflict
- secondary emotions
- stress

Running a successful healthcare organization requires leaders who understand and manage emotion, moods, and stress in themselves and among their workforce. Although not identical, emotions, moods, and stress are closely related concepts discussed in this chapter.

Emotions

Emotions are central to our personal and professional lives and inform all our relationships. An emotional disequilibrium underlies most anxiety and stress-related illnesses and is often the driving force behind positive and negative motivation.

emotions
Brief, intense episodes of a complex range of feelings that lead to physical and mental changes and influence actions and behaviors.

Emotions have been conceptualized as "transient events, produced in response to external or internal events of significance to the individual; they are typically characterized by attention to the evoking stimulus and changes in neurophysiological arousal, motor behavior, and subjective feeling state that engender a subsequent biasing of behavior" (Fink 2010, 3). They are also linked to the extent to which people value a variety of positive characteristics in themselves and others (Sznycer and Lukaszewski 2019).

Thus, emotions are brief, intense episodes of a complex range of feelings that lead to physical and mental changes and influence behaviors. Emotions are expressed through verbal, physiological, behavioral, and neural responses to events, actions, circumstances, or stimuli. Emotions and moods can be influenced by biological functions, such as levels of dopamine and serotonin. Likewise, cultural influences affect the types of emotions expressed. In addition, gender influences emotional processing and incidence of emotion-related illnesses, such as major depression, anxiety disorders, and posttraumatic stress (Maji 2018; Pessoa 2018).

Emotions Versus Moods

Moods are less intense than emotions but tend to last longer. Moods are also more pervasive than emotions and affect one's perception of life. They can be described as *background feelings*, though they remain tied to the transient emotions we feel. Completely separating mood from emotion can be difficult (Clark 2005). In fact, some propose the idea that moods are the end result of a whole emotion process with three levels. The first level is "either physiological or an automatic motor process" that surfaces in reaction to certain stimuli. The second level of this model suggests that we react to situations, at times, without even being aware of our reaction. The third level of the emotion process is more controlled or conscious. In this level our emotions show themselves and then we can begin to regulate them. Finally, our emotions become stable and form different moods (Kuang et al. 2019).

moods
The background feelings that are less intense but tend to last longer than emotions and affect one's perception of life.

Emotions in the Workplace

Emotions and moods can significantly affect individual worker and group behavior and the nature of workplace environments. Emotions drive how people and groups interact and the decisions they make. Negative emotions can damage relationships, reduce the effectiveness of decision-making, and cause health problems such as depression and anxiety disorders (Gregoire 2015).

Interestingly, positive emotions can lead to bad decision-making as well. For example, overconfidence can be as problematic as a lack of confidence. Medical misdiagnoses occur more frequently among physicians who exhibit overconfidence (Cassam 2017).

In any organizational setting, managers are challenged to foster positive emotions and appropriately regulate negative emotions. The ability to communicate emotions is critical to a properly functioning workplace. Relaying emotion can be as simple as smiling or as involved as constructively expressing concerns. Smiles, affirming tones, and encouraging gestures from a supervisor have been found to create a healthier supervisor–subordinate relationship. Those simple nonverbal cues can lead to greater employee well-being—expressed as pleasure on the job, feeling included, and relaxation (Jia, Cheng, and Hale 2017). Studies indicate that some individuals mimic the facial expressions and posture of others based on *emotional contagion*. Similar nonverbal communication has been identified in a variety of cultures around the world (Kuang et al. 2019). Expressing emotion effectively can directly affect managers' ability to successfully solve problems and negotiate. It also allows managers to more accurately identify emotions and understand how to harness their positive effects and minimize their potentially damaging results (Bucurean 2018).

Emotions have been categorized into six primary or basic emotions and multiple secondary emotions (exhibit 8.1). **Primary emotions** comprise love, joy, surprise, anger, sadness, and fear. Primary emotions are what people first experience in a situation. They are instinctive responses that may rapidly

primary emotions
The feelings people first experience as a response to a situation: love, joy, surprise, anger, sadness, and fear.

EXHIBIT 8.1
Primary and Secondary Emotions

Primary Emotion	Secondary Emotions
Love	Affection, lust, longing
Joy	Cheerfulness, zest, contentment, pride, optimism, enthrallment, relief
Surprise	—
Anger	Irritation, exasperation, rage, disgust, torment
Sadness	Suffering, disappointment, shame, neglect, sympathy
Fear	Horror, nervousness

Source: Adapted from Shaver et al. (2001).
Note: Interestingly, surprise does not have a secondary emotion.

---

secondary emotions
Longer-duration feelings that reflect an individual's mental processing of a situation and the primary emotions it elicited.

appear and then just as rapidly be replaced by **secondary emotions**, which more closely reflect an individual's mental processing of a situation and the primary emotions it elicited.

Primary emotions are almost impossible to prevent, as they are reactions to external events. People might feel sad or angry about a rude remark. However, they can learn to recognize this primary emotion of sadness or anger and steer it toward a more constructive secondary emotion, such as sympathy. Secondary emotions last longer than primary emotions. If negative secondary emotions linger too long, they may damage emotional well-being (Kuang et al. 2019; Seaward 2014).

The ability to express all emotions is helpful and healthy for maintaining positive personal and work relationships. Most people agree that feeling love and joy provides personal benefit. However, expressing surprise, anger, sadness, and fear can be valuable as well, especially if doing so motivates us to address a potentially harmful situation. For example, if you are walking on a road and a car careens into your path, you will feel fear that will motivate you to move out of harm's way.

emotional intelligence
The capacity to be aware of, to be in control of, and to express emotions as well as to handle interpersonal relationships with empathy and wisdom.

The ability to use emotions intelligently has become a popular management tool. **Emotional intelligence** (EI)—the capacity to be aware of, to control, and to express emotions as well as to handle interpersonal relationships with empathy and wisdom—is an important characteristic for business leaders. Organizations that value EI qualities such as integrity, empathy, self-awareness, creative thinking, passion, mental toughness, and the ability to think under pressure seem to build a culture of trust and thus have a higher tolerance for risk. These organizations seem to promote a better customer experience and elicit loyalty from their clients and customers. Data also suggest that when teams have high EI skills, generation differences seem to be less of a barrier. Reverse mentoring takes place such that older workers start to develop some of the traits of their younger team members (Harvard Business Review Analytic Services 2019).

EI has been found to be the biggest predictor of workplace performance—even more important than a leader's general intelligence (Pradhan, Jena, and Singh 2017). The EI of organizational leaders plays a key role in establishing the emotional climate in their organization by influencing how they handle themselves and their relationships. Workers take their emotional cues from their supervisors and top bosses (Goleman, Boyatzis, and McKee 2013). As illustrated by the vignette in the adjacent box, the CEO sets the climate of meetings, and a lack of emotional control can inhibit open discussion.

> **Lack of Emotional Control Sets Meeting's Climate**
>
> Brad was a driven CEO. He knew how to manage and get the best out of people. At least, he thought so. In his first month in the role, he "cleaned house" and fired three low-producing managers. He wanted input and ideas from his managers, and he held department meetings each month to obtain them. At one of the first meetings, he was clearly upset that hospital operations were doing poorly. He asked the managers to suggest solutions. Dan, the director of pharmacy, raised his hand and suggested that hospital costs could be reduced that year by decreasing or eliminating bonuses for members of the C-suite. Brad was shocked that someone would be so brash as to directly target his compensation. He then became angry, slammed his hand down on the table, and said loudly, "That is a stupid idea!" After that response, no one volunteered any further ideas. This made Brad even angrier. He flew into a rage and began to belittle the managers. He threatened that if they did not come up with solutions to solve the hospital's financial crises, he would do their job for them.
>
> What emotions did Brad feel? How did his primary emotion change to a secondary emotion? What could he have done to prevent his negative outburst?

Leaders who have high EI possess skills related to emotions, such as the following:

- Self-awareness—accurately perceiving one's own emotions.
- Other-awareness—accurately perceiving others' emotions.
- Applicability—harnessing emotions and applying them to solve problems.
- Regulation—managing emotions and regulating them to adjust to needs.

Controlling emotions can be difficult for many people. However, individuals can improve their ability to understand and manage emotions. Following are some suggestions for improving one's EI (*Dental Abstracts* 2019; Harvard Professional Development 2019):

- *Recognize emotions and name them.* Take time each day to ask, "What am I feeling right now?" Can you identify the emotions you are feeling? Provide uninterrupted time to think through your feelings.

- *Understand changes.* Recognize that emotions rise, fall, and fade.
- *Seek connections.* Seek connections between your feelings and other times when you felt the same.
- *Connect your thoughts with feelings.* Determine how your thinking connects with and affects your feelings.
- *Listen to your body.* Listen to how your body reacts to stress and interactions.
- *Track progress.* Rate yourself on your overall sense of well-being. On extreme days, note what ideas and associations may be connected to the feelings.
- *Record thoughts.* Write your thoughts and feelings in a journal.
- *Ask for feedback.* Ask managers, friends, or someone you can trust about how you respond to difficult situations. This can be a hard thing to do.
- *Learn your limits.* Learn when to take a break, change your setting, and shift your focus.

Stress

stress
The brain and body's response to any demand. "Any type of challenge—such as performance at work or school, a significant life change, or a traumatic event—can be stressful" (NIMH 2021).

Stress and emotion are tightly intertwined. At times, stress is incorrectly labeled an emotion (Knowlton 2020). However, the constructs are distinct. As described earlier, emotions such as love, anger, joy, or surprise are expressed through neural pathways as a response to a situation or the mental processing of a situation. The National Institute of Mental Health ([NIMH] 2021) describes stress as "how the brain and body respond to any demand" or challenge. Stress is a state of mental or emotional strain—a physical response when the body thinks it is under attack. The uncertainty and potential threat do not explicitly constitute emotion.

In the workplace, the ability to adapt and control emotions dictates the type of stress experienced. Dealing with unwarranted work stress has become a global challenge. Work in healthcare tends to be very stressful. Caregivers especially are exposed to highly stressful environments thick with heightened emotions. Improperly managed stress that promotes harmful behaviors and has a negative impact on physical and mental well-being can increase absenteeism and turnover (American Psychological Association [APA] 2012). Health professionals are also at greater risk of stress-related injuries than professionals in other industries. Chronic stress can manifest through physical symptoms such as headaches, muscle pain, increased blood pressure, increased heart rate, and other health problems; it disrupts all of the body's systems (Bennion, Olpin, and DeBelsio 2018; Olpin and Hesson 2016). Surveys show that nurses and physicians are more likely to show symptoms of burnout and be dissatisfied with their work–life balance, which often leads to physical injuries or emotional crises (some of which are described later in this chapter) (Hughes 2008; Shanafelt et al. 2012).

Burnout is a reaction to chronic high stress characterized by a physical or mental collapse, and may encompass emotional exhaustion, depersonalization, and reduced personal accomplishment (Hughes 2008). Burnout has become a serious problem for physicians. These highly trained providers are experiencing emotional exhaustion, cynicism, and a low sense of personal accomplishment, which together erode the degree of professionalism with which they practice, diminish the quality of care they provide, and increase the chance of committing medical errors. Physicians suffering from burnout also experience more broken relationships, alcohol misuse, and suicidal thoughts. Sadly, almost half of US physicians show symptoms of burnout (Shanafelt et al. 2012). Particularly frightening for healthcare professionals and their patients is that individuals experiencing high levels of burnout also experience compassion fatigue (Sweileh 2020).

burnout
A reaction to chronic high stress characterized by physical or mental collapse.

Early studies of the COVID-19 pandemic of 2020 indicated widespread stress and other mental health problems among healthcare workers. One study looked at 994 medical and nursing staff and found 36.9 percent had subthreshold mental health disturbances—conditions not meeting the full criteria for mental disorders, but still associated with significant problems (Kang et al. 2020). Another study surveyed staff from 41 hospitals and found that 50.4 percent reported symptoms of depression, 44.6 percent reported anxiety, 34 percent reported insomnia, and 71.5 percent reported distress (Lai et al. 2020). Frontline healthcare workers in 2020 did experience positive intellectual and emotional factors, but also reported stress, frustration, and personal fears (Mohindra et al. 2020).

Stress can be caused by a number of work-related factors, including the following (adapted from Agheli et al. 2017; Gujski et al. 2017):

- Lack of support
- Social contacts
- Uncertainty about duties
- Lack of control
- Conflict with team members
- High workload
- Encountering critically ill patients and witnessing their death
- Lack of reward and encouragement
- Professional conflict
- Lack of adequate equipment, supplies, facilities
- Invasive and aggressive behaviors

eustress
Positive stress that can motivate greater effort and focus and can result in improved productivity or mastery of a new skill.

distress
Negative, persistent, unresolved stress that may lead to anxiety, withdrawal, or depression.

On the other hand, stress is not always negative. Stress can motivate greater effort and focus and can result in improved productivity or mastery of a new skill. Positive stress has been termed **eustress**. It occurs when one responds positively to a stressor, allowing one to see the gap between actual and desired status or attainment. Too much stress or chronic stress, in contrast, causes **distress**—persistent, unresolved stress that may lead to anxiety, withdrawal, or depression (Branson et al. 2019).

Exhibit 8.2 shows the relationship between stress and performance. Increased stress augments performance (eustress) to a point, after which more stress begins to diminish performance and create distress. Ultimately, too much stress can lead to exhaustion, negative health effects, and burnout.

People react differently to varying amounts of stress. As shown in exhibit 8.3, both eustress and distress are affected by cognitive, behavioral, emotional, and physiological influences that are filtered by cultural expectations (Teng 2011). As can be seen from the arrows in the exhibit, each of these factors interacts with and jointly influences stress outcomes. People interpret events differently, so they also interpret stress differently. Cognitively, people examine stressors to determine whether they are direct threats, potentially harmful, or mere challenges, and then assess their own ability to cope. Those who interpret situations negatively may experience negative emotions that can lead to distress, whereas those who appraise or perceive challenges positively tend to feel eustress and achieve positive results (Branson et al. 2019).

EXHIBIT 8.2
Relationship Between Stress and Performance

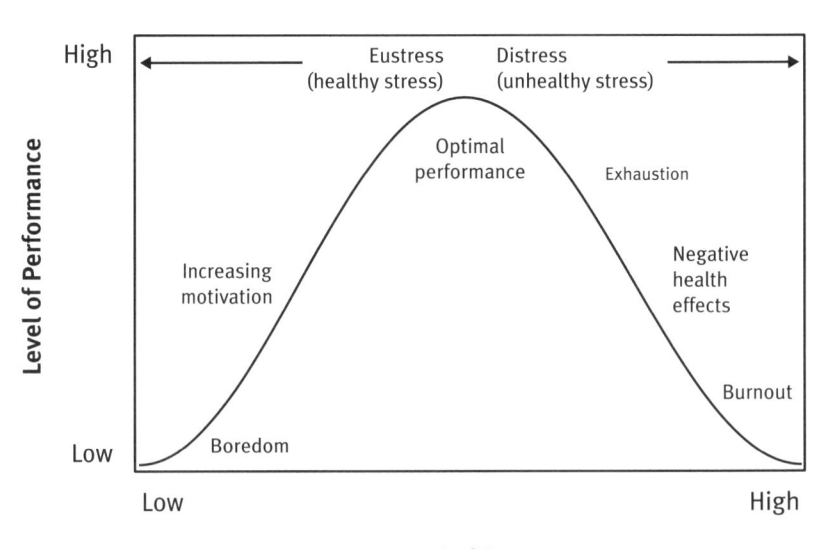

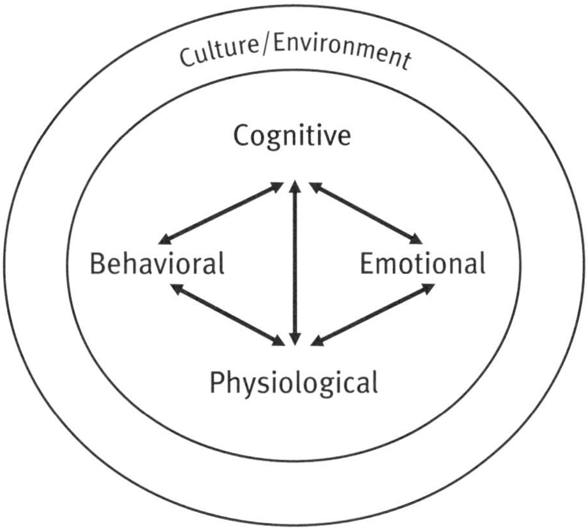
Culture/Environment
Cognitive
Behavioral
Emotional
Physiological

EXHIBIT 8.3
Influences on Stress

The choice of behaviors and actions also affects emotions and stress levels. Choosing to work long hours, limit sleep, avoid problems, and not exercise makes one prone to feeling negative emotions and increased distress. Also, frequent procrastination in making tough decisions can result in negative emotions and stress.

The amount of stress that motivates or distresses varies by person. Some people can endure tremendous stress and find the pressure stimulating. Others wilt under seemingly low levels of stress. Childhood experiences, family obligations, gender, genetic traits, immune disorders, and personality types all influence resilience and susceptibility to stress.

The ability to handle stress, or **hardiness**, represents a sense of control over one's life, a measure of commitment to an important endeavor, a notion of being challenged rather than threatened by change, and the desire to meet challenges. Individuals with a high hardiness factor experience a greater internal locus of control; they believe their own voluntary actions influence the outcomes they experience (Dobson and Dozois 2008).

hardiness
The ability to handle stress.

Locus of Control

A significant factor that affects individuals is locus of control—a person's perception of what influences or drives outcomes. People have either an internal or an external locus of control. An internal locus of control makes people feel they are in control of what happens to them; an external locus of control makes people believe outside factors (e.g., other people, circumstances) control their lives or their fate. Research has found that those with a strong internal locus of control are more satisfied with their jobs and have better coping strategies for minimizing stress than those whose locus of control is external (Nelson and Campbell 2012). Indeed, internal locus of control is associated with greater EI and more positive organizational citizenship behavior such as helping behaviors and doing good for the sake of the organization (Turnipseed 2017).

Sources of Stress

The APA conducted a 2019 survey on the topic of stress. Of note, overall levels of stress in the United States did not change much from the previous few years, but stress over specific issues rose. In particular, most adults in this survey expressed concern about mass shootings. Around 69 percent of those surveyed indicated concern about healthcare. Specifically, 71 percent of respondents with private insurance and 53 percent with public health insurance said healthcare costs caused them stress. Younger adults were also more likely to express concern about paying for and accessing healthcare than members of their parents' and grandparents' generations (APA 2019).

Reports of mass shootings in the United States were a source of stress across all races in the survey (APA 2019). Overall, 71 percent of adults reported this as a problem. Hispanic adults (84 percent) and Black adults (79 percent) were the most likely to report mass shootings as a significant source of stress. Following closely behind were Asian adults (77 percent), Native American adults (71 percent), and white adults (66 percent).

With the onset of the COVID-19 pandemic in 2020, the APA shifted from an annual to a monthly analysis of stressors and stress levels (APA 2020). By July 2020, Americans had been under some form of stay-at-home orders for four months. In addition, Americans faced a rise in the number of COVID-19 daily infections, increasing civil unrest, economic consequences of the pandemic, and significant discord between the two major political parties. Negative campaign ads filled the airwaves as the presidential campaign heated up, and debates among the candidates were deeply polarizing. Republicans pushed through a US Supreme Court nomination with total opposition from the Democrats, and presidential, state, and local elections took place.

So, in 2020, American stress levels related to the coronavirus pandemic held steady, but feelings of frustration, fear, and anger were on the rise (APA 2020). In addition to the pandemic, 2020 brought heightened concerns about police violence toward minorities, with 60 percent of adults reporting it as a significant source of stress and nearly two-thirds of Americans (64 percent) stressed about the government's response to protests. Black Americans, in particular, reported discrimination as a significant stressor and 78 percent said that being Black in America in 2020 was difficult. Exhibit 8.4 offers more findings from the 2019 and 2020 APA surveys.

Reported Stressors	Respondents (%)
August 2019	
Mass shootings	71
Cost of healthcare	69
Presidential election	56
Climate change	56
Sexual harassment	45
July 2020	
Contracting COVID-19	66
Economy	61
Police violence toward minorities	60
Money	58

EXHIBIT 8.4
Changes in Stressors for US Residents, 2019–2020

Source: Data from APA (2019, 2020).

Studies have shown that in healthcare organizations, inadequate staffing, excessive workload, poor leadership, lack of support, and lack of opportunity for development are significant stressors. Mental healthcare staff face the emotional challenges associated with caring for mentally unwell clients, high levels of violence, and the stress of caring for patients who not only refuse to comply with treatment but may harm themselves (Johnson et al. 2018).

Role ambiguity and role conflict commonly create stress for employees as well (Wu, Hu, and Zheng 2019). **Role ambiguity** is a lack of specificity and predictability about a job, role functions, or responsibilities resulting from insufficient, misleading, or restricted information about the work role. Role ambiguity occurs when workers do not clearly understand what is expected of them—because of unclear job descriptions, poor training, changing job requirements, or other reasons. **Role conflict**, on the other hand, is the dissonance that arises when employees are faced with two or more incompatible or contradictory job demands; for example, a nurse manager pushed to run the unit efficiently and save money yet still obligated personally and professionally to ensure staff achieve and maintain high-quality patient care.

Work-related stress itself can cause conflict among employees. Some behaviors that arise from work stress and create conflict include the following (Hospital Employees' Union 2000, 16–17):

- Getting mad at staff in another department because their work was shifted to yours.
- Accusing a co-worker of "not doing their share."

role ambiguity
A lack of specificity and predictability about a job, its functions, and its responsibilities because of unclear job descriptions, poor training, and changing job requirements.

role conflict
The dissonance that arises from being given two or more incompatible or contradictory job demands.

- Being afraid to speak out about work problems because co-workers may abuse or reject you.
- Talking behind someone's back, or starting rumors.
- Blaming your supervisor for work overload.
- Sabotaging a co-worker's job to get him or her in trouble.
- Making assumptions about someone's relationships at work and at home.
- Believing a co-worker has more power or privileges than he or she does.
- Becoming withdrawn and uncooperative—never smiling or even talking with co-workers.
- Ridiculing a person's appearance, speech, or personality.
- Giving up on trying to improve things or on getting along with coworkers.

Workplace stress, for some, does not end as they head home. For some, job stress bleeds into home life, resulting in moodiness that influences their personal life (Sharkey and Caska 2020).

Stress can also be produced from work overload and work underload, which can be either quantitative or qualitative. **Quantitative overload** consists of too much work to do in a given period; for example, a physician who has more patients in the waiting room than can be seen in one day. **Qualitative overload** arises when the work requires a skill that the employee does not yet feel comfortable using. This type of overload occurs often in training programs when new providers are assigned tasks and procedures they may have practiced only once.

Quantitative underload happens when too little work is available to handle in a period. For example, some shifts in hospital emergency departments see far fewer patients than they have the capacity to treat. **Qualitative underload** exists when the skill requirements for the job are far below the employee's training and ability. This situation may be experienced by a doctoral research assistant who is assigned tasks such as copying and faxing materials.

As stress levels grow and persist, strains can result. Strains occur in the psychological, physiological, and behavioral aspects of life. Psychological strains may lead to impaired cognitive function, depression, anxiety, and burnout; physiological effects may include illness, weight gain, high blood pressure, sweating, aches, and sleeplessness. Negative behaviors from excess strain include alcohol overconsumption, smoking, and suicidal actions (Barling, Kelloway, and Frone 2005).

Managing Stress

Organizations can take steps to manage the stress experienced by their employees. Factors that cause stress can be eliminated or reduced, and individuals can be taught to adapt to stress and lessen the negative stress they experience. Of course, stress will never be eliminated completely.

---

quantitative overload
Stress caused by having too much work to do in a given period.

qualitative overload
Stress caused by being required to use a skill that is not yet comfortable.

quantitative underload
Stress caused by having too little work to do in a given period.

qualitative underload
Stress caused by being assigned a job that requires skills far below the training and ability of the employee.

Reducing factors that create stress requires addressing issues surrounding job satisfaction and motivation. Many of the same changes that encourage motivation, discussed in chapter 7, can also prevent negative stress. For example, the absence of hygiene factors—such as good working conditions and job security—can create dissatisfaction, so hygiene factors should be introduced. Similarly, having enriching work, promoting mutual respect and appreciation, paying equitable salaries, and providing clear operational policies all help minimize workplace stress.

Firms can also train their employees to better adapt to stress. Many organizations provide individual, social, and work support to motivate positive action and decrease destructive stress. For instance, Eli Lilly, a large US pharmaceutical company, has been recognized for its enlightened treatment of workers. It offers employees a bonus program, fair compensation, good retirement plans, learning resources for career development, a flexible work structure that allows job sharing and teleworking, sponsorship of support groups, free gym membership or on-site fitness centers, and a "no-stress" dress code (Lilly 2020).

The Hospital Employees' Union (HEU) in British Columbia, Canada, created a document in 2000, still used today, suggesting that stress prevention policies be established in every healthcare organization. According to the HEU, a good policy would include the following:

- A definition of work-related stress.
- A statement by management that stress is an organizational problem that they are committed to tackling.
- An agreement on the key factors that cause/contribute to stress, such as excessive workload, lack of support, and lack of control over the job.
- A comprehensive list of stress symptoms, plus a willingness to add new symptoms.
- Techniques for assessing stressors, such as inspections, confidential surveys, audits, etc.
- Tools for assessing stress hazards, comparable to risk assessments for established hazards (e.g., manual lifting).
- Simple, clear procedures to use when a worker is showing stress symptoms. To encourage prompt reporting, the procedures should offer the worker ample representation and support.
- The right of every worker to receive training and ongoing information about workplace stress.
- A review of the policy at regular intervals.

Individual workers can be taught to self-regulate and improve EI; social support systems can be created; and the work environment can be structured to allow greater empowerment, autonomy, and responsibilities to employees. For example, Google, a leader in attending to the total well-being of its employees, offers a free course "designed to teach emotional intelligence through meditation" that focuses on improving one's attention, developing self-knowledge and self-mastery, and creating helpful mental habits. The course became so popular that it is now offered globally by a spinoff not-for-profit called the Search Inside Yourself Leadership Institute (Chain Reaction 2020).

Healthcare workers can also take personal actions to relieve stress and avoid burnout. Here are five ways to do so (Tottle 2020):

1. Pick a priority related to life goals or career change.
2. Set some goals.
3. Get better sleep.
4. Get more exercise.
5. Help others around you.

> **employee assistance programs**
> Benefit programs that generally provide confidential short-term counseling and referrals for employees who face challenges that, if left unmanaged, could seriously affect their work.

Most major organizations have created **employee assistance programs** (EAPs), which assist employees with personal problems that may trigger high and continuous stress. EAPs generally provide confidential short-term counseling and referrals for employees who face challenges that, if left unmanaged, could seriously affect their work. Some of the issues handled by EAPs include substance abuse, occupational and emotional stress, health and financial issues, and family problems.

The Value of Intervention

The well-being of healthcare staff and a reduction of their stress is often associated with the quality and outcomes of patient care (Hall et al. 2017; Johnson et al. 2017). What is not as clear is how these two sought-after outcomes play on each other. Staff not burdened with significant stress and burnout may offer high-quality care, but organizations that enjoy sufficient resources and processes that lead to quality patient care may also see less stress and burnout among their staff. Carefully crafted intervention may both decrease stress and improve patient outcomes (Johnson et al. 2017).

Chapter Summary

The ability to control and regulate emotions and stress is a critical competency for all individuals. Emotions and stress, although not identical concepts, are closely associated, and managing both can be improved by similar methods.

Emotions permeate daily activities as well as personal and work relationships, and they motivate both positively and negatively. Emotions and moods are related, but moods last longer, are less intense, and function as background feelings. Like emotions, moods can influence individual and group behaviors positively and negatively.

The six primary emotions are love, joy, surprise, anger, sadness, and fear. Primary emotions, which are almost impossible to prevent, are the first, instinctive responses experienced in situations. Primary emotions then transition to secondary emotions, which reflect a person's mental processing of the emotions and situations. Learning to understand and express emotions can help individuals manage their relationships and environment.

EI—the ability to use and control emotions intelligently, with empathy and wisdom—has been identified as a critical leadership competency. Organizational leaders set their working climate through their use of EI. Those with excellent EI have high self- and other-awareness, and they harness and regulate their own and others' emotions.

At times, stress is confused with emotion. Although they are closely related, stress often results from poorly handled emotions. Appropriately handling work stress has become a global challenge. Healthcare workers experience high degrees of stress, which results in increased rates of burnout and dissatisfaction. Stress is associated with many work-related factors.

Stress, however, does not need to be negative. Eustress, or positive stress, can motivate individuals and help them gain a sense of achievement. Distress, on the other hand, is negative stress that occurs when too much stress is experienced over too long a period. Individual traits may determine the amount of stress a person can endure and whether the stress is perceived as positive or negative. Cognitive, behavioral, emotional, and physiological factors interact with each other within the person's culture and environment to regulate the effects of stress.

Money, work, and family are major sources of stress. In the organizational context, role ambiguity and role conflict create stress for employees. Stress can also be caused by having too much to do (quantitative overload) or not having the requisite skills to do the job (qualitative overload). Similarly, not having enough to do (quantitative underload) and working under job requirements far below the skills of the employee (qualitative underload) also may cause stress.

Organizations can take actions to help employees manage stress. Work factors that increase stress can be altered, and individuals can be taught to reduce their stress. Most large employers offer EAPs to help employees deal with personal problems, which could lead to negative stress if left unresolved.

The appropriate intervention can both relieve stress and burnout in healthcare workers and improve the quality of patient care they offer.

Chapter Questions

1. What is the difference between a primary emotion and a secondary emotion?
2. Moods differ from emotions in what ways?
3. How has EI been found to be beneficial in a work setting?
4. Why could recording your thoughts and feelings in a journal increase your EI?
5. This chapter gives one definition of stress. Do you think it describes what stress is to you? Why or why not? Can you find another definition that more closely matches your perception of stress?
6. How does burnout differ from stress?
7. What are the indicators of eustress (positive stress)?
8. What are the five factors that influence stress?
9. How does role ambiguity relate to role conflict?
10. How can qualitative overload be addressed?
11. What are some ways employers can reduce stress for their employees?

Chapter Cases

Bad Driving—Road Rage

As human beings, we differ from animals in that we can determine our secondary emotions. Yet, interestingly, the initial reactions of animals and humans to stimuli are often similar. We both may get angry and fight or flee. However, humans have the ability to process our initial emotions and direct our perceptions and feelings to secondary emotions. One of my experiences while driving illustrates how perceptions and cognitive thoughts can influence emotions.

I was driving on a relatively crowded freeway, staying mostly in the passing lane because I was in a hurry and exceeding the speed limit. I came up on a group of cars traveling slowly in a caravan. The car in the left lane would not pull over to let me pass. In fact, the older woman in the driver's seat appeared completely unaware that I wanted her to move out of the lane. She was busy combing her hair and applying makeup.

Oh, I was angry! I immediately began constructing a nasty story about this woman. She was thoughtless and oblivious and probably did not even deserve to have a driver's license. My emotions started boiling over. I edged up on her car and turned on my bright lights. That finally got her attention, and she changed lanes.

I was now going to show her my disgust and anger by giving her my ugliest face as I passed her. As I drew alongside her car, to my surprise I saw my angelic Aunt Mildred behind the wheel. Oops! She was the perfect aunt, and always willing to volunteer at service organizations. My thoughts about the other driver changed dramatically. I also noticed my emotions change. Instead of being angry and combative, I was embarrassed and committed to being more careful about the stories I create about others.

Case Questions
1. What caused my initial emotions?
2. Could I have done something to have prevented these emotions?
3. What triggered my secondary emotions?
4. Given this example, what could you do to create more positive emotions?

Healing Hospital Conflict

A patient was admitted to the hospital for a stem cell transplant but seemed to be experiencing all the symptoms of a heart attack. Giving a person the drugs needed to perform a stem cell procedure is very risky if the patient is unstable. An electrocardiogram (EKG) had been recorded for the patient, but the cardiologist had not arrived by the time the oncology team came to see the patient.

The attending physician, an oncologist with a bad temper, was told about the patient's chest pain, glanced at the EKG, and told the nurse that the readings did not concern him. The nurse faced a dilemma: Should she try to delay the transplant until the cardiologist arrived, or go along with the oncologist?

Nurses are not licensed to order tests or medications, but they are the "final check" on the decisions doctors make for patients. The nurse chose the brave but more stressful option and asked for a delay. In the hallway, the oncologist yelled at her and arrogantly asked her why. To him, she was just a nurse.

Such confrontations increase the stress and tensions for nurses. Physicians hold more power than nurses do, so even if nurses are right, rude treatment by physicians will make them think twice before speaking up in the future. Generally, no structure is in place for nurses to resolve errors made by physicians. Most physicians recognize and correct mistakes if nurses point them out; however, if doctors refuse to change an order, nurses feel pressure to cooperate and implement the order. Even though nurses have a legal obligation to act, failing to implement the order risks the ordering physician's anger and even possible discipline or termination.

Some health systems are seeking to improve how physicians and nurses work together. The University of Virginia requires interprofessional education for all nursing and medical students. Training and courses are shared to allow nursing and medical students to learn together and gain respect for each other's areas of expertise and responsibilities. Teamwork is emphasized.

In this situation, the cardiologist arrived at the end of the oncologist's temper tantrum and, after examining the patient, determined that the patient was not having a heart attack and the procedure could continue.

Source: Adapted from Brown (2013).

Case Questions
1. How does the power differential in a healthcare setting increase the stress and tension for workers?
2. What organizational structures could be established to lessen the stress caused by conflict?
3. What could physicians do to diminish the stress and conflict in hospitals?

The CEO Case of Quantitative Overload and Qualitative Underload

Leon was recently promoted as the regional director for a large public health system. He was a conscientious and hard worker. His reputation as an excellent leader centered on his ability to understand in detail what was going on in his department and, after a series of earlier promotions, his agency. Now he oversaw multiple agencies across an expansive geographic area.

His philosophy could be expressed as, "Whatever one measures, improves." In this spirit, he designed a monthly report for all the managers to complete. The report took each manager about ten hours to finish and often reached 30 pages. He then held monthly conference calls during which he asked specific questions regarding the data. If managers were unable to answer his questions, they were frequently invited to "personal meetings." These meetings were rumored to often get tense, because Leon liked to "go for the jugular" and delve directly into the problem areas, at least as he perceived them.

After about six months, Leon had instilled a mixture of awe and fear in his managers. No one wanted to be called into his personal meetings. Leon had little authority to directly fire his managers, but he did reassign two of them to areas of lesser responsibility. The others wondered when they would be next. However, the managers' data collection and their readiness to answer even the most trivial questions had improved dramatically.

Overall, Leon felt that people had gotten his message and were managing better. Nevertheless, he had concerns about the high salary costs the organization was experiencing. The nursing clinics seemed to be operating efficiently, but the three hospitals over which he had control did not appear to be able to manage their worked staff hours well. The numbers seemed to fluctuate radically over the weekends. He had never worked in a hospital, but he felt that if he had enough information, he could reduce the overtime and excess staffing that continued at each hospital. In his conference calls, he had asked about the reasons for the weekend overages and had gotten conflicting information from the different hospital leaders. He had also met with each leader, and he still believed the leaders were not managing their worked staff hours appropriately on the weekends.

In frustration, Leon decided to devise a weekend monitoring report (shown after the Case Questions) to track the weekend staff-hour management. He required the CEO of each hospital to send him the report at 8:00 a.m. on Mondays so he could have the information on a timely basis. However, this meant each hospital's CEO, chief financial officer (CFO), and human resources director had to come in on Sunday evenings to collect and analyze the data, which took three to four hours. This added responsibility took valuable time away from the hospital leadership team's family time and heightened their frustration.

One of the CEOs, Steve, faithfully came into the office with his other executives for four weeks and submitted the reports. However, in week 5, the CFO of his hospital was sick and could not come in on Sunday evening. Rather than turn in a partial report, Steve did not turn in anything on Monday morning. He and his colleagues waited for the dreaded call from Leon asking for the data. The call never came. The next Sunday, they decided not to come in and did not turn in a report the following week.

After five weeks of not submitting a report, Steve received a call from Leon's administrative assistant asking if he and his team had overlooked sending the reports.

Case Questions
1. What type of qualitative and quantitative overload and underload were taking place in this case?
2. How did the reporting structure affect emotions and stress?
3. Could Leon's approach and the level of stress he imposed on his managers induce improved performance in the short term? In the long term?
4. After studying this chapter, what would you recommend to improve Leon's management style and, ultimately, the work environment and performance?

Weekend Staffing Report

	Worked Hours			Inpatient Census			Work/Workload Ratio		
	Friday Evening	Saturday	Sunday	Friday Evening	Saturday	Sunday	Friday Evening	Saturday	Sunday
Nursing Unit 1									
Nursing Unit 2									
Nursing Unit 3									
Nursing Unit 4									
Nursing Unit 5									
Nursing Unit 6									
Nursing Unit 7									
Nursing Unit 8									
Nursing Unit 9									
Nursing Unit 10									
etc.									

Workload Unit

Admitting
Dietary
Maintenance
Respiratory
Therapy
Radiology
Laboratory
Pharmacy
Other

Chapter Activities

Monitoring Your Emotional Intelligence

A key to good EI is understanding how you react to both negative and positive events in your life. To illustrate this, keep a journal for two weeks recording instances where you had a negative event. For example, if someone cuts in front of you while you are driving home, you would record the event, how it made you feel, what you did about it, and how you might have dealt with it better. You might create a table such as this one:

The Event	How I Felt	What I Did	How I Could Have Handled It Better
Some guy cut in front of me on the way home.	I was ticked. He should have slowed down and gotten behind me.	I called him a jerk. (No one was in the car with me.)	I should have just slowed down and let him in without worry. It really didn't slow me down.
The doctor yelled at me in the clinic today.	I haven't worked there that long. It made me feel like I wasn't good enough.	I was angry inside, but I didn't say anything. I was depressed most of the day.	I told myself that I'm good at what I do. I could better understand why the doctor was frustrated and see it from her point of view.

If you do this for a couple of weeks, you will begin to see a pattern of those events that cause you stress and how you could change your response, thereby reducing some of the stress in your life.

Measure Your Stress

Complete the free "Measure Your Stress" quiz at Psychologist World (www.psychologistworld.com/stress/stress-test). Then answer the following questions:

1. Which factors increase your stress level?
2. Which areas should you improve to manage your stress better?

References

Agheli, R., R. Roshangar, K. Parvan, P. Sarbakhsh, and S. Shafeh. 2017. "Work Stress and Organizational Citizenship Behaviors Among Nurses." *Annals of Tropical Medicine and Public Health* 10 (6): 1453.

American Psychological Association (APA). 2020. *Stress in America 2020: Stress in the Time of COVID-19, Volume 3*. Published July 28. www.apa.org/news/press/releases/stress/ (at Previous Stress in America Reports, tab "2020").

———. 2019. *Stress in America 2019: Stress Over Election, Health Care and Mass Shootings*. Published November 5. www.apa.org/news/press/releases/stress/ (at Previous Stress in America Reports, tab "2019").

———. 2012. *Stress in America: Our Health at Risk*. Published January 11. www.apa.org/news/press/releases/stress/2011/default.

Barling, J., E. K. Kelloway, and M. Frone. 2005. *The Handbook of Stress*. Thousand Oaks, CA: Sage.

Bennion, E., M. Olpin, and M. DeBelsio. 2018. "A Comparison of Four Stress Reduction Modalities on Measures of Stress Among University Students." *International Journal of Workplace Health Management* 11(1): 45–55.

Branson, V., E. Palmer, M. J. Dry, and D. Turnbull. 2019. "A Holistic Understanding of the Effect of Stress on Adolescent Well-Being: A Conditional Process Analysis." *Stress Health* 35 (5): 626–41, https://doi.org/10.1002/smi.2896.

Brown, T. 2013. "Healing the Hospital Hierarchy." *New York Times*, March 16. http://opinionator.blogs.nytimes.com/2013/03/16/healing-the-hospital-hierarchy/.

Bucurean, M. 2018. "The Effects of Moods and Emotions on Decision Making Process—A Qualitative Study." *Annals of the University of Oradea: Economic Science* 28 (1): 423–29. https://doaj.org/article/073addef61d647eab2bc918183c34f3d.

Cassam, Q. 2017. "Diagnostic Error, Overconfidence and Self-Knowledge." *Palgrave Communications* 3 (1): 17025. https://doi.org/10.1057/palcomms.2017.25.

Chain Reaction. 2020. "Google Developed a Mindfulness and Emotional Intelligence Course" (blog). Published Sept 16. www.chainreaction.life/blog/googlemindfulnesscourse.

Clark, A. 2005. *Causes, Role and Influence of Mood States*. Hauppauge, NY: Nova Biomedical Books.

Dental Abstracts. 2019. "Improving Emotional Intelligence" (conference abstract). *Dental Abstracts* 64 (5): 293–94. https://doi.org/10.1016/j.denabs.2019.05.009.

Dobson, K. S., and D. J. A. Dozois (eds.). 2008. *Risk Factors in Depression*. San Diego, CA: Elsevier.

Fink, G. (ed.). 2010. *Stress Consequences: Mental, Neuropsychological, and Socioeconomic*. San Diego, CA: Elsevier.

Goleman, D., R. Boyatzis, and A. McKee. 2013. *Leadership: Unleashing the Power of Emotional Intelligence*. Boston: Harvard Business Press.

Gregoire, C. 2015. "How Men and Women Process Emotions Differently." *Huffington Post*, January 25. www.huffingtonpost.com/2015/01/25/how-men-and-women-process_n_6510160.html.

Gujski, M., J. Pinkas, T. Junczyk, A. Pawelczak-Barszczowska, D. Raczkiewicz, A. Owoc, and I. Bojar. 2017. "Stress at the Place of Work and Cognitive Functions Among Women Performing Intellectual Work During Peri- and Post-Menopausal Period." *International Journal of Occupational Medicine and Environmental Health* 30 (6): 943–961. https://doi.org/10.13075/ijomeh.1896.01119.

Hall, L. H., J. Johnson, J. Heyhoe, I. Watt, K. Anderson, and D. B. O'Connor. 2017. "Exploring the Impact of Primary Care Physician Burnout and Wellbeing on Patient Care: A Focus Group Study." *Journal of Patient Safety*. https://doi.org/10.1097/PTS.0000000000000438.

Harvard Business Review Analytic Services. 2019. *The EI Advantage: Driving Innovation and Business Success Through the Power of Emotional Intelligence*. Research Report. https://hbr.org/sponsored/2019/08/the-ei-advantage-driving-innovation-and-business-success-through-the-power-of-emotional-intelligence.

Harvard Professional Development. 2019. "How to Improve Your Emotional Intelligence." Harvard Division of Continuing Education (blog). Published August 26. https://professional.dce.harvard.edu/blog/how-to-improve-your-emotional-intelligence/.

Hospital Employees' Union (HEU). 2000. "The Workplace Anti-Stress Guide." Accessed February 4, 2015. www.heu.org/sites/default/files/uploads/2008_healthsafety/HEU%20anti-stress%20guide.pdf.

Hughes, R. 2008. *Patient Safety and Quality*. Rockville, MD: Agency for Healthcare Research and Quality.

Jia, M., J. Cheng, and C. Hale. 2017. "Workplace Emotion and Communication: Supervisor Nonverbal Immediacy, Employees Emotion Experience, and Their Communication Motives." *Management Communication Quarterly* 31 (1): 69–87. https://doi.org/10.1177/0893318916650519.

Johnson, J., G. Louch, A. Dunning, O. Johnson, A. Grange, C. Reynolds, L. Hall, and J. O'Hara. 2017. "Burnout Mediates the Association Between Symptoms of Depression and Patient Safety Perceptions: A Cross-Sectional Study in Hospital Nurses." *Journal of Advanced Nursing* 73(7): 1667–1680. https://doi.org/10.1111/jan.13251.

Johnson, J., L. Hall, K. Berzins, J. Baker, K. Melling, and C. Thompson. 2018. "Mental Healthcare Staff Well-Being and Burnout: A Narrative Review of Trends, Causes, Implications, and Recommendations for Future Interventions." *International Journal of Mental Health Nursing* 27 (1): 20–32.

Kang, L., Y. Li, S. Hu, M. Chen, C. Yang, B. X. Yang, J. Hu, J. Lai, X. Ma, J. Chen, L. Guan, G. Wang, H. Ma, and Z. Liu. 2020. "The Mental Health of Medical

Workers in Wuhan, China Dealing with the 2019 Novel Coronavirus." *Lancet Psychiatry* 7 (3): E14. https://doi.org/10.1016/S2215-0366(20)30047-X.

Knowlton, S. 2020. "The Positive Effects of Stress." HealthGuidance.org (blog). Updated January 21. www.healthguidance.org/entry/15537/1/the-positive-effects-of-stress.html.

Kuang, B., S. Peng, X. Xie, and P. Hu. 2019. "Universality vs. Cultural Specificity in the Relations Among Emotional Contagion, Emotion Regulation, and Mood State: An Emotion Process Perspective." *Frontiers in Psychology* 10 (February 12): 186. https://doi.org/10.3389/fpsyg.2019.00186.

Lai, J., S. Ma, Y. Wang, Z. Cai, J. Hu, N. Wei, J. Wu, H. Du, T. Chen, R. Li, H. Tan, L. Kang, L. Yao, M. Huang, H. Wang, G. Wang, Z. Liu, and S. Hu. 2020. "Factors Associated with Mental Health Outcomes Among Health Care Workers Exposed to Coronavirus Disease 2019." *JAMA Network Open* 3 (3): e203976. https://doi.org/10.1001/jamanetworkopen.2020.3976.

Lilly. 2020. 2020 ESG Report at "Social: Employee Well-Being." https://esg.lilly.com/social#tab-control-tab4.

Maji, S. 2018. "Society and 'Good Woman': A Critical Review of Gender Difference in Depression." *International Journal of Social Psychiatry* 64 (4): 396–405. https://doi.org/10.1177/0020764018765023.

Mohindra, R. R., V. Suri, A. Bhalla, and S. M. Singh. 2020. "Issues Relevant to Mental Health Promotion in Frontline Health Care Providers Managing Quarantined/Isolated COVID19 Patients." *Asian Journal of Psychiatry* 51 (June): 102084. Published online April 7. https://doi.org/10.1016/j.ajp.2020.102084.

National Institute of Mental Health (NIMH). 2021. "5 Things You Should Know About Stress." NIH Publication No. 19-MH-8109. National Institutes of Health. www.nimh.nih.gov/health/publications/stress/index.shtml.

Nelson, D., and J. Campbell. 2012. *Organizational Behavior: Science, the Real World and You*, 8th ed. Mason, OH: South-Western.

Olpin, M., and M. Hesson. 2016. *Stress Management for Life: A Research-Based Experimental Approach*, 4th ed. Boston, MA: Cengage Learning.

Pessoa, L. 2018. "Embracing Integration and Complexity: Placing Emotion Within a Science of Brain and Behaviour." *Cognition and Emotion* 33 (1): 55–60. https://doi.org/10.1080/02699931.2018.1520079.

Pradhan, R. K., L. K. Jena, and S. K. Singh. 2017. "Examining the Role of Emotional Intelligence Between Organizational Learning and Adaptive Performance in Indian Manufacturing Industries." *Journal of Workplace Learning* 29 (3): 235–47. https://doi.org/10.1108/JWL-05-2016-0046.

Raudenská, J., V. Steinerová, A. Javurková, I. Urits, A. D. Kaye, O. Viswanath, and G. Varrassi. 2020. "Occupational Burnout Syndrome and Post-Traumatic Stress Among Healthcare Professionals During the Novel Coronavirus Disease 2019 (COVID-19) Pandemic." *Best Practice & Research Clinical Anaesthesiology* 34 (3): 553–60. https://doi.org/10.1016/j.bpa.2020.07.008.

Seaward, B. 2014. *Essentials of Managing Stress*. Burlington, MA: Jones & Bartlett Learning.

Shanafelt, T., S. Boone, L. Tan, L. Dyrbye, W. Sotile, D. Satele, C. West, J. Sloan, and M. Oreskovich. 2012. "Burnout and Satisfaction with Work–Life Balance Among US Physicians Relative to the General US Population." *JAMA Internal Medicine* 172 (18): 1377–85.

Sharkey, J., and B. Caska. 2020. "Work–Life Balance Versus Work–Life Merge: A Comparative and Thematic Analysis of Workplace Well-Being." *DBS Business Review* 3 (March). https://doi.org/10.22375/dbr.v3i0.59.

Shaver, P., J. Schwartz, D. Kirson, and C. O'Connor. 2001. "Emotional Knowledge: Further Exploration of a Prototype Approach." In *Emotions in Social Psychology: Essential Readings*, edited by G. Parrott, 26–56. Philadelphia, PA: Psychology Press.

Sweileh, W. M. 2020. "Research Trends and Scientific Analysis of Publications on Burnout and Compassion Fatigue Among Healthcare Providers." *Journal of Occupational Medicine and Toxicology* 15 (1): 23. https://doi.org/10.1186/s12995-020-00274-z.

Sznycer, D., and A. Lukaszewski. 2019. "The Emotion-Valuation Constellation: Multiple Emotions Are Governed by a Common Grammar of Social Valuation." *Evolution and Human Behavior* 40 (4): 395–404.

Teng, C. 2011. "Who Are Likely to Experience Flow? Impact of Temperament and Character on Flow." *Personality and Individual Differences* 50 (6): 863–68.

Tottle, S. 2020. "Reduce Stress at Work and Prevent Burnout—A Psychologist Explains How." *The Conversation*, February 7. https://theconversation.com/reduce-stress-at-work-and-prevent-burnout-a-psychologist-explains-how-129841.

Turnipseed, D. 2017. "Emotional Intelligence and OCB: The Moderating Role of Work Locus of Control." *Journal of Social Psychology* 158 (3): 322–36.

Wei, H., K. Sewell, G. Woody, and M. Rose. 2018. "The State of the Science of Nurse Work Environments in the United States: A Systematic Review." *International Journal of Nursing Sciences* 5 (3): 287–300.

Wu, G., Z. Hu, and J. Zheng. 2019. "Role Stress, Job Burnout, and Job Performance in Construction Project Managers: The Moderating Role of Career Calling." *International Journal of Environment Research and Public Health* 16 (13): 2394. https://doi.org/10.3390/ijerph16132394.

CHAPTER 9

PARADIGMS AND PERCEPTIONS

> Our views of the world, our beliefs and misbeliefs, help drive our behaviors. Toward the end of 2020, after almost a year of high unemployment, business shutdowns, and more than 200,000 deaths from COVID-19, vaccines began to be approved for public use. However, almost half of US adults polled in September indicated that they probably or definitely would not seek a vaccination. Conversely, just over 20 percent stated they would definitely get vaccinated. The speed at which companies developed the vaccines left many people concerned that the shots' safety and effectiveness would not be fully understood when they were introduced. Over three-quarters of Americans (77 percent) perceived the vaccines as being approved and used before they were known to be safe; about one in five believed that the approval process would be too slow. The differences in beliefs, and perhaps misbeliefs, positioned Americans for a long road to herd immunity to COVID-19 (Tyson, Johnson, and Funk 2020).

Learning Objectives

After studying this chapter, readers should be able to

- define the terms *paradigm* and *paradigm shift*;
- describe how attitudes and perceptions form and influence behaviors;
- discuss the fundamental attribution error and its impact on perceptions;
- explain stereotypes, halo effects, and similar-to-me effects and the damage they can cause if they are not recognized and addressed;
- summarize how the primacy and recency effects can influence decision-making; and
- compare different forms of commitment and their benefits.

Key Terms

- fundamental attribution error
- halo effect
- paradigm shift
- paradigms
- perceptions
- primacy effect
- recency effect
- self-fulfilling prophecy
- similar-to-me effect
- stereotype

How we perceive events is tied directly to our attitudes and cultural backgrounds. Furthermore, as discussed in the introduction, what we understand and perceive becomes our reality. This chapter discusses the ways we see events and experiences and the paradigms and filters that allow us to have distinct perspectives even when confronted by the same situation. Our way of thinking also creates potential biases that can negatively prejudice our decisions. Understanding how employees see the world and what affects their frame of reference allows managers to improve their decision-making and more fully engage employees.

Paradigms

All humans see the world through lenses crafted from their life experiences. These lenses are our **paradigms**, which filter how we perceive events (how we see the world) and affect how we make decisions. From our experiences, we make connections between actions and outcomes and develop expectations about how the world works. Paradigms color our expectations about people's behavior and direct our actions in organizations.

Paradigms help direct the focus of our attention and our interpretations of situations. According to Kuhn (2012), the way we see the world dictates

1. what we choose to study and research,
2. what types of questions we ask,
3. how we structure our questions, and
4. how we interpret results.

paradigms
The lenses through which people see the world, coloring their expectations of people's behavior and directing their actions in organizations.

Established paradigms facilitate decision-making by allowing us to determine in advance the relationship between cause and effect. For example, a sizable number of parents in the United States have refused to vaccinate their children for common communicable diseases. As a result, epidemics of childhood diseases such as measles have broken out in the country. Public health officials perceive that these parents endanger not only their own children but the health of the nation as well. Many parents who decide not to vaccinate are well educated, but allow their perception that vaccines may be linked to autism and other developmental maladies to dictate their thinking. One example of this comes from a *New York Times* report that in some schools in Orange County, California, 50–60 percent of kindergartners had not received the required vaccinations ("Vaccine Critics Turn Defensive over Measles," J. Healy and M. Paulson, January 30, 2015). These parents adopted a paradigm that assumes a dangerous, untrusting world thwarting their desire "to raise their children in a natural, organic environment" and are suspicious of pharmaceutical companies and big businesses. Much of their argument, however, is not based on science but on feelings forged by their experiences. As one parent stated, "Vaccines don't feel right for me and my family."

> **A Paradigm of Expected Physician Care**
>
> Good patient care has traditionally been about a close relationship between the patient and their primary care physician. When ill, a person would travel to their doctor's office, wait for a time, and then see their physician, which would result in face-to-face advice and often a prescription or a referral to a specialist.
>
> In the early 2000s, when one of the authors was working with a department of family practice in Indiana, a few physicians were experimenting with communicating with patients via e-mail, Skype, and phone. However, most doctors in the department and across the state felt very strongly that these interactions were inappropriate. They expressed concerns that patients could not be appropriately examined remotely.
>
> Today, millions of Americans are seeking care electronically with a physician. Healthcare systems and private companies such as Teladoc and Doctor on Demand provide doctors for consumers needing a remote consultation. This change in paradigm was supercharged in 2020 by the pandemic, which triggered an explosion in the use of telemedicine for care (Galewitz 2020). One company, CirrusMD, can connect a patient with a doctor in less than a minute, with most of the communication taking place through secure text messaging. Although some established physicians have expressed concerns about care quality provided using telemedicine, CirrusMD has more than 1 million people using their services (Murphy 2019).

Throughout our lives, we collect assumptions that construct our paradigms. A lack of awareness of these underlying assumptions can keep people from understanding others. Most of the time, at least initially, these assumptions help us to improve interactions and facilitate social and organizational interchange. However, problems arise when our assumptions, which we established in the past and no longer question (or even recognize), become mismatched with current reality and influence our behavior negatively. Improper or misaligned paradigms can cause incorrect perceptions and poor judgment.

As the story in the nearby box shows, even common experiences such as what is appropriate when seeing a doctor involve perceptions. Prior patient experiences clearly influence assumptions about the correct way to interact with a medical professional.

> **A Patient's Perspective**
>
> As a hospital CEO, I received many complaints from patients about the service they had experienced. Part of my improvement process was to meet with the heads of departments in which the services had been rendered to discuss patient complaints. Frequently, someone in the affected department would state that what the patient said did not really happen and then proceed to tell a totally different story. Again and again, I would remind staff that what actually happened from their perspective did not matter; what mattered—and had to be addressed—was the reality in the patient's mind.

Paradigms differ among humans because everyone perceives events and situations differently. We can view the same scene but come away with totally different concepts. As is the case with parents who refuse to have their children vaccinated, reality depends on the perspective of the beholder, and consequent actions and behaviors are directly tied to that reality. In healthcare, as illustrated by the vignette in the box, patients often have perspectives that differ from those of service providers. Even if the providers are certain they are right, the patients' perspectives are their reality and must be considered.

When beliefs fail to match reality, it is time to undergo a **paradigm shift**. Changing our paradigms can alter our decisions, prepare us for uncertainty, and enhance our ability to learn in the organizational setting (Covey 2004; Senge 2006).

Paradigm shifts occur when new information renders past accepted "facts" faulty or false. This facilitates the adoption of a new paradigm. The introduction of the internet, the widespread adoption of cell phones, and the COVID-19 pandemic all created environments that revolutionized how we behaved, worked, and interacted. As a result, our paradigms shifted to accommodate a new reality (Michelson 2020).

paradigm shift
The changing of a person's paradigms, which can alter their decisions, prepare them for uncertainty, and enhance their ability to learn in the organizational setting.

Perceptions

Exhibit 9.1 illustrates the ways in which stimuli, perceptions, and paradigms interact. **Perceptions** are the ways people experience, process, and interpret stimuli. These stimuli may originate from many sources—the weather, traffic, personal interactions, signs, and numerous others. Humans filter the stimuli through their paradigms and arrive at perceptions. The perceptions, in turn, provide feedback that helps modify or reinforce the paradigm.

perceptions
The ways people experience, process, and interpret stimuli.

Personal characteristics also affect what an individual perceives. Individuals' attitudes, motives, personality, education, interests, past experiences, and expectations can influence their perceptions. This filtering often results in differing or inaccurate perceptions. The fact that people can observe the

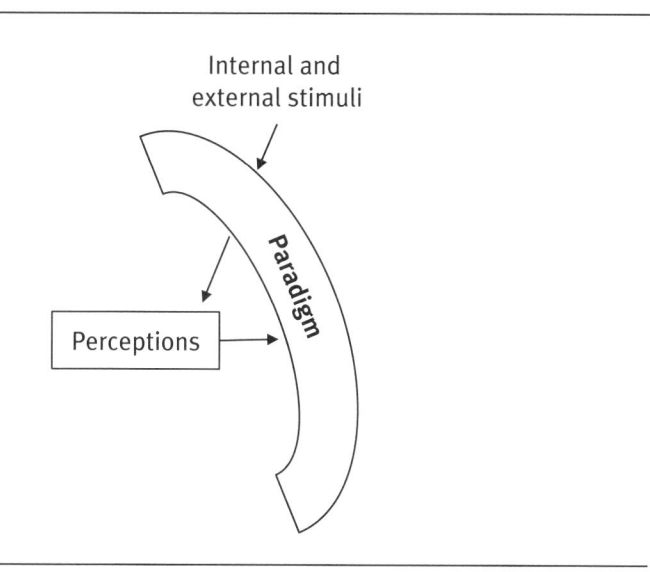

EXHIBIT 9.1
Interaction of Stimuli, Perceptions, and Paradigms

same situations or receive the same stimuli yet understand them in totally dissimilar ways has long been seen in healthcare organizations. For example, the perceptions of top managers tend to differ widely from those of staff personnel. High-level executives bring radically different paradigms to the work environment as compared with staff's, and each group can perceive the direction and success of their organization very differently (Walston and Chou 2011).

Generating perceptions is a multifaceted process. Living in a complex world that constantly bombards them with an extensive amount of information, individuals must select, organize, and interpret the stimuli. Experiences and paradigms guide them to select and ignore different information. Often, this process occurs without thought, as people hear and attend to only the stimuli that interest them or support what they seek. For example, people shopping at the grocery store are likely to buy much less food if they have eaten before visiting the store than if they shop while hungry. Likewise, an orthopedic surgeon may focus on surgery-related matters and ignore a patient's overall medical condition.

Once selected for attention, information is organized into recognizable patterns and interpreted. Some of the patterns may be opposites, while others may reflect cause-and-effect relationships. Opposites occur when we contrast one experience with another. We know how we have acted in certain circumstances and contrast that action with the behavior of others. Cause-and-effect patterns allow us to attach meaning to the source of the actions. Understanding cause and effect helps us explain the past, comprehend the present, and forecast the future.

People seek order and establish causal relationships. Of course, with our limited perspectives, our interpretations may not be accurate or may be interpreted differently by other parties. For example, in mid-2020 Republicans and Democrats were far apart in their views regarding the health risk posed by the COVID-19 pandemic. A wide majority of Democrats (85 percent) believed the coronavirus was a major health threat for Americans. Yet, only half as many Republicans (45 percent) thought the same. Party affiliation mattered to this assessment more than any other factor (Tyson 2020). As a result, Democrats were more likely to change their behaviors, states governed by Republicans were much less likely to impose restrictions, and more than half of Republican voters felt the threat of the virus was exaggerated. Significant factors in these differing perceptions included people's preferred source for news and Republicans' tendency to not trust scientists, the media, or the federal government (Brownstein 2020).

Part of the problem with our perceptions is that we never have complete information. Although we can perceive physical objects and the environment relatively objectively, information about people and social interactions is often subjective and open to personal interpretation. At best, our experiences and background provide fragmented evidence that we connect and from which we draw conclusions. As demonstrated in exhibit 9.2, we can interpret different outcomes from the information given. This drawing is made up of only short lines and circles, yet most who view the diagram perceive a three-dimensional cube embedded in the darkened box. We take the fragmented information presented and then extrapolate what we think we should see. Similarly, people tend to draw conclusions when presented with limited information.

EXHIBIT 9.2
Extrapolating from Limited Information

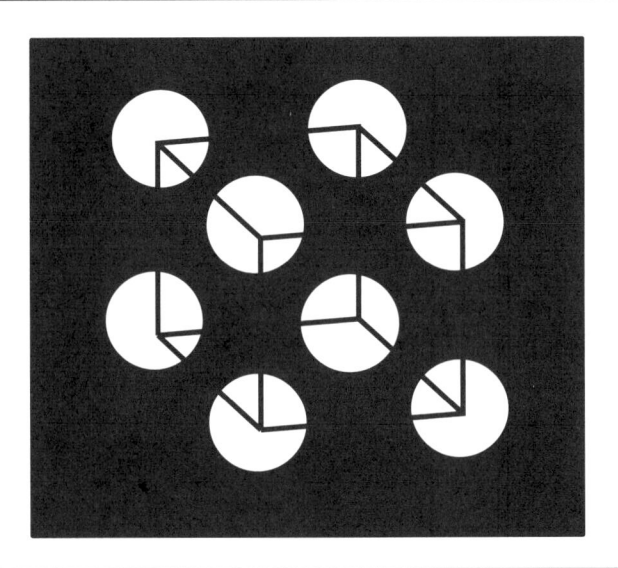

Patient Perceptions and Satisfaction

One perceptual area that has become increasingly important in healthcare is the measurement of patient satisfaction. For decades, healthcare organizations have surveyed their patients to ascertain their satisfaction with the services provided. National companies such as Press Ganey, National Research Corporation, Gallup, and HealthStream have made patient satisfaction surveys big business. These surveys became more important in 2006, when the Centers for Medicare & Medicaid Services (CMS) and the US Agency for Healthcare Research and Quality (AHRQ) collaborated to implement the Hospital Consumer Assessment of Healthcare Providers and Systems (HCAHPS) survey and tied the results to hospital compensation. HCAHPS is administered to a random sample of a hospital's adult patients 48 hours to 6 weeks after discharge and consists of 29 questions, most of which explore patients' hospital experiences, including issues of communication, responsiveness, cleanliness, and quietness of the hospital (CMS 2020).

Perceptual Biases

Perceptions can be helpful in making proper, prompt decisions. However, incorrect or misaligned perceptions can cause problems. Covey (2004, 200) estimated that "over 90 percent of all communication problems are caused by differences in either semantics or perceptions." Improper perceptions can wrongly bias our actions and behaviors. Too frequently, we establish patterns based on isolated or infrequent incidents that were random or accidental. Even the patterns we perceive may not be real. For example, we may flip a coin six times and encounter six straight heads. From this singular event, we may predict that the coin flip will always come up heads.

People also miscalculate their own abilities and those of others. Gamblers often say they can influence the game or have figured out how to beat the system. But casino games are based on averages and invariably win over the long term.

Following are common perceptual problems that can bias decisions:

- Fundamental attribution error
- Stereotypes
- Halo effect
- Similar-to-me effect
- Primacy effect
- Recency effect
- Self-fulfilling prophecies

Fundamental Attribution Error

fundamental attribution error
The tendency to attribute one's own success to personal traits and failure to external factors, while attributing others' success to external factors and their failure to personal traits.

Fundamental attribution error occurs because people tend to have different perceptions of how their own and others' behaviors are influenced (exhibit 9.3). People attribute their own success to personal traits (e.g., their wonderful personality, strong values, high motivation, unique ability), and attribute their failures to external factors (e.g., the work setting, organizational structure, the economy, bad luck). But when people consider the success or failure of others, the attributions switch: Success is primarily attributed to external factors, while failure is blamed on personal characteristics.

For example, say a nursing supervisor receives a report of a serious patient safety error. Through fundamental attribution error, the common tendency is to identify the person responsible, attribute fault, and administer punishment. The supervisor may attribute personal characteristics to explain the error: the person is irresponsible, doesn't think, or can't do the job. However, on committing a similar error, the supervisor may attribute the mistake to external factors such as a heavy workload or a confusing medication reporting system.

The healthcare quality improvement movement calls for shifting from a culture of blame (personal or internal attribution) to a system focus (external attribution), which indirectly addresses the problems of fundamental attribution error. Errors are almost always the result of system failures, not individual motivation or ability. As the Institute of Medicine (2000) suggests, casting blame on individuals does not correct problems, but causes the same error to reoccur. Managers need to recognize the normal attributional faults that exist and adjust their perspectives.

Stereotypes

stereotype
An oversimplified, prejudiced, or uncritical categorization of people on the basis of characteristics such as race, gender, age, religion, or occupation.

Perceptual difficulties can also arise from the use of **stereotypes**, defined by Merriam-Webster.com (2021) as "a standardized mental picture that is held

EXHIBIT 9.3
Fundamental Attribution Error

Source		My Success	My Failure	Others' Success	Others' Failure
Internal Attribution	Disposition, intelligence, character and personality traits, values, motivation, or ability	X			X
External Attribution	Physical setting, task difficulty, organizational structure, economy, or luck		X	X	

in common by members of a group and that represents an oversimplified opinion, prejudiced attitude, or uncritical judgment."

Stereotypes are not inherently bad; everyone establishes some stereotypes to simplify their perspective and reduce mental effort. Stereotyping is seen in every industry, including healthcare. Research has found, for example, that positive stereotyping results in physicians being seen as compassionate and nurses as being both compassionate and team players (Betra 2013). Adler (1991) noted that stereotypes can be helpful when they are

- consciously held;
- descriptive rather than evaluative;
- accurate;
- a first, best guess about a group before obtaining direct information; and
- modified when observation and experience are obtained.

Nevertheless, stereotyping can also contribute to work dissatisfaction and poor communication. Stereotypes are also commonly coupled with unconscious or implicit bias that can lead to discrimination and harmful prejudice (Agarwal 2018). Stereotypes toward people of color have been suggested as a major reason that proportionally many more of these populations suffered and died during the COVID-19 pandemic (Williams 2021). Additionally, people often express their cynical attitudes by stereotyping people. For example, individuals may describe "suits" (managers) as untrustworthy or a particular race as lazy.

An additional danger of stereotypes is that they often become embedded in a culture and become difficult to change. Stereotypes frequently are based on limited information, mostly anecdotes. Stereotypes are often found to be incorrect but are very resistant to being modified. Furthermore, they can lead individuals to make poor decisions, especially when issues of social justice and prejudice are involved (Osland et al. 2007; Talbot 2020).

Halo Effect

The halo effect can also influence decisions and behaviors. The **halo effect** is present when one characteristic or trait, positive or negative, dominates in the evaluation of people or products. For example, one study showed that patient perceptions of healthcare quality reflect "the halo effect of hospitality," with empty waste baskets and changed sheets directly impacting a person's perception of the clinical quality of care received (Glicksman 2020).

halo effect
The effect that occurs when one characteristic or trait dominates and affects the evaluation of people or products.

The halo effect may also occur in healthcare. For instance, obtaining a trauma center designation at a hospital emergency department can provide a halo effect on other services and result in significant financial and other operational benefits (Medicus Healthcare Solutions 2019). Similarly, when people are seen as very knowledgeable or highly respected in an area, their other traits may be perceived favorably. This effect is often seen with physicians and professors—their degrees and positions frame the opinions of others as, perhaps inappropriately, deferential.

Similar-to-Me Effect

The **similar-to-me effect** is at play when individuals and groups favor and select people who are physically and/or professionally similar to themselves. This effect can unintentionally influence hiring decisions, annual evaluations, and promotions. People relate to and can more easily communicate with others who share similar interests, values, experiences, and social backgrounds. Although this relatability can lead to greater cohesion, it can also result in homogeneous management teams that may discriminate against those with different characteristics and limit diverse opinions, which can stifle creativity (Hofmans and Judge 2019).

Managers need to understand that this bias occurs with everyone. Actions can be taken before and during the hiring, evaluation, and promotion processes to recognize the similar-to-me effect's potential and dampen its influence. Helpful steps in these situations include the following described by Knight (2017):

- Understand what hiring prejudices are and how they operate.
- Write job descriptions to be more inviting and inclusive.
- Review resumes without demographic characteristics such as names.
- Use work sample tests to evaluate applicants.
- Follow structured interviews with similar questions.
- If likability matters, assign a score to each applicant and weigh it the same as all other factors.
- Set diversity goals.

Primacy Effect and Recency Effect

The **primacy effect** and **recency effect** influence people's ability to recall information because they tend to remember most easily the first (primacy) and most recent (recency) items presented. In line with these effects, our perceptions are often dominated by the first or last impression we have of others. The old adage "You have only one chance to make a first impression"

---

similar-to-me effect
The effect that occurs when individuals and groups favor and select people who are physically or professionally similar to themselves.

primacy effect
The tendency to most easily recall the first information presented.

recency effect
The tendency to most easily recall the last information presented.

should be coupled with the thought that "Your last impression may be critical." Both the primacy effect and the recency effect should be recognized, and steps should be taken to moderate them.

The primacy effect may be a determinant in whether people achieve goals tied to rewards. Research has shown that the first reward given may have an oversized impact on future behaviors (Shea 2000; Shteingart, Neiman, and Loewenstein 2013).

This principle applies similarly to good communication about healthcare treatment choices. The most important messages should be positioned at the beginning of conversations and then restated at the end. If intermingled in the middle, the messages will not be readily recalled by the people to whom the message is directed. In choosing medical treatment options and in emergency and high-risk situations, understanding the primacy and recency effects can be particularly important (Bansback et al. 2014; Reilly and Markenson 2010).

Self-Fulfilling Prophecies

Perceptions and expectations can affect the results people produce. This phenomenon is called a **self-fulfilling prophecy** and can have either a positive or a negative effect. Setting positive expectations often leads to positive results (the Pygmalion effect) and, conversely, expecting the worst can result in poor performance (the Golem effect). Thus, leaders' expectations of and beliefs about their workers can become self-fulfilling prophecies of their outcomes. Leaders with positive expectations tend to provide greater emotional support and praise, while those with negative expectations frequently withhold praise and support. The leaders' behaviors cause employees to alter their actions. As hospital consultants can validate, employees' treatment of patients tends to reflect how the leaders interact with their employees.

Cultural Differences

Cultures dramatically affect perceptions and attitudes. We see and interpret situations through our distinct cultural perspectives, and cultural expectations differ significantly. Without an understanding of the different cultures at play in our environment, we may make incorrect judgments. For example, business interactions in the Northeast region of the United States tend to be formal and brusque, whereas businesspeople in the South often place great importance on social hospitality. Southerners doing business in New York City may initially be put off by the brash attitude their counterparts may display.

Symbols and numbers can also mean radically different things to different cultures. In Hong Kong's primary language, Cantonese, the word for

self-fulfilling prophecy
The effect that occurs when a person's results are predetermined by an observer's perception or expectation of them. Self-fulfilling prophecies may be positive as a result of higher expectations (the Pygmalion effect) or negative as a result of lower expectations (the Golem effect).

prosperity, *faat*, sounds like the English word *eight*. This connection once motivated a rich businessman to pay $5 million for a car license plate with just the numeral 8. The next year, Chinese people in Hong Kong were mystified when a European paid $4.8 million for a license plate with the number 7, as this numeral has little significance to Chinese culture or fortune (Adler 1991).

Perception is culturally determined and tends to be difficult to change. For example, one of the authors was once involved in a negotiation between a university and a Korean government entity that went on for almost a year. The parties were deciding on the language for a large loan that would not be paid back if the university did not become profitable within five years. Most of the terms had been agreed on, but the parties could not come to a consensus on language regarding the disposition of the loan. The university wanted the Koreans to "forgive" the loan if it was not able to pay it back. The Koreans refused to accept this contingency.

After significant discussion, the university realized that the Koreans' reluctance was based on their interpretation of the word *forgive*. Although this word is commonly used in the United States to denote that payment of owed money is no longer required, the Koreans were defining forgiveness as abandoning anger and blame—pardoning someone. Clearly, if the university did not pay back the loan, the Koreans would never forgive them; they might not collect the loan, but hard feelings and anger would exist. Once the different meanings were understood, a mutually acceptable term was introduced, and the negotiations proceeded.

Healthcare providers are increasingly treating multicultural patients. To ensure quality healthcare, physicians and other providers must understand the different cultural backgrounds and adjust their approach accordingly (Shepard 2020). The AHRQ (2020) recommends that providers better understand their patients' culture by respectfully asking questions such as these:

- Is there anything I should know about your culture, beliefs, or religious practices that would help me take better care of you?
- Do you have any dietary restrictions that we should consider as we develop a food plan to help you lose weight?
- Your condition is very serious. Some people like to know everything that is going on with their illness, whereas others may want to know what is most important but not necessarily all the details. How much do you want to know? Is there anyone else you would like me to talk to about your condition?
- What do you call your illness and what do you think caused it?
- Do any traditional healers advise you about your health?

Effects on Job Commitment

The perceptions and attitudes employees hold about their jobs affect the quality, efficiency, and effectiveness of their work. As described in chapter 5, job satisfaction strongly relates to job commitment and continuance among healthcare employees. How leadership and policies are perceived directly affects the level of engagement and other positive organizational behaviors (Manuti et al. 2020).

Involving employees in organizational processes has been found to create more positive attitudes toward their work and to increase their job commitment. Sadly, some studies show that especially nurses often have poor perceptions of aspects of their work, which can be exhibited in lower job satisfaction and higher stress (McGhan et al. 2020). However, greater involvement and participation of nurses in designing and improving their performance appraisals has led to more positive work attitudes and higher organizational commitment (Sepahvand et al. 2020).

Chapter Summary

Our decisions, actions, and behaviors are directed by how we see the world. Paradigms are lenses through which we perceive the world. Paradigms help us recognize situations and make decisions, but they can be harmful if mismatched with current reality. In these situations, we need to undergo a paradigm shift and realign our assumptions and perspectives.

Perceptions are the ways people experience, process, and interpret stimuli. Humans receive stimuli from numerous sources, which are filtered through their paradigms and lead to the formation of their perceptions, which in turn modify or reinforce their paradigms. Many factors influence what individuals perceive, including attitudes, motives, personality, education, interests, experiences, and expectations. People's perceptions vary widely as a result. One problem with our perceptions is the lack of complete information. This issue is especially prevalent in social interactions, where we almost always have to use fragmented and subjective assessments to form our perceptions. We then make judgments based on limited experiences and information, and those judgments are frequently incorrect.

Sources of bias include the application of the fundamental attribution error, stereotypes, the halo effect, the similar-to-me effect, the primacy and recency effects, and self-fulfilling prophecies. Each is the product of incomplete information and personal experience that may create biased, prejudiced outcomes.

Fundamental attribution error occurs when people attribute other people's success to external factors and their failures to personal characteristics, while reversing this framework for their own successes and failures.

Stereotypes can either serve an organization positively or create problems when people are categorized into groups based on their characteristics and behaviors, and traits are assigned to the groups. The dangers of stereotypes include their negative impact on social justice and reinforcement of prejudices and the fact that they become embedded in cultures and are difficult to change.

The halo effect takes place when one positive or negative characteristic overshadows the evaluation of a person or thing. Other traits, positive or negative, are subsumed by the dominant one. Therefore, people often make erroneous judgments as they extend their perceptions of one trait to elevate or diminish the others.

The similar-to-me effect also can introduce unintentional negative consequences. People relate to and communicate more easily with people like themselves. Therefore, managers tend to hire, promote, and give better evaluations to individuals with whom they share similarities. Unless managers make a conscious effort to be aware of and counteract this effect, it can skew their decisions about hiring, evaluations, and promotions.

The primacy effect and recency effect increase the influence of what is communicated first or last. The first and last information we receive tends to dominate our memory and have a greater effect on our perceptions. People also experience self-fulfilling prophecies in that their expectations, positive or negative, tend to result in similar outcomes.

Cultural differences significantly influence our perceptions and attitudes. Perceptions are culturally determined and can be difficult to change.

Perceptions and attitudes affect the relationships in and the outcomes of organizations. Managers need to understand the causes and underlying factors of their own and their associates' perceptions and attitudes. Managers can lead better if they recognize the biases that all humans experience to some degree. Managing revolves around establishing accurate and common perceptions that contribute to positive attitudes and outcomes.

Chapter Questions

1. How do paradigms filter what we perceive?
2. When is a paradigm shift necessary?
3. How do paradigms and perceptions interrelate?
4. How does the problem of incomplete and subjective information affect perceptions?

5. The fundamental attribution error concept suggests that we are far more critical of others' failures than our own. Why?
6. When can stereotypes be positive?
7. Why do management team members often seem so similar?
8. If you are invited to interview for a job, when should you request to be interviewed in the interview schedule? Why?
9. What can managers do to positively use the concept of a self-fulfilling prophecy?

Chapter Cases

Perceptions of Illness May Lead to Worse Results
Sam's throat bothered him, so he went to see his family doctor. After extensive tests his doctor sadly informed Sam that he had cancer that would eventually kill him. Sam was distraught and returned home to tell his family. Although the doctor had suggested that the cancer was still in its early stages, Sam passed away two weeks later. On receiving the autopsy report, the doctor found that the cancer had not spread past Sam's liver and one lung, clearly not enough to cause death. The doctor commented that Sam "died with cancer, but not from cancer."

Case Questions
1. How does Sam's situation suggest the concept of a self-fulfilling prophecy?
2. What might Sam's physician have done to improve this situation?

Employee Perceptions at HealthT Inc.
Connery is the corporate chief operating officer of HealthT, a new corporation with six regional divisions that operates a total of 82 hospitals in 28 states. He knows that the perceptions of HealthT employees and providers directly affect the organization's bottom line by influencing productivity and quality.

HealthT's wide dispersion creates unique management challenges for Connery. He wants to compare hospitals and identify the CEOs who are doing the best job. With hospitals in so many different environments, Connery wants to have an employee perception metric, as he believes strongly that this will highlight the best CEOs. He presented this idea to his management team, and the team agreed that having an employee perception survey would be beneficial. However, his team raised several questions that he had not considered:

- How much money has been budgeted for these surveys?
- How frequently should the survey take place?
- Who should conduct the survey?
- Should the provider and employee surveys be different and administered separately?
- Which areas of provider and employee perceptions are important to HealthT?
- How can the company ensure a high survey response rate?
- What kind of biased responses might result and need to be prevented?
- How should the survey results be used each year?

Each question was discussed in some detail. The company incurred a lot of bank debt during its formation, so limited funds are available for this survey. The human resources director, Pauline, indicated that only $500,000 has been allocated; that works out to $6,098 per hospital per year. Pauline checked with some prominent survey companies and found that most hospital employee surveys cost about $10,000 per survey, which would include a custom survey design, administration, and analysis. However, the survey firms generally offered a 30 percent volume discount if the same survey was administered at all of a system's hospitals.

Discussion then ensued about how frequently the survey should take place. Three members of Connery's management team previously worked at hospitals that conducted employee and provider surveys. Each was vocal about the need to survey more than once a year. They proposed semiannual surveys at a minimum, and believe quarterly surveys are ideal. As they explained, annual surveys did not provide adequate information for managers to act on, and became only a kind of report card. A heated discussion then erupted about why the surveys should be done in the first place, what their real value was, and how these factors might differ for corporate and hospital personnel.

The issue of who should conduct the surveys was less controversial. Most wanted a reputable national company to conduct them; however, one member of the team, who works at one of HealthT's largest hospitals, thinks the hospitals should have the option of doing their own surveys. The difficulties this suggestion presented were debated. Problems were identified, such as the potential lack of standardization, potential selection bias, and greater difficulty in collating data across all hospitals.

Everyone agrees that different surveys should be administered for employees and providers. The company employs only a small percentage of the physicians associated with HealthT hospitals; most are independent practitioners. The group believes that physicians often have different perspectives than employees, and that some of the survey questions should reflect those differences. Also, the system's intranet can provide electronic surveys for employees, but most physicians are not connected to it and will need to receive and return the surveys by mail. As the discussion wrapped up, the important employee and provider perceptions were decided.

Next, the managers contemplated what would need to be done to ensure a high response rate. Jack, the Western Region vice president, believes they need responses from at least 60 percent of all employees to avoid the bias that would occur if only the happiest and unhappiest responded. Pauline believes the response rate is not the best way to judge the survey's accuracy, but the representativeness of the response is critical.

The question of how the survey results should be used generated intense conversation. Connery, who originated the survey idea, wanted to use the survey as one indicator to find the top hospital CEOs in the organization. The regional vice presidents want to be able to use the data to set annual goals for their CEOs. Only Pauline asked how the surveys would be used by the CEOs to improve their hospital operations. Her comment made Connery realize that he had not thought about local use, and he could see from their previous discussion that greater response and support would result if employees could see the results used locally.

After three hours, the meeting concluded, and Connery asked Pauline to develop a report and recommendations based on the discussion within one week.

Case Questions
1. What are the conflicting aspects of putting together the employee and provider surveys?
2. How does perception affect the responses and response rate of employee surveys?
3. If you were Pauline, what would you recommend to Connery?

Chapter Activities

King for a Day
How we perceive each other's status becomes part of the paradigm that shapes our interactions. This activity explores those differences using a deck of playing cards with high-status cards (kings, queens, jacks), low-status cards (2s through 5s), and mid-level cards (6s through 10s).

Preparation

Create a deck of cards with equal numbers of high-status, low-status, and mid-level cards. For example, if there are 20 people in the group, create a 20-card deck: six or seven face cards (high status), six or seven low-status 2s through 5s, and the remainder mid-level 6s through 10s. You may use aces to make up any odd cards if you like (for instance, the 20-person group might use six face cards, six low cards, six mid-level cards, and two aces).

Instructions

1. Shuffle the deck and have each group member choose one card at random without looking at it.
2. Have each group member hold their card up to their forehead so everyone else can see it, but no one else can.
3. For ten minutes, use these cards to guide your interactions with other group members. Do not tell anyone what card they have, and do not let anyone tell you what your card is; simply interact and converse in ways that seem appropriate to other people's perceived status (based on their card).
4. At the end of the ten-minute period, stop the exercise and check your card. What status did you have? Could you tell by the way other people treated you? How did the cards change how you treated other people?

Change of View

Write down ten comments that you sometimes say to or about yourself. These comments can be about anything, such as a self-conception, an issue, a feeling, or an event. Everyone's list will be different, and you might have a mix of positive and negative comments such as these:

- I'm not good at this.
- I'm awesome at this.
- I give up.
- This is too hard.

Now, rephrase these statements in a more constructive way. For example, continuing with the previous list, you might expand your comments to provide room for learning:

- I'm not good at this—what am I missing?
- I'm awesome at this—I'm getting there, what's next?
- I give up trying to do this all at once—How can I tackle this one small step at a time?
- This is hard—This may take some time and effort.

The expanded comments provide the foundation for a paradigm shift that can change the way you think about these concepts, issues, feelings, or events.

References

Adler, N. 1991. *International Dimensions of Organizational Behavior*, 2nd ed. Mason, OH: South-Western.

Agarwal, P. 2018. "Unconscious Bias: How It Affects Us More Than We Know." *Forbes* (blog). Published December 3. www.forbes.com/sites/pragyaagarwaleurope/2018/12/03/unconscious-bias-how-it-affects-us-more-than-we-know/.

Agency for Healthcare Research and Quality (AHRQ). 2020. "Consider Culture, Customs, and Beliefs: Tool #10." *Health Literacy Universal Precautions Toolkit*, 2nd edition. Content last reviewed September 2020. www.ahrq.gov/health-literacy/improve/precautions/tool10.html.

Bansback, N., L. C. Li, L. Lynd, and S. Bryan. 2014. "Exploiting Order Effects to Improve the Quality of Decisions." *Patient Education and Counseling* 96 (2): 197–203. https://doi.org/10.1016/j.pec.2014.05.021.

Betra, K. 2013. "Stereotypes in Healthcare: Why Do They Exist and What to Do with Them?" *HOMER*. [Singapore] National Healthcare Group. Published July 4. www.nhgeducation.nhg.com.sg/homer/news-views/perspectives/stereotypes-in-healthcare-why-do-they-exist-and-what-to-do-with-them.

Brownstein, R. 2020. "Red and Blue America Aren't Experiencing the Same Pandemic." *The Atlantic*, March 20. www.theatlantic.com/politics/archive/2020/03/how-republicans-and-democrats-think-about-coronavirus/608395/.

Covey, S. 2004. *Seven Habits of Highly Effective People*. New York: Free Press.

Galewitz, P. 2020. "Telemedicine Surges, Fueled by Coronavirus Fears and Shift in Payment Rules." *Kaiser Health News*, March 27. khn.org/news/telemedicine-surges-fueled-by-coronavirus-fears-and-shift-in-payment-rules/.

Glicksman, E. 2020. "Hospital Ratings Often Depend More on Nice Rooms Than on Health Care." *Washington Post*, July 4. www.washingtonpost.com/health/hospital-ratings-often-depend-more-on-nice-rooms-than-on-health-care/2020/07/02/ac138fc8-b582-11ea-aca5-ebb63d27e1ff_story.html.

Healy, J., and M. Paulson. 2015. "Vaccine Critics Turn Defensive over Measles." Published January 30. www.nytimes.com/2015/01/31/us/vaccine-critics-turn-defensive-over-measles.html.

Hofmans, J., and T. A. Judge. 2019. "Hiring for Culture Fit Doesn't Have to Undermine Diversity." *Harvard Business Review* digital article, September 18. https://hbr.org/2019/09/hiring-for-culture-fit-doesnt-have-to-undermine-diversity.

Institute of Medicine. 2000. *To Err Is Human: Building a Safer Health System*. Washington, DC: National Academies Press. https://doi.org/10.17226/9728.

Knight, R. 2017. "7 Practical Ways to Reduce Bias in Your Hiring Process." *Harvard Business Review* digital article, June 12. https://hbr.org/2017/06/7-practical-ways-to-reduce-bias-in-your-hiring-process.

Kuhn, T. 2012. *The Structure of Scientific Revolutions: 50th Anniversary Edition*. Chicago: University of Chicago Press.

Manuti, A., M. Giancaspro, M. Molino, E. Ingusci, V. Russo, F. Signore, M. Zito, and C. Cortese 2020. "'Everything Will Be Fine': A Study on the Relationship between Employees' Perception of Sustainable HRM Practices and Positive Organizational Behavior during COVID19." *Sustainability* 12 (23): 10216. https://doi.org/10.3390/su122310216.

McGhan, G. E., N. Ludlow, C. Rathert, and D. McCaughey. 2020. "Variations in Workplace Safety Climate Perceptions and Outcomes Across Healthcare Provider Positions." *Journal of Healthcare Management* 65 (3): 202–15. https://doi.org/ 10.1097/JHM-D-19-00112.

Medicus Healthcare Solutions. 2019. "How Trauma Designation Creates a Halo Effect." *Medicus Healthcare Solutions* (blog). Published November 7. https://medicushcs.com/how-trauma-designation-creates-halo-effect/.

Merriam-Webster.com. 2021. "Stereotype." Accessed August 26. www.merriam-webster.com/dictionary/stereotype.

Michelson, J. 2020. "The COVID-19 Paradigm Shift—From Values to Careers to Whole Economies." *Forbes* (blog). Published May 5. www.forbes.com/sites/joanmichelson2/2020/05/05/the-covid-19-paradigm-shift--from-values-to-careers-to-whole-economies/.

Murphy, T. 2019. "Doctors Turn to Thumbs for Diagnosis and Treatment by Text." *Associated Press*, October 8. https://apnews.com/article/b3af57ee5d574a2db6a1a628eab1403b.

Osland, J., D. Kolb, I. Rubin, and M. Turner. 2007. *Organizational Behavior: An Experiential Approach*. Upper Saddle River, NJ: Prentice-Hall.

Reilly, M. J., and D. S. Markenson. 2010. *Health Care Emergency Management: Principles and Practice*. Burlington, MA: Jones & Bartlett Learning.

Senge, P. 2006. *The Fifth Discipline: The Art and Practice of the Learning Organization*. New York: Doubleday.

Sepahvand, F., F. Mohammadipour, S. Parvizy, M. Z. Tafreshi, V. Skerrett, and F. Atashzadeh-Shoorideh. 2020. "Improving Nurses' Organizational Commitment by Participating in Their Performance Appraisal Process." *Journal of Nursing Management* 28 (3): 595–605. https://doi.org/10.1111/jonm.12961.

Shea, M. 2000. *The Primacy Effect: The Ultimate Guide to Effective Personal Communication*. [US]: Orion Business.

Shepard, S. 2020. "Challenges of Cultural Diversity in Healthcare: Protect Your Patients and Yourself." The Doctors Company (blog). www.thedoctors.com/articles/challenges-of-cultural-diversity-in-healthcare-protect-your-patients-and-yourself/.

Shteingart, H., T. Neiman, and Y. Loewenstein. 2013. "The Role of First Impression in Operant Learning." *Journal of Experimental Psychology* 142 (2): 476–88.

Talbot, N. 2020. "'What Would You Do?' Addresses the Negative Impact of 'Positive' Stereotyping." *ABC News*, July 28. https://abcnews.go.com/US/addresses-negative-impact-positive-stereotyping/story?id=72033471.

Tyson, A. 2020. "Republicans Remain Far Less Likely Than Democrats to View COVID-19 as a Major Threat to Public Health." *Pew Research Center*, July 22. www.pewresearch.org/fact-tank/2020/07/22/republicans-remain-far-less-likely-than-democrats-to-view-covid-19-as-a-major-threat-to-public-health/.

Tyson, A., C. Johnson, and C. Funk. 2020. "U.S. Public Now Divided over Whether to Get COVID-19 Vaccine." *Pew Research Center*, September 17. www.pewresearch.org/science/2020/09/17/u-s-public-now-divided-over-whether-to-get-covid-19-vaccine/.

US Centers for Medicare & Medicaid Services (CMS). 2020. "HCAHPS: Patients' Perspectives of Care Survey." CMS.gov. Last updated February 11. www.cms.gov/Medicare/Quality-Initiatives-Patient-Assessment-Instruments/HospitalQualityInits/HospitalHCAHPS.

Walston, S., and A. Chou 2011. "CEO Perceptions of Organizational Consensus and Its Impact on Hospital Restructuring Outcomes." *Journal of Health Organization and Management* 25 (32): 176–94.

Williams, Z. 2021. "Racial Bias in Medicine: A Subconscious Barrier to COVID-19 Equity." *U.S. News & World Report*, January 14. www.usnews.com/news/health-news/articles/2021-01-14/racial-bias-in-medicine-a-barrier-to-covid-health-equity.

CHAPTER 10

DECISION-MAKING

> Leaders make many important and far-reaching decisions. Some seem to make sense but still fail miserably. Mergers of healthcare organizations, especially academic medical centers, involve complex, difficult decisions that frequently involve extensive analyses, intelligent leaders, expensive consultants, and oversized egos.
>
> In 1997 Stanford Health, one of the most prestigious medical centers in the United States, merged with UC San Francisco (UCSF) Medical Center. Both facilities are attached to prominent medical schools and sit about 30 miles from each other. At the time of the merger, which had been in negotiations for more than two years, leaders said that it would lead to the state's foremost academic health center and revolutionize the way academic healthcare was structured and provided. The merger was projected to increase revenues and new training opportunities (*Daily Bruin* 1997).
>
> Yet barely two years later leaders accepted that the merger had failed and the painful process of disentangling the two organizations began. Financial losses exploded and the differing cultures at the two hospitals conflicted. Clearly, the carefully laid decision made two years before had flaws that were not anticipated (Fagan 1999).

Learning Objectives

After studying this chapter, readers should be able to

- evaluate different decision-making models, including rational decision-making, bounded rationality, and garbage can models;
- distinguish the benefits and problems of heuristics;
- identify different forms of bias and what can be done to avoid them;
- appraise methods for improving decision-making; and
- describe groupthink and ways to avoid it.

Key Terms

- anchoring bias
- bounded rationality
- confirming-evidence bias
- framing bias
- garbage can model
- groupthink
- heuristics
- rational decision-making
- status quo bias
- sunk cost bias

Decision-making is the most important activity managers undertake. Great leaders tend to also be great decision makers (Kase 2010), but as shown in the failed merger of Stanford Health and UCSF Medical Center, decision-making is also risky and difficult. Managers decide where to allocate resources, whom to hire and fire, and what products and services to offer. Becoming the decider brings joy and frustration, blame and honor. Good decisions can further one's career, while poor decisions can derail it. Learning to make better decisions is a lifelong process. Determining who makes decisions and how they are made in an organization can fundamentally affect the extent to which a firm succeeds or fails.

Many people seem to make poor decisions on a frequent basis. For example, one survey showed that just 23 percent of attorneys and 58 percent of physicians thought that the cost of their education was worth their efforts (Hess 2018). Similarly, 14 percent of second-year medical students said that they made a bad decision by entering medical school (Dyrbye et al. 2018).

The decision-making process and outcomes can be demonstrated with a decision tree, as illustrated in exhibit 10.1. Decision trees can be helpful in

EXHIBIT 10.1
Decision Tree Example

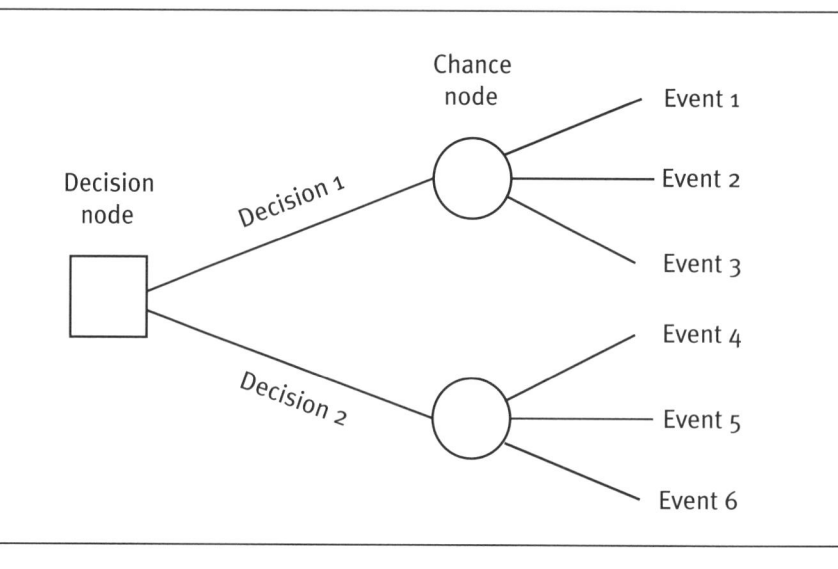

understanding links between alternatives and possible outcomes. This model also allows the decision maker to assign probabilities and quantify expected outcomes.

Models of Decision-Making

Rational Decision-Making

Early management scholars, including Max Weber and Henri Fayol, who are discussed in chapter 1, assumed that individuals and organizations make rational decisions. Thought leaders today warn against the failure to use rational decision-making and call for political leaders to use rational decision-making (Viguerie and Viguerie 2020).

Rational decision-making presupposes that there is a best decision. It involves (1) clearly defining the problem and decision to be made, (2) understanding and ascertaining the important criteria, (3) identifying and considering all possible solutions, (4) quantifying and determining the outcomes and effects of all solutions, and (5) choosing the best option. Some of these assumptions may not be realistic. Identifying all possible solutions is almost never practical or possible. In addition, knowing and quantifying the outcomes and consequences of one option is impractical. Rational decision-making, as defined here, also ignores participants' emotions and cognitive limitations.

However, we know from psychology and sociology that the unpredictable nature of individuals and groups can lead to irrationality in decision-making, often resulting in undesirable outcomes for individuals and organizations alike (Samuel 2020). For example, people who gamble often feel that they can beat the odds by using physical and mental tactics that realistically have no influence on the games they play (Greer 2005, 58):

rational decision-making
An approach to decision-making that emphasizes following a systematic path to analyze a problem and its possible solutions and logically select the best possible option.

> A craps player must roll an 11 to win his bet. Hoping to do so, he shakes his clasped hands vigorously then fires the two dice at the felt table. Instead, he rolls a four. On his next turn, the magic number is lower—three. He delicately cradles then gingerly tosses the dice. He gets a seven and loses.
>
> The gambler believes he can control the dice by how he throws them—a hard roll for a big number and a soft roll for a low number—even though the result is pure chance . . . a big cause should create a big effect . . . if I roll the die hard I'm more likely to get a big number. . . . Sometimes we are too eager to find connections, so we create them when none exist. And while using that bias at a craps game is relatively harmless, such thinking causes larger problems—from miscalculating quantity to choosing the wrong person for the job, psychologists say. What's worse, it's a tough bias to overcome.

Bounded Rationality

Recognizing the problems of the rational decision-making model, Herbert Simon (1976) proposed a **bounded rationality** model, which suggested that—given the limitations and costs of identifying all solutions and their corresponding information—people search not for optimal solutions but for a solution that will satisfy their needs. People accept a decision that is good enough, or that "satisfices." Individuals are still intentionally rational in the sense that they remain goal oriented and choose what they perceive is best for themselves, but their rationality is bounded by human cognitive limits and emotions as well as the costs of gathering and processing information (Ferasso and Bergamaschi 2020). Dating and marriage offer examples of bounded rationality. Instead of searching for the best, optimal partner in the world, we most often date and marry based on convenience and social networks. Dating continues until we find someone who may not be the perfect partner but whose being—including flaws—captures our emotions and clouds our judgment. As evidenced by high divorce rates, many people do not have a good track record in optimizing their marital partners.

The following elements are critical to making good decisions in an organizational context (McKinsey & Company 2019):

- Decisions are made at the right level in the organization.
- Decisions align with corporate strategy.
- Organizations commit to decisions once they are made.

Organizations that chronically make poor decisions allow biases to enter more freely than do firms that have mastered the organizational decision-making process.

Garbage Can Model

This model represents a chaotic form of decision-making that is practiced in some organizations. Characterized as existing in "organized anarchies" (firms that exhibit unordered and messy decision-making, such as some universities), the **garbage can model** is confusing and haphazard. Rather than have fixed preferences and clear goals, organizations that operate under a garbage can model have problematic, inconsistent, and ill-defined preferences caused by the fluid, frequent entry and exit of decision makers who lack clarity and understanding about how decisions are made (Cohen, March, and Olsen 1972).

The model is analogous to a garbage can because it hosts a haphazard mixture of problems, choices or decisions, participants, and solutions (as shown in exhibit 10.2). How these elements link to produce decisions can be capricious, depending on the current participants and the solutions available.

---

bounded rationality
The idea that individuals' decision-making is constrained by available information, their cognitive limits, and the time they have to make decisions.

garbage can model
A model for decision-making that is characterized by chaos caused by the fluid, frequent entry and exit of decision makers who lack clarity and understanding about how decisions are made.

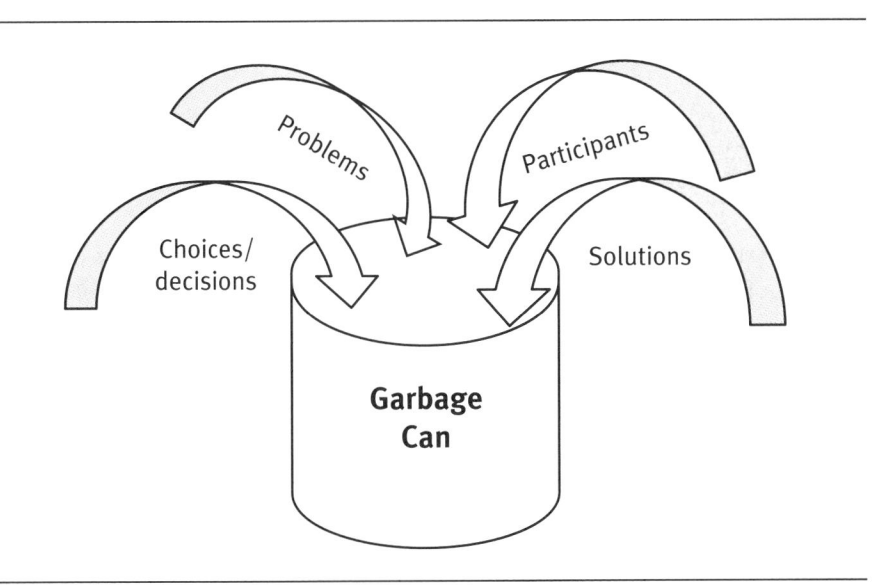

EXHIBIT 10.2
Garbage Can Model

This approach has been described as a "collection of choices looking for problems, issues and feelings looking for decision situations . . . solutions looking for issues . . . and decision-makers looking for work" (Cohen, March, and Olsen 1972, 2).

The garbage can model can clarify decision-making in complex and sometimes dysfunctional organizations. In these organizations, a set structure and established participants do not exist to deal with problems and identify solutions that lead to decisions; instead, many potential solutions exist by themselves and are connected to problems only when they arise. As mentioned, universities commonly follow this chaotic style of decision-making, but so do medical staffs. If one substitutes medical staff for university, as Cohen, March, and Olsen (1972, 11) stated,

> decision-making frequently does not resolve problems. Choices are often made by flight or oversight. . . . Problems, choices and decision makers arrange and rearrange themselves. In the course of these arrangements the meaning of a choice can change several times. . . . Problems are often solved, but rarely by the choice to which they are first attached. A choice that might, under some circumstances, be made with little effort becomes an arena for many problems.

As anyone who has worked in a dysfunctional organization can attest, such decision-making (or lack thereof) is exceptionally frustrating. In these circumstances, efforts should be made to frame the structures, goals, and processes in a rational and consistent manner. In some chaotic settings, such as emergency rooms, a variation of garbage can decision-making occurs frequently (All Answers Ltd. 2018).

Biases in Decision-Making

Even in rational organizations with highly educated leaders, poor decisions are made frequently. For example, flawed decisions have been linked to leaders with an increased sense of power that causes a failure to listen to advice. A perception of self-importance, overconfidence, and power diminishes the receptiveness to suggestions, which has been tied to poor decision outcomes (Light 2019).

In addition, we interject individual, group, and organizational biases—often unknowingly—into our decision-making. Biases creep into our judgments in several ways, including the use of **heuristics**. Heuristics are mental shortcuts or rules of thumb generated from personal experiences and used during problem-solving. Individuals and organizations typically rely on a small number of heuristics to make judgments. We often generalize personal experiences and apply them to a wide variety of situations that require decision-making. At times, these rules are extremely helpful in making fast, efficient decisions. However, if applied carelessly, heuristics can result in cognitive biases. Poor heuristics can "lead to problematic errors" and bad decisions (Krueger 2020). For example, research suggests that the wrong application of heuristics and cognitive biases may lead to errors in diagnoses up to 70 percent of the time (Saposnik et al. 2016).

We all would like to think that we make rational, objective decisions. However, we all have biases tied to our heuristics that can influence the choices we make. These biases can cloud our judgment (sometimes subconsciously) and cause us to make unwise or suboptimal decisions. The Joint Commission (2016) suggests that up to 17 percent of adverse events and 28 percent of diagnostic errors in hospitals result from cognitive biases. Some biases that impede our decision-making include the following:

heuristics
Mental shortcuts or rules of thumb generated from personal experiences and used during problem-solving.

anchoring bias
A bias that relies too heavily on the initial information received.

- **Anchoring bias**—bias toward the first information received. Our early impressions and data become references for future decisions. Thus, in making decisions, we begin from an initial point but reach a final decision by making judgments that are biased toward that point. Anchoring bias can occur in medical diagnoses, as mentioned previously. Croskerry (2013), writing in the *New England Journal of Medicine*, discussed a case where a 21-year-old man entered the emergency department of a hospital. He had been stabbed multiple times in his chest and most of the diagnoses concerned these wounds.

The physicians finally decided the abdomen was repaired, the man's wounds were sutured, and he was sent home. Five days later he returned to the emergency department and physicians discovered that a knife had penetrated the man's skull, which had not been detected earlier. The physicians' anchoring bias led to them focusing on the most significant injuries—those to the chest—without fully evaluating the head wound.

- **Status quo bias**—bias toward choices that perpetuate the status quo and the current situation. Leaving the status quo means acting and assuming responsibility, which can subject one to criticism and regret. Not surprisingly, people look for reasons to maintain the status quo and do nothing because that course carries less psychological risk (Hammond, Keeney, and Raiffa 2006). Redelmeier and Shafir (2020) suggest that the slow and unsteady response to the COVID-19 pandemic and resistance to public health guidelines to control its spread were partially caused by this bias. Status quo bias reflects the old saying "better the devil you know than the devil you don't."

- **Sunk cost bias**—bias toward investments that cannot be recovered. In decision-making, only costs and benefits that vary with the consequences of decisions should be included as factors. Sunk costs should not be considered because they are fixed and nonrecoverable. However, individuals often include sunk costs as major factors in their decisions. Physicians may at times fall victim to this bias when they are disinclined to stop a treatment that has been ineffective because they have spent so much time and efforts with it (Bajaj 2018).

- **Confirming-evidence (confirmation) bias**—bias toward information that supports or reinforces a position or belief. This bias affects where the evidence is obtained and how it is interpreted. For example, your political leaning may influence your decision to watch a news channel that delivers information and views in a way that matches your preference. As a result, you may discount the contrary information provided by other channels. Loaded with information that justifies and reinforces their existing beliefs, people may make uncompromising and potentially damaging decisions. This bias has contributed to the slow adoption of medical innovations and investments in questionable, unproven technologies (Elsbach and Stigliani 2019; Ubel and Asch 2015).

- **Framing bias**—bias toward a choice framed positively. The way a question is framed can strongly influence the choices made in response to it. People tend to be risk averse when making decisions and to reject options that present even the possibility of a small loss, even if the option is paired with a large potential gain. People are also much

status quo bias
A bias toward choices that perpetuate the current situation.

sunk cost bias
A bias toward investments that cannot be recovered.

confirming-evidence bias
A bias toward information that supports or reinforces existing positions or beliefs but against information that discounts or dismisses those beliefs.

framing bias
A bias toward information or choices presented in a positive frame.

more likely to accept a decision presented in a positive format than in a negative one. For example, in a study by Tversky and Kahneman (1981) individuals were asked to choose between two different treatments that were to be given to 600 people who suffered from a deadly disease. Treatment A was projected to result in 400 deaths, and Treatment B was predicted to lead to a 33 percent chance of survival but a 66 percent chance of death. When a positive frame was used (i.e., "Treatment A will save 200 lives"), 72 percent of participants chose Treatment A. However, when a negative frame was presented (i.e., "400 people will die with Treatment A"), only 22 percent of participants chose Treatment A.

- **Bandwagon effect**—bias toward doing something because others are doing it. Both healthcare clinicians and organizational leaders are susceptible to the bandwagon effect. Medical professionals may be influenced by the appearance of widespread adoption and visibility of a new treatment. Likewise, leaders frequently imitate strategic behavior when it has become popular (Kaissi and Begun 2008; O'Connor and Clark 2019). For instance, some observers have suggested that hospital mergers have occurred more because of the bandwagon effect than for objective purposes (Bate 2018; Schencker 2017).

bandwagon effect
A bias toward choosing to do something because others are doing it.

Groupthink

Another detriment to good decision-making is **groupthink**. Today's employees work extensively in groups, and leaders need to understand how group dynamics can affect decision-making. Although not explicitly considered a bias, groupthink can seriously affect important decisions. Groupthink occurs when people in a highly cohesive group are so motivated to make unanimous decisions that it restricts their ability to consider alternative courses of action. People in the grip of groupthink try not to upset the equilibrium of their group (Tabriz 2020).

When groupthink occurs, group members avoid raising controversial issues and stifle dissent because of their group cohesion, often arising from a lack of diversity among group members. Loyalty to perceived or actual group norms has priority over independent judgment. Individuals will often abstain from communicating their doubts and fears about the group decision.

The consequences of groupthink may include an incomplete survey of alternatives, failure to seriously recognize risks, a poorly applied search for supporting information and a biased analysis of it, and a lack of contingency plans. Groupthink can negatively affect clinical error rates and increase

groupthink
"The tendency for members of a highly cohesive group to seek consensus so strongly that they fail to do a realistic appraisal of other alternatives, which may be more correct" (Osland et al. 2007, 471).

serious patient safety issues when it impedes open communication and free discussion of problems (Mannion and Thompson 2014). Some believe that resistance to health mandates during the COVID-19 pandemic was caused primarily by groupthink (Forsyth 2020).

Decision-Making in Healthcare

The ability to make rational, effective, and efficient decisions is extremely important in healthcare. However, the challenges that leaders face in doing so continue to grow. Healthcare decision-making has become highly complex. In the beginning of the twentieth century, physicians had only to choose between a few simple tests to diagnose patients. When it was first published in 1899, the *Merck Manual*—one of the most famous comprehensive medical texts—had only 192 pages; its twentieth edition, published in 2018, comprised 3,500 pages. The critical nature of decisions in healthcare also highlights the importance of decision-making. Clinical healthcare decisions result in substantial consequences, important trade-offs, and significant uncertainties (Dionne and Mitton 2018).

A major issue that most countries grapple with is the wide disparity in health and healthcare among population groups. Decision-making biases are said to contribute to health disparities among racial and ethnic groups. Studies show that racial and ethnic minorities receive less accurate diagnoses and fewer treatment options, and have poorer clinical outcomes (Agrawal and Enekwechi 2020).

To help offset some of these issues, the Affordable Care Act encourages greater shared decision-making between patients and providers. Patients historically have not been adequately involved in their care. One survey showed that less than 10 percent of clinical decisions made in medical offices meet the government's minimum standards for informed decision-making. Providers are encouraged to offer written materials, videos, or interactive electronic presentations to inform patients and families regarding care options, outcomes, skills needed to perform procedures, and costs (Lee and Emanuel 2013).

Information technology has also become an important component in both clinical and administrative decisions in healthcare (Walston, Bennett, and Al-Harbi 2014). The Agency for Healthcare Research and Quality (2020) has found that clinical decision support and knowledge management systems may improve healthcare process results across diverse settings, but significant efforts are needed to ensure that these systems reach their potential.

Improving Decision-Making

Learning to make good decisions is a lifelong challenge. Good leaders constantly seek to improve their ability to make informed, well-thought-out decisions. However, they recognize that errors will be made, and these become learning experiences.

Good leaders also seek to understand their own and their employees' biases and create processes to guard against the influence of such biases. To avoid inappropriately interjecting one's biases in decision-making, Forbes Business Council (2020) recommends the following strategies:

- Acknowledge your own bias. Leaders need to be aware of their own biases to make good decisions.
- Step out of your perspective. Examine your decisions from a different viewpoint. Allow anonymous feedback to diminish the potential impact of biases.
- Set objective standards. Standards will minimize the detrimental impact of biases and allow equal application of judgment calls to all employees.
- Write down decision-influencing factors. This provides a way to recognize your own unconscious biases and allows you to recognize the factors that most influence your decisions.
- Focus on educating and building awareness. Increase exposure to new thinking and different perspectives, and embrace greater diversity.

Sometimes It Takes Courage

By Britt Berrett

A new CEO arrived to lead a hospital that was experiencing a 35 percent vacancy rate and 38 percent turnover in nursing services. A recent employee engagement survey had determined that 45 percent of the staff were "actively disengaged." An analysis by the hospital's human resources executive found that much of this dissatisfaction was due to the fact that nursing salaries were significantly under market standards and had been for almost two years.

In response, the executive team created a plan to be submitted to the division office for approval. Unfortunately, the division office's past behavior had been to reexamine, reanalyze, reconsider, and effectively delay any salary grade adjustments.

Sometimes it takes courage to effect positive change. The members of the executive team understood that if they proceeded without corporate approval, their jobs would be in jeopardy. But they also recognized a dysfunctional decision-making process that was creating a toxic and unsafe work environment.

Under the explicit direction of the CEO, the salary adjustments were implemented. The division office reacted by threatening to terminate the CEO. Other members of the executive team were shielded from corrective action, but the CEO was immediately put on disciplinary status and denied both a merit increase and an annual bonus.

Were the actions of the executive team painful? Unwise? Even stupid? Yes, yes, and yes. But they were courageous.

The implications were quickly communicated throughout the organization. The fairness of the executive staff was confirmed, and the organizational response was the first step in creating a world-class organization nationally recognized for its financial performance.

- Be proactive about team diversity. Ensure that teams and committees are composed of diverse individuals.

Leaders need to both make quality decisions and obtain their employees' acceptance and buy-in of their decisions. As discussed in chapter 18, organizational structure and information flows are critical to good decision-making.

Not only is decision-making a complicated and difficult task in most organizations, but it is also the key managerial duty that ultimately makes the difference between success and failure. Good leaders make—rather than avoid—the tough decisions. The adjacent box describes a real situation in which the CEO, at great personal risk, decided to increase nursing salaries when it became clear that doing so was the best decision for the organization.

Decision-Making in Meetings

Decision-making often occurs in meetings. For those working in a healthcare organization, sitting through the tenth poorly organized and seemingly pointless meeting of the week is both frustrating and fruitless. To improve the likelihood that decisions will be made in the meeting setting, meetings need to be appropriately facilitated to allow healthy conflict.

Effective meeting coordination includes careful preparation, organization, process, and follow-up. Agendas should be distributed beforehand, along with sufficient background materials, to inform participants of the upcoming topics. Meetings should start and end on time. Items that involve decisions should be noted. Minutes should be kept, assignments given, and responsibilities fulfilled. Meeting management should be seen as a cycle, as shown in exhibit 10.3. For subsequent meetings,

EXHIBIT 10.3
Meeting Cycle

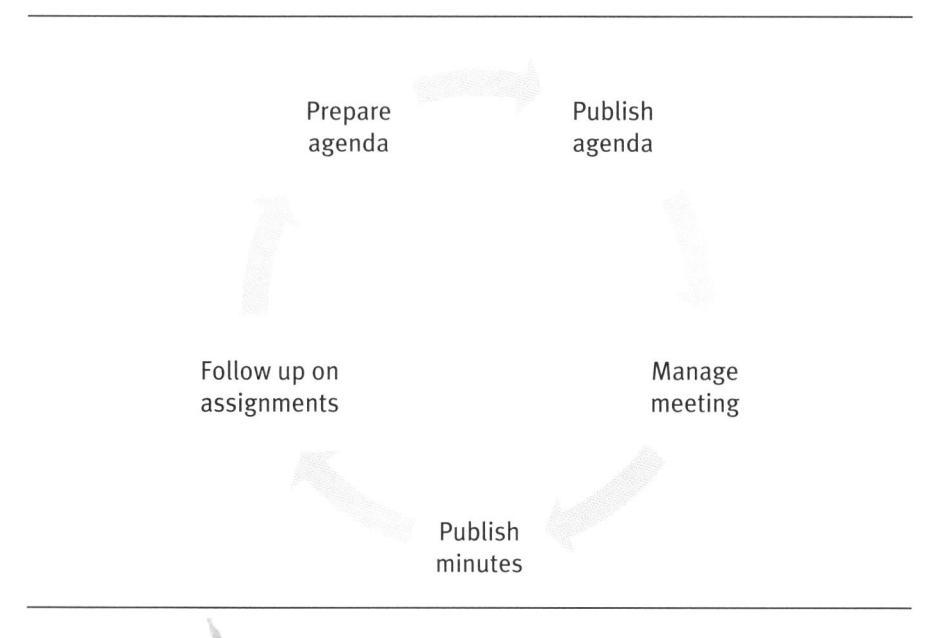

Prepare agenda → Publish agenda → Manage meeting → Publish minutes → Follow up on assignments → (Prepare agenda)

agendas should be published, meetings properly managed, minutes taken and published, assignments completed, and topics prepared for new discussions.

To make timely and informed decisions, each of these meeting guidelines requires effort and thought. An agenda should be considered a framework and a focal point, a means to guide and support the meeting. As such, it should reflect the critical topics that are relevant to the purpose of the meeting or committee. At a minimum, agenda items should be designated as requiring a decision and be accompanied by a note as to who will lead the discussion. Everyone with a stake in the given topic should be invited to the meeting. One person—generally the one in charge of the meeting—should be assigned to manage the agenda, schedule the meeting, and send out (at least 24 hours before the meeting) the agenda and any supporting materials. Generally, agendas contain the following elements:

- List of invited attendees
- Review of minutes from the previous meeting
- Follow-up on previous assignments
- New business (discussion of new topics, listing the name of presenter, time allotted, and desired outcomes)
- Date and time of next meeting

Successfully managing a meeting requires the work and cooperation of many. At least two roles should be established for each gathering: a meeting leader and a recorder of minutes. Before the meeting takes place, the method of making decisions (whether for the whole meeting or for specific items) must be established. Some groups use majority vote, others a supermajority, and others consensus. Either the meeting leader or a designated participant should keep people on track, involve everyone, and make certain that decisions are made. At the conclusion of the meeting, the recorder should summarize the actions to be taken.

Just because a meeting concludes does not mean that assignments will be completed. The meeting leader needs to follow up with those who have been assigned tasks to ensure timely completion. Some leaders take this action at the next step—while preparing the next meeting agenda. Requests for additional items and reminders of assigned activities can be given concurrently.

In short, running effective meetings facilitates decision-making, but meetings require structure and order to be effective. Using an organized agenda, involving all participants, and managing the meetings will help with making and implementing decisions.

Chapter Summary

Leaders are hired to make decisions, and good leaders tend to make good decisions. Learning to make good decisions and improving decision processes are a lifelong pursuit for most. Understanding the basic principles of decision-making and biases can directly affect the quality of decisions.

Three models of decision-making are presented in the chapter. The rational decision-making model was popular prior to the 1950s and assumed problems could be clearly defined, all options and their effects could be known, and a best solution could be chosen. Although ideal, this model has been found to be unreasonable in practice.

Offering an approach more reflective of reality, the bounded rationality model incorporates many of the constraints people experience in decision-making, including human cognitive limits and emotions and the costs of gathering and processing information. People do not seek the optimal solution but continue their search until they find a good-enough or satisfactory solution. Thus, decisions are "bounded" by human limitations.

The third decision model is the garbage can model, a chaotic form of decision-making that occurs in organized anarchies, or organizations that exhibit unordered and messy decision-making. This model involves the mixing of choices or decisions, participants, and solutions in a somewhat haphazard manner. The solutions selected can appear capricious, as they may depend on the current participants and available solutions.

Decisions can also be influenced by biases that exist at an individual, group, or organizational level. Often, we do not realize the effect of these biases on our thoughts and decisions. The use of heuristics is one way biases creep into our decisions. Heuristics are mental shortcuts or rules of thumb that help us make quick decisions yet can lead us terribly astray.

Many types of biases can influence our decision-making, including (1) anchoring bias, (2) status quo bias, (3) sunk cost bias, (4) confirming-evidence bias, and (5) framing bias. Each can cloud our judgment, and we need to understand and compensate for biases that may lead us to a poor decision.

Another detriment to good decision-making is the concept of groupthink. Groupthink occurs when members of a group seeking harmony or conformity make irrational or dysfunctional decisions. Groupthink often happens in homogeneous groups with limited diversity and when loyalty to group norms takes priority over independent judgment.

Learning excellent decision-making skills is extremely important in healthcare, as the level of complexity and challenges grows. Providers need to involve patients in decision-making; evolving information technology offers the ability to improve both clinical and administrative decisions.

Having effective meetings improves decision-making. Well-organized and -facilitated meetings allow topics to be appropriately discussed and timely decisions made.

Overall, decision-making is a challenging task for leaders and managers. Good leaders constantly seek to improve their decision-making abilities and guard against the influence of biases.

Chapter Resources

Following are several tools that can be used for creative problem-solving, along with a brief explanation and online information:

- *How-how diagram*—identifies ways to accomplish a goal or solve a problem by graphically displaying a range of solutions:
  - www.agric.wa.gov.au/improvement-tools-how-how-diagrams
  - http://creatingminds.org/tools/how_how.htm
- *Why-why diagram*—helps to creatively explore and consider multiple causes of a problem:
  - https://sustainableimprovement.weebly.com/why-why-diagram.html
  - www.cct.umb.edu/Why-WhyandHow-HowDiagrams.html
- *Fishbone (Ishikawa) diagram*—identifies many possible causes for an effect or a problem:
  - https://asq.org/quality-resources/fishbone
  - https://cornell.app.box.com/s/024dmt9rtv9tw9ctqumva7uqshkgyqpd
- *Kepner Tregoe decision-making*—aids in gathering and prioritizing information in a structured way:
  - www.decision-making-confidence.com/kepner-tregoe-decision-making.html
  - www.toolshero.com/problem-solving/kepner-tregoe-method/
- *Synectics*—encourages the use of the conscious and unconscious creative faculties:
  - www.ideaconnection.com/thinking-methods/synectics-00013.html
  - http://digitalcommons.buffalostate.edu/cgi/viewcontent.cgi?article=1035&context=creativeprojects

Chapter Questions

1. What are the major differences between rational decision-making and bounded rationality?

2. What characteristics does a university have that might be conducive to the garbage can model of decision-making?
3. What is the difference between a bias and a heuristic?
4. Why should one ignore sunk costs in decision-making?
5. I choose only to watch one news channel that matches my political persuasion. This is an example of which bias? Why?
6. Which of the biases discussed in this chapter could seriously affect a survey response? Why?
7. What could a leader do to reduce the possibility of groupthink?
8. How can healthcare decisions be improved?

Chapter Cases

Allocating Salary Increases and Effort

Pat and Chris were hired by Central O. District Hospital (CODH) as part of a three-year management contract with HCA Management Company. The hospital had been poorly run during the past decade, and numerous problems were evident. Pat and Chris were both young and energetic, but Pat's role as CEO meant greater visibility to the hospital board and community. Chris, the chief financial officer, was more operationally oriented and helped Pat make the tough decisions needed at the facility. They had learned to trust and depend on each other.

After the first year, they had made great progress. Instead of producing losses, CODH began to generate reasonable positive margins of 3 to 5 percent each month. New, badly needed equipment was purchased. The hospital seemed to be having one of its best years in decades. Pat, the CEO, received very positive news coverage in the local newspaper, which touted the "youthful turnaround" at CODH. A picture of Pat was prominently placed on the front page. Chris was exceptional with numbers but sometimes did not relate as well to others. However, the two were close friends, sometimes socializing after work, and had an extremely good working relationship.

The CODH board consisted of county residents, who were elected for four-year terms. Most were successful businesspeople with whom Pat could easily relate. The board had been displeased with the previous two CEOs it had hired. Both had financial backgrounds (one was a certified public accountant), had a hard time communicating with the board members, and were shy in approaching the public and media.

When it was time for Pat's and Chris's first-year evaluations, Rory, the regional vice president for the management company, visited the hospital to meet with the board. At the beginning of the board meeting, Pat presented a summary of the hospital's accomplishments during the past year. Afterward,

Pat and Chris left the room, and the board, with Rory present, met in an executive session. Rory offered a positive evaluation of the hospital's performance and rated both executives' overall work as exceptional. Considering their superior performance, Rory recommended to the board that both receive 6 percent increases in their base salaries.

After an extended debate, the hospital board decided, against Rory's advice, to divide the salary increase differently. Believing Pat was more responsible for the success of the hospital than Chris was, the board decided to give the former a 9 percent increase and the latter only 3 percent. When this information was shared, Pat was mortified and wondered how the board could have made such a decision.

Case Questions
1. Which biases may have entered the board's decision-making?
2. What might the board have done to minimize the effect of potential biases?

Seeing What We Want to See

Graham rules with an iron will. He feels that the only way to motivate his employees is to give them clear direction and have them keep him informed of their progress. He has full confidence in his own abilities, and believes that his employees respect and like his management style. This belief is validated in almost every meeting: He presents his agenda and states what needs to be done, and everyone always happily agrees with him. Well, almost always. Once, during a department head meeting, the new director of maintenance publicly disagreed with him. That discord was short lived, as Graham made it clear that his opinion on a topic would stand.

Recently, Graham and his sister were discussing a *Harvard Business Review* article titled "Three Tips for Overcoming Your Blind Spots" (Dame and Gedmin 2013). His sister, who is studying leadership, suggested that all leaders have blind spots which cause them to believe something other than reality. The article noted that blind spots may occur because of confirmation (or confirming-evidence) bias, selective memory, and groupthink. Graham thought the article was interesting but told his sister that his organization has no biases, that he can tell what his managers and employees feel about his suggestions, and that he can read in their faces and body language that they agree. Graham boasted that he has built a cohesive, well-oiled management team he knows like the back of his hand.

Case Questions
1. How is Graham's situation a possible example of confirming-evidence bias?

2. How could decisions made by Graham's management team be subject to groupthink?
3. What could you suggest to Graham to improve the decision-making process in his organization?

Chapter Activities

Who Will Live?

You are the CEO of Springfield Hospital. You have a small intensive care unit (ICU) designed to care for both medical and surgical patients. One bed is empty and staff are limited. Right now, there are four individuals in your emergency department:

- The first is a 78-year-old male who tests positive for COVID-19 and has significant breathing problems. His oxygen level is low and it is clear that he will die if his breathing is not assisted with a ventilator.
- The second individual is a 23-year-old woman who was in an auto accident. She is a student at a nearby university. She will need surgery, after which she will clearly need the support of the staff in the ICU.
- The third individual is a successful businesswoman. Her ethics are widely known to be shady, but she donates to the hospital and the university. She has suffered a heart attack, and she is still alive, but struggling. She, too, will undergo immediate surgery and needs to end up in the ICU.
- Finally, a local celebrity—much loved by all—is a victim of end-stage cancer. He will need the support of the ICU team for conditions caused by his cancer and its treatments.

As the CEO, your staff has come to you to decide which patient will get the last ICU bed. Using the principles discussed in this chapter, explain how that decision will be made and why.

Questions

1. As CEO, what is your final decision?
2. How did you arrive at this decision?
3. How did your own beliefs or background influence your decision?
4. Was your decision made individually or with a group? If you formed a group, who organized it and took charge of the process? Why?

What Prompted Me to Do That?

Consider the decisions you have made in the past few days and write them down. Compare the decisions you make without really thinking about it (e.g., your route home) to those where you compared choices or even researched alternatives (e.g., meals, clothing purchases). Now answer the following questions:

1. Which decisions are intuitive and which are subject to basic research? How might this translate to decisions made by leaders in a healthcare organization?
2. Which decision took the most time?
3. Which decisions involved a "committee"? (Perhaps you bounced some ideas off friends or family.) What are the advantages and disadvantages of using a committee?
4. Did you make any poor decisions? What makes them poor?
5. Do you think that you were biased in any of the decisions you made based on your background, values, or experiences? How so?
6. Did you use any sort of formal method to make your decision? For example, did you list pros and cons, write down or consider alternatives, use a diagram or tool to help, or research a decision online?

References

Agency for Healthcare Research and Quality. 2020. "Clinical Decision Support (CDS)." Digital Healthcare Research. https://digital.ahrq.gov/ahrq-funded-projects/current-priorities/clinical-decision-support-cds.

Agrawal, S., and A. Enekwechi. 2020. "It's Time to Address the Role of Implicit Bias Within Health Care Delivery." *Health Affairs* (blog). Published January 15. https://www.healthaffairs.org/do/10.1377/hblog20200108.34515/full/.

All Answers Ltd. 2018. "Leadership Competencies: Garbage Can Model." *NursingAnswers.net*. Published November. https://nursinganswers.net/essays/leadership-competencies-garbage-model-8023.php.

Bajaj, S. 2018. "Sunk Cost Fallacy in Medicine." *Doctor in Progress*. Published May 13. https://doctorinprogress.com/2018/05/13/sunk-cost-fallacy-in-medicine/.

Bate, D. 2018. "In the Midst of 'Merger Boom' Jefferson Moves Toward Acquiring Einstein Hospital Network." WHYY (Philadelphia), March 29. whyy.org/articles/in-midst-of-merger-boom-jefferson-moves-toward-acquiring-einstein-hospital-network/.

Cohen, M., J. March, and J. Olsen. 1972. "A Garbage Can Model of Organizational Choice." *Administrative Science Quarterly* 17 (1): 1–25.

Croskerry, P. 2013. "From Mindless to Mindful Practice: Cognitive Bias and Clinical Decision Making." *New England Journal of Medicine* 368 (26): 244548. https://doi.org/10.1056/NEJMp1303712.

Daily Bruin. 1997. "UC Regents Merge UCSF and Stanford." September 25. https://dailybruin.com/1997/09/25/uc-regents-merge-ucsf-and-stan.

Dame, J., and J. Gedmin. 2013. "Three Tips for Overcoming Your Blind Spots." *Harvard Business Review* digital article, October 2. https://hbr.org/2013/10/three-tips-for-overcoming-your-blind-spots/.

Dionne, F., and C. Mitton. 2018. "Health Care Trade-Offs: A Necessary Reality for Every Health System." *Health Affairs* (blog). Published March 20. https://www.healthaffairs.org/do/10.1377/hblog20180316.120106/full/.

Dyrbye, L., S. Burke, R. Hardeman, J. Herrin, N. Wittlin, M. Yeazel, J. Dovidio, B. Cunningham, R. White, S. Phelan, D. Satele, T. Shanafelt, and M. van Ryn. 2018. "Association of Clinical Specialty with Symptoms of Burnout and Career Choice Regret Among US Resident Physicians." *Journal of the American Medical Association* 320 (11): 1114–30. https://doi.org/10.1001/jama.2018.12615.

Elsbach, K., and I. Stigliani. 2019. "New Information Technology and Implicit Bias." *Academy of Management Perspectives* 33 (2): 185–206.

Fagan, K. 1999. "Hospital Merger Dead/Stanford Bails Out of Snakebit Joint Venture with UCSF." *SFGate*, October 29. Updated February 1, 2012. www.sfgate.com/health/article/Hospital-Merger-Dead-Stanford-bails-out-of-2899116.php.

Ferasso, M., and E. A. Bergamaschi. 2020. "Bounded Rationality Effect on Firm's Choices on R&D Investments: A Model for Decision-Making Effectiveness Analysis." *Journal of Research in Emerging Markets* 2 (1): 24–42. https://doi.org/10.30585/jrems.v2i1.449.

Forbes Business Council. 2020. "Addressing Unconscious Bias in Decision Making: 11 Strategies for Managers." *Forbes Business Council* (blog). *Forbes*, August 25. www.forbes.com/sites/forbesbusinesscouncil/2020/08/25/addressing-unconscious-bias-in-decision-making-11-strategies-for-managers/.

Forsyth, D. R. 2020. "Group-Level Resistance to Health Mandates During the COVID-19 Pandemic: A Groupthink Approach." *Group Dynamics: Theory, Research, and Practice* 24 (3): 139–52. https://doi.org/10.1037/gdn0000132.

Greer, M. 2005. "When Intuition Misfires." *Monitor on Psychology* 36 (3): 58.

Hammond, J. S., R. L. Keeney, and H. Raiffa. 2006. "The Hidden Traps in Decision Making." *Harvard Business Review* 84 (1): 118–26.

Hess, A. 2018. "Only 23% of Law School Grads Say Their Education Was Worth the Cost." CNBC, February 21. www.cnbc.com/2018/02/21/only-23-percent-of-law-school-grads-say-their-education-was-worth-the-cost.html.

Joint Commission. 2016. "Cognitive Biases in Health Care." *Quick Safety* Issue 28 (October 20). www.jointcommission.org/resources/news-and-multimedia/newsletters/newsletters/quick-safety/quick-safety-28/.

Kaissi, A. A., and J. W. Begun. 2008. "Fads, Fashions, and Bandwagons in Health Care Strategy." *Health Care Management Review* 33 (2): 94–102. https://doi.org/10.1097/01.HMR.0000304498.97308.40.

Kase, L. 2010. "Great Leaders Are Great Decision-Makers: Three Qualities to Take the Paralysis out of Decision Analysis." *Graziadio Business Review* 13 (4): 1–5.

Krueger, J. I. 2020. "Available Anchors and Errors." *Psychology Today* (blog). Published April 13. www.psychologytoday.com/ca/blog/one-among-many/202004/available-anchors-and-errors.

Lee, E., and E. Emanuel. 2013. "Shared Decision Making to Improve Care and Reduce Costs." *New England Journal of Medicine* 368 (1): 6–8.

Light, L. 2019. "Hubris Hammers Brands." *CMO Network* (blog). *Forbes*. Published February 21. www.forbes.com/sites/larrylight/2019/02/21/hubris-hammers-brands/.

Mannion, R., and C. Thompson. 2014. "Systematic Biases in Group Decision-Making: Implications for Patient Safety." *International Journal for Quality in Health Care* 26 (6): 606–12. https://doi.org/10.1093/intqhc/mzu083.

McKinsey & Company. 2019. "Decision Making in the Age of Urgency." Published April 30. www.mckinsey.com/business-functions/organization/our-insights/decision-making-in-the-age-of-urgency.

O'Connor, N., and S. Clark. 2019. "Beware Bandwagons! The Bandwagon Phenomenon in Medicine, Psychiatry and Management." *Australas Psychiatry* 27 (6): 603–6.

Osland, J., D. Kolb, I. Rubin, and M. Turner. 2007. *Organizational Behavior: An Experiential Approach*. Upper Saddle River, NJ: Prentice-Hall.

Redelmeier, D., and E. Shafir. 2020. "Pitfalls of Judgment During the COVID-19 Pandemic." *The Lancet* 5 (6): E306–8. https://doi.org/10.1016/S2468-2667(20)30096-7.

Samuel, S. 2020. "Is Rationality Overrated?" *Vox*, January 20. www.vox.com/future-perfect/2020/1/20/21068423/rationality-behavioral-economics-psychology-reasonable-decisions.

Saposnik, G., D. Redelmeier, C. C. Ruff, and P. N. Tobler. 2016. "Cognitive Biases Associated with Medical Decisions." *BMC Medical Informatics and Decision Making* 16 (November): 138. Published November 3. https://doi.org/10.1186/s12911-016-0377-1.

Schencker, L. 2017. "Chicago-Area Hospitals Have Merger Fever. Is It Good for Patients?" *Chicago Tribune*, October 25. www.chicagotribune.com/business/ct-biz-hospital-mergers-impact-1029-story.html.

Simon, H. A. 1976. *Administrative Behavior*. New York: Free Press.

Tabriz, A. 2020. "Healthcare Is Suffering from Groupthink Syndrome." *Being Well* (blog). *Medium*. Published August 29. https://medium.com/beingwell/healthcare-is-suffering-from-groupthink-syndrome-90848982285c.

Tversky, A., and D. Kahneman. 1981. "The Framing of Decisions and the Psychology of Choice." *Science* 211 (4481): 453–58.

Ubel, P. A., and D. A. Asch. 2015. "Creating Value in Health by Understanding and Overcoming Resistance to De-Innovation." *Health Affairs* 34 (2): 239–44. https://doi.org/10.1377/hlthaff.2014.0983.

Viguerie, P., and A. Viguerie. 2020. "We Need a Rational Approach to Reopening." *Harvard Business Review* digital article, May 27. https://hbr.org/2020/05/we-need-a-rational-approach-to-reopening.

Walston, S., C. J. Bennett, and A. Al-Harbi. 2014. "Understanding the Factors Affecting Employees' Perceived Benefits of Healthcare Information Technology." *International Journal of Healthcare Management* 7 (1): 35–44.

CHAPTER 11

CREATIVITY AND INNOVATION

> New healthcare knowledge and innovations are sometimes slow to spread among medical professionals. Other times, there may be a rush to adopt a supposed innovation on flimsy evidence. For example, when hydroxychloroquine was touted as a cure for COVID-19, more than 23 million doses were distributed from the Strategic National Stockpile. Just two months later, the US Food and Drug Administration (FDA) withdrew emergency authorization for the drug's use due to its potential adverse effects (Rowland, Cenziper, and Rein 2020).
>
> Adopting innovation without appropriate evaluation and translation can create significant problems and misallocations of resources. Models for testing and diffusing innovations have been developed that better coordinate and share new knowledge and innovations that can improve healthcare's practice, assessment, and management (Balas and Chapman 2018).

Learning Objectives

After studying this chapter, readers should be able to

- explain the value of creativity and innovation for an organization,
- appraise the methods to foster creativity and innovation,
- distinguish among different types of innovation,
- describe the diffusion of innovations throughout an industry and market, and
- compare the difference between disruptive innovation and sustaining innovation.

Key Terms

- creativity
- diffusion
- disruptive innovation
- innovation
- sustaining innovation

Although creativity and innovation have traditionally targeted the development of groundbreaking products and processes—new therapies, medical devices, and drugs in the healthcare industry, for example—they encompass much more than development. Healthcare leaders who encourage creativity and innovation in their organization must address a wide array of questions and seek to solve a multitude of problems. Drew Gilpin Faust, past president of Harvard University, observed that the industry

> has more than its share of very complex questions. How can we reduce costs and increase value, improve patients' experiences and outcomes, speed the translation of research into therapies and cures, make healthcare something that people can have access to here in the United States and, ultimately, around the world? (Forum on Healthcare Innovation 2015)

The global healthcare system has a great need to innovate and develop the creativity needed to address these issues, especially access to the "right" type of care. As enumerated by the Institute of Medicine (2001), care must be

1. *safe*—avoiding injuries to patients from the care that is intended to help them;
2. *effective*—providing services on the basis of scientific knowledge to all who could benefit and refraining from providing services to those not likely to benefit (avoiding underuse and overuse, respectively);
3. *patient-centered*—providing care that is respectful of and responsive to individual patient preferences, needs, and values and ensuring that patient values guide all clinical decisions;
4. *timely*—reducing wait times and harmful delays for those who receive and those who give care;
5. *efficient*—avoiding waste, including waste of equipment, supplies, ideas, and energy; and
6. *equitable*—providing care that does not vary in quality because of personal characteristics such as gender, ethnicity, geographic location, or socioeconomic status.

creativity
The ability to turn new ideas into new products, services, or devices.

innovation
A new idea, device, or method.

The Link Between Creativity and Innovation

Frequently, business leaders erroneously equate innovation with creativity. However, innovation is not creativity. Although the terms may mean different things to different people, **creativity** has been defined as the ability to turn new ideas into reality (Shulman 2020), while Merriam-Webster.com (2021) defines **innovation** as "a new idea, method, or device" itself. Anderson,

Potocnik, and Zhou (2014, 1298) offered a more elaborate definition of both terms:

> Creativity and innovation at work are the process, outcomes, and products of attempts to develop and introduce new and improved ways of doing things. The creativity stage of this process refers to idea generation, and innovation refers to the subsequent stage of implementing ideas toward better procedures, practices, or products. Creativity and innovation can occur at the level of the individual, work team, organization, or at more than one of these levels combined but will invariably result in identifiable benefits at one or more of these levels of analysis.

As shown in exhibit 11.1, creativity is often sparked by a changing environment and organizational challenges. Knowledge, leadership and culture, and technologies also spark creativity, which in turn generates new and useful ideas, stimulating innovation that then produces new products, processes, and services. Effective creative environments require strong knowledge bases from which employees can draw, leaders and a culture that promote investigation and imaginative exploration, and cutting-edge technologies (Dawson and Andriopoulos 2014).

Creative companies need to attract, reward, and retain employees who are risk takers. These are people who are willing to fail and operate in a culture that allows failures to be seen as a learning process. In addition, these employees should possess creativity-related cognitive skills and domain-specific knowledge, coupled with intrinsic motivation that drives employees' efforts forward. Because of the importance of employee characteristics, many creative organizations screen applicants for creative traits (Ayers 2018; Osland et al. 2007; Shieber 2020).

Creativity by itself is not sufficient, however. Creative organizations may generate many novel ideas, but unless the ideas are transformed into

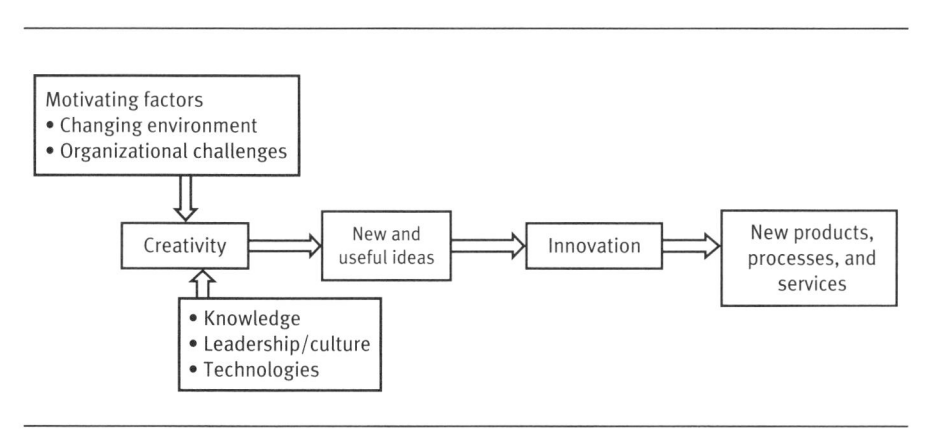

EXHIBIT 11.1
From Creativity to Innovation

Source: Adapted from Dawson and Andriopoulos (2014).

> **ReVision Optics**
>
> ReVision Optics was founded in 1996 with novel technology to correct presbyopia, a normal aging process when eyes lose the ability to see things up close. Their product, finally approved by the FDA in 2016, had a huge potential market with billions of aging people and the company raised $178 million in capital, but lasted only until 2018.
>
> ReVision developed a corneal inlay that required only minor surgery and a follow-up visit with the ophthalmologist. The company was able to have doctors perform more than 1,000 procedures with the innovative technology, but ophthalmologists felt that the procedure took too much time and effort. As ReVision's CEO, John Kilcoyne, stated, "Ophthalmic surgeons do not want to keep seeing their patients"; they preferred the prior surgery that did not require follow-up visits. ReVision had a great product, but even their best efforts could not keep their doors open (Haimovitch and Kirkner 2018).

usable, valuable products and services, a firm's creativity may ultimately be of little worth. As shown in the adjacent box, companies often fail to convert their creativity into innovation. Although ReVision was an innovative start-up and continued to tout its product, its inability to take its creative ideas to market and meet actual market needs contributed to its failure. Turning creative ideas into valuable, functional products, processes, and services requires innovative action.

Organizations that are creative and innovative do not copy other firms but instead develop unique products, processes, and services. Because healthcare systems across the globe require unique changes to address their many problems, successful healthcare innovation comes in the form of viable solutions to make patient treatments and care more accessible, affordable, and effective. As Muthu Krishnan, chief digital transformation officer at IKS Health, noted:

> Innovation is about finding solutions for tasks that we repeatedly do, that make them faster, better and cheaper. Innovation can be . . . incremental or radical, and transformative or disruptive. Every successful company that is also a learning organization, . . . is using one of the tools under the umbrella of innovation to solve their industry's problems. IKS has a two-pronged approach to innovation: innovate our processes and innovate our products/services. (Adams 2020)

Types of Healthcare Innovations

Healthcare innovations are segmented into three types:

1. *Consumer-focused innovations.* The way consumers buy and use healthcare is covered in this segment. For example, health plans may become more user-friendly and empower healthcare customers.
2. *Technology innovations.* Technological innovations in healthcare have long been known to be "directly related to the diagnosis and

treatment of disease" (Kimberly and Evanisko 1981). Today, these innovations include pharmaceutical breakthroughs; sophisticated drug-delivery systems; advanced information technology, such as artificial intelligence; and diagnostic devices that can be less costly to operate, allow less-invasive testing, and offer a less painful patient experience.

3. *Business model innovations.* Hospital and health system business models continue to evolve through the reorganization and improved integration of the healthcare activities of physicians, hospitals and nursing homes, and other providers (Herzlinger 2006; Kimble and Massoud 2017).

Changes to all or any of these three types of innovation may alter the future of healthcare. Consumer-focused innovation parallels the efforts of many healthcare organizations to become patient focused or provide patient-centered care. However, in the United States, the patient has long been outside the chief focus of healthcare providers. For example, although the following statement refers to pharmaceutical concerns, it is just as applicable to all other healthcare providers (Coleiro 2013):

> In healthcare, patients are often thought of as the passive recipients of what is manufactured by pharma companies, prescribed by their HCP [healthcare provider] and paid for by the insurance company or state funded system: not as decision-makers.

This focus is changing. For example, Microsoft Cloud for Healthcare has been introduced as an integrated health data solution to promote patient-centered healthcare. This service proposes to increase access to health information for both patients and providers. Patients will have additional digital tools to allow them to interact with their health providers. The product will also allow multiple healthcare providers to effectively engage and share patient information to provide better care with improved coordination (McGuinness 2020). In addition, the National Quality Forum (2020) released a report urging the US healthcare industry to improve safety, appropriateness, and focus on person-centered care. The report encourages standardized data systems, population health-based payments, and the adoption of advanced technologies.

Technology innovation is probably the best-known type of implemented creativity in healthcare. Examples include the discovery of penicillin and the development of MRI (magnetic resonance imaging) scanners. Throughout the twentieth century, technological innovations led to dramatic improvements in the quality of life and longevity of people across the globe. The continued advances in digital technology allow the development of more and increasingly user-friendly portable devices that empower patients and provide continuous monitoring and treatment.

Business model innovation is another type of innovation that can transform healthcare. A business model is "the core elements of an organization and how it is structured to deliver value to its customers and generate revenues" (Walston 2018, 46). It incorporates all parts of an organization and the way it operates, is funded, and relates to other organizational segments. Organizations with innovative business models may succeed, while others with better ideas and technology but a poor business model may fail.

Renowned Harvard professor Clayton Christensen (2016) suggested that innovation in healthcare can be a "game changer" and can drastically improve care and reduce costs. Writing for McKinsey & Company, Singhal (2020) listed six ways healthcare could innovate to fulfill Christensen's promise of game-changing creativity implementation:

1. *Business model transformation.* New business models in healthcare will create significant value for patients. The new business models must integrate the patient's care journey and align the continuum of care.
2. *Increased use of digital technology and artificial intelligence/machine learning.* Investors have contributed billions of dollars into health technology to create consumer-centric, personalized and integrated care.
3. *Major regulatory reform.* New regulations are needed to expand healthcare access and affordability in the United States, including provisions to increase the risk transfer to providers.
4. *Designed mergers and acquisitions.* Mergers and acquisitions need to be strategic to build capabilities and new businesses with new business models.
5. *Expanded use of socioeconomic factors to improve health.* In particular, innovators should integrate behavioral and physical health in the continuum of health.
6. *Controlled drug costs.* The industry should innovate methods across pharmacy supply chains and delivery models, and reshape the pharmacy benefit manager model.

Strategies for Increasing Creativity and Innovation

Companies vary dramatically in their creative and innovative abilities. Those that are creative frequently take proactive measures to boost that trait in their organization. At the same time, they minimize behaviors and actions that discourage creativity. As displayed in exhibit 11.2, the level of creativity

EXHIBIT 11.2 Activities That Encourage and Discourage Creativity and Innovation

	Encouraging Activities	**Discouraging Activities**
Employees and Culture	Screen job applicants for innovative characteristics	Limit turnover
	Employ staff with diverse backgrounds and skills	Retain a negative legacy culture
	Continually train and "retool"	
Jobs	Provide time to be creative	Encourage a high degree of competition
	Design complex jobs with significance, identity, variety, autonomy, and feedback	Place tight controls on information and decision-making
		Do not alleviate time pressures
	Allow extensive contact with customers	Emphasize status quo
Leaders and Rewards	Offer a clear vision and goals	Focus excessively on financial/extrinsic rewards
	Recognize and reward creativity	Set tight limits on staff
	Encourage risk taking	Micromanage
	Practice participative leadership	Allow political problems to perpetuate

Source: Adapted from Osland et al. (2007).

and innovation found in a firm is related to the types of employees, culture, jobs, leaders, and rewards. To have high levels of creativity and innovation, employers should screen new job candidates for specific innovative characteristics, established by leadership based on organizational needs and vision. In addition, hiring managers should diversify the backgrounds and skills of their employees and continually train them. Before embarking on a new hiring system, however, companies must be aware that limited turnover and a negative legacy culture that discourages change will cause problems for the new employees who would like to create and innovate.

Part of this problem can be avoided by better job design. Time should be built into the workday for employees to think creatively and implement creative concepts. Jobs should be relatively complex but (as reviewed in chapter 7) also significant and meaningful, lending identity, variety, autonomy, and

> **Innovation at Massachusetts General Hospital**
>
> Innovation occurs when problems are specifically addressed and people are organized to improve processes. To accomplish this, Massachusetts General Hospital has created a Healthcare Transformation Lab (HTL) that focuses on changing the way healthcare is delivered. Its mission is to improve the experience and value of healthcare through collaborative innovation and work to connect and inspire people to collaborate on ways to improve healthcare. HTL has worked to reduce the costs of cardiac catheterization, to create a device to detect body temperature to be used with telemedicine, and to design apps to obtain patient consent and allow providers to search for the optimal clinical specialist for a patient (HTL 2021.).

feedback to employees. Jobs that foment high degrees of competition, require tight controls on information and decision-making, involve excessive time pressures, and emphasize the status quo discourage new thought and innovation.

Last, leaders who articulate clear visions and goals, recognize and reward creativity, encourage risk taking, and engage their employees in participative leadership promote creativity and innovation. Conversely, leaders who place excessive focus on financial or other extrinsic rewards, set tight limits and micromanage, and foment political situations in their organization discourage creativity and innovation.

To promote innovation, many US health systems and even government bodies have created dedicated innovation centers. Three examples include the Mayo Clinic Center for Innovation, founded to "transform the experience and delivery of healthcare" (http://centerforinnovation.mayo.edu/); Massachusetts General Hospital's Center for Innovations in Care Delivery, established to bring teams together to innovate (www.mghpcs.org/Innovation/); and the Center for Medicare & Medicaid Innovation, part of the Centers for Medicare & Medicaid Services, created to test "innovative payment and service delivery models to reduce expenditures . . . while preserving or enhancing the quality of care" (https://innovation.cms.gov/about). The initiatives launched by these centers address a wide range of innovations, including digital health, mobile monitoring, products for rural practices, and advancing best practices.

As described in the box, if innovative efforts are organized and directed, they can have important, lasting effects on the improvement of patient care and organizational success.

Diffusion of Healthcare Creativity and Innovation

Not only are creativity and innovation important to every healthcare organization, but their widespread diffusion—both nationally and internationally—is also critical for improving overall patient outcomes and addressing healthcare costs. Most of the progress in health improvement in the second half of the twentieth century can be traced to the diffusion of innovations through public health and medical channels (Rust et al. 2010). However, much of the innovative medical technology adopted over the years has also been a major driver in increasing medical costs. Many healthcare innovations may only narrowly improve the performance of diagnoses and treatment, but dramatically affect costs. As shown in the box, eculizumab provided better medical treatment for patients, but at an extremely high cost. In addition, most healthcare innovations, even potentially effective ones, fail to be commonly accepted (Cahan, Kocher, and Bohn 2020). Therefore, new technology alone will not suffice to improve healthcare; a new wave of all types of innovations—and their diffusion—is required to open access to high-quality, low-cost care.

> **Eculizumab – A Highly Priced Innovation**
>
> In 2007, eculizumab was approved for the treatment of a serious blood disorder. The drug is a humanized monoclonal antibody that reduces the destruction of red blood cells and decreases the need for blood transfusions in people with paroxysmal nocturnal hemoglobinuria. This can be a very serious disease but occurs in only 1 person out of 10 million. Therefore, in the United States there may be only 30 to 40 people in need of eculizumab. However, the price of the antibody was set at more than $400,000 per treatment cycle, generating almost $4 billion revenues worldwide in 2019 (Alexion Pharmaceuticals 2020; Cahan, Kocher, and Bohn 2020).

While we define diffusion and explain its process in detail later in this section, some background is helpful at this point in the discussion. When we talk about diffusion, we mean that these innovative solutions must be not only locally discovered but also disseminated nationally or globally. Necessary changes defy simple solutions, and innovative designs are critical.

Newly created knowledge and innovations frequently are slow to spread across a healthcare community. Yet, at times medical professionals rush to adoption, based on limited evidence (Balas and Chapman 2018). Although many astonishing advances have occurred, concerns have been raised that the time required to diffuse innovations across healthcare systems is far too long and that most innovations ultimately fail to diffuse across their potential users (Darzi and Parston 2013; Dearing and Cox 2018). To promote diffusion, organizations such as the World Innovation Summit for Health (WISH) seek to promote and disseminate innovative evidence-based ideas and practices. To this end, the organization has sponsored forums (including an annual meeting), research, and reports, some of which help identify and document global innovations. Some of the many healthcare innovations WISH helped to promote and spread through their 2020 Virtual WISH event include:

- A DNA data bank to give individuals full control of their genomic data
- A solar-powered suitcase designed to provide lighting, communication, and power for small medical devices and emergency care in remote areas

- A smart assistant to help people who are blind recognize objects and other people
- An MRI simulation using virtual reality to prepare children for an MRI
- An affordable dialysis system that distills its own sterile water

Diffusion of healthcare innovation is complicated and facilitated by many issues. Two important factors that encourage adoption of new technology are (1) the perceived ease of use of the technology and (2) its perceived usefulness by its stakeholders (Thakur, Hsu, and Fontenot 2012). Stakeholders in healthcare may be the providers, managers, regulators, or patients. These people first need to be exposed to and learn about new technology, as its perceived ease and benefit of use is related to their knowledge of and experience with it (Walston, Bennett, and Al-Harbi 2014). Assuming a positive interaction, the more stakeholders are exposed to an innovation, the more likely it is to be adopted.

In addition to WISH, other organizations have founded exchanges and mechanisms to share innovation resources and ideas with healthcare stakeholders (*Becker's Hospital Review* 2019; Drees 2020):

- The Agency for Healthcare Research and Quality's Health Care Innovations Exchange expands efforts to spread innovations by sponsoring "learning communities" that collaboratively adapt and implement innovations that improve healthcare quality (www.ahrq.gov/innovations/index.html).
- University of Southern California's Lawrence J. Ellison Institute for Transformative Medicine collaborates with physicians and scientists across the world to discover ways to prevent, detect, and treat cancer.
- Providence Health & Services, based in Renton, Washington, opened a global innovation center in Hyderabad, India, in 2020, to drive the digital transformation of healthcare.
- Cleveland Clinic's Florida Research and Innovation Center facilitates translational research on immuno-oncology and infectious diseases.
- The Northwestern University Feinberg School of Medicine operates a Center for Primary Care Innovation dedicated to transforming the traditional primary care delivery practice.
- UPMC Enterprises focuses on generating translational science and novel digital solutions.

diffusion
The act of spreading and embedding innovation to transform an organization, an industry, or a system.

Diffusion is a social process that involves the act of spreading and embedding innovation through a social system (Dearing and Cox 2018). Exhibit 11.3 illustrates how creative ideas for innovation become

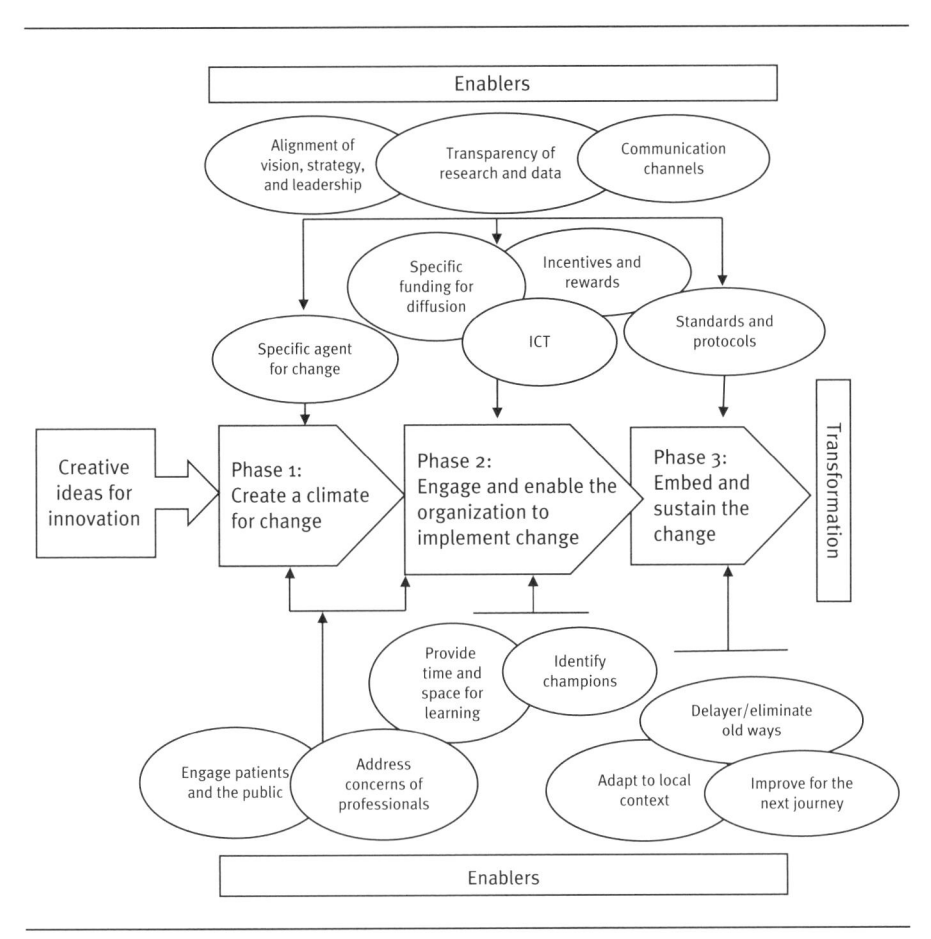

EXHIBIT 11.3
Enablers That Promote the Phases of Healthcare Innovation Diffusion

Source: Adapted from WISH (2015).
Note: ICT = information and communication technology.

transformational in three phases: creating a climate for change, engaging and enabling an organization to implement change, and embedding and sustaining the change. If these phases are completed, the innovation can become transformational and significantly affect the healthcare system.

The factors that enable the different phases are listed in exhibit 11.3. Across the full process, the presence of the following is crucial:

- Alignment of vision, strategy, and leadership to promote innovation and creativity
- Transparency of research and data that can be easily used for experimentation
- Communication channels to facilitate the transmittal of information

To create a climate for change in Phase 1, an organization should have the following:

- A specific agent to promote and shepherd the change
- A process to engage patients and the public
- A mechanism for addressing concerns healthcare professionals have about the change

To complete Phase 2, an organization must engage and enable implementation of the innovation. This phase is facilitated and enabled by the following components:

- Specific funding for diffusion of the innovation
- Incentives and rewards to encourage the implementation and dissemination of the innovation
- Appropriate information and communication technology (ICT)
- Adequate time and space for learning new concepts
- Champions who can promote and encourage innovation

Phase 3 consists of embedding and sustaining the change. It can be promoted by the following enablers:

- Presence of standards and protocols
- Efforts to "delayer" or eliminate old practices
- Adaptation of the innovation to the local context
- Improvement as a result of the initial innovation and preparation for the next change

disruptive innovation
Innovation that creates radical change and destroys existing organizational competencies.

sustaining innovation
Innovation that builds on past successes and organizational competencies and provides incremental improvements.

Disruptive Innovation and Sustaining Innovation

The concept of disruptive innovation, as championed by Harvard University professor Clayton Christensen, has become well known. Disruptive innovation differs from sustaining innovation in that **disruptive innovation** creates radical change and destroys existing organizational competencies, whereas **sustaining innovation** builds on past successes and organizational competencies and provides incremental improvements (Christensen 2016; Clayton and Martha 2009). Most innovations are sustaining, which helps existing organizations thrive. However, when disruptive innovation arises, firms frequently fail and are replaced by new companies (Christensen 2016).

Technological breakthroughs often engender disruptive innovation. Examples include the microprocessor, which created personal computers and doomed mainframes; the internet, which has largely supplanted traditional print news; and digital photography, which overwhelmed photo film companies. Disruptive technologies often drive exiting companies out of business. Companies that previously dominated markets—such as Polaroid and Kodak in photography, Blockbuster in movie rentals, Borders in the bookstore business, and many prominent newspaper organizations such as the Tribune Company (now part of Nexstar Media Group) and the *Minneapolis Star Tribune*—have filed for bankruptcy as a result of the influence of disruptive technologies (Thangavelu 2020).

Few dominant businesses survive disruptive innovation, as the value of much of their key competency is destroyed. For example, over the course of several decades, Kodak dominated the photography film market with expertise and competencies in chemical engineering. However, digital imaging destroyed the value of this competence, and thousands of chemical engineers employed by Kodak were eventually laid off. Electrical engineering skills were the competency needed for digital imaging, and Kodak, absent this platform, failed to survive (Walston 2018, 56).

Healthcare may now be experiencing disruptive innovation as Amazon, Apple, CVS Health, Google's parent company Alphabet Inc., Walgreens, and Walmart increase their activity in the healthcare sector. These companies have entered electronic personal health and expanded alternative sites for care (American Hospital Association 2020). Advances in genomics, gene therapy, and nanotechnology may have great potential for disruptive innovation in the diagnoses, treatment, and prevention of disease (Sounderajah et al. 2020).

However, information technology remains a key facilitator for innovation in healthcare. The ability to transmit healthcare images and data globally using a data infrastructure offers an opportunity to radically transform the healthcare industry and allow for new ways to deliver care around the world (Tas and Kimpen 2020). As discussed in chapter 15, leaders must provide a vision and exhibit transformational traits to achieve this transformation.

Chapter Summary

Creativity and innovation are critically important for healthcare to address the many challenges that exist today. Creativity may be the precursor to innovation and involves idea generation, whereas innovation refers to the implementation of ideas. Creativity can be motivated by changes in the business environment and organizational challenges. It can also be facilitated by increased knowledge, proper leadership and culture, and cutting-edge technologies.

Creativity is necessary for an agile business, but it is not sufficient. Creative ideas must be converted through innovation into usable, valuable products, processes, and services to be of worth. In healthcare, innovation is needed to create viable solutions to improve the treatment of patients and make care more accessible and cheaper than it is currently. Healthcare innovation can be segmented into three types: (1) consumer-focused innovations, (2) technology innovations, and (3) business model innovations.

Companies that are creative and innovative consistently take measures to increase these competencies. The types of employees, culture, jobs, leaders, and rewards directly affect the levels of creativity and innovation in a firm. Excessive focus on financial and extrinsic rewards, managers who micromanage, and adverse political situations all discourage creativity and innovation. To promote innovation, many healthcare organizations have established dedicated innovation centers.

The diffusion of innovation is also important, especially in healthcare. Most of the progress in health improvement in the latter part of the twentieth century resulted from the diffusion of public health innovations; however, many recent medical innovations have also greatly increased healthcare costs. Diffusion is facilitated by the perceived usefulness of the innovation. To dramatically improve worldwide healthcare, more rapid diffusion of healthcare advances needs to occur. To this end, organizations have been established to promote diffusion of healthcare innovations.

Several enablers of innovation have been identified, which differentially affect the three phases of moving an innovation toward a transformative outcome. Critical to the process are the alignment of vision, strategy, and leadership; transparency of research and data; and open communication channels.

Disruptive innovation—innovation that creates radical change and destroys existing organizational competencies—is facilitated by technological breakthroughs and frequently drives incumbent, dominant firms out of business. Mid-level providers, retail clinics, genomics, and information technology have the potential to develop into disruptive healthcare innovations.

Chapter Questions

1. Can an organization have innovation without creativity?
2. The creation and operation of a single-organ-focused hospital is what form of healthcare innovation?
3. What can organizations do to discourage the ability to be creative and to innovate?

4. Examine two of the innovation centers listed in the chapter. How are they similar? Different? Do they focus on any different aspects of healthcare innovation?
5. What two factors encourage the diffusion of an innovation? Why? What can be done to encourage these two factors?
6. What organizational enablers will best assist in creating a climate for change in a company?
7. What is the difference between disruptive innovation and sustaining innovation?
8. Name some potential disruptive innovations in healthcare. Why might they be disruptive?

Chapter Cases

UCLA Health's Introduction to Innovation

UCLA Health, the healthcare system of the University of California at Los Angeles, appointed a chief innovation officer, Molly Coye, MD, to reinvigorate its innovation efforts. Past initiatives seemed to have flagged, and a new focus and energy were needed. Although the system had many past successes, it recognized that it had to overcome many current and future challenges if it was to fulfill its mission to educate future healthcare providers, effectively and efficiently treat patients, and promote research.

During her first week in the position, Coye met with the department chairs. Over the course of the two-hour discussion, she was asked, "Isn't innovation mostly about technology, and doesn't it fit with the research part of our mission?"

To this, she replied that almost all innovations were enabled by technology but having a culture that promoted innovation and implementing change was even more important than technological invention.

This answer confused some of the chairs, one of whom said that he thought invention and innovation were the same concept. Coye then pointed out that the scientists at UCLA invented things almost daily, but few of those inventions were actually used to affect patients' care. Innovation was the piece that provided value creation, she added.

Then one of the doctors asked what she meant by changing the culture. She explained that healthcare must move to more evidence-based and personalized medicine, along with a culture that supported both. This shift involved more predictive systems; greater preventive efforts; increased participation by all stakeholders, especially patients; and more personalized care.

The chairs were interested in how innovations would be implemented. Coye stated that the institute she would be heading would scan innovations and select those with the best chance of advancing the system's transformation. When candidate innovations were selected, they would be brought to an innovation leadership council and ultimately to the executive group to charter. A pilot project would then be initiated. If successful, commitments would be made to deploy the innovation across the system.

Coye was then asked which areas of innovation the system would be seeking to develop. She stated that the innovation portfolio would be broad and include drug discovery, neuromodulation, primary care-integrated care coordination, and patient relations. In addition, to remain fresh and cutting edge, UCLA had joined other national organizations focused on innovation, including the Institute for Healthcare Improvement, the Innovation Learning Network, and the Health Technology Forum: Los Angeles.

The chairs were impressed, but many withheld judgment until they could see the results.

Source: Adapted from Gamble (2013).

Case Questions
1. According to this chapter, creativity and innovation are different concepts. How does this case address creativity? Innovation?
2. What other factors discussed in the chapter could Coye implement to enable greater creativity and innovation?

The Future of Biotechnology, Gene Therapy, and Computer-Assisted Diagnostics

Biotechnology, gene therapy, and computer-assisted diagnostics continue to advance, but what will this progress mean to the healthcare industry? Yesterday's science fiction is today's reality when it comes to gene therapy and biotechnology. Advanced human trials are now being conducted, and governments will begin approving gene therapy treatments for diseases such as prostate cancer, metastatic melanoma, artery failure in limbs, neurodegenerative diseases, early-onset blindness, and metabolic syndromes.

Gene therapy may present disruptive innovation to many medical fields. This revolution could affect every level of society—doctors especially. The new drugs, treatments, and technologies will mean a new model of medicine that will destroy past competencies.

As genetic therapies advance, a genetic revolution is predicted. Tools now widely used in animals provide tomorrow's scientists with the power to alter every aspect of life on earth, even the possibility of redesigning the human race. Although such knowledge raises serious ethical issues, it also promises wonderful results.

Gene therapy is not a single entity, however. It may be divided into three areas:

1. Replacing a defective or maladaptive gene that is responsible for some monogenic disease (e.g., cystic fibrosis, sickle cell anemia)
2. Altering or killing an aberrant cell (e.g., infected by HIV, cancerous)
3. Inducing production of a therapeutic protein (e.g., treating hepatitis C by promoting secretion of interferon by other cells)

In addition, some experts predict that combining computerization and gene therapy will produce many bionic enhancements. Advances have been made that link computer chips to human cells and nerves to help those who are paralyzed to move or walk. Soon, providers will be able to implant biochips that control blood sugar levels, benefiting people with diabetes. Biochips may also be implanted directly on the brain to potentially restore sight, hearing, and movement, and even enhance memory and heighten intelligence. Preliminary work has already been completed in animals that fused living nerve tissue with the surface of a chip, allowing nerve impulses to activate a computer pathway and, in turn, a computer to activate brain cells directly.

Computer-aided diagnostics and genetic therapies are two promising technologies for twenty-first-century medicine. Both may be used to create healthier, stronger people, with enhanced characteristics. Processes may include cloning for needed body parts; cures for cancers; new drugs from microbes; viruses that correct genetic defects; genetically modified foods that contain vaccines; and continuous biomonitoring of indicators such as blood sugar levels by means of implanted electrical devices that last a lifetime.

Instead of having the freedom to diagnose and treat by themselves, doctors will need to consult computers for advice before prescribing important treatments. These diagnostic computers will offer expert opinions, with malpractice consequences if those opinions are ignored. Medical training will also shift from emphasizing what individuals know to methods of obtaining accurate data from computer-based information sources.

Some specialties, such as surgery, will remain in demand, as accidents and aging will provide many opportunities for their use. However, surgeons will add remote surgery to their routine, along with teleconferencing to advise surgical teams. Disease-related specialties that have a relation to genetics—such as cancers, blood disorders, allergies, and cardiac problems—will radically decrease in number, diminishing the need for physician specialists in their areas.

Will biotechnology, computer-assisted diagnostics, and gene therapy become disruptive innovations in healthcare? Will medical competencies established over centuries be destroyed? Time will tell.

Sources: Adapted from McCain (2005); additional information from Dixon (2016).

Case Questions
1. Which medical specialties may experience the most disruption from future innovation, such as: biotechnology, gene therapy, or computer-assisted diagnostics? How might this occur?
2. What can medical professionals do to adapt to the new technologies?

Chapter Activities

Video Diary
With your smartphone or other device, create a 1-minute film on the healthcare topic you are most excited about learning. You can do this in any way that is ethical and legal, but you cannot just walk into a hospital and start filming. Your institution may have some guidance on what is allowed or not allowed for projects such as this. When you share your completed video with the class, tell them why you made this film. Explain the creative choices that led to this outcome.

Innovation Exploration
Visit the WISH website (www.wish.org.qa) and explore the current Innovation Hub. Read about one of the listed innovations and write a summary report. Explain why this is an innovation, what its potential impact on healthcare could be, and which factors might prevent its diffusion and practical use.

References

Adams, K. 2020. "10 Big Ideas in Healthcare Innovation." *Becker's Hospital Review*, September 25. www.beckershospitalreview.com/digital-transformation/10-big-ideas-in-healthcare-innovation.html.

Alexion Pharmaceuticals. 2020. "Alexion Reports Fourth Quarter and Full Year 2019 Results" (press release). Published January 30. https://ir.alexion.com/news-releases/news-release-details/alexion-reports-fourth-quarter-and-full-year-2019-results.

American Hospital Association. 2020. *Disruption in Health Care*. AHA Center for Health Innovation. www.aha.org/center/emerging-issues/market-insights/disruptive-innovation/disruption-in-health-care.

Anderson, N., K. Potocnik, and J. Zhou. 2014. "Innovation and Creativity in Organizations: A State-of-the-Science Review, Prospective Commentary, and Guiding Framework." *Journal of Management* 40 (5): 1297–333.

Ayers, R. 2018. "Want Innovative Employees? Use These 6 Innovative Hiring Methods." Innovation Management (blog). Published April 12. https://innovationmanagement.se/2018/04/12/want-innovative-employees-use-these-6-innovative-hiring-methods/.

Balas, E. A., and W. W. Chapman. 2018. "Road Map for Diffusion of Innovation in Health Care." *Health Affairs* 37 (2): 198–204. https://doi.org/10.1377/hlthaff.2017.1155.

Becker's Hospital Review. 2019. "40+ Hospitals and Health Systems with Great Innovation Programs." September 27. www.beckershospitalreview.com/lists/innovation-centers-to-know-2019.html.

Cahan, E. M., B. Kocher, and R. Bohn. 2020. "Why Isn't Innovation Helping Reduce Health Care Costs?" *Health Affairs* (blog). Published June 4. https://www.healthaffairs.org/do/10.1377/hblog20200602.168241/full.

Christensen, C. 2016. *The Innovator's Dilemma: When Technologies Cause Great Firms to Fail*. Boston: Harvard Business School Press.

Clayton, M., and E. Martha. 2009. "Good Days for Disruptors." *MIT Sloan Management Review* 50 (3): 67–70.

Coleiro, D. 2013. "Carving an Identity Through Customer-Focused Innovation." PMLiVE. Published June 12. www.pmlive.com/pharma_news/carving_an_identity_through_customer-focused_innovation_482409.

Darzi, L., and G. Parston. 2013. *Global Diffusion of Healthcare Innovation: Report of the Global Diffusion of Healthcare Innovation Working Group 2013*. Wish Foundation. Accessed July 30. www.wish-qatar.org/app/media/503.

Dawson, P., and C. Andriopoulos. 2014. *Managing Change, Creativity, and Innovation*, 2nd ed. Thousand Oaks, CA: Sage.

Dearing, J. W., and J. G. Cox. 2018. "Diffusion of Innovations Theory, Principles, and Practice." *Health Affairs* 37 (2): 183–90. https://doi.org/10.1377/hlthaff.2017.1104.

Dixon, P. 2016. "The Future of Medicine and Health Care." GlobalChange.com. www.globalchange.com/medicine.htm.

Drees, J. 2020. "13 Hospitals, Health Systems Launching Innovation Centers in 2020." *Becker's Hospital Review*, August 6. www.beckershospitalreview.com/digital-transformation/13-hospitals-health-systems-launching-innovation-centers-in-2020.html.

Forum on Healthcare Innovation. 2015. "5 Imperatives: Addressing Healthcare's Innovation Challenge." Harvard Business School and Harvard Medical School. www.hbs.edu/healthcare/Documents/Forum-on-Healthcare-Innovation-5-Imperatives.pdf.

Gamble, M. 2013. "How Ideas Become Innovations: Roundtable with Healthcare Innovation Leaders from UCLA, Ohio State." *Becker's Hospital*

Review, August 28. www.beckershospitalreview.com/hospital-management-administration/how-ideas-become-innovations-roundtable-with-healthcare-innovation-leaders-from-ucla-ohio-state.html.

Haimovitch, L., and R. M. Kirkner. 2018. "A Look Behind ReVision Optics' Shuttered Door." Ophthalmology Innovation Summit (OIS). Published February 14. https://ois.net/look-behind-revision-optics-shuttered-door/.

Healthcare Transformation Lab (HTL). 2021. "Who We Are." Accessed July 30. http://healthcaretransformation.org/who-we-are/.

Herzlinger, R. 2006. "Why Innovation in Health Care Is So Hard." *Harvard Business Review* 84 (5): 58–66, 156. https://hbr.org/2006/05/why-innovation-in-health-care-is-so-hard.

Institute of Medicine. 2001. *Crossing the Quality Chasm: A New Health System for the 21st Century*. Washington, DC: National Academies Press. https://doi.org/10.17226/10027.

Kimberly, J., and M. Evanisko. 1981. "Organizational Innovation: The Influence of Individual, Organizational, and Contextual Factors on Hospital Adoption of Technological and Administrative Innovations." *Academy of Management Journal* 24 (4): 689–713.

Kimble, L., and M. R. Massoud. 2017. "What Do We Mean by Innovation in Healthcare?" *European Medical Journal Innovations* 1 (1): 89–91. www.emjreviews.com/innovations/article/what-do-we-mean-by-innovation-in-healthcare/.

McCain, J. 2005. "The Future of Gene Therapy." *Biotechnology Healthcare* 2 (3): 52–60. www.ncbi.nlm.nih.gov/pmc/articles/PMC3564347/.

McGuinness, T. 2020. "Creating a Resilient Patient-Centered Healthcare System." Microsoft Industry Blogs. Published September 22. https://cloudblogs.microsoft.com/industry-blog/health/2020/09/22/creating-a-resilient-patient-centered-healthcare-system/.

Merriam-Webster.com. 2021. "Innovation." Accessed August 26. www.merriam-webster.com/dictionary/innovation.

National Quality Forum. 2020. *The Care We Need: Driving Better Health Outcomes for People and Communities*. https://thecareweneed.org/.

Osland, J., D. Kolb, I. Rubin, and M. Turner. 2007. *Organizational Behavior: An Experiential Approach*. Upper Saddle River, NJ: Prentice-Hall.

Rowland, C., D. Cenziper, and L. Rein. 2020. "White House Sidestepped FDA to Distribute Hydroxychloroquine to Pharmacies, Documents Show. Trump Touted the Pills to Treat COVID-19." *Washington Post*, October 31. www.washingtonpost.com/business/2020/10/31/trump-hydroxychloroquine-stockpile-pharmacies/.

Rust, G., D. Satcher, G. Fryer, R. Levine, and D. Blumenthal. 2010. "Triangulating on Success: Innovation, Public Health, Medical Care, and Cause-Specific US Mortality Rates over a Half Century." *American Journal of Public Health* 100 (51): S95–S104.

Shieber, J. 2020. "Wondering About Getting a Job at SpaceX? Elon Musk Says Innovation Is the Main Criterion." *TechCrunch*, February 28. https://techcrunch.com/2020/02/28/wondering-about-getting-a-job-at-spacex-elon-musk-says-innovation-is-the-main-criterion/.

Shulman, R. D. 2020. "This Is What Happens When We Close Doors on Creativity in the Classroom" *Forbes* (blog). Published March 10. www.forbes.com/sites/robynshulman/2020/03/10/this-is-what-happens-when-we-close-doors-on-creativity-in-the-classroom/.

Singhal, S. 2020. "Seven Healthcare Industry Trends to Watch in 2020." *McKinsey & Company* (blog). February 6. www.mckinsey.com/industries/healthcare-systems-and-services/our-insights/seven-healthcare-industry-trends-to-watch-in-2020.

Sounderajah V., V. Patel, L. Varatharajan, L. Harling, P. Normahani, J. Symons, J. Barlow, A. Darzi, and H. Ashrafian. 2020. "Are Disruptive Innovations Recognized in the Healthcare Literature? A Systematic Review." *BMJ Innovations* 7 (1): 208–16. https://doi.org/10.1136/bmjinnov-2020-000424.

Tas, J., and J. Kimpen. 2020. "Health Systems Are in Need of Radical Change; Virtual Care Will Lead the Way." *MIT Technology Review*, April 30. www.technologyreview.com/2020/04/30/1000818/health-systems-are-in-need-of-radical-change-virtual-care-will-lead-the-way/.

Thakur, R., S. Hsu, and G. Fontenot. 2012. "Innovation in Healthcare: Issues and Future Trends." *Journal of Business Research* 65 (4): 562–69.

Thangavelu, P. 2020. "Companies That Failed to Innovate and Went Bankrupt." *Investopedia*. Updated June 5. www.investopedia.com/articles/investing/072115/companies-went-bankrupt-innovation-lag.asp.

Walston, S. 2018. *Strategic Healthcare Management: Planning and Execution*, 2nd ed. Chicago: Health Administration Press.

Walston, S., C. Bennett, and A. Al-Harbi. 2014. "Understanding the Factors Affecting Employees' Perceived Benefits of Healthcare Information Technology." *International Journal of Healthcare Management* 7 (1): 35–44.

World Innovation Summit for Health (WISH). 2015. "Global Diffusion of Healthcare Innovation." www.wish-qatar.org/summit/2015-summit/global-diffusion-of-healthcare-innovation.

CHAPTER 12

GROUP BEHAVIOR

> As Scott walked into the lunchroom seating area with his tray of food, he found his usual lunch group. He had enjoyed eating with Julian and his assistant, Patty, for a few years now. Scott worked in a different department and Julian was older—almost ready to retire—but the three had worked together on a project and hit it off. Looking around, Scott noticed other small groups who had formed bonds at work and were eating together. At one table, he saw a group of Iranian immigrants who had all moved to the United States in the 1970s—friends and relatives who worked in a variety of departments. A group of nurses sat together at another table. It occurred to Scott that if he really wanted to get things done at the hospital, he just needed to tap into these informal groups.

Learning Objectives

After studying this chapter, readers should be able to

- evaluate the importance and use of groups in today's workforce;
- distinguish among different types of groups;
- compare and contrast the types of interdependence and the environments in which they exist;
- understand and describe groupthink and group shift;
- discuss group polarization, social facilitation, and social loafing; and
- evaluate the advantages and disadvantages of group decision-making.

Key Terms

- command groups
- formal groups
- group
- group polarization
- group shift
- groupthink
- informal groups
- pooled interdependence
- reciprocal interdependence
- social facilitation
- social loafing
- task groups

group
Collection of individuals who interact with each other and share common interests or characteristics.

informal groups
Groups that are self-formed as a result of or for the purpose of work and social interactions.

formal groups
Groups prearranged by an organization as a command or task entity.

command groups
Groups formed to give directions and orders within their organization.

task groups
Groups organized for a specific job or undertaking.

Working in groups has become the norm in today's workplace. Groups exist in almost every facet of work. **Groups** are collections of individuals who interact with each other and share common interests or characteristics. People come together in both informal and formal groups. **Informal groups** are self-formed, rather than prearranged by an organization, and may evolve from work and social interactions. Examples include people who meet outside work to exercise, golf, or volunteer at a soup kitchen.

Formal groups involve both command and task entities. **Command groups**, such as an executive team, are units that can give directions and orders within their organization. **Task groups** are organized for a specific job or undertaking and may be structured on the basis of individual expertise and not hierarchical position.

In healthcare, task groups include patient care teams and project groups. Such groups are often organized into either task forces or standing committees. Task forces are formed for a limited time, usually until the completion of a project or an objective; a standing committee continues indefinitely. Healthcare systems generally have a handful of standing committees as part of their governance structures. For example, as of April 2021, the website of Cook County Health in Chicago lists five standing committees comprised by its board of directors: (1) audit and compliance, (2) finance, (3) human resources, (4) quality and patient safety, and (5) managed care.

Group identity is an important aspect of human existence. Personal security, companionship, and behavior all relate to group identity. Individuals are acculturated into groups through interactions, stories, and rituals. The core of group commitment is strengthened by the greater emotional intensity of group experience and collective rituals, which include religious ceremonies, festivals, rallies, commemorations, weddings, sporting events, and even holidays (Thye and Lawler 2010). The stronger the initiation, the stronger the group commitment.

Groups also form through professional organizations. Professional organizations allow individuals with similar backgrounds and interests to interact and develop their skills. They impart group norms that establish acceptable and unacceptable behaviors. A 2017 Pew Research survey reported that 16 percent of all Americans participated in a professional organization (Sandstrom and Alper 2019). A few of the more prominent in healthcare include the following:

- AcademyHealth (www.academyhealth.org)
- American Cancer Society (www.cancer.org)
- American College of Healthcare Executives (www.ache.org)
- American Heart Association (www.heart.org)

- American Hospital Association (www.aha.org)
- American Medical Association (www.ama-assn.org)
- American Public Health Association (www.apha.org)
- America's Essential Hospitals (https://essentialhospitals.org)
- Association of University Programs in Healthcare Administration (www.aupha.org)
- Association of State and Territorial Health Officials (www.astho.org)
- Healthcare Financial Management Association (www.hfma.org)
- Medical Group Management Association (www.mgma.com)
- Mental Health America (www.mentalhealthamerica.net)
- National Association of County and City Health Officials (www.naccho.org)
- National Association of State Mental Health Program Directors (www.nasmhpd.org)
- National Environmental Health Association (www.neha.org)

As discussed in chapter 6 with regard to the American College of Healthcare Executives, members of a professional group agree to the ethical codes espoused by the organization. These groups establish behavioral expectations, and their educational activities provide socialization opportunities.

Groups Versus Teams

Often the terms *group* and *team* are used interchangeably. However, teams are evolved groups that have task orientation, purpose, interdependence, structure, and social familiarity. Work teams will be studied in chapter 13.

Interdependence

The type of interdependence that exists in a work setting strongly dictates the need for group or team characteristics. Thompson (1967) proposed three types of interdependence:

1. Pooled
2. Sequential
3. Reciprocal

Here, we discuss pooled and reciprocal interdependence in more depth.

As suggested in exhibit 12.1, the need for a team relationship increases as the type of interdependence moves from pooled (least interdependent) to

EXHIBIT 12.1
Type of Interdependence and Need for Relationship

	Type of Interdependence		
	Pooled	**Sequential**	**Reciprocal**
Description	Members make separate, independent contributions	Tasks completed in a sequence and handed off to other team members	Work moves back and forth among members
Sports Examples	Golf, wrestling	Relay race/track	Soccer, football
Healthcare Examples	System-owned hospitals dispersed across the country, multidisciplinary teams	Hospital admission process	Intensive care or trauma care unit, interdisciplinary teams
Spectrum	Group ⬌ Team		
	Multidisciplinary team		Interdisciplinary team

reciprocal (most interdependent). Groups function better with limited interdependence. **Pooled interdependence** requires that members make only discrete, independent contributions, such as within a group of hospitals owned by a healthcare system and dispersed across the United States. Each hospital may be operated independently, and its finances and capital resources may be "pooled" in the system headquarters.

Reciprocal interdependence requires members to have a team relationship because their work is highly interactive and necessitates immediate responses. Reciprocal work settings in healthcare that do not display team characteristics can negatively affect the quality and efficiency of care, with serious consequences (Baker, Day, and Salas 2006).

Conformity and Norms

Adolescents struggle to be individuals, while still conforming to norms set by their friends. People learn social skills at a young age by observing others. They copy the behavior of some and avoid that of others. As individuals age, the pressure to conform to group norms intensifies (McAndrew 2020). Conformity is the response of individuals to people around them. It affects attitudes, beliefs, and behaviors. Conformity is partially to blame for decreased

pooled interdependence
A type of interdependence that requires members to make only discrete, independent contributions to their group.

reciprocal interdependence
A type of interdependence that requires members to have a team relationship as their work is highly interactive and necessitates immediate responses.

support for political compromise (Ryan 2016) and even expresses itself in individual trial jurors, who relinquish their moral responsibility by conforming as groups who desire to punish. These individuals become less cautious and more impulsive, amplifying the value they place on punishment (Son, Bhandari, and FeldmanHall 2019). Consider, for example, the Salem witch trials in colonial Massachusetts (Baker 2014).

> **Behavior in Groups**
>
> During 2020 and in years past, the news media reported on protests accompanied by looters and rioters. Research more than 100 years old (Le Bon 1895) and verified in recent studies (Borek and Abraham 2018) supports the idea that some of those looters would likely have behaved differently on their own. Le Bon suggested that individuals act differently when they are part of crowds. Borek and Abraham point out the positive effect of groups promoting good health. Conversely, Zaretsky (2016) argued that groups form in response to specific events and individuals voluntarily join a group that embraces a collective identity. These views are not mutually exclusive. Both illustrate the behavior of groups and their members.

Groups in the workplace, whether formal or informal, persuade members and outsiders to conform though praise, criticism, or bullying, or by modeling certain behaviors the group deems appropriate. Dress codes or expected behaviors are examples of conforming on the job. Some norms or expectations were challenged or shattered during the 2020 pandemic when many workers stayed home. They wore what they wanted, started the work day when they wanted, mixed work with household chores at times, and participated in meetings by only listening to some of the discussions while multitasking, which sometimes included caring for their children.

Conformity to crowds has been cast in a negative light for many years, and more than one study suggests the evils of peer pressure (Cialdini 2003; Latané and Darley 1968; Prentice and Miller 1993). Prosocial conformity, however, leads to group norms that inspire people to be helpful, donate to charity, act fairly, protect the environment, or even vote. Some conformity to prosocial behaviors can even prompt individuals to behave in a positive way at a different time and context. Empathy, a strong force in healthcare, produces kind and generous behaviors, suggesting that empathy and prosocial behavior are deeply intertwined within individuals (Nook et al. 2016). Leaders would be wise to investigate the association of social influence or conformity and prosocial behaviors anchored in their organization.

Norms are the acceptable standards of behavior shared by the group. In a healthcare organization some of these would be performance norms (how a person should do their job), appearance norms (e.g., dress codes, facial hair, hair styles, body art, piercings), social arrangement norms (expected behaviors), and resource allocation norms (e.g., assignment of human resources, availability of raw materials, acceptability of working overtime) (Tutorials Point 2020a).

EXHIBIT 12.2

AACN's Six Essential Standards

- Skilled communication
- True collaboration
- Effective decision-making
- Appropriate staffing
- Meaningful recognition
- Authentic leadership

Source: Adapted from AACN (2021).

The American Association of Critical-Care Nurses (AACN) has developed a set of standards they recommend for creating a healthy work environment (AACN 2021). Exhibit 12.2 lists their six standards. AACN supports the establishment of these norms through education and assessment. For example, one standard promotes enough staffing to take adequate care of patients. AACN argues that nurses get more work done when staffing is appropriate. AACN offers an assessment tool to help healthcare organizations determine if this is a norm in their system.

Cohorts and Reference Groups

Some healthcare workers look to their local or corporate leaders and wish they could have that sort of lifestyle. They envision nice homes, nice clothes, travel, and all the rest that they assume comes with those positions. Some leaders look to their staff and wish they could just do an eight-hour shift, go home, and not worry about the job until the next day. Others will look at a group and say to themselves, "I don't want anything to do with that group." Such are the concepts of the aspirational, primary, and dissociative reference groups. The aspirational group is the one a person wants to join. The primary reference group is the group an individual is around most of the time, such as coworkers, family members, and friends. The dissociative group is the one a person sees as the opposite of everything they are or want to be—the one an individual actively avoids (Tutorials Point 2020b).

Some informal and formal groups form around similar traits. These cohorts might share a similar age, gender, religion, or length of service in an organization—characteristics called *demographics*. Generational cohorts, for example, have been the focus of much research and are discussed in chapter 3. Health experts look at cohorts in high-risk professions to promote screenings or good health practices (Soriano et al. 2020). Common to healthcare organizations are cohorts of individuals who work in the same clinical area and who began their work around the same time. Nurses, for example, who began their jobs together on being licensed and who work in the same unit often form tight bonds. Cohort experiences make it easier for these new employees to get to know and support one another.

While they share similar characteristics, cohorts may have different reference groups. Not all Gen Xers, for example, strive for the same lifestyle. The great task of a healthcare manager is to understand the individual cohort or to group members together to achieve organizational goals and tasks. Supervisors who understand their employees' aspirations build on that knowledge to increase productivity and growth (Al-Masri 2015).

Groupthink and Group Shift

On January 28, 1986, the NASA space shuttle Challenger launched with its seven-person crew, including Christa McAuliffe, the first participant in NASA's Teacher in Space program. Just 73 seconds into the flight the shuttle exploded; all those on board lost their lives. The explosion was caused by a leak in the booster resulting in an uncontrolled mixture of liquid oxygen and liquid hydrogen. The source of the leak was a faulty O-ring, known to be sensitive to cold. The temperature that morning was only 36 degrees Fahrenheit—well below the safety range for the critical part. The infamous decision to launch Challenger when experts knew the likelihood of disaster is a result of an incredible lack of information and a phenomenon labeled *groupthink* (Teitel 2019).

Introduced in 1971 by Irving Janis, the theory of **groupthink** suggests that individuals within groups tend to refrain from expressing doubts and shy away from disagreeing with group decisions. Group members may actually ignore ethical or moral consequences of their decisions. Exhibit 12.3 includes eight symptoms Janis described as reflecting groupthink (Janis 1972, 1991).

The dynamics around the Challenger disaster suggest incomplete and misleading information, pressure from NASA officials to launch, and a failure of engineers at Morton Thiokol, who manufactured the O-ring, to speak up as definitively as they should have. Morton Thiokol leadership was worried about satisfying NASA. NASA was worried about its public image and wanted to launch flights more often; the Challenger mission had already been delayed for several months. And NASA managers insulated top NASA officials from debate on the integrity of the O-rings (Teitel 2019; Janis 1991).

While groupthink focuses on the idea that group members make decisions based on the pressures they feel from the group, **group shift** refers to a condition where individual group members shift to a more extreme position or opinion because of the influence of the group. Group shift would explain, for example, why some individuals adopt a more discriminatory

groupthink
"The tendency for members of a highly cohesive group to seek consensus so strongly that they fail to do a realistic appraisal of other alternatives, which may be more correct" (Osland et al. 2007, 471).

group shift
The tendency of individual group members to shift to a more extreme position or opinion due to the influence of the group.

EXHIBIT 12.3
The Symptoms of Groupthink

Illusion of invulnerability	Group members are assured that everything will work out.
Belief in the inherent morality of the group	Members assume the rightness of their cause.
Collective rationalization	The group rationalizes away any problems—"hear no evil, see no evil, speak no evil."
Out-group stereotypes	Group members possess stereotypical views of outsiders.
Self-censorship	Group members do not speak out against the consensus of the group.
Illusion of unanimity	The prevailing assumption is that everyone in the group supports the decision.
Direct pressure on dissenters	Group members experience pressure to conform (actual or perceived).
Self-appointed mindguards	Group's leaders are protected from troublesome ideas.

Source: Adapted from Janis (1972).

response to stereotyped individuals who are not part of the group (Smith and Postmes 2011). Healthcare administrators may experience group shift as they consider what resources and funding to put into a new service line. Individual decision makers faced with pressure from the leadership team or board of directors may shift from a balanced approach to making an extreme high-risk decision with a significant commitment of resources. The average response of some individuals will shift as they are part of a group (Mannion and Thompson 2014).

Group Polarization

group polarization
A situation in which groups are driven to take sides and accept extreme positions.

While group shift suggests an individual may change behavior when faced with pressure from the group, **group polarization** illustrates how the group may move to an extreme decision even though individual members of the group have a different view. Consider a popular GEICO television commercial, "Horror Movie: It's What You Do" (https://youtu.be/uQ-hlcux66s). The characters, running from a typical Hollywood villain, are debating where to hide. One member of the group points to a car idling nearby and asks, "Why can't we just get in the running car?" Another protests, "Are you crazy?" and points to a nearby shed. "Let's hide behind the chainsaws." They pause and consider. "Smart," says a third group member, and they all rush to the shed.

An example of group polarization in healthcare involves the decision by one practice group that the preferences of clients using cognitive behavioral therapy should be factored into their mental health care. Over

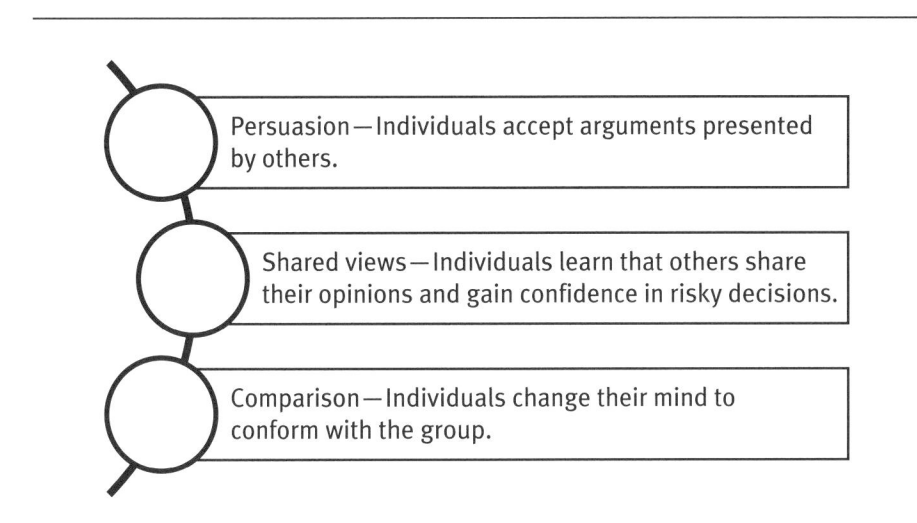

EXHIBIT 12.4
Three Key Reasons for Group Polarization

- Persuasion—Individuals accept arguments presented by others.
- Shared views—Individuals learn that others share their opinions and gain confidence in risky decisions.
- Comparison—Individuals change their mind to conform with the group.

six months of policy meetings, the group shifted from the idea that it was important to understand the client's feelings to the development of a client questionnaire that would be completed before treatment. Ten months later, nurses and physicians refused to use the survey, which took 30 minutes to an hour to complete and led to no real changes in clinical practice (Mannion and Thompson 2014).

Exhibit 12.4 lists three reasons for group polarization: persuasion, shared views, and comparison. *Persuasion* suggests that group members change their minds when they listed to arguments from others in the group. When group members learn that others have similar ideas, those *shared views* may give group members more confidence in making risky decisions. *Comparison* describes those who change their minds to fit in with group norms (Mannion and Thompson 2014).

Obedience

In a study conducted by Martin and Bull (2008), midwives completed a questionnaire about best practices and procedures in delivering a baby. Later, a more senior midwife and supervisor asked the subjects to do something they had indicated in the questionnaire that they opposed. Most of the junior midwives followed the orders of their supervisor and went against their own beliefs. This obedience was a change in the nurses' behavior in order to comply with someone in authority. "I'm just doing what I was told," is the excuse one might use.

A well-known study of obedience was conducted by Stanley Milgram (1963), in which he found that subjects were willing to shock confederate "learners" when they gave the wrong answers to a series of test questions.

The learners were not actually shocked, but the participants did not know that. As the learners continued to give incorrect answers, the participants were told to shock them at increasing 15-volt increments. At times the learners would groan, complain of heart trouble, and beg the participants to stop, yet 65 percent of the participants continued to shock the learners to a supposed maximum of 450 volts. They did this because they were asked to by someone in authority. They obeyed.

Obedience is important. At times, supervisors must be able to ask subordinates to do something without question. Obedience can be educative or even result in acts of charity and kindness. Understanding obedience is a study in values and ethics. What does an individual do if an authority figure makes a request believed to be incorrect or unethical? These are moral questions. Most individuals are social people, and social psychologists argue that much of what we do is strongly influenced by those around us (Burger 2020).

Social Facilitation and Social Loafing

social facilitation
A phenomenon explaining why some individuals perform better when an audience is watching.

social loafing
A phenomenon explaining why individuals sometimes exert less effort when working in a group.

Two final subtopics of a discussion about groups are somewhat opposite of each other. **Social facilitation** suggests an individual performs better when an audience is watching, while **social loafing** explains that individuals sometimes exert less effort when working in a group. For example, in a game of tug-of-war, some players will barely hold the rope and will let the strongest members of their group do all the work.

Social facilitation is often included in theories of health behavior change (Ajzen, Albarracin, and Hornick 2007; Greene and Yedidia 2005; Jenerette and Phillips 2006; Ryan 2009). These theories suggest that along with knowledge, beliefs, and self-regulation, social facilitation, which includes social influences, social support, and collaboration of family and friends, greatly enhances an individual's ability to see desired outcomes. Exhibit 12.5 illustrates the Integrated Theory of Health Behavior Change, emphasizing social facilitation as a key component (Ryan 2009).

Social facilitation tends to have a bigger effect on those who are familiar with the task. When individuals face something more difficult or are new to a task, they may shy away from an audience or show a more impaired performance (McLeod 2020). Social facilitation may manifest in front of just one or two coactors. Social facilitation is thought to involve cognitive factors (individuals pay more attention to the task if someone is watching), affective factors (people concerned about being evaluated), and physiological factors (a drive or excitement about achieving the task).

One example of social loafing concerns a senior nurse who took a hands-off approach to a clinical audit of recordkeeping. The nurse assumed

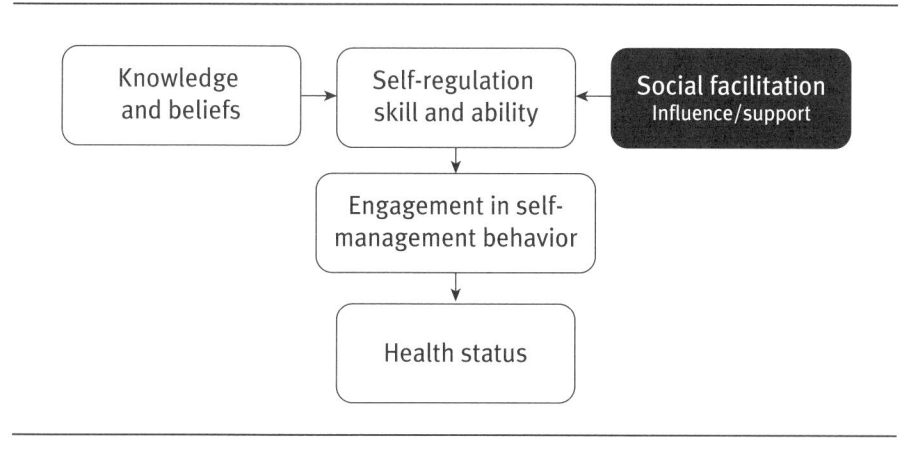

EXHIBIT 12.5 Integrated Theory of Health Behavior Change

```
Knowledge          Self-regulation         Social facilitation
and beliefs   -->  skill and ability  <--  Influence/support
                          |
                          v
                   Engagement in self-
                   management behavior
                          |
                          v
                     Health status
```

Source: Adapted from Ryan (2009).

that her three deputies would pick up the task of collecting audit data and she was not motivated to question that, but no data had been collected for the past eight months. When questioned by the auditor, the senior nurse indicated that "keeping your head down" had been her strategy in terms of maintaining her long tenure as a hospital employee (Mannion and Thompson 2014).

Managers may consider four strategies to limit social loafing on the job (Mannion and Thompson 2014):

1. Limit workers' ability to hide in a crowd. Giving group members specific assignments and asking them to report is one strategy to increase recognition.
2. Limit the size of the group. Smaller groups make it tougher for an individual to get lost.
3. Strengthen group cohesiveness. When members of groups bond together and share similar goals, they are less likely to pass their role in the group off to other members.
4. Allow individuals to choose their tasks or roles. This gives group members more buy-in and greater motivation to be involved.

Advantages and Disadvantages of Group Decision-Making

An old proverb tells us there is only one way to eat an elephant: a bite at a time. Another way would be to assign the process to a group and ask them to share the tasks among themselves. Greater capacity to complete complicated tasks is one advantage of delegating tasks to a group; another is the group members' ability to brainstorm or bounce ideas off one another. Group members can hold one another accountable to get the job done. They can create good examples for new employees and provide opportunities to learn new skills or take on new tasks.

Groups who are not careful may create an environment prone to groupthink. When this happens, the outcomes can be devastating. Another challenge groups face is strong personalities that limit feedback from other group members. Social loafing or an unequal division of labor can create conflict in a group. Some individuals may feel undervalued as members of a group. Even informal groups can undermine the culture and mission of an organization.

Chapter Summary

People today work primarily in groups, which can be formal or informal, permanent or temporary, and may take the form of committees, work groups, or task forces. Healthcare organizations manage extensively through committees. Professional groups also exert significant influence in healthcare by establishing behavioral expectations and creating socialization opportunities.

Groups may work independently from one another and pool their contributions to achieve success in an organization or system. Sequential interdependence requires one group to complete a task before handing it off to the next. Reciprocal work is handed back and forth from group to group.

Norms or standards of behavior established by organizations include everything from dress codes to complex healthcare procedures. Conformity to norms affects attitudes, beliefs, and behaviors. Conformity is often portrayed in a negative light, but can generate positive outcomes. Newly hired employees learn professionalism and standards of care, for instance, by watching others and conforming to their example. Individuals are sometimes pressured to conform through praise, modeling, criticism, or even bullying.

Groups often form around similar traits such as age, gender, religion, or length of service in an organization. Individuals hope to be part of an aspirational primary group who have a lifestyle or position they want to attain. Most are part of a primary reference group with similar demographics and jobs. Cohorts such as these allow individuals to support and learn from one another. Primary reference groups also include family and friends.

When groups form such strong bonds that they begin to lose a sense of vulnerability and group members stop any sort of dissension, they are likely experiencing groupthink. Group members may actually ignore negative outcomes or the ethics of decisions under the influence of this phenomenon.

Groupthink focuses on pressures—real or imagined—placed on group members to conform. Group shift occurs when an individual shifts from more moderate beliefs to an extreme position or opinion taken by the group. Individuals faced with pressure by their supervisors, for example, may shift from a balanced approach to one involving a more extreme belief or greater risk. Groups can also shift, as a whole, to making unwise decisions as they convince one another through discussion. Group polarization happens via persuasion, shared views, and comparisons that encourage conformity.

Obedience is another aspect of individual and group behavior that leads to positive outcomes, but may be abused. Supervisors often need their employees to complete tasks when asked—sometimes without question. But studies have shown people will behave unethically or even destructively when asked to do so by an authority figure.

Finally, some individuals will hang back and let their fellow group members do most of the work. This social loafing involves a sense of anonymity or hiding in a crowd, but can be minimized by reducing the size of a group, assigning group members specific tasks, strengthening group cohesiveness, and allowing group members to choose their tasks or roles. Social facilitation is somewhat the opposite of social loading: Group members occasionally do better when they are being watched. Extra attention enables them to perform, or they may feel they are being evaluated and focus more on the job at hand.

Chapter Questions

1. How does a team differ from a group?
2. How do professional organizations emphasize group identity for healthcare professionals?
3. Why can groups function better in situations of pooled interdependence than in reciprocal interdependence?
4. How was conformity affected by the COVID-19 pandemic of 2020?
5. Give an example of a primary reference group, including cohort demographics.
6. When engineers of the O-ring responsible for the Challenger disaster failed to speak up about the dangers of launching in cold weather, what aspect of groupthink were they exhibiting?
7. What are the dangers of group shift and group polarization?
8. Is obedience always a bad thing? Explain.
9. How is social loafing like a game of tug-of-war?
10. How is social facilitation like being on stage?

Chapter Cases

The Laundry Group

For many years, the small Midwestern hospital has housed its own laundry services in a building adjacent but not connected to the main hospital. While the laundry supervisor was born and raised in the local town, nearly all the laundry team members immigrated to the United States from Laos in the late 1970s and became naturalized citizens a few years later. A few speak English, but most only understand and speak Lao.

Conrad Petersen, the hospital CEO, badly wants to help the group feel more part of the hospital team. He has invited them to several social functions without success. He has worked with the laundry supervisor, Jill McCurry, to brainstorm ideas, but try as they might the group shows up for work, gets things done, and then goes home at the end of their shift without much interaction with anyone else at the hospital.

Case Questions

1. If you were acting as an adviser to Conrad or Jill, what might be your first question?
2. What theories or aspects of groups do you see in play here?
3. What would be potential concerns with this sort of group?
4. If you were Conrad, what would you do to support or strengthen the group?

Cardiac Risk at Pineview Hospital

Olivia Clark is only a year into her job as CEO of Pineview Hospital, a 100-bed community hospital. From the first board meeting she attended, she felt pressure from the group to open a large cardiac care center in the facility. To do so meant purchasing very expensive diagnostic and treatment equipment, adding or reassigning dedicated hospitals beds—including cardiac intensive care services—and recruiting and paying physicians and staff to support the services. It was a significant expense for a midsize facility such as Pineview, but board members insisted the need was there. The community was aging. Heart disease was the number one cause of death in the population. Board members felt the increased business would more than cover the costs. Although she initially felt the financial risk to Pineview was too high, Olivia eventually shifted her view and joined with the board to support the plan.

It was not long before the original budget for the new services had to be nearly doubled to cover the costs of facilities, equipment, supplies, and personnel. Now that the new cardiac wing has opened, Olivia and the board members are facing a lot of criticism from external auditors and the community for spending so much.

Case Questions
1. What caused Olivia to shift her level of financial risk?
2. What might the board have done as they faced such a risky decision?

The Story of James, Bill, and the Treatment Team

The infusion center at Carbondale Regional Hospital provided transfusion services for a number of patients. Today, James Williams was coming for a treatment. James suffered from sickle cell anemia, an inherited red blood cell disorder that causes significant pain. He received a blood transfusion every few weeks, and each time he was unruly, unkempt, and mean to the nursing staff. Knowing James was coming, the unit manager, Rachel, decided she would personally meet him this time as he came to the center, to get to know his side of things a bit better and shield the nursing team from his usual behavior.

Rachel walked into the unit only to find James already there and upset. It was not long before Bill, the hospital's manager of patient relations, was notified that James was unhappy and he also arrived on the scene. James told Bill that the nurses had refused to treat him and told him that he would have to come back another day. James had paid transportation to get to the hospital and now would have to come up with the money to return. In addition, because the transfusion takes much of the day, James had been offered a meal to eat during the procedure; but the staff member who brought it had stuck her thumb in the food as she served it. James was not happy.

Bill offered James meal and transportation vouchers for his return visit. He vowed to find out why James had been refused treatment and offered to get in touch with James the next day to see what could be done.

That afternoon, Bill met with Rachel and the staff of the unit to learn their side of the story and to support them where he could. He barely made it into the room before the staff was complaining loudly of Bill's actions. They reported that James was again threatening and mean when he arrived. Only one of the nurses was even willing to work with him. They said he had waited too long to come in after being checked to see if the blood he was getting was the right match and that he would have to be tested again—hence the delay in services. They also argued that no one put their thumb in James's food; the employee's thumb was only on the tray holding the food. The staff were angry that Bill had supported James and not them. Rachel, who normally supports Bill and his work, was supportive of her clinical team and was among the loudest of the group as they voiced their concerns.

Case Questions
1. What are some of the group dynamics that you see happening in this case?
2. What could Bill have done to improve the situation?

Chapter Activities

Visual Scavenger Hunt
For this activity, you will form a task group and use your experiences with the group to explore some of the concepts discussed in this chapter.

Preparation
With your classmates, separate into four or five evenly sized groups. Each group should have at least one way of taking or downloading photos—smartphones will do.

Activity
1. Working as a group, collect photographs that best define your university. You may use photos you find online or take your own. Your instructor will give you a time limit—usually 30–45 minutes.
2. After collecting your photos, create a short presentation for the class explaining what your photos mean and why you chose them. Choose one person from your team to make the presentation.
3. As a class, vote on the best presentation.

Cohorts and Reference Groups
Cohorts are common in high schools. With your classmates, list the names given to the cohorts in your high school (e.g., jocks, brains, gamers, goths). What are the traits of each of these groups? Discuss your association with those cohorts. Often, we are members of informal groups that include individuals from a variety of cohorts. How do the traits of those blended informal groups differ?

Cohorts found in healthcare administration often share similar characteristics and join to solve a number of problems or to support one another. Informal groups are also common at the workplace and differ from the bigger cohorts.

References

Ajzen, I., D. Albarracin, and R. Hornick (eds.). 2007. *Prediction and Change of Health Behavior: Applying the Reasoned Action Approach.* Mahwah, NJ: Lawrence Erlbaum Associates.

Al-Masri, S. 2015. "Managing Staff Aspirations: Three Ways to Drive the Growth of Both Your Human Capital and Your Company." *Entrepreneur Middle East* (blog), March 25. https://www.entrepreneur.com/article/244264.

American Association of Critical-Care Nurses (AACN). 2021. "Healthy Work Environments." www.aacn.org/nursing-excellence/healthy-work-environments.

Baker, D., R. Day, and E. Salas. 2006. "Teamwork as an Essential Component of High-Reliability Organizations." *Health Services Research* 41 (4): 1576–98.

Baker, E. W. 2014. *A Storm of Witchcraft: The Salem Trials and the American Experience*. New York: Oxford University Press.

Borek, A. J., and C. Abraham. 2018. "How Do Small Groups Promote Behavior Change? An Integrative Conceptual Review of Explanatory Mechanisms." *Applied Psychology: Health and Well-Being* 10 (1): 30–61. https://doi.org/10.1111/aphw.12120.

Burger, J. M. 2020. "Conformity and Obedience." In *Noba Textbook Series: Psychology*, edited by R. Biswas-Diener and E. Diener. Champaign, IL: DEF Publishers. http://noba.to/hkray8fs.

Cialdini, R. B. 2003. "Crafting Normative Messages to Protect the Environment." *Current Directions in Psychological Science* 12 (4): 105–9. https://doi.org/10.1111/1467-8721.01242.

Greene, J., and M. J. Yedidia. 2005. "Provider Behaviors Contributing to Patient Self-Management of Chronic Illness Among Underserved Populations." *Journal of Health Care for the Poor and Underserved* 16 (4): 808–24. https://doi.org/10.1353/hpu.2005.0097.

Janis, I. L. 1991. "Groupthink." In *A First Look at Communication Theory*, edited by E. Griffin, 235–46. New York: McGrawHill.

———. 1972. *Victims of Groupthink: A Psychological Study of Foreign-Policy Decisions and Fiascoes*. Boston: Houghton Mifflin.

Jenerette, C. M., and R. C. S. Phillips. 2006. "An Examination of Differences in Intra-Personal Resources, Self-Care Management, and Health Outcomes in Older and Younger Adults with Sickle Cell Disease." *Southern Online Journal of Nursing Research* 3 (7): 1–24.

Latané, B., and J. M. Darley. 1968. "Group Inhibition of Bystander Intervention in Emergencies." *Journal of Personality and Social Psychology* 10 (3): 215–21. https://doi.org/10.1037/h0026570.

Le Bon, G. (1895) 2002. *The Crowd: A Study of the Popular Mind*. New York: Dover.

Mannion, R., and C. Thompson. 2014. "Systematic Biases in Group Decision-Making: Implications for Patient Safety." *International Journal for Quality in Health Care* 26 (6): 606–12. https://doi.org/10.1093/intqhc/mzu083.

Martin, C. J. H., and P. Bull. 2008. "Obedience and Conformity in Clinical Practice." *British Journal of Midwifery*. 16 (8): 504–9. https://doi.org/10.12968/bjom.2008.16.8.30783.

McAndrew, F. 2020. "The Eternal Challenge of Conformity Pressure." *Psychology Today* (blog). Published June 8. www.psychologytoday.com/us/blog/out-the-ooze/202006/the-eternal-challenge-conformity-pressure.

McLeod, S. A. 2020. "Social Facilitation." *Simply Psychology*. Updated June 24. www.simplypsychology.org/Social-Facilitation.html.

Milgram, S. 1963. "Behavioral Study of Obedience." *Journal of Abnormal and Social Psychology* 67 (4): 371–78.

Nook, E. C., D. C. Ong, S. A. Morelli, J. P. Mitchell, and J. Zaki. 2016. "Prosocial Conformity: Prosocial Norms Generalize Across Behavior and Empathy." *Personality and Social Psychology Bulletin* 42 (8):1045–62. https://doi.org/10.1177/0146167216649932.

Osland, J., D. Kolb, I. Rubin, and M. Turner. 2007. *Organizational Behavior: An Experiential Approach*. Upper Saddle River, NJ: Prentice-Hall.

Prentice, D. A., and D. T. Miller. 1993. "Pluralistic Ignorance and Alcohol Use on Campus: Some Consequences of Misperceiving the Social Norm." *Journal of Personality and Social Psychology* 64 (2): 243–56. https://doi.org/10.1037/0022-3514.64.2.243.

Ryan, P. 2009. "Integrated Theory of Health Behavior Change." *Clinical Nurse Specialist* 23 (3): 161–72.

Ryan, T. 2016. "No Compromise: Political Consequences of Moralized Attitudes." *American Journal of Political Sciences* 61 (3): 409–23. https://doi.org/10.1111/ajps.12248.

Sandstrom, A., and B. A. Alper. 2019. "Americans with Higher Education and Income Are More Likely to Be Involved in Community Groups." *FactTank*. Pew Research Center, February 22. www.pewresearch.org/fact-tank/2019/02/22/americans-with-higher-education-and-income-are-more-likely-to-be-involved-in-community-groups/.

Smith, L. G. E., and T. Postmes. 2011. "The Power of Talk: Developing Discriminatory Group Norms Through Discussion." *British Journal of Social Psychology* 50 (2): 193–215.

Son, J.-Y., A. Bhandari, and O. FeldmanHall. 2019. "Crowdsourcing Punishment: Individuals Reference Group Preferences to Inform Their Own Punitive Decisions." *Scientific Reports* 9 (August): 11625. https://doi.org/10.1038/s41598-019-48050-2.

Soriano, C. T., T. J. McGarrity, J. Zhu, J. Loloi, L. P. Peiffer, and J. Cooper. 2020. "An Electronic Questionnaire to Survey Colorectal Cancer Screening Status and Identify High-Risk Cohorts in Large Health Care Organizations." *American Journal of Medical Quality* 36 (3): 163–70. https://doi.org/10.1177/1062860620937236.

Teitel, A. S. 2019. "Challenger Explosion: How Groupthink and Other Causes Led to the Tragedy." *History*. Updated December 13. www.history.com/news/how-the-challenger-disaster-changed-nasa.

Thompson, J. 1967. *Organizations in Action*. New York: McGraw-Hill.

Thye, S. R., and E. Lawler. 2010. *Advances in Group Processes*. Bingley, UK: Emerald Group.

Tutorials Point. 2020a. "Group Structure." www.tutorialspoint.com/individual_and_group_behavior/group_structure.htm.

———. 2020b. "Consumer Behavior—Reference Groups." www.tutorialspoint.com/consumer_behavior/consumer_behavior_reference_groups.htm.

Zaretsky, R. 2016. "Donald Trump and the Myth of Mobocracy." *The Atlantic*, July 27. www.theatlantic.com/international/archive/2016/07/trump-le-bon-mob/493118/.

CHAPTER 13

WORK TEAMS

> Jennifer Anderson, CEO of St. Thomas Hospital, knew she needed to work on a community health assessment and find a way to support her community's population health needs. She did not want to tackle this alone. In fact, she did not have the time to do what was needed. She knew the perfect candidate to head up the team, though. John Johnson, a member of the hospital's marketing team, was heavily involved in the community action programs. Jennifer knew that he could lead a team to get the ball rolling. She set up a meeting with John and the director of the local health department. It was the beginning of what would become the hospital's brilliant population health campaign.

Learning Objectives

After studying this chapter, readers should be able to

- distinguish among different types of teams;
- evaluate team composition;
- discuss team formation, socialization, and development;
- describe team effectiveness, processes, and enhancement; and
- recognize team leadership and motivation.

Key Terms

- forming
- interdisciplinary teams
- multidisciplinary teams
- norming
- performing
- storming
- teams

The Nature of Teams

teams
Evolved groups that have great task orientation, purpose, interdependence, structure, and social familiarity.

As discussed in chapter 12, the terms *group* and *team* are often used interchangeably. However, **teams** are evolved groups that have great task orientation, purpose, interdependence, structure, and social familiarity. Teams work together to accomplish shared goals and mutually bear the responsibility for their own success. As exhibit 13.1 shows, teams coordinate tasks and activities; focus on producing outcomes; and, as a result, are more interdependent than groups are. Teams are also generally smaller than groups; the membership of groups can range into the millions (e.g., Hindus, women). The optimal team size depends on many factors and continues to be debated. In general business, teams with fewer than ten people may be more successful than larger teams (Harter 2020); in healthcare, the optimal team size seems to be 8–12 individuals (West 2018).

The difference between groups and teams can also be seen in sports. Well-functioning teams are essential for successful football, basketball, and soccer clubs. Often in these sports, the winning team is not the one with the best players but the one that plays best together. Players have positions and roles with distinct contributions and require great interdependence; they need to execute their tasks effectively and act and react simultaneously to their team members' actions. Sports organizations that have exceptional individual players but fail to work as a team frequently lose. Dallas Cowboys linebacker Jaylon Smith cited this factor when discussing the team's lack of success in 2020, telling *Sports Illustrated*, "We weren't playing together as a team. . . . You've got a bunch of dominant, elite players individually. You've got to come together as a team" (Fisher 2021).

EXHIBIT 13.1
Differences Between Groups and Teams

Groups	Teams
Focused leadership	Shared leadership
Individual accountability	Individual and team accountability
Individual work outcomes	Team work outcomes
Desire for efficient meetings	Desire for open discussion and problem-solving
Effectiveness measured by indirect influence	Effectiveness measured by collective work output
Discussion, decision, and delegation	Discussion, decision, and working together on output

Source: Adapted from Katzenbach and Smith (2005).

On the other hand, individual sports—such as track, wrestling, and golf—require little teamwork. The interdependence among "team" members is often minimal, and these teams consist more of groups of players than of teams in the true sense.

Team Composition

Healthcare uses interprofessional teams extensively. Properly functioning interprofessional teams are essential to providing safe and high-quality care to patients. The Institute of Medicine defines an interdisciplinary (interprofessional) team as "composed of members from different professions and occupations with varied and specialized knowledge, skills, and methods" (Greiner and Knebel 2003, 54).

Interprofessional team members work together as colleagues to deliver quality, individualized care for patients. These teams can consist of interdisciplinary groups of nurses, physical therapists, occupational therapists, and patient care assistants who work together to reduce the incidence of immobility-associated complications. They can be composed of physical, occupational, speech and language, and exercise physiology therapists providing wellness and prevention interventions to people who are homeless or have chronic illnesses. A number of healthcare educational institutions have begun to recognize the need to jointly train different professionals and have changed their curriculum to create interdisciplinary teams (Johnson 2019). Schools of public health and their professional association and accreditation bodies now promote interdisciplinary education (Petersen, Finnegan, and Spencer 2015). Medical schools such as the University of Minnesota train using collaborative and coordinated care (Davis and Gonzalo 2019).

Multidisciplinary and Interdisciplinary Teams

In addition to highly interdependent teams, healthcare operations function best with multidisciplinary and interdisciplinary teams, which also can be arrayed across the interdependence spectrum.

Multidisciplinary teams are composed of professionals from multiple disciplines—such as medicine, nursing, nutrition, physical therapy, respiratory therapy, and pharmacy—who work to provide a great breadth of services to patients. Traditionally, most healthcare has been organized this way. Even though a multidisciplinary team's members work with representatives of other disciplines, they tend to perform independently and interact formally. Multidisciplinary teams allow members to act as they deem best with little or

multidisciplinary teams
Teams composed of professionals from multiple disciplines who tend to work independently and interact formally.

no awareness of services or efforts outside their disciplines, as experts from different professions may treat components of a patient's case relatively independently. Rather than reflect an integration of care, patients' ailments are segmented and treated simultaneously by distinct providers.

On the other hand, an **interdisciplinary team** is defined as

> a group of persons who are trained in the use of different tools and concepts, among whom there is an organized division of labor around a common problem with each member using his own tools, with continuous intercommunication and re-examination of postulates in terms of limitations provided by the work of the other members and often with group responsibilities for the final product. (Clark, Spence, and Sheehan 1987)

This team is composed of professionals who work interdependently in the same setting. Separate assessments may still be performed, but patient information is shared and issues are resolved systemically, involving other team members. Interdisciplinary teams require greater interdependence and integration of the involved medical disciplines.

The interdisciplinary nature of healthcare makes the ability to successfully work in teams even more critical. However, the many professional groups required to provide high-quality patient care often express mistrust and difficulty relating to each other. These groups—including dietitians, laboratory technologists, respiratory therapists, occupational therapists, pharmacists, nurses, and physicians—develop their own social identity, as individuals are socialized into their professional communities of practice. The mixing of professionals with diverse backgrounds and perspectives frequently causes intragroup conflict, which may negatively affect the quality of care and constrain the spread of valuable innovations (Bartunek 2011).

> **interdisciplinary teams**
> Teams composed of a coordinated group of professionals from different fields who work interdependently but share information and resolve problems systematically and together.

Diversity

Does filling a team with diverse individuals make a difference? When it comes to gender diversity, companies in the top quartile are 15 percent more likely to outpace their peers (Hunt, Layton, and Prince 2015). A study of 2,400 companies found that those with at least one woman on the board of directors yielded higher return on equity and higher net income growth (Rock and Grant 2016).

Team members from diverse backgrounds tend to frame issues in a variety of ways. They raise more issues and make fewer factual errors. Diverse teams are more likely to avoid groupthink (discussed in chapter 12) by objectively questioning members' actions. They become more aware of their own potential biases, thus make more objective decisions (Rock and Grant 2016). Teams who are diverse in personality and gender can be very synergistic, as members together cover all the skills needed to accomplish a task.

The challenge to managers, of course, is to create teams with sufficient diversity but appropriate competencies. Some advocate the creation of teams by determining personality traits and grading competencies (Andrejczuk et al. 2019). Others support the idea of manually creating teams based on personalities and genders (Winsborough and Chamorro-Premuzic 2017) or simply building teams based on competencies (Leishman 2017). Putting people together in a room, however, is not forming a team. Team formation is a more involved process.

Team Formation

Teams progress through four predictable stages (as seen in exhibit 13.2):

1. Forming
2. Storming
3. Norming
4. Performing

Effective results occur in the fourth stage, highlighting the importance of moving efficiently through the first three stages.

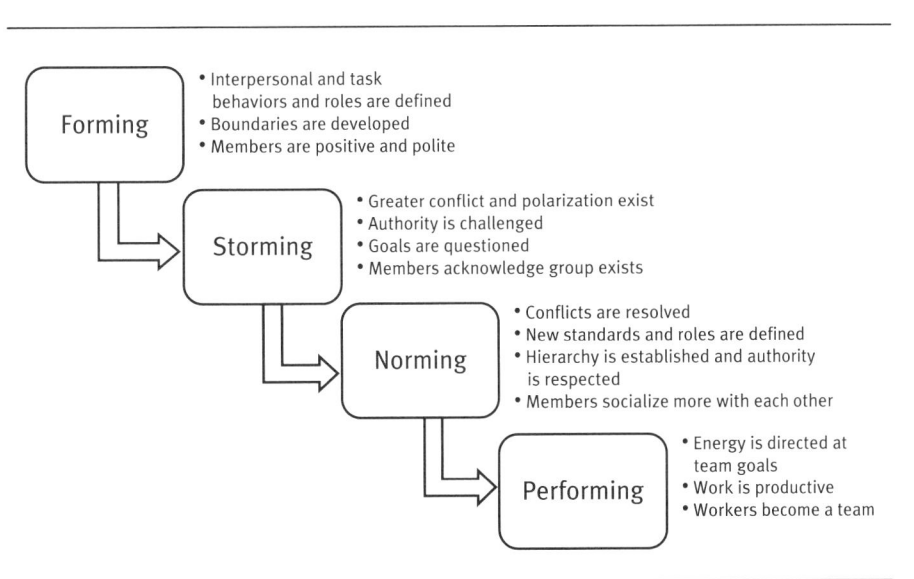

EXHIBIT 13.2
Four Stages of Team Building

Forming
- Interpersonal and task behaviors and roles are defined
- Boundaries are developed
- Members are positive and polite

Storming
- Greater conflict and polarization exist
- Authority is challenged
- Goals are questioned
- Members acknowledge group exists

Norming
- Conflicts are resolved
- New standards and roles are defined
- Hierarchy is established and authority is respected
- Members socialize more with each other

Performing
- Energy is directed at team goals
- Work is productive
- Workers become a team

Source: Adapted from Tuckman (1965).

forming
The first stage of team building, when a team comes together and an individual transitions into a team member.

storming
The second stage of team building, when members begin to resist collaboration with other members and to experience conflict.

norming
The third stage of team building, when members establish group rules, which usher in harmony and team cohesion.

performing
The fourth stage of team building, when members have learned their roles and accepted each other's strengths and weaknesses.

Forming occurs when a team comes together. Members are usually excited, and this becomes a stage of transition from individual to member status. **Storming** may be the most difficult stage for any team. Members may determine that the task is more difficult than they had realized and begin to resist collaboration with other team members, perhaps becoming defensive and arguing over noncritical issues. Team building is especially critical in this stage.

Next comes **norming**, which involves establishing group rules for the team. Harmony begins to replace conflict, and the team develops common goals and a sense of team cohesion. Finally, at the **performing** stage, relationships and expectations are settled. Team members have accepted each other's strengths and weaknesses and learned their roles. Members can prevent or work through group problems and begin to function as a cohesive, efficient team.

Teams in the forming stage can benefit from team-building exercises. For example, activities that introduce team members to each other can open lines of communication and create team bonding. Many types of activities can be used for team bonding, including the following exercises:

- *Two truths and a lie.* Team members tell three stories about themselves, of which two are true and one is a lie. After each member tells three stories, the other members vote on which story they believe is the lie.
- *First jobs.* Each member tells the others about their first job. The team member then answers the following three questions:
  - What parts of the job did you find most difficult?
  - What impression did you have of the bosses? What did you learn from them?
  - What did you learn most about that job?
- *Superlatives.* Each team member writes answers to a list of questions. Once the individuals complete their answers, the team comes together to compare and determine who the extreme member in each category is. Here are sample questions:
  - How old are you?
  - How many children do you have?
  - How many homes have you lived in?
  - How many years have you attended school?
  - How old was your father when you were born?
  - How many brothers and sisters do you have?
- *Conversation starters.* Before the meeting, a list of incomplete topic sentences is created and posted for team members to review. At the meeting, team members take turns starting a conversation on one of

the posted topics, focusing on their personal experiences. Following are some examples of incomplete sentences to introduce:
- Anybody will work hard if . . .
- People who run things should be . . .
- I would like to be . . .
- One thing I like about myself is . . .
- Nothing is as frustrating as . . .
- The teacher I liked best was a person who . . .
- Ten years from now, I . . .
- Every winning team needs . . .
- I take pride in . . .
- If you want to see me get mad . . .
- A rewarding job is one that . . .

- *If I were at my job right now.* Team members share what they would be doing if they were not in the meeting. They should go into detail, or they can be prompted for more detail. Once everyone has spoken, members are asked to forget about their usual job responsibilities until the meeting ends.

Team Building

High-functioning teams are the result of a healthy organizational culture and periodic training in team building (see exhibit 13.3). Building excellent, effective teams requires effort and management attention. Whenever a team is formed—whatever its nature—the following guidelines are helpful:

- *Define a clear purpose, goals, and priorities.* Teams need to understand clearly what they are trying to accomplish and for what purpose. The goals and priorities should be linked to the larger organizational goals or mission and be seen as adding value to patients, staff, and the organization as a whole.
- *Set appropriate time frames.* Establish schedules for important team deliverables to achieve the goals and priorities. Attach dates to the important milestones.
- *Select members who offer the best contributions.* When forming a new team or replacing team members, choose individuals who have the knowledge and ability to contribute. Having equal representation by discipline or hierarchical level is not necessary. Although people directly involved with the issue or problem should be selected, sometimes

EXHIBIT 13.3
Successful Team Characteristics

When 21 articles in a special issue of *American Psychologist* were reviewed and key findings about working in teams were summarized, the results revealed that successful teams share several distinct characteristics:
- Team members have personalities, values, and abilities that help achieve team goals.
- Teamwork (cooperation among members) rather than taskwork (completing individual assignments) takes place.
- Healthcare teams, in particular, are fluid, with clear roles and goals.
- Team members communicate.
- Team members bring a diversity of thoughts and ideas.
- Members are well trained.
- Team members trust one another.

Source: Adapted from Weir (2018).

    inviting someone from outside may provide a fresh and unique perspective.
- *Define the roles for team members.* Unless previously established by job descriptions or other means, set forth the roles for the team. Team roles may relate to decision-making and process facilitation (e.g., team leader, coach, facilitator) or to functional duties (e.g., scribe, interteam liaison, task worker).
- *Have a sponsor or champion within the organization.* Successful teams require organizational support and a go-to sponsor or champion. This individual may be the leader to whom a work team reports or a champion positioned to facilitate the implementation of a team's recommendations.
- *Establish ground rules.* Agree on how team members should treat and interact with each other. Set rules for how decisions are made, what level of participation is acceptable, and what degree of formality is followed. Creating ground rules helps establish a nonthreatening environment that encourages open communication and avoids personal attacks, greatly facilitating team building.

    Team building and breaking down barriers among professional groups are both critical to ensuring the delivery of high-quality healthcare. As mentioned, groups of healthcare professionals are consistently placed together; but if left alone, many professionals will remain in groups and not develop into cohesive teams. Bereft of guidance, groups may also become dysfunctional and produce workers full of anger, mistrust, and cynicism. Team building can allow teams to produce results quickly and achieve high levels of openness, participation, and creativity. Team building can be important for temporary teams, such as task forces, and for permanent work units, such as patient treatment teams.

Team building is often designed around improving team problem-solving and processes. Efforts to build teams should include the following components (adapted from Buller 1986):

- Planned intervention with known objectives or desired accomplishments
- Facilitation by a third party, if potential emotional and personality barriers are present
- Inclusion of necessary team members; do not begin the team-building process if key members are absent
- Identification of barriers and skill gaps to improve problem-solving

Because many teams bring together members from diverse departmental and educational backgrounds, some of the team members may lack knowledge of domains that are central to accomplishing the team goals. Training may be needed to educate members regarding the operational processes, technology, and the organizational interface of the problem or issue under evaluation. For example, if a team has been formed to evaluate the pharmacy distribution system, some of its members—such as representatives from materials management, information technology, or administration—may not understand the operation and function of the pharmacy. Education for this team might cover the hospital's formulary, purchase contracts, and existing distribution system, among other aspects of pharmacy distribution. This shared knowledge is essential to evaluating and improving the existing system.

When individuals form teams, undercurrents of conflicting emotions and loyalties often seem to get in the way of efficient progress. If left unattended, these undercurrents can impede effective team performance. Addressing team dynamics and group processes can dramatically improve team performance.

Teams often underestimate the need for their own development. Frequently, they do not recognize that teams do not automatically function at high levels of performance. They must spend time working on both their processes and the feelings among members, which frequently are only indirectly related to their team's outcomes.

Team building should also focus on strengthening relationships. High-performing teams most often develop strong bonds to the team, among team members, and to their organization. These relationships can be categorized as personal identity with the team, identity with other team members, and identity with the organization:

- *Identity with the team.* Team members relate to and feel part of the team.
- *Identity with other team members.* Proper, congenial interactions, which are critical to performance, exist among team members.
- *Identity with the organization.* Effective team members usually identify strongly with their own department and organization.

Teams that gain a strong sense of team identity are effective, and their members feel that the team is distinctive, valued, and important. Team identity can be strengthened in many ways, especially by distinguishing and highlighting the team's importance. Following are five approaches that can help teams achieve this (Butterfield 2011):

1. *Create a team name.* A name distinguishes the group and creates a sense of identity.
2. *Develop a team logo.* A logo can help establish a brand for the team, increase team visibility, and foster morale.
3. *Adopt slogans, songs, or cheers.* In some work cultures, these elements are effective in promoting team pride.
4. *Develop signs and reminders.* Create images to reinforce the purpose and processes of the team.
5. *Create branded apparel.* Such items can be used both as incentives and as methods for highlighting the importance of the team.

Ultimately, effective team members learn to trust and respect each other. They interact both formally and informally and generate synergies that allow them to accomplish much more than when working as a group or as individuals.

Signs of an Effective Team

How can you tell if your team is effective? An effective team involves its members and has a leader who is approachable and listens. When an effective team meets, shared discussion takes place—not a monologue or faction-dominated conversation. In addition, team members communicate freely and openly among themselves. They are unafraid to provide difficult feedback, and they use appropriate problem-solving tools as needed.

Members of effective teams willingly volunteer and complete tasks. They are task focused yet innovative, and they do not allow personal differences to interfere with task achievement. Members also take responsibility for team decisions and positively communicate their team's efforts to outside stakeholders.

An assessment for team effectiveness is provided in exhibit 13.4. Think of a team with which you have worked. Score each category and then add up the points, for a total of 75 possible points. Teams that score more than 60 points can be considered well-functioning teams.

EXHIBIT 13.4 Team Assessment Tool

Instructions: Grade your team using the following criteria. Teams that score higher than 60 points are likely functioning well.

Criteria					
Goals	Unknown		Unclear		Clear
	1	2	3	4	5
Commitment to goals	None		Marginal		Great
	1	2	3	4	5
Meetings	Unproductive		Somewhat productive		Very productive
	1	2	3	4	5
Implementation of decisions	None		Periodic		Consistent
	1	2	3	4	5
Trust among team members	None		Some		High
	1	2	3	4	5
Work distribution	Unfair		Mixed		Fair
	1	2	3	4	5
Communication	Poor		Adequate		Excellent
	1	2	3	4	5
Respect among team members	None		Adequate		Excellent
	1	2	3	4	5
Innovation	None		Adequate		Excellent
	1	2	3	4	5
Involvement of members	Little		Adequate		High
	1	2	3	4	5

(continued)

EXHIBIT 13.4
Team Assessment Tool (Continued)

Instructions: Grade your team using the following criteria. Teams that score higher than 60 points are likely functioning well.

Criteria

(continued from previous page)

Progress checks	None		Some		Consistent
	1	2	3	4	5
Attendance	Poor		Adequate		Excellent
	1	2	3	4	5
Harmful conflict	Always		Sometimes		Never
	1	2	3	4	5
Task assignments	Unclear		Known		Clear
	1	2	3	4	5
Collaboration	None		Adequate		Excellent
	1	2	3	4	5

Source: Adapted from Dyer (1987, 42–43).

Conflict

Conflict can be positive or negative for teams. Conflict is natural when people work together. Many people perceive conflict negatively and associate it with tension and anger, but it can be valuable to a team's functioning as well. Conflict, if appropriately managed, can increase a team's vitality and creativity and lead to effective solutions. Managed conflict also minimizes the potential for groupthink, as discussed in chapter 12. Conflict can be positive if a team uses it to perform team building and the tension is appropriately resolved. However, team leaders need to be aware of group dynamics and respond to unresolved conflict. Following are some guidelines (Brett and Goldberg 2017):

- *Respond as a mediator rather than the boss.* Team members in conflict are more likely to react well to a decision if they are part of it.
- *Meet separately first with those in conflict.* Build empathy. Listen and gain an understanding of the individual's view. Use subsequent meetings to resolve the conflict.
- *Set rules in the first meeting together.* Make clear that decisions will have everyone's buy in. Set rules, such as all team members showing respect for one another and listening without interruption.
- *Move forward with a few options for agreement.* Offer a solution with a limited duration; try something for a while and see how it goes. Offer

a solution that does not set a precedent. Suggest that a new discussion will take place if the same problem occurs in the future. Make agreements contingent on a few outcomes happening (or not) in the future.

High-functioning teams can also help resolve conflict. As illustrated by the adjacent box, teams—especially those within a professional group—can form a united front to discipline even a person with higher authority. In this situation, the nurses created an announced "code white" to summon others to witness and, ultimately, shame a physician into behaving appropriately.

Team Viability

Team viability is defined as a team's capacity for sustainable growth and success. Viability is important for teams that tackle ongoing problems, those that are likely to undergo change such as new members, and long-term organizational teams (Bell and Marentette 2011). Teams that are highly adaptable are more viable (Cooperstein 2017).

As new teams develop, their ability to continue working as a team is related to performance improvement, the time team members spend working

---

Doctors Behaving Badly

By Britt Berrett

The newly arrived Dr. Lira found tremendous professional satisfaction in belittling the clinical staff. He created a difficult and dysfunctional work environment as he leveled his wrath at clinicians who did not meet his expectations or did not agree with his clinical direction. He cornered such staff members in private moments, when they would be the sole recipient of his anger.

Having long endured similar antics, nursing staff in general are uniquely aware of bad physician behavior. A nursing supervisor initially addressed Dr. Lira's behavior, but he failed to respond to this early intervention. The issues escalated as more individual nurses and therapists became the target of his tirades.

The nurse manager and director called a meeting with Dr. Lira to discuss his behavior. Insulted by the efforts of leadership to intervene, he continued his attacks—now even more carefully and deviously delivered. Months passed, and additional incidents involving the doctor created an almost intolerable environment. The CEO inserted himself into the corrective plan of action, summoning Dr. Lira to his office to discuss employee complaints about him and to provide specific direction on the doctor's future behavior. The poor behavior improved for a time, but eventually the caustic interactions reemerged.

The final and most effective strategy was deployed by several imaginative nurses. Aware of Dr. Lira's propensities, the nursing team was on high alert for clues of potential escalating behavior. Once his rage was detected, the nurses would call a "code white," and all nurses on the unit would gather as quickly as possible to encircle the doctor during a tirade. No words would be exchanged; the nurses would simply stand in solidarity with their colleagues and stare at Dr. Lira.

This ingenious strategy became known throughout the hospital and was a source of tremendous embarrassment for not only Dr. Lira but also other physicians on staff. Culturally, the nurses had succeeded in redefining appropriate and acceptable behavior. Despite policies and procedures and committees and interventions, group dynamics effectively dictated organizational norms and expectations.

together, and the greater familiarity they develop toward one another. Positive affect (moods and emotions) has been linked to team viability. Teamwork engagement, enthusiasm, and energy are important (Costa, Passos, and Barata 2015).

A 2020 study by Cao and colleagues found that team viability comes from active engagement among team members, even those teams who meet virtually. The message to managers is that when some team members are left out or not involved, managers need to step in and address the problem by changing work patterns. Healthcare managers who understand the patterns and interaction of viable teams can use the knowledge to help other teams be more successful.

Chapter Summary

While the terms *group* and *team* are used interchangeably, teams tend to be more independent and task oriented, and team members become more socially familiar with one another. Teams often have shared leadership and outcomes. As in sports, team members have distinct roles and contributions to accomplish such outcomes.

Healthcare systems comprise many interprofessional and multidisciplinary teams, including clinical teams of nurses, physicians, therapists, and pharmacists and support teams that keep the grounds and facilities functional and safe. Schools of public health, medicine, and allied health now promote interprofessional education and teamwork. Multidisciplinary teams work to provide a great breadth of services to patients. Interdisciplinary teams labor around a common problem. Professionals who work interdependently in the same setting form these teams. For example, different team members make separate assessments of a patient and then share the results in order to treat the individual.

Diversity among team members has been proven to yield greater outcomes. Team members from different backgrounds frame issues in a variety of ways. They raise awareness of more issues and make fewer factual errors. Diverse teams make objective decisions, building on team members' strengths and backgrounds to be very synergistic. The challenge for managers lies in building diverse teams, finding individuals with a variety of backgrounds, personality traits, and competencies.

Effective, high-functioning teams have clear goals and purposes; they understand what needs to be achieved and by when. Such teams include members who take needed roles and have the knowledge and ability to contribute and treat each other with respect.

Team-building efforts can be effective in helping groups become well-functioning teams. This process may involve only singular interventions or a consistent, multiyear process. Unified team members identify with the team, other team members, and their organization.

Team building follows four stages: forming, storming, norming, and performing. Forming begins when a team comes together, which then transitions into storming. Storming often is the most difficult stage, and team-building efforts are critical during this time. During norming, the team sets rules and goals, which then enables performing.

Effective teams can be identified by how they interact and handle difficult problems. They generally have leaders who are approachable and listen and members who communicate openly. Members volunteer willingly and complete tasks.

Conflict can be positive or negative for teams. If handled appropriately, conflict can engender team vitality and creativity. Leaders should not overreact or underreact to conflict and should deal with chronic and serious disruptions directly.

Team viability—the capacity for continued growth and success—comes from active engagement among team members. They work together and become familiar with one another. Teamwork enthusiasm and energy is important. Healthcare leaders build on this to promote team viability.

Chapter Questions

1. How does a team differ from a group?
2. Why might interdisciplinary teams, as defined in this chapter, be more efficient than multidisciplinary teams?
3. Describe a few qualities of diverse teams that make them more successful.
4. What is the most difficult stage in team development and why?
5. Why is establishing team ground rules a good initial step? In which stage of team building might this be helpful?
6. How do problems help build teams?
7. What are ways to increase team identity?
8. Use exhibit 13.4 to assess a team you belong to. Where has the team done well? Poorly? What could be done to improve the team's performance?
9. Although conflict is normal, often people see it as negative. Why is this the case?
10. Name a few keys of team viability.

Chapter Cases

Dr. Handly and the Multidisciplinary Team

Sue Handly, MD, was recently recruited into a multispecialty group of 40 physicians. The clinic offers a wide scope of services, including a relatively sophisticated radiology department, physical therapy, and a same-day surgery unit. The clinic has been growing and employs highly trained healthcare providers.

In addition to her medical degree, Sue completed a master's degree in health administration while she was practicing in South Carolina. She always wanted to return home to Texas and, after an extensive search, found this group in a suburb of Austin, which was relatively close to her hometown. She thoroughly enjoyed the time she spent with the health system's organizational development team during management training, which performed team building with different system groups and committees to improve their performance.

During her first week in the new practice, Sue noticed that the staff and physicians worked like a multidisciplinary team. Each practiced reasonably good medicine but did not interact or communicate well with one another; the staff and physicians worked together but did not feel like team members. Sue wanted to change this, so she obtained the permission of the clinic's executive group to lead a team-building effort. A team-building steering committee was created, and over the course of several meetings, they established the following mission statement and goals:

1. Overall organizational mission statement: Improvement of patients' health
2. Goals:
    a. Reduction in barriers to access to care
    b. Improvement in practice's financial performance
    c. Enhancement of physician and staff satisfaction

The committee then set specific, measurable operational objectives (adapted from Bodenheimer 2007):

- At least 80 percent of patients with diabetes in the practice will have hemoglobin A1c lower than 8.
- At least 90 percent of nonurgent requests will receive an appointment within one week.
- The practice will achieve $1.2 million in revenue per month.
- Each team member will establish an explicitly identified goal for personal professional development.

- Physicians' and staff members' roles will be reevaluated and reconfigured in the next six months.
- Eighty percent of staff will be cross-trained to substitute for other roles.

Sue knows that this was just a start, but she is happy to have established these goals. Now for the next steps.

Case Questions
1. How would you evaluate what Sue has done so far? What is positive? Negative?
2. What would you recommend for her next steps?

A Brief History of Primary Care Teams

Teams are especially needed in primary care. Primary care offices offer many different services, and patients, especially elderly patients, can present with multiple diagnoses and be prescribed handfuls of medications. To simplify the delivery of care, some primary care offices have decreased their number of staff and have the physician perform most of the care. However, this approach is not efficient.

The primary care / general practitioner in the early twentieth century was a solo operator. Carrying his equipment in a black bag, he often treated patients in their homes. Gradually, more patients were treated in an office setting, often by a husband-and-wife team, with the wife serving as receptionist, nurse, billing clerk, and bookkeeper. Later, seeking more efficiencies, nonphysician tasks were segmented into separate positions for nurses, receptionists, medical assistants, billing clerks, radiology technologists, and so on—a pattern found in myriad small practices dotting the United States.

Concurrently, many groups sought to introduce and develop primary care teams. In 1915, teams of physicians, health educators, and social workers were developed at outpatient areas of Massachusetts General Hospital. Efforts to create functional primary care team models continued at New York's Montefiore Hospital in 1948 and at Yale in 1951. Then, in the 1960s, neighborhood health center programs sought to establish primary care teams in area clinics.

However, the use of primary care teams did not become dominant because of several barriers. One barrier was the tension between physicians and nurses regarding their respective responsibilities, authority, and knowledge. Another obstacle resulted from payment systems that primarily paid only for physician-related services and failed to reimburse nonphysician work. In addition, team relationships during the 1960s and 1970s were vaguely defined and not based on training or clear divisions of labor. Team meetings became drawn-out, unproductive affairs.

Large teams were difficult to manage in primary care. Some experts assert that optimal primary care teams should include 6–12 people. Even in teams of this size, however, decision-making can be problematic.

The activity of building new teams involves creating alternative systems of care delivery. Processes must be changed and decision-making must be transformed. These efforts do not occur overnight and may take years to accomplish fully. But ultimately, the rewards of improved quality and patient satisfaction will be worth the effort.

Source: Information from Bodenheimer (2007).

Case Questions
1. What were the barriers to forming primary care teams?
2. Why might the forming of teams be more difficult in primary care settings than in single-specialty physician offices or other businesses?
3. What could have been done to strengthen teams over the history of healthcare delivery?

Chapter Activities

Marshmallow Towers
This activity will give you an opportunity to experience and discuss team formation, team building, and team viability concepts.

Materials
Each team of four or five individuals will need

- a bag of miniature marshmallows and
- a box of toothpicks.

Activity
You have 20 minutes to work with your team to build the tallest structure in your class. Your structure must stand on its own for at least 15 seconds with no support of any kind.

Are You a Team Player?
Take the *Psychology Today* Team Player Test (www.psychologytoday.com/us/tests/career/team-player-test). Identify those areas where you are better and worse at working in a team.

References

Andrejczuk, E., F. Bistaffa, C. Blum, J. A. Rodríguez-Aguilar, and C. Sierra. 2019. "Synergistic Team Composition: A Computational Approach to Foster Diversity in Teams." *Knowledge-Based Systems* 182 (October 15): 104799. https://doi.org/10.1016/j.knosys.2019.06.007.

Bartunek, J. 2011. "Intergroup Relationships and Quality Improvement in Healthcare." *BMJ Quality & Safety* 20 (Suppl. 1): i62–i66.

Bell, S. T., and Marentette, B. J. 2011. "Team Viability for Long-Term and Ongoing Organizational Teams." *Organizational Psychology Review* 1 (4): 275–95. https://doi.org/10.1177/2041386611405876.

Bodenheimer, T. 2007. "Building Teams in Primary Care: Lessons Learned." California Health Care Foundation. Published July 17. www.chcf.org/publication/building-teams-in-primary-care-lessons-from-15-case-studies/ (document download).

Brett, J., and S. B. Goldberg. 2017. "How to Handle a Disagreement on Your Team." *Harvard Business Review* digital article, July 10. https://hbr.org/2017/07/how-to-handle-a-disagreement-on-your-team.

Buller, P. 1986. "The Team Building–Task Performance Relation: Some Conceptual and Methodological Refinements." *Group & Organization Studies* 11 (3): 147–68.

Butterfield, J. 2011. *Team Building*. Boston: Cengage Learning.

Cao, H., V. Yang, V. Chen, Y. J. Lee, L. Stone, N. J. Diarrassouba, M. E. Whiting, and M. S. Bernstein. 2020. "My Team Will Go On: Differentiating High and Low Viability Teams Through Team Interaction." *Proceedings of the ACM [Association for Computer Machinery] on Human-Computer Interaction* 4 (CSCW3; January 2021): Article 230. https://doi.org/10.1145/3432929.

Clark, P. G., D. L. Spence, and J. L. Sheehan. 1987. "A Service/Learning Model for Interdisciplinary Teamwork in Health and Aging." *Gerontology & Geriatrics Education* 6 (4): 3–16. https://doi.org/10.1300/J021v06n04_02.

Cooperstein, J. N. 2017. "Initial Development of a Team Viability Measure." *College of Science and Health Theses and Dissertations* 202. https://via.library.depaul.edu/csh_etd/202.

Costa, P. L., A. M. Passos, and M. C. Barata. 2015. "Multilevel Influences of Team Viability Perceptions." *Team Performance Management* 12 (1/2): 19–36. https://doi.org/10.1108/TPM-03-2014-0020.

Davis, C. R., and J. D. Gonzalo. 2019. "How Medical Schools Can Promote Community Collaboration Through Health Systems Science Education." *AMA Journal of Ethics* 21 (3): E239–47. https://doi.org/10.1001/amajethics.2019.239.

Dyer, W. G. 1987. *Team Building: Issues and Alternatives*. Reading, MA: Addison-Wesley.

Fisher, M. 2021. "Jaylon on Cowboys Problem: 'We Didn't Play as a Team.'" *Sports Illustrated*. Published February 3. www.si.com/nfl/cowboys/news/jaylon-smith-on-dallas-cowboys-problem-we-didnt-play-as-a-team.

Greiner, A. C., and E. Knebel (eds.). 2003. *Health Professions Education: A Bridge to Quality*. Washington, DC: National Academies Press.

Harter, J. 2020. "What's the Ideal Team Size? It Depends on the Manager." *Workplace* (blog). *Gallup*, February 28. www.gallup.com/workplace/286997/ideal-team-size-depends-manager.aspx.

Hunt, V., D. Layton, and S. Prince. 2015. "Why Diversity Matters." *McKinsey & Company* (blog). January 1. www.mckinsey.com/business-functions/organization/our-insights/why-diversity-matters.

Johnson, K. F. 2019. "Preparing 21st Century Counselors and Healthcare Professionals: Examining Technology Competency and Interprofessional Education Comfort." *Journal of Counselor Preparation and Supervision* 12 (4): Article 7. https://repository.wcsu.edu/jcps/vol12/iss4/7.

Katzenbach, J., and D. Smith. 2005. "The Discipline of Teams." *Harvard Business Review* 83 (4): 162–71.

Leishman, C. 2017. "Building a Powerful Team with Competencies." Human Resource Systems Group (blog). Published November 28. https://resources.hrsg.ca/blog/building-a-powerful-team-with-competencies.

Petersen, D., J. Finnegan, and H. Spencer. 2015. "Anticipating Change, Sparking Innovation: Framing the Future." *American Journal of Public Health* 105 (Suppl. 1): S46–S49.

Rock, D., and H. Grant. 2016. "Why Diverse Teams Are Smarter." *Harvard Business Review* digital article, November 4. https://hbr.org/2016/11/why-diverse-teams-are-smarter.

Tuckman, B. 1965. "Development Sequence in Small Groups." *Psychological Bulletin* 63 (6): 384–99.

Weir, K. 2018. "What Makes Teams Work?" American Psychological Association 49 (8): 46. www.apa.org/monitor/2018/09/cover-teams.

West, M. 2018. "Does Team Size Matter?" Affina Organisation Development (blog). Published July 3; updated March 7, 2019. www.affinaod.com/article/does-team-size-matter/.

Winsborough, D., and T. Chamorro-Premuzic. 2017. "Great Teams Are About Personalities, Not Just Skills." *Harvard Business Review* digital article, January 25. https://hbr.org/2017/01/great-teams-are-about-personalities-not-just-skills.

CHAPTER 14

COMMUNICATION

> Todd, a nurse working on a surgical floor, had graduated from nursing school only seven months ago. He was bright, but still somewhat intimidated by some of the general surgeons. Dr. Black especially almost always seemed angry and did not like to stop to listen. Often he would hurry through the nursing floor, glance at the charts, see his patients, and depart without saying much to the nurses. If a nurse tried to speak with him, the doctor seemed irritated and impatient.
>
> Todd was taking care of Mr. James, who had received an appendectomy from Dr. Black the previous day. Mr. James was not feeling well and had started having abdominal pains, which Todd noted on the chart. But when Dr. Black came on the floor, Todd did not catch him to explain that his patient was experiencing abdominal pains and had a low red blood cell count, which could be indicative of internal bleeding. Sadly, Mr. James later died from the internal hemorrhage that could have been addressed.

Learning Objectives

After studying this chapter, readers should be able to

- recognize the importance and components of organizational communication,
- identify problems and barriers that can occur in communication,
- distinguish and apply the differences between information richness and message complexity and importance,
- explain the value of nonverbal communication, and
- learn and apply methods to improve communication and dialogue.

Key Terms

- communication
- communication channel
- decoding
- dialogue

- encoding
- feedback
- information richness
- noise
- nonverbal communication

Despite all their intelligence and degrees, healthcare professionals tend to be very poor at communicating. Too frequently, doctors fail to talk to doctors, researchers do not talk to government regulators, and electronic health records (EHRs) do not talk to anyone or anything. Poor communication has been blamed for many of the flaws and failures of the US health system. Bad communication among medical caregiving teams causes about 30 percent of malpractice cases. In addition, it has been estimated that hospitals waste $12 billion per year because of poor communication. Sadly, even though EHRs are a multibillion-dollar business, communication between EHR platforms exists only on a limited basis (Fisher 2017).

Good communication skills are paramount for any manager in business today. The ability to conceptualize an idea and have others understand it is a core function of leaders. It is impossible to become an effective leader without excelling in communication skills. Effective communication is critical for professional success, whether it is interpersonal, group, or organizational (Landry 2020). Leaders spend as much as 80 percent of their day communicating—speaking, listening, reading, and writing to interact with others, solve problems, and plan strategies (Zandan 2020). Yet, miscommunication occurs far too often, and, sadly, many organizational problems occur because of the poor communication skills of a firm's leaders.

The general population also recognizes that good communication skills are essential to succeed. The vast majority of people (85 percent) see communication as a critical skill (Parker and Rainie 2020). Likewise, as shown in exhibit 14.1, American parents rank communication skills as the most important to their children's success in life.

Communication Process

communication
The process of transmitting information and meaning from one individual or group to another.

Communication is the two-way process of transmitting information and meaning from one individual or group (the sender) to another (the receiver). As exhibit 14.2 shows, this process starts with the sender, or encoder, having a thought or an idea, which is encoded and then transmitted through some mode of communication to the receiver. The receiver decodes the message; gives it meaning; encodes a response; and provides feedback to the sender, who decodes the response. All the while, the communication is surrounded by noise that can impede the accurate exchange of information.

EXHIBIT 14.1
Life Skills Children Need

Skill	Percentage of Survey Respondents
Communication	90
Reading	86
Math	79
Teamwork	77
Writing	75
Logic	74
Science	58
Athletics	25
Music	24
Art	23

Source: Data from Goo (2015).

The communication process may appear simple, but clearly communicating an idea or a thought is often difficult. A problem with any portion of the transmission can reduce communication effectiveness.

The first step in communication is **encoding**—or transforming a message into signs or symbols—and it can misfire. How the message is encoded depends on the sender's evaluation of the receiver's capability.

encoding
The communication step that transforms a message into signs or symbols.

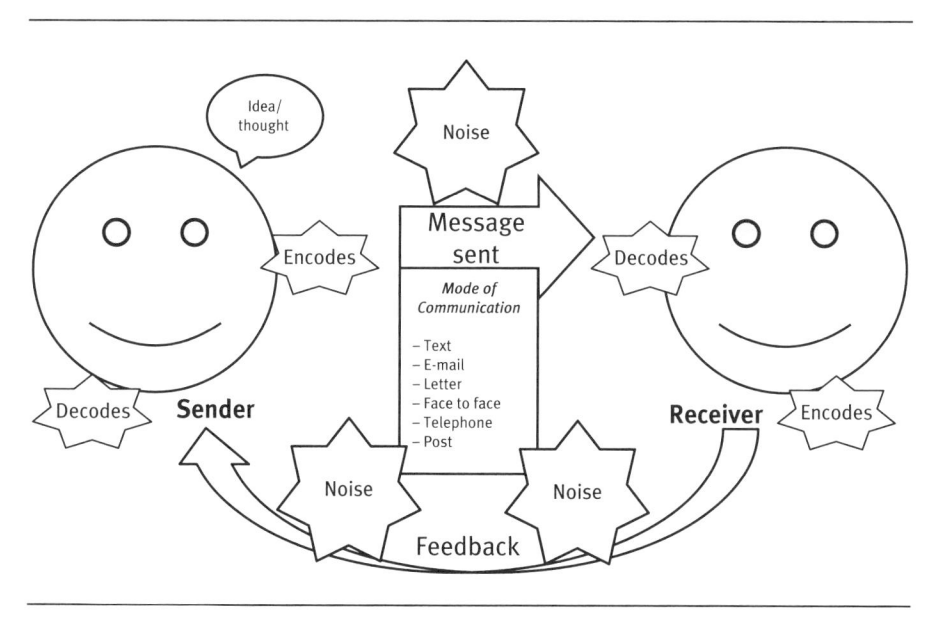

EXHIBIT 14.2
The Communication Process

> **Doctor–Patient Miscommunication**
>
> Jim grew up in Alabama and moved to Utah in his early twenties, where he worked in a mill and married a local woman. Now close to retirement, he sometimes had trouble breathing and also was experiencing terrible pain in his right ear. At his wife's urging, he finally visited a doctor, who ordered a series of tests and X-rays.
>
> After these were completed, Jim met with the doctor, who informed him, "You have a mass in your left lung, and the cancer tests came back positive. You also have an infection in your right ear that needs to be treated."
>
> The doctor asked Jim if he understood. Jim said, "Yow," which was his way of saying yes. The doctor then wrote a prescription for the ear infection that Jim was to take to the nurse to administer. The prescription stated, "This patient may be S.O.B. Take care, but please place the medication in the R.ear."
>
> Jim called his wife immediately, relieved that although he had something big in his lung, the test was positive so he must be good to go. He was upset that the doctor had called him an S.O.B. and planned to tell off the doctor at his next visit. However, Jim was so glad about the "positive" cancer test that he must not have heard the doctor say the nurse would be making him lie down and putting the medication in his rear. Needless to say, Jim's ear infection did not improve, and he was surprised when he was called to come in to start chemotherapy the following week.

However, people who formulate messages often encode their thoughts into words, gestures, and symbols that cannot be interpreted by or may mean something different to the receiver (Bradberry 2020; Soffar 2020).

As the box describes, erroneous encoding of a message can easily occur with both verbal and written communication. Almost half of US adults report having trouble understanding and remembering what their doctor tells them (Heath 2018). Doctors use words patients may not understand up to 70 times in each visit. Many patients do not comprehend the meaning of *bowel*, *colon*, *screening test*, or *blood in the stool* (Davis et al. 2001), and 95 percent of patients with advanced cancer reportedly had difficulty understanding their prognosis (Cabral-Isabedra 2016). In addition, many people have no understanding of the multitude of acronyms and abbreviations used in healthcare. For instance, "the patient needs an EKG because of the MI, but before going to the cath lab, get a CBC and coags and make the patient NPO" (Pitt and Hendrickson 2019). Proper encoding requires the sender to know the receiver's background and abilities.

Furthermore, hospital executives suggest that the lack of communication skills among healthcare service providers results in increased costs and avoidable medical errors. At times, doctors do not communicate well with hospital personnel or patients, with miscommunication resulting in almost 2,000 patient deaths in five years and factoring in about 30 percent of medical malpractice cases (Bailey 2016). The Joint Commission recognizes communication's importance in healthcare and has established it as a critical focus for patient safety and sees good communication as leading to increased patient satisfaction, decreased emotional stress, improved patient adherence, better health outcomes, and less burnout (Joint Commission 2020).

In addition, cultural differences and translations from one language to another can dramatically increase encoding errors. Written language that makes sense to the one who wrote it can convey completely different meanings. For instance, the following examples are from actual signs around the world:

- On an office door: "Head Transplant Surgery"
- Over a kiosk in an airport: "Declaration for Livestock-Related Persons"
- At a buffet over chopped celery: "Salary Mix"
- On a sign on a fence: "If caught you will be trespassed!"

Each of these signs involves an inexact translation and encoding into English. The signs may be humorous, but they also illustrate the difficulties in conveying meaning.

Beyond ensuring that the communication itself is understandable, a communicator must select a workable **communication channel**—the medium through which a message is sent and received. Among the many possible modes are face-to-face, videoconferences, phone calls, voicemails, texts, e-mails, letters, policy statements, newspapers, and formal written reports. And these do not even begin to cover the nonverbal channels such as eye contact, body position, movements, and symbols (Conor 2020).

The selection of a communication channel should relate to the complexity and importance of the message, which dictates the degree of **information richness** required. As displayed in exhibit 14.3, channels of

communication channel
The medium through which a message is sent and received.

information richness
The degree of nonverbal or verbal communication used to convey the complexity and importance of a message.

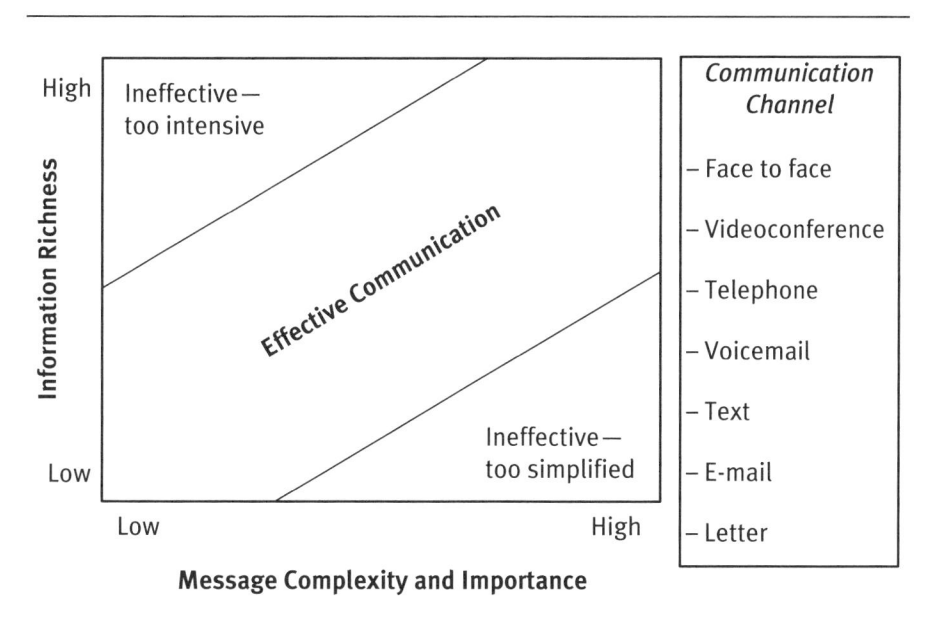

EXHIBIT 14.3
Information Richness and Complexity

Source: Adapted from Daft and Lengel (1984).

communication vary in their capacity to relay information-rich content and messages in their full complexity and importance. High degrees of information richness convey more nonverbal information, which allows for improved understanding and feedback regarding the message. Effective communication occurs when the right degree of information richness is used, given the complexity and importance of the message.

Highly important and complex messages, for example, should be transmitted through face-to-face conversations. However, face-to-face conversations for trivial and noncomplex messages may result in an ineffective meeting because the communication is too intense. On the other hand, using a communication channel with a low degree of information richness for a complex, important message may result in an ineffective and oversimplified interaction. Most have experienced this ineffective messaging after sending a misunderstood e-mail only to realize a richer channel should have been selected.

Choosing the correct channel of communication can be challenging. Low-richness channels—such as letters, e-mails, and texts—should be used for only routine and low-urgency matters, whereas high-richness channels are recommended for complex communication. High-richness channels, which allow opportunities for feedback, are also recommended for first meetings, where each party places high value on a clear impression of the other.

The next step in communication is **decoding**, the process by which the receiver assigns meaning to the message that is, with luck, consistent with the sender's original intent. Decoding creates meaning from language and nonverbal behavior, but it fails frequently. As with encoding, decoding is highly influenced by the receiver's self-identity, background, mood, culture, and behavior. In addition, the receiver may lack knowledge about or misinterpret the meaning of the symbols (verbal and nonverbal) used by the sender. As illustrated by the story in the box, improper decoding can create serious problems.

decoding
The communication step that assigns meaning to the message.

noise
Distractions that diminish the effectiveness of the communication process.

Each of the aforementioned components of communication—the sender, the receiver, and communication channels—is subject to noise. **Noise** consists of distractions that diminish the effectiveness of the communication process. Distress, self-consciousness, environmental conditions, personal status, and feelings, among other factors, can act as noise and

---

Noise in Healthcare Communication

Employees in hospital settings are subject to a great deal of noise that impedes good communication. Staff members face competing tasks, fatigue, and cultures that can discourage questioning and increase the risk of decoding errors. "For instance, the physician may ask a resident to pull a chest tube, but perhaps the patient has two tubes and the resident translates this message to mean the right-sided one, without confirming this interpretation with the attending."

Source: Salas and Frush (2013, 59).

impede communication (Quester et al. 2007). As demonstrated in the box, noise is ever-present in healthcare settings and, if care is not taken, can result in care delivery errors.

Cell phones and other personal communication devices add another dimension of noise to our lives. Each of us has attempted to speak with someone who was checking e-mail or reading social media posts or texts during the conversation. Such noise distracts from and hinders good communication.

Another crucial aspect of communication, often overlooked in real life, is **feedback**. Feedback refers to the "acknowledgment and reaction of the receiver to the sender after receiving the message. Feedback enables the sender to ensure that the message is being properly communicated to the receiver" (Kumar 2010, 472).

feedback
The process in which the sender and receiver engage to validate the message sent and received.

In other words, feedback is the process in which the sender and receiver engage to validate the message sent and received. It allows the receiver to reverse roles with the sender to verify whether the message was interpreted accurately. In this way, information is shared, recycled, and fine-tuned to achieve mutual understanding by creating a circular mechanism to clarify meaning. Feedback tells the sender how the receiver interpreted the message, thus accommodating adjustments to perceptions and interpretations.

Communication without feedback can lead to erroneous results. One-way communication can leave the sender thinking that the message was adequately conveyed when, in reality, the receiver may be confused and frustrated. An example of one-way communication is an intercom announcement, which can come across garbled in speech and meaning. One-way communications also frequently occur between individuals who reside in different authority levels of an organization. Bosses often tell (send) and fail to listen (receive) for feedback.

In healthcare, two-way communication involving feedback is critical. If one-way communication is employed, feedback is lacking and the interpretation of the intended message can be radically different, with potentially tragic consequences. Patient safety processes among healthcare professionals are entwined thoroughly with feedback—from double-checking patient identities, surgical sites, and medications to encouraging and framing

> **Surgical Time-Outs**
>
> Most hospital surgical departments have adopted surgical time-outs to improve communication and thereby eliminate errors. In 2003, the Joint Commission instituted a universal three-step protocol to eliminate wrong-site surgery. Performed before surgery, the protocol consists of a time-out, or pre-procedure verification process, involving all members of the procedure team to validate the correct procedure for the correct patient at the correct site. The process requires communication among all members of the surgical or procedure team and should be initiated by a designated team member. No procedure should begin if any member of the team has concerns.
>
> *Sources*: Joint Commission (2016); Pellegrini (2017).

clear questions. Physicians also need feedback from nurses, pharmacists, and others to ensure proper communication so that the correct service, medication, and treatment are provided. Clearly, feedback is highly important in healthcare (Institute for Healthcare Improvement 2020; Salas and Frush 2013).

Verification is a process to increase feedback and ensure that the information has been received accurately. Verification can be achieved by asking the receiver to repeat the message. Joint Commission International, the prominent accreditation body for healthcare organizations worldwide, encourages providers to include verification in their healthcare processes. The Joint Commission also, as part of their accreditation, requires the use of at least two patient identifiers when caregivers provide services (Joint Commission 2021). The accreditation requirements mandate verification and time-outs (explained in the box on page 289) to direct open communication and ensure consensus of surgical team members before invasive procedures begin.

Nonverbal Communication

nonverbal communication
The process of communicating without words.

As mentioned earlier, much is communicated nonverbally, without words. Nonverbal cues add significant information for the receiver to interpret messages, and these cues are present in all communications. In fact, **nonverbal communication** may more accurately represent the actual message than the words used. In many cases, at the very least, the nonverbal information can overshadow the verbal message and comprise more than half of the meaning conveyed (Arnold and Boggs 2016; Nobilo 2020). As the adjacent box shows, nonverbal communication impeded by medical personal protective equipment can severely hamper communication in healthcare.

Nonverbal communication can be provided in

Nonverbal Communication Challenged by COVID-19

Patients better understand instructions and empathy from their healthcare workers through nonverbal communication. Caregivers do things such as touching, head nodding, smiling, and direct eye contact. The caregiver's body language quickly establishes the setting and atmosphere for the visit. Positive nonverbal communication decreases patient anxiety and improves outcomes. Patients become more trusting, compliant with directions, and communicative.

However, the face coverings required by COVID-19 limit the ability of both the caregiver and patient to understand nonverbal communication. This has especially been true with hospitalized patients. An emergency room doctor in Florida commented that he acutely felt the barriers to communication. "Masks on both sides significantly limits our ability to interpret emotions and a patient's feelings. Not hearing each other through layers is frustrating. Expressing feelings with masks, goggles, face shield and gowns is seriously challenging" (Nobilo 2020). To compensate for this loss, some doctors resorted to drawing smiling faces on their gowns.

many different ways, which can be categorized under the following seven forms (adapted from Pedersen, Miloch, and Laucella 2007):

1. *Physical touching.* Touch can convey a set of meanings. Shaking hands in Western culture communicates hospitality and openness. Likewise, embraces, touching someone's arm, or patting another person's hand all contribute meaning to a message. Touching people can also facilitate their health and recovery (Nobilo 2020).
2. *Gestures.* Movement of the hands, eyes, and body can aid in communication. Gestures express meaning, such as an index finger over one's mouth or a wink. Facial expressions tend to reveal emotional states.
3. *Space.* Proximity may indicate the relationship between parties, through designated personal space, private territory, and seating arrangements. Greater personal space and private territory may signify greater power differentiation. In addition, the distance between individuals suggests the degree of interpersonal relationship. Personal space for close, intimate relationships, reserved for the most trusted and loved ones, may be less than two feet; social space for business communication may range from 5 to 12 feet (Nobilo 2020).
4. *Physical characteristics.* Body size and shape and the type of clothing worn may provide significant nonverbal cues. Assumptions are made regarding people, their occupation, and their status based on their physical characteristics.
5. *Environmental factors.* Physical settings may communicate status, authority, position, and even personality characteristics. Office, work, and home environments influence communication.
6. *Tone:* The tone of speech carries particular messages through speed, volume, intonation, rhythm, rate, and fillers (e.g., *er, um*). Each tends to relay information about the speaker and the message beyond the content of the speech. For instance, impressions of age, personality, occupation, emotional state, and temperament can be conveyed through tone.
7. *Time perception.* How time is perceived and used by people provides added meaning. Who shows up on time, who tends to be late, and how much time people spend with each other all reveal priorities and convey meaning.

A medical provider's body language communicates much to patients and can improve healthcare outcomes. Positive nonverbal communication decreases patient anxiety and gives a patient confidence that a physician better understands. Because of this, patients are more trusting and communicative with their provider. However, providers who do not smile and lack direct eye contact have the opposite effect and have worse patient outcomes. Patients with only a common cold whose doctors provided positive nonverbal communication recovered faster (Nobilo 2020).

Barriers to Effective Communication

Most of us want to be good communicators, but too often our efforts to truly communicate go astray. Effective communication and mutual understanding can be stymied repeatedly along the way. Following are some major barriers:

- *Poor relationships.* Damaged relationships and poor communication go hand in hand. If we do not feel safe with another person our conversation will be guarded, and we will not provide open, understandable feedback.
- *Lack of clarity.* The encoded message may not accurately reflect the intended message. The encoder may fail to consider how the audience will perceive the message and may load the message with ambiguous language and jargon. Never assume your meaning is obvious to others.
- *Individual differences in encoding and decoding.* An individual's experiences, personality traits, and abilities strongly influence how messages are encoded and decoded. Ignoring these factors creates barriers to mutual understanding.
- *Gender.* Overall, women focus on connecting with others and relationship building, while men tend to emphasize status and dominance in conversations. If these tendencies are not adjusted for, communication across genders can be compromised.
- *Perceptions.* Individuals give selective attention to messages and interpret them subjectively, often according to their own preconceived understandings.
- *Culture.* As described later in the chapter, differences in cultural backgrounds inhibit the ability to communicate effectively. Some environments (e.g., Germany, Switzerland, the United States) have low-context cultures that rely on clear verbal communication to transfer intent and meaning, whereas high-context cultures (e.g., some Asian and Latin American cultures) transmit more meaning through physical and relational contexts, social norms, and historical context beyond the verbal message.
- *Silence.* The meaning of silence differs across cultures, but its frequent use as a means to punish and leverage conversations is unconstructive. A communicator who readily moves to silence, and a party's

inability to break that silence, can be a significant barrier to effective communication.
- *Misinterpretation of nonverbal communication.* As discussed earlier, nonverbal communication produces significant meaning, often overshadowing transmitted words. For instance, a message sender may interpret a pursing of lips by the receiver to mean anger rather than deep thought.
- *Defensiveness.* People who feel defensive stop listening and frequently misinterpret messages. Defensive people spend most of their time protecting themselves and justifying their positions rather than achieving understanding.
- *Lack of feedback and clarification.* Assumptions that the message's meaning is obvious and clear often lead to little or no feedback. Absence of consistent feedback methods, such as asking for clarification or paraphrasing the sender's words, can create serious barriers to communication.
- *Seeking to place blame.* If people seek to place blame and determine who is at fault when poor communication occurs, the communication will inevitably break down further.

Impact of Culture on Communication

The relationship between communication and culture is well established. Edward Hall (1959, 169) asserted that "culture is communication and communication is culture." One person taking part in a message cannot hope to enjoy effective communication without understanding the other's culture. Ignoring cultural differences seriously hinders communication.

Nonverbal communication, in particular, can be easily misunderstood and impede the accurate flow of meaning. For example, a gesture as common as smiling or making eye contact can carry far different meanings in different cultures. In Western cultures, smiling signifies happiness, but some Chinese smile when they are discussing a sad or an uncomfortable topic. Likewise, people from Western cultures tend to feel that a lack of eye contact conveys disrespect. Yet some Native American and Asian cultures may deem eye contact—especially with an authority figure—disrespectful (Acello and Hegner 2015). Tossing one's head in the United States usually means a direction, but in Mediterranean countries and most of the Middle East it means "no." Likewise, nodding one's head in the United States means "yes" but in Greece and Bulgaria it signifies "no" (US Department of State 2020).

Managers often have a hard time discerning the source of communication problems because they are not aware of others' cultures. In addition, cultural contrasts vary widely. For example, cultural differences between the United States and many European countries exist but are minimal in comparison to the dissimilarities between US and Asian cultures. As one correspondent explains:

> While you are likely to have some cultural mix-ups as an American visiting European countries, it's nothing compared to Asia, where the proper etiquette or behaviour often seems to be the complete opposite of what it is in America. . . . It is rude to ask new friends or business partners for things directly, to criticise someone in front of their peers, or to contradict or upstage someone. (Jacobs 2019)

Clearly, communication requires mutual understanding. Somewhat counterintuitively, the increasing cultural diversity and globalization of our communities may make achieving this understanding more difficult. However, to successfully communicate, we must not only learn about but also appreciate and respect our differences. Recognizing that people are different and being open minded and accepting of our differences are paramount. In ambiguous settings where you do not know what the cultural norms are, be tentative and follow cues from those with whom you are interacting.

Virtual Communication

Across the globe today, work has increasingly shifted to virtual work groups. The COVID-19 pandemic accelerated this trend, and more and more organizations have adopted virtual work as their norm (Roberts 2020). However, virtual work groups have greater communication challenges because of the physical distance and reduced frequency of interactions among workers. Communication among virtual work groups can suffer as group members have limited nonwork interactions, speak less frequently with each other, and are less attuned to the nonverbal cues of colleagues. Although videoconferencing, as shown in exhibit 14.3, has high information richness, research suggests that video calls do not facilitate good communication within virtual teams. Leaders who manage virtual teams should be aware of the following (Raffoni 2020):

- Interpersonal dynamics are harder to manage. Both for technical reasons and because people are harder to read over video, the appropriate affect, tone, pacing, and facial expressions that we rely on for effective communication in person are more difficult to give and receive virtually, especially in group settings.
- You can easily lose people's attention. It is challenging enough to engage people in a face-to-face meeting, but virtual meetings often come with a plethora of new distractions that you have little control over.

- New skills are required from you. Whether it is managing tech, maintaining strong facilitation skills, or rethinking agendas, virtual is different than in-person.

Successful Communication

Good communicators possess a heightened awareness of their situation and context. They are highly skilled listeners and observers. They can sense the moods, attitudes, and concerns of their audience. In addition, they adapt their messaging to their environment. They know that the ability to communicate successfully is not about the messenger but about the needs and expectations of the recipients and the degree of existing trust and credibility. Positive perceptions of empathy, openness, commitment, and competence will greatly improve communication (Tumpey, Daigle, and Nowak 2018).

Moreover, because people can practice ways to improve their communication, good leaders constantly seek to develop their communication skills. Some of these approaches include the following (Myatt 2012):

- Increase the level of trust. Trust can be earned by always being honest in your communication and following through on your commitments.
- Make your conversations personal and engaging. Demonstrate your concern about your subordinates by addressing their needs.
- Be specific and clear by using simple and concise language. Communicate well so that people not only understand but also cannot misunderstand the message.
- Focus on transferring your key ideas, aligning mutual expectations, and inspiring action.
- Be open minded. Update your assumptions as you obtain more information.
- Listen extensively, especially to different opinions.
- Show empathy for others, be authentic, and demonstrate transparency.
- Seek to understand the underlying message that may not be communicated with words.
- Be a technical expert on the subject being communicated.
- Speak to groups as individuals.
- Be willing and prepared to change the message if necessary.

Successful communication moves a conversation to **dialogue**—the free flow of meaning between two or more people. The more people share their ideas, feelings, thoughts, and opinions, the greater their understanding and shared meaning. Greater meaning can be shared when trust and a

dialogue
The free flow of meaning between two or more people.

sense of safety exist. When people feel unsafe and at risk, they are not secure enough to deal with difficult conversations. To make others feel safe, establish mutual purpose, trust, and respect (Tumpey, Daigle, and Nowak 2018).

Chapter Summary

Communication—the transmission of information and meaning from one individual or group to another—is a critical skill for any manager or leader and is a primary function of the position. The communication process involves a two-way method whereby a sender encodes and transmits information to a receiver, who decodes the message, gives it meaning, and provides feedback to the sender. Although the process appears simple, communicating with others is a challenge for all of us. Poor communication engenders stress in relationships and can lead to errors in process or outcomes. Healthcare professionals frequently use terms that patients fail to understand. This and other communication shortcomings often lead to the errors that occur in hospitals and other healthcare settings.

The communication channel should match the complexity and importance of the message and the information richness required. High degrees of information richness convey more nonverbal information. Highly important and complex messages should be transmitted through information-rich channels, such as face-to-face meetings.

Decoding takes place when the receiver assigns meaning to a message. As with encoding, decoding is highly influenced by the receiver's personal characteristics and traits, which may lead to misinterpreting the sender's true meaning. Noise surrounds the entire communication process and distracts and diminishes the effectiveness of communication.

Feedback is essential for successful communication. Conveyed through a two-way process, feedback allows the sender and receiver to acknowledge that the message was properly transmitted. It informs the sender about how the receiver interpreted the message and permits timely adjustments to clarify and validate the message's intended meaning. Communication without feedback leads to a one-way conversation that may cause serious problems. Patient safety processes require two-way communication to ensure that proper, high-quality services, medications, and treatments are provided.

Nonverbal messages make up a lot of any interpersonal communication. Some experts suggest that almost two-thirds of perceived meaning comes from nonverbal communication. The seven forms of nonverbal communication are physical touching, gestures, space, physical characteristics, environmental factors, tone, and time perception.

Many barriers can impede good communication. Some of the major barriers include poor relationships, lack of clarity, individual differences in encoding and decoding, gender, perceptions, culture, silence, misinterpretation of nonverbal communication, defensiveness, lack of feedback and clarification, and seeking to place blame. Any or all of these can prevent successful communication.

Differing cultures between senders and receivers can create significant challenges to communication. Ignoring cultural differences often seriously hinders communication. Cultures can differ in many ways, especially regarding nonverbal communication. Facial expressions, eye contact, and many other behaviors have a variety of meanings depending on the communicators' culture. Successful communicators recognize such differences and act accordingly.

More and more work is being accomplished through virtual work groups. Virtual work groups may increase communication challenges, as distance between members leads to less formal and practically no informal contact. Virtual work groups must make efforts to increase their interpersonal interactions to create a team identity. This sense of affiliation may be accomplished, in part, with available social media.

Successful communicators possess a heightened awareness of their situation and context. They listen and observe. They sense their audience's moods, attitudes, and concerns and adapt their messages accordingly. Good leaders should constantly strive to improve their communication skills. They should seek to improve trust, engage people in their conversations, work to deliver specific and clear messages, and focus on transferring key ideas. They should also be open minded, listen, and show empathy for others' points of view. In addition, good leaders speak to groups as individuals and, more than any other characteristic, are willing and prepared to change their message as needed.

Successful communication moves a conversation to dialogue, which brings people to a mutual understanding and shared meaning. Mutual understanding and shared meaning can only exist when trust and safety are present.

Unsafe communication environments place people at risk, which diminishes their ability to operate effectively. Mutual purpose, trust, and respect should be established to create a safe environment in which communication and dialogue can reside.

Chapter Questions

1. What is the difference between two-way communication and one-way communication?
2. What problems can occur with encoding a message?
3. How does the selection of a communication channel relate to information richness?

4. How is the speed to convey a message related to information richness?
5. How has today's environment increased the amount of noise that can impede communication?
6. How has feedback been incorporated in patient safety processes?
7. Why is nonverbal communication misinterpreted?
8. How can the lack of trust destroy communication?
9. How can communication problems within virtual work groups be addressed?
10. In what ways can you improve your communication skills?

Chapter Cases

Disloyal Support of Change?

St. John's Hospital is in the middle of major changes to reposition the organization in their market. Its operating margin has steadily deteriorated over the last few years; last year the hospital experienced a 4.5 percent loss. The previous CEO retired two years ago and Peter, the new CEO, has decided that drastic action is needed. After reading about a new style of change management focused on rapid process improvement, he decided to organize and implement major changes to put the hospital back in the black.

Peter created four nine-person committees, one to redesign each of the hospital's primary processes—financial, ancillary, nursing, and support. He hired a consulting firm to work with the committees and set the goal of a 20 percent cost reduction in all areas. Because Peter wanted novel ideas, he refused to allow area leaders and supervisors to participate in the committees and the redesign discussions. Each team was given 60 days to develop their recommendations.

About 40 days into the committee process, draft recommendations began circulating in the hospital. Many of the department managers became very concerned that the proposals they were seeing were not feasible. For instance, one committee was proposing that materials purchasing be decentralized and each major department take responsibility for their own purchases. When the director of purchasing, Fred, first raised his concerns about this in a department meeting, Peter told him not to worry, everything would work out.

Two weeks later, the committees had started making formal presentations on their proposals, and yet no material changes had been made. At the department meeting after the first presentation, Fred again raised his concerns. This time Peter became red and tense. Quietly and calmly, Peter said that only loyal managers should be working at their hospital, and that leaders needed to get on or off the bus. Those speaking against the changes would be considered disloyal.

After the department meeting this week, Peter is now certain that everyone agrees with him. There have been no further concerns voiced over his proposed changes.

Case Questions:
1. What did Peter communicate during the first department meeting?
2. In the second department meeting, what verbal and nonverbal communication occurred? Even though Peter's voice was calm, what message was sent by his nonverbal communication?
3. In the third department meeting, did Peter communicate well with his department leaders? Was the lack of feedback a sign of positive communication? Why?

Unsafe Patient Care — The Result of Poor Communication

Healthcare organizations have invested in many tools to promote patient safety, but are they effective without good communication skills? Checklists, handoff protocols, warning systems, severity indexes, and other tools alone may not address the patient safety issues that face our healthcare system. Nurses, especially in critical care areas, are confronted by these challenges daily. Often, because of the political and emotional stress that occurs when nurses raise issues with physicians, the resulting silence "undermines the effectiveness of current safety tools." The choice to avoid a conversation can create organizational silence that leads to unfavorable results.

A 2010 study conducted by VitalSmarts, the American Association of Critical-Care Nurses, and the Association of periOperative Registered Nurses showed that more than half of nurses had experienced situations in which they felt unsafe to speak up or unable to get others to listen to them, with almost 20 percent encountering this situation multiple times a month. The incidents fell into three general categories: dangerous shortcuts, displays of incompetence, and demonstrations of disrespect. These issues were reported by more than 80 percent of nurses.

Although dangerous shortcuts and incompetence clearly may harm patients, disrespect is also important because it prevents nurses from presenting their opinion and communicating their concerns and problems. Only a small number of nurses (less than 15 percent) reported speaking up. One of the stories from the report illustrates the depth of the problem:

> During the surgical safety checklist, we realized the permit and the scheduled surgery did not match (wrong side). We tried to stop the doctor (plastic surgeon) and he said the permit was wrong. The patient was already asleep and he proceeded

to do the wrong side against what the patient had verified, which had matched the permit. We could not get any support from the supervisor or anesthesiologist. The surgeon completed the case. Nothing was ever done. We felt awful because there was no support from management to stop this doctor. What is the point of having a checklist when it is not consistently followed? We felt absolutely powerless to being an advocate for the patient. (Maxfield et al. 2015, 5)

Breaking the silence that surrounds these incidents is critical for improving patient care. Specific recommendations were made in the report to create a culture of safety that invites communication and allows people to express their concerns. These recommendations included the following:

1. Identify crucial moments that put safety protocols at risk.
2. Define vital behaviors that keep patients safe.
3. Develop a playbook as a strategy to implement vital behaviors.

The ability to improve quality of patient care and ensure patient safety goes beyond the presence of safety tools and hinges primarily on the organizational culture that permits communication regarding difficult issues. Nurses, in particular, face these challenges in our healthcare system, and efforts need to be made to address these needs.

Source: Adapted from Maxfield et al. (2015).

Case Questions
1. How does poor communication result in silence? How does this happen in healthcare?
2. How do patient safety tools become ineffective when employees do not feel free to fully communicate?
3. What should an organization do to improve its culture of open communication?

Chapter Activity

The first step in improving communication skills is understanding where you are starting. These activities should get you thinking deeply about your current skill set, strengths that will help you, and areas you should begin to improve.

1. Take the MindTools communication quiz "How Good Are Your Communication Skills?" (www.mindtools.com/pages/

article/newCS_99.htm). Write a one-page paper describing your communication strengths and weaknesses.
2. Take the Science of People "Body Language Quiz" (www.scienceofpeople.com/quiz/) on nonverbal communication. Write a one-page paper about the body language in the quiz. Do you agree with the answers provided by the quiz? Did you miss any questions? Why?

References

Acello, B., and B. Hegner. 2015. *Nursing Assistant: A Nursing Process Approach*, 11th ed. Boston: Cengage Learning.

Arnold, E., and K. Boggs. 2016. *Interpersonal Relationships: Professional Communication Skills for Nurses*, 7th ed. St. Louis, MO: Saunders.

Bailey, M. 2016. "Communication Failures Linked to 1,744 Deaths in Five Years, US Malpractice Study Finds." *STAT*, February 1. www.statnews.com/2016/02/01/communication-failures-malpractice-study/.

Bradberry, T. 2020. "8 Ways to Read Someone's Body Language." *Inc.* (blog), May 4. www.inc.com/travis-bradberry/8-great-tricks-for-reading-peoples-body-language.html.

Cabral-Isabedra, C. 2016. "Only 5 Percent of Patients with Advanced Cancer Understand Their Prognosis." *Tech Times*, May 24. www.techtimes.com/articles/160537/20160524/only-5-percent-of-patients-with-advanced-cancer-understand-their-prognosis.htm.

Conor, A. 2020. *Body Language: Body Language and Non-Verbal Communication*. N.p.: Red Kite Publishing.

Daft, R., and R. Lengel. 1984. "Information Richness: A New Approach to Managerial Behavior and Organizational Design." In *Research in Organizational Behavior*, edited by L. Cummings and B. Staw, 191–233. Homewood, IL: JAI Press.

Davis, T., N. Dolan, M. Ferreira, C. Tomori, K. Green, A. Sipler, and C. Bennett. 2001. "The Role of Inadequate Health Literacy Skills in Colorectal Cancer Screening." *Cancer Investigation* 19 (2): 193–200.

Fisher, N. 2017. "10 Ways Lack of Communication Is Ruining Healthcare." *Forbes* (blog). Published May 2. www.forbes.com/sites/nicolefisher/2017/05/02/10-ways-lack-of-communication-is-ruining-health-care/.

Goo, S. K. 2015. "The Skills Americans Say Kids Need to Succeed in Life." *Pew Research Center*, February 19. http://pewrsr.ch/17uuKR8.

Hall, E. 1959. *The Silent Language*. New York: Random House.

Heath, S. 2018. "Patient Recall Suffers as Patients Remember Half of Health Info." *Patient EngagementHIT*, March 26. https://patientengagementhit.com/news/patient-recall-suffers-as-patients-remember-half-of-health-info.

Institute for Healthcare Improvement. 2020. "Provide Feedback to Front-Line Staff." *Changes* (blog). www.ihi.org/resources/Pages/Changes/ProvideFeedbacktoFrontLineStaff.aspx.

Jacobs, H. 2019. "15 Culture Clashes I've Had as an American Traveling in Asia." *Business Insider*, December 17. www.businessinsider.com/culture-clashes-american-traveling-in-asia-china-japan-korea-indonesia-2019-5.

Joint Commission. 2021. "National Patient Safety Goals January 2021." www.jointcommission.org/-/media/tjc/documents/standards/national-patient-safety-goals/2021/npsg_chapter_hap_jan2021.pdf.

———. 2020. "Quick Safety 29: Advancing Patient–Provider Communication and Activating Patients." www.jointcommission.org/resources/news-and-multimedia/newsletters/newsletters/quick-safety/quick-safety-issue-29-advancing-patientprovider-communication-and-activating-patients/advancing-patient-provider-communication-and-activating-patients/.

———. 2016. "Universal Protocol." www.jointcommission.org/standards_information/up.aspx.

Kumar, R. 2010. *Basic Business Communication*. New Delhi: Excel.

Landry, L. 2020. "8 Essential Leadership Communication Skills." *Business Insights* (blog). Harvard Business School Online. https://online.hbs.edu/blog/post/leadership-communication.

Maxfield, D., J. Grenny, R. Lavandero, and L. Groah. 2015. "The Silent Treatment: Why Safety Tools and Checklists Aren't Enough to Save Lives." Accessed July 23.

Myatt, M. 2012. "10 Communication Secrets of Great Leaders." *Forbes* (blog). Published April 4. www.forbes.com/sites/mikemyatt/2012/04/04/10-communication-secrets-of-great-leaders/.

Nobilo, B. 2020. "Coronavirus Has Stolen Our Most Meaningful Ways to Connect." CNN. https://edition.cnn.com/interactive/2020/06/world/coronavirus-body-language-wellness/.

Parker, K., and L. Rainie. 2020. "Americans and Lifetime Learning in the Knowledge Age." *Trend* (Spring 2020). Published April 13. https://pew.org/2JiTqle.

Pedersen, P., K. Miloch, and P. Laucella. 2007. *Strategic Sport Communication*. Champaign, IL: Sheridan.

Pellegrini, C. A. 2017. "Time-Outs and Their Role in Improving Safety and Quality in Surgery." *Bulletin of the American College of Surgeons*, June 1. https://bulletin.facs.org/2017/06/time-outs-and-their-role-in-improving-safety-and-quality-in-surgery/.

Pitt, M. B., and M. A. Hendrickson. 2019. "Eradicating Jargon-Oblivion—A Proposed Classification System of Medical Jargon." *Journal of General Internal Medicine* 35: 1861–64. https://doi.org/10.1007/s11606-019-05526-1.

Quester, P., R. McGuiggan, W. Perreault, and J. McCarthy. 2007. *Marketing: Creating and Delivering Value*, 5th ed. North Ryde, Australia: McGraw-Hill/Irwin.

Raffoni, M. 2020. "5 Questions That (Newly) Virtual Leaders Should Ask Themselves." *Harvard Business Review* digital article, May 1. https://hbr.org/2020/05/5-questions-that-newly-virtual-leaders-should-ask-themselves.

Roberts, M. 2020. "Reconfiguring the Modern Office: Making the Shift to Virtual Long Term" *Communications Council* (blog). *Forbes.* June 4. www.forbes.com/sites/forbescommunicationscouncil/2020/06/04/reconfiguring-the-modern-office-making-the-shift-to-virtual-long-term/.

Salas, E., and K. Frush. 2013. *Improving Patient Safety Through Teamwork and Team Training.* New York: Oxford University Press.

Soffar, H. 2020. "Principles of Communication in Healthcare: Encoding, Decoding and What Do We Communicate?" *Online Sciences* (blog). Published July 8. www.online-sciences.com/health/principles-of-communication-in-healthcare-encoding-decoding-what-do-we-communicate/.

Tumpey, A. J., D. Daigle, and G. Nowak. 2018. "Communicating During an Outbreak or Public Health Investigation." *CDC Field Epidemiology Manual.* Last reviewed December 13. www.cdc.gov/eis/field-epi-manual/chapters/Communicating-Investigation.html.

US Department of State. 2020. "Cross-Cultural Communication" (at "Gestures"). So You're an American? A Guide to Answering Difficult Questions Abroad. www.state.gov/courses/answeringdifficultquestions/html/app.htm?p=module3_p2.htm.

Zandan, N. 2020. "How Much of Our Workdays Do We Spend Communicating?" *Quantified Communications* (blog). www.quantifiedcommunications.com/blog/how-much-of-our-workday-do-we-spend-communicating.

CHAPTER 15

LEADERSHIP THEORIES AND STYLES

> Midwest Regional Physician's Clinic had many CEOs in its long history, but this one was different. Almost immediately, Leroy Paul gained the trust of his employees. He listened intently. He followed through with things he could change and was honest about those he could not. He was transparent with his board, his management team, and his staff. No one seemed to be surprised by Leroy's decisions, because he made his intentions clear. Even the clinic's physicians seemed to get behind him. He was far from perfect, but Leroy had a vision and most of the stakeholders at Midwest had bought in. It was no surprise to the community that when the COVID-19 pandemic hit home, Leroy was able to rally the troops to protect the clinic's healthcare workers and patients, get the personal protective equipment they needed, and set up a center that soon tested thousands of individuals in the fight against the disease.

Learning Objectives

After studying this chapter, readers should be able to

- appraise the five major leadership theories and their leadership styles,
- discuss the importance of having a clear vision for transformational leaders,
- summarize the difficulty in precisely defining leadership,
- distinguish trait theory from other leadership theories,
- explain the Blake and Mouton managerial grid,
- identify the differences between leaders and managers,
- explain the components of contingency theory,
- discuss transactional leadership and path–goal theory,
- appraise transformational leadership and its current importance in management thought,
- recognize the unique challenges of leading millennials,
- describe the role leadership played in the COVID-19 pandemic,

- state the critical importance of charisma in transformational leadership, and
- explain the need for succession planning in transformational leadership.

Key Terms

- authentic leadership
- behavior theory
- contingency theory
- ethical leadership
- great man theory
- leader–member exchange theory
- path–goal theory
- servant leadership
- situational leadership
- trait theory
- transactional leadership
- transformational leadership

The healthcare industry needs good leaders. Escalating costs, concerns regarding quality of care, and limited access for some patient populations plague healthcare internationally. Greater competition and regulation, coupled with demands for increased accountability, are common challenges, and leadership is desperately needed to change existing structures and processes and adapt to the new demands and conditions. Too often, organizations maintain cumbersome bureaucracies and embedded, powerful, self-interested groups. Dynamic leaders are required to create agile, patient-focused, and cost-effective systems of care.

The perspective of what leadership is and where it originated has evolved over the past century. Understanding the development of leadership theory allows us to see the evolution in our understanding of who leaders are and what creates them. Since the turn of the twentieth century, the study of leadership theory has included five major schools of thought (Antonakis, Cianciolo, and Sternberg 2004):

1. Trait
2. Behavior
3. Contingency, contextual, or situational
4. Transactional
5. Transformational

Each theory is reviewed in this chapter, and the last—transformational theory—is considered in more depth to address its unique and highly applicable insights.

Defining Leadership

Originally, a leader was someone who held a title, such as a head of state, monarch, magistrate, or military commander. The concept of a *leader* is ancient. Great literary and religious volumes—such as those written by Aristotle, Aśoka, Confucius, Plato, Shakespeare, and Tennyson, along with texts describing the lives of numerous pharaohs and Greek heroes—ruminated on the role, characteristics, and nature of the leader (Northouse 2007). Historically, one constant prevails: The leader's position differentiates this individual from the other members of society.

The term *leadership*, however, is a relatively new addition to the English language. It first appeared only within the past 200 years (Yukl 1981) and denotes a set of characteristics or behaviors unique to a leader. Although a relatively new concept, leadership has become a prominent area of business study. For example, a survey conducted by Burns (1995) identified more than 130 definitions of leadership; the world-famous New York Public Library has tens of thousands of biographies, monographs, and newspaper clippings on the topic.

However, defining *leadership* has been difficult. Many years ago, Warren Bennis wrote:

> Always, it seems, the concept of leadership eludes us or turns up in another form to taunt us again with its slipperiness and complexity. So we have invented an endless proliferation of terms to deal with it . . . and still the concept is not sufficiently defined. (Bennis 1959, 260)

An older definition that remains applicable is, "Leadership may be considered as the process (act) of influencing the activities of an organized group in its efforts toward goal setting and goal achievement" (Stogdill 1950, 3). As seen in the theories discussed throughout this chapter, the concept of influencing a group of people toward achieving goals is thoroughly intertwined with leadership.

Contemporary leadership study can be divided into five overlapping periods, which align with the five types of theory introduced earlier: the trait period (1920s to 1940s), the behavioral period (1940s to 1960s), the contingency or situational period (1960s to present), the transactional period (1970s onward), and the transformational period (1980s onward) (Antonakis, Cianciolo, and Sternberg 2004; Van Maurik 2001). A study of 752 articles led Dinh and colleagues (2014) to rank transformational leadership as the theory most often studied among the papers they reviewed.

Trait Theory

Trait theorists of the 1920s defined leaders as those endowed with superior characteristics and traits that differentiate them from their followers. These traits resulted in behaviors found in successful leaders (Cherry 2021). The conventional wisdom during this period held that "history is handmaiden to men; great men actually change the shape and direction of history" (Van Wart 2005, 6).

The common reference to the **great man theory** (Antonakis, Cianciolo, and Sternberg 2004) ascribed the shaping of history to exceptionally gifted individuals with certain dispositional characteristics (Zaccaro, Kemp, and Bader 2004). The traits most prominently mentioned in early literature include physical characteristics (e.g., height, appearance, energy level), personality (e.g., self-esteem, dominance, emotional stability), and ability (e.g., verbal fluency, intelligence, originality, social insight) (Yukl 1981).

Critics of **trait theory** suggested that leadership traits might be effective on the battlefield or in public life but not necessarily in other settings (Chemers 1995). Ultimately, most felt that traits had only a weak impact on determining whether people become leaders. One study attempted to identify superior traits of performers but concluded that the single unique characteristic was that they were tall (Van Maurik 2001).

Today, the popular literature still frequently considers the question of whether a leader is born rather than made (nature versus nurture) and explores specific traits exhibited by contemporary leaders. For instance, Sir Bernard Ingham, president of the British Franchise Association, in a 2001 interview, attributed the success of former UK prime minister Margaret Thatcher to five qualities or traits: ideological security, moral courage, constancy, iron will, and low need for love. Some have even hinted at the existence of a leadership gene (Van Maurik 2001).

great man theory
A perspective that exceptionally gifted individuals with prominent traits—such as physical characteristics, personality, and ability—have affected history.

trait theory
The theory that personality traits and characteristics result in certain successful leadership behaviors.

Behavior Theory

By the 1940s, the focus of leadership theory shifted from a leader's traits to a leader's behavior, which marked the beginning of **behavior theory** in the study of leadership. The great man perspective was replaced by ranges of leadership styles available to a manager. Following the sudden entry of the United States into World War II, the military needed to train officers and noncommissioned officers as quickly and effectively as possible (Van Maurik 2001). The military presumed that leadership could be taught, so it engaged theorists to identify the ideal leadership behaviors.

behavior theory
The theory that proposes two categories of leadership behaviors: employee-oriented leadership and production-oriented leadership.

Work by researchers at Ohio State University and the University of Michigan resulted in a large-scale, comprehensive analysis of leadership behaviors. The Ohio State researchers broadly defined two categories of behavior: employee-oriented (consideration) leadership and production-oriented (initiating) leadership (Antonakis, Cianciolo, and Sternberg 2004; Van Wart 2005).

The University of Michigan study also categorized leadership behaviors, and separated relationship-oriented behaviors in a third category, called *participative leadership*. Participative leadership was described as "managing group processes constructively, especially information flow, meetings, and decision-making" (Van Wart 2005, 352).

The intent of these two studies was to discover what leadership behaviors lead to effective group performance (Schriesheim and Kerr 1976; Yukl 1981). Blake and Mouton (1965) built on these works and presented one of the first theories that applied a behavioral orientation to leadership. Their theory used two dimensions—concern for people and concern for production—on a "managerial grid" (exhibit 15.1). The ideal leader displays high levels of concern in both dimensions, while impoverished leaders show little concern for either (Van Maurik 2001). To ascertain numerical scores, individuals answer survey questions that represent their level of concern for people and production.

Henry Mintzberg (1973) added to the study of behavior theory by defining leadership roles that exist within a team, such as figurehead, leader,

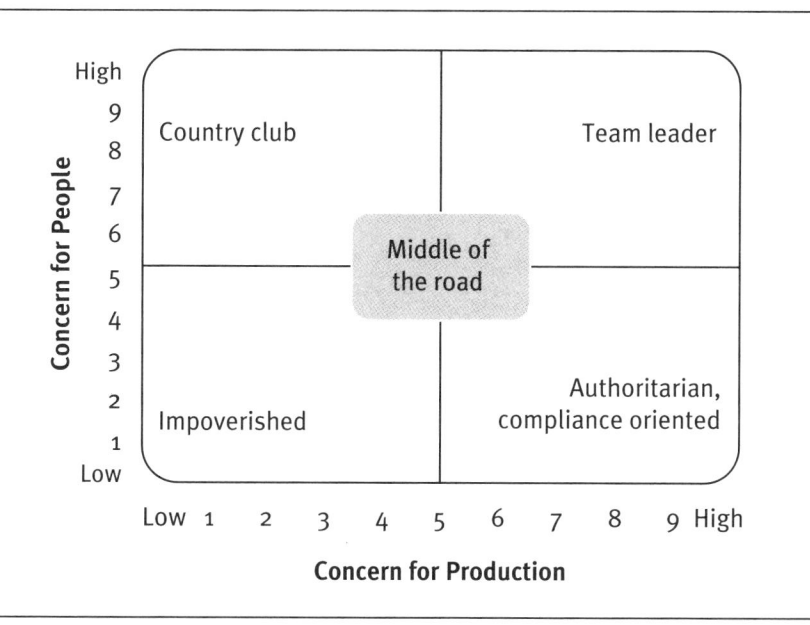

EXHIBIT 15.1
Blake and Mouton's Managerial Grid

Source: Adapted from Blake and Mouton (1965).

liaison, monitor, disseminator, spokesperson, entrepreneur, disturbance handler, resource allocator, and negotiator. Mintzberg's work also highlighted the differences between managers and leaders. Leadership and management are frequently seen as complementary, but require different competencies. Managers have subordinates; leaders have partners. Managers seek to do what is right, plan and budget, organize and staff, control and solve problems, and produce order. Leaders, on the other hand, desire to do what is right, establish a vision of the future, innovate, inspire, motivate, and produce change (Porter-O'Grady and Malloch 2016).

Contingency Theory

contingency theory
The theory that the best leadership style should be considered for the situation and context.

By the 1960s, leadership theorists began to focus on the situation and environment in which a leader functions (Antonakis, Cianciolo, and Sternberg 2004). **Contingency theory** suggests that the best leadership style depends on the situation and context (Chemers 1995). Different situations require different kinds of leadership (Northouse 2007). Three situational features include leader–member relations, task structure, and position power (Schriesheim and Kerr 1976). Contingency-oriented leadership theories also address leadership decision-making style as it relates to group performance and morale. The most effective style of leadership is dictated by the characteristics of the situation (Antonakis, Cianciolo, and Sternberg 2004; Chemers 1995; Yukl 1981). As shown in the box, leader–member relations and position power leadership styles can be assessed through a variety of means.

Pop leadership literature began to emerge when Kenneth Blanchard translated earlier work on leadership theory into stylized contingency theory wrapped in popularized writings, publishing such titles as *The One Minute Manager*, *High Five!*, and *Whale Done!* Blanchard suggested that the leader's style is most effective when it meets the demands of the situation confronting the leader (Van Maurik 2001).

Ayman (2004, 163) summarized the premise of contingency theory as follows: "Most of the theories and models in the contingency approach consider the situation as the contingent factor that interacts with the leader's characteristics, be they traits or behaviors." Furthermore, effective leadership is said to be contingent on

> **An Informal Indicator of Leadership Style**
>
> As part of consulting engagements, one of the authors would often visit hospitals. In preparation for these trips, he would request to view the healthcare organization's newsletters for the previous six months. Although not a scientific approach to fact-finding, the frequency with which the hospital CEO's picture appeared in the publication was an uncannily accurate way to quickly gauge leadership style. Those executives with few photos often were much more participative, and conversely, those who appeared frequently were more authoritarian.

the ability of a leader to match style and situation. The right leader needs to be in place for the situation (Northouse 2007).

Transactional Leadership and Situational Leadership

Transactional leadership embraces a more sophisticated approach to situational and contingency variables. This theory examines the influence and behaviors of those being led (Wren and Swatez 1995) and their interactions with leaders. Transactional theorists recognize that people are at different levels of motivation and they hold different degrees of power potential. They suggest leaders understand and use that in pursuit of a common purpose (Burns 1995). However, the use of rewards and power in transactional exchanges is rooted in the principles of contingency theory (Pearce, Yoo, and Alavi 2004).

> **transactional leadership**
> The theory that examines the influences and behaviors of those being led and their interactions with leaders through both rewards and punishments.

Leadership study pioneer James MacGregor Burns observed that most leadership research was focused on transactional interactions:

> Leadership, unlike naked power-wielding, is thus inseparable from followers' needs and goals. The essence of the leader–follower relation is the interaction of persons with different levels of motivation and of power potential, including skill, in pursuit of a common or at least joint purpose. (Burns 1978, 17)

The environment was thought to play an important role in the emergence of a leader and organizational leadership (Bass 1990).

Situational leadership theories help direct leaders in how to behave in different circumstances. Situational leadership suggests that effective leaders need to understand their environment or situation and respond with a style that matches the existing need. Much of modern leadership training has been based on this concept. According to the work of Hersey and Blanchard (1969), the core premise of this theory is that effective leaders must adapt their leadership style to their organizational context, and that to do so they must be capable of using different leadership styles and aligning them appropriately with the situation. Key environmental factors include subordinates' abilities, maturity, relationships, and motivations and the nature of the tasks and goals confronting them (Hersey, Blanchard, and Johnson 1996). As discussed in chapter 20, leaders delegate differently depending on their subordinates' needs, situations, and abilities.

> **situational leadership**
> The theory that effective leaders need to understand their environment or situation and respond with a style that matches the existing need.

Different leadership theories have evolved from situational and transactional leadership perspectives. A few that have received significant attention are Fiedler's contingency theory (1964), the path–goal theory (House 1996), the leader–member exchange theory (Graen and Uhl-Bien 1995), and equity theory (Adams 1965).

Fiedler's contingency theory integrates the people, process, and situation to suggest that effective leaders balance task and relationship motivation depending on three situational elements: (1) the leader–follower relationship, or the extent to which the leader demonstrates friendliness with subordinates and gains their trust and respect; (2) the degree of structure in the work; and (3) the position power of the leader, which entails the amount of formal power and influence to reward and punish (Fiedler 1964). The theory proposes that the autocratic decisions and directive styles by which leaders tell followers what to do are more likely to work when the leaders know exactly what to tell their subordinates (Chemers 1995).

The **path–goal theory** of leadership explores how leaders motivate subordinates to accomplish designated goals. It considers both employee and environmental factors to suggest which leadership style would be most effective. According to this theory, a leader's primary role is to set clear goals and remove obstacles that impede those goals (House 1977). It suggests the following four leadership styles that a leader can employ depending on the situation (Barker 1992; Rue and Byars 2009):

path–goal theory
The theory that considers both employee and environmental factors to suggest which leadership style would be most effective.

1. *Directive*—sets clear expectations and goals for employees; suggested for ambiguous tasks
2. *Supportive*—shows concern for employees; suggested for stressful and unpleasant work environments
3. *Participative*—seeks input and suggestions for decisions; suggested for when employees are highly invested and decisions or work may be ambiguous
4. *Achievement oriented*—sets goals for and demonstrates confidence in subordinates; suggested for work that is nonrepetitive and unclear

Good leaders recognize and fill in what is missing in the environment or their subordinates. In effect, successful leaders adjust their leadership behaviors to meet their employees' abilities contingent on the nature of work and group dynamics (exhibit 15.2). Behaviors may include setting and clarifying the goals and standards as well as the rewards for achieving them, mentoring and coaching, supporting through concern and friendly behavior, encouraging teamwork, inviting participative decision-making, representing the group, and providing a vision.

leader–member exchange theory
The theory that presents a complex, relationship-based approach to leadership, making the interaction between leader and member the focal point of the leadership process.

A unique view of the transactional interchange between leaders and members is part of the **leader–member exchange theory**. This theory presents a complex, relationship-based approach to leadership, making the interaction between leader and member the focal point of the leadership process. Group members make contributions and continue with these interactions because they perceive a mutual benefit (Graen and Uhl-Bien 1995).

EXHIBIT 15.2
House's Path–Goal Leader Behaviors

Leader's Behaviors	Leader's Actions
Path–goal clarifying	Communicates what is expected, sets performance standards, schedules activities, rewards positively or negatively on the basis of performance
Achievement oriented	Sets challenging goals, drives improvement and excellence, demonstrates confidence in employees' abilities, encourages pride in work
Work facilitation	Mentors and coaches to improve employees' skills, removes barriers, facilitates and empowers employees' work
Supportive	Acts friendly, shows concern for employees, treats them as equals
Interaction facilitation	Communicates and encourages teamwork, resolves conflict, promotes positive relationships among employees
Group-oriented decision-making	Invites decision-making participation, obtains and shares needed information for decisions
Representation and networking	Acts as a representative for the organization, fills ceremonial roles, develops and maintains relationships with influential parties
Values-based	Creates and shares a vision, demonstrates confidence to achieve the vision, provides feedback

Source: Adapted from House (1996).

Both equity theory and expectancy theory, discussed in chapter 7, attempt to determine the conscious choices made by both leaders and followers, and the rewards they expect. These leadership theories provide insights into how leaders interact and function. The dynamics of transactional leadership have been expressed as a psychological contract between the leader and followers that depends on both parties' expectations and actions. The leader contributes value to those who are led, and in exchange, members return value to the leader. The degree and significance of this social exchange is the foundation of transactional leadership theory (Hollander 1987).

Transformational Leadership

Many contemporary observers felt that transactional theory did not transcend self-interest in leadership. Transformational leadership has been seen as the bridge to cover that gap.

transformational leadership
The theory that leaders inspire and motivate followers to pursue outcomes centered on a sense of purpose and an idealized mission.

In contrast to leadership theories positing that leaders and followers enter transactional relationships to effect change, **transformational leadership theory** suggests that leaders inspire and motivate followers to pursue outcomes centered on a sense of purpose and an idealized mission (Sashkin 2004). This theory better addresses the skills needed to lead today's workforce, with its focus on visionary, charismatic, and inspirational leader characteristics. Transformational leadership theory has been used extensively by modern researchers to explore why some organizations create high-performing work environments and some do not (Kouzes and Posner 2006).

Burns's (1978) early work expanded transactional leadership theory to develop the transformational leadership framework (Antonakis, Cianciolo, and Sternberg 2004). He stressed that transforming leaders empower individuals and organizations to embrace the mission and vision. In so doing, leaders champion and inspire their followers (Burns 2003). The nature of this effect is important, as transformational leaders engage in activities that not only change performance but also change the very essence of the organization.

Although no grand or unifying theory provides common direction for researchers on transformational leadership, most scholars agree that one central and unique theme defines the practice of transformational leadership: the creation of a vision (Antonakis, Cianciolo, and Sternberg 2004). A vision is an organizational goal or state of being that transcends previously held conceptual frameworks (Kouzes and Posner 2006). Today, the

---

HCA STORY

By Britt Berrett

In 2005, Hospital Corporation of America (HCA) was the largest private hospital company in the world, with 189 hospitals and outpatient facilities throughout the United States and Europe. Hospitals owned and operated by HCA performed hundreds of thousands of inpatient procedures and treated millions of patients, employing and credentialing almost a quarter million healthcare providers.

As part of an extensive internal study of organizational performance conducted that year, HCA evaluated its 189 hospitals to determine the characteristics of top performers. The goal of the study was "to identify best practices that could increase employee engagement, patient satisfaction, and physician satisfaction throughout the HCA system" (Wolf 2008, 39). It was theorized that high-performing facilities (HPFs) could be identified and performance characteristics could be effectively shared throughout the organization. Eleven HPFs were identified through a performance matrix that included employee engagement, patient satisfaction, nursing measures, employee turnover, and comparative financial measures:

- Greenview Hospital, Bowling Green, Kentucky
- Hendersonville Medical Center, Hendersonville, Tennessee
- Horizon Medical Center, Dickson, Tennessee
- Medical Center of Plano, Plano, Texas
- Medical City Dallas Hospital, Dallas, Texas
- Methodist Ambulatory Surgery Hospital North West, San Antonio, Texas
- Redmond Regional Medical Center, Rome, Georgia
- Round Rock Medical Center, Austin, Texas

(continued)

study of transformational leadership and its acceptance in healthcare is a natural extension of the study of organizational behavior, theory, and design in the industry.

Bass, who extended the idea of transformational leaders, wrote that the way leaders are deemed transformational is measured by the motivation of the followers (Albritton 1998). These followers feel trust and loyalty to such leaders. In other words, transformational leaders embrace a dynamic relationship that elevates both leader and subordinate. Their interactions are more than transactions; they transform each party. As illustrated by the box that tells the HCA Story, top-performing hospitals have visionary leaders who develop deep relationships with their employees, communicate effectively with them, and motivate them.

Charisma

Transformational leadership explains how leaders inspire others to perform beyond expected standards, by developing an emotional attachment between themselves and their followers (Avolio and Yammarino 2002). Originally conceived by Max Weber (1958, 77) in his work on charismatic

---

(continued from previous page)
- Skyline Medical Center, Nashville, Tennessee
- Texas Orthopedic Hospital, Houston, Texas
- West Houston Medical Center, Houston, Texas

Each of these facilities demonstrated top levels of performance overall and with consistency in a three-year period from 2002 to 2004 (Wolf 2008).

HCA undertook a series of on-site visits to these hospitals, conducting nearly 160 personal interviews with senior leadership and directors or managers, 64 focus groups that included more than 700 staff, and almost 2,000 surveys (Wolf 2008). From these sources, the HCA team identified seven central characteristics of HPFs: (1) visionary leadership, (2) consistent and effective communication, (3) selection for fit and ongoing development of staff, (4) agile and open culture, (5) service as job one, (6) constant recognition and community support, and (7) solid physician relationships.

HPFs have significantly higher employee engagement scores, with almost four times as many engaged employees as at low-performing hospitals (5.68 versus 1.63). (The term *engaged employee* is defined by Gallup as an individual who is actively involved in the organization's success and performance [Coffman and Gonzalez-Molina 2002].) Engaged employees are more profitable, more customer focused, safer, and more likely to withstand temptations to leave than nonengaged employees are.

HPFs also see significantly greater employee retention, enjoying 7 percent lower turnover than low performers do. Turnover from 2000 to 2004 decreased by 3.9 percent in HCA's HPFs, and increased 1.4 percent in their low-performing counterparts. Notwithstanding the financial impact of staff turnover, the cultural implications represent a significant issue for an organization (Wolf 2008).

Finally, on average, HPFs enjoy superior financial performance, exceeding low performers over the course of the study by a 5 percent margin. The identification of these characteristics of HPFs makes this study a significant contribution to the literature.

According to a separate internal report (HCA 2005), HPFs generated $15 million more in average profits than their low-performing counterparts, measured by earnings before interest, taxes, depreciation, and amortization (EBITDA) per facility; achieved $32,000 more in revenue per bed; and achieved higher average EBITDA as a percentage of net revenue by six basis points compared to low performers (Wolf 2008).

leadership, this view contends that the leader can inspire followers to an "attitude that is revolutionary and . . . transcends everything."

Charismatic leadership is central to the theory of transformational leadership, as leaders command strong emotional ties that excite, motivate, and inspire their subordinates (Bass 1995). The elements that characterize charismatic leaders are present in transformational leaders. However, transformational leaders are more than inspirational, as they also play the roles of teacher, mentor, coach, reformer, and revolutionary. The transformational leader seeks to engage the full person of the follower and, in so doing, elevates those influenced to a higher level of performance (Bass 1995). Thus, transformational leaders can attract, retain, and promote others, and thereby create a succession of transformational leaders. Conger and Kanungo (1998) concluded that charismatic leaders are perceived as more effective, are given higher performance ratings than other leaders, and have followers who are more motivated and satisfied.

Components of Transformational Leadership

Transformational leadership comprises the following specific characteristics (adapted from Antonakis and House 2002; Bass 1995):

- *Charismatic leadership (or idealized influence)*. Transformational leaders behave in ways that make them role models for their followers. These leaders are admired, respected, and trusted. Followers identify with them and want to emulate them; the leaders are viewed by their followers as having extraordinary capabilities, persistence, and determination. The leaders are willing to take risks and are consistent rather than arbitrary. They can be counted on to do the right thing, demonstrating high standards of ethical and moral conduct.
- *Inspirational motivation*. Transformational leaders behave in ways that motivate and inspire those around them by providing meaning and challenge to their followers' work. Team spirit is aroused. Enthusiasm and optimism are displayed. Leaders involve followers in envisioning attractive future states; they clearly communicate expectations that followers want to meet, and they demonstrate commitment to goals and the shared vision.
- *Intellectual stimulation*. Transformational leaders stimulate their followers' innovative and creative impulses by questioning assumptions, reframing problems, and approaching old situations in new ways. Creativity is encouraged. Individual members are not publicly criticized for their mistakes. Followers are included in the process of addressing problems and finding solutions. Followers are encouraged to try new

approaches, and their ideas are not criticized because they differ from the leaders' ideas.

- *Individualized consideration.* Transformational leaders pay special attention to each follower's needs for achievement and growth by acting as coach or mentor. Followers and colleagues are developed to achieve successively higher levels of potential. Individualized consideration is practiced when new learning opportunities are created and a supportive climate is in place. Differences in individual needs and desires are recognized. The leader's behavior demonstrates acceptance of individual differences (e.g., some employees receive more encouragement, some more autonomy, others firmer standards, and still others more task structure). A two-way exchange in communication is encouraged, and the leader is often found in workspaces, practicing "management by walking around." Interactions with followers are personalized (e.g., the leader remembers previous conversations, is aware of individual concerns, sees the individual as a whole person not just as an employee). The considerate leader listens effectively and delegates tasks as a means of developing followers. Delegated tasks are monitored to see if the followers need additional direction or support and to assess their progress; ideally, followers do not feel they are being checked on.

Transformational leaders can motivate subordinates to higher levels of performance by raising the importance of certain goals, demonstrating the means by which to achieve them, and enticing subordinates to transcend their self-interests to fulfill those goals (Conger and Kanungo 1998). Such leaders transform the needs, values, preferences, and aspirations of followers from self-interests to organizational interests (Shamir, House, and Arthur 1993) because they can motivate and convince their followers to invest additional work and energy into accomplishing extraordinary things (Fuller et al. 1996). Leaders who possess the attributes described in transformational leadership theory experience the staff's heightened enthusiasm for and excitement about shared organizational priorities. Not only are transformational leaders better performers themselves, the people associated with them are better performers and are more satisfied with the performance of their leaders (Cross, Baker, and Parker 2003).

Healthcare today requires strong transformational leaders. The rapid change and uncertainty in the industry creates a need for flexible, competent, charismatic leaders to move their organizations forward. As discussed earlier, the needed changes will only occur with skilled leaders who can establish and maintain a long-term vision that moves their organization to manage the health of populations (Buell 2011). Even financial executives are now expected to provide "a clear vision of success," become inspirational leaders to motivate teams, and actively engage coworkers at every level (Madden

2015, 42). To this end, the American College of Healthcare Executives (ACHE 2021) has developed a competencies assessment tool, which is subdivided into the following competencies:

- Communication and relationship management
- Leadership
- Professionalism
- Knowledge of the healthcare environment
- Business skills and knowledge

Transformational Leadership for a Millennial Workforce

As more and more millennials join the workforce, the effectiveness of transformational leadership is coming into question. Some researchers have begun examining and questioning the differences between millennials and their older colleagues. Three propositions, in particular, should cause leaders to consider how they influence their younger team members (Anderson et al. 2017).

First, millennials tend to focus more on individual goals than organizational goals. Transformational leadership is less focused on how leaders balance the need to achieve corporate goals with employees' personal goals.

Second, millennial employees tend to put less focus on work and more on work–life balance. Transformational leadership doesn't prepare managers to influence such workers.

Third, millennials place more value on extrinsic rewards; they tend to expect rapid promotion, they value rewards and recognition, and are generally willing to

---

COVID-19 and Leadership

Healthcare Executive, published by ACHE, included an article in the November/December 2020 issue suggesting that COVID-19 created "a defining moment for leadership." The author, Jessica Squazzo (2020), asked several healthcare CEOs to describe how they led their organizations during the pandemic. Broad themes emerged from the discussions, such as agility and adaptability, managing uncertainty, shifting to a contingency style of leadership, emotional intelligence, nurturing trust, and leading with humility.

The leaders interviewed for the article described how established culture supported communication and trust, allowing for better response to the pandemic. These leaders found that, rather than making all the decisions themselves, they relied on their employees and team members who were committed to the care of their patients and the mission of the organization. Some of the organizations had learned how to adapt quickly through their experience with previous natural disasters. Many of the executives had developed communication skills, emotional intelligence, and other competencies that they could draw on to tackle the challenges of the pandemic.

Routine workdays changed during the pandemic. Leaders discontinued unimportant meetings. They had to make quick decisions—sometimes without much information or data. They became very focused and did not consider other issues. Face-to-face gatherings were replaced by virtual meetings. Leadership competencies were enhanced as a result, and executives learned to draw on expertise and practices from outside the field of healthcare. Virtual skills were enhanced, and telecommunication will likely be used more in the future.

move from job to job to meet their expectations. They are less likely to be motivated by an inspirational talk or an idealized vision. (Anderson et al. 2017).

Healthcare leaders and researchers need to be aware of these and other shortfalls of transformational leadership theory as they attempt to manage younger employees. These leaders must be able to learn and adapt—skills that became more urgent as the COVID-19 pandemic struck in 2020.

Succession Planning

To sustain an organization, transformational leaders embrace succession planning as a critical element of their leadership behavior. Effective succession planning results from an organization's ability to discern which employees will develop and meet organizational needs and which will not fulfill the company's desired return on its investment.

The value of succession planning is discussed in a report by Development Dimensions International (DDI), a nationally recognized leader in human resource development. It found that the workforce recognizes and appreciates the organization's efforts to promote from within and develop its own people. Employee morale improves, and staff are encouraged to take on responsibility, assume risk, measure outcomes, and grow through their achievements. The DDI report concluded that "growing from within allows an organization to meet both long-term and emergency leadership needs at all levels—it ensures continuity of management" (Byham 2008, 3).

In addition, a 2003 report by the US Government Accountability Office stated that "leading organizations identify, develop, and select successors who are the right people, with the right skills, at the right time for leadership and other key positions" (Mihm 2003, 1). This report identified key practices for effective succession planning that will strengthen current and future organizational capacity. Six of those practices are as follows (adapted from Mihm 2003):

1. *Ensure the active support of top leadership.* Effective succession planning and management have the support and commitment of top leadership. Top leaders not only use these programs to develop, place, and promote individuals but also demonstrate support through adequate funding and staff resources to operate effectively over time.
2. *Link to the strategic plan.* Succession planning and succession management are viewed as strategic tools that focus on current and future needs and develop high-potential staff to meet the organizational mission over the long term. These efforts are integrated with strategic planning.
3. *Identify talent from multiple organizational levels, early in careers, or with critical skills.* High-performing employees are identified at

multiple levels in the organization. Succession planning efforts develop knowledge and skills that are critical in the workplace.

4. *Emphasize developmental assignments in addition to formal training.* Succession planning highlights development or "stretch" assignments in addition to more formal training components. Assignments place candidates in new roles or unfamiliar job environments to strengthen their skills and competencies and broaden their experience.
5. *Address specific human capital challenges, such as diversity, leadership capacity, and retention.* Leading organizations are aware of changing organizational needs and demands. Shifting workforce demographics require agility in responding to diversity needs as well as anticipation of impending retirements. The retention of high-potential staff is important to succession planning.
6. *Facilitate broader transformation efforts.* Succession planning and related management efforts provide resources for organizations to implement change by selecting and developing candidates who embrace a change agenda.

All five theories of leadership add value and assist in understanding what leadership is and how it functions. Exhibit 15.3 provides a brief summary of each theory, along with servant, authentic, and ethical leadership models (discussed in the next section).

EXHIBIT 15.3 Summary of Leadership Theories and Models

Theory/Model	Period	Key Style Factors	Related Concepts
Trait	1920s to 1940s	Leaders are endowed with superior characteristics and traits.	Great man
Behavior	1940s to 1960s	Leaders are characterized by how they behave regarding employee orientation, production, and relations.	Managerial grid
Contingency/ Situational	1960s onward	Leaders apply different styles of leadership in different situations.	"One-minute manager"
Transactional	1970s onward	Leaders are examined in terms of the influence and behaviors of those being led and their interactions with leaders.	Path–goal theory, leader–member exchange theory, equity theory

(continued)

Theory/Model	Period	Key Style Factors	Related Concepts
(continued from previous page)			
Transformational	1980s onward	Leaders use the strength of their vision and personality to inspire followers to change expectations, perceptions, and motivations to achieve common goals.	Charisma, succession planning
Servant	1970s onward	Leaders seek to serve and improve the lives of their employees, customers, and stakeholders.	Vision, trust, charisma
Authentic	2000s onward	Leaders exhibit a positive moral perspective characterized by high ethical standards that guide their decision-making and behavior, as well as consistency among their values, beliefs, and actions.	Self-awareness, self-regulation, transparency, authentic behavior
Ethical	2000s onward	Leaders demonstrate ethical conduct through their personal actions and relationships and promote such conduct to subordinates.	Credibility, authenticity, ethically appropriate

EXHIBIT 15.3 Summary of Leadership Theories and Models *(Continued)*

Emerging Theories

As mentioned early in this chapter, Dinh and colleagues (2014) reviewed 752 articles written prior to 2014 dealing with leadership theory. The research team suggested that emerging theories of leadership fit under broad topics such as strategic leadership; team leadership; contextual, complexity and system perspectives of leadership; and ethical/moral leadership. This final category includes servant, authentic, and ethical leadership theories.

Servant Leadership

Considered by some an extension of transformational leadership and participative management, **servant leadership** is a more values-based view of leaders' optimal behavior and motivations than traditional leadership theory. Rather than leadership being a tool for self-aggrandizement, this theory

servant leadership A values-based view of leadership that views service as the core function of leadership and a moral and ethical imperative.

considers service the core function of leadership and a moral and ethical imperative (Russell and Stone 2002). Servant leadership requires decision makers to let a moral perspective guide their behaviors. "Becoming servant leaders engages us in personal, internal self-change and changes our outward behavior" (Fairholm 1997, 149).

The concept of servant leadership has existed for millennia. Lao-tzu, a Chinese philosopher who lived in the sixth century BCE and is considered the founder of Taoism, admonished leaders to serve. He is credited with saying, "The highest type of ruler is one of whose existence the people are barely aware. . . . The Sage is self-effacing and scanty of words. When his task is accomplished and things have been completed, all the people say, 'we ourselves have achieved it'" (Heskett 2013).

In the modern era, the servant leadership concept began to receive attention after Robert Greenleaf's essay "The Servant as Leader" was published in 1970 (Greenleaf 2003). Leaders who practice this leadership style tend to be more highly regarded by their subordinates, be more productive, and feel better about themselves and their work, compared with leaders who are not "servants" (Grant 2014). Some believe servant leadership is the best model through which to address the many dysfunctional facets of the US healthcare system. Healthcare leaders using a servant leadership style typically engender trust and teamwork among stakeholders that enables lower-cost and more efficient healthcare delivery (Trastek, Hamilton, and Niles 2014).

However, practicing servant leadership can be difficult, and some observers claim that it is rarely done (Heskett 2013). Often, leaders' rewards and incentives encourage self-promotion rather than selfless service. Yet great transformational leaders who leave important legacies encapsulate the principles of servant leadership. Iconic leaders such as Abraham Lincoln, Martin Luther King Jr., Mahatma Gandhi, and Nelson Mandela sacrificed their personal comfort and goals for the good of their countries. They were other-centered, rather than self-centered, and were respected and honored. Leaders can achieve results with autocratic behaviors, which may

---

Unfortunate Legacy of an Autocratic Style

People exhibit different styles of leadership, and the memories they leave often reflect not just the results they achieved but also the way they treated their subordinates. Those not exhibiting the values and traits embodied in servant leadership may end up with an unfortunate legacy.

In the 1950s, Harry Cohn was the president of Columbia Pictures. He was known as an extreme autocrat and managed through intimidation. He was accused of being an absolute monarch and of deploying listening devices to spy on his employees. He screamed at employees and sexually harassed stars. When he died in 1958, over 2,000 people reportedly attended his funeral, many of whom are said to have commented that they attended not to honor Cohn but to confirm that he was really dead.

Source: Chadwick (2015).

seem an easier approach, but as shown in the box, subordinates may end up celebrating the passing of autocratic leaders.

Authentic Leadership and Ethical Leadership

Other, more recent models of leadership that have emerged from the desire for more positive forms are authentic leadership and ethical leadership (Brown, Trevino, and Harrison 2005; George 2003). Without explicit models that establish standards for authenticity and ethics, some believe that holding leaders ethically accountable is difficult (Folger and Cropanzano 2001). Both authentic and ethical leadership models build on many aspects of transformational and servant leadership and extend the emphasis on values-based leadership performance.

Authentic leadership, although still formative, has been defined as

> a pattern of leader behavior that draws upon and promotes both positive psychological capacities and a positive ethical climate, to foster greater self-awareness, an internalized moral perspective, balanced processing of information, and relational transparency on the part of leaders working with followers, fostering positive self-development. (Walumbwa et al. 2008, 94)

authentic leadership An approach to leadership that emphasizes honest relationships with followers and a positive ethical climate.

Ethical leadership continues to be refined from previous leadership models. This general framework has focused primarily on a leader's behavior toward subordinates (Bass and Bass 2008) and has been defined as "the demonstration of normatively appropriate conduct through personal action and interpersonal relationships, and the promotion of such conduct to followers through two-way communication and decision-making" (Brown, Trevino, and Harrison 2005, 120).

ethical leadership A model of leadership that emphasizes trustworthy, fair, and honest personal conduct to promote ethical behaviors in followers.

Like other leadership models, ethical leadership is characterized by those who demonstrate trustworthy, fair, and honest behaviors, but it expands the ethical focus by promoting ethical conduct in employees and colleagues. An ethical leader is "both a moral person and a moral manager" (Brown and Trevino 2006, 597). Ethical leadership has been identified as important for our struggling, often amoral business environment (Frisch and Huppenbauer 2014).

Chapter Summary

Leadership is a group phenomenon involving the interaction between two or more people. The interaction includes a process of influence whereby the leader exerts intentional influence over the followers.

Leadership study comprises five recognized theories or schools of thought: trait theory, behavior theory, contingency theory (or situational leadership), transactional leadership, and transformational leadership. Transformational leadership has become increasingly accepted today, as leadership roles focus on inspiring and motivating followers. Followers are empowered and inspired by the organizational mission and vision under transformational leadership.

The concept of leadership has changed over time. Originally, leaders were monarchs, magistrates, or military commanders whose positions and titles differentiated them from others. In the English language, the word *leadership* is relatively new and denotes characteristics or behaviors of leaders, but it has been difficult to define.

Trait theory was popular in the 1920s and suggested that leaders possessed superior characteristics and traits. "Great men" were born and changed history. These individuals had greater physical and mental prowess than others. Many observers still attribute leadership success to superior traits, even though the theory has fallen out of favor with most.

Behavior theory became accepted in the 1940s and focused on the behaviors of leaders. To fulfill the military's desire to train leaders for World War II, academics developed a range of leadership styles for practice. Leadership behavior that led to effective group performance was identified. One popular framework for behavior theory was Blake and Mouton's managerial grid, which examines the level of leader concern for both people and production. The differences between a manager's and a leader's behaviors were also described.

In the 1960s, contingency or situational theories became widespread. This set of leadership theories recognized that different leadership styles were needed for different situations and that effective leadership depends on matching a leader's style and characteristics to the given circumstances.

Transactional leadership theory, which emerged in the 1970s, dealt with the leader–follower relationship and levels of motivation, power, and skill. Other models arose under transactional theory, such as the path–goal theory, leader–member exchange theory, and equity theory.

Transformational leadership evolved from previous leadership theories and embraced the process of empowerment to allow leaders to transform and inspire followers. Under this theory, leaders and followers work together to improve their motivation and ethics. This dynamic becomes a transforming relationship, elevating both leader and subordinate. Charisma is a central aspect of a leader with transformational style, as it emotionally bonds followers and leaders. Charismatic leaders profoundly affect employees because of the force of their personalities. Aside from charisma, transformational leadership includes inspirational motivation, intellectual stimulation, and individualized consideration. Transformational leaders can motivate employees to higher performance and align followers' needs, values, preferences, and aspirations with organizational interests. Succession planning is a critical element of transformational leadership.

Millennials pose a unique challenge for the use of transformational leadership. They are more likely to pursue individual goals over corporate goals, and they want a work–life balance that shifts their focus away from company vision. They are also more extrinsically motivated and less interested in inspirational ideals.

The COVID-19 pandemic required unique leadership skills, with managers relying on their experience and their coworkers to get through the many challenges they faced.

A concept that has evolved from participative and transformational leadership is servant leadership. Servant leaders are other-centered, rather than self-centered, and lead from a values and ethics perspective. This style rejects the concept of leadership as a tool for self-aggrandizement, and considers service the core function of leadership and a moral and ethical imperative. Leaders should examine their motives and seek to provide long-term benefit to their stakeholders.

Two additional leadership models—authentic leadership and ethical leadership—have emerged since 2000. Both build on past models and present ideal values-based leadership characterized by transparent, credible, and genuine behaviors.

Chapter Questions

1. Why do you think people highlight leadership traits to explain the success of leaders?
2. What is the central theme of transformational leadership? Why do you think this is the critical aspect of the theory?
3. Why is it difficult to define leadership?
4. Under trait theory, can leadership be taught? Why or why not?
5. How does behavior theory overlap with transformational leadership?
6. How did the United States' entry into World War II affect research and beliefs about leadership?
7. What is an optimal position on the Blake and Mouton managerial grid? Why?
8. What is the major premise of contingency theory?
9. Path–goal theory considers that leadership characteristics are modified by what factors?
10. Why is charisma so important to transformational leadership?
11. How is servant leadership an extension of transformational leadership?

Chapter Cases

It's All About the Title—but It's Not

By Britt Berrett

Angie was an exceptional catheterization laboratory technician who was respected by her teammates. When the director of the cath lab took another job, Angie was the natural choice to take the director's position. She was asked to step into the role but with an interim title.

Within days, she was in my office to discuss why her coworkers would not follow her direction. She believed that she needed the permanent title for anyone to listen to her. She kept having to tell people, "This is what we will do, because I am the boss." They would nod their heads as if they agreed, but often they did what they wanted anyway.

I explained that, instead of using the interim title as a stick to beat over their heads, Angie should look for common challenges and frustrations that they could solve as a team. Most certainly, there would come a time when tough decisions would need to be made and her role and title would be necessary, but day-to-day collaboration was the best way to solve problems and make decisions. The team would learn to trust her judgment, and when a crisis came, they would respect her decision about how to handle it.

Angie returned to the cath lab and brainstormed with her team about their frustrations. She began working with and listening to the employees. With their input, she established a vision of where the department should go and what they all could do to improve patient satisfaction and clinical quality. Over time, she built a reputation as a team player and an advocate for staff. Many employees commented that she seemed to gain a lot of charisma and looked to her for advice and expertise. Annoying issues that had plagued the cath lab were addressed, and she soon became the permanent director of the department—title and all.

Case Questions
1. Why did people not obey Angie initially?
2. What leadership style did Angie adopt in the beginning?
3. What did she do to change the attitude of the employees?
4. What leadership theories might apply in this case?

Inspiring Employees: The Turkey Entitlement

Every year, the hospital provided free turkeys to employees during the Thanksgiving holiday. Eventually, the tradition became an entitlement and a significant financial obligation. Rather than perpetuate the entitlement mentality, the executive team transformed this time-honored tradition into a meaningful and purposeful event.

Instead of distributing gift coupons for staff to cash in at the local grocery store, the organization arranged for a refrigerated semi to be parked in front of the hospital during Thanksgiving week. Wearing freezer mitts and warm jackets, each member of the executive team personally participated by handing a frozen turkey to each employee. In return, to impress on staff the importance of gratitude, employees had to write down something they were thankful for before receiving a turkey. Not only was this perceived as a cherished interaction and discussion between employee and executive during the distribution, but the activity was used as a tracking process to ensure that only one turkey was distributed per employee.

A tense moment occurred one year when a belligerent employee arrived at the table in front of the turkey truck. She was not going to write down what she was thankful for and demanded her "damn" turkey. The CEO was covering that shift and graciously refused to give her a turkey, inviting her to head on home. She was stunned. So were the other employees gathered around. But the word quickly spread throughout the organization that this activity represented the season of gratitude and was not an entitlement. To be sure, the CEO smiled and was kind, but the message was clear.

As a result, many employees who had previously skipped the Thanksgiving tradition requested that their free turkeys be donated to a local food bank. A table was set up and their turkeys were set aside with a note of gratitude from the food bank.

After the event, the expressions of gratitude were stapled onto the wall adjacent to the cafeteria. The expressions were priceless, giving thanks for parents, children, servicemen and -women, bosses, teammates, faith, friends, and so on. Soon, the area became a congregating point and a source of inspiration and appreciation.

What had evolved into an entitlement for employees was transformed into an expression of gratitude and an inspiration to do more for others.

Case Questions
1. How was this CEO a transformational leader?
2. What was required to achieve what he did?
3. How did his actions inspire others? What were the results?

The Case of the Bad Boss

Perry was one of the worst bosses Lia had ever worked for. Perry had arrived from the main corporate office only six months ago to become the regional vice president for clinical operations, but already many staff members had polished their resumes and were looking for other work. It was hard for Lia to identify exactly what bothered her about Perry until she read an article that listed "Ten Things Only Bad Bosses Say" (Green 2013):

1. "You're lucky even to have a job."
2. "Just figure it out."
3. "I received an anonymous report . . ."
4. "I don't have time for your performance evaluation, but you're doing fine."
5. "That's a dumb idea."
6. "That dress really flatters your figure."
7. "Just do what I tell you to do."
8. "What's wrong with you?"
9. "Your job is what I say it is."
10. "You're so much better at this than Bob is."

Many of these statements reminded Lia of Perry. Then, a specific incident one December day crystalized the problem. Lia's company operated satellite offices in Asia, and one of her responsibilities was to arrange and allocate housing for expatriates working at one of these satellite sites. Employee turnover and shortages of good apartments seemed to be constant issues on this campus, so senior personnel were often placed in a smaller apartment with the promise that they would be moved to a larger and better senior housing unit when it became available. Lia felt she did a good job of juggling the needs and sensibilities of senior staff with cost concerns.

Six months earlier, Scott, a senior-level orthopedist, had agreed to relocate to the site with his spouse, and they were told they could have the only apartment available in the senior housing unit. But three weeks before they were to arrive, a senior administrator decided to transfer to the campus and moved into the promised apartment. Scott and his spouse were placed in a much smaller and older apartment near the site and were promised a better apartment as soon as one became available.

When the next senior-level apartment became available, Lia submitted the request to move Scott and his spouse into it. However, Perry told her he had already promised it to a young couple he was friendly with—two junior employees who had impressed Perry by recently completing their master's degrees. This, he said, was in compliance with his new policy that couples who both worked for the company would receive priority treatment. Lia was flabbergasted. She reviewed both parties' contracts and found that only Scott, the senior employee, was promised the larger apartment. The young couple's contracts did not even mention the size or type of apartment they were to be housed in.

Lia presented the terms of the contracts to Perry, emphasizing that the firm was contractually obligated to give the larger apartment to Scott. She also mentioned that allocating apartments was her job. Perry reddened and told her, "Your job is what I tell you it is." Lia tried to convince Perry that what he had promised was not correct. Perry eventually realized he should not have promised the apartment to the young couple, but he had already announced his decision. He told Lia, "Just do what I tell you to do."

Lia tried one more strategy. She suggested the company might face legal problems if Perry persisted in his decision. Perry replied, "What's wrong with you? I'm the boss, and this is the way it is!"

Case Questions
1. What characteristics did Perry lack that prevented him from being a transformational leader?
2. What is wrong with using the ten "bad boss" sayings listed in the case?
3. Why does it take strength to admit one is wrong? Why must a transformational leader be willing to admit responsibility?

Chapter Activities

My Best Manager
Working alone, list the behavioral attributes of the best manager you have ever had. This could be someone you worked for in a full-time or part-time job, a summer job, a volunteer role, or even a student organization.

Next, form groups as assigned by your instructor, or work with a classmate. Share your list of attributes and read or listen to the lists of others. Discuss your lists in detail, asking clarifying questions and commenting on items of special interest. Work together to create a list that combines the unique attributes of the best managers experienced by members of your group.

Have a spokesperson from your group share your leadership list with the class. (Your instructor may adapt this portion for work with a virtual group or an asynchronous class).

Finally, compare your group's list with the leadership theories discussed in this chapter. See if you can identify how the attributes you listed relate to these theories.

Leadership Role-Play
In this activity, you will role-play hospital leadership roles: CEO, chief nursing officer, chief medical officer, vice president of human resources, director of supply chain management, head of maintenance and housekeeping, director of safety and security, patient relations director, head of social work, public relations director, and any other significant leadership role that might be considered.

Using the scenario of the spread of COVID-19 (or another significant event), discuss its impact on your hospital, the role each leader plays, the leadership challenges associated with that role, and the experience needed to meet and manage the crisis. Following are some questions you might consider:

- What is the focus of the individual during the pandemic?
- Who are the team members and close partnerships associated with that role?
- What are the top five or more biggest challenges that individual faces?
- How would you approach those challenges?
- Who would you go to for help or support if you needed it?
- How would you motivate those who report to you?

The Ideas of the Joint Commission

Review the Governance Institute's white paper *Leadership in Healthcare Organizations: A Guide to Joint Commission Leadership Standards* (P. M. Schyve, 2009, The Governance Institute: www.jointcommission.org/assets/1/18/wp_leadership_standards.pdf). Compare the white paper's proposals for leadership in healthcare organizations with the leadership theories presented in this chapter. How are they similar and different?

References

Adams, J. 1965. "Inequality in Social Exchange." In *Advances in Experimental Psychology*, edited by L. Berkowitz, 267–99. New York: Academic Press.

Albritton, R. L. 1998. "A New Paradigm of Leader Effectiveness for Academic Libraries: An Empirical Study of the Bass (1985) Model of Transformational Leadership." In *Leadership and Academic Librarians*, edited by T. F. Mech and G. B. McCabe, 66–82. Westport, CT: Greenwood Press.

American College of Healthcare Executives (ACHE). 2021. *Healthcare Executive Competencies Assessment Tool*. www.ache.org/career-resource-center (at "Competency Assessment").

Anderson, H. J., J. E. Baur, J. A. Griffith, and M. R. Buckley. 2017. "What Works for You May Not Work for (Gen)Me: Limitations of Present Leadership Theories for the New Generation." *The Leadership Quarterly* 28 (1): 245–60. https://doi.org/10.1016/j.leaqua.2016.08.001.

Antonakis, J., and R. House. 2002. "The Full-Range Leadership Theory: The Way Forward." In *Transformational and Charismatic Leadership: The Road Ahead*, edited by B. Avolio and F. Yammarino, 3–33. Oxford, UK: Elsevier Science.

Antonakis, J., T. Cianciolo, and R. Sternberg (eds.). 2004. *The Nature of Leadership.* Thousand Oaks, CA: Sage.

Avolio, B., and F. Yammarino. 2002. *Transformational and Charismatic Leadership: The Road Ahead.* Oxford, UK: Elsevier Science.

Ayman, R. 2004. "Situational and Contingency Approaches to Leadership." In Antonakis, Cianciolo, and Sternberg 2004, 148–70.

Barker, A. M. 1992. *Transformational Nursing Leadership.* Burlington, MA: Jones & Bartlett Learning.

Bass, B. M. 1995. "The Meaning of Leadership." In *The Leader's Companion: Insights on Leadership Through the Ages*, edited by J. T. Wren, 37–38. New York: Free Press.

———. 1990. *Handbook of Leadership: Theory, Research, and Managerial Applications*, 3rd ed. New York: Free Press.

Bass, B. M., and R. Bass. 2008. *The Bass Handbook of Leadership: Theory, Research, and Managerial Applications.* New York: Free Press.

Bennis, W. 1959. "Leadership Theory and Administrative Behavior: The Problem of Authority." *Administrative Science Quarterly* 4 (4): 259–301.

Blake, R. R., and J. Mouton. 1965. *The Managerial Grid.* Houston, TX: Gulf Publishing.

Brown, M. E., and L. K. Trevino. 2006. "Ethical Leadership: A Review and Future Directions." *Leadership Quarterly* 17 (6): 595–616.

Brown, M. E., L. K. Trevino, and D. A. Harrison. 2005. "Ethical Leadership: A Social Learning Perspective for Construct Development and Testing." *Organizational Behavior and Human Decision Processes* 97 (2): 117–34.

Buell, J. 2011. "Key Skills Help Put the Pieces in Place." *Healthcare Executive* 26 (6): 8–16.

Burns, J. M. 2003. *Transforming Leadership: A New Pursuit of Happiness.* New York: Atlantic Monthly Press.

———. 1995. "The Crisis of Leadership." In Wren 1995, 8–10.

———. 1978. *Leadership.* New York: Harper & Row.

Byham, W. 2008. "Taking Your Succession Management Plan into the 21st Century." Development Dimensions International. Accessed July 10, 2016. www.ddiworld.com/ddi/media/white-papers/gyol_wp_ddi.pdf.

Chadwick, D. 2015. *It's How You Play the Game.* Eugene, OR: Harvest House.

Chemers, M. 1995. "Contemporary Leadership Theory." In Wren 1995, 83–99.

Cherry, K. 2021. "Understanding the Trait Theory of Leadership." *Very Well Mind*, March 8. www.verywellmind.com/what-is-the-trait-theory-of-leadership-2795322.

Coffman, C., and G. Gonzalez-Molina. 2002. *Follow This Path.* New York: Warner Books.

Conger, J., and R. Kanungo. 1998. *Charismatic Leadership in Organizations.* Thousand Oaks, CA: Sage.

Cross, R., W. Baker, and A. Parker. 2003. "What Creates Energy in Organizations?" *MIT Sloan Management Review* 44 (4): 51–56.

Dinh, J. E., R. G. Lord, W. L. Gardner, J. D. Meuser, R. C. Liden, and J. Hu. 2014. "Leadership Theory and Research in the New Millennium: Current Theoretical Trends and Changing Perspectives." *The Leadership Quarterly* 25 (1): 36–62. http://dx.doi.org/10.1016/j.leaqua.2013.11.005.

Fairholm, G. W. 1997. *Capturing the Heart of Leadership: Spirituality and Community in the New American Workplace*. Westport, CT: Praeger.

Fiedler, F. 1964. "A Contingency Model of Leadership Effectiveness." *Advances in Experimental Social Psychology* 1: 149–90.

Folger, R., and R. Cropanzano. 2001. "Fairness Theory: Justice as Accountability." In *Advances in Organization Justice*, edited by J. Greenberg and R. Cropanzano, 1–55. Stanford, CA: Stanford University Press.

Frisch, C., and M. Huppenbauer. 2014. "New Insights into Ethical Leadership: A Qualitative Investigation of the Experiences of Executive Ethical Leaders." *Journal of Business Ethics* 123 (1): 23–43.

Fuller, J. B., C. Patterson, K. Hester, and D. Stringer. 1996. "A Quantitative Review of Research on Charismatic Leadership." *Psychological Reports* 78 (1): 271–87.

George, B. 2003. *Authentic Leadership: Rediscovering the Secrets to Creating Lasting Value*. San Francisco: Jossey-Bass.

Graen, G. B., and M. Uhl-Bien. 1995. "Relationship-Based Approach to Leadership: Development of Leader–Member Exchange (LMX) Theory of Leadership over 25 Years: Applying a Multi-level, Multi-domain Perspective." *Leadership Quarterly* 6 (2): 219–47.

Grant, A. 2014. *Give and Take: Why Helping Others Drives Our Success*. New York: Penguin.

Green, A. 2013. "10 Things Bad Bosses Say." Yahoo! Finance. Published August 21. https://finance.yahoo.com/news/10-things-bad-bosses-131630776.html.

Greenleaf, R. K. 2003 (1970). "The Servant as Leader." In *The Servant-Leader Within: A Transformative Path*, 29–74. New York: Paulist Press.

Hersey, P., and K. H. Blanchard. 1969. "Life Cycle Theory of Leadership." *Training and Development Journal* 23 (5): 26–34.

Hersey, P., K. Blanchard, and D. E. Johnson. 1996. *Management of Organizational Behavior: Utilizing Human Resources*, 7th ed. Englewood Cliffs, NJ: Prentice-Hall.

Heskett, J. 2013. "Why Isn't 'Servant Leadership' More Prevalent?" *Forbes* (blog). Published May 1. www.forbes.com/sites/hbsworkingknowledge/2013/05/01/why-isnt-servant-leadership-more-prevalent/.

Hollander, E. P. 1987. "College and University Leadership from a Social and Psychological Perspective: A Transactional View." Presented at the Invitational Interdisciplinary Colloquium on Leadership in Higher Education, National Center for Postsecondary Governance and Finance, Teacher's College, Columbia University, May.

Hospital Corporation of America (HCA). 2005. The High Performance Facility Study. Nashville, TN: HCA.

House, R. 1996. "Path–Goal Theory of Leadership: Lessons, Legacy, and a Reformulated Theory." *Leadership Quarterly* 7 (3): 323–52.

———. 1977. "A 1976 Theory of Charismatic Leadership." In *Leadership: The Cutting Edge,* edited by J. G. Hunt and L. L. Larson, 189–207. Carbondale, IL: Southern Illinois University Press.

Kouzes, J., and B. Posner. 2006. *Leadership Legacy.* San Francisco: Jossey-Bass.

Madden, M. 2015. "Soft-Leadership Competencies for Today's Healthcare Finance Executives." *Healthcare Financial Management* 69 (5): 42–45.

Mihm, J. C. 2003. "Human Capital—Success Planning and Management Is Critical Driver of Organizational Transformation." Testimony before the Subcommittee on Civil Service and Agency Organization, Committee on Government Reform. Washington, DC: US Government Accountability Office.

Mintzberg, H. 1973. *The Nature of Managerial Work.* New York: Harper & Row.

Northouse, P. 2007. *Leadership Theory and Practice*, 4th ed. Thousand Oaks, CA: Sage.

Pearce, C. L., Y. Yoo, and M. Alavi. 2004. "Leadership, Social Work, and Virtual Teams: The Relative Influence of Vertical Versus Shared Leadership in the Nonprofit Sector." In *Improving Leadership in Nonprofit Organizations*, edited by R. E. Riggio and S. S. Orr, 180–203. San Francisco: Jossey-Bass.

Porter-O'Grady, T., and K. Malloch. 2016. *Leadership in Nursing Practice: Changing the Landscape of Health Care.* Burlington, MA: Jones & Bartlett Learning.

Rue, L. W., and L. Byars. 2009. *Management Skills and Application.* New York: McGraw-Hill/Irwin.

Russell, R., and A. G. Stone. 2002. "A Review of Servant Leadership Attributes: Developing a Practical Model." *Leadership & Organization Development Journal* 23 (3): 145–57.

Sashkin, M. 2004. "Transformational Leadership Approaches." In Antonakis, Cianciolo, and Sternberg 2004, 171–96.

Schriesheim, C., and S. Kerr. 1976. "Theories and Measures of Leadership: A Critical Appraisal of Current and Future Directions." In *Leadership: The Cutting Edge*, edited by J. G. Hunt and L. L. Larson, 9–56. Carbondale, IL: Southern Illinois University Press.

Shamir, B., R. J. House, and M. B. Arthur. 1993. "The Motivational Effects of Charismatic Leadership: A Self-Concept Based Theory." *Organizational Science* 4 (4): 577–94.

Squazzo, J. 2020. "A Defining Moment for Leadership." *Healthcare Executive* (November/December): 20–28.

Stogdill, R. M. 1950. "Leadership, Membership and Organization." *Psychological Bulletin* 47 (1): 1–14.

Trastek, V., N. W. Hamilton, and E. Niles. 2014. "Leadership Models in Health Care—A Case for Servant Leadership." *Mayo Clinic Proceedings* 89 (3): 374–81.

Van Maurik, J. 2001. *Writers on Leadership.* London: Penguin Group.

Van Wart, M. 2005. *Dynamics of Leadership in Public Service.* Armonk, NY: M.E. Sharpe.

Walumbwa, F. O., B. J. Avolio, W. L. Gardner, T. S. Wernsing, and S. J. Peterson. 2008. "Authentic Leadership: Development and Validation of a Theory-Based Measure." *Journal of Management* 34 (1): 89–126.

Weber, M. 1958. *From Max Weber: Essays in Sociology,* translated and edited by H. Gerth and C. Mills. Oxford, UK: Oxford University Press.

Wolf, J. A. 2008. "Health Care, Heal Thyself! An Exploration of What Drives (and Sustains) High Performance in Organizations Today." *Performance Improvement* 47 (5): 38–45.

Wren, J. T., and M. Swatez. 1995. "The Historical and Contemporary Contexts of Leadership: A Conceptual Model." In *The Leader's Companion: Insights on Leadership Through the Ages,* edited by J. T. Wren, 245–52. New York: Free Press.

Yukl, G. 1981. *Leadership in Organizations.* Englewood Cliffs, NJ: Prentice-Hall.

Zaccaro, S., C. Kemp, and P. Bader. 2004. "Leader Traits and Attributes." In Antonakis, Cianciolo, and Sternberg 2004, 101–24.

CHAPTER 16

POWER, POLITICS, AND INFLUENCE

> A nationally recognized physician drugged and then sexually assaulted a patient in his hospital's emergency department. All the staff at the hospital thought the doctor was exceptional and liked working with him. He was a "superstar," and this power, prestige, and sense of invincibility made him feel that he could exploit others and get away with it. Abuse in medicine is sadly common, with more than a third of medical trainees reporting some form of harassment and discrimination by senior doctors.
>
> Serious power problems exist in academic medicine. Too many doctors have too much power with too little oversight to check the power. In addition, the outstanding superstars often are unlikely to experience negative consequences for their abusive actions (Karan 2019).

Learning Objectives

After studying this chapter, readers should be able to

- distinguish between power and influence,
- understand influence tactics and the different sources of power,
- discuss how referent power can be gained,
- describe the zone of indifference and its meaning to organizational trust,
- discern the short- and long-term advantages and problems with using both positive and negative influence tactics,
- appraise the function and antecedents of organizational politics, and
- understand the negative effects of abuse of power and sexual harassment.

Key Terms

- coercive power
- expert power
- formal authority
- harassment

- influence
- organizational politics
- power
- referent power
- reward power
- sexual harassment
- zone of indifference

Many people crave power and influence, but they often carry negative connotations in today's work environment. As shown in the introduction, powerful physicians too often use their power to abuse patients and students. Those who lead must hold sufficient power and influence to get things done. Power and influence can create access to needed resources and key decision makers. But power and influence can become troublesome and even destructive if poorly managed. Thus, knowledge, understanding, and successful application of power and influence are critical to managerial skill.

Power and Influence Defined

Power and influence are connected, and at times the terms are used synonymously. However, they are not the same. **Power** often is portrayed as the capacity to influence others by control over valued resources. Individuals with power have the ability to get others to do what they want. Anderson and Brion explained it this way:

power
The capacity to influence others by control over valued resources.

> Power is broadly defined as asymmetric control over valued resources. Power, as most commonly defined, is therefore inherently relational, in that power exists only in relation to others, whereby low-power parties depend on high-power parties to obtain rewards and avoid punishments. (Anderson and Brion 2014, 69)

Because "power exists only in relation to others" and involves the ability to control rewards and punishments, the greater the power, the greater the influence. **Influence**—the process of persuading others to do something—is triggered when power is exercised. Influence, then, becomes effective only when the entity possessing it concurrently holds enough power.

influence
The process of persuading others to do something; it occurs when power is exercised.

Exhibit 16.1 illustrates the conceptual difference between power and influence. Power, as the capacity to influence (a person or people), is the amount of water stored in the tank. Influence is the pressure of water behind the spigot, which depends on the height and quantity of water in the tank. As with water pressure, the degree of influence depends on the amount of power.

Having power is critical to being an effective leader. It provides increased job security and the ability to successfully influence others. Those without power often lack autonomy and control; they can be susceptible to

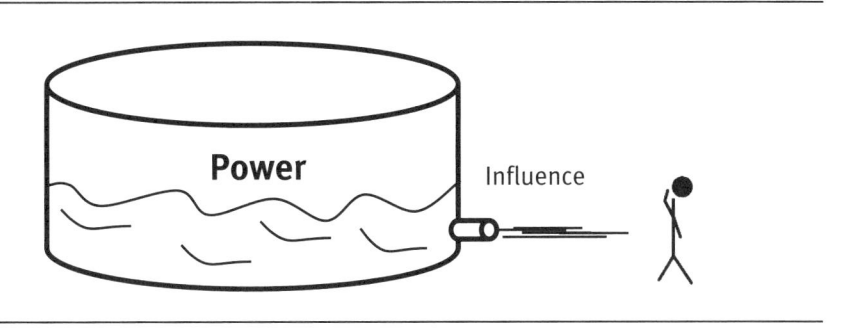

EXHIBIT 16.1
Power Versus Influence

unfair treatment and experience low job satisfaction and morale. Power comes from gaining control over resources, which can be very broadly defined as

> anything of value on which others depend, such as money, information, access to important people, or decisions. It can also apply to personal characteristics. That is, individuals can be construed as controlling a valued resource if they possess personal skills, knowledge, or expertise that others need. (Anderson and Brion 2014, 69)

formal authority
The right to influence someone.

Thus, resources can include both physical assets, such as money and employees, and intangible assets such as formal authority, relationships in social networks, or valuable individual traits (e.g., skills, knowledge, expertise). Greater power is obtained as more of these assets are gained.

Holding a position of authority does not necessarily equate to power. **Formal authority** refers to the right to influence someone. However, as shown in the box a person may hold a position of formal authority but have no or little real power. On the other hand, most positions in an organization convey some level of power (if that power is not squandered).

Big Desk but No Power

Amir had finally finished his master's degree in healthcare quality. He joked that the past three years were the best two years of his life. He did have a lot going on and had to retake a couple classes. Done was done, however. His father owned a midsize healthcare consulting firm, and he had been promised a job when he finished his degree.

As promised, the week after graduation, his father appointed him as the regional director of offices located in three Middle Eastern countries. The firm conducted a fair amount of business in each of the three countries and employed five consultants and staff in these areas, who would report to Amir.

Amir was excited, especially when his father showed him his office, which had a very big desk. Amir had arrived! But he quickly found that the consultants, although polite, often ignored his directives and failed to inform him of their activities. They seemed to have a back channel with his father, and if Amir pushed his authority too far, his father intervened and told him to let the consultants do what they wanted.

One month into his new job, Amir realized he had a very nice desk but not much influence. He could spend the morning reading the paper and often would collate the activity files from the staff to report to his father. Well, that desk really looked good, anyway.

coercive power
The ability to use the threat of force to make someone compliant.

reward power
The ability to promise positive incentives, such as bonuses, raises, promotions, and time off.

The degree of power derived from formal authority depends on the strength of a manager's coercive power and reward power, which can be exercised by either positive or negative incentives. Managers can coerce employees with negative, punitive actions; this **coercive power** uses the threat of force to make someone compliant. Punishments can range from fines to demotions to public scoldings to loss of raises and bonuses. Coercive power generally has the benefit of generating fast results.

Reward power, on the other hand, consists of the promise of positive incentives for work well done, such as bonuses, raises, promotions, and time off. The use of reward power may take longer to yield results. The extent to which a boss implements both coercive and reward power dictates the boss's level of power.

Likewise, power can be garnered from the strength of personal relationships in social networks, political coalitions, and alliances. Although these relationships may be tied to or initiated through a formal position, the power comes from the strength of the relationships with other powerful individuals. Relational power produces **referent power**, which originates from being trusted and respected and motivates people to do what the person in power wants done.

referent power
The ability to influence followers because of the trust and respect of others.

expert power
The ability to influence followers because of one's experiences, skills, talents, or knowledge.

Furthermore, power can come from individual characteristics and abilities. Referred to as **expert power**, this type of power arises from experiences, skills, talents, or knowledge. Often, people demonstrate their expertise through graduation certificates, reputation, or membership in respected associations and groups. The degree of expert power a person holds is directly related to others' recognition of that individual's expertise.

Zone of Indifference

The ability to influence is also affected by which tasks employees are asked to perform. The range of acceptable tasks employees are willing to do without questioning the rationale of the direction is called the **zone of indifference**. For example, duties that are clearly written in a job description usually fall into the zone of indifference. However, tasks outside of the job description, such as personal shopping for the executive and "volunteering" at a leader's favorite charity, may or may not enter the zone of indifference.

zone of indifference
The range of acceptable tasks employees are willing to do without questioning the rationale of the direction.

As shown in exhibit 16.2, the zone of indifference varies according to the degree of trust an employee extends to the employer. A trusting employee may have a large zone, while a cynical, mistrustful employee may have a very small zone. Chester I. Barnard described the zone of indifference this way:

> If all the orders for actions reasonably practicable can be arranged in the order of their acceptability to the person affected, it may be conceived that there are a number which are clearly unacceptable, that is, which certainly will not be obeyed;

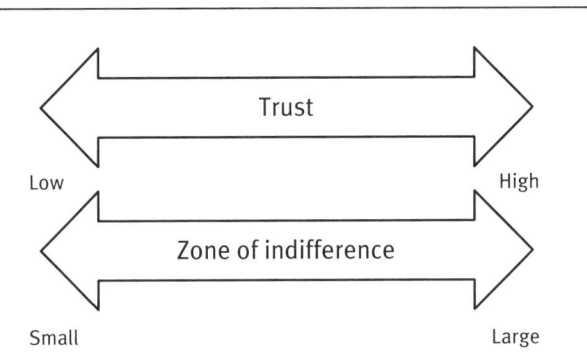

EXHIBIT 16.2
Trust and the Zone of Indifference

```
         Trust
Low                High

    Zone of indifference
Small              Large
```

there is another group somewhat more or less on the neutral line ... and a third group unquestionably acceptable. This last group lies within the "zone of indifference." The person affected will accept orders lying within this zone and is relatively indifferent as to what the order is so far as the question of authority is concerned. (Barnard 1938, 168–69)

The zone of indifference may be affected by the level of power a leader wields. In general, the greater the power of and trust in the leader, the more tasks employees will accept. As mentioned earlier, this relationship may be the result of the use of rewards and punishments.

Influence Tactics

A critical determinant of managerial effectiveness resides in the capacity to influence subordinates. To a large extent, a leader's success rests on the ability to influence those in an organization. The breadth of an individual's influence varies, as discussed earlier, not only by the amount of power held but also by the influence tactics the leader learns and exercises. Leaders may use several influence tactics, both positive and negative. Yukl (2002) identified a few influence tactics and categorized them as either positive or negative.

Positive influence tactics include the following:

- Rational persuasion—using logical arguments and factual information.
- Inspirational appeals—using emotional requests or proposals to arouse enthusiasm by appealing to values and ideals.
- Consultation—seeking participation in decision-making or planning.
- Exchange—offering to share potential rewards and/or reciprocate favors.
- Personal appeal—drawing on a person's loyalty or friendship.

Negative influence tactics include the following:

- Ingratiation—using pleasant words or friendly behavior to make someone feel positive toward something.
- Pressure—using demands, threats, inspections, and intimidation to encourage behavior.
- Coalition—using support and aid from others to persuade.
- Legitimacy or upward appeals—using approval from higher management to gain compliance.

Wise leaders assess each situation as it occurs and choose among the tactics that are most effective at influencing those targeted. Picking an appropriate influence tactic can strongly affect desired outcomes. Positive influence tactics tend to not harm relationships when used. Leaders using positive influence tactics have also been shown to have greater success and to be more inspirational (Feser 2016). Conversely, negative influence tactics can strain relationships and damage reputations. However, the use of both can influence behavioral changes and actions in others (Chatterjee and Pollock 2017). As shown in the box, opportunities to choose tactics occur in both our business and personal lives. Negative tactics often seem to be more direct and take less time to yield results, but they can harm relationships. Positive tactics, on the other hand, frequently take more time, are messier, and invite visible conflict.

After a leader chooses an influence tactic, the response of the subordinate determines the tactic's success or failure. The subordinate may resist by refusing to change behaviors, ignoring the leader, making excuses, seeking out a higher authority to pull rank on the leader, delaying action, or

---

Which to Use: Positive or Negative Tactics?

Jeff is a polished healthcare executive who uses the participative management approach extensively with his employees. When he needs to influence the physicians on his medical staff, he generally begins with rational persuasion and then moves to inspirational appeals and consultation. He has been successful with this style and has been promoted recently as a result.

He and his spouse, along with their four preteen children, are now driving 1,200 miles to relocate for his new position. It is almost noon, and they need to stop for lunch. Last night Jeff asked his children where they wanted to eat for dinner, which resulted in four opinions and a 15-minute argument. He tried rational persuasion and consultation, but finally told the upset children that the car was stopping at the next restaurant no matter what it served. Later that night, he and his wife talked about the problem of trying to gain consensus with four stubborn children.

Jeff and his wife need to decide what form of influence they should use to avoid a repeat of the earlier conflict. They could just make all the decisions, pressure the children with threats, or even try ingratiation, but these tactics always seem to backfire with the children. Yet positive tactics invite visible conflict and take a long time. What should Jeff do?

pretending to comply but quietly seeking to sabotage the outcome. The follower can also choose to be unenthusiastic or apathetic regarding the requested change. The follower may behave as desired, but the activity may be undertaken with a sullen or cynical attitude. Of course, the ideal result is the follower's full commitment: the follower accepts the influence and voluntarily does what is asked.

Depending on the perspective of the manager and the situation, the last two results might both be considered successes—at least in the short term. The requested behaviors are accomplished in both scenarios. In certain circumstances, this situation might be acceptable; all too often, though, it results in visible compliance but inappropriate behaviors when the employee is unsupervised.

Influence Principles

Exhibit 16.3 displays six influence principles leaders can use to affect their followers' behaviors. Leaders should recognize the different principles and understand the situations in which they might be used. Furthermore,

EXHIBIT 16.3 Six Influence Principles

Influence Principle	Definition	Example
Reciprocity	People return a favor.	Pharmaceutical companies offer gifts to physicians.
Consistency/ Commitment	If people commit to an idea or goal, they are more likely to comply.	Ask those making reservations to call if plans change and wait for a response.
Social proof	People are more likely to do things they see others do.	Parents are more likely to vaccinate their children if all other children in a school are vaccinated.
Consensus	People look to the actions and behaviors of others to determine their own.	Show a list of neighbors who already contributed to a fund.
Authority	People tend to obey authority figures.	Having higher-level titles and wearing proper attire for leadership can signal authority.
Scarcity	Perceived scarcity increases demand.	Use phrases such as "limited time only" or "limited supply" for persuasive messaging.

Source: Adapted from Cialdini (2020).

learning these principles allows leaders to realize when these principles are being used to persuade them.

All organizational members, leaders, managers, and staff use persuasive strategies and power to influence people and achieve both personal and organizational goals. At times, as suggested, this behavior can be adopted for personal gain and result in harm to others. However, the outcome depends on the motives and skills of the individual exercising the influence strategy.

Organizational Politics

organizational politics
The informal means of gaining power other than through merit or luck.

An inherent part of power and influence that commonly occurs in organizations is organizational politics. **Organizational politics** has been defined as "a variety of activities associated with the use of influence tactics to improve personal or organizational interests" (Jarrett 2017, 3). Most people see organizational politics negatively, as often those using it are seeking personal gain. Self-serving behaviors may include circumventing the chain of command to obtain project approval, following inappropriate channels to gain special treatment, or directly lobbying a manager prior to a promotion decision. These political activities can undermine perceived fairness, and employees not politicking may feel jealous and resentful if they receive an unfair allocation of the organization's rewards and recognition.

Organizational politics repeatedly manifests in the conflicts, power plays, and interpersonal intrigues that frequently replace constructive organizational activity. Politicking is continuous in almost every organization, but it is mostly invisible to all but those directly involved. Most firms today tacitly sponsor political behavior because of the competition embedded in their systems and structures. Employees are expected to collaborate in pursuit of a common goal yet compete with others for limited resources, status, and career advancement. Political behavior is a normal response to the tensions produced between employees and their organizations. Politics is almost always a factor when work standards and budgets are being set, during daily supervision, and in the pursuit of opportunities and careers—all of which can invite sophisticated forms of gamesmanship and political maneuvering (Morgan 1996). Politicking often arises around the allocation of scarce resources, such as promotions, budgets, and perquisites. Many organizations manage in a competitive environment, which arrays individuals in rivalry, disagreeing about how to allocate the resources.

However, politics can be used ethically and profitably. Sustainable organizational politics does not require winning at any cost; rather, it revolves around maintaining positive relationships while still achieving results. People with political skill also have greater personal power and manage stress and job demands better (Jarrett 2017). Potentially destructive organizational politics clearly exist, and the skilled manager will seek to minimize their negative effects, such as the amount of time individuals can waste on political behavior.

Negative organizational politics is more likely during significant organizational change or when times of scarcity breed competition among organizational groups. To curtail overly political behavior, leaders should be open with information, model cooperative behavior, and make clear that political machinations are not rewarded or tolerated. Furthermore, clear and open feedback to employees about their performance helps diminish organizational politics (Schooley 2021).

Overall, the level of politics in an organization is affected by both individual and organizational factors. Both sets of factors determine the degree to which organizational politics occurs in a company (exhibit 16.4). Individual factors include the political skills people possess, their internal locus of control, how invested they are in their firm, and their expectations of how successful they will be. The level of organizational politics increases as individual factors rise in intensity.

Likewise, organizational factors influence the degree of organizational politics. The scarcity of resources, such as when financial incentives or promotions are limited, makes organizations more political. Increases in role ambiguity also create organizational politics: Ambiguity about job responsibilities, performance evaluations, and promotions leads to political actions

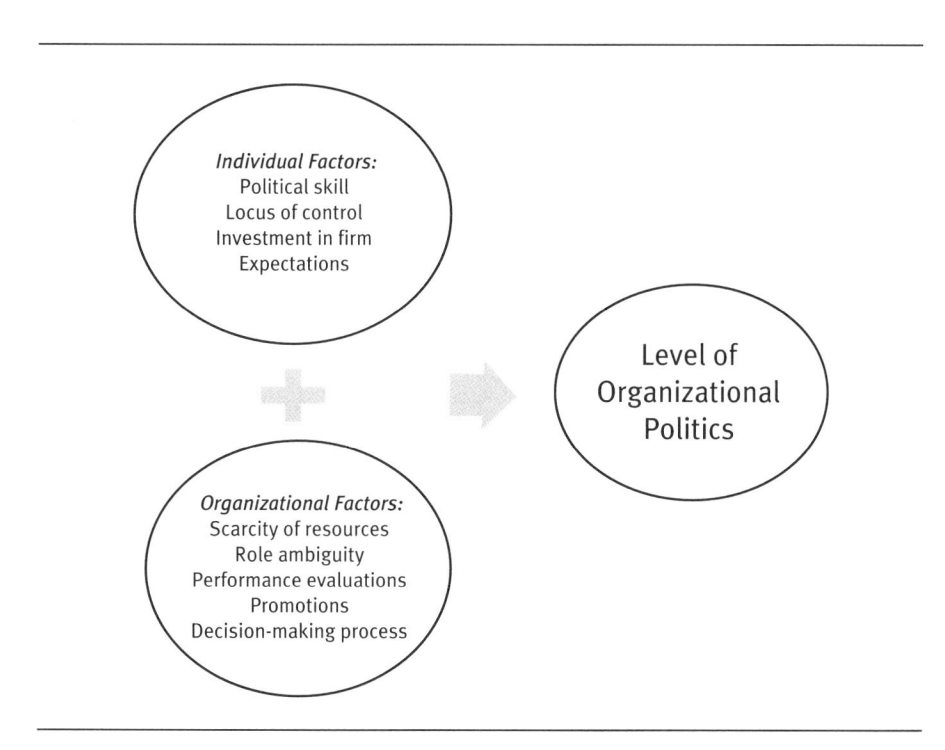

EXHIBIT 16.4
Individual and Organizational Factors That Lead to Organizational Politics

Individual Factors:
Political skill
Locus of control
Investment in firm
Expectations

Organizational Factors:
Scarcity of resources
Role ambiguity
Performance evaluations
Promotions
Decision-making process

→ Level of Organizational Politics

such as impression management, which involves people seeking to actively manage and control the impressions others form of them.

Democratic decision-making can augment political behavior. As many people participate in the decision-making processes of a firm, more people are available to be influenced and political behavior increases (Luthans, Luthans, and Luthans 2021).

Abuse of Power and Sexual Harassment

The accumulation of power can be a great motivator for many managers. However, all too often, managers abuse their power. Such behavior creates a hostile work environment that causes fear, low initiative, turnover, and poor performance. Sadly, abusive bosses rarely recognize their contributions to the problems and react by escalating the abusive behavior, which may spiral into more severe employee problems followed by greater abuse (Foulk et al. 2018; Pinder 2008).

Continued abusive behavior can become **harassment**, which sadly is a common occurrence in the healthcare workplace (Adams and Bryan 2021). The term *harassment* refers to both psychological harassment and sexual harassment. Psychological harassment has been given many names, such as bullying, victimization, and generalized workplace abuse (Aquino 2000; Einarsen et al. 2003). Overall, harassment refers "to repeated and systematic hostile acts, which are primarily of a verbal or nonverbal, rather than physical, nature" (Salin 2009, 27). Sexual harassment has three dimensions: gender-based harassment, unwanted sexual attention, and sexual coercion. Gender harassment involves negative treatment because of one's gender that could include sexist remarks and degrading stories and materials. Unwanted sexual attention can include leering, ogling, and unwanted touching. Sexual coercion is pressuring or bribing one to engage in a sexual act. Although these problems have been addressed for years, many workers continue to experience them (Johnson et al. 2019).

What one supervisor might think is funny and friendly teasing can be highly offensive to another staff member. For example, one aging manager frequently called the only Black staff supervisor in the organization "dwarf." The offending manager thought his name calling was humorous, while the supervisor tried to act as though it did not bother her. (The manager retired before a harassment claim was filed against him.) Harassment can take many forms and come from a variety of sources, and may include actions on social media that contribute to creating a hostile work environment.

As mentioned previously, an important subset of harassment is **sexual harassment**. The US Equal Employment Opportunity Commission (EEOC) (2020a) defines sexual harassment as "unwelcome sexual advances, requests for sexual favors, and other verbal or physical harassment of a sexual nature."

harassment
A set of hostile activities that are repeated and systematic, and which are usually verbal or nonverbal rather than physical.

sexual harassment
Unwelcome sexual conduct or advances that subtly or blatantly threaten a person's job or sense of personal safety; all forms of sexual harassment are illegal.

For example, a supervisor may make sexual advances toward a subordinate, whose job may be implicitly or explicitly threatened if the advances are refused. Sexual harassment can occur between parties of any gender, as well as between colleagues. All forms of sexual harassment are illegal in the United States and in most other countries, and can severely damage a work environment.

Sexual harassment is one of the worst abuses of power in organizations. Primarily a power disparity issue, sexual harassment often happens because a person with more power uses it to obtain or to try to obtain sexual favors from someone with less power. In most nations, the employing organization is legally responsible for the actions and behaviors of its managers and bears the risk for their misbehavior. As can be seen in the story relayed in the box, employers can be held liable for harassment and may be required to compensate employees for back pay and damages. A workplace can become a hostile environment due to sexual harassment if employees (managers especially) use sexual innuendoes and jokes, place inappropriate pictures where they can be seen, fondle staff members, use crass gestures, or make unwanted sexual overtures. Sexual harassment is more likely to occur under the following five conditions (Strauss 2019):

1. The workplace appears to tolerate such misconduct.
2. Men outnumber women in the workforce or in leadership, or women are working in perceived atypical jobs.
3. Extensive hierarchical power structures are in place.
4. There is symbolic compliance with laws through documentation, but little organizational discussion.
5. Leaders avoid addressing misconduct.

Eliminating sexual harassment in the nursing profession is seen as one of the most challenging tasks for healthcare leaders. Organizations should have a zero-tolerance policy for this type of behavior and have fair and confidential avenues for reporting it (Ross et al. 2019).

To combat sexual harassment, companies should have a written policy that clearly prohibits all forms of

> **Harassment of Nurses**
>
> A pediatric medical practice was found to have violated federal law for retaliating against a nurse, who had complained that a doctor had inappropriately touched her twice. Her supervisor agreed that the incident was inappropriate and referred her to human resources. After the complaint, her employer transferred her to another site with lower pay and working conditions that she deemed intolerable, which caused her to resign. The case was referred to the EEOC, who found that the organization had punished the nurse for reporting the physician's harassment. The EEOC filed suit seeking "back pay, compensatory and punitive damages" for the nurse (EEOC 2020b).

abusive behavior. For example, a portion of the sexual harassment policy at Hospital Corporation of America (HCA) as of November 2020 is displayed in exhibit 16.5. This policy clearly expresses that sexual harassment is not tolerated and describes examples of prohibited behaviors.

EXHIBIT 16.5
HCA's Sexual Harassment Policy

PURPOSE: To define sexual harassment, outline responsibilities and requirements for reporting violations of this policy, and to ensure treatment in accordance with the mission and values of the organization and compliance with federal, state and local regulations and statutes.

RESPONSIBILITIES: Colleagues have the right to work in an environment free of harassment and disruptive behavior. Sexual harassment will not be tolerated. Sexual harassment may include any unwelcome sexual advances, requests for sexual favors, and all other verbal or physical conduct of a sexual nature, especially where:

a. Submission to such conduct is made either explicitly or implicitly a term or condition of employment;
b. Submission to or rejection of such conduct is used as the basis for decisions affecting an individual's employment; or
c. Such conduct has the purpose or effect of creating an intimidating, hostile, or offensive working environment.

    Behaviors that engender a hostile or offensive work environment will not be tolerated. These behaviors may include but are not limited to offensive comments, jokes, innuendoes, and other sexually-oriented statements, printed material, material distributed through electronic media, or items posted on walls or bulletin boards.

REQUIREMENTS: Each member of management is responsible for creating an atmosphere free of sexual harassment. Further, each employee is responsible for respecting the rights of coworkers.
    If an employee experiences any conduct or activity that is reasonably believed to be considered sexual harassment, the employee should promptly report the incident to the employee's supervisor, who will investigate the matter and take appropriate action, including reporting it to the Human Resources Department. If an employee believes it would be inappropriate to discuss the matter with the employee's supervisor, the employee may bypass the employee's supervisor and report it directly to the Human Resource Business Partner. An employee may also call the Ethics Line at 1-800-455-1996. The complaint will be kept confidential to the maximum extent possible.
    If it is determined that an employee is guilty of sexual harassment of another individual, appropriate disciplinary action will be taken against the offending employee, up to and including termination of employment. Any form of retaliation against any employee for filing a bona fide complaint under this policy or for assisting in a complaint investigation is prohibited.

Source: Reprinted with permission from HCA (2020).

Chapter Summary

Power and influence function both positively and negatively in most firms. Leaders must have sufficient power and influence to achieve results. Having power is critical to being an effective leader.

Power and influence are related but not interchangeable concepts. Power is the capacity to influence others, while influence occurs when power is exercised. Power comes from gaining control over resources and demonstrating superior individual characteristics.

An individual who holds a position of authority does not necessarily have power. Formal authority from a position conveys the right to influence someone. However, the degree of power depends on the actual strength of a manager's coercive and reward power. Coercive power is a motivation approach that relies on threats of fines, demotions, public scoldings, and loss of monetary rewards. Reward power motivates through promises of bonuses, raises, promotions, and other awards for good results. Power can also come from referent and expert power. Referent power arises from the strength of relationships with other powerful individuals. This interpersonal power motivates people to act because of their respect for the power holder. Likewise, expert power motivates compliance through people's respect for the experiences, skills, talents, and knowledge of the power holder.

Influence operates in a zone of indifference, which consists of the tasks employees are willing to do without question. Tasks outside of this zone may be objectionable to the employee. The scope of the zone of indifference varies according to the degree of trust the employee has in the supervisor and the amount of power the supervisor holds.

Managerial effectiveness is tightly tied to the capacity to influence subordinates. Skilled managers use influence tactics to appropriately motivate employees. As with power, influence tactics can be both positive and negative. Positive tactics include rational persuasion, inspirational appeals, consultation, exchange, and personal appeal. Negative tactics include ingratiation, pressure, coalition, and legitimacy or upward appeals. The proper influence tactic for the given situation should be used, as negative tactics tend to strain relationships and damage reputations.

Six influence principles are recommended for affecting subordinates' behaviors: reciprocity, consistency and commitment, social proof, consensus, authority, and scarcity. All organizational members use influence strategies. Their outcomes often depend on the motives and skills of the individual who exercises the influence strategy.

Organizational politics is an inherent part of power and influence. Organizational politics can be self-serving and undermine perceived fairness. It repeatedly manifests in conflicts, power plays, and other intrigues in organizations, and is implicitly sponsored by the competitive nature of most firms. Politics frequently becomes a factor in disagreements over the allocation of scarce resources and during significant organizational change. The degree of organizational politics varies by individual and organizational factors.

Harassment is a dysfunctional abuse of power. This behavior, which happens far too often, creates a hostile work environment, and increases fear, turnover, and poor performance. Harassment refers to repeated and systematic hostile acts and can take many forms. One important subset of harassment is sexual harassment—one of the worst abuses of power that can occur in an organization. To prevent sexual harassment, organizations should establish written policies that prohibit all forms of abusive behavior and should not tolerate this type of behavior. Employees should be informed to report any instance of sexual harassment, and firms should establish written policies for handling the reporting, investigation, and disposition of harassment complaints.

Chapter Questions

1. What is the difference between power and influence?
2. Why is power so important to leaders?
3. How does authority become power?
4. What are the downsides of using coercive power? What are its benefits?
5. How does having extensive social networks help garner power?
6. Who establishes a zone of indifference for employees?
7. How are coercive power and negative influence tactics related?
8. When should different influence strategies be used?
9. In what ways can organizational politics be destructive?
10. In your opinion, why do abusive bosses often fail to recognize their role in the abuse?

Chapter Cases

The Proposed Metropolitan Hospital Restart
One year ago, Teresa, a hospital CEO, approached her supervisor, Kent, the health system's regional vice president, with an idea to build a new hospital in an adjoining community. She explained the many advantages to him. For example, locating a hospital in the suburban area would allow the

parent system to better negotiate managed care contracts and attract a larger population to its services. Teresa also explained that several physicians in the metropolitan area had approached her to ask why the system had not already established a hospital in that community. She recognized that planning, designing, and constructing a new hospital would require a lot of up-front work on her part, including the need to affiliate with many of the physicians in the area and other surrounding communities.

Kent responded enthusiastically and authorized seed money to begin the development. Teresa understood that final funding would depend on the financial projections and on obtaining commitments from local physicians to admit to the new hospital. Over the next four months, Teresa refined her projections and gathered letters of support from 25 of the 30 physicians she personally visited, spending significant time on the project. Many of the physicians also gave Teresa checks—in amounts ranging from $20,000 to $50,000—to invest in the new hospital. In total, she held almost $400,000 worth of checks in a safe deposit box, to be retained until the system decided and either invested the money in the project or returned it to the physicians.

After many hours spent with the strategic planner, the hospital's chief financial officer, and regional personnel, Teresa developed the following pro forma for the hospital. She felt confident that her estimates were conservative, as she had carefully vetted her assumptions with all key personnel. The hospital would show a loss its first year, effectively break even its second year, and then make a significant profit thereafter.

As Teresa was finalizing the proposal, Kent announced that he was stepping down, and a new regional vice president, Chris, was appointed. Chris had been a peer of Teresa's, and the two had even dated, but she broke off the relationship after a short time when she felt he was too controlling. She dreaded meeting with him now that he was her boss.

During Teresa's first meeting with Chris, she presented the proposal for the new hospital. He did not seem impressed, but at the end of the meeting he suggested that if she went to dinner with him, she could probably convince him of the proposal's merits. As politely as she could, Teresa refused. In response, he requested that she send him all her information and said he would "have to think hard about it." Later, he called to tell her to return the checks to the physicians and said his staff would review her numbers and reevaluate the proposal.

Teresa was incensed but followed her new boss's direction. She told the physicians when she returned their checks that Chris might visit them later to talk about investing. She felt she had been undercut and her credibility was diminished in the eyes of the physicians. She was also concerned that acceptance of her work might be conditional on her relationship with Chris.

Metropolitan Hospital Proposed 5-Year Pro Forma

		Year 1	Year 2	Year 3	Year 4	Year 5
Gross revenues						
	Inpatient	17,500,000	19,250,000	21,175,000	23,292,500	25,621,750
	Outpatient	22,000,000	26,400,000	31,680,000	38,016,000	45,619,200
Deductions						
	Inpatient	10,500,000	11,550,000	12,705,000	13,975,500	15,373,050
	Outpatient	8,360,000	10,032,000	12,038,400	14,446,080	17,335,296
Net revenues						
	Inpatient	7,000,000	7,700,000	8,470,000	9,317,000	10,248,700
	Outpatient	13,640,000	16,368,000	19,641,600	23,569,920	28,283,904
TOTAL NET REVENUE		20,640,000	24,068,000	28,111,600	32,886,920	38,532,604
	Salaries and wages	8,250,000	8,910,000	9,622,800	10,392,624	11,224,034
	Benefits	2,722,500	2,940,300	3,175,524	3,429,566	3,703,931
	Contracts	4,050,000	4,252,500	4,465,125	4,688,381	4,922,800
	Supplies	6,125,000	6,492,500	6,882,050	7,294,973	7,732,671
	Other	1,288,000	1,378,160	1,474,631	1,577,855	1,688,305
TOTAL EXPENSES		22,435,500	23,973,460	25,620,130	27,383,400	29,271,742
PROFIT (LOSS)		(1,795,500)	94,540	2,491,470	5,503,520	9,260,862
Margin		(0.087)	0.004	0.089	0.167	0.240

Six months later, having validated Teresa's projections, Chris sent his assistant to visit the physicians who had initially contributed checks to the project. Surprisingly, only three of the physicians showed any interest, and the visits generated less than $75,000 in potential investment. Chris was upset and could not figure out what went wrong.

Case Questions
1. What went wrong?
2. Could Chris's behavior be considered sexual harassment? If so, what should Teresa do?
3. What application does this case have to power and influence?

The ER Physician and the ER Nurse

Dr. P was a great emergency room (ER) physician. He had worked at Eastern Hospital for about ten years and now was serving as the president of his six-member ER group. He had the type of personality that put patients and staff members at ease. He was a devoted father and active in his church. Therefore, it came as a shock to the hospital CEO when the ER director pulled him aside to inform him that Dr. P was having an affair with one of the ER staff nurses. By all accounts it was consensual, but the ER director wanted to know if she should take any action. After discussing the matter for a few minutes, both concluded that because the affair was consensual and Dr. P did not really supervise the nurse, the only thing they could do was try not to have them work the same shift. However, both felt uncomfortable speaking with either Dr. P or the nurse. They felt the relationship was really "none of their business."

The affair appeared to go on for about six months, until Dr. P's wife found out and issued an ultimatum. After deep emotional struggles, Dr. P agreed to terminate the relationship. The nurse was upset, as she felt she had been promised marriage as soon as Dr. P divorced his wife. She became even angrier when Dr. P, who primarily worked the day shift, asked that the nurse be scheduled only nights so that he would not work at the same time, as he had promised his wife.

As surprised as he had been by Dr. P's workplace relationship, the CEO was even more surprised when, a week after the duty shifts were reshuffled, he received notice that the nurse had filed a sexual harassment case with the hospital's human resources department and the EEOC. She claimed she only continued the sexual relationship because of implicit threats Dr. P made, and that by reassigning her to nights the ER director had contributed to the harassment.

Case Questions
1. Was this sexual harassment?

2. What should the CEO have done when he found out that a person with quasi-supervisory authority had a relationship with a subordinate?
3. Why might the ER director think the charge of sexual harassment was unfair?

Power of a Contract

IHD was an international hospital company with hospitals in three Central and South American countries. Cliff, IHD's chief operating officer, had worked for the corporation for more than eight years and invested countless hours making the hospitals profitable. IHD was a privately held company with big plans but minimal financial backing. Cliff had built and was supervising ten hospitals that offered general acute care. The hospitals differentiated their care from that of their competitors by offering an "American"-style clinic practice, hiring only US-trained physicians, and obtaining Joint Commission accreditation. Over time, this strategy was successful.

Cliff was dedicated to helping his company succeed. For instance, when he had to terminate a CEO in one of the larger hospitals he could not find the right replacement immediately, so he moved to the location for six months to take the reins until he felt most of the major problems had been addressed and a competent CEO was found. He also traveled extensively and was on the road about 40 percent of the time, visiting different hospitals in all three countries. Cliff was the linchpin that made the company successful. At least this is what he was told many times by the majority owner and CEO.

Cliff had a good relationship with the CEO. They frequently met to talk about the hospitals' operations and challenges. The CEO also gave Cliff the highest possible evaluations, and significant bonuses when money was available. Cliff felt he could trust his boss.

In Cliff's ninth year with IHD, the company began seriously considering divesting the six hospitals it owned in one country because of the activities of corrupt officials there. This concerned Cliff, as it would leave him only four hospitals to run. While these discussions were ongoing, Cliff was approached by another US company that was buying a system of 11 hospitals in Chile and asked if he might be interested in becoming its divisional CEO and supervising its international facilities. After doing due diligence, and given the uncertainty with IHD, Cliff could see that this would be a great opportunity for him, as he would have a significant increase in salary and prestige.

Before accepting the offer, Cliff decided to meet with his boss to let him know about the planned move. He explained the circumstances, the offer, and his plan to resign and take the new position. The CEO responded by thanking him for his efforts but then pulled out Cliff's employment contract, which included a noncompete clause. The CEO threatened to sue Cliff to enforce the contract and even enjoin the other company if he accepted the position, claiming that IHD would lose all its investment in him if he left.

Cliff was shocked that the CEO would treat him this way. The contract did have a noncompete clause for areas surrounding the company's hospitals, but Chile was a long way from any of its current markets. He met with an employment attorney for advice and was told that the noncompete clause was probably not enforceable, because of the geographical distance involved. However, the lawyer told Cliff that a recent client in a similar situation had been sued, along with the hiring company. Rather than fight in court, the hiring company terminated the client's offer of employment, which left him without a job. Cliff now had a dilemma. He needed to continue to work, but he felt betrayed by his boss.

Case Questions
1. Was this a misuse of power by the CEO?
2. How do the principles of power apply in this case?
3. What should Cliff do?

Chapter Activities

Lessons from #MeToo
Read "Lessons from #MeToo for Health and Health Care Improvement" (by Jo Ann Endo, for the Institute of Healthcare Improvement blog: www.ihi.org/communities/blogs/lessons-from-metoo-for-health-and-health-care-improvement). Write a one-page paper on how you can prevent workplace harassment and support those who have experienced it.

Power Dynamics
Read "Power and Physician Leadership" (by Saxena et al. for *BMJ Leader*: https://doi.org/10.1136/leader-2019-000139). Working with a small group of classmates, develop a list of things physicians do and can do to exercise power (1) appropriately and (2) inappropriately.

References

Adams, L., and V. Bryan. 2021. "Workplace Harassment: The Leadership Factor." *Healthcare Management Forum* 34 (2): 81–86. https://doi.org/10.1177/0840470420978573.

Anderson, C., and S. Brion. 2014. "Perspectives on Power in Organizations." *Annual Review of Organizational Psychology and Organizational Behavior* 1 (March): 67–97.

Aquino, K. 2000. "Structural and Individual Determinants of Workplace Victimization: The Effects of Hierarchical Status and Conflict Management Style." *Journal of Management* 26 (2): 171–93.

Barnard, C. 1938. *The Functions of the Executive*. Cambridge, MA: Harvard University Press.

Chatterjee, A., and T. Pollock. 2017. "Master of Puppets: How Narcissistic CEOs Construct Their Professional Worlds." *Academy of Management Review* 42 (4): 703–25.

Cialdini, R. 2020. "The Principles of Persuasion Aren't Just for Business." Influence at Work (blog). Updated July. www.influenceatwork.com/principles-of-persuasion/.

Einarsen, S., H. Hoel, D. Zapf, and C. Cooper. 2003. "The Concept of Bullying at Work: The European Tradition." In *Bullying and Emotional Abuse in the Workplace: International Perspectives in Research and Practice*, edited by S. Einarsen, H. Hoel, D. Zapf, and C. Cooper, 3–30. London: Taylor & Francis.

Feser, C. 2016. *When Execution Isn't Enough: Decoding Inspirational Leadership*. Hoboken: NJ: Wiley.

Foulk, T., K. Lanaj, M. Tu, A. Erez, and L. Archambeau. 2018. "Heavy Is the Head That Wears the Crown: An Actor-Centric Approach to Daily Psychological Power, Abusive Leader Behavior and Perceived Incivility." *Academy of Management Journal* 61 (2): 661–84.

Hospital Corporation of America (HCA). 2020. Sexual Harassment Policy, HR.ER.024. Accessed November 26, 2020. https://hcahealthcare.com/ethics-compliance/policies/hr.dot.

Jarrett, M. 2017. "The 4 Types of Organizational Politics." *Harvard Business Review* digital article, April 24. https://hbr.org/2017/04/the-4-types-of-organizational-politics.

Johnson, S. K., K. Keplinger, J. F. Kirk, and L. Barnes. 2019. "Has Sexual Harassment at Work Decreased Since #MeToo?" *Harvard Business Review* digital article, July 18. https://hbr.org/2019/07/has-sexual-harassment-at-work-decreased-since-metoo.

Karan, A. 2019. "Medicine's Power Problem." *Voices* (blog). *Scientific American*. November 9. https://blogs.scientificamerican.com/voices/medicines-power-problem/.

Luthans, F., B. C. Luthans, and K. W. Luthans. 2021. *Organizational Behavior: An Evidence-Based Approach*, 14th ed. Charlotte, NC: Information Age Publishing.

Morgan, G. 1996. *Images of Organization*, 2nd ed. Thousand Oaks, CA: Sage.

Pinder, C. 2008. *Work Motivation in Organizational Behavior*, 2nd ed. New York: Psychology Press.

Ross, S., P. Naumann, D. V. Hinds-Jackson, and L. Stokes. 2019. "Sexual Harassment in Nursing: Ethical Considerations and Recommendations." *Online

Journal of Issues in Nursing 24 (1): Manuscript 1. https://ojin.nursingworld.org/MainMenuCategories/ANAMarketplace/ANAPeriodicals/OJIN/TableofContents/Vol-24-2019/No1-Jan-2019/Sexual-Harassment-in-Nursing.html.

Salin, D. 2009. "Organizational Responses to Workplace Harassment: An Exploratory Study." *Personnel Review* 38 (1): 26–44.

Schooley, S. 2021. "Politics Destroying Your Business? Here's How to Fix It." *Business News Daily*, April 7. www.businessnewsdaily.com/6374-fix-workplace-politics.html.

Strauss, S. 2019. "Overview and Summary: Sexual Harassment in Healthcare." *Online Journal of Issues in Nursing* 24 (1): Overview. https://ojin.nursingworld.org/MainMenuCategories/ANAMarketplace/ANAPeriodicals/OJIN/TableofContents/Vol-24-2019/No1-Jan-2019/OS-Sexual-Harassment-in-Healthcare.html.

US Equal Employment Opportunity Commission (EEOC). 2020a. Sexual Harassment, www.eeoc.gov/sexual-harassment. Accessed November 25, 2020.

———. 2020b. "EEOC Sues Pediatric Health Care Alliance for Retaliation over Harassment Complaints." June 22. www.eeoc.gov/newsroom/eeoc-sues-pediatric-health-care-alliance-retaliation-over-harassment-complaints.

Yukl, G. 2002. *Leadership in Organizations*, 5th ed. Englewood Cliffs, NJ: Prentice-Hall.

CHAPTER 17

CONFLICT MANAGEMENT AND NEGOTIATION

> Clinic 3 was a challenge. One group of physicians worked from opening until noon, when a second group came on board and worked until 6 p.m. The problem was that the nurses, assistants, and clerks worked the entire day and were not getting much of a lunch break—or any other break, for that matter. Morale was low and Jill, the clinic manager, had to do something. She was spending too much time dealing with complaints and employee turnover was rising. She needed to get the physicians and team leaders together to deal with the conflicts that had arisen. They had to collaborate and come up with something that would be a benefit to all. Jill was certain that if morale improved, the physicians would be happier with the support they received from the staff.

Learning Objectives

After studying this chapter, readers should be able to

- appraise the meaning and application of conflict to organizations,
- recognize and differentiate among the types of conflict,
- describe the issues surrounding polarization, and
- summarize the skills involved in negotiation.

Key Terms

- BATNA
- conflict
- interests
- intergroup conflict
- interpersonal conflict
- intragroup conflict
- intrapersonal conflict
- nontask organizational conflict
- polarization
- positions
- process conflict
- relationship conflict
- task conflict
- zero-sum games

Conflict and negotiation are present daily in healthcare. Anyone who says differently has either never stepped into a hospital or physician's office or has never been part of a team with challenging output goals. If managed appropriately, conflict can improve decision-making and further an organization's mission. However, if poorly managed, conflict can quickly become destructive. Organizations that manage conflict well can succeed, while those that do not can become dysfunctional collections of competing individuals. The need for negotiation—a component of conflict management—arises when conflict surfaces. Negotiation skills facilitate the successful use of conflict. This chapter addresses both.

Conflict Basics

conflict
A situation that arises when two or more parties have opposing views, positions, needs, or interests that are perceived as incompatible.

Although a consistent, accepted definition is lacking, the more challenging aspect of **conflict** has been defined as a "competitive or opposing action of incompatibles" (Merriam-Webster.com 2021). Another definition describes conflict as

> a process that begins when an individual or group perceives differences and opposition between itself and another individual or team about interests and resources, beliefs, values, or practices that matter to them. (De Dreu and Gelfand 2008, 6)

As suggested, conflict arises when two or more parties have opposing views, positions, needs, or interests that are perceived as incompatible. In other words, negative conflict is said to occur when one party faces the potential of gaining something at the expense of another. It can originate from a variety of sources, such as differing values, assumptions, and goals. Situations of conflict often feature the following elements:

- Parties (groups or individuals) have opposing interests and hold the perception that only one interest can be met.
- Opposing parties often do not recognize and acknowledge opposing interests.
- Opposing parties believe the other side will seek to achieve its own interest at the expense of the other.
- Existing relationships of opposing parties are a reflection of their past interactions.
- Actions are taken or efforts are made to gain the parties' interests.

Although conflict was initially seen as an evil that should be eliminated from organizations, more recent management scholars have highlighted conflict's productive potential (Rahim 2011). In other words, conflict can result in positive as well as negative outcomes. Positive outcomes from conflict that facilitate organizational goals include the following (Rahim 2011):

- Innovation, creativity, and positive change
- Improved organizational decision-making
- Discovery of synergistic solutions
- Increased individual and group performance
- Enhanced clarity and understanding of assumptions and intentions of parties
- Displays of actual values and belief systems of an organization
- Increased group cohesiveness

Exhibit 17.1 illustrates the potential for positive and negative outcomes of conflict. Positive conflict is constructive and may improve the quality of decisions, foster new ideas, create a chance to learn new skills, and guard against groupthink (discussed in chapter 12). Relationships are actually strengthened and productivity improved when conflict occurs at appropriate levels (Boyle 2017).

Leaders help make conflict positive by creating a vision that team members work to achieve. A good leader helps to set common goals and supports open and honest communication. Such culture is set by leadership and supports the notion of a win–win environment rather than focusing on differences (Gosnell 2019).

Of course, conflict can escalate and quickly produce dysfunctional outcomes, such as the following):

- Job stress, burnout, and employee dissatisfaction
- Diminished communication between and among employees and groups

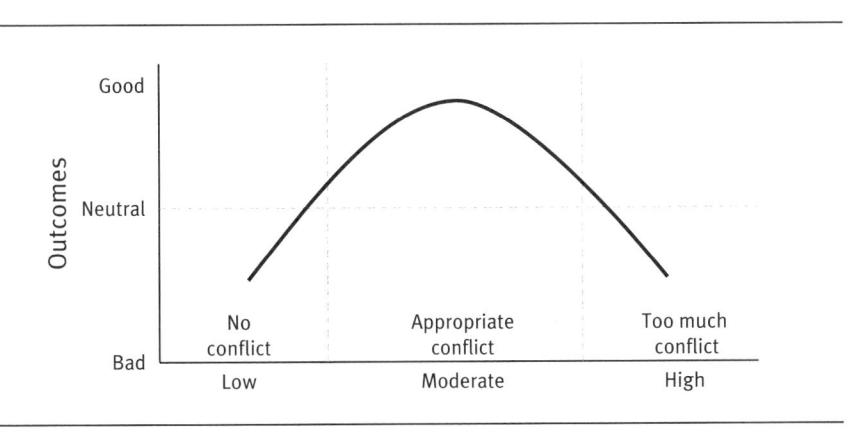

EXHIBIT 17.1
Conflict Is Not All Bad

- Heightened distrust and suspicion
- Damaged relationships
- Decreased job performance
- Increased resistance to change
- Diminished employee loyalty and organizational commitment

Conflict in healthcare organizations has also led to patient safety errors, poor morale, and distrust (Grubaugh and Flynn 2018). The determination of whether organizational conflict becomes positive or negative rests largely with the employees' skills, abilities, and conflict management capabilities. As such, conflict management is one of the major roles of all healthcare managers as they deal with the many healthcare professionals who work in their organization.

Types of Work-Related Conflict

Four types of work-related conflict are discussed in this chapter: (1) task conflict, (2) process conflict, (3) relationship conflict, and (4) nontask organizational conflict. **Task conflict** occurs when different opinions arise about work details and goals—that is, about what is to be accomplished. **Process conflict**, on the other hand, involves disagreements about how a job gets done. **Relationship conflict** results from differences in values, personality, political beliefs, and style. **Nontask organizational conflict** develops from disputes regarding "company policies, hiring decisions, benefits, organizational culture, organizational leadership or power" (Bruk-Lee, Nixon, and Spector 2013, 340).

task conflict
Conflict that occurs regarding work details and goals.

process conflict
Conflict that occurs regarding how a job gets done.

relationship conflict
Conflict that occurs regarding values, personality, political beliefs, and style.

nontask organizational conflict
Conflict that occurs regarding corporate policies, hiring decisions, benefits, culture, leadership, or power.

Escalation from Conflict to Assault

A doctor became frustrated when he called a nursing unit at lunchtime and no one immediately answered the phone. After eight rings, he slammed the phone down, stomped over to a nurse standing nearby, and demanded that she go to the nursing floor to see what was going on. The nurse, who worked in a different nursing unit, told the doctor that she was not going to that floor but would pass on his message once she arrived at her own nursing station. This response further enraged the doctor, who grabbed the nurse's arm and began yelling at her. The nurse then lost her temper, jerked her arm away from him, and made a derogatory remark about his ethnic heritage. The doctor then really "lost it" and slapped the nurse. She backed away and called the police, who soon arrived and charged the doctor with assault.

Poorly managed, these four types of conflict can needlessly stress employees. Relationship and nontask organizational conflict, in particular, can generate anger and frustration that can increase physical strain and cause health problems, including stress, burnout, and depression (Tafvelin, Keisu, and Kvist 2019). Relationship conflict can engender negative emotions, damage working relations between and among people, hurt overall morale across the company, and make future interactions difficult.

Conflicts that escalate often produce **polarization**, whereby people—even those who may initially have been neutral—are driven to take sides and adopt extreme positions. When people become polarized, little room is left for agreement. Individuals and groups drift to increasingly radical poles, which makes compromise and resolution increasingly difficult. As shown in the box, issues can quickly escalate and create detrimental results for an organization.

> **polarization**
> A situation in which people are driven to take sides and accept extreme positions.

Dealing with Conflict

While individuals and organizations use more than one style to resolve conflict, a combination of five of the following methods is common. These ideas have been around since the mid-1970s (Thomas and Kilmann 1974):

1. Individuals fight for their own interests in the *competing* style, often at the expense of others. It is defending the right to wear or not wear a mask during the COVID-19 pandemic, or to keep businesses open or closed. Simply trying to win is another characteristic of the competing style.
2. *Accommodating* is the exact opposite of competing. Here the individual forgets selfish interests in order to satisfy someone else. Giving in to another person's point of view or denying one's own beliefs illustrates this style.
3. When people decide they just do not want to deal with the conflict, they practice the *avoiding* style. Evading, postponing, or walking away are forms of avoidance.
4. *Collaborating* is a combination of being assertive and cooperative. It involves understanding different viewpoints, breaking down the issues, and working together to solve them. The collaborating style is an attempt to meet the needs of all involved parties.
5. *Compromising* is an attempt to find a mutually acceptable solution and often means all the needs or desires of the involved parties are not completely met. Concessions are offered in order to come to an agreement.

Another model suggests individuals use a combination of styles based on their concern in meeting their own goals versus their willingness to support the goals of others (Rahim 1985, 2002). Exhibit 17.2 illustrates the possible combinations and outcomes of using the conflict management styles of integrate, force, dominate, avoid, and compromise.

EXHIBIT 17.2
Rahim's Conflict Management Styles

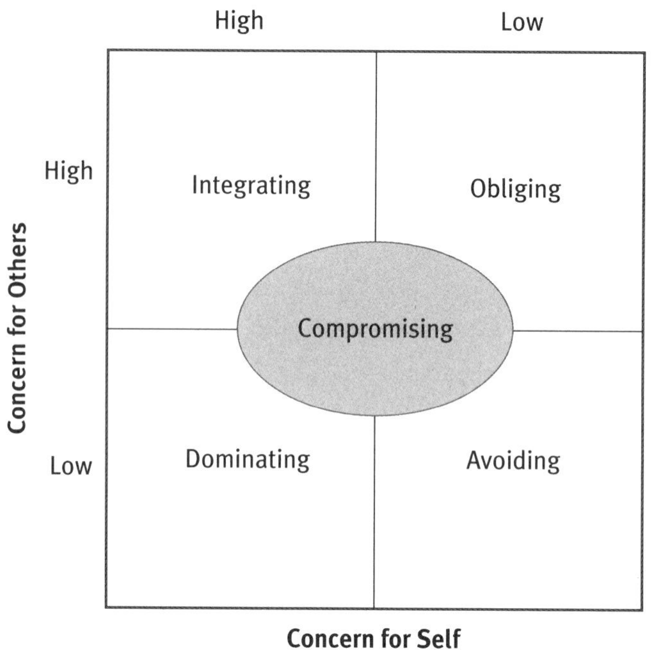
High
Low
High
Integrating
Obliging
Concern for Others
Compromising
Low
Dominating
Avoiding
Concern for Self

Contributing Factors to Conflicts in Healthcare

intrapersonal conflict
Conflict that arises because of an individual's roles, values, or goals.

interpersonal conflict
Conflict between two or more individuals that may be caused by personality, values, and style differences.

intergroup conflict
Conflict between two or more groups.

intragroup conflict
Conflict among members of a group.

Conflict exists at different levels, as exhibit 17.3 illustrates. **Intrapersonal conflict** arises because of an individual's roles, values, or goals. At this individual level, a focus on self over others exists and the individual is stretched by a lack of resources (Kim et al. 2016; Osland et al. 2007). **Interpersonal conflict** occurs between two or more individuals and may be caused by personality, values, and style differences. Four factors contribute to interpersonal conflict: bias from earlier experiences, a dehumanization of coworkers, power dynamics (see chapter 16), and a lack of communication (Kim et al. 2016). **Intergroup conflict** occurs between two or more groups, such as different departments, and **intragroup conflict** happens among members of a group.

Conflict emerges in the workplace for many reasons. Opposing feelings, competitive pressures, power struggles, big egos, jealousy, compensation issues, or just having a bad day may trigger conflict. While some might think almost any situation could create conflict, poor communication and the inability to control one's emotions are often the triggers (Kokemuller 2018; Program on Negotiation 2021). Communication—or rather, its absence—is a perennial problem in all organizations (see chapter 14) and directly affects conflict. Communication breaks down when people inappropriately interject their uncontrolled emotions in work relationships and decisions. Such

EXHIBIT 17.3
Levels of Conflict

Level	Involved Parties
Intrapersonal	Self
Interpersonal	Two or more people
Intergroup	Two or more groups
Intragroup	Single group

communication breakdowns frequently lead to angry confrontations and an escalation of conflict. Expressions of anger during conflict often result in damaged work relationships and inability to communicate.

Organization factors contribute to challenges in healthcare organizations. Difficulties navigating within these complex systems lead to conflict. Roles and responsibilities, procedures, workflow, and a lack of adequate resources can all create challenges (Kim et al. 2016). These conflict triggers, described in more detail in the following list, exist because of the nature of healthcare (Marcus 1995):

- *Ambiguity.* Healthcare information and outcomes can be interpreted in different ways by different people through the lens of their own knowledge, expectations, values, and experiences.
- *Complexity.* Healthcare organizations bring together a large number of people, who are involved in and affected by the numerous decisions made.
- *Competition.* Different healthcare departments, professions, and organizations often compete for limited resources, power, prestige, and status.
- *Obligatory cooperation.* Information must be rapidly and accurately exchanged for the care of patients. Responsibility for patient care is transferred across shifts and from one provider to another.
- *Time pressures.* Time is critical in healthcare decision-making. Adverse consequences can result if tests, communications, and care are late.

Small Business Is Not Exempt from Conflict

Small businesses such as medical groups or clinics must deal with conflict and tailor their conflict resolution system to meet their unique internal dynamics. Experts would argue, however, that a badly managed system of dispute or grievance resolution could be worse than having no system at all. The key is constant feedback, or what some call using a "What's Working and What's Not Working" model of evaluation (Burr 2016).

Small businesses that create a culture with a strong vision and common goals will find added benefits from a system designed to manage conflict.

- *Change.* Changes in technology, reimbursement methods and rates, professional responsibility, social expectations, knowledge, and information are constantly occurring in healthcare.

Interpersonal conflict is a leading source of employee stress and a significant reason for employee turnover among healthcare workers (Loes and Tobin 2018). Conflict plagues even the executive levels of healthcare, sometimes called the *C-suite*. The relationship between CNOs (chief nursing officers), CFOs (chief financial officers), and CEOs (chief executive officers) has been strained historically due to different priorities and communication challenges. Nurses in one study felt unable to deliver the care their patients needed due to a lack of collaboration among the health team (Ingwell-Spolan 2018).

A properly functioning organization experiences a moderate amount of conflict that encourages improved solutions and decision-making. Enlightened managers design methods to introduce conflict in critical processes. Why don't more managers inject conflict in their organizations? Conflict often is unpleasant, and many managers seek to avoid it—even if its long-term effects could be positive.

zero-sum games Competitions in which one party wins at the expense of the loser.

Zero-Sum Games and Competition

One aspect of society that promulgates conflict is the degree of competition that occurs in a culture. Cultures that encourage competition, such as in the United States, produce winners and losers, thereby engendering conflict. As can be seen in many sports, winning becomes paramount, and coaches and players may even engage in unethical and illegal behaviors to beat their opponents. Purely competitive contests result in **zero-sum games**, where one party wins at the expense of the loser. Almost all sports contests are designed to end with one winner and one or more

---

Cheating Athletes

Athletics almost always involves winners and losers. "To the victors go the spoils" is apt; the winners of high-profile contests can earn millions of dollars in salary, bonuses, awards, or endorsements. Often, those who come close but do not win receive relatively little. For example, *Golf Digest* reported in its coverage of the 2020 US Open golf tournament that the third-place finisher, Louis Oosthuizen, received about one-third of the amount the winner, Bryson DeChambeau, took home (Herrington 2020).

The pressure to win, unfortunately, encourages cheating—sometimes in sophisticated ways that are difficult to discover. One example is Lance Armstrong, who won the Tour de France bicycling race seven times before race officials proved that he cheated by using performance-enhancing drugs, or "doping," to gain a competitive edge in his racing. Once his cheating was discovered, Armstrong was stripped of his titles and banned from competitive cycling for life. This is just one example, among many, of athletes and teams who have been compelled to win at any cost—be it through doping or deflating balls to below-regulation standards, as occurred in the National Football League in 2015 (Hume 2015).

losers. Likewise, business activities such as seeking employment and bidding for contracts often become competitive zero-sum games.

Competition also frequently occurs among groups. This is especially true in healthcare, where professional group loyalties are strong. Physicians, therapists, nurses, and most other clinical groups value their group's priorities and point of view more highly than those of outsiders. Professional differences lead to competition when "turf battles, differences of knowledge level and experience, and rare opportunities for group conversation lead to a competitive atmosphere where everyone is struggling" (Geradi 2003). What often results is a cycle of competition, hostile interaction, and escalation, followed by more competition (Osland et al. 2007).

As the "Cheating Athletes" box discusses, when beating the competition becomes the sole focus, dysfunctional competition is likely. Dysfunctional competition occurs when individuals and groups seek to finish ahead of others and "win" instead of focusing primarily on self-improvement.

Healthcare is not immune to the "win at any cost" mindset. Large egos bereft of humility often pit intelligent people against each other in a competition for limited resources. As a result, conflict can occur and easily escalate. In addition, some healthcare providers commit fraud, which is now estimated at billions of dollars per year. As with the athletes described in the box, some providers feel they must cheat to win. But many eventually get caught and ultimately lose (Piper 2016).

However, competition among groups is not always dysfunctional. It can encourage individuals and groups to achieve higher goals than might otherwise be set. As long as all parties are good sports and efforts are focused on playing by the rules while pushing for continuous self-improvement, competition functions well. As implied earlier, conflict in healthcare is unavoidable. However, if they manage it properly, organizations can learn from conflict. It becomes a means to "help us better perceive ourselves, the people we work with, and what we are trying to achieve together" (Marcus 1995, 57).

Conflict and COVID-19

The coronavirus pandemic of 2020 brought with it a new way of doing business. Organizations that could do so asked employees to work from home. Healthcare organizations, for the most part, did the opposite—they sought more workers to come and help. Some caregivers were asked to shift from their usual unit to help with patients affected by the virus. This change, and a high demand on resources, resulted in a magnified threat of conflict.

The US Centers for Disease Control and Prevention (2020) recommended that people wash their hands often, maintain a six-foot distance from others (both inside and outside), and cover the nose and mouth with a mask in public. Not everyone agreed with these precautions, resulting in coworkers being upset with one another or voicing anger. All of the aspects of waiting for a vaccine, fear of contracting COVID-19, fear of death from the disease, social isolation, and family dynamics added to the conflict. In addition, 2020 was a presidential election year in the United States and a year of social unrest in the form of protests against police brutality and racially motivated violence (see chapter 3).

What was the advice given to healthcare and other leaders to manage conflict during the pandemic? The overarching principal was to recognize potential conflict and then put policies in place to reduce it. Employers were advised to put COVID-19 prevention strategies in place, communicate regularly with employees about the issues, consistently stick with the policies and respond to employee concerns (Nagele-Piazza 2020).

Conflict management experts offered a few key suggestions to prevent conflict during a crisis (Pollack Peacebuilding Systems 2020):

- Make certain employees' needs are met
- Communicate
- Stop conflict when early signs suggest it is coming
- Keep team members focused on their mission and common goals
- Maintain strong leadership

In general, the idea of managing conflict was heightened during the pandemic, which required the use of the principles of conflict management.

Managing Conflict

To offset the inherently difficult nature of healthcare, effective healthcare leaders learn to properly manage conflict. One survey reveals that managers spend about a quarter of their time dealing with conflict (Acuna 2013). One prominent business commentator wrote, "if you cannot or will not address conflict in a healthy, productive fashion, you should not be in a leadership role" (Myatt 2012). Those who habitually avoid conflict will fail in the long run. Conflict rarely diminishes and becomes positive if left to itself. Benefiting from positive conflict requires good managers who can recognize conflict, diagnose its cause(s), and intervene to resolve or moderate it. With this understanding, many companies have initiated training to provide their managers with conflict resolution skills.

Training can involve many aspects of conflict and focus on a variety of topics. Best practices often include tying the training to the employee's work circumstances and situation. For example, conflict resolution training for physicians could connect to their clinical experience and practice among interdisciplinary teams. Teamwork and inclusion become key to decision-making and conflict resolution (Greengard 2018). Overall, training should help people accomplish the following (Myatt 2012):

- *Define acceptable behavior.* The way people should treat each other must be clearly articulated.
- *Address conflict proactively.* Leaders should actively seek out potential conflict and proactively intervene. They must understand the tensions in the workplace and work to moderate concerns before they flare into conflict.
- *Understand the involved parties' motivations.* Leaders should learn what those involved in the issues want to accomplish and take action to help all achieve their goals.
- *Use conflict as an opportunity for learning and growth.* Leaders who properly use conflict can stimulate innovation and open new perspectives.

One large medical center's efforts to manage conflict are described in the box. As recommended earlier, the organization's first step was to define in detail those behaviors that were

---

Maimonides Medical Center's Approach to Reducing Hospital Conflict

Conflict occurs daily in hospitals. Big egos, critical life-and-death decisions, a high level of work interdependence, strong professional identities, and gender differences combine to produce an environment of sometimes-extreme conflict and distrust. This conflict increases medical errors and poor morale. To address employee conflicts, Maimonides Medical Center, a large urban hospital in Brooklyn, New York, created a process to change behaviors that lead to conflict.

Maimonides has known its share of organizational conflicts. Heavily unionized, it endured a three-week-long nurses' strike in 1998, for example. In an effort to improve physician relationships and engender mutual respect, the hospital and unions created the physician-written Code of Mutual Respect in 2005, updated in 2009, which established seven key principles of expected behavior: (1) professionalism, (2) respectful treatment, (3) appropriate language, (4) appropriate behavior, (5) prompt, direct, and constructive feedback, (6) confidentiality, and (7) communication. To enforce employee compliance with the code and deal constructively with violators, the hospital added the following five complementary strategies, which were implemented by both labor and management:

1. Formal and informal leadership development
2. A respect hotline for reporting violations
3. Trained managers and leaders to mediate issues with code violators
4. Crucial-conversations training
5. Measurement of compliance to the code

Training physicians to investigate alleged code violations by other physicians helped to more quickly resolve problems and lessen hospital conflicts. Physician commitment to the Code of Mutual Respect (which can be found in its entirety at https://maimo.org/wp-content/uploads/2020/09/codeofmutualrespectrev709.pdf) has contributed to improved communication and patient safety. Maimonides is making a long-term effort to embed these changes, which requires continued buy-in and collaboration from all stakeholders.

Source: Adapted from Givan (2010).

acceptable and the consequences for those who chose to behave outside these guidelines.

Conflict management has been referred to as the process of negotiating differences (Tinsley 2001). Simply defined, a *negotiation* is a discussion aimed at reaching an agreement between two parties. *Conflict management* usually refers to a proactive approach to handling conflict. High-functioning organizations do not simply wait for workplace disputes to erupt and then decide how to resolve them. Instead, they implement conflict management policies and procedures that are consistent with organizational goals and objectives (Hu, Wu, and Gu 2019). Organizations that successfully negotiate differences avoid harmful conflict, reach agreements, and produce consistently positive results.

Negotiation Skills

Considering the close association between conflict and negotiation, negotiation skills are critical for any leader or manager in healthcare. Negotiation is a constant in healthcare organizations and is vital to preempting and resolving conflict. Everything from simple schedules to organization-changing strategies can involve some degree of negotiation. Successfully negotiated agreements not only solve a problem but also improve the parties' relationship.

Many books and guidelines have been published describing the art of negotiation. However, only a few basic tenets are required to engage in successful negotiation. They include the following:

- *Focus on the issues, not personalities and people.* Separate the issues at hand from the people involved in the negotiation. Too often, people become personally invested in a negotiation, become emotional, and make personal attacks. To focus on the issues, both parties must seek to understand how the other perceives the situation, avoid assigning blame, and employ active listening. Having a good relationship before the negotiation is one of the best ways to begin a negotiation.
- *Do not bargain over positions.* There is a big difference between positions and interests. **Positions** are the expressed desires or presented proposals of the parties involved, whereas **interests** are a party's real needs, desires, fears, and goals. Interests are, in effect, the underlying objectives that a given position should achieve. However, stated positions often do not reflect the real desires, so positions can clash with interests.

Begin negotiations by clarifying the interests of both parties; this allows the parties to work together to address the real problem and come up with solutions that are satisfactory to both. Conversely,

positions
In negotiations, the expressed desires or presented proposals of the parties involved.

interests
In negotiations, a party's real needs, desires, fears, and goals.

starting negotiations with positions may result in greater resistance to alternatives. Seeking to align interests leads to win–win outcomes and prevents parties from moving to confrontation and conflict.

- *Establish ground rules for negotiating.* For any significant negotiation, the parties need to agree on the process, timing, participants, and conduct. Establishing a common framework facilitates successful negotiations and prevents parties from taking their grievances to the press (Jensen 2013), as demonstrated by the example provided in the box "Negotiating in the Press."
- *Generate novel win–win solutions.* Separate the solution-generating stage from the evaluation stage. Agree that options will be explored first. This stage may be undertaken in a brainstorming session or through other means. After multiple options have been generated, evaluation of potential solutions should begin.
- *Use objective criteria.* If interests seem opposing, set objective criteria that can resolve differences. Establish parameters that are legitimate and practical, and search for scientific and professional standards that both parties can accept.
- *Understand the BATNA.* **BATNA** stands for "best alternative to a negotiated agreement." Each party should begin by establishing its BATNA and be ready to consider its next choice if the current negotiation fails. The more valuable the BATNA is to a party, the stronger the negotiating position that party holds. For example, if you are negotiating for a new job, how hard you push for a higher salary than the one offered depends on your BATNA. Without a clear idea of your BATNA, you negotiate in ignorance. Recognizing your negotiating power comes from understanding your BATNA. Furthermore, knowing your BATNA

BATNA
The best alternative to a negotiated agreement.

Negotiating in the Press

Negotiating managed care contracts has become difficult in the past decade. Rather than hammering out agreements privately, many healthcare organizations take their contract complaints to the public, where they paint their opponent as unreasonable and exert external pressure to gain power in the negotiation.

In Tennessee, Hospital Corporation of America (HCA) took part in a very public disagreement during its 2003 negotiations with BlueCross of Tennessee. HCA took out full-page newspaper ads that claimed BlueCross was not fair in offering only 5.9 percent rate increases while raising its rates 15 percent in the previous three years. BlueCross responded publicly that HCA's rates were already so high that if BlueCross awarded the requested rate increase, HCA's rates would be 20 percent higher than those of other hospitals and thus would significantly increase BlueCross's costs. One BlueCross executive was quoted as saying, "With hospitals across the state experiencing the same financial difficulties and challenges, we just can't understand why HCA's rates are so out of line." HCA responded with data that showed its revenue per patient was actually lower than at other hospitals.

allows you to know when to walk away from the negotiation: You leave once your BATNA becomes better than the potential result of the negotiation (Osland et al. 2007).

Many people regard negotiations as stressful. Negotiation places people in a situation of mutual dependence, bereft of total control. People negotiate because they cannot mandate what they want and must come to an agreement with other parties. In addition, negotiating is unpredictable. It is difficult to predict how others will react and the eventual result. This uncertainty brings a significant amount of stress. Other parties may be uncooperative and competitive. They may inject strong emotions into the process. Negotiating also is stressful because of the lack of feedback on the negotiator's performance. Even if you reach an agreement, knowing if it was the best result or if you damaged relationships may be difficult (Leary, Pillemer, and Wheeler 2013).

Stressed negotiators are less effective in reaching successful agreements than are negotiators who remain physiologically stable. O'Connor, Arnold, and Maurizio (2010) found that negotiators who felt threatened and experienced more stress reached lower-quality deals. A primary way to manage stress is to be prepared and become skillful in managing emotions. This skill can be achieved by reacting to needs and not to expressed emotions. People need to be emotionally prepared to negotiate, even if they expect no problems. Anxieties, hurt feelings, and resentments may be hidden, ready to burst forth. Negotiators should prepare for others' emotions, and their own, and deal with them productively (Leary, Pillemer, and Wheeler 2013).

At times, as shown in the box, parties will try to use emotions and stress to their advantage. If the hospital negotiators in this case had allowed the union representative's negative emotions to infect the bargaining session, the results could have been very undesirable.

Allowing negative emotions to dominate negotiations injects tension and distrust in the process, minimizing communication and options; and parties in the

---

Deceptive Emotions in Negotiations

A hospital's service workers' labor contract had expired, and the dreaded time arrived to open negotiations with the labor union. The union was known for its tough and often nasty tactics. Predictably, the union presented a demand for a high salary increase of 18 percent over two years, whereas the hospital proposed 7 percent over three years. The lead union negotiator became angry and accused the hospital of negotiating in bad faith. After the hospital team tried to positively engage him for about 15 minutes, he got up, hurled a curse word at them, and left the room. The other union negotiators remained in the room and almost immediately suggested reaching an agreement before the lead negotiator returned. The hospital team soon realized that the antics were mostly for show and an attempt to manipulate the negotiations. The hospital team proceeded by examining the real needs of both parties and ignored the inappropriate behavior of the union's lead negotiator.

grip of negative emotions may even reject potential agreements that are better than their BATNA. On the other hand, encouraging positive emotions permits greater collaboration and cooperation, open communication, more options, and the potential for the best agreement, as long as it exceeds the BATNA (Marchi et al. 2020).

Ultimately, successful negotiations should produce agreements that all parties feel good about over time. People need to perceive that the negotiated outcomes were fair and mutually beneficial. In addition, the parties involved in the negotiations should, at a minimum, depart with their personal relationships undamaged and, one hopes, improved. Following are some ways to ensure solidified relationships (O'Hara 2015; Thompson 2013):

- *Make small talk, and give people space to tell their stories.* New information can come to light, and people, if upset, should be able to vent. This space can also help with establishing rapport.
- *Be professional and, if needed, challenge people respectfully.* Use nonjudgmental language such as "I think" or "it seems to me." Stress what the parties have in common, and use *we* much more often than *I* to constructively engage the other party. Avoid demeaning words that might trigger strong emotions, such as "you wouldn't understand," "you never," "calm down," "what's your problem?" or "why don't you be reasonable?"
- *Approach the negotiation as a joint problem-solving effort.* Be creative in developing positive, innovative solutions.
- *Ask questions and listen.* Watch body language to better understand the emotions behind the words.
- *Be aware of cultural values and biases.* Your biases might cause you or the other party to view the situation as different from what it really is.

Chapter Summary

Conflict and negotiation are common occurrences for healthcare leaders. Appropriately managed, both can contribute to improved decision-making and to meeting the organization's goals. However, poorly managed conflicts and negotiation can become destructive. Conflict begins when parties perceive differences between or among themselves related to important resources, beliefs, values, and practices. Conflict can arise from many sources and can contribute positively or negatively to an organization's operations. Positive conflict can improve innovation, creativity, decision-making, performance, communication, and group cohesion. Negative conflict can produce stress, burnout, dissatisfaction, damaged communication, distrust, poor job performance, resistance, and diminished loyalty and commitment.

Conflict in healthcare has also resulted in patient safety errors and poor morale. Although many healthcare professionals lack the basic skills to resolve conflict, conflict management is a critical function of healthcare managers.

Different types of work-related conflict include task conflict, which occurs regarding work details and goals; process conflict, regarding how to do a job; relationship conflict, regarding values, personality, political beliefs, and style; and nontask organizational conflict, regarding policies, benefits, culture, leadership, and power. Poorly managed, these conflicts can cause stress and even health problems for employees. Escalating conflicts can also create polarization, driving parties to take extreme positions.

Interpersonal conflict leads to employee stress and turnover. Potentially more than half of employee retention problems result from poorly handled conflict. This trend is also seen for top managers in healthcare, with more than one-quarter of CNOs reporting they left their positions because of conflicts with their CEOs.

Good managers understand that a moderate level of conflict should be maintained in their organization. They recognize when and where positive conflict can be engendered. However, many managers avoid introducing conflict, as it may be an unpleasant experience.

The culture in the United States promotes competition that frequently produces winners and losers. These zero-sum games occur when one party wins at the expense of the other. Almost all sports contests engage in zero-sum games. Likewise, among professional groups in healthcare, competition can become a destructive cycle of conflict. When winning—or finishing ahead of all other competitors—becomes the primary goal, competition can be dysfunctional. However, competition can be positive if the rules are clear and participants are good sports focused on self-improvement.

Conflict also exists at different levels. These include intrapersonal conflict, interpersonal conflict, intergroup conflict, and intragroup conflict. In these categories, conflict happens for many reasons, but it most frequently occurs as a result of poor communication and poorly controlled emotions.

In healthcare, conflict results because of the structure of the work environment. Healthcare work settings involve a great deal of ambiguity, complexity, competition, obligatory cooperation, time pressure, and change. All these factors contribute to conflict in an organization and require leaders to become masters of conflict management. Conflict management can be facilitated by training, which many firms have instituted.

The COVID-19 pandemic that began in 2020, along with an election and civil unrest, resulted in a heightened threat of conflict. Strong leaders who successfully navigated the challenges of the pandemic were those who recognized the potential for conflict, established clear policies, and communicated well.

Conflict management refers to the process of negotiating differences, while negotiating means reaching agreements. Organizations that are proactive and resolve potential conflicts with successful negotiations produce better results than those that address conflict as it arises. Basic components to negotiation include focusing on issues, not personalities; bargaining about interests, not positions; establishing ground rules for negotiating; generating novel win–win solutions, using objective criteria; and understanding the BATNA, or the best alternative to a negotiated agreement.

Many people find negotiating stressful, as it places them in a situation of mutual dependence, is unpredictable, may involve strong emotions, and could end in difficult-to-understand results because of the common lack of feedback. However, highly stressed negotiators are less effective in reaching successful agreements; negotiators need to be prepared and become skillful in managing emotions. Allowing negative emotions in a negotiation can create tension and distrust and allow suboptimal choices to be made.

To create an environment that encourages successful negotiations and improved relationships, parties should consider making small talk, acting in a professional and respectful manner, looking at negotiation as a joint problem-solving effort, asking questions and listening, and being aware of potential cultural values and biases.

Overall, conflict and negotiations are daily events at most healthcare organizations. Those who master conflict management and negotiation bring a strong skill set to their work setting.

Chapter Questions

1. Why does conflict develop?
2. What can individuals and groups do to make conflict positive?
3. From your own experiences, identify examples of (a) task conflict, (b) process conflict, (c) relationship conflict, and (d) nontask organizational conflict.
4. How can healthcare professional differences increase the probability of negative conflict?
5. Along with the COVID-19 pandemic, what aspects of the year 2020 heightened the threat of conflict?
6. All leaders face conflict. What should you do to prepare yourself to improve your skills in managing conflict?
7. In negotiation, what is the difference between positions and interests?
8. What is a BATNA? State the BATNA you identified in one of your recent negotiations.

Chapter Cases

Negotiating Medical Staff Privileges

Dr. Garrett, the chief medical officer of a busy tertiary medical center, was having a good day until Dr. Daer, a leading cardiologist at the hospital, approached him in the doctors' lounge and insisted on speaking with him about an urgent quality problem. After retiring to Dr. Garrett's office, Dr. Daer stated that a certain primary care physician (PCP) was, in his opinion, incompetent at reading EKGs (electrocardiograms). Dr. Daer claimed that this PCP's incorrect reading of EKGs led to the recent death of a patient.

Dr. Daer said that he and all his partners were planning to propose that only cardiologists be credentialed to read EKGs or, as a concession, that all EKGs would be "over-read" or reread after a noncardiologist looked at them—and that the hospital would pay for these over-readings. This was a matter of such importance, Dr. Daer stressed, that he and his partners were ready to present the proposal to the medical executive committee, or even to take it to the hospital's board of directors if necessary.

Dr. Garrett, now having a bad day, thanked Dr. Daer for the information, asked him to hold off on presenting his proposal to the medical executive committee or the board, and promised to follow up on his concern and get back to him within the next week.

Once alone, Dr. Garrett called the chair of the hospital's quality improvement committee to see what quality issues had been reported from PCPs reading their own EKGs. The chair informed Dr. Garrett that this issue had been an ongoing battle between the cardiologists and PCPs. Five years earlier, new credentialing criteria were established for all physicians seeking EKG reading privileges. However, the cardiologists were surprised to discover that many of the PCPs met the criteria, and the cardiologists responded by voicing their concerns. Overall, the quality improvement committee had not found evidence that warranted taking this privilege away from PCPs. However, because of the friction the conflict had caused, the chair told Dr. Garrett, several PCPs had started to refer their patients who needed a cardiologist to other groups that practiced at other hospitals.

Clearly, Dr. Garrett had a serious problem to resolve. He thought about the situation and recognized that a distinction existed between the positions and the interests expressed. The positions—what people were demanding—were contrary. The cardiologists' position of reading all EKGs was incompatible with the PCPs' position of being allowed to read their own patients' EKGs. The interests of both parties—their goals—were not incompatible, however. Both groups desired the continued long-term relationship among the medical staff and high-quality patient care.

To approach the issue effectively, Dr. Garrett realized that he needed to involve key stakeholders: the hospital's executive administrative team, the medical staff president, and key cardiologists and PCPs. He made appointments to meet with each of them the following week.

Dr. Garrett's challenge was to open lines of communication, reduce the ongoing conflict, and reach a win–win solution. For the negotiation, he had to determine how to align the seemingly contradictory interests of the two groups of medical staff to meet not only their needs but also the needs of the hospital overall, as well as maintain a high quality-of-care standard. To proceed, Dr. Garrett established the following key guidelines:

- *Ensure that communication takes place.* Establish a way for real communication to begin between the two groups of physicians.
- *Build relationships.* Bring the groups together to establish trust and long-term connections.
- *Get people off their positions.* Explore the parties' interests or goals to move them away from their expressed positions.
- *Facilitate effective negotiation.* During meetings, ensure that professional language is used and appropriate engagement occurs. Keep the process moving, steer away from collisions and intimidation, and use the position of authority to ensure a safe environment.
- *Provide a reality check.* Make certain the physicians understand the possible negative outcomes if a successful negotiation does not take place.
- *Bring workable new ideas.* Come up with win–win ideas, but do not present them to both sides until the ideas are vetted by each side separately.
- *Consider an outside mediator.* If failure remains a possibility, consider bringing in an outside mediator.

Now he just needed to move ahead with this task.

Source: Adapted from Mellman and Dauer (2007).

Case Questions
1. What did Dr. Garrett identify as the critical issues to be addressed?
2. What else might he do to facilitate the conflict resolution?

The CEO and the Physician

Methods Hospital enjoyed a near-monopoly position in its midsize, conservative, Midwest community of 350,000 people. Methods was a tax-exempt, 325-bed tertiary care hospital in a system that historically had been very successful. For the past 75 years, the hospital board had prided itself on having a great relationship with its employees and medical staff. Every year for more than 25 years, an annual holiday party was held that almost everyone attended. However, two years ago, in the midst of reimbursement reductions, the hospital hired a new CEO, Stacy, who instituted many changes—one of which was to cancel the holiday party.

Almost concurrently, two large physician groups began talking about the need to be entrepreneurial and to create profitable healthcare services to maintain their income. One group was the largest local orthopedic practice in the system, generating 15 percent of the hospital's revenues and 25 percent of its profits. The orthopedists engaged an architect and showed other physicians their drawings of an imaging and surgical center to elicit interest. One set of drawings was left on a table in the hospital's doctors' lounge and was subsequently seen by a hospital employee, who showed it to Stacy.

The other group consisted of the hospital-based emergency department (ED) physicians and pathologists, who began planning a series of walk-in clinics and blood-drawing stations in conjunction with a local pharmacy chain. These plans had been rumored for the past year, but recently a member of the board of trustees had commented to Stacy that a local pharmacy had mentioned getting close to signing a contract with the physicians.

Stacy inherited other problems when she became CEO—one of which was a serious disagreement with the community over reproductive rights. The hospital had quietly allowed contraception services, sterilizations, and selective abortions to be performed at its location for the past 30 years. However, a change in population demographics and local politics created a battle over the provision of these services. Although the majority of the community and employees supported the hospital's stance on offering reproductive procedures, an increasingly vocal minority had been trying to make the hospital eliminate them.

When Stacy became CEO, she publicly announced her support for continuing to offer reproductive services in that market, and she verbally sparred with the more conservative orthopedists in general medical staff meetings about the issue, damaging her relationship with them. After the last encounter, one of the orthopedists—the oldest and most eccentric of the group—wrote a letter to the system's board of trustees, demanding that it fire Stacy and threatening to personally lead a protest outside Methods clinics to get rid of this "abortion activist" if the board did not acquiesce. Later, two other orthopedists stopped Stacy in the hallway and assured her that, although they held different personal opinions regarding reproductive rights, they supported her as CEO for all the other good decisions she had made.

The hospital-based ED physicians and pathologists had contracted with the hospital for more than 15 years. One of Stacy's first acts as CEO was to renegotiate those existing contracts, which she felt provided much higher compensation to the ED clinicians and pathologists than either should reasonably expect. Both sets of negotiations were tense and did not result in new agreements. In light of the failed negotiations with the pathologists, Stacy drew up a tentative contract with an outside pathology group, which she shared with the current group. She also invited two national ED physician companies to visit and offer proposals. These actions induced the existing groups to agree to new contracts that effectively lowered their overall earnings by about 20 percent. As might be expected, neither physician group was happy. A few members of both groups remained cordial with her, but most of the physicians avoided even speaking with her.

With rumors now surfacing that both the orthopedists and the ED physicians and pathologists were close to executing contracts to proceed with their new ventures, Stacy felt she had about two weeks to devise a strategy to avert their actions. She believed it was critical to intervene, as the plans by both groups to compete with Methods could halve the hospital's bottom line. She assessed her options: (1) threaten to punish the groups by bringing in other orthopedic groups and placing the hospital-based contracts up for bid when they expired in eight months, (2) ignore their actions and beef up marketing to counter the impact on the hospital's revenue, (3) threaten a joint venture with other physicians to build another surgical center, or (4) create a joint venture with the two current groups.

Case Questions
1. What conflict management techniques could Stacy have tried earlier?
2. What process might you use to increase the probability of a successful negotiation?
3. What mistakes might Stacy have made?
4. Which option would you take, and why?

Chapter Activities

Explore Your Negotiating Style

1. Take the "What's Your Negotiation Style?" quiz (Nursing Times 2011, www.nursingtimes.net/quiz-yourself-whats-your-negotiation-style/5032100.fullarticle). Write an outline of your style and its strengths and weaknesses.
2. Play the "Two Dollar Game" with your classmates (Rowe 2011, MIT Open Courseware, https://ocw.mit.edu/courses/sloan-school-of-management/15-667-negotiation-and-conflict-management-spring-2001/lecture-notes/). Start by reading the General Instructions (PDF) on that page, and download the other resources as required. This game illustrates negotiation and conflict management.

References

Acuna, A. 2013. "How Much Time Do Managers Spend on Conflict?" Learning4Managers. Published May 21. https://learning4managers.com/dir/conflict_management/.

Boyle, K. 2017. "5 Benefits of Workplace Conflict." Queens University IRC. December 5. https://irc.queensu.ca/5-benefits-of-workplace-conflict/.

Bruk-Lee, V., A. Nixon, and P. Spector. 2013. "An Expanded Typology of Conflict at Work: Task, Relationship and Non-task Organizational Conflict as Social Stressors." *Work & Stress* 27 (4): 339–50.

Burr, M. W. 2016. "Organizational Conflict Management Systems in Small Business." *Cornell HR Review*. https://ecommons.cornell.edu/bitstream/handle/1813/73012/CHRR_2016_Burr_Org_Conflict.pdf.

De Dreu, C. K. W., and M. J. Gelfand (eds.). 2008. *The Psychology of Conflict and Conflict Management in Organizations*. New York: Erlbaum.

Geradi, D. 2003. "Conflict Management Training for Health Care Professionals." Mediate.com. Published November. www.mediate.com/articles/gerardi4.cfm.

Givan, R. 2010. "The Maimonides Medical Center Model: Conflict Resolution Through Mutual Respect and Conflict Resolution Through Mediation." *Dispute Resolution Journal* 65 (4): 11–56.

Gosnell, S. 2019. "Positive Conflict in the Workplace." *Exude* (blog). Published August 18. www.exudeinc.com/blog/positive-conflict-in-the-workplace/.

Greengard, S. 2018. "Turning Conflict into Improvement." *Physician Leadership Journal* 5 (5): 28–32.

Grubaugh, M., and L. Flynn. 2018. "Relationships Among Nurse Manager Leadership Skills, Conflict Management, and Unit Teamwork." *Journal of Nursing Administration* 48 (7/8): 383–88. https://doi.org/10.1097/NNA.0000000000000633.

Herrington, R. 2020. "U.S. Open 2020: You Won't Believe How Much the Prize Money Payout Is at Winged Foot." *Golf Digest*. Published September 19. www.golfdigest.com/story/us-open-2020-here-is-the-prize-money-payout-for-each-golfer-at-winged-foot.

Hu, N., J. Wu, and J. Gu. 2019. "Cultural Intelligence and Employees' Creative Performance: The Moderating Role of Team Conflict in Interorganizational Teams." *Journal of Management and Organization* 25 (1): 96–116. https://doi.org/10.1017/jmo.2016.64.

Hume, M. 2015. "Condensing Six Months of the DeflateGate-Tom Brady-NFL Circus into Five Essential Questions and 25 Links." *Washington Post*, July 30. www.washingtonpost.com/news/sports/wp/2015/07/30/condensing-six-months-of-the-deflategate-tom-brady-nfl-circus-into-five-essential-questions-and-25-links/.

Ingwell-Spolan, C. 2018. "Chief Nursing Officers' Views on Meeting the Needs of the Professional Nurse: How This Can Affect Patient Outcomes." *Healthcare* 6 (2): 56. https://doi.org/10.3390/healthcare6020056.

Jensen, K. 2013. "You Can't 'Win' Negotiations Without Rules of the Game." *Forbes* (blog). Published September 3. www.forbes.com/sites/keldjensen/2013/09/03/you-cant-win-negotiations-without-rules-of-the-game/.

Kim, S., E. Buttrick, I. Bohannon, R. Fehr, E. Frans, and S. Shannon. 2016. "Conflict Narratives from the Healthcare Frontline: A Conceptual Model." *Conflict Resolution Quarterly* 33 (3): 255–77. https://doi.org/10.1002/crq.21155.

Kokemuller, N. 2018. "How Does a Lack of Communication Cause Conflict in the Workplace?" *Business Operations* (blog). Bizfluent, December 27. https://bizfluent.com/13362276/how-does-a-lack-of-communication-cause-conflict-in-the-workplace.

Leary, K., J. Pillemer, and M. Wheeler. 2013. "Negotiating with Emotion." *Harvard Business Review* 91 (1–2): 96–103.

Loes, C. N., and M. B. Tobin. 2018. "Interpersonal Conflict and Organizational Commitment Among Licensed Practical Nurses." *Health Care Manager* 37 (2): 175–82. https://doi.org/10.1097/HCM.0000000000000208.

Marchi, S., N. Targi, P. Liston, and O. Parlangeli. 2020. "The Possible Role of Empathy and Emotions in Virtual Negotiation." *Ergonomics* 63 (3): 263–73. https://doi.org/10.1080/00140139.2019.1685678.

Marcus, L. J. 1995. *Renegotiating Health Care*. San Francisco: Jossey-Bass.

Mellman, D., and E. Dauer. 2007. "Negotiation: The CMO's Indispensable Skill." *Physician Executive* 33 (4): 48–51.

Merriam-Webster.com. 2021. "Conflict." Accessed July 29. www.merriam-webster.com/dictionary/conflict.

Myatt, M. 2012. "5 Keys of Dealing with Workplace Conflict." *Forbes* (blog). Published February 22. www.forbes.com/sites/mikemyatt/2012/02/22/5-keys-to-dealing-with-workplace-conflict/.

Nagele-Piazza, L. 2020. "How to Resolve Co-Worker Conflicts over Coping with COVID-19." SHRM (Society for Human Resource Management). Published September 16. www.shrm.org/resourcesandtools/legal-and-compliance/employment-law/pages/-co-worker-conflicts-over-coping-with-covid-19.aspx.

O'Connor, K., J. Arnold, and A. Maurizio. 2010. "The Prospect of Negotiating: Stress, Cognitive Appraisal, and Performance." *Journal of Experimental Social Psychology* 46 (5): 729–35.

O'Hara, C. 2015. "How to Negotiate Nicely Without Being a Pushover." *Harvard Business Review* digital article, April 9. https://hbr.org/2015/04/how-to-negotiate-nicely-without-being-a-pushover.

Osland, J., D. Kolb, I. Rubin, and M. Turner. 2007. *Organizational Behavior: An Experiential Approach*. Upper Saddle River, NJ: Prentice-Hall.

Piper, C. 2016. *Healthcare Fraud Investigation Guidebook*. Boca Raton, FL: CRC Press.

Pollack Peacebuilding Systems 2020. "Tips to Prevent Workplace Conflict During COVID-19 Crisis: Online Panel Discussion." Pollack Peacebuilding Systems. March 19 (recording online). https://pollackpeacebuilding.com/blog/tips-to-prevent-workplace-conflict-during-covid-19-crisis/.

Program on Negotiation. 2021. "How to Control Your Emotions in Conflict Resolution." *Program on Negotiation* (blog). Harvard Law School. Published February 9. www.pon.harvard.edu/daily/conflict-resolution/check-your-emotional-temperature/.

Rahim, M. A. 2011. *Managing Conflict in Organizations*, 4th ed. New Brunswick, NJ: Transaction.

———. 2002. "Towards a Theory of Management of Organizational Conflict." *International Journal of Conflict Management* 13 (3): 206–35.

———. 1985. "A Strategy for Conflict Management in Complex Organizations." *Human Relations* 38 (1): 81–89.

Tafvelin, S., B.-I. Keisu, and E. Kvist. 2019. "The Prevalence and Consequences of Intragroup Conflicts for Employee Well-Being in Women-Dominated Work." *Human Service Organizations: Management, Leadership & Governance* 44 (1): 47–62. https://doi.org/10.1080/23303131.2019.1661321.

Thomas, K. W., and R. H. Kilmann. 1974. *Thomas-Kilmann Instrument in Conflict Mode*. Smoking, NY: Xicom.

Thompson, G. 2013. *Verbal Judo: The Gentle Art of Persuasion*. New York: HarperCollins.

Tinsley, C. 2001. "How Negotiators Get to Yes: Predicting the Constellation of Strategies Used Across Cultures to Negotiate Conflict." *Journal of Applied Psychology* 86 (4): 583–93.

US Centers for Disease Control and Prevention. 2020. "How to Protect Yourself and Others." COVID-10 (Coronavirus Disease). Updated November 27, 2020. www.cdc.gov/coronavirus/2019-ncov/prevent-getting-sick/prevention.html. Accessed December 22, 2020.

CHAPTER 18

ORGANIZATIONAL DESIGN AND STRUCTURE

> Healthcare organizations, as the environment changes, must adapt their organizational structures. Efficient organizational structures have multiple connections to facilitate the free flow of information across the organization. Traditional functional structures that cluster like professions in departments often block these information flows and create "silos" that can impede good decision-making. Silos separating people and work areas increase the risk of errors and harmful choices. The viability and strength of a healthcare organization depends on the confluence of culture, behaviors, practices, and a supporting organizational structure that provides excellent governance, decision-making, and direction. However, transitioning to a new organizational structure can be problematic. A study from McKinsey & Company suggested that restructuring may be successful less than 10 percent of the time (Huffman 2017; McKinsey & Company 2014).

Learning Objectives

After studying this chapter, readers should be able to

- compare the meaning and use of chains of command in organizations;
- differentiate between organizational structure and organizational design;
- apply principles of organizational design to improve work settings;
- explain the concepts of division of labor and chain of command;
- discuss the differences between organic organization and mechanistic organization;
- relate how integration and differentiation function in organizations;
- distinguish among types of organizational structures, including functional, multidivisional, and matrix;
- summarize the problems transfer pricing can create; and
- illustrate the different healthcare organizational structures that may address future demands, including horizontal and network structures.

Key Terms

- accountable care organizations
- chain of command
- corporation
- division of labor
- functional organizations
- matrix organizations
- mechanistic organizations
- multidivisional organizations
- network structures
- organic organizations
- organizational design
- organizational structure
- span of control
- transfer pricing

No organizational structure is universally optimal or inherently superior to another. However, as the introduction states, an organization's structure can facilitate or impede important decisions, and changing structures can be problematic. The best organizational structure is one that is crafted to support the organizational strategies and mission. How the reporting relationships are designed and function should adapt as needed to "new economic realities without diminishing core capabilities" (SHRM 2015).

Healthcare companies are organized in many ways, the structuring of which involves choices about services, relationships, locations, and ownership types. For example,

> hospitals, physicians, and other providers, such as post-acute care providers, are structurally and contractually organized in diverse arrangements, with varying levels of autonomy. . . .
> . . . They vary in terms of their origins, included providers and services, care management functions, and governance. . . . Different models relate to various local market pressures, payment policies, and provider regulations in the United States. (Heeringa et al. 2020: 1, 6)

Corporations

corporation
A legal structure that allows a group of people to act as a single entity and provides limited liability to its owners.

Large businesses most often have corporate structures. A **corporation** is a legal structure that is separate and distinct from its owners. It has most of the rights and responsibilities of individuals in that it can enter contracts, borrow and loan money, sue other entities and be sued, hire people, own assets, and pay taxes. A corporation limits liability for its shareholders and may be for-profit or not-for-profit (Investopedia 2020). The owners of the corporation are liable only to the extent of their investment in the corporation. As

Chapter 18: Organizational Design and Structure   383

healthcare organizations have increased in size, many have adopted a corporate structure.

Healthcare corporations have become extremely important to the US economy. In fact, 11 of the 70 largest for-profit companies are healthcare corporations. The largest of these 11 companies, CVS Health, reported almost $260 billion in revenues in 2019 and operated about 9,900 retail locations and 1,100 MinuteClinics as of 2021, according to the company website. In contrast, the largest US for-profit and not-for-profit healthcare systems are HCA Healthcare, with 186 hospitals, and Ascension Health, which operates 151 hospitals (*Becker's Hospital Review* 2020).

Corporations often comprise a very large conglomeration of different units, products, and services. As such, their organizations can be subdivided into three structural levels: the corporate level, the business unit level, and the functional unit level. As seen in exhibit 18.1, which presents a simplified view of CVS Health's structure, the corporate level involves the CEO and board, who decide what business the organization should be in (or should exit), how to raise and allocate financial capital, and how to direct and monitor the overall company. The business unit level involves the strategic business units, which focus on the development, marketing, and provision of products or services. The functional unit level includes the functions that support the business unit and corporate levels. These may include human resources (HR), legal, financial, and other administrative services.

Companies can be either for-profit or not-for-profit. For-profit organizations exist to provide goods and services to financially benefit their owners, and they pay taxes. Not-for-profit organizations are tax exempt and exist to provide some type of community benefit. Their "profits," or excess earnings, cannot be given or accrue to individuals. Licensed healthcare

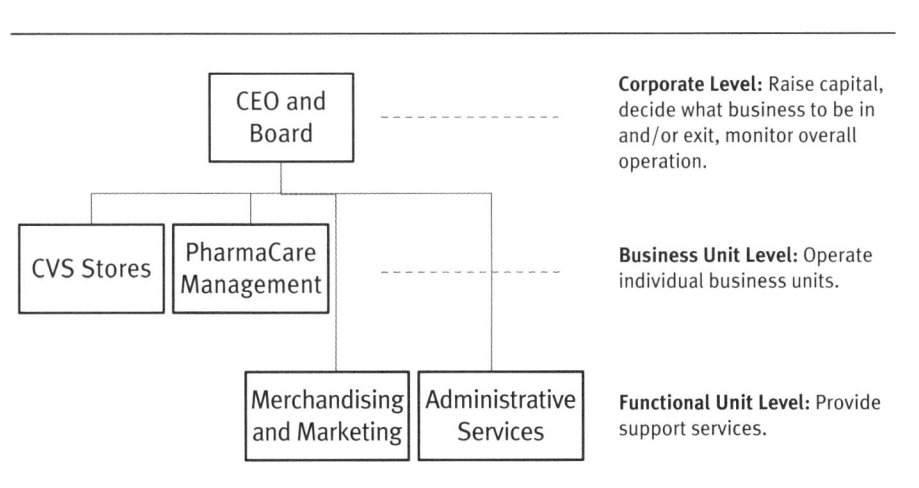

EXHIBIT 18.1
CVS Health's Three Levels of Organization

Corporate Level: Raise capital, decide what business to be in and/or exit, monitor overall operation.

Business Unit Level: Operate individual business units.

Functional Unit Level: Provide support services.

Organizational chart:
- CEO and Board
  - CVS Stores
  - PharmaCare Management
    - Merchandising and Marketing
    - Administrative Services

EXHIBIT 18.2
Healthcare Organizations by Percentage of Ownership

Organization Type	For-Profit (%)	Not-for-Profit (%)	Government (%)	System Affiliated (%)
Nursing homes	69	24	7	58[a]
Hospitals	24	57	19	57[b]
Home health agencies[a]	81	15	5	—
Hospices[a]	63	23	14	—

Source: Data from Kaiser Family Foundation (2019) except as noted.
[a]Data from Centers for Disease Control and Prevention (2020); figures are for 2015–16 (latest available).
[b]Data from American Hospital Association (2021).

professionals, such as doctors and dentists, often organize into professional corporations.

Healthcare organizations may also be owned and operated by various parties, where ownership type varies by the industry segment. As can be seen in exhibit 18.2, except for hospitals, the majority of healthcare organizations are for-profit entities. Home health agencies have the highest percentage of for-profit businesses, at 81 percent, while only 24 percent of hospitals are for-profit.

Organizational Structure and Organizational Design

organizational structure
The way a company arranges its tasks, work, and people to create a product or service and achieve its goals.

organizational design
The alignment of the organizational structure, including its roles and processes for formal reporting relationships, with organizational mission and goals.

Organizations choose how to structure their reporting relationships in several different ways. **Organizational structure** describes the way a company arranges its tasks, work, and people to create a product or service and achieve its goals. An organization's structure depends on its culture, management preferences, company size, geographic dispersion, and array of products and services (Walston 2018). A similar term, **organizational design**, normally refers to the alignment of an organization's structure—including its roles and processes for formal reporting relationships—with its mission and goals. Organizational design includes deciding what the organization will make internally versus buy from others, breaking jobs into optimal subtasks, designating roles, acquiring or developing technology, and instituting and enforcing policies toward achievement of its mission.

The role and scope of duties can vary substantially from organization to organization. Small organizations, such as single-physician practices, may have all staff report to a single person—be it an office manager or the physician—and may give staff many overlapping and shared duties. As organizations grow and more employees are added, duties become more specialized and responsibilities divided.

Division of Labor

Prior to the Industrial Revolution, most businesses were small entities run by artisans who handled the full creation of a product. However, the Industrial Revolution introduced new technologies, which created factories that required more workers to run them efficiently. As more employees clustered in organizations, employers sought greater productivity by specialization through a division of labor. **Division of labor** is the segmentation of tasks and roles into smaller components that are performed by separate individuals or groups. A prime example is the assembly line, which segregates work into simple repetitive tasks to reduce unnecessary motion and labor. Workers in these environments become specialized and perform more limited duties.

An American who contributed greatly to the concept of division of labor and today's business structures was Frederick W. Taylor. He argued that the "principal object of management" was to maximize the economic benefits for the employer. To this end, he applied science to maximize employees' efficiency, using time-and-motion studies to reduce unnecessary movements, eliminate waste, and standardize processes and practices. Scientific management was one of the first theories to address management as a scientific problem. As a result, businesses sought to optimize their work by altering how their organizations were structured. As discussed in chapter 1 and 2, Taylor became known as the father of scientific management (Kanigel 2005).

Healthcare extensively follows the principle of division of labor. For example, in a hospital operating room, the roles are clearly and narrowly defined. Surgeons, anesthesiologists, scrub and circulating nurses, and technicians work together to "produce" a successful operation. Each has specified roles. For example, scrub nurses and circulating nurses have distinct jobs. Scrub nurses, wearing sterile gowns and gloves, monitor and provide equipment to the surgeon, whereas circulating nurses, who are not "scrubbed in," perform duties such as retrieving supplies and assisting with documentation. Although assembly lines do not exist in the provision of healthcare, healthcare jobs are segmented. Each role generally requires different education and training, and most workers would have difficulty performing another's duties.

Division of labor has benefits. Specialization allows employees (providers, in healthcare) to gain expertise in their own narrow area. Training can be better coordinated, and professional standards can be established and maintained. However, coordination of patient care can become more difficult. Division of labor requires that a great deal be coordinated and that the

division of labor
The segmentation of tasks and roles into smaller components that are performed by separate individuals or groups.

> **Who Is in Charge of Healthcare?**
>
> During a seminar with a group of healthcare administrators, we asked the participants to diagram the cycle of service that ensues when a patient is wheeled off for, and eventually brought back from, a series of medical tests. After several minutes of discussion about the place of aides, nurses, doctors, and lab technicians in the cycle, the task was completed. As they sat admiring their handiwork, one of the administrators said aloud—as much to himself as to the group—"My goodness! No one is in charge." His insight proved to be a valuable one that we have since seen in other organizations. His explanation went like this: Our hospital is organized and managed by professional specialty—by functions such as nursing, housekeeping, security, pharmacy, and so on. As a result, no single person or group is really accountable for the overall success and quality of the patient's experience. The aides are accountable for a part of the experience, the nurses for another, the lab technicians for another, and so on. There are a lot of people accountable for a part of the service cycle, but no one has personal accountability for an entire cycle of service.
>
> *Source*: Reprinted from Albrecht and Zemke (2008, 38).

product (in healthcare, often the patient) be "handed off" to other personnel. As the box shows, however, care coordination often fails, and no one seems to be in charge.

Some healthcare organizations use liaisons, case managers, task forces, and other personnel to seek coordination across specialized positions. Others have sought to "reengineer" the processes, duties, and relationships and collapse the many fragmented positions into fewer, less specialized jobs (Walston, Lazes, and Sullivan 2004).

Span of Control

Another structural decision that managers must make is how many individuals should report to a manager. This concept is known as **span of control**. The effective size of a span of control depends on a number of factors, including the complexity of the work, the skills and competencies of both the manager and subordinates, employee retention rates, and the geographic clustering of employees and work.

span of control
The number of subordinates who report to a supervisor.

For instance, a complex work environment such as an emergency department or intensive care unit may warrant a lower span of control than a long-term care facility where the work is more routine. Also, seasoned healthcare leaders can manage more individuals and a larger span of control. Likewise, larger spans of control can exist when employees are experienced and highly motivated and require minimal supervision. Having lower turnover allows greater stability in relationships and competencies that may allow expanded spans of control. Spans of control can also be larger when work and employees are clustered in relatively close geographic proximity; while more dispersed work locations lend themselves generally to smaller spans of control.

Finding a span of control that matches the work context is important. Some research suggests that nursing unit managers who have very large spans of control and high turnover suffer from lower patient satisfaction (Sherman 2013).

Chain of Command

A management concept that is complementary to span of control is **chain of command**. A chain of command forms the hierarchy—the formal reporting structure—and delineates the direction for formal company communication and decision-making. In this way, employees know who is responsible for what decisions and to whom they report. All organizations have some form of a chain of command.

Traditionally, healthcare, like many industries, operated with a relatively small span of control and a clear chain of command in a very hierarchical organization. For example, exhibit 18.3 shows Mercy Health's organizational chart as of 2015, which displays its span of control. Mercy Health employs more than 6,500 people and provides a wide variety of hospital and nonhospital care in Australia. As seen in the exhibit, all supervisors have a relatively small span of control; nine people report to the group CEO, and each area CEO or executive director has between three and five direct reports.

Contrast this chart to the US Department of Veterans Affairs (VA) organizational chart in exhibit 18.4. The VA has a much more hierarchical structure for its almost 400,000 employees and over $200 billion budget.

> **chain of command**
> The hierarchy, or formal reporting structure, that delineates the direction for formal company communication and decision-making.

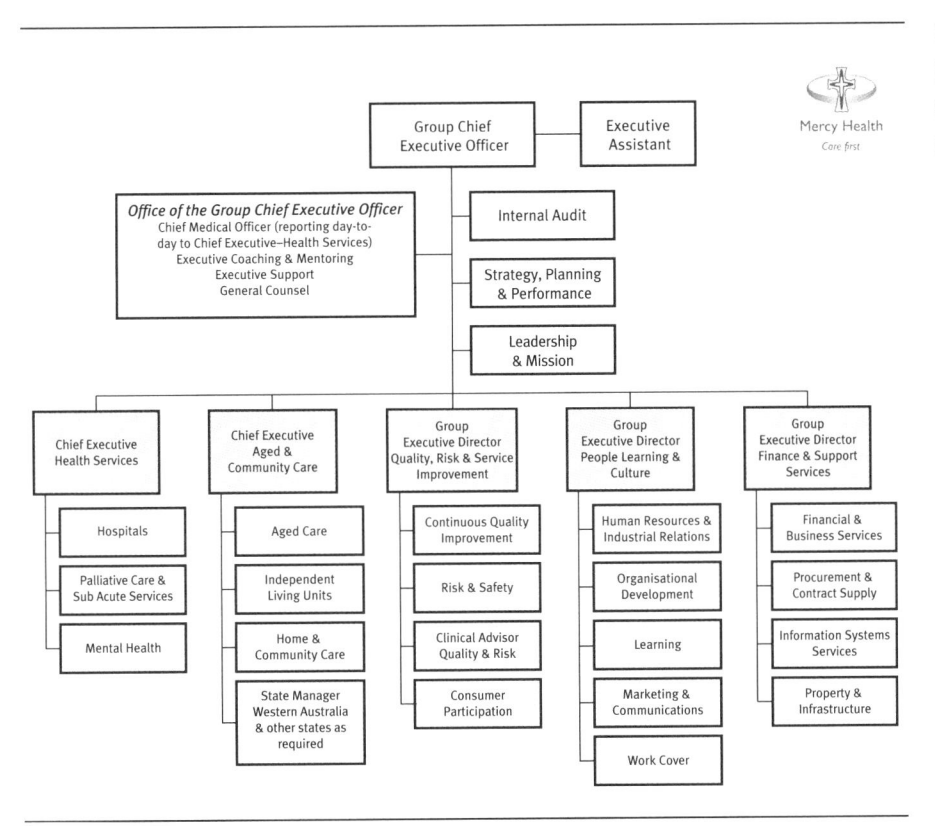

EXHIBIT 18.3
Mercy Health Organizational Chart

Source: Reprinted from Mercy Health (2015).

EXHIBIT 18.4
US Department of Veterans Affairs Organizational Chart

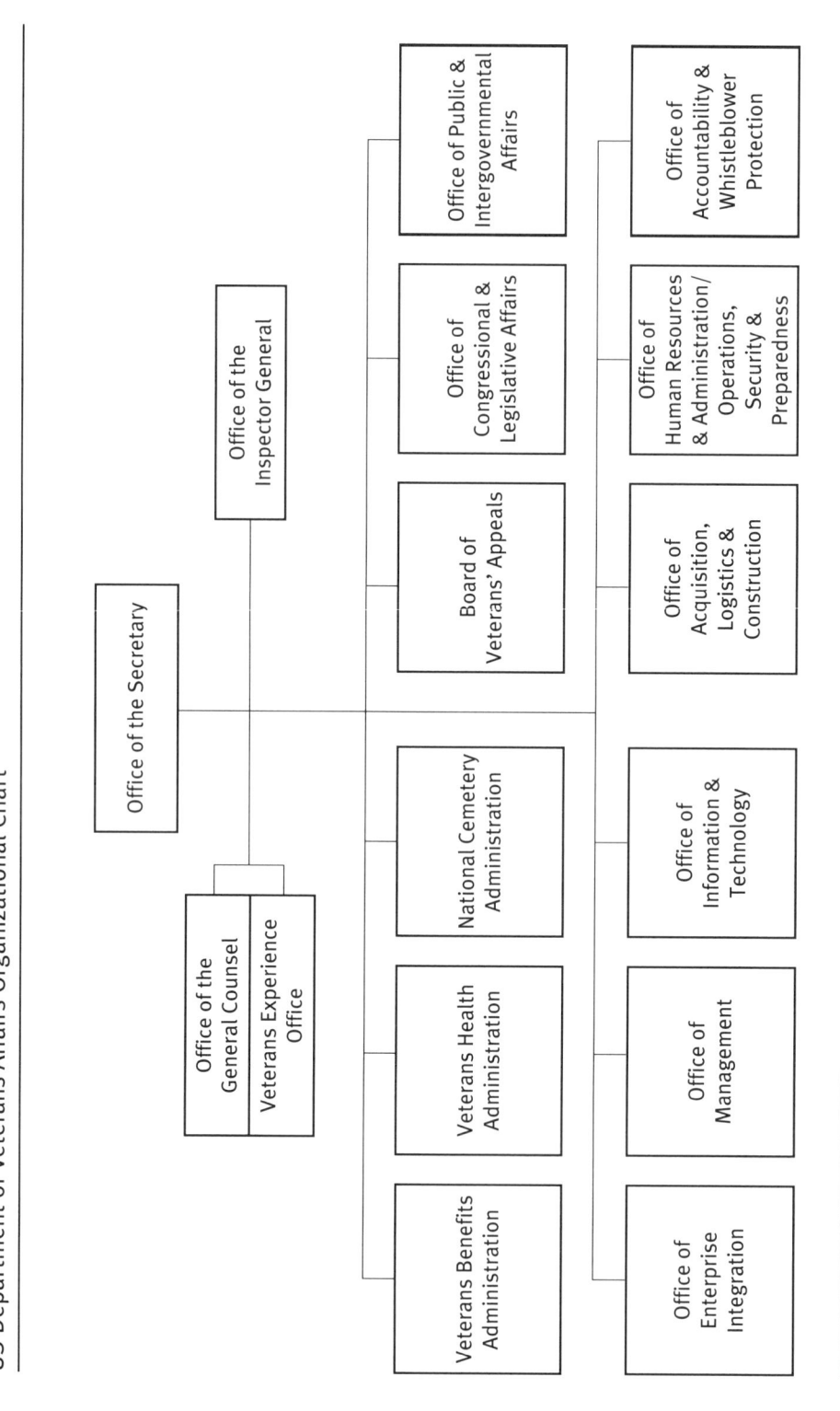

- Office of the Secretary
  - Office of the Inspector General
  - Office of the General Counsel
  - Veterans Experience Office
  - Veterans Benefits Administration
  - Veterans Health Administration
  - National Cemetery Administration
  - Board of Veterans' Appeals
  - Office of Congressional & Legislative Affairs
  - Office of Public & Intergovernmental Affairs
  - Office of Enterprise Integration
  - Office of Management
  - Office of Information & Technology
  - Office of Acquisition, Logistics & Construction
  - Office of Human Resources & Administration/Operations, Security & Preparedness
  - Office of Accountability & Whistleblower Protection

Source: Reprinted from US Department of Veterans Affairs (2020).

Many organizations, however, within and outside healthcare, have attempted to expand their spans of control and delete layers of management. For example, one of the authors once worked for a large hospital company, HealthTrust Inc., that sought economies of scale by combining regions, thus forming a very flat, nonhierarchical structure with 21 hospital CEOs reporting to a regional vice president (see exhibit 18.5).

Flat organizations with larger spans should reduce costs by reducing the number of managers and increase the responsibility, autonomy, and authority of the remaining managers and increase company agility and innovation. Some firms—such as W. L. Gore & Associates (Caulkin 2019) and Nike (Goins 2018)—have had success operating with flat, nonhierarchical structures. Effective, large spans of control empower employees and decentralize decision-making. W. L. Gore, with sales of more than $3.5 billion and about 10,000 employees, operates with only three hierarchical levels and many self-managing teams of 8 to 12 members (Caulkin 2019). To this point, W. L. Gore's website (www.gore.com, "Working at Gore") states:

> There are no traditional hierarchies at Gore, but we're not a completely flat organization. Our lattice structure guides how we operate and communicate; through this structure, Associates engage with whomever is needed to get our work done.

However, other successful companies, such as Amazon, use mostly a hierarchical structure with several levels of management across their departments (Nouri 2019). In 2020 Amazon employed more than 647,000 people managed by 14 senior vice presidents (two called CEOs of their areas) and 12 vice presidents (Dudovskiy 2020).

Traditionally, a span of control of no more than seven or eight employees was recommended; however, US businesses have had an average span of control of 11 in service industries, and 16 in healthcare organizations (Davison 2003). Nurse managers in hospitals and other inpatient facilities often have spans of control exceeding 40 people (Ellrich 2018).

Flat organizations are still relatively rare ("Employee Performance Reviews" 2020). They present problems such as limited advancement potential, the formation of informal cliques, expressions of unprofessional attitudes, and limited workplace diversity that may occur because of the selection of personnel who "fit" the organizational culture (Finley 2014). Flattened structures may also have unintended consequences, such as increasing the

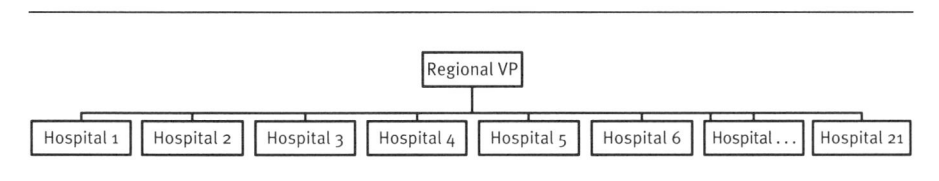

EXHIBIT 18.5
HealthTrust Inc. Regional Structure

Regional VP — Hospital 1, Hospital 2, Hospital 3, Hospital 4, Hospital 5, Hospital 6, Hospital…, Hospital 21

centralization of decision-making, diminishing the desired autonomy, and decreasing communication (Craig 2018).

Flat structures have been found to be more appropriate when the environment is rapidly changing and requires constant innovation. Rapidly changing environments necessitate swift communication and flexibility. Some believe that healthcare organizations must move to flat structures with few administrative levels between patients and executives to achieve the quality improvements recommended by the Institute of Medicine's report *Crossing the Quality Chasm* (Cowen et al. 2008). However, flat organizations by themselves, as indicated earlier, do not guarantee an optimal structure; appropriate coordinative mechanisms, information technologies, and cultures need to be in place.

organic organizations
Organizations characterized by decentralized and participative decision-making, loosely defined roles, and frequent adaptation that brings in new skills and modified roles.

Organic and Mechanistic Organizations

To properly function, flat organizations need the organic characteristics that Burns and Stalker (1961) attributed to **organic organizations**. As shown in exhibit 18.6, organic organizations are characterized by decentralized and

EXHIBIT 18.6
Comparison of Organic and Mechanistic Organization Characteristics

Characteristic	Organic	Mechanistic
Structure	Flat, less specialization	Hierarchical, specialized jobs
Communication	Lateral, diffused	Mostly vertical
Span of control	Wide	Narrow
Decision-making	Decentralized	Centralized
Information flows	Diffused throughout	Concentrated at top, flows downward
Ideal environment	Uncertain, dynamic	Stable, unchanging
Levels of management	Relatively few	Many
Advantages	Free flow of information, feeling of teamwork, wider span of control, able to respond quicker to customer needs	Specialization, discipline, less supervision cost, quick decision-making for company-wide issues, clear lines of responsibility
Disadvantages	High cost of coordination, complex decision-making, high administrative cost, joint specialization, unpredictable work processes, difficult to control	Heavy manager workload, autocratic leadership, rigidity, greater formalization, communication problems

participative decision-making, loosely defined roles, and frequent adaptation that brings in new skills and modified roles. They are fluid and flexible, with employees performing a variety of tasks as dictated by circumstances. On the other hand, more traditional organizations are described as **mechanistic organizations**, with greater job specialization, narrow spans of control, and increased centralization of decision-making.

> **mechanistic organizations**
> Traditional organizations characterized by greater job specialization, narrow spans of control, and increased centralization of decision-making.

Integration and Differentiation

Many companies seem to be constantly reorganizing their structures, seeking the perfect organizational framework. However, no structure is perfect. The best an organization can hope to do is create an organization that responds to the needs of its external environment and reflects its culture. Companies periodically face tensions between the forces of integration (centralization) and differentiation (decentralization). As discussed decades ago by Lawrence and Lorsch (1967), companies often seek to gain synergies through centralization and direct control of organizational functions.

Centralizing functions and decision-making allows managers to make quicker company-wide decisions, establishes clear lines of authority, and provides greater standardization. Executives in centralized organizations often feel more in control because they are constantly making decisions, however trivial. On the other hand, decentralization permits lower-level decision-making, which can allow quicker responses to customer needs. In decentralized organizations, executives serve more as coordinators and facilitators to decision-making.

Structure Types

Although most organizations exhibit variations, they tend to fall under one of three fundamental types of organizational structure: functional, multidivisional, and matrix.

Functional Organizations

Functional organizations divide departments by common duties, tasks, services, or roles. Healthcare is often organized in a functional structure. Many hospitals extend the functional structure even into their C-suite, which may have a chief nursing officer, a chief financial officer, a chief information officer, a chief learning officer, and other executive officers who focus in specialized areas. Functional areas—such as marketing, accounting, business office, maintenance, food services, housekeeping, pharmacy, nursing, laboratory, radiology, and emergency services—are often broken into their own units. Mercy Health, charted in exhibit 18.3, is an example of a functional organization. As can be seen, it is segmented into units for

> **functional organizations**
> Organizations that divide departments by common duties, tasks, services, or roles.

hospitals, palliative care, mental health, finance, procurement, information systems, and so on.

The main advantage of a functional structure is the value that comes with specialization by concentrating similar activities, which develops greater knowledge and skills for specialized personnel and thus higher quality and efficiency. For example, physicians specialize and are grouped into medical departments to concentrate on a smaller skill set and provide a higher quality of care. Specialization allows the physician (and other providers) to complete many more procedures in their specialty, the repetition of which their professional organizations have deemed necessary to maintain competency in that area. For example, the American Board of Surgery (www.absurgery.org) training and certification requirements for physicians seeking to be certified in general surgery include performing at least 850 surgical procedures and having at least 54 months of clinical surgical experience, among many other criteria. Only by specializing in that function can physicians attain the level of activity necessary to meet these targets and maintain their skills.

A functional organization can also readily standardize processes and products, as specialized tasks are centralized in departments that have responsibility for company-wide processes. In this manner, the processes for functions such as finance, marketing, manufacturing, and purchasing are centralized and standardized for their company.

The main disadvantage of a functional structure is the potential for poor communication and coordination among departments. Departments that operate in isolation from each other can become siloed, and competition may even arise that can lead to inefficiencies, conflicting goals, and poor quality. To address the many points of interaction, companies must engage a facilitator or liaison, although this position increases coordination costs (Walston 2018).

The potential problems of a functional structure can be amplified in healthcare with its many professions and their individual professional standards and guidelines. Adherence to these differing professional tenets can lead to misunderstandings and even competition among organizational members; information might be withheld, or inefficiencies and conflict can result. In addition, the many units in a functional organization can delay the transfer of timely information and hinder decision-making. Functional structures are especially prone to impeding the horizontal flow of information and making coordination difficult (Luke, Walston, and Plummer 2004).

As explained by Fiorio, Gorli, and Verzillo (2018), the functional structure in hospitals can be wasteful, due to its

> severe shortcomings, consisting mainly of economic and organizational inefficiencies. In fact, the functional organization often lacks the capability to control

the workflow across departments and thus the coordination of the care activities within a patient care trajectory. Moreover, in the functional organization, resources tend to be duplicated, causing waste, and the autonomy in using the specialty's resources often prevails over accountability, in some cases reducing the effectiveness of treatments.

As functional companies expand across geographic regions and increase the number of products they make, their organizational complexity escalates and the information needs and communication demands on managers intensify. At a certain point, executives feel overloaded and unable to appropriately address the heavy demands to coordinate such a large functionally organized structure. It has long been suggested that information overload because of organizational growth moved many firms to abandon a functional structure and reorganize as a multidivisional company (Chandler 1962).

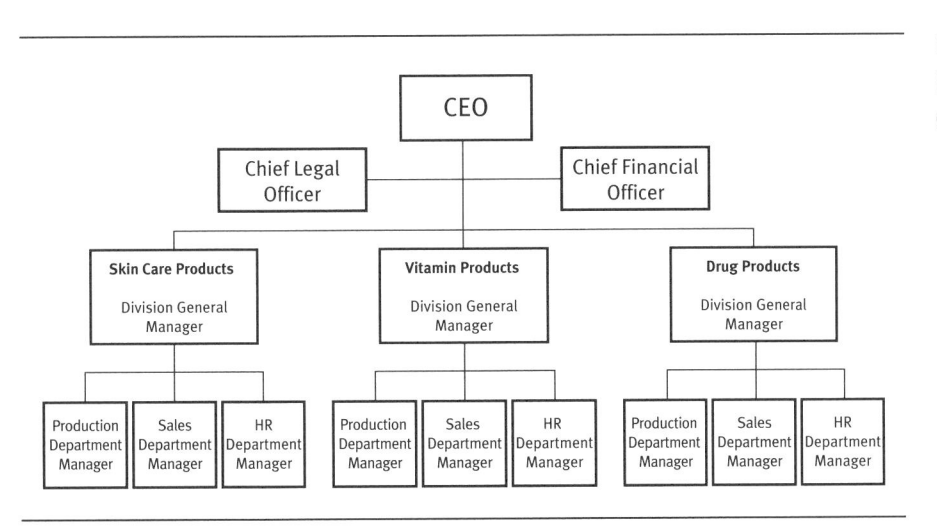

Multidivisional Organizations

Multidivisional companies are popular in large businesses today. Commonly known companies such as Disney, McDonald's, General Motors, and Microsoft use variants of the multidivisional form. In **multidivisional organizations**, a parent company is divided into segments or divisions made up of separate businesses or profit centers so that day-to-day operations occur at a divisional level, allowing the units to act independently. As shown in exhibit 18.7, similar functions are placed in each business unit. For example, instead of having one centralized HR department, each division may have its own HR department.

Divisional leaders, under the parent company's direction, manage and organize their business units. They control and direct their day-to-day divisional resources and operations. Tasks performed in functional

multidivisional organizations Organizations divided into segments or divisions made up of separate businesses or profit centers so that day-to-day operations occur at a divisional level to allow units to act independently.

EXHIBIT 18.7
Multidivisional Organization

multidivisional organizations are duplicated and performed in each division. The greater autonomy encourages innovation and responsiveness to localized needs and frees corporate executives to focus on overall strategy, company direction, and overall divisional operations. Executives can use the similar statistics from their divisions to compare and evaluate performance across the company. This ability facilitates company-wide understanding regarding the performance of divisional products and services and allows parent-company executives to make better decisions about allocation of money and resources to competing divisions.

One advantage of a multidivisional structure is the ability it affords the organization to better allocate financial capital, based on general management's evaluation of division recommendations. Williamson (1975, 148) and other observers have suggested for many years that the parent company's improved ability to "assign cash flows to high yield uses is the most fundamental attribute" and the primary advantage of the multidivisional organization.

Multidivisional structures are created not just to accommodate size but also to expand into dispersed geographic areas where the cultures, markets, customer preferences, politics, and regulations may vary significantly. These companies may establish a multidivisional structure that features international, country-specific, or geography-specific divisions. For example, Baxter International—a very large healthcare supply company with manufacturing facilities in 20 countries making products that are sold in over 100 countries—divides its company into three geographic segments according to the company's 2019 *Form 10-K*: Americas (North and South), Europe/Middle East/Africa, and Asia/Pacific.

Organizations can also be divided by products and service lines if the products and services differ significantly from each other by customer and content. For instance, Johnson & Johnson has divisions dedicated to consumer healthcare, medical devices and diagnostics, and pharmaceuticals. Each division requires different skills and has distinct customers, competitors, and markets. The division leaders can more easily address their specific consumer needs and better develop strategies for their specific markets than might be possible in a different type of organizational structure.

Likewise, hospitals and health systems are organized as multidivisional structures around service lines such as general surgery, cardiovascular, geriatrics, plastic surgery, and orthopedics. Creating divisions around service lines has become common and is seen to reduce costs, increase patients, and improve quality by increasing success rates and patient satisfaction (Druckenmiller 2018). Using service lines permits healthcare organizations to create effective metrics, protocols, and care pathways to reduce costs and improve patients' experiences. In healthcare, this type of division leadership generally includes a physician–hospital partnership arrangement. The box illustrates one method for partnering with physicians in a service line organization that has resulted in improved quality and lower costs.

The decentralization of functions to a multidivisional setting eliminates many in-division coordination problems but may introduce other company-wide coordination challenges. In-division coordination of functional activities (e.g., finance, HR, marketing, engineering, research and development) is facilitated because the activities are located together and controlled by divisional leaders. However, this structure divides and duplicates functions among divisions. Coordination and standardization by the parent company thus become difficult to accomplish. As a result, differing systems and duplicated efforts negatively affect costs and quality. The duplication, unless appropriately managed, may result in inefficiency, redundancy, and uneven quality.

> **Service Line Divisions at Ridgeview Medical Center**
>
> Ridgeview Medical Center, in Waconia, Minnesota, restructured by organizing around service lines. Each of its eight service lines is managed by an administrative lead who partners with at least one physician. Representatives from each line serve on the medical staff executive committee. Unlike a formal co-management arrangement, Ridgeview's approach does not include a management fee nor performance bonuses. Instead, physicians who engage in service line work are paid an hourly stipend to compensate for time spent away from their practices.
>
> Giving physicians a voice in service line management has made doctors, particularly those in independent practice, more willing to engage in quality and efficiency projects. For example, the three competing obstetric groups, two of which are independent, are working together to reduce inductions at fewer than 39 weeks' gestation.... The service lines' focus on implementing evidence-based practices results in less variation in care, and that means improved processes for staff and consistency for patients and their families. Quality improvement translates not only to better care but also reduced readmission rates and lengths of stay.
>
> *Source*: Reprinted from Aston (2015).

Transfer pricing can also be a common problem in multidivisional organizations. Transfer pricing refers to the price set for goods and services that are transferred between divisions of the same company. Divisional units frequently sell services and products to other divisions in the same firm. Establishing a fair transfer price is difficult. As mentioned, one advantage of a multidivisional organization is the increased ability to hold divisions accountable for their performance, which can generate competition among divisions. However, when transference of goods and services occurs across divisions, contradictory incentives and unproductive competition may result. The division producing the good or service desires the highest transfer price, yet the receiving division desires the lowest. Transfer prices may be set at market prices, costs, or somewhere in between. Few companies ever fully eliminate this tension among divisions (Duhaime, Stimpert, and Chesley 2012; Friis 2020).

transfer pricing
The price set for goods and services that are transferred between divisions of the same company.

Matrix Organizations

matrix organizations
Organizations with multiple reporting relationships, generally to both a functional manager and a product or service line manager, that allow horizontal and vertical coordination to concurrently occur.

Matrix organizations involve multiple reporting relationships, allowing horizontal and vertical coordination to occur concurrently. As can be seen in exhibit 18.8, employees in this structure are organized into both functional departments and project or service line groups and have two bosses, generally a functional manager and a product or service line manager. The departmental managers handle the traditional vertical relationships, and the project managers address horizontal relationships that cut across the functional departments. In this way, matrix organizations can incorporate the strengths of both the functional and multidivisional structures while compensating for their weaknesses.

Most large organizations use some variant of matrix structures, and these structures are common in project-driven industries such as construction, aerospace, and telecommunications. Prominent companies such as Boeing, Philips, Digital Equipment Corporation, Procter & Gamble, IBM, Nokia, Unilever, and Cisco have often used matrix structures (Hattangadi 2018).

Many hospital clinical care areas also have adopted the matrix structure. Decades ago, about one-fourth of all large teaching hospitals in the United States reported using matrix structures "to promote the coordination and integration of functional department personnel" (Burns and Wholey 1993, 108). This arrangement superimposes a clinical manager on top of the functional structure such that, as mentioned earlier, employees report to both a unit manager and their functional supervisor. This structure builds in the necessity for interaction, lateral communication, and interchange between the clinical and support personnel, which is critical to improving coordination and breaking down silos. It allows a company to obtain the efficiencies of

EXHIBIT 18.8
Matrix Structure

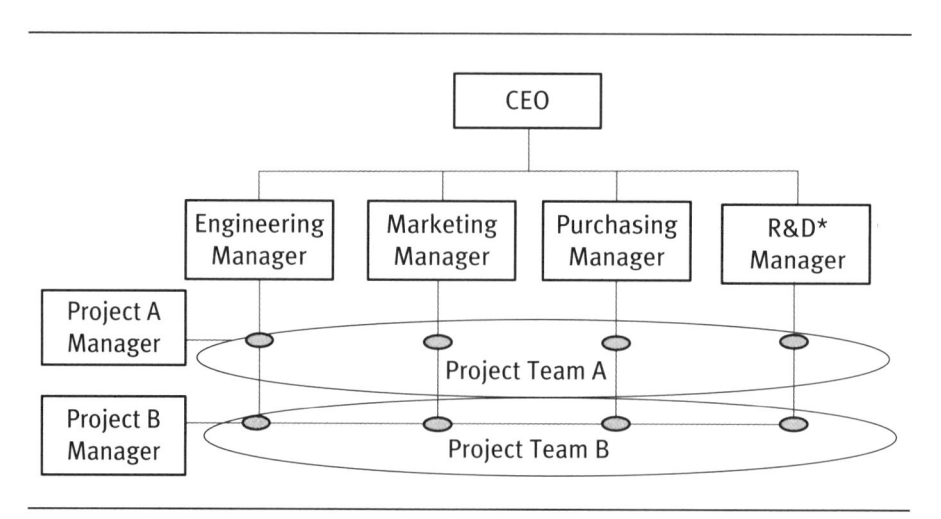

Source: Walston (2018).
*R&D = research and development.

a functional structure while permitting a mechanism to coordinate programs and projects across the departments. Matrix structures in healthcare also provide managers the authority to oversee clusters of patients whose clinical management can then be tracked and treated across the care continuum (Persily 2013). Hospitals seeking to integrate care across professions and service may use matrix management (Axelsson et al. 2014).

Matrix structures tend to work best in companies that develop innovative, project-based products. Diverse staff from disciplines that normally would not work together may form a project team to develop a new drug, airplane, or automobile. Instead of being assigned a cross-departmental task that requires coordination and cooperation across an organizational boundary and then returning results to the department that assigned the task, staff in matrix organizations function as cross-departmental teams to jointly and collaboratively accomplish their work. Efforts are focused on completion of a project or product development, not on the specialized duties of functional units.

Many healthcare companies have adopted at least partial matrix structures because of the increasing market pressures and complexity of healthcare delivery. They believe that only through a matrix structure can they achieve the quality improvements needed in patient care. As such, they have used a matrix structure in organizing interprofessional teams, which brings together members of different departments to work on specific objectives. As healthcare moves into accountable care organizations, which require coordination of care rather than traditional treatment of illness, matrix arrangements may engender the needed cooperative behavior among providers and producers of healthcare (Axelsson et al. 2014; Persily 2013).

Matrix structures can create problems, however. Any time two people are jointly responsible for anything, cooperative behavior can quickly be tested, as when the two bosses have divergent goals. Power struggles can erupt and hinder performance. Employees may also be unclear about which of their bosses has responsibility for which decisions or duties. The two-boss challenge runs contrary to traditional command-and-control management and has been difficult for many organizations to adopt successfully. The matrix organization, although popular in the 1970s, was declared a fad by some management experts, who suggested that its complexity caused too much confusion and could become detrimental to innovation (Peters and Waterman 1982).

Of course, the success or failure of a matrix structure depends substantially on how it is implemented. Ambiguity, poor communication, and lack of accountability in matrix structures cause conflict and diminished performance:

> Addressing the role ambiguity that pervades matrixed companies is a critical priority for their leaders . . .

> It is also imperative to maintain day-to-day lines of communication to root out and dispel ambiguity and ensure that everyone is consistently on the same page. . . .
>
> Last, the matrix structure is notorious for frequently obscuring lines of accountability, so leaders and managers should ensure that all employees understand whom they answer to and the duties for which they are responsible. (Bazigos and Harter 2016)

The amount of authority given to a project or service line manager can significantly affect the success of using a matrix structure. At one extreme, the project manager may be given no budgetary control or authority over employees and serve as a liaison and team leader while the functional manager has authority and responsibility for the performance, costs, and evaluation of employees. Under this approach, the project manager's primary responsibilities are documenting milestones and communicating the project's progress to functional managers. Without authority, the project manager becomes essentially a cheerleader, whose lack of authority can substantially delay projects and key decisions.

A more moderate approach gives project managers budgetary control over the project and the authority to recruit resources from different functional units as the functional managers act in a supporting role but remain responsible for evaluating the performance of their employees who are assigned to projects. This option provides greater authority to project managers, but employees remain tied to their departments, which is where their evaluations take place.

A third approach permits project and functional managers to share financial responsibility. Shared responsibility accentuates the critical need for a good relationship between the two managers, as they must be able to collaborate, share decision-making, and communicate well to make this option work. This is often the structure used, as previously mentioned, in large medical centers where administrators and clinicians share responsibility for a program or project. McKinsey & Company suggests a similar interlocking model called a "helix organization" that divides traditional matrix manager duties into value-creation and capabilities (De Smet, Kleinman, and Weerda 2019).

Advantages and Disadvantages of Different Structures

All organizational structures offer both advantages and disadvantages. No ideal organizational structure exists, but some work better than others in certain conditions. Exhibit 18.9 displays each structure and the environmental conditions for which it is best suited. For example, a functional structure may be ideal in stable markets for small firms that are centralized geographically and deliver a relatively small number of products and services.

As shown, use of a multidivisional structure may benefit large organizations positioned in geographically dispersed markets that hold distinctive consumer preferences. This structure also may be applicable for

EXHIBIT 18.9
Advantages and Disadvantages of Functional, Multidivisional, and Matrix Structures

Structure	Advantages	Disadvantages	Most Suitable Conditions
Functional	• Specialization and standardization across company	• Growth-induced information overload on top executives • Creation of silos and lack of communication among departments	• Small firms that are geographically centralized and produce a modest number of products and services • Stable markets
Multidivisional	• Adaptability to local conditions • Uniform monitoring and comparisons among divisions • Reduction of information overload on top executives • Focus on allocation of capital and overall strategies	• Duplication of functions • Inefficiency • Less standardization among units	• Large firms with divisions in geographically dispersed, distinct markets that may change independently
Matrix	• Collaboration and interaction among departments	• Two-boss challenge • Inefficiency • Difficult to manage	• Firms that are developing products and projects • Uncertain markets with changing technology and consumer tastes

Source: Walston (2018).

conglomerates that operate business units, which offer diverse products and services. On the other hand, matrix structures appear best suited for companies that seek to develop new products and services for changing markets. In particular, matrix structures may be more successful for product- and project-oriented firms that exist in markets that are rapidly changing as a result of technological innovation. In addition, they are more effective than the other structures if their customers' tastes and preferences are also shifting.

However, few organizations use only one type of these structures; combinations and amalgams of the structures are most common. For instance, a functional structure might be used for support departments such as accounting and finance to ensure consistent, standardized oversight across the organization. Yet at the same organization, a multidivisional geographic structure might be employed for product sales to allow for customization as needed by customers in different markets. Healthcare corporations often exhibit such mixed structures, with the functional support areas of information technology, patient accounts, purchasing, payroll, and credentialing services centralized, while patient care services are decentralized into multidivisional units.

Possible Future Structures in Healthcare

Current and future changes in the US healthcare system, including mandates of the Affordable Care Act (ACA), are altering the way healthcare will be provided, which may necessitate modifications to governance structures. In part, the ACA establishes **accountable care organizations** (ACOs), defined by the Centers for Medicare & Medicaid Services (CMS) (2020) as "groups of doctors, hospitals, and other health care providers, who come together voluntarily to give coordinated high-quality care." In addition, most groups will be paid for services by some type of adjusted capitation reimbursement. These changes will considerably alter the relationships among patients, providers, and payers.

Structures will need to change as well, as ACOs must be accountable for the quality, cost, and care of the defined ACO population; affiliate with a legal structure that can receive and distribute bundled shared-savings payments; include primary care physicians; implement clinical and administrative management systems; and ensure coordination of care (Pierce-Wrobel and Micklos 2018). This transition has been difficult for many healthcare organizations that have historically been organized in primarily functional structures that have generally operated independently.

Future organizational structures will have to be more inclusive and expand to allow local provider organizations to have the authority and

---

accountable care organizations
"Groups of doctors, hospitals, and other healthcare providers who come together to give coordinated high-quality care" (CMS 2020).

ability to better manage care. Possible new structures include group practice arrangements, networks of individual practices, partnerships and joint ventures between providers, and other hybrid arrangements. Although hospitals were predicted to be at the forefront of ACO creation, physician groups have increasingly led the formation and operation of these organizations (Muhlestein, Tu, and Colla 2020; National Association of ACOs 2020). Integration of the functional and matrix forms of governance will be critical to the success of ACOs.

Changing structures to meet the needs of ACOs is expected to be difficult. Many of an ACO's structural requirements appear to resemble the integrated delivery systems that were created, and mostly failed, in the 1990s. These structures needed to align physicians, other providers, and hospitals to properly coordinate patient care, which proved to be very challenging. Designing a structure that accomplishes such alignment will be critical to the success of ACOs ("ACOs and CINs" 2019; Burns and Pauly 2012).

Team-Based Structures

Increasingly, companies are focused on and working within teams. Rather than being directed by the traditional hierarchical structures, firms are moving to autonomous or semiautonomous cross-functional work teams within a flatter organization centered around processes. As previously discussed, traditional hierarchical structures have vertical reporting structures and work is divided into functional specialties. Team-based structures, however, focus on a mutual goal through interdependent actions and accountability. Team-based structures in healthcare are being used to improve patient outcomes and team members' well-being (Armstrong 2013).

One global survey reported that almost one-third (31 percent) of large firms performed most or almost all of their work in team-based structures, which appeared to improve performance. Companies using work teams include Cisco, Google, and Liberty Mutual (Volini et al. 2019). Healthcare has also shifted to more team-based structures, with physician practices and other clinical care providers moving to greater functional and cultural integration (Kyle, Aveling, and Singer 2020). Healthcare providers are beginning to understand the importance of team-based care. However, challenges of reimbursement, leadership and culture exist that create barriers to this shift (Hupke 2016).

Modular or Network Structures

Network structures, also called modular or virtual organizations, allow for flexibility and decentralization. In this structure, managers coordinate and direct relationships both internal and external to their company. Modular companies focus on their core competencies and rely on other firms to

network structures
Organizational structures, also called modular or virtual organizations, that allow for flexibility and decentralization.

perform noncore activities. For instance, a company may partner with external firms for development, production, and sales. Nike is a good example of this type of structure; it acts like a virtual organization through the companies with which it contracts to produce most of its almost 100 million shoes annually. Nike owns no manufacturing facilities and links networks through technology. Internal functions focus on marketing and design, with most other functions outsourced (Gallimore 2020). Network organizations require network partners to establish trusting relationships so that the network companies can concentrate on what they do well and subcontract tasks outside their competencies to others. Such relationships minimize the need for administrative overhead and function well in uncertain and changing markets.

Organizational Structure and the Environment

Although an optimal structure will never exist, the choice of organizational structure should relate to the internal and external environments of a company. Each structure has pluses and minuses, but the degree of complexity and uncertainty in and surrounding a firm suggests which structure may be best for the organization to use. Complexity increases as a firm grows in size and spreads geographically. Likewise, increased market competition creates a more complex environment. Uncertainty can arise from technological advances, legislation and policy changes, and other factors.

Low levels of complexity and uncertainty diminish the need for organizational flexibility and allow centralization. As shown in exhibit 18.10, functional organizations may be preferred for low-complexity and low-uncertainty situations. As complexity and uncertainty increase, the other structures should be considered, with the horizontal and network structures being ideal in environments with high complexity and uncertainty.

Governing Boards

Most businesses are overseen by a governing board—a board of directors in for-profit organizations or a board of trustees in not-for-profit settings. The same is true in the healthcare industry. A properly functioning board is critical for a successful organization. Simply stated, a board's primary responsibilities are to provide overall policy direction and oversight and to select the organization's CEO, who generally reports to the board.

Governing boards widely vary in their composition, structure, and operation. According to a 2019 Governance Institute survey, hospital or

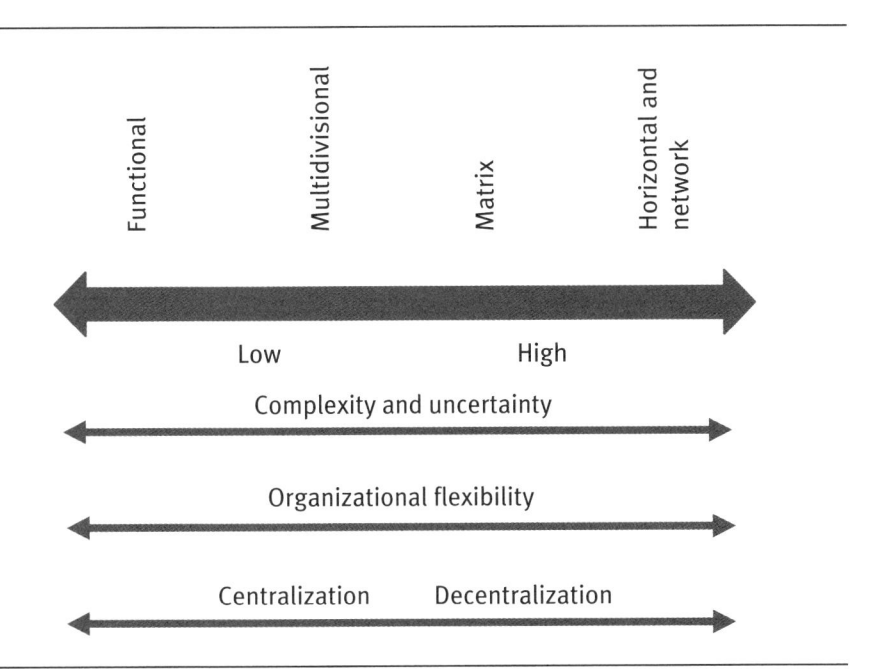

EXHIBIT 18.10
Organizational Structures and Environment

```
Functional    Multidivisional    Matrix    Horizontal and network
   <──────────────────────────────────────────────>
              Low                  High
              Complexity and uncertainty
         <────────────────────────────────>
              Organizational flexibility
         <────────────────────────────────>
              Centralization   Decentralization
         <────────────────────────────────>
```

health system boards in the United States average 12.4 members, while 10 to 15 members is recommended as an ideal size for most (National Research Corporation 2020). Healthcare system boards have become more important by exercising fiscal and strategic responsibilities beyond their traditional scope (Grossbart 2019). As local authority and governance increase in importance, the role and proper functioning of governing boards will likewise become more important. Governing boards will need to include members with the necessary skills and competencies in an array of areas to appropriately plan, evaluate, and execute. The increasing complexity of healthcare systems will require careful selection and training and greater participation of board members.

Chapter Summary

The way organizations are structured varies widely. No one structure stands out as always better than others; instead, an organization's structure should be crafted to fit its environment and assist in meeting its mission and goals. All organizations have some form of a chain of command, which is the official channel for reporting and formal communication. Large businesses most often use a corporate structure, which allows a group of people to act as a single entity and limits their liability. Healthcare corporations are among the biggest firms in the United States. Corporations can be segmented into three structural levels: corporate, business unit, and functional unit. Each has different roles, with the corporate role deciding the overall business portfolio; the business unit level directing the development, marketing, and provision of products and services; and the functional unit level supporting the other two levels.

Companies can be either for-profit or not-for-profit. For-profit organizations pay taxes and exist to make profits for their owners. Not-for-profits are tax exempt and provide some type of community benefit. Healthcare organizations may be either for-profit or not-for-profit; the percentage of each type varies according to the industry segment.

Organizational structure involves how a company arranges its tasks, work, and people, while organizational design refers to the alignment of an organization's structure. The role and scope of employees' duties vary widely, depending on the size of the organization and many other factors. Prior to the Industrial Revolution, most businesses were small, and individual artisans handled all aspects of product creation. As companies grew with the introduction of new technologies, greater specialization and a division of labor occurred. Scientific management, promoted by Frederick W. Taylor, fostered specialization and time-and-motion efficiencies.

Healthcare workers are highly specialized. Specialization permits enhanced expertise, training, and professionalization. However, coordination often becomes problematic. The lack of coordination remains a problem in healthcare. Healthcare organizations use liaison positions and committees to coordinate across specialized departments.

Another structural concept is span of control, which refers to the number of subordinates who report to a manager. The effective size of a span of control depends on the abilities of the manager and subordinates, retention rates, and variability of work. Complementary to this is the concept of chain of command, which is the formal reporting structure of a company. Traditionally, healthcare has had a relatively small span of control and clear chain of command. However, in the past few decades, more organizations have experimented with flat structures with larger spans of control. Flat structures are effective in rapidly changing environments that require consistent innovation if appropriate coordinative mechanisms are in place to ensure seamless functioning.

Flat organizations can be considered organic organizations, with decentralized decision-making, loosely defined roles, and fluid and flexible reporting structures. Traditional organizations are often described as mechanistic organizations.

Organizations constantly struggle with tensions between centralization and decentralization. Centralizing operations allows relatively quick company-wide decisions, clear lines of authority, and standardization. However, decentralization permits lower-level decision-making, aiding in responsiveness to customers' needs.

Three fundamental organizational structures exist: functional, multidivisional, and matrix. Functional organizations divide their structures by function, such as marketing, accounting, and housekeeping. Their advantages include specialization, by concentrating similar activities, and standardization of processes and products. However, poor communication and coordination may arise as functions are separated, which often occurs in healthcare.

As companies grow bigger and more complex, most move to a multidivisional organization that divides the company into segments or divisions encompassing separate businesses or profit centers. This type of organization allows increased flexibility and independence for day-to-day operations at a divisional level and frees corporate managers to focus on strategic decisions. However, it also duplicates functions across the organization. Divisions can be based on geography (e.g., international versus domestic) or on product or service lines. In healthcare, many organizations are structuring around service lines such as cardiovascular, geriatrics, and orthopedics.

Although multidivisional structures help with coordination among functions, they do divide and duplicate functions across the parent company. Coordination and standardization across the full company can become difficult and result in inefficiencies, redundancies, and uneven quality. In addition, transfer pricing—the price set for goods and services transferred between divisions—can create competition and tension among divisions.

Matrix organizations involve multiple reporting relationships to both functional and product or service line managers, which allows horizontal and vertical coordination. Most large companies and many hospital clinical areas use some type of matrix structure. This structure builds in the need for lateral communication and interchange between both clinical and support personnel to improve tracking and treatment of patients.

Matrix structures can cause difficulties. The two-boss challenge can create tension and power struggles. Its success or failure can be attributed to the amount of authority the project or service line manager is given.

Advantages and disadvantages exist for all organizational structures. However, functional structures may work well in stable markets for smaller firms that deliver a small number of products and services. Likewise, multidivisional structures may benefit larger organizations dispersed geographically. Matrix structures may be best for product- and project-oriented firms whose markets are rapidly changing, along with their customers' tastes and preferences.

A result of ongoing changes in the US healthcare system may be the establishment of the accountable care organization as the primary means to provide care, for which innovative healthcare structures may be required. New frameworks may include networks, partnerships, joint ventures, and integrated forms of functional and matrix structures. Any or all of these may rely on aspects of horizontal and network structures.

Organizational structures should adapt to the level of companies' complexity and uncertainty. Low-complexity and low-uncertainty environments call for functional structures, more rigidity, and centralization. High levels of these factors set the stage for greater flexibility and decentralization.

As stated, no optimal structure exists. The choice and successful use of any structure depends on numerous factors, both internal and external to the organization. Understanding those influences and the needs of the alternative structures can greatly assist and benefit a healthcare manager.

Governing boards are in place in most public and private healthcare organizations. They have responsibility for overall company policies, oversight, and selection and evaluation of the organization's CEO. Properly functioning governing boards are essential to the success of healthcare organizations.

Chapter Questions

1. How do chains of command exist in every organization?
2. What does it mean to be a for-profit healthcare organization?
3. What are the advantages and disadvantages of division of labor?
4. What factors influence the optimal size of a span of control?
5. Although flat organizational structures reduce layers to improve communication, what are some of the problems they can create?
6. What are the primary differences between an organic organization and a mechanistic organization?
7. What is the advantage to healthcare organizations of using functional structures?
8. How does transfer pricing affect multidivisional organizations?
9. In what situation might it be best to use a matrix structure?
10. What types of structures may be needed to confront the challenges of a changing healthcare market?

Chapter Cases

The Fragmented University Healthcare Venture

One university had a great opportunity to establish an international healthcare campus in Asia. The host government had invited selected universities from around the world to create a global healthcare campus and would provide subsidies and loans for five years, which should be sufficient to attract an adequate number of students to become self-supporting. The satellite campus was to be both a training and a clinical site.

It was unclear who would be in charge of the satellite campus. A few years earlier, the university had established an office of global engagement to increase the school's international presence. The vice president (VP) of global affairs was a former dean and reported directly to the university president. At the same time, the VP of the university's health system was technically in charge of all healthcare provision. Both executives seemed to have responsibility for establishing this venture.

It seemed that the decision to proceed with the venture was much easier than organizing it. In addition to the global VP and health system VP, the VP of student affairs and the provost for academic affairs on the main campus demanded a presence and commensurate authority. Policies and procedures on the satellite campus, including admission criteria, were to be the same as on the main campus, with little input from those working at the satellite campus. However, the individual who had been hired as satellite campus president wanted full authority to run the remote operation and wished to report directly to the main university president, because he almost immediately clashed with the global VP, to whom he was scheduled to report. As a result of the poor relationship, the satellite campus president was given responsibility for only a portion of the satellite campus functions, and a satellite campus provost for academic affairs was hired, as a peer of the satellite campus president, who was to report to the global VP. Neither the global VP nor the health system VP had a direct relationship with the university provost or the VP of student affairs. All reported directly to the president of the university, who had made the decision to establish the satellite campus but would not be involved in developing operational processes and strategies.

The chain of command for this structure was complicated, with individuals reporting to multiple bosses. For example, the satellite campus provost, although technically a direct report of the university provost, also reported to the global VP, the health system VP, and the head of his faculty department. Most of his reporting and coordination took place through the global VP, but his evaluation was conducted by his department head. Plus, the major areas at the satellite campus reported to different supervisors on the main campus, so ultimately the university president was the only person to have everyone report to him. Therefore, when disagreements arose that could not be settled among peers, the only person in the university who could resolve them was the university president, who rarely took the time to do it. As a result, most areas of disagreement were not addressed at all.

Standing committees were established to govern the satellite campus. These included three at a general level and three at a campus level. The general committees were Leadership, Academic Affairs, and Student Affairs, and the campus committees were Recruitment, Clinical Affairs, and Operations. The composition and responsibilities of each committee were as follows:

Leadership Committee
Role: Coordinate activities of the satellite campus, and resolve problems and formulate policy
Composition: Health system VP, global VP, assistant VP student affairs, campus president, campus provost, assistant global VP for finance, six department heads
Chair: Assistant global VP for finance

Academic Affairs Committee
Role: Discuss and recommend academic policies for the satellite campus
Composition: Campus provost, recruitment personnel, registrar office personnel, six department heads
Chair: Jointly chaired by the campus provost and a department chair

Student Affairs Committee
Role: Discuss and recommend student affairs policies for the satellite campus
Composition: Campus provost, assistant VP student affairs, satellite campus and main campus recruiting personnel
Chair: Assistant VP student affairs

Campus Operations Committee
Role: Oversee the physical and operational decisions at the satellite campus
Composition: Campus president, campus provost, campus finance officer, campus operations manager
Chair: Campus president

Campus Clinical Affairs Committee
Role: Ensure clinical quality and safety
Composition: Clinic manager, campus provost, campus finance officer, operations manager, three healthcare staff
Chair: Clinical manager

Campus Recruitment Committee
Role: Direct and conduct student recruitment activities
Composition: Campus recruitment personnel, campus president, campus provost, three campus faculty
Chair: Campus recruitment director

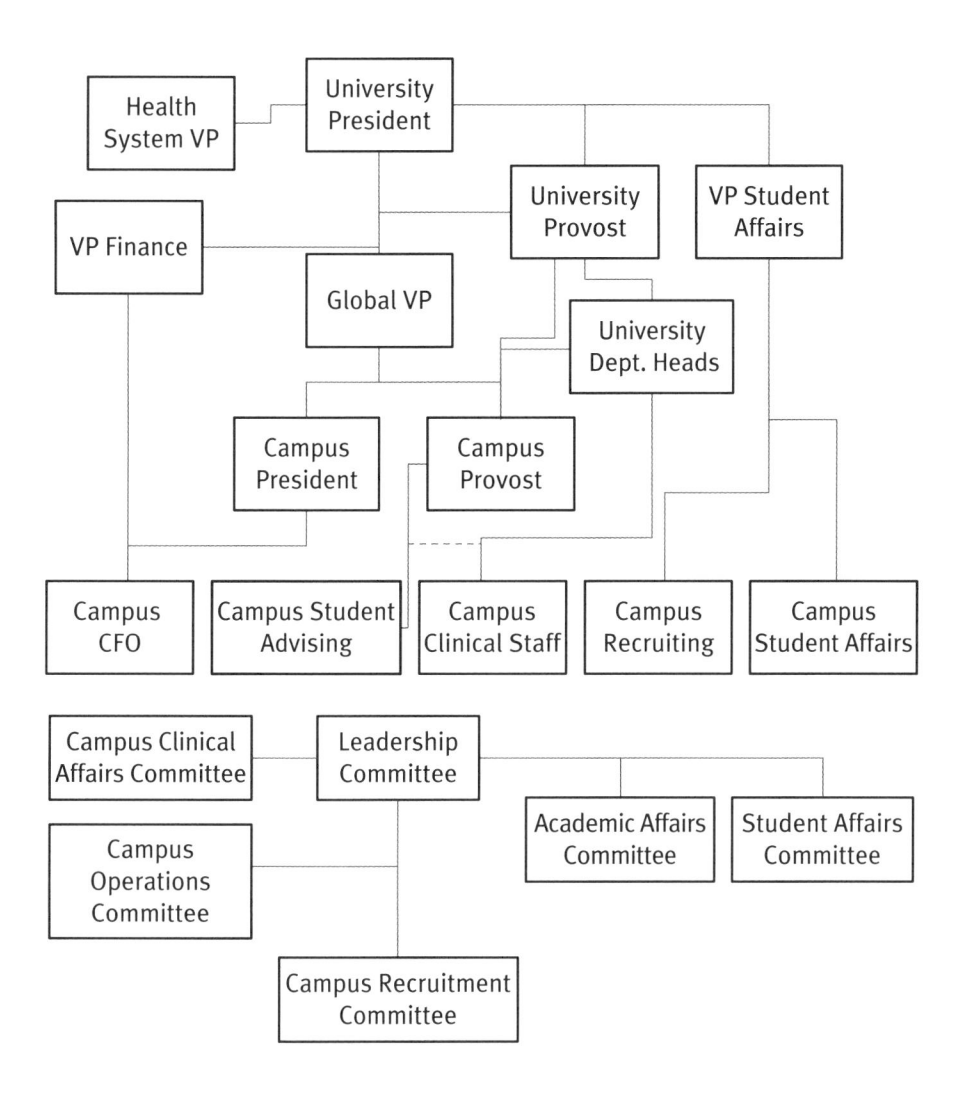

Chapter 18: Organizational Design and Structure

```
                    ┌─────────────┐
                    │ University  │
       ┌────────────│ President   │────────────┐
       │            └─────────────┘            │
┌──────────────┐           │          ┌──────────────┐
│   Health     │           │          │ VP Student   │
│  System VP   │    ┌─────────────┐   │   Affairs    │
└──────────────┘    │ University  │   └──────────────┘
                    │  Provost    │
┌──────────────┐    └─────────────┘
│  VP Finance  │           │
└──────────────┘    ┌─────────────┐   ┌──────────────┐
                    │  Global VP  │   │  University  │
                    └─────────────┘   │ Dept. Heads  │
                                      └──────────────┘
            ┌──────────────┐  ┌──────────────┐
            │    Campus    │  │    Campus    │
            │  President   │  │   Provost    │
            └──────────────┘  └──────────────┘
```

| Campus CFO | Campus Student Advising | Campus Clinical Staff | Campus Recruiting | Campus Student Affairs |

| Campus Clinical Affairs Committee | Leadership Committee | | Academic Affairs Committee | Student Affairs Committee |

| Campus Operations Committee | | | |

| | Campus Recruitment Committee | | |

The committees were to meet monthly to conduct business. However, because of the 14-hour time difference between the main campus and the satellite campus, scheduling and holding the meetings consistently was difficult. The Student Affairs and Campus Recruitment Committees each met once, were not sure what they were to accomplish, and never met again. The Campus Operations Committee met only sporadically. The Academic Affairs, Clinical Affairs, and Leadership Committees did meet monthly, but reports seemed hurriedly prepared and abbreviated for the Leadership Committee because the agenda was always long and key people frequently did not attend.

Many, including the VP of global affairs, felt it essential that the committees meet monthly as previously planned. The issue was raised several times in the Leadership Committee, where those involved tacitly agreed but always found excuses not to hold the committee meetings. The VP of global affairs did not want to raise the issue to the university president, so the meetings were not held.

Likewise, making decisions and creating policies became a big challenge. Campus administrators frequently had difficulty deciding where decisions needed to go. To be certain all bases were covered, the issues were often taken to multiple parties, resulting in multiple, contrary decisions. For example, the campus administrators convinced the VP of global affairs that a major change in the admission criteria was necessary. However, the health system VP and the VP for student affairs, who were responsible for recruitment on the main campus, refused to consider any change. The proposal was ultimately referred to and died in a main campus committee. As a result, campus administrators failed to bring up many issues that needed to be addressed, and those that were brought forth often languished for months before being decided on. Campus administrators continued to act but were regularly frustrated.

Case Questions
1. Why are committee structures often superimposed over organizational structures?
2. Why did the committee structure fail to fully function? What could be done to make it work?
3. What structural changes would you recommend? Why?

The Case of a Flat Structure but Centralized Control

Although a flat structure has been promoted to decentralize decision-making, decentralization does not necessarily occur. The style of decision-making and the way information flows through an organization can be distinct from the type of structure used. Conversely, tall, hierarchical organizations can decide to decentralize decision-making without altering their structure.

HealthBest Inc. decided to eliminate two regions and one layer of management, predicting that these changes would reduce costs and speed decision-making. The Western Region was created, with 21 hospital CEOs reporting directly to the regional VP. All CEOs met with key regional and corporate managers shortly before the structural changes were to be announced. The corporate chief operating officer, Hud, explained the rationale, stressing the need for quicker decisions as the company faced more aggressive competition. He showed a slide that stated, "A flatter structure for a more competitive environment." All the CEOs seemed to be positive about the changes.

At the end of the meeting, a question-and-answer session was held. One CEO asked which decisions the CEOs were going to be able to make now that they could not before and wondered if they would change the six-month budget preparation process or alter their signatory authority. Currently, each CEO could approve costs of up to $25,000, and the regional

VPs up to $100,000. Hud appeared embarrassed and finally replied that the regional VP would clearly decentralize the decision-making, but no changes in the budget process or signatory authority were contemplated. He explained that the decentralization would occur as the regional VP saw fit, but that this would be a very challenging year for the company, and everyone was going to have to perform at a much higher level.

Hud then went on to discuss the new incentive structure, which allowed CEOs and regional VPs to earn a bonus of up to 80 percent of their base salary if they achieved certain objectives—mostly financial. Hud felt certain that these could be achieved with the new, flat structure.

On returning to their hospitals, the CEOs did not see many differences in their relationship with their regional VP, except that more data were required weekly. Reports on staffing hours, patient satisfaction, quality indicators, and projected monthly financial data were added to the CEOs' duties. In addition, the regional VP could be expected to call at any time—sometimes several times a week—to ask questions about the submitted data. On the other hand, if the CEOs needed an approval or had a situation that required the regional VP's input to resolve, it could take days to reach her.

Case Questions
1. What was the relationship between a flat structure and the decision-making process for the region?
2. What would need to occur to change the decision-making process? Did the overall structure need to become flat for this change to take place?
3. What else should the region do to become more efficient?

Chapter Activities

1. Identify two of the healthcare organizations in your area. These can be hospitals or healthcare systems, large clinics, post-acute care organizations, or others. In small teams, do some research to locate their organizational chart and analyze the organization's structure. Is it flat or hierarchical? Is it a multidivisional organization? Does it have any characteristics of a matrix organization? Where is the largest span of control in the organization? Compare what you learn with what others have found.
2. Read the first two chapters in *The Guide to Good Governance for Hospital Boards* (American Hospital Association Center for Healthcare Governance, https://trustees.aha.org/sites/default/files/trustees/09-guide-to-good-governance.pdf). Write a one- to two-page paper on the duties and roles of hospital boards.

3. Read "COVID-19 Pandemic Could Result in Permanent Governance Changes at Hospitals" (Jeff Legasse, Healthcare Finance, April 14; www.healthcarefinancenews.com/news/covid-19-pandemic-could-result-permanent-governance-changes-hospitals) which discusses the potential changes for hospital governance caused by the COVID-19 pandemic. What recommendations does this article call for? What factors are causing these potential changes?

References

"ACOs and CINs: Past, Present, and Future." 2019. *Health Catalyst*, May 14. www.healthcatalyst.com/insights/acos-cins-past-present-future.

Albrecht, K., and R. Zemke. 2008. *Service America! Doing Business in the New Economy*. San Diego: Karl Albrecht International.

American Hospital Association. 2021. "Fast Facts on U.S. Hospitals, 2021." www.aha.org/statistics/fast-facts-us-hospitals.

Armstrong, J. 2013. "Leadership and Team-Based Care." AMA Journal of Ethics, *Virtual Mentor* 13 (6): 534–37. https://doi.org/10.1001/virtualmentor.2013.15.6.msoc2-1306.

Aston, G. 2015. "Service-Line Management: A Behind the Scenes Road to Value." *Hospitals & Health Networks*, January 13. www.hhnmag.com/articles/3757-service-line-management-a-behind-the-scenes-road-to-value.

Axelsson, R., S. G. Axelsson, J. Gustafsson, and J. Seemann 2014. "Organizing Integrated Care in a University Hospital: Application of a Conceptual Framework." *International Journal of Integrated Care* 14: e019. https://doi.org/10.5334/ijic.1529.

Bazigos, M., and J. Harter. 2016. "Revisiting the Matrix Organization." McKinsey & Company, January 1. www.mckinsey.com/business-functions/organization/our-insights/revisiting-the-matrix-organization.

Becker's Hospital Review. 2020. "100 of the Largest Hospitals and Health Systems in America/2020." November 5. www.beckershospitalreview.com/lists/100-of-the-largest-hospitals-and-health-systems-in-america-2020.html.

Burns, L. R., and D. R. Wholey. 1993. "Adoption and Abandonment of Matrix Management Programs: Effects of Organizational Characteristics and Interorganizational Networks." *Academy of Management Journal* 36 (1): 106–38.

Burns, L. R., and M. V. Pauly. 2012. "Accountable Care Organizations May Have Difficulty Avoiding the Failures of Integrated Delivery Networks of the 1990s." *Health Affairs* 31 (11): 2407–16. https://doi.org/10.1377/hlthaff.2011.0675.

Burns, T., and G. M. Stalker. 1961. *The Management of Innovation*. London: Tavistock.

Caulkin, S. 2019. "WL Gore: The Company Others Try and Fail to Imitate." *Financial Times*, August 2. www.ft.com/content/aee67fe0-ac63-11e9-b3e2-4fdf846f48f5.

Centers for Disease Control and Prevention. 2020. "Long-Term Care Providers and Services Users in the United States, 2015–2016." Appendix III. Detailed Tables, table V, www.cdc.gov/nchs/fastats/home-health-care.htm.

Centers for Medicare & Medicaid Services (CMS). 2020. "Accountable Care Organizations (ACOs)." www.cms.gov/Medicare/Medicare-Fee-for-Service-Payment/ACO.

Chandler, A. D. 1962. *Strategy and Structure: Chapters in the History of the Industrial Enterprise*. Cambridge, MA: MIT Press.

Cowen, M., L. Halasyamani, D. McMurtrie, D. Hoffman, T. Polley, and J. Alexander. 2008. "Organizational Structure for Addressing the Attributes of the Ideal Healthcare Delivery System," *Journal of Healthcare Management* 53: 407–18.

Craig, W. 2018. "The Nature of Leadership in a Flat Organization." *Forbes* (blog). Posted October 23. www.forbes.com/sites/williamcraig/2018/10/23/the-nature-of-leadership-in-a-flat-organization/.

Davison, B. 2003. "Management Span of Control: How Much Is Too Wide?" *Journal of Business Strategy* 24 (4): 22–29.

De Smet, A., S. Kleinman, and K. Weerda. 2019. "The Helix Organization." *McKinsey Quarterly* 2019 (4). www.mckinsey.com/business-functions/organization/our-insights/the-helix-organization.

Druckenmiller, G., Jr. 2018. "How to Grow High-Value Service Lines Effectively." Healthcare Financial Management Association. Published July 5. www.hfma.org/topics/hfm/2018/july/61155.html.

Dudovskiy, J. 2020. "Amazon Organizational Structure: A Brief Overview." *Business Research Methodology*, March 24. https://research-methodology.net/amazon-organizational-structure-2-2/.

Duhaime, I., L. Stimpert, and J. Chesley. 2012. *Strategic Thinking: Today's Business Imperative*. New York: Routledge.

Ellrich, M. 2018. "How to Reduce Spans of Control in Nursing." *Workplace* (blog). *Gallup*, March 16. www.gallup.com/workplace/236024/reduce-spans-control-nursing.aspx.

"Employee Performance Reviews in a Flat Organizational Structure." 2020. *Trakstar* (blog). Published September 18. www.trakstar.com/blog-post/employee-performance-reviews-flat-organizational-structure/.

Finley, K. 2014. "Why Workers Can Suffer in Bossless Companies Like Github." *Wired*, March 20. www.wired.com/2014/03/tyranny-flatness/.

Fiorio, C. V., M. Gorli, and S. Verzillo. 2018. "Evaluating Organizational Change in Health Care: The Patient-Centered Hospital Model." *BMC Health Services Research* 18 (1): 95. www.ncbi.nlm.nih.gov/pmc/articles/PMC5806258/.

Friis, I. 2020. "Preservation of Incentives Inside the Firm: A Case Study of a Quasi-Market for Cost-Based Transfer Pricing." *Journal of Management Accounting Research* 32 (2): 137–57. https://doi.org/10.2308/jmar-52562.

Gallimore, D. 2020. "Nike's Approach to Outsourcing." The Outsourcing Accelerator (blog). Published March 30. www.outsourceaccelerator.com/articles/nikes-approach-to-outsourcing/.

Goins, J. 2018. "Nike's Flat Organizational Structure." *BizFluent*, December 4. https://bizfluent.com/facts-6887850-nike-s-flat-organizational-structure.html.

Grossbart, S. 2019. "Engaging Health System Boards of Trustees in Quality and Safety: Six Must-Know Guidelines." *Health Catalyst*, June 5. www.healthcatalyst.com/insights/healthcare-boards-quality-safety-pivotal-role.

Hattangadi, V. 2018. "Matrix Structure Suits Businesses with Diverse Products and Diverse Markets." drvidyahattangadi.com. Published August 6. http://drvidyahattangadi.com/matrix-structure-suits-businesses-with-diverse-products-and-diverse-markets/.

Heeringa, J., A. Mutti, M. F. Furukawa, A. Lechner, K. A. Maurer, and E. Rich. 2020. "Horizontal and Vertical Integration of Health Care Providers: A Framework for Understanding Various Provider Organizational Structures." *International Journal of Integrated Care* 20 (1): 2. https://doi.org/10.5334/ijic.4635.

Huffman, K. 2017. "Ask These Five Key Questions Before Restructuring Your Healthcare Organization." *Becker's Hospital Review*, August 8. www.beckershospitalreview.com/hospital-transactions-and-valuation/ask-these-five-key-questions-before-restructuring-your-healthcare-organization.html.

Hupke, C. 2016. "Team-Based Care: Moving from Ideas to Action." Institute for Healthcare Improvement (blog). Published January 29. http://www.ihi.org/communities/blogs/_layouts/15/ihi/community/blog/itemview.aspx?List=7d1126ec-8f63-4a3b-9926-c44ea3036813&ID=192.

Investopedia. 2020. *s.v.* "Corporation." www.investopedia.com/terms/c/corporation.asp.

Kaiser Family Foundation. 2019. State Health Facts database. Specific data sets: Distribution of Certified Nursing Facilities by Chain-Owned Affiliation; Distribution of Certified Nursing Facilities by Ownership Type; Hospitals by Ownership Type. https://www.kff.org/state-category/providers-service-use/.

Kanigel, R. 2005. *The One Best Way: Frederick Winslow Taylor and the Enigma of Efficiency*. Cambridge, MA: MIT Press.

Kyle, M. A., E.-L. Aveling, and S. J. Singer. 2020. "Establishing High-Performing Teams: Lessons from Health Care." *MIT Sloan Management Review* Research Highlight, February 25. https://sloanreview.mit.edu/article/establishing-high-performing-teams-lessons-from-health-care/.

Lawrence, P., and J. Lorsch. 1967. "Differentiation and Integration in Complex Organizations." *Administrative Science Quarterly* 12 (1): 1–47.

Luke, R., S. Walston, and P. Plummer. 2004. *Healthcare Strategy: In Pursuit of Competitive Advantage.* Chicago: Health Administration Press.

McKinsey & Company. 2014. "Health-Focused Redesign: Creating a Payor Organization for the Future." February 1. www.mckinsey.com/industries/healthcare-systems-and-services/our-insights/health-focused-redesign-creating-a-payor-organization-for-the-future.

Mercy Health. 2015. "Organisational Structure." Published April. www.mercyhealth.com.au/au/ourorganisation/Pages/Organisational%20Structure.aspx.

Muhlestein, D., T. Tu, and C. H. Colla. 2020. "Accountable Care organizations Are Increasingly Led by Physician Groups Rather than Hospital Systems." *American Journal of Managed Care* 26 (5): 225–28. www.ajmc.com/view/accountable-care-organizations-are-increasingly-led-by-physician-groups-rather-than-hospital-systems.

National Association of ACOs (NAACOS). 2020. "ACOs and the Future of Health Care." www.naacos.com/acos-and-the-future-of-health-care.

National Research Corporation. 2020. "The Governance Institute Releases 2019 Biennial Survey Results Highlighting Governance Structures in Hospitals and Health Systems" (press release). *Intrado Global Newswire,* February 5. www.globenewswire.com/news-release/2020/02/05/1980281/0/en/The-Governance-Institute-Releases-2019-Biennial-Survey-Results-Highlighting-Governance-Structure-in-Hospitals-and-Health-Systems.html.

Nouri, C. 2019. "Hierarchical vs. Flat Organizational Structure and Benefits of Each." *Pingboard* (blog). Published November 4. https://pingboard.com/blog/hierarchical-vs-flat-organizational-structure-and-benefits-of-each/.

Persily, C. 2013. *Team Leadership and Partnering in Nursing and Health Care.* New York: Springer.

Peters, T., and R. Waterman. 1982. *In Search of Excellence: Lessons from America's Best Run Companies.* New York: Harper & Row.

Pierce-Wrobel, C., and J. Micklos. 2018. "How the Most Successful ACOs Act as Factories of Innovation." *Health Affairs,* January 29. www.healthaffairs.org/do/10.1377/hblog20180124.514403/full/.

Sherman, R. O. 2013. "Span of Control in Nurse Leader Roles." *The Emerging RN Leader,* June 27. www.emergingrnleader.com/span-of-control-in-nurse-leader-roles/.

Society for Human Resource Management (SHRM). 2015. "Understanding Organizational Structures." November 30. www.shrm.org/resourcesandtools/tools-and-samples/toolkits/pages/understandingorganizationalstructures.aspx.

US Department of Veterans Affairs. 2020. Functional Organizational Manual Version 6.0. www.va.gov/VA-Functional-Organization-Manual-2020-4.pdf.

Volini, E., J. Schwartz, I. Roy, M. Hauptmann, Y. Van Durme, B. Denny, and J. Bersin. 2019. "Organizational Performance: It's a Team Sport." Deloitte Insights, April 11. www2.deloitte.com/us/en/insights/focus/human-capital-trends/2019/team-based-organization.html.

Walston, S. 2018. *Strategic Healthcare Management: Planning and Execution*, 2nd ed. Chicago: Health Administration Press.

Walston, S., P. Lazes, and P. Sullivan. 2004. "Improving Hospital Restructuring: Lessons Learned." *Health Care Management Review* 29 (4): 309–19.

Williamson, O. 1975. *Markets and Hierarchies.* New York: Free Press.

CHAPTER 19

PERFORMANCE MANAGEMENT

> Jack walked through the clinic's waiting room on his way to visit with some of the staff. Jack's managerial style included getting regular feedback from the employees. He felt it was important to visit with them, build trust, and try to prevent problems that might occur. Today, however, a patient in the waiting room stopped him. "Can you help me?" The patient appeared to be an older woman, and looked quite distressed. "Sure," Jack replied. "How can I help?" The patient told him she had been waiting for 45 minutes and no one had helped her. "Have you spoken to the receptionist?" Jack asked. No, she hadn't. She didn't know to go up to the registration desk and ask; she just walked into the room and sat down. No one had said anything to her. No one had even noticed she was there. Jack looked around the waiting room. It wasn't that crowded.
>
> Jack was shocked. He personally helped the patient get through the check-in process and into an exam room. He was determined this would never happen again. He immediately set out to create a way to monitor how long patients had to wait in the waiting room and the exam room once ushered in. His new goal was to get wait times down.

Learning Objectives

After studying this chapter, readers should be able to

- appraise the value of performance management;
- identify tools to chart performance management, including key performance indicators, Gantt charts, and balanced scorecards;
- analyze numerical rating systems, and explain the difficulties with implementing forced distributions and stacked or forced ranking systems;
- evaluate the concept of a 360-degree feedback appraisal system and its challenges; and
- apply a competency-based appraisal system.

Key Terms

- balanced scorecard
- competency-based appraisal systems
- forced distribution (stacked ranking or forced ranking)
- Gantt charts
- key performance indicators
- numerical rating systems
- performance management
- 360-degree feedback appraisal system

performance management
The process of establishing individual and corporate goals through planning, reviewing, assessing, and developing the skills and abilities of the workforce.

Performance management is a critical function for any firm. Performance management is a process of setting individual and corporate goals. It involves planning, reviewing, assessment, and developing the skills and abilities of the workforce (Armstrong 2017). Performance management encompasses the critical management function of controlling, mentioned in chapter 1.

Performance management occurs at multiple levels in an organization, from corporate to individual (exhibit 19.1). In this chapter, we discuss the mechanisms used to manage performance across these levels.

Providing constructive feedback and monitoring performance in organizations is a critical function, yet many firms struggle with it. Most large firms establish goals, monitor outcomes, and provide feedback through episodic performance reviews and reports. Performance management systems can be used to support many different company systems, including profitability, efficiency, pay and promotion, employee development, and even staff reductions. Performance management systems vary, and no one type of system is best suited for all situations. The optimal performance system should be determined by the business needs and culture of the organization.

Successful organizations hold their employees accountable. As illustrated by the story in the box, this enforcement of accountability might

EXHIBIT 19.1
Levels at Which Performance Management Occurs

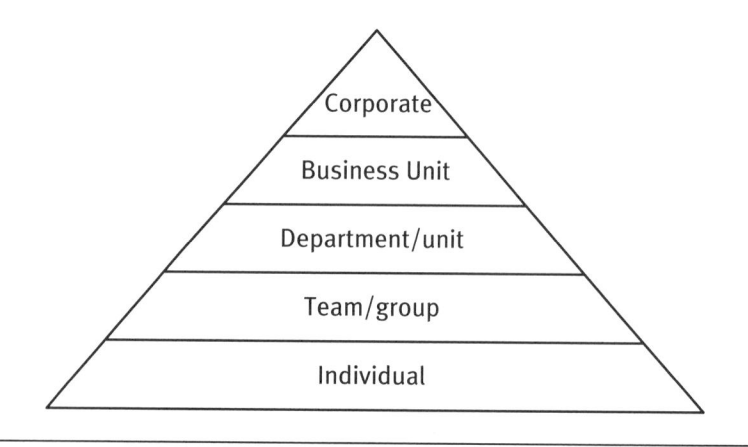

(Pyramid from top to bottom: Corporate / Business Unit / Department/unit / Team/group / Individual)

include ending an employment relationship if the expectations of the job are not being, or cannot be, met. Although helping employees gain needed skills and designing mechanisms to motivate are both important, at times a leader must have the courage to terminate an employee. The inability to take such action can have negative ramifications for the leader, who will lose credibility. Enforcing later decisions and correcting future problems will become more and more difficult if the initial issue was not dealt with appropriately.

Performance management requires regular monitoring efforts. Regular monitoring allows management to understand what progress is being made, recognize whether any areas are underperforming, and determine which areas need adaptation and adjustment. Most healthcare organizations establish metrics for gauging progress on their goals. However, a 2018 survey suggests many healthcare organizations are not satisfied with their own processes (Seargeant and Spence 2018). Analysis of responses from more than 350 senior finance executives of US hospitals and health systems revealed the following:

- Only 25 percent were "very confident" that they could shift strategies and plans easily and quickly.
- Only 8 percent were "very satisfied" with performance management reporting at their organization.
- Yet, 73 percent believed performance management to be critical.

Sometimes It's OK to Say Goodbye

By Britt Berrett

The medical director of the rehabilitative unit was challenged by the new CEO to provide a plan to increase volume and profitability. Unwilling to assume responsibility for growing the business, the medical director claimed that the aged physical appearance of the unit was minimizing its ability to attract new business.

In response to his request for funding, the hospital board committed capital for a new unit, and within six months, a new, modern, and physically appealing unit was completed. Expecting increased volume, the CEO scheduled a meeting with the medical director to review his plan of action. But there was no plan. In fact, the medical director refused to meet with the strategy and planning team. The CEO gave the medical director an ultimatum: Define a plan of action or resign.

In the ensuing weeks, the medical director rallied the political influence of key medical staff leaders to continue supporting him, under threat that his departure would create an organizational and clinical catastrophe.

On the appointed date, the medical director decided not to provide a plan of action and instead threatened to resign. Despite potentially overwhelming political fallout, the CEO accepted the medical director's resignation and swiftly made plans to replace him. The initial reaction from the medical staff was surprise, shock, and anger, but calm eventually ensued.

Subsequent strategy and planning sessions with physician leaders in key critical areas included overwhelming support and involvement by the strategy and planning department, resulting in key alignment and commitment of resources to build volume and improve profitability.

Sometimes it's OK to say goodbye.

Handled properly, performance management offers an opportunity to

- efficiently achieve goals and objectives,
- evaluate the progress toward mission and vision,
- assess the level of efficiency in using resources,
- encourage ongoing improvement, and
- provide a continued basis for informed decision-making and planning.

Performance Management Tools

Key Performance Indicators

Monitoring requires both the right data and the right processes. Thus, goals and their measures must be carefully established. Metrics used in performance management that are directly tied to strategic organizational goals are often called **key performance indicators** (KPIs). A few such indicators in healthcare settings are patient wait time, bed or room turnover, employee wages, number of mistake events, childhood immunization rates, time between symptom onset and hospitalization, patient versus staff ratio, and overall satisfaction. Organization management identifies the KPIs most meaningful to their strategic process.

Critical to the success of performance management is the consistent, periodic evaluation of these goals and objectives at weekly, monthly, or quarterly intervals.

An interesting example of KPIs is provided by one tool used to assess the maintenance management of clinic facilities. The experts used seven indicators: (1) annual maintenance expenditure; (2) the age of the building; (3) patient density, or number of patients seen; (4) a building performance indicator; (5) the efficiency of maintenance (performance/investment); (6) how much maintenance was outsourced; and (7) the number of employees in the maintenance department (Shohet and Nobili 2017).

Gantt Charts

Gantt charts can be used to quickly determine a project's status. A Gantt chart is a bar chart that shows the schedule and progress of one or more projects. Supporting tasks are presented in a specialized graph format that shows their start and end dates, along with the current percentage of completion. Gantt charts can also indicate critical dependencies and key beginning and ending points. A simple example is shown in exhibit 19.2.

Balanced Scorecards

Many leading healthcare organizations have instituted a performance management system called a **balanced scorecard**—a reporting mechanism that

---

key performance indicators
Metrics used in performance management that are directly tied to strategic organizational goals.

Gantt charts
Bar charts that show the schedule and progress of one or more projects.

balanced scorecard
A reporting mechanism that incorporates financial and nonfinancial aspects of performance to allow a comprehensive, balanced perspective of organizational results.

EXHIBIT 19.2
Gantt Chart Example

Item	Task	Dependencies	Start Date	Days	% Done	Jul 1–15	Jul 16–31	Aug 1–15	Aug 16–31	Sep 1–15	Sep 16–30	Oct 1–15	Oct 16–31
1	Mission and vision	None	Jul 1	31	0	▓	▓						
2	Environmental analysis	None	Jul 1	62	0	▓	▓	▓	▓				
3	Strategic priorities	1 and 2	Sep 1	15	0					▓			
4	Strategic programs	1, 2, and 3	Sep 16	15	0						▓		
5	Strategic plan	1 and 2	Aug 16	60	0				▓	▓	▓	▓	
6	Board evaluation and approval	1, 2, 3, 4, and 5	Oct 16	15	0								▓

Source: Reprinted from Walston (2014).

incorporates financial and nonfinancial aspects of performance, such as customer satisfaction and business processes, to allow a comprehensive, balanced perspective of organizational results. All too often, healthcare organizations focus almost exclusively on financial results—or, perhaps, finance first and quality second—with each area reviewed separately without regard for interrelationships. Balanced scorecards have become popular because of their capability to show these relationships, and have been implemented across a wide array of healthcare organizations (Gonzalez-Sanchez, Broccardo, and Martins Pires 2017).

A balanced scorecard usually extends monitoring to include the following measures (Gonzalez-Sanchez, Broccardo, and Martins Pires 2017):

- *Financial.* Potential measures include profits, revenue growth, return on investment, and expense reductions.
- *Customer/stakeholder.* Potential measures include customer acquisition, retention, and satisfaction.
- *Internal business processes.* Potential measures include production costs and volumes.
- *Learning and growth.* Potential measures include new services, employee satisfaction, and retention.

The balanced scorecard metrics interact with each other and paint a picture of how well an organization is fulfilling its mission and vision (exhibit 19.3). Healthcare organizations have modified these dimensions to include healthcare quality, outcomes, and access (Gonzalez-Sanchez, Broccardo, and Martins Pires 2017). Presenting and evaluating performance on multiple criteria provides a more informed and global perspective.

EXHIBIT 19.3
Relationships Between Balanced Scorecard Metrics and Firm Mission and Vision

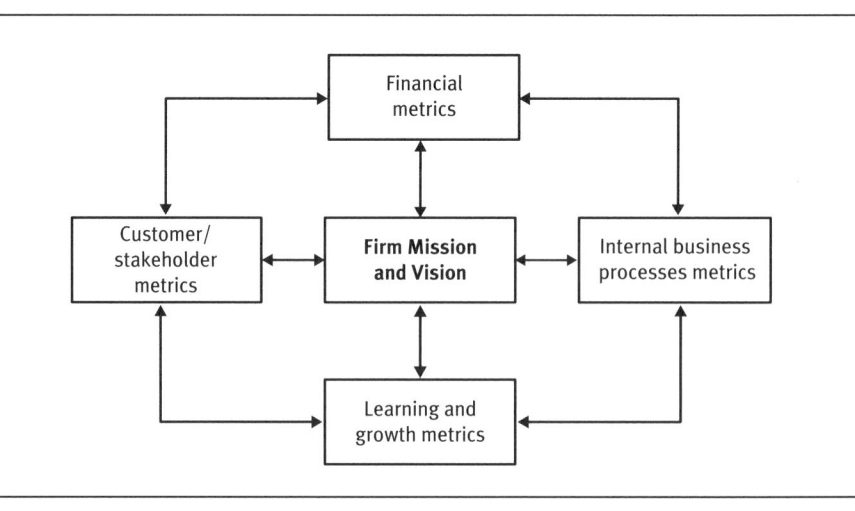

To create a visual representation of balanced scorecards, healthcare and other organizations have created strategy maps—single-page tools that clearly communicate a strategic plan. Using a strategy map provides several benefits (Lucco 2020):

- It is a clean, visual representation of the balanced scorecard.
- It ties together all of the goals of the strategic plan.
- It is shared with employees and provides them with a vision related to their tasks.
- It outlines key goals.
- It allows users to find areas that need improvement.
- It helps identify the importance of key elements.

Organizations seeking to implement company-wide performance management systems such as the balanced scorecard often find that aligning goals across the company to expressed strategies can be a challenge. Likewise, ill-defined measures can lead to unintended outcomes.

Individual Performance Management

Individual performance management systems also widely vary. In addition to the purposes of corporate performance management systems, individual performance management systems seek to

- clarify job responsibilities and expectations;
- enhance individual and group productivity;
- develop employee capabilities through effective feedback and coaching;
- drive behavior to align with the organizational values, goals, and strategies;
- provide the metric for performance pay increases;
- improve communication between employees and managers; and
- select employees for promotion, termination, and career development.

However, accomplishing all of these goals simultaneously can challenge the best organization. Performance management systems, which should motivate and improve performance, are considered the Achilles' heel of human resources management. Both employees and managers regularly lament their flaws and ineffectiveness. Pulakos, Mueller-Hanson, and Arad (2019) suggest the performance management process is of little value, although organizations continue to experiment with assessment and driving

> **A Culture of Feedback**
>
> When patients walk into a hospital or clinic, a patient service representative (PSR) or a clerk at the front desk is there to greet them. These frontline staff contribute to the quality of the patient experience and influence the patient's perceptions of the organization. Managers contribute to the exchange between PSRs and their customers by communicating performance expectations, giving staff the opportunity to develop the standards of the job, and providing feedback and coaching (Kennedy, Anastos, and Genau 2019).
>
> Challenges in the form of inadequate resources for the ideal performance monitoring and feedback get in the way. Healthcare leadership prefers to monitor data and numbers rather than human performance. Some supervisors find it difficult to initiate individual feedback. The stigma associated with this one-on-one critique suggests the staff member did something wrong (Kennedy, Anastos, and Genau 2019).
>
> The answer is to create service standards and monitor performance against such standards. An established culture of one-on-one check-ins—short visits to praise staff and give feedback—removes the stigmas.

performance improvement. Annual performance evaluations do not seem to improve performance, yet nearly 90 percent of firms around the globe continue with annual performance reviews that directly affect compensation decisions (Ewenstein, Hancock, and Komm 2016). The cause of many problems lies not in the poorly developed tools and processes but in the nature of performance management, which is highly personal and can be seen as threatening for both managers and employees.

The implementation of individual performance management usually takes place in the form of performance appraisals, frequently as annual evaluations. Individual performance appraisals are not one of the activities managers like to do (Richards 2019). These appraisals become problematic when

- managers are not properly trained,
- different managers are not consistent with ratings or scores (one might say performance is good, when another thinks it is poor), or
- the appraisal does not help to improve performance or is not meaningful.

Some of the problem lies in the dual goals many companies establish for performance appraisals by using them for both allocation of rewards and identification of developmental needs. For example, performance systems that focus heavily on numerical outcomes may crowd out employee development. While a performance management system can conceivably address both decision-making and employee development needs, this combination can be difficult to establish in practice. **Numerical rating systems**—mechanisms for rating employee performance on a numeric scale—are used

numerical rating systems
Mechanisms for rating employee performance on a numeric scale.

in most performance management systems but may detract from employee development efforts, as employees may be overly concerned about their ratings and rank compared with others and will work to appear excellent in all areas. Therefore, rather than identifying areas for employee development, the discussion centers on performance outcomes and their resultant rewards (Cappelli and Tavis 2016).

One large firm, Deloitte, has ditched 360-degree reviews and cascading goals that apply to everyone in the organization. Instead of having employees answer numerous questions in their annual self-evaluations, the company developed four simple statements to be assessed at the end of every project (or once a quarter for employees who have long-term assignments). Managers respond to the first two statements using a five-point scale, and to the last two with a simple yes or no (McGregor 2015):

1. Given what I know of this person's performance, and if it were my money, I would award this person the highest possible compensation increase and bonus. (1 – strongly agree to 5 – strongly disagree)
2. Given what I know of this person's performance, I would always want him or her on my team. (1 – strongly agree to 5 – strongly disagree)
3. This person is at risk for low performance. (Yes or No)
4. This person is ready for promotion today. (Yes or No)

Forced Distribution or Stacked Ranking Appraisals

Potentially compounding the pressures on the numerical scoring are the **forced distribution** appraisal systems (also called *stacked ranking* or *forced ranking*) that some companies use. Forced distribution systems require managers to rank their employees across a distribution, much like grading on a curve. In a forced distribution appraisal, a certain percentage of employees must be rated unsatisfactory (often 10 percent) and only a set percentage can be ranked excellent or outstanding (again, often 10 percent). About 30 percent of all major US corporations have used some form of forced distributions, including General Electric and Microsoft (Mathis, Jackson, and Valentine 2014).

Advocates of forced distribution claim that without it, "rater inflation" increases and it is impossible to differentiate and accurately reward performance. They also say it also brings "disciplined rigor to the management process" and forces managers to address difficult performance-related issues (Lipman 2012). Yet forced ranking can create significant employee problems, because objectively ranking employees is fraught with subjectivity. Furthermore, especially for those in the bottom tier,

forced distribution Mechanisms for rating employee performance that require managers to rank their employees across a distribution, much like grading on a curve. Also called *stacked ranking* or *forced ranking*.

the threat of dismissal can destroy an organization's open culture and damage team cooperation. The forced ranking appraisal system has even been suggested as a cause of Microsoft's competitive struggles since 2000 (Eichenwald 2012):

> At the center of the cultural problems was a management system called "stack ranking." Every current and former Microsoft employee I interviewed—*every one*—cited stack ranking as the most destructive process inside of Microsoft, something that drove out untold numbers of employees. The system—also referred to as "the performance model," "the bell curve," or just "the employee review"—has, with certain variations over the years, worked like this: every unit was forced to declare a certain percentage of employees as top performers, then good performers, then average, then below average, then poor.
>
> "If you were on a team of 10 people, you walked in the first day knowing that, no matter how good everyone was, two people were going to get a great review, seven were going to get mediocre reviews, and one was going to get a terrible review," said a former software developer. "It leads to employees focusing on competing with each other rather than competing with other companies."

Interestingly, because of the problems it created, Microsoft discontinued forced ranking in 2013—at the same time that Yahoo adopted it (Brustein 2013).

Finding the correct form for providing appropriate feedback and appraisals to employees continues to be a struggle. In 2015, Accenture—one of the world's largest companies, employing 330,000 people—completely discontinued its annual performance review and moved to more ongoing, timely feedback from managers following assignments (Cunningham 2015). By 2016, about 16 percent of surveyed companies had eliminated the rating scale from their annual performance evaluation (McGregor 2016). As noted by Ewenstein, Hancock, and Komm (2016), other companies are experimenting with different approaches, including

- focusing exclusively on only very high or very low performing employees and not seeking to differentiate those in the middle,
- collecting more objective performance information through automated analyses,
- breaking the link for most employees between their performance evaluation and compensation or only linking them for high and low performers, and
- moving to more frequent evaluations on an as-needed basis instead of annual reviews.

Guidelines for Providing Performance Feedback Effectively

Although providing constructive performance evaluations can be difficult, some practices can improve their effectiveness. Greene (2018) offers seven tips:

1. Set meaningful goals with employees up front.
2. Don't wait until the annual evaluation to offer feedback. Give it regularly.
3. Make sure employees know what is expected of them and how they will be evaluated.
4. When a performance problem occurs, give feedback immediately.
5. Give positive feedback. Don't focus solely on problems.
6. When employees struggle, help them to succeed.
7. Focus on the performance, not on the person.

For annual performance appraisals to be effective, they must be part of a continuous feedback cycle. Immediate and proximate feedback for both good and poor performance should be given to employees throughout the year. Research has shown that frequent feedback—at least quarterly and perhaps monthly—generates better results. One human resources executive pointed out that the speed of work today frequently exceeds the speed of human resources processes, such as annual evaluations, and noted that "the idea of an annual performance review or six-month performance review just doesn't make sense any more" (McGregor 2016). Successful performance appraisals summarize ongoing feedback and set goals to help the employee. The aim of the annual appraisal system should be to improve performance, not punish employees. Managers should never store up employee problems throughout the year and unload them on the employee at the annual evaluation.

The University of Texas at Dallas (UT Dallas) follows this model closely, providing resources to improve performance communication, implement annual performance appraisals, and develop performance improvement plans. The UT Dallas website directs managers that the annual appraisal process should be

> a small part of the appraisal process. In its most productive form, performance appraisal is actually a continuous, year-round practice of exchanging information between the supervisor and employee that begins and ends with the formal annual performance appraisal meeting. The most highly motivated, productive employees are those who know what they are supposed to do and how well they are doing it, who participate in planning how their work will be accomplished and who have open, honest rapport with their supervisor. Supervisors are strongly encouraged to make the annual review meetings participative and collaborative. (UT Dallas 2015)

EXHIBIT 19.4

Performance Rating Numerical Scale Example

A 360-degree performance appraisal form might have a few subheadings such as skills and knowledge, teamwork and collaboration, accountability, and leadership, with three or four criteria in each area. Scores are then awarded as follows:

5 – Exceeds expectations—goes beyond the expected norms or standards.
4 – Meets expectations—meets the expected norms or standards.
3 – Meets most expectations—Needs some improvement, but meets the average.
2 – Needs improvement—While some averages are met, needs serious improvement in other areas.
1 – Unsatisfactory—General performance is below expectations and averages.

	Self	Supervisor/ Board	Direct Report	Other	Average
Demonstrates effective skills					
Collaborates with other team members					
Gets the job done					
Follows through on commitments					

Source: Adapted from HR HelpBoard (2017).

Performance Rating Scales

Although a numerical scale is not always warranted, organizations often use one to help them compare employees, units, departments, and divisions. Exhibit 19.4 shows an example of a performance rating scale that relates the numerical value to behaviors in communication practices and business results. Additional categories should be included to reflect the job responsibilities and organizational values. Job responsibilities might include important behaviors, such as customer interaction, while organizational values should reflect those usually expressed in conjunction with the organizational mission and vision. The values criteria might include categories of teamwork, integrity, innovation, and compassion, among others.

360-Degree Feedback Appraisal Systems

Traditionally, annual employee evaluations have been completed by a superior, with limited input from the employee and based mostly on the superior's experiences and perceptions of the employee. This singular perspective frequently interjects bias into the appraisal process. To provide more representative feedback to both the rater and the employee, the **360-degree feedback appraisal system** has been introduced in many companies. In healthcare, organizations are recommending 360-degree appraisals even for physicians (Dubinsky et al. 2010).

The 360-degree system seeks feedback from stakeholders who have frequent contact with the employee being appraised. These stakeholders, whose responses are confidential, are asked to evaluate the employee on a broad array of job behaviors, skills, and competencies. The employee is asked to complete the same survey. All the evaluations are given to the supervisor performing the appraisal, who is expected to use at least a composite of the responses during the final evaluation. The feedback from others can be compared with the employee self-evaluation, which helps the supervisor or employee quickly identify areas for improvement.

The anonymous nature and multiple sources of the 360-degree system provide more comprehensive and accurate feedback than a traditional evaluation because they cannot be as easily attributed to bias, thus improving appraisal results. For example, this tool has been used successfully in healthcare to improve physicians' emotional intelligence (Hammerly, Harmon, and Schwaltzberg 2014).

However, some human resources experts caution against using 360-degree appraisals, especially when the outcome affects pay and promotion. This process has been seen as most effective when used as a development tool and not a rating tool. Other potential problems arise when organizations fail to determine which competencies should be reviewed before implementing the evaluation and do not maintain the anonymity of reviewers (Chopra 2017). In addition, some organizations see the time required to perform a 360-degree evaluation as prohibitive. Scheduling multiple stakeholders to complete the evaluations, collecting and collating the data, and presenting the review can be a significant time burden. As a result, some organizations perform 360-degree appraisals only every few years, conducting traditional evaluations in between. For example, Texas Health Resources, based in Dallas, has its managers undergo a 360-degree evaluation every three years. In addition, some university medical centers have implemented 360-degree reviews to provide more complete feedback to residents and medical students than can be gathered by traditional student evaluations.

To make 360-degree appraisal systems successful, Jackson (2012) suggested that managers

- seek the involvement and support of the employee's direct supervisor;
- make the questions specific enough to provide actionable information;

360-degree feedback appraisal system
A mechanism for evaluating employee performance that seeks feedback from stakeholders who have frequent contact with the employee being appraised.

- keep the comments and process constructive, not personal;
- set an improvement plan to change behaviors;
- revisit the recommendations with the employee periodically (at least quarterly);
- keep the information and process confidential; and
- focus the evaluation and plan on both strengths and weaknesses.

Competency-Based Performance Systems

competency-based appraisal systems
Mechanisms for evaluating employee performance on the basis of required competencies established for the employee's position.

Most contemporary appraisal systems are based on competencies, which can be broken down into behaviors to be measured. **Competency-based appraisal systems**—mechanisms for evaluating employee performance on the basis of required competencies established for the employee's position—are intended to facilitate recognition, reward, and correction of behaviors; they are now required for hospitals to be accredited by the Joint Commission (Daniels and Ramey 2005). In addition, this type of evaluation has been recommended for use in appraising boards of trustees (Jarousse 2014).

The key advantages of establishing behavior-related competencies are setting clear employee work expectations and translating them into criteria that can be used to assess and develop employees. This process helps establish criteria to appropriately recruit, select, and evaluate employees.

Competency models appraise individuals on the skills, knowledge, and characteristics that are important for attaining positive job outcomes. Generally, five to ten key competencies derived from strategic objectives, organizational values, and key job success factors are used for evaluations. (The number should be limited to ten competencies because too many can overload the raters, who may need to complete many appraisals.)

Although a competency-based evaluation tool can be constructed in many ways, one requirement for any such tool is to have a matching scale for common organization-wide and department-wide competencies to allow comparison of employees across different units. Once the common competencies have been set, additional competencies should be established for specific job requirements.

As described in the preface, the American College of Healthcare Executives offers the *Healthcare Executive Competencies Assessment Tool* (www.ache.org/career-resource-center/at "Competency Assessment"), which can be used to assess a healthcare leader's expertise. This assessment framework categorizes competencies into five critical domains:

1. Communication and Relationship Management
2. Leadership

3. Professionalism
4. Knowledge of the Healthcare Environment
5. Business Skills and Knowledge

Healthcare executives are expected to demonstrate competence in all aspects of these domains.

Healthcare organizations that seek to develop a competency-based evaluation for their managers could use this document to establish performance measures centered on these competencies. As shown in the following list, each of the major domains is subdivided into categories, which contain evaluative questions that can be used for appraisals:

- Communication and Relationship Management
  - Relationship Management
  - Communication Skills
  - Facilitation and Negotiation
- Leadership
  - Leadership Skills and Behavior
  - Organizational Climate and Culture
  - Communicating Vision
  - Managing Change
- Professionalism
  - Personal and Professional Accountability
  - Professional Development and Lifelong Learning
  - Contributions to the Community and Profession
- Knowledge of the Healthcare Environment
  - Healthcare Systems and Organizations
  - Healthcare Personnel
  - The Patient's Perspective
  - The Community and the Environment
- Business Skills and Knowledge
  - General Management
  - Financial Management
  - Human Resource Management
  - Organizational Dynamics and Governance
  - Strategic Planning and Marketing
  - Information Management
  - Risk Management
  - Quality Improvement
  - Patient Safety

Chapter Summary

Performance management is an important organizational control function that should occur from the corporate tier to the individual level. However, developing and maintaining a constructive feedback and performance appraisal system is a challenge for most companies. Performance management should assist firms in achieving their goals, evaluate progress toward meeting their mission and vision, assess their efficiency, and encourage constant improvement.

Tools used as performance monitors include KPIs, Gantt charts, and balanced scorecards. KPIs are the critical metrics used to evaluate the progress of each key goal. Gantt charts provide a visual way to quickly monitor the progress of projects. Balanced scorecards use multiple key metrics to monitor performance.

Individual performance management systems are used in most organizations. They vary widely, but their primary purposes include improving employee skills and aligning employee behaviors with desired organizational outcomes.

Unfortunately, many companies struggle to maintain productive employee evaluation systems, often performed as annual evaluations. Instead of inspiring greater work efforts and motivation, individual evaluations can strain relationships and create excessive stress on both employees and managers. The dual, contrasting nature of the evaluation goals causes many of these problems. Individual evaluations can support both decision-making and employee development.

Numerical rating systems that rank employees allow for differentiated salary increases, promotions, firings, and bonuses. Forced distribution systems (stacked or forced ranking) are one example of a numerical rating system that ranks employees. In this system, managers are required to place a certain percentage of their employees in the highest and lowest categories for each evaluation. The pressure to score better than peers to achieve the related rewards has caused many firms to discontinue using this system.

Effective performance feedback exists across a time continuum. Prior to the formal evaluation meeting, clear, measurable expectations should be set, along with needed job skills and training. Feedback and coaching should be continuous. Likewise, the evaluation should be conducted in a private location and provide immediate, positive, developmental feedback. The employee should not be surprised by the feedback and should be allowed the opportunity to provide input to identify issues and develop a constructive plan for improvement.

If numerical scales are used for appraisals, they should include a 5- or 7-point scale. Rating items and scales should be created for each important employee behavior and area of responsibility.

A 360-degree feedback system can be used to obtain a more comprehensive, representative appraisal from multiple stakeholders, which can be compared with employees' perceptions of their own work.

Most contemporary appraisal systems use competency-based performance criteria. Appraisal systems based on job-related competencies allow management to set clear job performance expectations and provide constant criteria for evaluations. Such systems appraise individuals on the skills and knowledge required for positive job outcomes. Generally, five to ten competencies should be used for the evaluation.

Chapter Questions

1. Why would it be important to have a performance management system linked to strategic goals and implemented relatively consistently across all levels in an organization?
2. How could one tell whether the metrics used for performance evaluations were KPIs?
3. Describe two ways that a balanced scorecard may be superior to more traditional monitoring systems.
4. List four reasons why companies have so many difficulties with individual performance appraisal systems.
5. What are the advantages of a forced distribution in employee evaluations (a stacked or forced ranking system)?
6. Why should employee appraisals be conducted more than once a year?
7. Give two reasons the 360-degree feedback appraisal system improves an employee evaluation. Offer two reasons that 360-degree feedback may make the evaluation more difficult.
8. How do competency-based appraisal systems provide "consistency, transparency, and fairness"?

Chapter Cases

A Surprising Performance Evaluation

Enrique had worked very hard the past four years. He had consistently exceeded the job expectations listed in his employee manual and had received exceptional job evaluations for the first three years. His fourth annual performance appraisal was now scheduled in a few minutes, and he was certain that, although circumstances had changed, he would still receive a good evaluation.

Enrique had been hired as a home health program director four years earlier. He knew that the program was dramatically underfunded, and before he accepted the role, his manager, Rosa, had promised to increase funding and provide more organizational support. Enrique trusted Rosa and accepted the position.

His first two years managing the program went well. Rosa did come up with additional resources, although the need for more was still significant. After two years, however, Rosa quit for a job in another state, and the new manager, Ruben, was brought in from the organization's operation in another city. Ruben liked to threaten employees and bragged in many manager meetings that he would "get those slackers and troublemakers" in his group at their annual evaluations. He stated he would make sure they got less than the usual 3 percent merit increase—that would show them what he thought of them!

During the first year of Ruben's reign, he and Enrique did not get along well. Ruben felt no obligation to honor the commitments that Rosa had made. He cut Enrique's budget back to what it was when Enrique took the position, and he made Enrique move his office—from one close to the physicians he worked with into the general offices close to Ruben. He also took away Enrique's expenditure authority for any costs above $50. In addition, he wanted to reduce the pay differentials Enrique had been receiving for two regional duties he had been appointed to. Enrique reminded Ruben that he had been appointed to these regional positions by the regional vice president and offered to resign from them if he were not paid for them. Ruben finally backed off, but he was not happy about it.

Even with this battle, Enrique persevered. The work outcomes and customer satisfaction ratings remained high. However, he began to voice his concerns privately to close friends, and going to work became painful. Finally, in September, Enrique had had enough, and he resigned his responsibilities as program director. In response, Ruben radically lowered Enrique's salary—by not just taking away his director's pay differential but also dropping him three steps in the pay scale. After a lengthy discussion with the human resources department, Enrique's original base pay was reinstated. Ruben took over the program director duties.

A month later, the organization sponsored a home health program retreat, which Ruben was not planning to attend. Outside stakeholders were invited, and a facilitator was hired to run the meeting. The ground rules for the meeting called for an open and frank discussion of the program's strengths and problems. Enrique was invited, participated actively, and pointed out the problems, especially those caused by Ruben's poor management decisions. The meeting minutes were dutifully recorded and submitted to both Ruben and the regional vice president. Enrique continued working in the program and received high praise from customers and coworkers.

In December, Ruben was transferred to a different department, and Carlos was appointed in his place. Carlos seemed more fair-minded than Ruben and announced he would begin a search for a new program director in March. However, annual evaluations were due in February. Enrique was anxious but thought Carlos would treat his situation reasonably.

When Carlos and Enrique met to discuss Enrique's annual evaluation, Enrique was shocked to receive a very low overall rating. He demanded an explanation and was told he was a "disloyal" employee whose comments at the program retreat were seen as offensive and inappropriate. No amount of arguing could change the rating. Even though he had performed well in every other category, his rating for the year was "very low," which meant he would receive no merit increase.

The day after his evaluation, Enrique began sending out his resume. Three months later, he left to take another position.

Case Questions
1. According to this chapter, what went wrong with the annual performance evaluation?
2. What should Carlos have done to improve the annual evaluation process?

Mixed Use of Performance Management System Steals Its Effectiveness

Riverside Health System had two goals for its annual employee performance evaluations: (1) to motivate employees to work hard and (2) to identify areas in which employees could improve Riverside Health. To support these goals, Riverside Health decided to implement a performance management system that required managers and their employees to simultaneously complete an evaluation of the employee's activities throughout the year. The evaluation form contained seven separate areas in which the employee could be rated from "1—totally unsatisfactory" to "7—outstanding." Then, managers would meet with each employee, discuss the individual ratings, and come up with a composite form that would be submitted for significant bonuses. Although the amount of bonus changed each year, the potential bonus this year was a hefty 25 percent of base salary. The problem, as most employees knew, was that the hospital had only budgeted an average of 8 percent for the bonus payout.

Peter had joined Riverside Health System three years earlier as a maintenance engineer. His wife was recovering from cancer, which had stressed them financially this past year. He had worked hard and felt that his performance this year was exceptional, especially compared to that of the other maintenance engineers. Peter was sure that if anyone deserved the bonus this year, it was him. Last year, he had been told that only those with an average score of 6.6 or higher received the maximum bonus, so when he completed his evaluation, he rated himself with mostly 6s and 7s.

Peter's boss, Henry, liked Peter and appreciated his hard work. However, he wanted Peter to improve in a few areas, especially in communication and in two technical areas. Scoring Peter lower in these areas would justify recommending him for further training; the hospital had internal classes on communication and could send Peter to the local community college for additional technical training.

Peter and Henry's meeting did not go well. Peter was upset that Henry scored him low in these areas, while Henry became frustrated that Peter was not willing to receive constructive criticism and seek improvement. After an hour of discussion, they both became angry, and Henry decided to end the meeting and reschedule it for a time when each might rethink the other's evaluation.

Case Questions
1. What went wrong with the evaluation meeting?
2. What could be done to motivate employees and yet support training and development needs?

Setting Medical Office Staff Performance Measures

Jill was hired as the manager of a 40-member multispecialty medical practice with 180 support staff. The practice's five clinics were generally prosperous, but a few of them appeared to be poorly staffed. The physician committee that hired her said that only a few of the clinic workers were stars and the rest needed to be motivated or asked to leave. They added that the medical practice's current annual performance system for employees was deplorable and needed to be revised. Annual bonuses had always been tied to these appraisals, which made them important for everyone. Unfortunately, the annual evaluations were due in just six weeks.

Jill was excited, though, and knew she could whip this group into shape. She had just graduated with a master's degree in health administration and had three years of experience working for a smaller clinic. She felt she had the talent, dedication, and energy to succeed. She recognized, however, that if she were to have a functional evaluation tool completed in six weeks, her energy and talent would be tested.

She began by examining the medical practice's values, which included integrity, initiative, respect, communication, quality, and teamwork. She created three questions to identify adherence to these values, basing them on a 5-point scale. To these she added questions about the workers' essential job functions. These questions encompassed their duties and responsibilities, health and safety, professionalism, and efficiency and effectiveness.

Jill also designed a performance improvement plan to allow managers and employees to address and resolve performance issues. The plan required a set time (generally 90 days) for re-review, after which time a written warning would be given to the employee if performance had not improved. If a second period ended without employee improvement, the employee would receive a second and final warning. At the end of the third period without improvement, the employee would be dismissed.

Bonuses had been generously allocated to most of the employees before the change. The average rating for employees across the clinic was good to excellent, or 4.1 on a 5-point scale. Considering all of the complaints from the medical staff about the employees' behaviors, Jill was certain the high ratings were the result of lazy clinic managers, and she had to create a mechanism to make the evaluations more reflective of actual performance. She decided that a forced rating system would be the best way to make her managers assess their employees fairly. In her plan, only the excellent employees would receive the full bonus. A graduated, lesser amount would be given to the other employees who still exceeded the average rating. Those below the average rating would receive no bonus for the year. Finally, those who were ranked in the bottom 20 percent were to have strict performance improvement plans, and they would be terminated if they remained in the bottom 20 percent for two years.

The doctors were enthusiastic about Jill's new appraisal system and encouraged her to implement it immediately. However, when she presented the new system to the clinic managers, she heard a lot of grumbling. A few asked her if she had ever used a forced ranking system. She had to admit that she had not, but almost 30 percent of major companies used one, so it had to be a good method. The managers left, unconvinced, and many complained that their employees were going to be mad if they did not get their bonuses. A few were heard quietly threatening to resign if they had to rank all their employees.

The next month flew by, and when the evaluations were completed and the bonuses were distributed, 20 staff resigned. The problem was, only one of the staff members who left had been ranked in the bottom 20 percent, and five were top performers. Jill was perplexed.

Case Questions

1. What went wrong with Jill's performance appraisal system?
2. What could have been done better?
3. How does forced ranking help improve performance? What changes could Jill implement to make the forced ranking system work?

Chapter Activities

Designing Better Appraisals

Read the *TLNT* article "The Top 50 Problems with Performance Appraisals" (John Sullivan, PhD, January 31, 2011; www.eremedia.com/tlnt/the-top-50-problems-with-performance-appraisals/2011). According to the principles discussed in this chapter, what steps can be taken to address the first five problems mentioned in the article?

Role-Playing a Performance Evaluation

1. Form groups of 6–8 people. The person in each group whose birthday falls closest to December 25 will be the supervisor for this activity. The rest of the group will be subordinates.
2. Subordinates have ten minutes to plan a celebration of National Hospital Week. Your task is to list the activities that will take place and assign departments to be responsible for key assignments.
3. Supervisors should rate each subordinate's performance on a scale of 1–5 (1=poor, 5=excellent). Share your rankings with each subordinate. Rewards can be given to those with high rankings (4 or 5).

References

Armstrong, M. 2017. *Armstrong's Handbook of Performance Management: An Evidence-Based Guide to Delivering High Performance*, 6th ed. Philadelphia, PA: KoganPage.

Brustein, J. 2013. "Microsoft Kills Its Hated Stack Rankings. Does Anyone Do Employee Reviews Right?" *Bloomberg Business*, November 13. www.bloomberg.com/bw/articles/2013-11-13/microsoft-kills-its-hated-stack-rankings-dot-does-anyone-do-employee-reviews-right.

Cappelli, P., and A. Tavis. 2016. "The Performance Management Revolution." *Harvard Business Review* 94 (10): 58–67. https://hbr.org/2016/10/the-performance-management-revolution.

Chopra, R. 2017. "360 Degree Performance Assessments: An Overview." *Global Journal of Enterprise Information System* 9 (3): 102–5. https://gjeis.com/index.php/GJEIS/article/view/316.

Cunningham, L. 2015. "In Big Move, Accenture Will Get Rid of Annual Performance Reviews and Rankings." *Washington Post*, July 21. www.washingtonpost.com/blogs/on-leadership/wp/2015/07/21/in-big-move-accenture-will-get-rid-of-annual-performance-reviews-and-rankings/.

Daniels, S., and M. Ramey. 2005. *The Leader's Guide to Hospital Case Management*. Burlington, MA: Jones & Bartlett Learning.

Dubinsky, I., K. Jennings, M. Greengarten, and A. Brans. 2010. "360-Degree Physician Performance Assessment." *Healthcare Quarterly* 13 (2): 71–76.

Eichenwald, K. 2012. "Microsoft's Lost Decade." *Vanity Fair*, July 24. www.vanityfair.com/news/business/2012/08/microsoft-lost-mojo-steve-ballmer.

Ewenstein, B., B. Hancock, and A. Komm. 2016. "Ahead of the Curve: The Future of Performance Management." *McKinsey Quarterly*, May 16. www.mckinsey.com/business-functions/organization/our-insights/ahead-of-the-curve-the-future-of-performance-management.

Gonzalez-Sanchez, M. B., L. Broccardo, and A. M. Martins Pires. 2017. "The Use and Design of the BSC in the Health Care Sector: A Systematic Literature Review for Italy, Spain, and Portugal." *International Journal of Health Planning and Management* 33 (1): 6–30. https://doi.org/10.1002/hpm.2415.

Greene, L. 2018. "Seven Tips for Effective Employee Performance Evaluation." *Training Journal*, March 2. www.trainingjournal.com/articles/features/seven-tips-effective-employee-performance-evaluation.

Hammerly, M., L. Harmon, and S. Schwaltzberg. 2014. "Good to Great: Using 360-Degree Feedback to Improve Physician Emotional Intelligence." *Journal of Healthcare Management* 59 (5): 354–65.

HR HelpBoard. 2017. "360 Degree Performance Appraisal, Feedback System and Its Review." www.hrhelpboard.com/performance-management/360-degree-performance-appraisal.htm.

Jackson, E. 2012. "The 7 Reasons Why 360 Degree Feedback Programs Fail." *Forbes* (blog). Published August 17. www.forbes.com/sites/ericjackson/2012/08/17/the-7-reasons-why-360-degree-feedback-programs-fail/.

Jarousse, L. 2014. "Transforming Governance: Leading in an Era of Reform." *Hospitals & Health Networks*, March 11. www.hhnmag.com/articles/5040-transforming-governance-leading-in-an-era-of-reform.

Kennedy, D. M., C. T. Anastos, and M. C. Genau. 2019. "Improving Healthcare Service Quality Through Performance Management." *Leadership in Health Services* 32 (3): 477–92. https://doi.org/10.1108/LHS-02-2019-0006.

Lipman, V. 2012. "The Pros and Cons of Forced Rankings: A Manager's Perspective." *Forbes* (blog). Published July 19. www.forbes.com/sites/victorlipman/2012/07/19/the-pros-and-cons-of-forced-rankings-a-managers-perspective/.

Lucco, J. 2020. "Strategy Maps: 6 Benefits for Your Company." *ClearPoint Strategy* (blog). Published November 2. www.clearpointstrategy.com/software-banks-insurance-balanced-scorecard-strategy-maps/.

Mathis, R., J. Jackson, and S. Valentine. 2014. *Human Resource Management*, 14th ed. Boston: Cengage Learning.

McGregor, J. 2016. "This Big Change Was Supposed to Make Performance Reviews Better. Could It Be Making Them Worse?" *Washington Post*, June 7. www.washingtonpost.com/news/on-leadership/wp/2016/06/07/this-big-change-was-supposed-to-make-performance-reviews-better-could-it-be-making-them-worse/.

———. 2015. "What If You Could Replace Performance Evaluations with Four Simple Questions?" *Washington Post*, March 17. www.washingtonpost.com/blogs/on-leadership/wp/2015/03/17/deloitte-ditches-performance-rankings-and-instead-will-ask-four-simple-questions/.

Pulakos, E. D., R. Mueller-Hanson, and S. Arad. 2019. "The Evolution of Performance Management: Searching for Value." *Annual Review of Organizational Psychology and Organizational Behavior* 6 (January): 249–71.

Richards, L. 2019. "What Are the Problems with Performance Appraisals?" Small Business. *Houston Chronicle*, March 6. https://smallbusiness.chron.com/problems-performance-appraisals-1913.html.

Seargeant, D., and J. Spence. 2018. "4 Strategies to Unlock Healthcare Performance Management Constraints." *Healthcare Financial Management Association* (blog). Published April 1. www.hfma.org/topics/hfm/2018/april/60139.html.

Shohet, I. M., and L. Nobili. 2017. "Application of Key Performance Indicators for Maintenance Management of Clinics Facilities." *International Journal of Strategic Property Management* 21 (1): 58–71.

University of Texas at Dallas (UT Dallas). 2015. "Performance Management." Accessed April 24. www.utdallas.edu/hr/er/performance/.

Walston, S. 2014. *Strategic Healthcare Management: Planning and Execution*. Chicago: Health Administration Press.

CHAPTER 20

DEVELOPING EMPLOYEES THROUGH MENTORING, COACHING, AND DELEGATION

> Mentors provide critical support for healthcare workers, especially during a crisis. During the COVID-19 pandemic in 2020, this was manifest in many healthcare settings. Doctors, nurses, and many others worked for months short-staffed and at risk for contracting the virus. Many looked to a mentor for emotional support; often this was not their manager, who was overwhelmed just trying to keep the organization functioning.
>
> To mentor someone who is providing healthcare you should
>
> - fortify yourself to have the strength to help others,
> - address your mentee's emotional well-being,
> - practice reflective listening,
> - offer reassurance and appreciation, and
> - share tactics for supporting your mentee's well-being.
>
> Crises, often traumatic, require continued connections and meaningful coaching and mentoring. One person's contact and interest can make a lasting difference (Fessell, Chopra, and Saint 2020).

Learning Objectives

After studying this chapter, readers should be able to

- differentiate between coaching and mentoring,
- appraise the value and importance of coaching and mentoring,
- describe the different types of coaching,
- apply the concept of delegation to improve organizational decision-making,
- distinguish between responsibility and authority, and
- explain the different levels of delegation and the best time to apply them.

Key Terms

- coaching
- delegation
- gofer delegation
- mentoring
- stewardship delegation

Leadership development remains a significant challenge in today's healthcare environment. Around the world, healthcare systems are changing and requiring new and complex skills to successfully lead. In addition, as healthcare leaders age the next generation must be prepared to manage in this difficult environment. This chapter deals with two important leadership development mechanisms: (1) mentoring and coaching and (2) delegation.

Mentoring and Coaching

Mentoring and coaching are important means to empower employees and increase the skills and abilities of healthcare managers. Mentoring and coaching both seek to develop healthcare leaders by increasing the caliber and quality of personnel, reducing turnover, and improving performance (Marton, Wright, and Pister 2019). Greater complexity and increased stakeholder demands require better leaders to be prepared in new and creative ways. Development of leadership skills often involves an array of activities, including coaching and mentoring (Berriman 2007). Effective leadership development often engages existing and prospective leaders in programs that integrate training, coaching, and mentoring.

The terms *coaching* and *mentoring* are frequently used synonymously. The concepts are closely related but differ in their temporal dimensions. **Coaching** tends to focus mostly on the transfer or improvement of specific skills over a short period, whereas **mentoring** involves long-term employee growth and nurturing to improve leadership capabilities (Schraeder and Jordan 2011). More than 70 percent of the largest companies offer some type of coaching (Johnson, Smith, and Haythornthwaite 2020). Coaching primarily aims to help people work out solutions for specific problems and "to think clearly about the . . . actions needed to address specific practical issues, and understand the unconscious processes that may be sabotaging their success"; mentoring, on the other hand, emphasizes sharing experience, advice, and wisdom for "the development of the learner [and thus] is personalized and domain-specific" (Stout-Rostron 2014, 53).

Coaching and mentoring are critical tools for developing leaders, as the importance of leaders' roles in the development process has increased

---

coaching
Instruction or training focused mostly on the transfer or improvement of specific skills over a short period.

mentoring
Advising or training for long-term employee growth and nurturing to improve leadership capabilities.

dramatically in recent years. The great value of coaching and mentoring lies in a person's capacity to take traditional, often theoretical, classroom training and translate it into actual leadership behaviors, bridging the gap between training and practice in the workplace (Taie 2011). Coaching and mentoring can fully engage new executives to complete the knowledge transfer that instruction and book learning begin. Providing coaching or mentoring can help people advance their careers while reducing turnover and increasing employee engagement (St. John 2019). Stevens and Frazer (2005, 8–9) explain that coaching and mentoring serve

> a mission-critical role for learners—transferring skills from the learning experience to regular workplace practice. . . . The purpose of coaching is to provide higher level direction or fine-tuning that enables the learner to extend the general learning of process and procedure to those idiosyncratic performance settings of the workplace.

Effective coaching and mentoring become a natural complement to training and leadership development programs and are especially critical in new executives' first years. Thus, successful coaching and mentoring should be part of an organization's leadership development program. Mentoring is a crucial component of meaningful leadership development efforts (Ayoobzadeh and Boles 2020; Bawany 2014).

The ability of organizations to buck predicted turnover trends in healthcare also necessitates better use of coaching and mentoring. The CEO position in the healthcare industry—especially in hospitals—presently experiences constant, chronic turnover of 14–20 percent, averaging 18 percent from 2014 to 2019. Plus, more and more hospital CEOs are arriving at retirement age (American College of Healthcare Executives [ACHE] 2020a). This continued and accelerating turnover will require greater vigilance in identifying and developing future leaders.

In addition, millennials tend to change their jobs more frequently; at any given time, about half are seeking other employment (Adkins 2020). Thus, turnover rates are likely to increase. Today's C-suite must mentor new leaders to retain talented employees and ensure competent long-term organizational leadership.

A coach's focus is not to provide solutions or address business problems, as a consultant might. Instead, a coach asks penetrating questions that challenge the person being coached, prompt insights, and shift awareness and perspective (Koonce 2010). A coach may work for the same organization as the person being coached, or may be an independent coach from an outside organization. Firms often tap their senior executives to coach and mentor junior executives and prospective leaders.

> **Chief of Anesthesia Training with an Executive Coach**
>
> When Dr. Waronker became the chief of anesthesia in his clinic, he realized his clinical training and clinical practice did little to prepare him for his administrative responsibilities. He now had to shift between the patient bedside and budget meetings. To gain a better understanding of his expanded role and how better to work collaboratively with others, he started meeting weekly with an executive coach to learn the leadership skills needed to deal with his large, traditional organization.
>
> Before coaching, Dr. Waronker's approach had been "go on offense, play hard and don't compromise." As a result, some found him abrasive and difficult to work with. His executive coach helped him "listen more, talk less, compromise" and diminish his prior intimidating approach to issues. He felt the coaching helped with both his job and home life (Tyler 2020).

Coaching is globally recognized as a critical method for preparing leaders. The primary reasons people seek coaching are to increase self-confidence, improve work–life balance, and expand career opportunities (Tyler 2020). Many independent professional executive coaches are in practice today, and many professional associations represent and certify executive coaches. Some of these organizations are listed in exhibit 20.1.

Executive coaching has become a prevalent strategy in most industries to improve leadership performance in companies. Some large healthcare organizations have found coaching essential in developing their upcoming leaders (Balser 2019).

On his popular coaching website, internationally recognized leadership coach John Mattone has outlined "The 5 Essential Components of Successful Coaching" (John Mattone Global 2019):

1. *The coach–client relationship.* Productive coaching requires a strong relationship between the coach and client.
2. *Problem identification and goal setting.* The client and coach must identify strengths and skill gaps, and then establish goals to improve executive competencies.

EXHIBIT 20.1
Professional Associations for Coaching

Association for Coaching: www.associationforcoaching.com
Association for Professional Executive Coaching and Supervision: www.apecs.org
Association of Coach Training Organizations: www.actoonline.org
Association of Corporate Executive Coaches: https://acec-association.org/
International Authority for Coaching & Mentoring: https://coach-accreditation.services/
International Association of Coaching: www.certifiedcoach.org
International Coaching Community: www.internationalcoachingcommunity.com
International Coaching Federation: https://coachingfederation.org/

3. *Problem-solving.* A roadmap should be created to move the client toward the new skill set. The coach and client work together to identify ways to achieve the desired skill improvement.
4. *Transformational processes.* The coach and client work together to make the changes, focusing on long-term improvements, not just short-term gains.
5. *Outcome definition and measurement.* To know that goals are being achieved, the coach and client must define success and establish metrics to measure it.

While coaching focuses on skill development, mentoring assists in socializing new or junior members in an organization. Rather than building specific skills, mentors focus on building relationships as they share their experiences, knowledge, and insights. While mentoring may not lead to immediate actions and change, those who receive mentoring are more likely to obtain promotions, higher salaries, and greater job satisfaction than those who do not (Lester et al. 2011; Sindell and Sindell 2016). Women healthcare executives who receive mentoring are more likely to become CEOs and advance in their careers (Banwell, Kerr, and Stirling 2020; Sexton, Lemak, and Wainio 2014). Furthermore, integrating coaching and mentoring with leadership development has assisted the positive transformation of hospitals' cultures by increasing innovation and improving leadership competencies (Hicks and McCracken 2013). ACHE (2020b) explains that healthcare leaders seek out mentoring to improve self-confidence, critical thinking skills, visibility, and presence, and to "clarify long-term career goals."

Although mentoring is used in many settings, programs without clear guidelines and direction often fizzle out. Established ground rules greatly assist in the successful application of mentoring functions. First, the involved parties should become acquainted both personally and professionally. Understanding each other's work styles, personalities, and personal backgrounds can build confidence and trust, which increases the value of mentoring. Second, the parties should agree to ground rules about the following items:

- *Availability.* When, how, and how often will the parties meet and how long will the mentorship continue?
- *Access.* How can the parties communicate questions or concerns outside scheduled meetings?
- *Agenda.* What topics will be covered in each meeting?
- *Accountability.* How will the parties record action items and completed actions?

Some participants in the mentoring process have found that scheduling a year's worth of mentoring meetings is valuable just by itself (Landry and Lewiss 2020).

Leaders should carefully design mentoring programs to positively contribute to their subordinates' growth, as poorly contrived mentoring programs can be worse for employees than no program at all. Establish a selection process to choose only mentors who have high levels of emotional intelligence and integrity. Then provide mentor training to teach skills such as listening, affirmation, feedback, networking, among others. Properly selecting and preparing mentors will set the foundation of the mentoring program and allow significant contributions to the development of employees (Johnson, Smith, and Haythornthwaite 2020).

Both coaching and mentoring provide psychosocial support for junior managers by exposing them to role models they can imitate. In addition, positive coaching and mentoring experiences provide mutual support and encouragement that validates the junior manager's efforts and achievements.

Furthermore, counseling for personal and professional problems can be provided to assist in promoting self-esteem and self-image. Finally, some of these relationships develop into long-lasting friendships that span decades and careers (Osland et al. 2007).

Delegation

delegation
The act of authorizing another to perform a task or duty and, in doing so, allocating and sharing responsibilities to increase productivity and empowerment.

A critical tool that successful leaders use to empower and develop subordinates is **delegation**. If mastered and used well, delegation can motivate employees and increase the productivity of an organization.

Effective delegation allocates and shares responsibilities to increase productivity and empower employees. Good delegators direct their focus and energy to high-leverage activities that only they can do. In the process, subordinates are provided opportunities to be challenged and to grow, while superiors gain free time to pursue critical activities. Stephen Covey (2004, 179), a prominent leadership consultant, captured the importance of this skill: "Effective delegation is perhaps the best indicator of effective management simply because it is so basic to both personal and organizational growth." Appropriate delegation also imbues jobs with meaning, which directly impacts how empowered employees feel, their skills, and their productivity (Atanacio 2020).

Although most would concur that effective delegation remains a key leadership function, many managers merely dump duties and tasks on subordinates. If delegation provides so many benefits, why do so many managers fail to delegate appropriately? Following are some common reasons (Lloyd 2020):

- Lack of training in effective delegation
- Belief that workers cannot do the job as well
- Belief that delegating will take longer than doing the work
- Lack of trust in workers' drive or diligence
- Need to be indispensable
- Enjoyment of the work
- Guilt associated with delegating to overworked employees

Merriam-Webster.com (2021) defines delegation as "the act of empowering to act for another." However, in management contexts, parameters must be added to this definition. In the nursing context, for example, delegation is defined as "transferring to a competent individual the authority to perform a selected nursing task in a selected situation. The nurse retains the accountability for the delegation" (LaCharity, Kumagai, and Bartz 2014). The importance of competence and accountability is highlighted here. For our purposes, delegation is the act of authorizing another to perform a task or duty and, in doing so, allocating and sharing responsibilities to increase productivity and empowerment.

Some who have considered delegation believe it entails a loss of control (Shin and Strausz 2014). However, when executed well, delegation establishes better controls. Furthermore, as stated, a key principle of delegation is that no matter the task delegated, accountability remains with the supervisor.

Delegation entails four key concepts:

1. Responsibility
2. Authority
3. Accountability
4. Trust

Responsibility always ultimately resides with the supervisor. Jobs and work can be delegated, but responsibility for a task always comes back to the supervisor who delegated it. Therefore, it is imperative that managers monitor delegated activities to ensure proper outcomes are achieved.

Note that the supervisor's responsibility for the delegated task does not remove the subordinate's accountability for the processes, activities, and results. Furthermore, accountability for results is key: If subordinates feel they are judged on movement and process alone, they might move rapidly

> **No Trust, No Delegation**
>
> Steve once served as an executive consultant in a large medical center, working with the CEO. The medical center had almost 1,000 beds and employed nearly 9,000 people. The CEO was exhausted. He had been working six or seven days a week for more than two years, often beginning his day at 6:00 a.m. and finishing after 10:00 p.m. He had asked for help becoming more productive.
>
> Steve quickly diagnosed many of the CEO's problems. Although more than 20 employees reported to him, he was reluctant to delegate even the simplest tasks. He had a long list of decisions that he had to approve and sign. These included vacation requests, expenditures greater than $5,000, pay increases, and many others. Frequently, he and his administrative assistant were still in the office signing documents at 7:00 p.m. when others had gone home. One evening, he proudly showed Steve his desk, which had three 6-inch piles of papers awaiting his review.
>
> When Steve presented his analysis and suggested solutions for the CEO's lack of productivity, he demurred to the opinion that he had centralized far too many decisions and needed to delegate some to his subordinates. Rather than review the detailed report prepared for him, the CEO stated that he could not see how he could delegate to those reporting to him as he "DID NOT TRUST THEM!" Now, that raised another issue . . .

and give the appearance of activity but not accomplish what is important.

Authority must be given to the individual entrusted with the task if the task is to be completed successfully. Delegation does not imply the surrender of overall authority but rather the transfer of the authority needed for task completion.

Accountability is an essential part of delegation and ties back to responsibility. The person receiving the delegation must understand the outcomes the supervisor seeks and the level of periodic reporting that must occur. Regular feedback is crucial. Delegation still requires supervision, and offering timely assessments periodically will make delegation more successful.

Over time, *trust* becomes the foundation of delegation. Supervisors who do not trust their subordinates will delegate few assignments. Successful delegation builds trust, which allows more delegation and greater growth.

Delegation may take up more of the supervisor's time at first. Some people use this expectation as an excuse to avoid delegating tasks, and often say they could do the job faster than they could explain it. However, as with the CEO described in the box, these managers soon accumulate too many tasks to complete on their own and then have even less time to begin delegating.

Others claim that delegated tasks often do not get done correctly and thus must be redone. Again, delegating does take more time at first. However, as Covey noted long ago, supervisors who refuse to delegate

> end up leading harassed lives, putting in fourteen-hour days, neglecting their families and their health, and undermining the vitality of the entire organization. . . . Time spent delegating in the long run, is our greatest time saved. (Covey 1992, 237)

Levels of Delegation

Delegation has been categorized in different ways. Covey (2004) suggested two basic kinds: gofer delegation and stewardship delegation. **Gofer delegation** is a cute term that signifies the delegation of specific, detailed actions—such as "go for" this and "go for" that—to a person or team who, after completing the tasks, must immediately return, report, and then wait for another assignment. As can be imagined, gofer delegation requires a lot of direct, one-on-one supervision and a small span of control.

Stewardship delegation, on the other hand, is focused on outcomes instead of processes. It empowers people or teams to choose how they will complete their assigned activities and be responsible for results.

Gofer and stewardship delegation involve different levels of empowerment, different frequencies (or times) of required reporting back to the boss, and different focuses on outcomes. Even within stewardship delegation, the degree of these factors may vary. As displayed in exhibit 20.2, the levels of delegation—from lowest to highest—include (1) wait until told, (2) assess and report, (3) recommend a course of action, (4) follow an action plan, (5) make decisions and report, and (6) own and report periodically.

1. *Wait until told.* This is the best example of gofer delegation. It involves very little empowerment and no growth potential. The leader simply

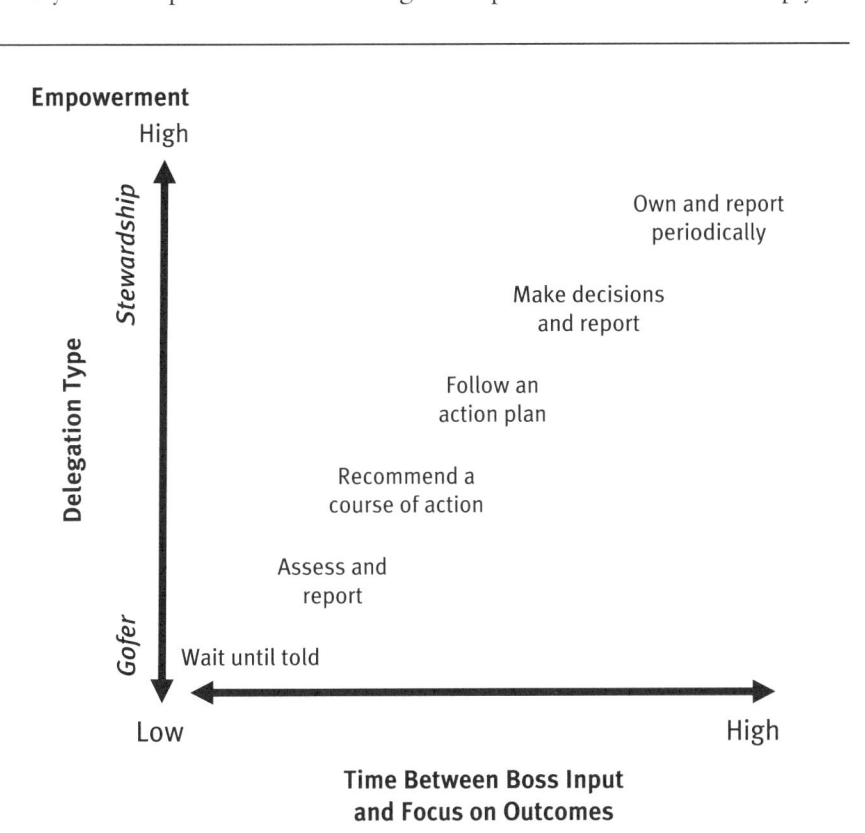

gofer delegation
The act of delegating specific, detailed actions to a person or team who, after completing the tasks, must immediately return, report, and then wait for another assignment.

stewardship delegation
The act of delegating that empowers the person or team assigned a task to choose how to complete activities and be responsible for results.

EXHIBIT 20.2
Levels of Delegation by Empowerment, Reporting Time, and Focus on Outcomes

tells a person or team what to do. The individual or team rushes off, completes the task, and then waits for the next command. This is the lowest level of delegation, and often the most common in many organizations. The advantage of this low level of delegation lies in that it is quick, efficient, and effective in the short term. However, in the long term it is ineffective and wastes time, in part because the subordinates learn dependence and lose initiative.

2. *Assess and report.* People on the receiving end of this level of delegation are given something to evaluate and told to report their findings so that the boss can tell them what to do next. This type of delegation is a form of gofer delegation, although it provides a small amount of responsibility to the subordinates. Little growth and development are seen with this form of delegation. A slight increase in productivity may occur, as the person or team evaluates issues, but the leader performs the thinking and takes responsibility for the next steps.

3. *Recommend a course of action.* This is the first level that begins to approach stewardship delegation. Responsibility becomes more shared in that subordinates are expected to evaluate an issue and recommend a course of action, although they must still obtain approval before initiating the solution. The responsibility for determining and suggesting a plan of action has been transferred to the person or team that will carry it out. Both parties can learn and grow at this level of delegation; the subordinate grows by performing the delegated tasks, and the leader grows by taking a supporting role to allow the subordinate to develop. This can be an early leadership development activity that allows leaders to learn to trust their thinking and decision-making. As self-trust grows, these leaders can move to higher levels of stewardship delegation, as can their subordinates.

4. *Follow an action plan.* At this level, the leader and subordinate agree on an overall plan of action and the subordinate carries it out. The person or team has limited authority to make decisions and engage across the general action plan. Once the assignment is completed, the subordinate notifies the leader, and the action plan is renewed.

5. *Make decisions and report.* This level comes close to full stewardship delegation, as most responsibility has been transferred to the subordinate. The person or team now has an area of responsibility to oversee and provides updates to the leader relatively frequently.

6. *Own and report periodically.* This level represents full stewardship delegation in that responsibility has been transferred completely. The subordinate owns the area, figuratively speaking, and has accountability for the outcomes it produces. These outcomes are reported to the superior at predetermined intervals, such as monthly or quarterly. The leader trusts the subordinate's decisions.

Managerial Key Points Regarding Delegation

The ability to delegate depends on the level of trust between the supervisor and subordinate. In a new relationship, where trust may not exist, it may be best to start delegation at the "recommend" or "follow an action plan" level. This allows the parties to gain experience with each other and learn to trust each other. The subordinate can be engaged in the thought process and learn from the leader. As trust builds over time, the leader can transfer increasing levels of delegation to the subordinate.

Beware of Micromanaging

Micromanaging is the worst form of gofer delegation. Micromanagers display a lack of trust by constantly asking the status of tasks, and an extreme focus on details of the process rather than on outcomes. Micromanaging also takes an inordinate amount of both the leader's and the subordinate's time, causing inefficiencies for both. To diminish micromanagement, leaders should avoid making excuses and blaming employees for their micromanaging. Likewise, leaders should focus on strategic issues and measure the desired outcomes rather than processes (Rappleye 2014). Farrer (2020) advises that leaders can tell if they are micromanaging if most of the following are present:

- Requirements for constant reporting from subordinates
- Overscheduling of workers with detailed itineraries
- Meetings that consist primarily of manager monologues
- Leader involvement in all decisions
- Excessive monitoring of employees
- Step-by-step instructions that are very inflexible
- Undermining of independent troubleshooting by telling employees "call me any time you have a question"

Communicate Clearly When Delegating

One of the authors' earliest bosses, who was a key mentor, consistently counseled him that it is "not good enough to be understood, but to communicate well enough that others could not misunderstand you." This is especially true for communicating when delegating.

Lack of clarity is a main issue in dysfunctional delegation. Often, the objective and level of delegation are muddled (Lipman 2013). Called

> **Dump-and-Run Delegation**
>
> Your boss calls to tell you, "I need a quick competitor analysis of surgical centers in the United States." You can tell she is at the airport and has only a few minutes before she boards a plane. She swiftly assigns the task to you and Fred, your coworker, but makes it clear that this is a high priority for her boss, the company's CEO. She concludes by expressing her trust that you will complete the task successfully.
>
> You are taken by surprise by the call and assignment, and the urgency and impatience in your boss's voice concern you. What did she really mean? Are you to prepare a one-page summary, a PowerPoint presentation, a 20-page report? And what is the analysis about? Revenue potential? Earnings? Market share? Advertising? You are also not certain who is in charge of the project—Fred or you. In addition, what does "quick" mean? Is it required by tomorrow? Next week? In a month?
>
> You remember a previous time when your boss called you at 8:00 a.m. the day after delegating a similar task to you, demanding to know where the analysis was. She was irritated that it wasn't finished because she was going into a meeting with the CEO in ten minutes. With that experience in mind, you decide to stay late tonight to finish the analysis, just in case. You inform Fred of the assignment but tell him you will handle all of it, even if it takes all night.

"dump-and-run" delegation, as described in the box, a boss hurriedly passes off an assignment without clearly defining the expectations, scope, deadlines, or parameters of authority. The subordinate is left solely responsible for completing the assignment, receiving no support or guidelines.

Eight Steps to Effective Delegation

Many of the steps listed here are similar to those for goal setting discussed in chapter 7. Much like for goals, the level and extent of delegation need to be clearly defined and appropriate processes must be established to coordinate efforts between the leader and the subordinate. As noted by Bloom (2016), the delegation steps are as follows:

1. *Clearly define what you can and cannot delegate.* Determine what work others should take on to make your time more effective and to help develop the person receiving the work.
2. *Have a prioritized delegation plan.* Specify which tasks will be delegated to which employee, along with the importance and visibility of the delegated tasks.
3. *Give clear instructions and defined expectations.* Determine (a) who is ready, with the appropriate skills, competencies, and motivation for the task, or (b) who needs the challenge and will develop the required skills. If additional skills or competencies are needed, make certain the means to obtain them is established.
4. *Provide appropriate level of management support.* Allocate resources, training, time, and instructions as necessary.
5. *Give employees the room to complete their delegated tasks.* Do not micromanage, but still stay involved.

6. *Continue mentoring and teaching.* Use delegation to teach and train employees.
7. *Give credit for work delegated to employees.* Use delegation to praise and compliment employees for their contributions.
8. *Solicit feedback.* Speak to employees regarding what is delegated and how. Look for ways to adjust your delegation to improve performance.

Successful delegation comes from practice and experience. Be willing to reflect on your behaviors in terms of what level of delegation you provide and receive. As a boss, seek to build trust concurrent with increasing levels of stewardship delegation. As a subordinate, constantly build trust by meeting and exceeding expectations, and talk to your boss about taking on more stewardship responsibilities.

Chapter Summary

Mentoring, coaching, and delegation provide valuable tools to develop healthcare leaders. These processes assist in training and empowering employees to cultivate leadership skills and build their confidence. Although the terms *coaching* and *mentoring* are often used synonymously, coaching generally involves short-term support and skill transfer whereas mentoring is characterized by long-term relationships geared toward growing and nurturing leadership capabilities. The wide popularity of executive coaching today is demonstrated by the many professional executive coaching organizations.

Mentoring can greatly assist in socializing new and junior members of an organization. Research shows that those mentored are more likely to receive promotions and enjoy job satisfaction than those who are not. Mentoring and coaching can also have a positive impact on transforming a hospital's culture. To be successful, a mentoring program must establish goals and ground rules.

Delegation needs to be appropriately practiced, empowering and developing subordinates, to motivate employees and increase productivity. Delegation encompasses (1) responsibility, (2) authority, (3) accountability, and (4) trust. Even though the ultimate responsibility resides with the supervisor, employees should be delegated specific areas of responsibility to achieve results and not just carry out processes and actions. Authority, accountability, and trust are likewise essential for successful delegation. If any of these are lacking, the delegation will be ineffective and both superior and subordinate will become frustrated. Effective delegation may take more time up front to establish, but once functioning, it will free time for the supervisor to execute more important tasks.

The different levels of delegation can be classified into gofer delegation and stewardship delegation. Gofer delegation involves employees carrying out detailed directions and waiting for the next assignment. Stewardship delegation frees employees to think, generate ideas, and implement solutions.

The ability to delegate depends greatly on the level of trust that exists between the supervisor and subordinate. This trusting relationship takes time and effort to develop. Good delegation also requires clear communication and comes from practice and experience.

Chapter Questions

1. What are the major differences between mentoring and coaching?
2. How can coaching be different from having a consultant assist a healthcare leader?
3. Visit the website of one of the professional coaching organizations listed in exhibit 20.1 and describe the services it provides to its members.
4. How might mentoring increase an employee's job satisfaction?
5. What guidelines could be established for mentoring?
6. Are there times when delegation should not occur?
7. How does delegation help establish trust?
8. What is positive and negative about gofer delegation?
9. What is micromanagement, and why is it destructive?

Chapter Cases

Take-Care-of-It Delegation

Early in my career as a 26-year-old assistant administrator at a hospital, I was on administrative call for the weekend. Our hospital provided the only obstetric service for the county, and its three anesthesiologists and five certified registered nurse anesthetists took turns providing call coverage for the hospital. At that time, I was unaware that one of the anesthesiologists was abusing drugs and often would inform his colleagues that he was "sick" when he was scheduled to provide call coverage.

The weekend I was on administrative call, it was the drug-abusing anesthesiologist's turn to provide anesthesia call coverage. However, early that Saturday afternoon, he reported that he was unable to cover the hospital and one of his partners would have to do so instead.

Chapter 20: Developing Employees Through Mentoring, Coaching, and Delegation

His partners had all left town. Not one was available. The nursing shift supervisor was worried about having no anesthesia coverage for the hospital, which could have serious medical and legal implications. When I received her call, I became alarmed and wondered what to do. I called the hospital CEO, explained the situation, and asked for his advice.

The CEO was a direct and trusting person who believed in delegating and having me take responsibility for my duties. He listened intently, and when I was done talking he said, "Fix it. Let me know Monday what you did." Then he hung up.

Despite feeling stressed by the situation, I did find a solution and was able to arrange for an anesthesiologist from another hospital to cover the weekend. I promised him whatever compensation it took for him to cover the call duty.

On Monday morning, I reported to the CEO what actions I had taken, and he thanked me for my efforts. He complimented what I did and did not criticize the amount I paid the other doctor to cover call.

Looking back, I see this as a significant learning experience in my career that taught me the importance of proper delegation. I never went to the CEO without a solution to a problem and frequently solved issues without his input. I grew more confident, and both of us became much more productive.

Case Questions
1. How did the CEO's actions involve both mentoring and delegation?
2. What did I learn from the way the CEO handled my call?
3. What else could the CEO have done to emphasize stewardship delegation?

When Are We Going to Lunch?

The CEO of a large health system with more than 9,000 employees, 20 of whom reported to her, liked to be involved in decisions, even if they were trivial. In fact, she often put off making a big decision because she was too busy making small ones. Effectively, she was a great "firefighter," resolving crises daily, but a poor leader, as she refused to delegate much to her managers.

The effort to get approval for many activities was excessive, as the CEO required a paper trail and expected to sign off on even the most trivial decisions in writing. For example, during a strategic planning effort, the organization had brought in two prominent international consultants. Combined, they were being paid more than $10,000 per day. At noon on the first day of their visit, the director of strategy asked if they would like to join him for lunch in the organization's premier dining room. The director, however, had forgotten to obtain the CEO's approval for this expenditure, which was about $15 per person, and he was unable to take the consultants to the dining area without written approval. The director apologized and asked the consultants to sit in his office until he could get the approval. The two consultants sat, wondering whether they were going to eat that day. About 45 minutes later, the approval form was finally signed and the three left for a late lunch.

Case Questions
1. Why do people such as this CEO want to be involved in trivial decisions?
2. What are the consequences when bosses spend most of their time on nonstrategic decisions?
3. What could the director of strategy do to assist his boss in focusing on more strategic issues?

I Thought We Already Made That Decision

By Britt Berrett

If the CEO must make all the decisions, then no one makes decisions. At one organization, it had been the previous CEO's custom to analyze and critique every decision. Rather than support important decisions made by his subordinates, the CEO insisted that proposals were to be submitted, reviewed, modified, and authorized only by him.

The benefit of this practice was that the CEO owned each decision. The problem was that members of the executive team refrained from making decisions themselves.

This situation was challenged when a talented vice president (VP) needed to upgrade the Gamma Knife equipment in the imaging department. The department could either upgrade the existing equipment for a nominal expense or replace it at a significant cost. Both options had benefits, including increased capability and improved operational performance. The intricacies of the decision required insights and opinions at the operational level, well outside the expertise of the CEO.

The VP presented the issues and awaited the CEO's decision. His response? "It's your call. I will support your decision."

This unexpected answer called for a new process. Returning to his office, the VP struggled to make the decision—upgrade or replace—because he assumed that eventually the CEO would tell him what to do. Regrettably, he could not accept that he owned the decision.

The VP forwarded several additional reports to the CEO and awaited a written directive. The decision about the Gamma Knife languished for months. Finally, the VP returned to the CEO's office to request that a

Chapter 20: Developing Employees Through Mentoring, Coaching, and Delegation

decision be made. The CEO, attending to other issues, looked up and said, "I thought we already made that decision."

It was a turning point in the dynamic of the executive team. The team finally recognized that the CEO was starting to delegate operational-level decision-making with unquestioning support.

Case Questions
1. Why was the VP reluctant to make the final decision, even though he was told to do so?
2. How could the delegation have been more clearly defined?
3. What do you think the CEO and VP should have done to clarify the delegation issue?

Chapter Activities

Delegation Quiz
Take the MindTools test "How Well Do You Delegate?" (www.mindtools.com/pages/article/newTMM_60.htm). What did you learn from the test? How good are your delegation skills?

Delegation Video
Watch the ten-minute EntreLeadership video "How to Delegate" (https://youtu.be/DMsHHS-Gs_o). Write a one-page paper pointing out the principles discussed in this chapter and in the video. What points does the presenter emphasize?

Find a Mentor
Identify someone nearby who is currently working in an occupation and role that interests you. Make an appointment and visit with that individual. During your visit, ask the person (1) how they prepared for the job, and the background that brought them to this point; (2) what advice they might have to help you prepare for a similar role; (3) if they would be willing to mentor you, or at least let you come back for guidance occasionally, as you progress in your career.

References

Adkins, A. 2020. "Millennials: The Job-Hopping Generation." *Business Journal* (blog). *Gallup* (n.d.). www.gallup.com/workplace/231587/millennials-job-hopping-generation.aspx.

American College of Healthcare Executives (ACHE). 2020a. "Hospital CEO Turnover Rate Shows Small Decrease" (press release). September 15. www.ache.org/about-ache/news-and-awards/news-releases/hospital-ceo-turnover-2020.

———. 2020b. "Leadership Mentoring Network." www.ache.org/career-resource-center/advance-your-career/leadership-mentoring-network.

Atanacio, A. 2020. "The Importance of Delegating Effectively." *Forbes* (blog). Published June 15. www.forbes.com/sites/theyec/2020/06/15/the-importance-of-delegating-effectively/.

Ayoobzadeh, M., and K. Boles. 2020. "How Mentoring Improves the Leadership Skills of Those Doing the Mentoring." *Phys.org.* October 19. https://phys.org/news/2020-10-leadership-skills.html.

Balser, J. 2019. "The Case for Executive Coaching in Academic Medicine." *Consulting Psychology: Practice and Research* 71 (3): 165–69.

Banwell, J., G. Kerr, and A. Stirling 2020. "Benefits of a Female Coach Mentorship Programme on Women Coaches' Development." *Sports Coaching Review*, May 18. https://doi.org/10.1080/21640629.2020.1764266.

Bawany, S. 2014. "Mentoring & Leadership Development." *Leadership Excellence Essentials* 31 (8): 52.

Berriman, J. 2007. "Can Coaching Combat Stress at Work?" *Occupational Health* 59 (1): 27–29.

Bloom, E. 2016. "8 Steps to Maximize Your Managerial Delegation Effectiveness." *Lab Talk* 44 (02E): 20–21.

Covey, S. 2004. *Seven Habits of Highly Effective People.* New York: Free Press.

———. 1992. *Principle-Centered Leadership.* New York: Simon and Schuster.

Farrer, L. 2020. "12 Signs of a Virtual Micromanager." *Forbes* (blog). Published August 4. www.forbes.com/sites/laurelfarrer/2020/08/04/12-signs-of-a-virtual-micromanager/.

Fessell, D. P., V. Chopra, and S. Saint. 2020. "Mentoring During a Crisis." *Harvard Business Review* digital article. October 29. https://hbr.org/2020/10/mentoring-during-a-crisis.

Hicks, R., and J. McCracken. 2013. "Popcorn Coaching." *Physician Executive* 102 (1): 85–87.

John Mattone Global. 2019. "The 5 Essential Components of Successful Coaching." Published November 1. https://johnmattone.com/blog/the-5-essential-components-of-successful-coaching/.

Johnson, W. B., D. G. Smith, and J. Haythornthwaite. 2020. "Why Your Mentorship Program Isn't Working." *Harvard Business Review* digital article, July 17. https://hbr.org/2020/07/why-your-mentorship-program-isnt-working.

Koonce, R. 2010. "Executive Coaching: Leadership Development in the Federal Government." *Public Manager* 39 (2): 44–51.

LaCharity, L., C. Kumagai, and B. Bartz. 2014. *Prioritization, Delegation, and Assignment: Practice Exercises for the NCLEX Examination.* St. Louis, MO: Elsevier.

Landry, A., and R. E. Lewiss. 2020. "What Efficient Mentorship Looks Like." *Harvard Business Review* digital article, August 25. https://hbr.org/2020/08/what-efficient-mentorship-looks-like.

Lester, P., S. Hannah, P. Harms, G. Vogelgesang, and B. Avolio. 2011. "Mentoring Impact on Leader Efficacy Development." *Academy of Management Learning & Education* 10 (3): 409–29.

Lipman, V. 2013. "The Secret to Effective Delegation." *Forbes* (blog). Published June 3. www.forbes.com/sites/victorlipman/2013/06/03/the-secret-to-effective-delegation/.

Lloyd, S. 2020. "Managers Must Delegate Effectively to Develop Employees." *SHRM*. www.shrm.org/ResourcesAndTools/hr-topics/organizational-and-employee-development/Pages/DelegateEffectively.aspx.

Marton, K., C. Wright, and K. Pister. 2019. "3 Keys for Effective Physician Leadership." *Physician Leadership Journal* 6 (2): 46–49.

Merriam-Webster.com. 2021. "Delegation." Accessed August 26. www.merriam-webster.com/dictionary/delegation.

Osland, J., D. Kolb, I. Rubin, and M. Turner. 2007. *Organizational Behavior: An Experiential Approach*. Upper Saddle River, NJ: Prentice-Hall.

Rappleye, E. 2014. "4 Strategies to Mitigate Micromanagement." *Becker's Hospital Review*, November 13. www.beckershospitalreview.com/hospital-management-administration/4-strategies-to-mitigate-micromanagement.html.

Schraeder, M., and M. Jordan. 2011. "Managing Performance: A Practical Perspective on Managing Employee Performance." *Journal for Quality and Participation* 34 (2): 4–10.

Sexton, D., C. Lemak, and J. Wainio. 2014. "Career Inflection Points of Women Who Successfully Achieved the Hospital CEO Position." *Journal of Healthcare Management* 59 (5): 367–83.

Shin, D., and R. Strausz. 2014. "Delegation and Dynamic Incentives." *Rand Journal of Economics* 45 (3): 495–520.

Sindell, T., and M. Sindell. 2016. "'Mentoring' and 'Leadership Coaching' Are Not the Same. Do You Know the Difference?" *Entrepreneur*, August 23. www.entrepreneur.com/article/280275.

St. John, A. 2019. "Who's Mentoring the Future?" *Chief Learning Officer*, December 4. www.chieflearningofficer.com/2019/12/04/whos-mentoring-%E2%80%A8the-future/.

Stevens, G., and G. Frazer. 2005. "Coaching: The Missing Ingredient in Blended Learning Strategy." *Performance Improvement* 44 (8): 8–13.

Stout-Rostron, S. 2014. *Business Coaching International: Transforming Individuals and Organizations*, 2nd ed. London: Karmac.

Taie, E. 2011. "Coaching as an Approach to Enhanced Performance." *Journal for Quality and Participation* 34 (1): 34–38.

Tyler, K. 2020. "Executive Coaches Ease Leadership Transitions." *HR Magazine* 59 (9). www.shrm.org/hr-today/news/hr-magazine/pages/0914-executive-coaching.aspx.

CHAPTER 21

ORGANIZATIONAL CULTURE

> Cultures of blame and denial are predominant in healthcare organizations. Afraid of the consequences, many healthcare cultures shift blame to others, fail to report errors, and experience incivility and conflict. Physicians traditionally have been seen as the "captain of the ship," giving directions to all of their subordinates. Yet, providing healthcare requires team-based approaches and a culture of engagement and shared decision-making to provide patient-centered care, assure quality, and improve the health of populations. To move to a healthier culture, the American College of Cardiology (ACC) created a program called "Leadership Saves Lives." As part of this effort, the ACC produced a Leadership Saves Lives Toolkit that includes tools and insights on how hospitals can transform their cultures (Association of Schools and Programs of Public Health 2018; Chen 2018; Moore and Bates 2020).

Learning Objectives

After studying this chapter, readers should be able to

- summarize the components of organizational culture;
- relate how rituals, routines, and stories help create and reinforce a culture;
- appraise the concept of power distance and its relative importance in different cultures;
- identify the concept and application of uncertainty avoidance among cultures;
- distinguish cultures that stress individualism from those that stress collectivism;
- contrast between masculine and feminine organizational behaviors and preferences; and
- analyze cultural assessments and the way cultural change takes place.

Key Terms

- cultural assessment
- individualism (versus collectivism)
- indulgence
- masculinity (versus femininity)
- organizational culture
- power distance
- rituals and routines
- stories
- symbols and structures
- temporal orientation
- uncertainty avoidance

organizational culture
"The pattern of basic assumptions that . . . have worked well enough to be considered valid and . . . the correct way to perceive, think, and feel" (Schein 1984, 3) for members of a given group.

Organizational culture is a critical element in organizational performance and in the success or failure of a business. Establishing and maintaining a positive culture has become a major task for organizations today. The primary purpose of a corporate culture is to help guide actions and decisions of all employees (Sull, Turconi, and Sull 2020). The values and mission of a company should be the foundation of its culture. However, many firms fail to ingrain their written values and mission into the actual behaviors and actions of their employees and end up with a culture that distracts from what they want to accomplish. As can be seen in the story of HealthSouth (see the box), the toxic culture created by former HealthSouth CEO Richard Scrushy fostered an environment that led to massive and endemic fraud, which almost shuttered the company and led to criminal convictions for most of the company's senior managers.

Although **organizational culture** is an important factor in the functioning of any group, the concept lacks a universally accepted definition. For our purposes, organizational culture is the pattern of basic assumptions that a given group has invented, discovered, or developed in learning to cope with its problems of external adaptation and internal integration, and that have worked well enough to be considered valid and, therefore, to be taught to new members as the correct way to perceive, think, and feel in relation to those problems. (Schein 1984, 3)

Simply put, culture can be considered the set

A Toxic Culture at HealthSouth

After nearly two decades of growth and the appearance of success at HealthSouth, a large for-profit chain of rehabilitation clinics, almost its entire management team was found guilty of fraud, conspiracy, obstruction of justice, and money laundering. The toxic culture that allowed corruption to occur in the company provides an interesting window into the effects of culture on organizational performance.

Richard Scrushy, the founder and first CEO of HealthSouth, ruled by intimidation. Each Monday morning, he called a meeting that his employees called the "Monday morning beating" because it almost always deteriorated into an opportunity for Scrushy to publicly berate someone for a perceived failure. Interviews with associates of Scrushy, government officials, and former employees, as well as a review of the litigation history of HealthSouth, painted a picture of an executive who

(continued)

of a group's shared beliefs and values that establishes the context for the proper way to behave in an organization (SHRM 2020). Culture creates the "background music" that directs employee decisions and delineates what is acceptable and unacceptable in a firm (King and Demarie 2014). Members of organizations tend to think and act similarly and often exhibit common personality traits that are persistent over time. For example, the HealthSouth culture during Scrushy's tenure did not allow for frank and open conversations with him regarding problems facing the company. Employees accepted the unwritten directives to hide bad news and never contradict the boss. Their actions were consistent over time, and only dismissal of most of the top managers altered the prevailing culture.

> *(continued from previous page)*
>
> ruled by top-down fear, threatened critics with reprisals, and paid loyal subordinates well (Abelson and Freudenheim 2003). For example, he would criticize staff about missed profit goals and would demand two-minute presentations from them, complete with numbers. Afterward (if he allowed them to finish), he would launch into hard-nosed questions and frequently utter the dreaded phrase, "That was the stupidest thing I ever heard" (Helyar 2003). This behavior was also exhibited toward physicians and others if they crossed him. He had no tolerance for criticism and responded quickly when he perceived a personal slight. After leading HealthSouth for 19 years, he had almost single-handedly molded the organizational culture into one of compliant, cowering, and excessively eager-to-please managers.
>
> Scrushy felt a need to honor his name and donated liberally to schools and communities, which named facilities and programs after him. He built a small museum in HealthSouth's Birmingham, Alabama, headquarters to pay tribute to his hard work, featuring the furniture he used when he founded the company and a life-sized statue of himself. He owned multiple mansions, airplanes, and boats; jewelry worth several million dollars; and property worth more than $22 million (Farrell 2004).
>
> In 2006, his life changed dramatically when he was found guilty of conspiracy, bribery, and mail fraud in a federal court, which sent him to prison for almost seven years. A separate civil case brought by HealthSouth investors regarding accounting fraud resulted in a $2.9 billion judgment. Today, he continues to blame many of his problems on those who reported to him and claims he is innocent. It is interesting to speculate how a healthy culture might have resulted in different decisions at HealthSouth.

Components of Organizational Culture

Understanding and managing organizational culture are important skills for leaders. Competence in these skills includes knowing the answers to the following questions:

- What makes up organizational culture?
- How is it created?
- How can it be maintained?
- What causes it to change?

> **Values Are the Basis of Any Organizational Culture**
>
> After laying off more than 10 percent of their employees in 2016 following their CEO's unexpected death, SurveyMonkey sought to reset their culture. They first surveyed their workforce, which resulted in five employee values: Be accountable, trust the team, prioritize health, listen to the customers, celebrate the journey. These values were used as the basis for change in their culture and they sought to put them into action and align them with how their employees worked. Once aligned, they began to increase their recruiting and ramp up their new products. As a result of this realignment, the company has enjoyed great success (Lurie 2019).

Organizational culture develops and is maintained through symbols, heroes, rituals, and values (Hofstede, Hofstede, and Minkov 2010; SHRM 2020). Over time, organizational members develop similar values and beliefs, as they share similar experiences. Likewise, organizations tend to retain those employees who hold or develop similar values and act in similar ways.

Groysberg and colleagues (2018) identified four generally accepted attributes of organizational cultures:

1. *Shared.* Groups share culture through their behaviors, values, and assumptions.
2. *Pervasive.* Culture is broad and deep in an organization, permeating actions and mindsets.
3. *Enduring.* Culture becomes self-reinforcing, as organizations attract and retain employees that "fit" with the established culture.
4. *Implicit.* People recognize and respond to culture instinctively.

rituals and routines Collective social activities that reinforce organizational values by engendering active participation from organizational members.

stories Narratives that describe the culture's values in action or demonstrate the violation of stated values.

Values, linked with organizational ethics and moral codes, form the core of culture and drive the norms for what actions are accepted and not accepted. Organizational values must direct the goals that should be pursued and the appropriate standards for behaviors and processes to achieve the goals. Strong, effective cultures exist when employees' actions are aligned with organizational values. As indicated in the box, when this alignment occurs, strong cultures create highly functioning companies and produce outstanding outcomes (Patnaik 2011).

Rituals and routines are collective social activities that reinforce organizational values by engendering active participation from organizational members. Rituals and routines consist of ordinary actions and protocols (e.g., coffee breaks, greetings, dress codes, conduct of meetings), as well as infrequent events (e.g., retirement ceremonies, office sports betting pools, retreats). Rituals help build social bonds among members, and to that end, many organizations have some type of initiation ritual and routine.

Values are also supported or damaged by the stories told in an organization. **Stories** describe the culture's values in action or demonstrate the violation of those values. For example, for many years, employees in one organization told the story of the day the chief financial officer hit a patient's husband during an argument and the story of the chief operating officer seen mowing his lawn on a workday during a spate of financial cutbacks in the organization. Negative stories such as these detract from expressed values. On the other hand, positive stories—such as one about a top leader stopping in a busy airport to help carry a young mother's luggage—reinforce a company's caring values.

symbols and structures Images, events, activities, objects, and workplace structures that express or represent an idea or quality, among others.

Storytelling has been recognized as an important vehicle for instilling values, as it can highlight examples of service and devotion. People remember stories more easily than written values or mission statements. Stories also carry more emotional context and can more significantly influence individuals. Organizational members who wish to be influential leaders, then, should learn to tell positive, constructive stories.

In addition, storytelling can be an effective means of promoting culture by differentiating between the organization and its competitors, conveying a sense of member identity, enabling a sense of commitment, shaping member attitudes and behaviors, and enhancing the stability of the organization (Brady and Haley 2013). Stories contribute to self-worth and self-knowledge and create positive cultures (Verghese 2019).

Similarly, **symbols and structures** are meaningful to culture. Symbols include images, events, activities, or

---

Korean Culture Structures Stifle Productivity

The culture in Korea is very strong but can be detrimental to productivity. In fact, as of 2019, Korea had one of the lowest productivity ratings among the 37 nations of the OECD (Organisation for Economic Co-operation and Development). Its culture influences how organizations are structured and how workers communicate and project busyness.

In Korea, corporate reporting structures are top-down and rigid. Organizations are structured much like military units, with authoritarian leadership that demands constant and often unnecessary reports to senior directors. Work teams are required to brief their department heads weekly, and if a director wants to know something—no matter its relevance—a team leader is forced to report on it. The constant cycle of impromptu reporting creates an environment with little strategic work and a lot of paper shuffling, firefighting, and endless audits and presentations.

Corporate communication in Korea is also affected by culture. Most workers feel pressured to eat and drink with each other and with customers well past work hours. This socialization among small groups leads to factions within companies, fueling suspicion, competition, and poor communication across teams and units. In addition, the wide availability of fast internet and technology has eliminated much verbal conversation, as electronic messages prevail. One poll showed that more than 40 percent of employees regularly used work time for games, internet surfing, texting, and phone calls.

The Korean culture also encourages people to look busy. Therefore, Korean employees remain on-site beyond regular hours to give the impression of working hard, but staying late is a test of loyalty, social pressure, and performance. Actual work often slows to fill the expected overtime. This is how a culture can create visible forms and functions and still produce suboptimal outcomes.

Source: Adapted from Kocken (2014).

EXHIBIT 21.1
Components of Organizational Culture

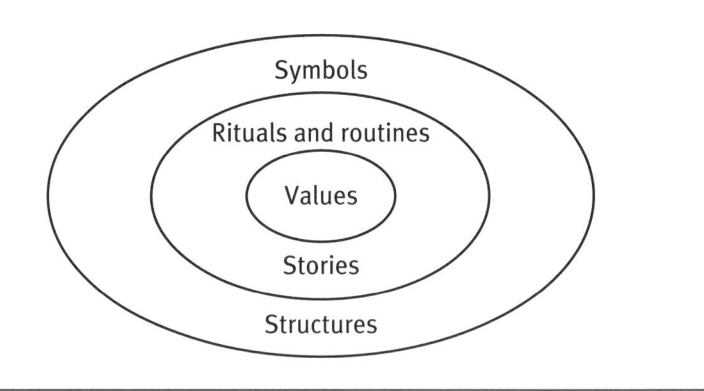

Diagram: concentric ovals labeled (outermost to innermost): Symbols; Rituals and routines; Values; Stories; Structures

objects that help identify, characterize, or represent an entity, an idea, or a quality and are woven into the fabric of most organizations. Organizational symbols may include the type of clothing worn on-site, the size or physical layout of offices, the pictures or other images placed in the environment, or the nature of personal interactions that take place in it. They acquire meaning in organizations by their repeated connection to values, as viewed through the eyes of organizational members. Symbols often tell us much of what we understand about our own organization.

Structures can also reflect and influence culture. The choice of structure defines how people are divided, grouped, controlled, and coordinated. A company can choose a tall, hierarchical reporting structure that may have small spans of control and highly centralized decision-making, or it can opt for a flat, decentralized reporting structure defined by large spans of control and more decentralized decision-making.

All these components of organizational structure, shown in exhibit 21.1, affect expectations and reporting requirements and may generate barriers to communication and productivity (see the box on page 465).

power distance
The way power is distributed and the degree to which individuals accept the inequity of power distribution.

uncertainty avoidance
The degree to which members feel uncomfortable in ambiguous and uncertain situations and take action to avoid them.

Cultural Differences

Comparing cultures can be difficult, but certain dimensions have been identified that allow an understanding of differences. Power distance, uncertainty avoidance, individualism (versus collectivism), temporal orientation, indulgence, and masculinity (versus femininity) are dimensions often used to examine country cultures, but are also applicable to business cultures. These dimensions are defined as follows (Hofstede 2020):

- **Power distance**—the way power is distributed and the degree to which individuals accept the inequity of power distribution. Low power distance equates to high power distribution and equality. High power distance results in powerful bosses, leader-only problem resolution, and top-down direction. Many East Asian countries have a high power distance.

- **Uncertainty avoidance**—the degree to which members feel uncomfortable in ambiguous and uncertain situations and take action to avoid them. Groups with high uncertainty avoidance tend to have inflexible codes of conduct and exhibit intolerance toward unorthodox behaviors and ideas.
- **Individualism**—the preference for personal gain (individualism) over benefits for the group (collectivism). Individualism exists in a loosely knit social framework in which responsibility is primarily to the self, whereas collectivism is seen in a tightly knit society whose members look after each other.
- **Temporal orientation**—the degree to which members are willing to defer satisfaction and focus on achieving long-term, rather than short-term, outcomes.
- **Indulgence**—the amount of freedom to act on one's impulses and pursue personal enjoyment, as opposed to duty and obligation.
- **Masculinity**—the preference for achievement, heroism, assertiveness, or material rewards (masculinity) over cooperation, modesty, caring, and quality of life (femininity).

The Hofstede Centre uses these dimensions to compare national cultures.

Many companies use a **cultural assessment** to compare their culture with their mission and values. A gap analysis, which uncovers areas of organizational culture that do not align with organizational mission and values, can be conducted and action plans can be developed to rectify these problem areas. As discussed, cultures are complex, and changing a culture is a multidimensional process that may take many years to yield desired results. However, the effort is worthwhile, as organizations that achieve a compatible culture are more likely to meet the expectations set by their mission and values.

Leaders can ascertain the proper alignment with the following questions, using a Likert-type scale from 1 (not at all) to 5 (all of the time) (adapted from Osland et al. 2007):

- Can people in the organization easily identify its dominant values?
- Does the hiring process consistently select people who fit into the company culture?
- Do socialization and training occur for new employees to help them quickly understand the culture and values?

---

individualism
The preference for personal gain (individualism) over benefits for the group (collectivism).

temporal orientation
The degree to which members are willing to defer satisfaction and focus on achieving long-term, rather than short-term, outcomes.

indulgence
The degree to which a culture emphasizes personal freedom and enjoyment over duty and obligation.

masculinity
The preferences for achievement, heroism, assertiveness, or material rewards (masculinity) over cooperation, modesty, caring, and quality of life (femininity).

cultural assessment
A tool for comparing organizational culture with organizational mission and values to identify needs and appropriate interventions.

- Are employees who do not live the organizational values asked to leave?
- Are people rewarded for following the key organizational values?
- Do leaders and managers signal the desired values and norms by their behaviors and actions?
- Do managers measure and hold people accountable for key values?

Cultures must adapt to and yet maintain alignment with an organization's values as well as its environment. Firms that do not adjust their cultures to new environmental challenges can falter. For example, Uber was highly successful, but ran into trouble related to its culture, which included a lack of internal transparency, a tendency to avoid regulations, and a climate of sexual harassment. These were published as "risks" when Uber went public in 2017 (Wong 2019). Likewise, successful healthcare systems have been faced with significant challenges in employee relations. Those instituting layoffs and exhibiting a profit-oriented culture have scored much poorer than other systems with more employee-centric cultures. For instance, as can be seen in exhibit 21.2, employee ratings of hospital CEOs in Dallas, Texas, on the jobs site Glassdoor ranged from only 20 percent approval to 88 percent approval (Schnuman 2019).

Healthcare is now pressured to improve on many fronts, and numerous healthcare organizations are trying to change their cultures to meet the new demands. Structural changes have not been, and will not be, adequate to achieve the improvements needed in healthcare; they must be coupled with appropriate cultural change. The many interconnections that define complexity in healthcare make these changes difficult, because healthcare contains both organizational and professional cultures. However, studies have demonstrated, for example, that improving aspects of physicians' professional culture and relationships is more likely to produce positive, desired changes than offering physicians economic incentives to align with organizational culture (Janus 2014; Navathe et al. 2016).

EXHIBIT 21.2 Glassdoor Approval Ratings for Dallas Hospital CEOs

	Favorable Employee Reviews (%)
Methodist Health System	88
Texas Health Resources	87
UT Southwest	82
Baylor, Scott & White	66
Tenet Healthcare	20

Source: Adapted from Schnuman (2019).

One transcendent effect of organizational culture is its impact on organizational justice through the perceived value of fairness. As discussed in chapter 6, distributive, procedural, and interactional justice make up organizational justice. Within a culture, members develop an understanding of what constitutes fairness. Note that fairness only exists in the context of culture. If power distance is high, mandates from higher authorities may be accepted as fair. This concept is evident in some East Asian cultures, where old age and high position are respected. In this type of structure, a leader's directive, even if arbitrary, may be accepted in the culture as fair and just and thus followed without hesitation. In cultures with lower power distance, the same action may be deemed unacceptable and unfair. Arbitrary decisions may be protested and resisted in these cultures. Leaders should understand the culture and make certain employees feel they are treated fairly, as employees who perceive the presence of organizational justice are happier and are more likely to remain at a firm. In an unjust organization, employees who do not quit often take more sick days and may even resort to workplace violence, theft, sabotage, or other counterproductive behaviors (Osland et al. 2007; Prive 2019).

Companies may likewise see otherwise valuable employees as a poor fit for the culture and terminate them for cultural insensitivity, of which the employees may not even be aware. For example, the leading 2015 scorer in the Korean Basketball League, American Davon Jefferson, was released from his contract two days after he was seen stretching while the Korean national anthem was played before a playoff game; all the other players were standing at strict attention (*Korea Times* 2015).

With cultures often having different perceptions of organizational justice, it is not surprising to learn that organizations frequently have serious problems merging employees from different firms and their contrasting cultures. Differing cultures account for more than 30 percent of failed mergers. Some of the mega-mergers that have failed because of dissimilar cultures include automakers Daimler and Chrysler, software companies Novell and WordPerfect, communication giants AOL and Time Warner, telecommunication firms Sprint and Nextel, and computer makers Hewlett Packard and Compaq (Jacobsen 2012). One executive discussing the AOL-Time Warner merger remarked later:

> I remember saying at a vital board meeting where we approved this, that life was going to be different going forward because they're very different cultures, but I have to tell you, I underestimated how different. . . . It was beyond certainly my abilities to figure out how to blend the old media and the new media culture. (Arango 2010)

The same phenomenon has occurred in healthcare—one prominent example being the failure of the merger of Stanford Medical Center and the

> **Stupid Boss + Stupid Employee**
>
> The CEO of a large personnel staffing company read a news article about how workers become unproductive if they do not balance family and work life. She was so impressed that she sent out a company-wide e-mail along with an attachment that showed the equation
>
> A Stupid Boss + A Stupid Employee = Overtime.
>
> She then called a meeting at which she stated that the organization's culture needed smart bosses and smart employees, stressed the importance of work–life balance, and explained how this balance, or lack of it, directly affected efficiency at the workplace. Most employees came away from the meeting excited that the company was now publicly committed to recognizing that they had lives away from work and efforts needed to be made to change the company's culture to balance these sometimes-conflicting demands.
>
> A month later, staff were given the forms to use for their annual performance evaluations. They were surprised to see that two of the key criteria were "What time does the employee leave work?" and "On average, how many hours per day are worked?" The more hours and the longer days an employee worked, the higher the number of points given. These questions clearly conveyed what was important: not *what* you do but *how long* you stayed at work.
>
> This seemed unfair and inconsistent with what the CEO had recently said. In response, someone wrote on the anonymous company board: "If stupid boss + stupid employee = overtime, then why are we rewarding the stupid people?"
>
> The CEO was, of course, upset about this message but could not verbally express her anger because it would directly contradict what she had previously communicated to staff. Instead, she called a meeting of all employees and made a passionate speech about the importance of sacrifice and how there was no room at the company for those who did not love to work and spend extra time at work.
>
> So much for work–life balance.

UC–San Francisco Medical Center after just two years. *Stanford Magazine* (2000) later commented that "the venture's biggest downfall may have been that it never managed to bind the two institutions together with a common culture."

Companies that seek to merge should seriously consider their cultural differences and plan for integration teams to handle the task of reducing or eliminating culture clashes. Those healthcare firms that managed their cultural mergers well have succeeded (Morse 2020).

Changing a Culture

Organizational leaders have a primary role in fostering a productive, vibrant culture in their company. As previously stated, cultures are embedded deeply in the fabric of organizations and are difficult to change. The change process can last years, but the formation and maintenance of a culture is an ongoing process.

Rather than seek to change cultural values, experienced change agents first change behaviors. Addressing culture change begins when leaders define "the things we want to do, establish the ways we want to behave and want others to behave, provide training and do what is necessary to reinforce those behaviors" (Shook 2010). In effect, an organization seeks to reframe their culture in new practices (Deloitte 2016). As appropriate behaviors are adopted across and up and down the organization, attitudes and values follow.

To be effective, leaders must be fully engaged and lead cultural change by example. Change comes to those areas that leaders consistently pay attention to, measure, allocate resources to, and control; what employees see as being constantly addressed communicates which values are really important. As the box shows, lip service—or telling employees what is important—is not sufficient.

Employees quickly recognize the actual values and the resultant expected behaviors by the criteria their bosses use for employee evaluations, the types of questions their leaders ask, the items placed on agendas, which emotions their leaders express in which settings, and the way crises are managed.

The US Department of Veterans Affairs (VA) has, for many years, sought to improve its culture but seems constantly battered by controversy and scandal (Pearson 2014; Stafford 2020). Many observers believed a negative culture existed in the organization, "with bad habits building up to create a bureaucratic mess unique in the federal government" (Brodey 2015). The solution to change this culture offered by the US Congress was to make it easier to fire employees. It is unclear whether this adjustment will eventually result in a positive shift in the VA's work culture.

That said, cultures can and do change. Numerous books have been written promoting cultural change processes by placing a focus on leaders building and embedding the appropriate values and beliefs in their organizations. Rather than firing "bad" employees, Schein (2010) suggested providing leaders with six primary and six secondary approaches to effect cultural change. Leaders can apply the following primary levers to directly affect their organizational culture:

1. *Pay attention to, measure, and control those behaviors and outcomes important to change.* Leaders cannot focus on everything, so select the key indicators that signal the desired changes and then track, trend, monitor, and reward or discipline on the basis of these indicators.
2. *React to critical incidents and crises with a view of how management's behavior will affect the culture.* Reacting with consistent, values-laden actions emphasizes and reinforces the desired cultural behaviors.
3. *Allocate resources to the effort to enhance organizational change.* Give personnel the means and resources to motivate and drive the desired changes. Generate surveys and data that will help leaders understand the progress and perceptions of employees and other stakeholders.
4. *Model, teach, and coach the desired behaviors and culture.* Know that the leader is the "barometer" of the organization, and people watch leaders to gauge how well things are going. Take time to teach and coach individuals, groups, and teams.

5. *Allocate rewards and status to encourage cultural change.* Provide rewards—both monetary and intrinsic—to those who model the desired cultural behaviors.
6. *Recruit, select, and promote employees who foster the desired culture and "excommunicate," or terminate, those who distract from it.* Establish hiring mechanisms that test for cultural fit of new employees. Also, be willing to act decisively and terminate employees who refuse to live the desired cultural values.

The six secondary approaches, if applied meaningfully and appropriately, serve as mechanisms that assist in changing and embedding culture in an organization. These mechanisms do not necessarily require specific behaviors and actions by leaders; they do involve employee processes, stories, and statements that can effect cultural change. They include the following:

1. Design and structure of an organization
2. Systems and procedures used in an organization
3. Company rites and rituals
4. Design of the physical space, facades, and buildings
5. Stories, legends, and myths told in the organization
6. Formal statements containing organizational philosophy, values, mission, and vision

Too often, leadership direction is not identified in cultural change, and organizations seem—culturally speaking—to randomly wander. To be effective, leaders must select those mechanisms and levers that encourage proper behavioral and cultural change. In this way, subordinates can identify with and adopt their organizational values and beliefs.

Chapter Summary

Organizational culture is a significant factor in the success or failure of a firm. Culture is composed of patterns of basic assumptions that groups make, as well as acceptable behaviors and actions. Over time, organizational members develop similar values and beliefs that form the core of their culture. Strong, effective cultures exist when employees' actions are aligned with their firm's values. Rituals and routines are collective social activities that reinforce organizational values and culture. In addition, the stories that organizations generate and the symbols they create can instill values.

Cultures can be classified into the dimensions of power distance, uncertainty avoidance, individualism (versus collectivism), temporal orientation, indulgence, and masculinity (versus femininity). These factors can provide a means to compare organizations as large as countries or as small as groups.

Cultural assessments can be conducted on organizations to ascertain areas that align and do not align with the desired organizational mission and values. Changing a culture to the ideal model is difficult and takes time. Companies that do not adapt their cultures to new environments or operational climates are especially prone to failure. Healthcare faces many pressures today that require cultural realignment in many organizations.

An important aspect of a healthy culture is the presence of organizational justice. Companies that promote distributive, procedural, and interactional justice embed the concept of fairness, which leads to a positive culture. Employees who feel fairly treated are more likely to remain at the organization, take fewer sick days, and act appropriately.

Differing organizational cultures also account for the failure of many mergers. An estimated 30 or more high-profile mergers failed as a direct result of cultural differences. Companies seeking to merge should seriously consider potential cultural clashes and design means to integrate the different cultures.

Leaders have a primary role in improving their organization's culture, which is a continuous, complex process. Defining appropriate, healthy behaviors can be an important step in beginning to change a culture. Leaders also must demonstrate new behaviors by example and use both primary and secondary mechanisms to motivate change.

Chapter Questions

1. What happens to an organization's culture if the actions of its leaders differ from their expressed, written values and mission?
2. How do behaviors reflect an organizational culture?
3. How do values interact with an organization's culture?
4. How can positive storytelling help a culture?
5. How do uniforms serve as symbols?
6. Why does the acceptable power distance vary across different cultures?
7. What would a cultural assessment gap analysis contain?
8. Provide an example of a firm whose culture may have contributed to its deteriorating market position, as its environment changed but its culture did not adjust to match the new environment.
9. Many academic medical centers have merged with community not-for-profit hospitals and struggled to combine their workforces. Think of three ways the cultures of these two types of organizations might differ.
10. What is the difference between the primary and secondary mechanisms that Schein (2010) suggested?

Chapter Cases

A Culture of Violence

Eastern Medical Center (EMC) struggled with its quality indicators, consistently ranking in the bottom quartile of its corporation's quality measures. Several interventions—training, motivational talks by respected authorities, and financial incentives—were offered. A consulting firm brought in to work with the quality improvement employees noted that the organization's culture did not support quality. However, the consultants' proposed interventions were too expensive to implement, far exceeding the medical center's budget, so nothing more was done. As expected, no change occurred in the dismal quality outcomes.

The CEO was frustrated. He had a favorite saying that people should "man up" and deal directly with problems. One year after the consulting firm's visit, the CEO took his own advice and fired the chief nursing officer (CNO) and quality leader. After a national search, a new CNO and quality leader were hired. The CEO had great expectations, and during the first six months after the new employees' arrival, the quality indicators did record a small increase. However, beginning in the seventh month, the indicators fell back to the previous year's levels. As a result, the EMC board met and fired the CEO.

Sally was hired three months later as the new CEO. The board stressed that changing the medical center's culture was a top priority. Sally had previous experience in organizational development and felt she had the right skills to create a healthy culture at EMC. She also recognized the challenge and difficulty in changing a culture.

After only three weeks, an incident occurred that made Sally realize just how damaging EMC's culture was. She was visiting the medical imaging department when an overhead page called her "stat" to the operating room (OR). This was the first time in her career that she had been paged "stat" in a hospital. She quickly walked to the OR to see what the urgent call was about.

Steve, the OR director, met her at the entrance and escorted her into his office. He explained that a few minutes earlier, an orthopedic surgeon had become enraged at one of the circulating nurses in an operating suite. The surgeon swore at the nurse, and when the nurse did not move fast enough, the surgeon threw a scalpel at her and threatened her with another. The nurse was now out of the room and out of danger, and the surgeon was expected to finish the procedure in about 15 minutes. Steve was angry and wanted to know what Sally was going to do about the situation.

Sally quickly called her assistant and found out that this surgeon was known to have a bad temper and to frequently berate employees and create problems. One time, he was not happy with what had been dictated in the nursing notes for one of his patients, so he tore out the notes, crumpled them up, and threw them in the trash. He also was consistently behind in his dictation, and his Medicare billings were always months late. However, he was the third-highest revenue producer in the hospital, friends with many of the EMC board members, and considered "untouchable."

Sally felt strongly that she had to address the issue, but she had a couple of decisions to make. First, should she confront the surgeon when he finished the procedure? If so, what should she say? Should she inform the medical staff and use their disciplinary procedures?

She also wondered whether allowing this type of behavior had directly affected the inability of the previous leadership to change EMC's culture and quality outcomes.

Sally met with the surgeon after he finished the procedure and asked him what had happened. The doctor explained his anger toward the nurse and said he inadvertently let a scalpel slip out of his hand, which landed close to the nurse. He did not intend to hit her; he just wanted to get her to act more efficiently, he said. Before the meeting, Sally had called the chief medical officer and asked him to investigate the case. Sally informed the surgeon that such behavior was not appropriate and that the medical staff would be investigating the incident and making disciplinary recommendations.

The surgeon was shocked. How could they do this to him? He stressed that he was his patients' advocate and was only trying to get better care for them. This type of public scrutiny would embarrass him, he said. "Maybe," he threatened, "I should take my practice to one of the other hospitals in town." Sally calmly reassured the surgeon that he was appreciated but said he could not yell, use vulgar language, or threaten the employees.

The medical staff recommended a six-month probationary period for the surgeon, along with anger management training. Any further incident would result in his full suspension from the EMC medical staff. Perhaps not surprisingly, not only did his behavior improve, but so did that of many other physicians who practiced at EMC. Soon after, the quality indicators began to rise.

Case Questions
1. How does the way physicians are treated in a healthcare organization reflect the organization's culture?
2. In this situation, what could Sally do to actively change the culture?
3. How do cultures become dangerous, as in this case?

The Need for a More Egalitarian Hospital Culture

Hospitals' policies frequently treat different classes of people differently. A hospital trainee once commented that "The hospital is like an elephant. When she goes to the right, you must go to the right. When she goes to the left, you must go that way, too." Doctors, nurses, and cafeteria workers, among others, are often treated differently in a hierarchical culture. Nurses can feel powerless and executives little involved in patient care. Studies have shown that all this negatively impacts patient care.

A main issue in changing this culture is that large teaching hospitals are the big elephants of the healthcare jungle that train and spread their hierarchical cultures. Yet, hospital cultures can change when physician attitudes move from "because I said so" directives to the staff to focusing on the *why*s and asking for input. Staff begin to feel that they can voice their concerns and that they have a more equal role in providing patient care. Negative behaviors such as excessive deference to authority, placing blame, and empty promises with no follow-through all diminish. Hospitals that change to a more equalitarian culture find that patient outcomes improve.

Case Questions
1. What components of culture are discussed in this case?
2. How do changed actions in the hospitals affect their cultures?
3. Why would a more open, equalitarian culture improve patient care?

Chapter Activities

1. Read the 2014 GLOBE CEO Study (https://globeproject.com/study_2014). Select three countries and write a two- to three-page paper on the differences in their cultural perspectives on leadership.
2. In small groups, identify the culture of the university department of which you are part. Is it totally serious or do you have fun? Can you communicate freely with professors? How about the department chair? Does the department have any stories or rituals that set it apart? Are there any annual routines or activities unique to the department? In what other ways might you identify your department's culture? Share your ideas with others in the class.
3. Review the Health Systems Culture 500 data and the nine "most talked about cultural values in the industry" compiled by *MIT Sloan Management Review* and Glassdoor (https://sloanreview.mit.edu/culture500/industry/Ind16/Health_Systems). Click on the Integrity value and write a one-page paper that compares three of the healthcare companies. Why do you think some companies rank higher on integrity than others? What factors might influence the rankings?

References

Abelson, R., and M. Freudenheim. 2003. "The Scrushy Mix: Strict and So Lenient." *New York Times*, April 20. www.nytimes.com/2003/04/20/business/the-scrushy-mix-strict-and-so-lenient.html.

Arango, T. 2010. "How the AOL-Time Warner Merger Went So Wrong." *New York Times*, January 10. www.nytimes.com/2010/01/11/business/media/11merger.html.

Association of Schools and Programs of Public Health. 2018. "Yale: New Leadership Saves Lives Toolkit Available." *Connect* (blog). Published February 22. www.aspph.org/yale-new-leadership-saves-lives-toolkit-available/.

Brady, W., and S. Haley. 2013. "Storytelling Defines Your Organizational Culture." *Physician Executive* 39 (1): 40–43.

Brodey, S. 2015. "Can the VA Fire Its Way out of Its Problems?" *Minneapolis Post*, November 10. www.minnpost.com/dc-dispatches/2015/11/can-va-fire-its-way-out-its-problems.

Chen, P. 2018. "A More Egalitarian Hospital Culture Is Better for Everyone." *New York Times*, May 31. www.nytimes.com/2018/05/31/well/live/doctors-patients-hospital-culture-better-health.html.

Deloitte. 2016. "Culture Shift: Changing Beliefs, Behaviors, and Outcomes." *CFO Insights*, November 2016. www2.deloitte.com/us/en/pages/finance/articles/cfo-insights-culture-shift-beliefs-behaviors-outcomes.html.

Farrell, G. 2004. "Former HealthSouth CEO Scrushy Turns Televangelist." *USA Today*, October 25. http://usatoday30.usatoday.com/money/industries/health/2004-10-25-scrushy-cover_x.htm.

Groysberg, B., J. Lee, J. Price, and J. Cheng. 2018. "The Leader's Guide to Corporate Culture." *Harvard Business Review* 96 (1): 44–52.

Helyar, J. 2003. "The Insatiable King Richard." *Fortune* 148 (1): 76–81.

Hofstede, G. 2020. *Geert Hofstede*. https://geerthofstede.com/culture-geert-hofstede-gert-jan-hofstede/6d-model-of-national-culture/.

Hofstede, G., G. J. Hofstede, and M. Minkov. 2010. *Culture and Organizations: Software of the Mind—Intercultural Cooperation and Its Importance for Survival*, 3rd ed. New York: McGraw-Hill.

Jacobsen, D. 2012. "6 Big Mergers That Were Killed by Culture (and How to Stop It from Killing Yours)." *Workhuman*. Published September 26. www.workhuman.com/resources/globoforce-blog/6-big-mergers-that-were-killed-by-culture-and-how-to-stop-it-from-killing-yours.

Janus, K. 2014. "The Effect of Professional Culture on Intrinsic Motivation Among Physicians in an Academic Medical Center." *Journal of Healthcare Management* 59 (4): 287–303.

King, D., and S. Demarie. 2014. "Tuning Up Organizational Culture." *Industrial Engineer* 46 (11): 26–30.

Kocken, M. 2014. "Seven Reasons Why Korea Has the Worst Productivity in the OECD." *BusinessKorea*, March 17. www.businesskorea.co.kr/news/articleView.html?idxno=3698.

Korea Times. 2015. "Thou Shalt Not Stretch During National Anthem! LG Cuts Leading Scorer in Middle of Playoffs." March 20, 2015. www.koreatimesus.com/thou-shalt-not-stretch-during-national-anthem-lg-cuts-leagues-top-scorer-in-middle-of-playoffs/.

Lurie, Z. 2019. "Surveymonkey's CEO on Creating a Culture of Curiosity." *Harvard Business Review* 97 (1): 35–39. https://hbr.org/2019/01/surveymonkeys-ceo-on-creating-a-culture-of-curiosity.

Moore, M., and V. V. Bates. 2020. "Going from a Culture of Blame and Denial to a Culture of Safety." *Health Management* 20 (2): 122–25. https://healthmanagement.org/c/healthmanagement/issuearticle/going-from-a-culture-of-blame-and-denial-to-a-culture-of-safety.

Morse, S. 2020. "Mergers in 2020 Expected to Be More Strategic Than Financial in Nature." *Healthcare Finance*, January 23. www.healthcarefinancenews.com/news/mergers-2020-expected-be-more-strategic-financial-nature.

Navathe, A. W., A. P. Sen, M. B. Rosenthal, R. M. Pearl, P. A. Ubel, E. J. Emanuel, and K. G. Volpp. 2016. "New Strategies for Aligning Physicians with Health System Incentives." *American Journal of Managed Care* 22 (9): 610–12. www.ajmc.com/view/new-strategies-for-aligning-physicians-with-health-system-incentives.

Osland, J., D. Kolb, I. Rubin, and M. Turner. 2007. *Organizational Behavior: An Experiential Approach*. Upper Saddle River, NJ: Prentice-Hall.

Patnaik, J. 2011. "Role of Work Culture in Improving Organizational Health." *Amity Journal of Applied Psychology* 2 (1): 40–48.

Pearson, M. 2014. "The VA's Troubled History." *CNN*, May 30. www.cnn.com/2014/05/23/politics/va-scandals-timeline/.

Prive, T. 2019. "4 Devastating Consequences of a Toxic Workplace Culture." *Inc.com*, November 3. www.inc.com/tanya-prive/4-devastating-consequences-of-a-toxic-workplace-culture.html.

Schein, E. H. 2010. *Organizational Culture and Leadership*, 4th ed. San Francisco: Jossey-Bass.

———. 1984. "Coming to a New Awareness of Organizational Culture." *Sloan Management Review* 25 (2): 3–16.

Schnuman, M. 2019. "Somebody Break It to the Boss: Morale's a Problem at Tenet Healthcare." *Dallas News*, January 15. www.dallasnews.com/opinion/commentary/2019/01/15/somebody-break-it-to-the-boss-morales-a-problem-at-tenet-healthcare/.

Shook, J. 2010. "How to Change a Culture: Lessons from NUMMI." *MIT Sloan Management Review* 51 (2): 63–68.

Society for Human Resource Management (SHRM). 2020. "Understanding and Developing Organizational Culture." www.shrm.org/ResourcesAndTools/tools-and-samples/toolkits/Pages/understandinganddevelopingorganizationalculture.aspx.

Stafford, M. 2020. "Veterans Affairs Says Agency Is Changing Troubled Culture." *U. S. News & World Report*, July 2. www.usnews.com/news/best-states/virginia/articles/2020-07-02/veterans-affairs-says-agency-is-changing-troubled-culture.

Stanford Magazine. 2000. "The Anatomy of a Failed Hospital Merger." *Stanford Magazine* (January/February). https://stanfordmag.org/contents/the-anatomy-of-a-failed-hospital-merger.

Sull, D., S. Turconi, and C. Sull. 2020. "When It Comes to Culture, Does Your Company Walk the Talk?" *MIT Sloan Management Review*, July 21. https://sloanreview.mit.edu/article/when-it-comes-to-culture-does-your-company-walk-the-talk/.

Verghese, A. 2019. "Building a Storytelling Culture in Organizations with Internal Communications." *Institute for Public Relations* (blog). Published March 26. https://instituteforpr.org/building-a-storytelling-culture-in-organizations-with-internal-communications/.

Wong, J. 2019. "Disgruntled Drivers and 'Cultural Challenges': Uber Admits to Its Biggest Risk Factors." *The Guardian*, April 12. www.theguardian.com/technology/2019/apr/11/uber-ipo-risk-factors.

CHAPTER 22

HUMAN RESOURCES POLICIES AND PRACTICES

> New to the job as manager of a satellite clinic—part of a large medical group management organization—Steve would face his first big challenge. A physician at the clinic met him in the hallway. In front of the staff and patients, the physician began yelling at Steve, informing him of everything wrong at the facility. Steve knew that yelling back would not help in this situation, but he listened calmly, and eventually suggested to the physician that they should meet later. The physician stormed off, leaving Steve to look around at the staff members and patients staring at him. What was his next move? He decided it would be a visit to Human Resources.

Learning Objectives

After studying this chapter, readers should be able to

- describe the connection between organizational behavior and human resource management;
- develop job descriptions and job specifications;
- discuss the pros and cons of performance simulation and tests;
- describe key elements of an employment interview;
- identify elements of training;
- explain the importance of implementing anti-harassment initiatives and training, and enforcing anti-harassment policies; and
- summarize the leadership role of human resource departments.

Key Terms

- behaviorally anchored rating scales (BARS)
- career ladder
- ethics training
- human resource management
- job description

- job specification
- performance simulation
- personality tests
- sexual harassment
- structured interviews
- workplace bullying

human resource management
The formal system within an organization that staffs, monitors, establishes policies for, and trains members of the work team.

Organizational behavior is defined in chapter 1 as the way people interact in groups and their impact on the organization. The central concept of the study of organizational behavior suggests evidence for a scientific approach that allows for the efficient and effective management of people. **Human resource management** is the formal system within an organization that staffs, monitors, establishes practices, and trains members of the work team. It has the capacity to influence the human behavior in an organization and support the achievement of corporate goals and objectives (Mehwish et al. 2019). The human resources (HR) department is focused on these activities, but many individuals or groups within an organization help create practices in support of employees.

Job Descriptions and Specifications

HR experts work with healthcare managers to determine the staffing needs of the organization. They conduct a job analysis to determine the specific tasks, activities, and responsibilities of a position. A useful job analysis differentiates between jobs based on the following characteristics (adapted from SHRM 2021):

job description
Formal documentation of the duties, responsibilities, and functions of a specific job, including title, working conditions, and a summary description.

- Knowledge, skills, and abilities required to do the job
- Job tasks and technology used
- Performance standards
- Cost or budget implications
- Working conditions
- Who reports to the jobholder
- Who supervises the jobholder

The job analysis allows for the development of both a job description and a job specification.

The **job description** includes the duties, responsibilities, and functions of a specific job. A complete job description should include the job title, working conditions, and a summary of the job. In addition to hiring, management can use job descriptions to evaluate job performance and to help define training an employee may need (Trueick 2018).

job specification
Formal documentation of the minimum qualifications, capabilities, and traits a candidate needs to perform a specific job.

The **job specification** states the minimum qualifications, capabilities, and traits a candidate needs to perform the job, such as level of

> **EXHIBIT 22.1**
> Job Position Details for a Registered Nurse
>
> **Job title:** Clinical Nurse (RN)
> **Reports to:** Director of Nursing
>
> **Position summary:**
> - The RN demonstrates clinical competency by using the nursing process to assess, plan, implement and evaluate patient care . . .
>
> **Qualifications:**
> - Licensed registered nurse in the State of . . .
> - Bachelor's degree (BSN) required.
> - One year experience . . .
>
> **Job duties:**
> - Perform all nursing duties in accordance with the State Nursing Act.
> - Monitor patient progress . . .
> - Assist physicians and all healthcare professionals . . .
> - Perform routine nursing care for assigned patients . . .
>
> **Physical requirements:**
> - Must be physically able to lift 50 pounds, bend, stoop, and sit for long . . .
> - Must have sufficient visual acuity to . . .
> - Must have hearing acuity to hear spoken communications . . .
>
> **Work conditions:**
> - Often exposed to infectious diseases and chemicals . . .
> - Shifts include nights, weekends and holidays . . .

experience, communication skills, physical skills, or even emotional traits. Job specifications help applicants judge whether or not they are the right individual for the job. Exhibit 22.1 demonstrates how a job description and job specification come together as a position is created and advertised for a registered nurse.

Performance Simulation

The manager responsible for a job is typically responsible for recruiting and hiring someone to fill the position. The manager works with HR to develop a job position or advertisement for the position and uses job boards, social media, newspapers, recruitment agencies, and employee referrals to find qualified candidates.

The process of selecting an individual involves reviewing job applications; conducting interviews by phone, online, or face-to-face; collecting references from people who know the candidates; and sometimes conducting tests and simulations.

> **A Successful Job Simulation**
>
> Armed with a new graduate degree in marketing, Hayden Clark confidently made his way to the office of the marketing director for the R. M. Thomas Medical Center. The director, Lisa Petersen, asked a number of questions and shared her vision for the marketing team. One of the tactics used by the marketing group was a social media campaign, complete with a weekly online newsletter and blog. Lisa wanted to know if Hayden could contribute and sent him on an impromptu simulation to let him show what he could do.
>
> Hayden's assignment was to visit with Rachel Clark, the director of the radiology department, who had worked at the hospital for some time. After a long internal campaign, she had won approval for a new diagnostic wing in the hospital, complete with state-of-the-art equipment. The hospital was to celebrate its fifteenth anniversary soon, and the launch of the new diagnostic wing would be part of the associated marketing campaign.
>
> Hayden and Rachel visited for an hour, after which Hayden wrote an article about the center and some of the great work the diagnostic team was doing. He even took the initiative to interview Patrick Siirila, MD, a radiologist in the department.
>
> Lisa was impressed with Hayden's writing and the initiative he took in getting the interview. She found a few grammatical errors in the article—something Hayden could learn from—but eventually Hayden got the job.
>
> The interview and article represented only a small aspect of Hayden's new job in marketing. He would be involved in a number of initiatives and marketing efforts early in his career. That recruitment activity, however, allowed the marketing director to get a sample of Hayden's work and showed her his drive and initiative. Hayden also got an opportunity to sample the culture of the organization and get to know his prospective boss better as she reviewed his work and offered some constructive criticism.

Simulation of clinical experiences is generally used in the education of health professionals. These simulations have been demonstrated to be highly effective for developing clinical competency, building confidence, and preparing students to enter the healthcare workforce (Beyea, von Reyn, and Slattery 2007). Similarly, **performance simulation** places a candidate in a highly realistic employment experience. The use of simulation in recruiting results in shorter training times, less employee turnover, and an increase in productivity. Simulation allows employers to make accurate, informed decisions about those they hire. Candidates undergo a fair and equal test to demonstrate their skills in a simulation. Simulations also let participants experience job conditions and see if they have the needed skills. These experiences are highly engaging and lead to greater job satisfaction and productivity (Sefcik 2020).

performance simulation
A preemployment evaluation that places a candidate in a highly realistic employment experience to assess potential job performance.

Additional Testing Techniques

Performance simulation is not the only method HR uses to select the workforce. Tests of intelligence or cognitive ability, personality, and even emotional intelligence are sometimes used.

Written tests are commonly used to understand an individual's knowledge level. Traditional advanced cardiac life support courses, for example, administer both written and simulation exams. One study found the written exam scores of a study group to be higher than the simulation scores and concluded that simulation may be more discriminating (Strom et al. 2015). Low-fidelity simulation in hiring is similar. Recruiters present a verbal or written description of a scenario to candidates, who then describe how they would respond to the situation. Situational interview questions and a written healthcare management situation are both examples of low-fidelity simulations (Havighurst et al. 2003). These types of assessments tend to be less expensive and do not need the equipment used in performance simulations. However, they tend to be less realistic.

Personality tests have grown popular over the past several decades and are used for executive coaching, team building, hiring, and promotion. Hundreds of personality tests exist. These instruments collect self-reported information about an individual's personality traits. Test takers typically answer questions about their personality or select items that describe themselves (American Psychological Association 2020). Those who use personality tests argue that they promise higher retention rates and increased objectivity in hiring. Candidates and their potential employers look to these tools as a way to determine whether an applicant will fit in a potential job and organization (Youngman 2017). More than six decades of research have led many personality psychologists to believe there are five basic personality traits (exhibit 22.2). Imagination, insight, and a broad range of interests characterize *openness*. *Conscientiousness* includes thoughtfulness, impulse control, and goal-directed behaviors. *Extraversion* is exhibited by sociability, assertiveness, and high emotional expression. Trust, altruism, kindness, and affection illustrate *agreeableness*. Finally, *neuroticism* is the trait that includes sadness and moodiness (Cherry 2020).

personality tests
Instruments that collect self-reported data about an individual's personality traits.

EXHIBIT 22.2
The Big Five

- Openness
- Conscientiousness
- Extraversion
- Agreeableness
- Neuroticism

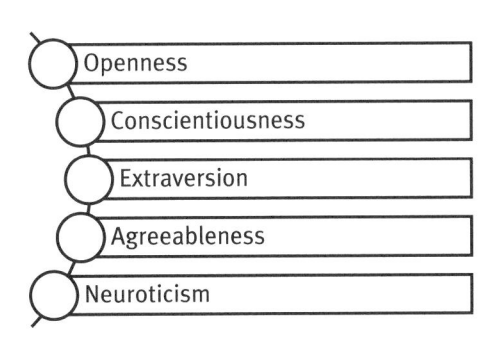

More than six decades of research have led many personality psychologists to believe these are the five basic personality traits.

Source: Adapted from Cherry 2020.

Critiques of personality tests suggest they do not capture a full range of personality variance and are thus not an accurate representation of an individual's personality. Evidence points to personality scores changing as the same individual retests; in other words, test–retest reliability has mixed results. Others note that personality tests—and hundreds exist—are not equal in their ability to predict job performance. Self-reported questionnaires can be faked, as individuals may attempt to place themselves in the outcome they deem most valuable to the job (Moyle and Hackston 2018). Some argue that employers—whether on purpose or not—may discriminate among job applicants by using personality profiles (Youngman 2017).

Interviews

Job interviews are among the HR practices used for decades to improve employee performance and company profits. Some argue that interviews are not as effective as testing (Moore 2017). Nevertheless, research indicates that **structured interviews** (versus interviews without a specific set of questions) could significantly enhance hiring outcomes (Huffcutt and Arthur Jr. 1994; Levashina et al. 2014; Lubbe and Nitsche 2019) and reduce the chance of hiring someone not suited for the job (Huffcutt and Roth 1998; Williamson et al. 1997).

Structured interviews include a number of components related to the content and evaluation of the interview. Among the key elements according to researchers is ensuring that all applicants receive the same questions based on a job analysis. Researchers also recommend that the same interviewers question and review all the applicants; taking notes and discussing their opinions only after all the interviews are completed (Levashina et al. 2014; Williamson et al. 1997). Other components of a structured interview, according to these authors, include the following:

- Interviewers should not prompt the candidates on what to say.
- Longer interviews are better.
- Candidates should ask their questions at the end of the interview.
- Candidate performance should be measured against specific performance scales.
- Multiple interviewers are better than just one.
- Interviewers should resist discussing the candidates between interviews.

The goal of an interview is to find candidates with the right skills and behaviors for a particular job. Many HR experts believe behavioral questions result in the most effective interviews. These questions focus on a candidate's

structured interviews
A job interview practice in which all candidates are reviewed by the same interviewers and asked the same questions, which are based on a job analysis.

predicted behavior in a particular situation. When every candidate is asked the same questions, bias and ambiguity are reduced. Candidates also get a better idea of what the job may entail if behavioral questions are realistic and honest (SHRM 2016).

Behavioral questions are associated with **behaviorally anchored rating scales** (BARS). BARS rate candidates according to their expected or exhibited behaviors in an interview. As illustrated in exhibit 22.3, BARS give examples of a response or performance at along a continuum of behaviors. This evaluation tool is associated with greater success in hiring qualified candidates, with less bias involved in the process (Harrison et al. 2017).

Job interviews take place via a variety of mediums, including the telephone, video-based interviews, and face-to-face meetings. While telephone interviews offer some protection against bias due to ethnicity, some research suggests discrimination occurs in interviews based on ethnicity, gender, or both (Dean, Roth, and Bobko 2008; Kraiger and Ford 1985). A field experimental study of more than 13,000 job applications found that majority applicants received 53 percent more callbacks, or invitations to interview, than did minority applicants. The same study reported that the majority applicants received 145 percent more job offers (Quillian, Lee, and Oliver 2020).

Evidence also exists of discrimination based on facial attractiveness of the applicants, with "unattractive faces" needing to submit 33 percent more applications to get an interview (photos were included with fictitious candidates) than their attractive counterparts. In that study of 24,192 submitted applications, women received more callbacks than did men (Maurer-Fazio and Lei

behaviorally anchored rating scales
Evaluation scales that use example behaviors to "anchor" ratings.

EXHIBIT 22.3
Behaviorally Anchored Rating Scales (BARS)

Question:
Consider a situation in which a patient is upset with you because you did not respond to her call for help quick enough. How would you most likely react?

Rating scale:

Rating	Description
5	Could be expected to discern and discuss the broader concern of the patient.
4	Could be expected to truly empathize with the patient.
3	Could be expected to make eye contact and ask how the patient's needs could be met.
2	Could be expected to enter and ask, "What is the problem?"
1	Could be expected to ignore or even yell at the patient.

2015). A similar study found that attractive women had a callback rate of 54 percent versus 7 percent for unattractive women. Attractive men were offered an interview at a rate of 47 percent, while only 24 percent of their unattractive counterparts were asked to come in (Busetta, Fiorillo, and Visalli 2013).

History has shown that LGBTQ individuals have been targets of discrimination, including at the workplace and job interviews (Lindsey et al. 2013). Even when interviewers were given information about affirmative action procedures, a study found them to rate gay applicants less positively than non-gay applicants. No differences were seen among interviewers' self-reported and implicit heterosexist attitudes. Only those in the study held accountable—they would have to verbally explain their ratings—showed no bias in their interviews (Nadler et al. 2014).

HR staff and managers need to be aware of potential bias and do what they can to control it. Evidence just presented would suggest that holding the interviewers accountable is one measure of protection (Nadler et al. 2014). Multiple interviewers and structured interviews help control racial bias (de Kock and Hauptfleisch 2018). Chapter 3 includes discussion and evidence of the value of diversity in a healthcare workforce. Organizations should do all that they can to promote it and support it via less-biased interview processes.

Training

As discussed in chapter 15, the American College of Healthcare Executives (2021) focuses on five competency categories important to healthcare leaders: communication and relationship management, leadership, professionalism, knowledge of the healthcare environment, and business skills and knowledge. Certainly, many healthcare workers must have the appropriate clinical or technical skills. Analytical skills are important to some and creativity is important to many. Many organizations offer training after candidates get the job and to other employees.

career ladder
Formal programs supporting employees with training and development so they can move into more advanced positions.

Career ladder programs in healthcare organizations have included compensated education and training with the idea that nurses and other workers move to more advanced positions, thus reducing turnover, improving patient care, and addressing staff shortages (Custodio, Gard, and Graham 2009; Lerman, McKernan, and Riegg 2004; Waldman et al. 2004). Workforce training leads to more responsibility and competency, and provides increased job satisfaction (Smith 2019; Swedberg et al. 2015). Success in these types of programs is contingent on the support of employee leaders, frontline management, education leaders, community need, and educational policies (Dill, Chuang, and Morgan 2014).

Training seeks to enhance job knowledge and skills by standardizing on the job and classroom or online learning. In addition, licenses or certification are required of some workers. Partnerships with education institutions support the preparation and examinations to earn those credentials (Dill, Chuang, and Morgan 2014). Training teaches a variety of skills, including basic skills needed for the job, technical skills, and problem-solving skills. Interpersonal skills and diversity training might be part of a formal program.

Healthcare workers are sometimes shifted from a frontline service role to that of a supervisor or manager—many without any leadership training. The public health sector found this to be an issue. Yeager and colleagues reported in 2019 that 28 percent of public health workers indicated they needed management and leadership skills. Communication skills were next on their list (21 percent). Moving from direct practice to a new management role can leave workers feeling unprepared for the new job. The perceived pressure to perform makes it hard for some to admit their doubt and uncertainty and they may not ask for help (Patterson 2015).

An online search for the best training of new managers outside of a formal degree yields empirical research or ideas from the field of healthcare. *Becker's Hospital Review* (2012), for example, offers these best practices:

- Programs should include material for several different learning styles.
- Engage learners with less lecture.
- Make training specific to a hospital or health system. Personalize it.
- Assess the effectiveness of the training.

Training is most effective when it takes place over time and it should include all the traditional healthcare domains. It should be inclusive of all the activities a new leader may undertake and be applicable to a number of interprofessional programs (Sonnino 2016). Exhibit 22.4 lists the elements of management training in healthcare.

The COVID-19 pandemic that began in 2020 pushed healthcare institutions to the limit. Reports of hospital intensive care units (ICUs) at maximum capacity were common. As a result,

> **What Would You Do?**
>
> Lakeside Regional Hospital's ICUs were full, as was its emergency department. Paramedics waited outside with more patients suffering the effects of COVID-19. The hospital had moved patients around and created as many beds as it could to treat all who needed care. Resources were down to nothing, including the staff required to care for everyone.
>
> Russ, the hospital CEO, had to make some decisions. He was not alone, however. He consulted with his leadership team and the hospital's ethics committee about the choices they had to make. Should they admit new patients (when beds became available) on a first-come, first-served basis? Should they admit only those patients who had the best chance for recovery? Maybe they should admit the community leaders and VIPs first. They could consider the role of the individual (a mother with several children versus an elderly grandfather). Or they could admit younger individuals simply because they have more years to live.
>
> If you were Russ, what would you do?

EXHIBIT 22.4
Elements of New Leadership Training

Early career training prepares workers to move from direct care to management roles. Outcomes research suggests that training should include the following:

Finance and budgeting	Team building
Communication skills	Negotiation and conflict management
Empathy and awareness	Ethics and justice
Stewardship	Delegation and time management
Healthcare regulations and legal issues	Mentoring and coaching
	Networking
Problem solving	Emotional Intelligence
Professionalism	

Source: Adapted from Sonnino (2016).

healthcare teams faced difficult decisions such as what to do for uninfected patients who needed an ICU bed if the ICU was full of COVID-19 patients. Family visits were prohibited or strictly limited. Some institutions debated the need to accelerate withdrawal of life support or prioritize ICU beds for patients with the best prognosis (Robert et al. 2020). Ethical dilemmas have always been present in healthcare and training staff who face them is another function of HR.

Ethics should be a basic element for any training offered in healthcare. Components of such training include ethical reasoning and decision-making. Simulation (already presented in this chapter) is an important education tool and effective in **ethics training**. Some have used standardized patients (subjects trained to present or act out the issues) who bring their ethical problems to trainees. The standardized patients are taught to be as realistic as they can while interacting with the trainees. The trainees are debriefed after the experience, so they can explore their emotions and reactions to the simulation. Studies show that those involved in simulation training find it very meaningful (Buxton, Phillippi, and Collins 2014).

Another approach to ethics training includes case review, where trainees discuss the ethical issues related to a given scenario (Thiel et al. 2013). Such approaches ask trainees to consider organizational and personal values, consult resources and information available to help them make a decision, and then resolve the situation. This method has been shown to be effective and engaging (Laditka and Houck 2006).

Some organizations, even higher education, spend a significant amount of time and resources on what are sometimes called "soft" skills, including interpersonal skills, civility, diversity awareness, and cultural sensitivity.

ethics training
Training that includes elements such as ethical reasoning and decision-making and prepares employees to resolve ethical dilemmas.

Schools and training programs attempt to measure students' competencies. Most researchers looking at these competencies differentiate the more effective from the less effective managers in terms of the performance of the firm or the abilities of the individual manager. Additionally, research has shown improvement in interpersonal skills via corporate training programs. (Hunt and Baruch 2003). As of 2021, work is underway to use virtual humans and immersive virtual reality technology to provide interpersonal skills training in organizations (Schmid Mast et al. 2018).

In 2017, the US Equal Employment Opportunity Commission launched two training programs focused on respectful workplaces. These programs were the result of a 2016 study of harassment in the workplace. Two forms of workplace harassment have garnered a significant amount of research and training: bullying and sexual harassment.

Workplace bullying can take many forms: practical jokes, denial of requests for time off without a valid reason, verbal abuse, humiliation, or even unjust criticism. A 2009 study found that 27 percent of nurses surveyed had experienced workplace bullying (Johnson and Ruth 2009). Bullying is persistent, frequent hostility and drains the coping resources of the victim. Emotional exhaustion then leads to poor performance and turnover (Peng et al. 2016). Research has even identified bullying as a risk factor for cardiovascular disease (Xu et al. 2019).

workplace bullying
Persistent, frequent hostility in the workplace.

Interestingly, even those one might consider in the upper levels of the healthcare workforce can be subject to bullying. In a study of Australian surgeons, 47 percent reported being a victim of bullying and 68 percent reported witnessing it (Ling et al. 2016). This is typically a result of bullies in senior leadership positions. Bullying represents one of the ways a surgeon experiences loss of control and leads to burnout and even suicide (Pei and Cochran 2019). Bullying can take place at all levels of an organization's workforce.

Sexual harassment has been described as a "chronic occupational health problem" where "harassers and aggressors destroy lives, leaving long legacies of suffering" (Quick and McFadyen 2017, 286). Even though the #MeToo movement, which took hold in 2017, increased focus on sexual harassment, evidence would suggest harassment in healthcare is common and

> **Bullying in Healthcare**
>
> In a meeting of the oncology surgery department at a large academic medical center, a young resident, Dr. Oliver, reports on a case involving a patient suffering from colon cancer. When asked a question by a senior surgeon, Dr. Oliver becomes flustered. At that point, the senior surgeon continues to interrupt and ridicule Dr. Oliver during her report. The bullying surgeon repeats this behavior whenever Dr. Oliver participates in department meetings (adapted from Pei and Cochran 2019).
>
> Bullying in healthcare occurs not only among junior staff, but at all levels of the healthcare workforce. It is not enough for organizations to set policies prohibiting such behaviors; they must also work hard to enforce those policies.

has not decreased with time (Rihal et al. 2020). Nearly one-third of female clinician-researchers in academic medical centers reported having experienced sexual harassment in the workplace (Jagsi et al. 2016). Another study found one-third of nurses have experienced physical assault, were bullied, or were injured, and 25 percent were sexually harassed (Spector et al. 2007). Even patients or clients can be the cause of sexual harassment of healthcare workers (Vincent-Höper et al. 2020), including those providing home care (Clari et al. 2020).

Sadly, literature suggests many employees remain silent about workplace mistreatment, in large part due to the employees' dysfunctional relationships with their superiors (Greenberg and Edwards 2009; Morrison 2014; Rai and Agarwal 2018). An individual's personal and professional resources—workplace friends, specifically—may be their only recourse and help with workplace bullying (Rai and Agarwal 2018). Managers must work hard to develop trust. They must create a friendly environment that makes anti-harassment policies part of the organization's culture. Even the courts are saying it is not enough for employers to merely set policy and provide training prohibiting sexual harassment; they must also enforce it (Morris Jr., Hoerner, and Smith 2018).

The Leadership Role of HR

HR is involved in all of the issues discussed in this chapter. HR officials are the link between management and the employee workforce. They have specific leadership roles in at least six areas:

- Recruiting, selecting, and retaining new employees
- Communicating HR practices
- Designing and administering benefits programs
- Drafting and enforcing employment policies
- Managing work–life conflicts
- Mediations, terminations, and layoffs

These roles and others are the subject of entire textbooks devoted to HR. This chapter has focused on the organization behavior aspects of HR. HR departments have the potential to influence the entire climate of an organization, promoting its values and mission and assisting managers to do the same. These departments have the potential to make positive change. They can create a values-based framework to make decisions and set policy. At the same time, they contribute to quality output and the positive bottom line of an organization (Frye 2020).

Chapter Summary

Human resource (HR) management staffs, monitors, trains, and supports employees of an organization such that they have a positive work life experience. At the very beginning of that experience HR determines the roles and needs of a job, and then helps create a job description, complete with job specifications. This document helps a candidate understand the tasks, activities, needed skills, and expectations of a job and describes potential supervisory relationships.

Some hiring processes include a performance simulation that provides a realistic employment experience. Both clinical and nonclinical jobs can use performance simulations. These simulations allow managers to make accurate and fair candidate evaluations while candidates experience realistic job conditions and gain a better understanding of the skills needed.

In addition to simulations, some employers may have candidates complete written tests, licensing exams, or even personality tests. The latter have been used for many years and have both supporters and detractors. Employers use personality tests to determine an applicant's fit for a potential job and as part of a team.

Job interviews are another tool used in hiring new employees. Structured interviews that use a specific set of questions, a set number of interviewers, and specific performance scales for assessments tend to be most effective. Studies also suggest behavioral questions are important, especially when associated with behaviorally anchored rating scales (BARS) that identify performance using example behaviors placed along a continuum.

Once a candidate is hired, training becomes important to the success and retention of the new employee. Training includes support of clinical and technical skills, communication and relationships, professionalism, leadership, and other business skills and knowledge. Training is important to workers who have shifted from a service role to that of supervisor or manager. These new managers learn to deal with former coworkers while meeting the demands of their own supervisors.

Some of the best training provides material for different learning styles, interactive work rather than just lectures, personalization specific to the hospital or health system, and assessment of training effectiveness.

Training for what some call "soft" skills includes the subjects of ethics and anti-harassment. Ethics training includes ethical reasoning and decision-making. Simulations are a valuable tool for such training, allowing individuals to understand and feel some of the difficult aspects of choices that have to be made in healthcare. Studies show simulated ethics training to be very meaningful to those who participate.

Harassment—in the form of bullying and sexual harassment—is common in healthcare organizations. Bullying takes the form of practical jokes, denial of requests for time off without a valid reason, verbal abuse, humiliation, and even unjust criticism. It tends to be persistent and leads to emotional exhaustion, poor performance, and turnover.

Sexual harassment takes place at all levels of the healthcare workforce and has been called a "chronic occupational health problem" (Quick and McFadyen 2017, 286). As much as a third of women in the healthcare workforce have experienced harassment, including that coming from patients and clients.

Managers must work hard to build trust and establish an environment that is free from harassment and bullying. The courts have determined that establishing a policy prohibiting harassment is not enough; organizations must also enforce it.

HR departments can influence the climate of an organization. They can make positive change. They should establish a values-based framework to make decisions and set policy.

Chapter Questions

1. Outline the differences between a job description and a job specification.
2. Why is performance simulation effective for assessing a potential employee?
3. What are the positive aspects of a personality test? What are the negative aspects?
4. Name five elements of a good structured interview.
5. Why are behavioral questions in an interview effective?
6. What are BARS?
7. What does evidence suggest about bias during job interviews?
8. What are career ladder programs?
9. What is the value of ethics training?
10. What do the courts say are the responsibilities of organizations regarding workplace harassment, including sexual harassment?

Chapter Cases

Patty's Personality Profile
All finalist candidates for positions at Valley View Care Center completed a personality profile. The profile included statements such as "I love making new friends" and "Accuracy is important to me." Results of the test indicated where candidates fell in terms of four areas: confidence and a focus on the

bottom line, emphasis on relationships and persuading others, dependability and tendency to cooperate, and focus on accuracy and quality outputs. Results typically indicated strength in one area over another, but could show strong tendencies in more than one category.

Patty was applying for the marketing director role and was happy to complete the test. In fact, she was curious what the results would tell her about herself. When she got the results back, Patty learned that she had the highest tendencies in the area of cooperation and dependability. Her next highest category was building relationships and persuading others. She was marked lowest in the area of focus on accuracy and quality outputs. She was not sure she completely agreed with the results, but she got the job.

One day, while in the copy room, Patty overheard a conversation in the hallway and was surprised to realize the two individuals were talking about her. "Oh, she scored high in the area of cooperation. Her creativity scores were much lower. She's probably not right for that assignment," her coworker said. The two were talking about plans for a new service and who would work on the project. Patty was disappointed. She knew personality profiles had their advantages, but they were far from being accurate predictors of work outcomes.

Case Questions
1. List some of the pros and cons of personality profiles. In this case, why might the company choose to use them in hiring candidates?
2. How were the outcomes of Patty's test misused?
3. How might Patty best use her personality profile?

What Should Mike Do?

Mike was the new manager at Riverside Clinic in northern Washington. The clinic was part of a large medical group management organization. Riverside had a number of family practitioners, obstetricians/gynecologists, and internal medicine physicians, a few specialists, and some physician assistants. Staff includes 10 clerks, 3 radiology technicians, 4 lab technicians, 6 medical assistants, and 14 registered nurses. Human resources and other administrative support staff are located at the organization's headquarters.

Mike was responsible for managing Riverside's staff. He interviewed everyone soon after he joined the clinic, so he could get to know them. His goal was to build trust and maintain open lines of communication. In general, the clinic ran smoothly. Minor disagreements or personnel problems happened from time to time, but Mike was happy that he did not have many major issues to overcome—at least not for a while.

Two of the medical assistants, Liz and Joe, seemed to get along well with one another. Both single, they often ate lunch together and generally shared the events happening in their lives. They communicated via social media when not at work. Mike was surprised, however, when one of his clerks asked to visit with him about Liz. The clerk indicated that Liz was open with everyone about her sex life. She seemed to take pride in sharing with many of the other staff members, especially the other medical assistants and clerks. According to his clerk, the lab and radiology techs had even heard Liz's stories. The clerk was not asking to make a formal complaint, she said, but she wanted Mike to know about it. She seemed to be uncomfortable with Liz's conversations.

The next day, as Mike was contemplating what he should do, Liz walked into his office. She wanted to make a complaint, she said. Joe had been coming on to her—touching her on the arm and back, and joking inappropriately—and she was uncomfortable. "Have you asked him to stop?" Mike asked. "No," Liz responded.

"What would you like me to do?" Mike asked.

"I don't know," Liz replied, "but I don't think I can work around him anymore."

Case Questions:
1. If you were Mike, what would you do next?
2. Should Mike terminate Liz or Joe?
3. What are some of Mike's options at this point?

Chapter Activities

Personality Testing Pros and Cons

Many personality profile tests are available online for free. Complete a personality test that interests you, such as the NERIS Type Explorer (www.16personalities.com/free-personality-test/) or the DISC personality test at 123test (www.123test.com/disc-personality-test/). Once you have reviewed your test results, research the "pros and cons of personality tests" online, and consider them in light of your results.

Finally, discuss the pros and cons of personality tests with your class. Did your test results provide an accurate reflection of your personality? What did you learn from your research about the accuracy and applicability of personality testing?

Behavioral Interview Design

Working in small groups, come up with five behavioral questions that could be given in a job interview. Here is an example: "You are stressed because you are late for a meeting. Two people show up on the spur of the moment to talk with you and they say it is important. How would you handle this situation?"

Once each small group has five questions, share your ideas with the rest of the class. Which ones are you most likely to consider using in future interviews? Why? You could even vote on your favorites.

References

American College of Healthcare Executives. 2021. *Healthcare Executive Competencies Assessment Tool.* www.ache.org/career-resource-center (at "Competency Assessment").

American Psychological Association. 2020. *APA Dictionary of Psychology.* https://dictionary.apa.org/personality-test.

Becker's Hospital Review. 2012. "7 Best Practices for Hospitals' Training and Development Programs." December 12. www.beckershospitalreview.com/hospital-management-administration/7-best-practices-for-hospitals-training-and-development-programs.html.

Beyea, S. C., L. K. von Reyn, and M. J. Slattery. 2007. "A Nurse Residency Program for Competency Development Using Human Patient Simulation." *Journal for Nurses in Staff Development* 23 (2): 77–82. http://dx.doi.org/10.1097/01.NND.0000266613.16434.05.

Busetta, G., F. Fiorillo, and E. Visalli. 2013. "Searching for a Job Is a Beauty Contest." MPRA Paper No. 49825. September 2013. https://mpra.ub.uni-muenchen.de/49825/.

Buxton, M., J. C. Phillippi, and M. R. Collins. 2014. "Simulation: A New Approach to Teaching Ethics." *Journal of Midwifery & Women's Health* 60 (1): 70–74. https://doi.org/10.1111/jmwh.12185.

Cherry, K. 2020. "The Big Five Personality Traits." Verywell Mind. Published July 13. www.verywellmind.com/the-big-five-personality-dimensions-2795422.

Clari, M., A. Conti, A. Scacchi, M. Scattaglia, V. Dimonte, and M. Gianino. 2020. "Prevalence of Workplace Sexual Violence Against Healthcare Workers Providing Home Care: A Systematic Review and Meta-Analysis." *International Journal of Environmental Research and Public Health* 17 (23): 8807. http://dx.doi.org/10.3390/ijerph17238807.

Custodio, R., A. Gard, and G. Graham. 2009. "Health Information Technology: Addressing Health Disparity by Improving Quality, Increasing Access, and Developing Workforce." *Journal of Health Care for the Poor and Underserved* 20 (2): 301–7. http://dx.doi.org/10.1353/hpu.0.0142.

De Kock, F., and D. Hauptfleisch. 2018. "Reducing Racial Similarity Bias in Interviews by Increasing Structure: A Quasi-Experiment Using Multilevel Analysis." *International Perspectives in Psychology* 7 (3): 137–54. http://dx.doi.org/10.1037/ipp0000091.

Dean, M. A., P. L. Roth, and P. Bobko. 2008. "Ethnic and Gender Subgroup Differences in Assessment Center Ratings: A Meta-Analysis." *Journal of Applied Psychology* 93 (3): 685–91.

Dill, J. S., E. Chuang, and J. C. Morgan. 2014. "Healthcare Organization–Education Partnerships and Career Ladder Programs for Health Care Workers." *Social Science & Medicine* 122 (December 2014): 63–71. https://doi.org/10.1016/j.socscimed.2014.10.021.

Frye, E. Y. 2020. "The Role of HRD in Influencing Ethical Behavior and Corporate Social Responsibility Within Organizations." *New Horizons in Adult Education and Human Resource Development* 32 (7): 62–66. https://doi.org/10.1002/nha3.20277.

Greenberg, J., and M. S. Edwards (eds.). 2009. *Voice and Silence in Organizations.* [UK]: Emerald Group Publishing.

Harrison, J., M. Martin-Raugh, L. Carney, P. Inglese, L. Chen, and G. Feng. 2017. "Exploring Methods for Developing Behaviorally Anchored Rating Scales for Evaluating Structured Interview Performance." ETS Research Report Series. December 2017. https://doi.org/10.1002/ets2.12152.

Havighurst, L. C., L. E. Fields, and C. L. Fields. 2003. "High Versus Low Fidelity Simulations: Does the Type of Format Affect Candidates' Performance or Perceptions?" IPMAAC Conference on Personnel Assessment, Baltimore, Maryland, June 2003. (Unpublished). http://annex.ipacweb.org/library/conf/03/havighurst.pdf.

Huffcutt, A. I., and P. L. Roth. 1998. "Racial Group Differences in Employment Interview Evaluations." *Journal of Applied Psychology* 83 (2): 179–89. http://dx.doi.org/10.1037//0021-9010.83.2.179.

Huffcutt, A. I., and W. Arthur Jr. 1994. "Hunter and Hunter (1984) Revisited: Interview Validity for Entry-Level Jobs." *Journal of Applied Psychology* 79 (2): 184–90. http://dx.doi.org/10.1037/0021-9010.79.2.184.

Hunt, J. W., and Y. Baruch. 2003. "Developing Top Managers: The Impact of Interpersonal Skills Training." *Journal of Management Development* 22 (8): 729–52.

Jagsi, R., K. A. Griffith, R. Jones, C. R. Perumalswami, P. Ubel, and A. Stewart. 2016. "Sexual Harassment and Discrimination Experiences of Academic Medical Faculty." *Journal of the American Medical Association* 315 (19): 2120–21. https://doi.org/10.1001/jama.2016.2188.

Johnson, S. L., and R. E. Ruth. 2009. "Workplace Bullying: Concerns for Nurse Leaders." *Journal of Nursing Administration* 39 (2): 84–90. https://doi.org/10.1097/nna.0b013e318195a5fc.

Kraiger, K., and J. K. Ford. 1985. "A Meta-Analysis of Ratee Race Effects in Performance Ratings." *Journal of Applied Psychology* 70 (1): 56–65.

Laditka, S., and M. Houck. 2006. "Student-Developed Case Studies: An Experiential Approach for Teaching Ethics in Management." *Journal of Business Ethics* 64 (March): 157–67.

Lerman, R. I., S. McKernan, and S. Riegg. 2004. "The Scope of Employer-Provided Training in the United States: Who, What, Where, and How Much?" In *Job Training Policy in the United States*, edited by C. J. O'Leary, R. A. Straits, and S. A. Wander, 211–44. Kalamazoo, MI: W. E. Upjohn Institute. https://doi.org/10.17848/9781417549993.ch7.

Levashina, J., C. J. Hartwell, F. P. Morgeson, and M. A. Campion. 2014. "The Structured Employment Interview: Narrative and Quantitative Review of the Research Literature." *Personnel Psychology* 67 (1): 241–93. https://doi.org/10.1111/peps.12052.

Lindsey, A., E. King, T. McCausland, K. Jones, and E. Dunleavy. 2013. "What We Know and Don't: Eradicating Employment Discrimination 50 Years After the Civil Rights Act." *Industrial and Organizational Psychology: Perspectives on Science and Practice* 6 (4): 391–413. https://doi.org/10.1111/iops.12075.

Ling, M., C. J. Young, H. L. Shepherd, C. Mak, and R. P. Saw. 2016. "Workplace Bullying in Surgery." *World Journal of Surgery* 40 (11): 2560–66. https://doi.org/10.1007/s00268-016-3642-7.

Lubbe, D., and A. Nitsche. 2019. "Reducing Assimilation and Contrast Effects on Selection Interview Ratings Using Behaviorally Anchored Rating Scales." *International Journal of Selection and Assessment* 27 (1): 43–53. https://doi.org/10.1111/ijsa.12230.

Maurer-Fazio, M., and L. Lei. 2015. "As Rare as a Panda: How Facial Attractiveness, Gender, and Occupation Affect Interview Callbacks at Chinese Firms." *International Journal of Manpower* 36 (1): 68–85. https://doi.org/10.1108/IJM-12-2014-0258.

Mehwish, J., A. Amir, A. Bashir, and T. Hasan. 2019. "Human Resource Practices and Organizational Commitment: The Mediating Role of Job Satisfaction in Emerging Economy." *Cogent Business & Management* 6 (1): 1608668. Published online May 6. https://doi.org/10.1080/23311975.2019.1608668.

Moore, D. A. 2017. "How to Improve the Accuracy and Reduce the Cost of Personnel Selection." *California Management Review* 60 (1): 8–17. https://doi.org/10.1177/0008125617725288.

Morris, F. C., Jr., J. Hoerner, and K. Smith. 2018. "Second Circuit Decision in Sexual Harassment Case Shows Heightened Risk for Health Care Employers." *Employee Relations Law Journal* 44 (1): 5–9.

Morrison, E. W. 2014. "Employee Voice and Silence." *Annual Review of Organizational Psychology and Organizational Behavior* 1 (1): 173–97. http://dx.doi.org/10.1146/annurev-orgpsych-031413-091328.

Moyle, P., and J. Hackston. 2018. "Personality Assessment for Employee Development: Ivory Tower or Real World?" *Journal of Personality Assessment* 100 (5): 507–17. https://doi.org/10.1080/00223891.2018.1481078.

Nadler, J., M. R. Lowery, J. Grebinoski, and R. G. Jones. 2014. "Aversive Discrimination in Employment Interviews: Reducing Effects of Sexual Orientation

Bias with Accountability." *Psychology of Sexual Orientation and Gender Diversity* 1 (4): 480–88.

Patterson, F. 2015. "Transition and Metaphor: Crossing a Bridge from Direct Practice to First Line Management in Social Services." *British Journal of Social Work* 45 (7): 2072–88. https://doi.org/10.1093/bjsw/bcu034.

Pei, K. Y., and A. Cochran 2019. "Workplace Bullying Among Surgeons: The Perfect Crime." *Annals of Surgery* 269 (1): 43–44. https://doi.org/10.1097/sla.0000000000003018.

Peng, Y.-C., L.-J. Chen, C.-C. Chang, and W.-L. Zhuang. 2016. "Workplace Bullying and Workplace Deviance: The Mediating Effect of Emotional Exhaustion and the Moderating Effect of Core-Self Evaluations." *Employee Relations* 38 (5): 755–69. https://doi.org/10.1108/ER-01-2016-0014.

Quick, J. C., and M. A. McFadyen. 2017. "Sexual Harassment: Have We Made Any Progress?" *Journal of Occupational Health Psychology* 22 (3): 286–98. http://doi.org/10.1037/ocp0000054.

Quillian, L., J. J. Lee, and M. Oliver. 2020. "Evidence from Field Experiments in Hiring Shows Substantial Additional Racial Discrimination After the Callback." *Social Forces* 99 (2): 732–59. https://doi.org/10.1093/sf/soaa026.

Rai A., and U. A. Agarwal. 2018. "Workplace Bullying and Employee Silence: A Moderated Mediation Model of Psychological Contract Violation and Workplace Friendship." *Personnel Review* 47 (1): 226–56. http://dx.doi.org/10.1108/PR-03-2017-0071.

Rihal, C. S., N. A. Baker, B. E. Bunkers, S. J. Buskirk, J. N. Caviness, E. A. Collins, J. C. Copa, S. N. Hayes, S. L. Hubert, D. A. Reed, S. R. Wendorff, C. H. Fraser, G. Farrugia, and J. H. Noseworthy. 2020. "Addressing Sexual Harassment in the #MeToo Era: An Institutional Approach." *Mayo Clinic Proceedings* 95 (4): 749–57. http://dx.doi.org/10.1016/j.mayocp.2019.12.021.

Robert, R., N. Kentish-Barnes, A. Boyer, A. Laurent, E. Azoulay, and J. Reignier. 2020. "Ethical Dilemmas Due to the COVID-19 Pandemic." *Annals of Intensive Care* 10: 84. https://doi.org/10.1186/s13613-020-00702-7.

Schmid Mast, M., E. P. Kleinlogel, B. Tur, and M. Bachmann. 2018. "The Future of Interpersonal Skills Development: Immersive Virtual Reality Training with Virtual Humans." *Human Resource Development Quarterly* 29 (2): 125–41. https://doi.org/10.1002/hrdq.21307.

Sefcik, J. T. 2020. "4 Reasons to Use Simulations in Your Hiring Process." Employment Technologies Corporation. https://employmenttechnologies.com/4-reasons-use-simulation-hiring-process/.

Smith, T. 2019. "Technology Implementation and Training in New Systems: As Related to Healthcare Workers' Job Satisfaction." D. Ed. diss., University of St. Francis.

Society for Human Resource Management (SHRM). 2021. "Performing Job Analysis." SHRM Toolkits. www.shrm.org/resourcesandtools/tools-and-samples/toolkits/pages/performingjobanalysis.aspx.

———. 2016. "A Guide to Conducting Behavioral Interviews with Early Career Job Candidates." www.shrm.org/LearningAndCareer/learning/Documents/Behavioral%20Interviewing%20Guide%20for%20Early%20Career%20Candidates.pdf.

Sonnino, R. E. 2016. "Health Care Leadership Development and Training: Progress and Pitfalls." *Journal of Healthcare Leadership* 2016 (8): 19–29. https://doi.org/10.2147/JHL.S68068.

Spector, P. E., M. L. Coulter, H. G. Stockwell, and M. W. Matz. 2007. "Perceived Violence Climate: A New Construct and Its Relationship to Workplace Physical Violence and Verbal Aggression, and Their Potential Consequences." *Work & Stress* 21 (2): 117–30. https://doi.org/10.1080/02678370701410007.

Strom, S., C. Anderson, L. Yang, C. Canales, A. Amin, S. Lotfipour, C. McCoy, and M. Langdorf. 2015. "Correlation of Simulation Examination to Written Test Scores for Advanced Cardiac Life Support Testing: Prospective Cohort Study." *Western Journal of Emergency Medicine* 16 (6): 907–12.

Swedberg, L., H. Michélsen, E. Hammar Chiriac, and I. Hylander. 2015. "On-the-Job Training Makes the Difference: Healthcare Assistants' Perceived Competence and Responsibility in the Care of Patients with Home Mechanical Ventilation." *Scandinavian Journal of Caring Sciences* 29 (2): 369–78. https://doi.org/10.1111/scs.12173.

Thiel, C. E., S. Connelly, L. Harkrider, L. D. Devenport, Z. Bagdasarov, J. F. Johnson, and M. D. Mumford. 2013. "Case-Based Knowledge and Ethics Education: Improving Learning and Transfer Through Emotionally Rich Cases." *Science and Engineering Ethics* 19 (1): 265–86. https://doi.org/10.1007/s11948-011-9318-7.

Trueick, A. 2018. "4 Differences Between a Job Description and a Job Specification." Cpl Resources, Inc. (blog). Published March 2018. www.cpl.com/blog/2018/03/4-differences-between-a-job-description-and-a-job-specification.

US Equal Employment Opportunity Commission. 2017. "EEOC Launches New Training Program on Respectful Workplaces" (press release). www.eeoc.gov/newsroom/eeoc-launches-new-training-program-respectful-workplaces.

Vincent-Höper, S., M. Adler, M. Stein, C. Vaupel, and A. Nienhaus. 2020. "Sexually Harassing Behaviors from Patients or Clients and Care Workers' Mental Health: Development and Validation of a Measure." *International Journal of Environmental Research and Public Health* 17 (7): 2570. https://doi.org/10.3390/ijerph17072570.

Waldman, J. D., F. Kelly, S. Arora, and H. L. Smith. 2004. "The Shocking Cost of Turnover in Health Care." *Health Care Management Review* 29 (1): 2–7.

Williamson, L. G., J. E. Campion, S. B. Malos, M. V. Roehling, and M. A. Campion. 1997. "Employment Interview on Trial: Linking Interview Structure with

Litigation Outcomes." *Journal of Applied Psychology* 82 (6): 900–12. https://doi.org/10.1037/0021-9010.82.6.900.

Xu, T., L. L. Magnusson Hanson, T. Lange, L. Starkopf, H. Westerlund, I. E. H. Madsen, R. Rugulies, J. Pentti, S. Stenholm, J. Vahtera, Å. M. Hansen, M. Virtanen, M. Kivimäki, and N. H. Rod. 2019. "Workplace Bullying and Workplace Violence as Risk Factors for Cardiovascular Disease: A Multi-Cohort Study." *European Heart Journal* 40 (14): 1124–34. https://doi.org/10.1093/eurheartj/ehy683.

Yeager, V. A., J. Wisniewski, T. Chapple-McGruder, B. Castrucci, and E. Gould. 2019. "Public Health Workforce Self-Identified Training Needs by Jurisdiction and Job Type." *Journal of Public Health Management and Practice* 25 (2): 181–90. http://dx.doi.org/10.1097/PHH.0000000000000830.

Youngman, J. 2017. "The Use and Abuse of Pre-Employment Personality Tests." *Business Horizons*, 60 (3): 261–69.

CHAPTER 23

STRATEGY AND CHANGE MANAGEMENT

> Change is often difficult, but it is most successful if mission driven. In 2010, Atlantic Health System recognized a need to change. It began with the addition of four words to the organization's mission statement: "Deliver high-quality, safe, affordable, patient care *within a healing culture*." However, the words had to be put into action. Atlantic Health's board of trustees and executives quickly set to work to turn the mission into a healing movement for the system. To make the mission actionable, Atlantic defined a healing culture as:
>
> - Sharing responsibility for healing with patients, families and the community;
> - Demonstrating respect for diversity through cultural competence;
> - Embracing synergies among physical, emotional and spiritual connections; and
> - Recognizing optimal well-being, prevention and health promotion as parts of the healing process.
>
> A Healing Culture Council was then formed and tasked with beginning initiatives and programs to make their healing culture operational. Over the next five years, the council grew to over 100 members and met at least ten times a year. The effort was a great success, thanks to top-down commitment from Atlantic Health's executives, involvement from all levels of the organization, and a focus on action. Major initiatives dramatically improved both patient and staff experiences.
>
> *Source*: Adapted from *Becker's Hospital Review* (2015).

Learning Objectives

After studying this chapter, readers should be able to

- articulate the importance of and interrelationships between an organization's strategy (including its values, mission, vision, and strategic direction), behaviors, and activities;

- identify the difference between a mission and vision;
- realize the critical function of leaders in directing change;
- apply methods to overcome resistance and implement planned change; and
- state the role of leaders in a change effort.

Key Terms

- gap analysis
- mission
- values
- vision

Organizations are formed to accomplish a purpose efficiently and effectively for their stakeholders. Company purposes vary greatly. A profit-oriented company might seek to maximize wealth for its shareholders, while a service organization might provide healthcare to the poor. Establishing and instilling a purposeful direction for an organization is a critical function of organizational leaders. As suggested in the introduction, embedding this purpose throughout an organization can be a long and challenging process, and can involve both organizational development and change management efforts.

The purpose of an organization is often expressed through its values, mission, and vision statements. If appropriately used, these statements identify the stakeholders the organization serves, how it serves them, and what type of relationship it expects to have with them. These statements become commitments and help define how the organization will measure success, what it will do, and its desired outcomes (Walston 2018).

These declarations should be accurate, convincing, and explicit, and should reflect the principles and desires of the organization's key stakeholders, who might be the owners, shareholders, trustees, or community leaders. Properly crafting and adhering to the values, mission, and vision statement can be critical to organizational success; organizations that fail to do so may not achieve the synergies of a dedicated and mission-driven workforce.

values
Overarching principles or standards that signal how people should behave.

mission
The organization's ideals and purpose—why it exists.

Values, Mission, and Vision

As exhibit 23.1 illustrates, the values of an organization are the foundation of its mission and vision. **Values** are overarching principles or standards that signal how people should behave; an organizational values statement defines acceptable and unacceptable conduct for employees. The **mission** should

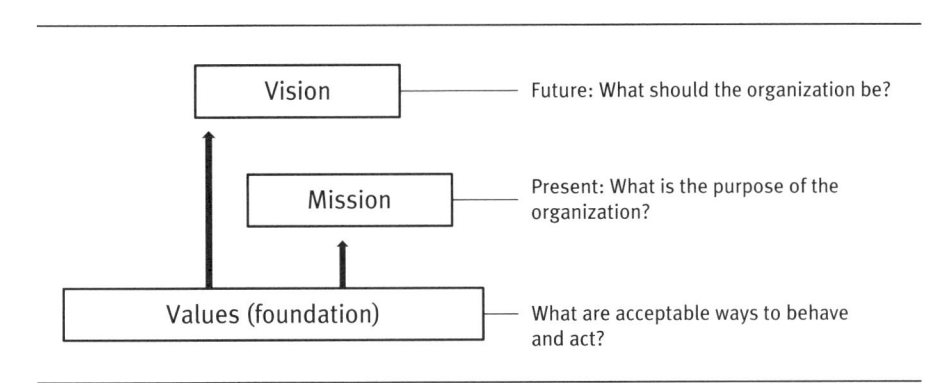

EXHIBIT 23.1
Relationships Between Values, Mission, and Vision

- Vision — Future: What should the organization be?
- Mission — Present: What is the purpose of the organization?
- Values (foundation) — What are acceptable ways to behave and act?

mirror these values in articulating the organization's ideals and purpose—why it exists. The **vision** depicts the organization's desired future state. As can be seen, values, mission, and vision are highly interrelated and, if suitably constructed, allow stakeholders to comprehend and express the organization's desired behaviors, purpose, direction, and priorities.

vision
The organization's desired future state.

Values

Most successful organizations are values based and practice clear, relevant values. Almost 75 percent of companies have between three and seven values, with five being the most common number (Sull, Turconi, and Sull 2020). To be effective values need to be fully incorporated into the organization's decisions and processes, which should include employee hiring and firing, performance reviews, promotions, and incentive structures. In addition, values define the ethics that guide decisions, actions, processes, and resolution of conflicts. If observed, values become essential guiding principles for all company actions and are the foundation of organizational culture. All internal and most external stakeholders should know the values, accept them in their hearts and minds, and incorporate them into their behaviors and actions; values statements should not be written just to hang on a wall (Thomas 2018; Walston 2018).

Appropriately lived values through engaged employees in hospitals may be a key factor in lowering patient mortality rates (Brooks Carthon et al. 2019; Curry et al. 2011). This finding supports the notion that values should endure across time. Organizational strategies will adapt, but values should remain consistent.

An organization's values should be the ultimate measure to determine whether it has succeeded or failed. Just achieving goals, while necessary, is not sufficient. If goals are attained but values are compromised, the outcomes should be considered a failure. For example, as shown in the box, physicians may have succeeded in making money, but they did so by violating their

> **Prominent Physician Guilty of Fraud, Conspiracy, and Identity Theft**
>
> A prominent Florida physician pled guilty to a $29 million fraud involving 56 counts of conspiracy and identity theft. Dr. deGraft-Johnson owned and operated a heart institute in Tallahassee and performed unneeded invasive surgical procedures on patients but altered his medical records to falsely indicate they were needed. He also admitted submitting false insurance claims for as many as 3,000 surgical procedures. In one case he claimed to have performed 14 procedures in only a seven-hour period (Ellison 2020).
>
> **Prominent Cardiologist Sentenced for $19 Million Billing Fraud Scheme**
>
> On November 20, 2013, Jose Katz, of Closter, New Jersey, was sentenced to 78 months in prison and three years of supervised release and ordered to pay $19 million in restitution. Katz, a well-known cardiologist and the founder, CEO, and sole owner of two large medical services companies in New Jersey and New York, pleaded guilty to one count of conspiracy to commit healthcare fraud. He also pleaded guilty to one count of Social Security fraud arising from a separate scheme to give his wife a "no show" job and make her eligible for Social Security benefits. According to court documents, from 2004 through 2012, Katz conspired to bill Medicare Part B, Medicaid, Empire BCBS, Aetna, and others for unnecessary tests and unnecessary procedures based on false diagnoses and for medical services rendered by unlicensed practitioners (US Department of Justice 2013).

professional values, making their efforts not just a failure but also unethical or illegal. Similarly, when organizations realize stellar financial goals but disregard their values in the process, their supposed success is exposed as fraud or abuse. Whether or not they engaged in criminal activity, compromised values can have a devastating impact on employee morale.

Too frequently, organizations create nice value statements but fail to root them in their culture. Value statements become marketing slogans and window dressing—visible on a wall but ignored in practice. One of the authors once worked for a company that espoused written values of service, honesty, and respect, but everyone who worked there knew that financial outcomes were all that mattered, and the stated values were disregarded. Ultimately, ignoring the stated values badly damaged the company's culture, reputation, morale, and long-term viability. As a result, they ended up paying huge fines and removing their corporate name from all of their facilities.

People need strong moral values to remain motivated. Few employees can be highly motivated and engaged for a long time if the primary reason for their firm's existence is—implicitly or explicitly—profit maximization. Emphasizing only profits has long been seen as flawed and unsustainable (Drucker 1959). Seeking to maximize profits must occur in the context of other values; otherwise, an organization will lose its direction and employee support over time (D'Angelo 2018).

Mayo Clinic, widely respected as among the best healthcare organizations in the world, states that its values guide its actions, define its existence, and express the vision and intent of their founders. These values, which appear on the organization's "About Mayo Clinic" webpage, comprise the following:

Primary Value: The needs of the patient come first.

Respect
Treat everyone in our diverse community, including patients, their families and colleagues, with dignity.

Integrity
Adhere to the highest standards of professionalism, ethics and personal responsibility, worthy of the trust our patients place in us.

Compassion
Provide the best care, treating patients and family members with sensitivity and empathy.

Healing
Inspire hope and nurture the well-being of the whole person, respecting physical, emotional and spiritual needs.

Teamwork
Value the contributions of all, blending the skills of individual staff members in unsurpassed collaboration.

Innovation
Infuse and energize the organization, enhancing the lives of those we serve, through the creative ideas and unique talents of each employee.

Excellence
Deliver the best outcomes and highest quality service through the dedicated effort of every team member.

Stewardship
Sustain and reinvest in our mission and extended communities by wisely managing our human, natural and material resources.

Mission

Most organizations establish written mission and vision statements. Successful organizations are steadfast and unfailing in following their missions (MacLeod 2016). A healthcare mission statement provides the guiding force for defining an organization's ongoing purpose and its products and markets

(Kern 2018). This mission should drive organizational strategies and should be founded on organizational values. In addition, the mission should suggest factors that highlight an organization's success, such as goals and key performance indicators. Basically, the mission needs to tell what the organization does, why it does what it does, for whom it does it, and what value it delivers (Walston 2018). In other words, a mission statement should define the organization's products or services, standards and values, customers or service population, and unique contributions. In addition, a mission statement should describe what the organization does differently or better than others (Walston and Chou 2011). For example, the mission statement of the University of Utah Health states in the "About Us" section of its website that its purpose is to provide patient care, educate, and conduct research to improve the health and quality of life for the people of Utah and beyond in an excellent and compassionate manner:

Our Mission
The University of Utah Health serves the people of Utah and beyond by continually improving individual and community health and quality of life. This is achieved through excellence in patient care, education, and research; each is vital to our mission and each makes the others stronger.

- We provide compassionate care without compromise.
- We educate scientists and health care professionals for the future.
- We engage in research to advance knowledge and well-being.

However, mission statements, like values, have little worth if they are not properly expressed and lived. Mission statements often fail to accurately communicate their essential elements. Frequently, they are too similar among organizations, are too vague, are not rooted in reality, are too lengthy, and do not distinguish the organization from its competitors (Bourgeois, Duhaime, and Stimpert 1999; DeLapa 2020). Some missions do not seem to care what business they are in. For instance, Albertsons, a chain of grocery stores, once used the following mission statement: "To create a shopping experience that pleases our customers; a workplace that creates opportunities and a great working environment for our associates; and a business that achieves financial success" (Zetlin 2013). Even though these goals were laudable, one would have difficulty understanding the company's primary business.

Although 85 percent of large companies have one, it has been estimated that only 10 percent of mission statements "say something meaningful" or establish why the firm should be chosen over others (Holland 2007). Healthcare mission statements too frequently include meaningless declarations such as "providing world-class services" and "the highest quality of care."

Some mission statements are concise and terse; others are long and wordy. They should be long enough to contain the necessary components but short enough to be remembered. If a mission rambles on and on, employees will not remember it or use it to guide their actions. Shorter mission statements are easier to remember and communicate. The general recommendation is for mission statements to be between one and three sentences long. Long mission statements that extend for multiple paragraphs are often incomprehensible, unfocused, and useless.

> **Novartis Mission Statement**
>
> Our purpose is to reimagine medicine to improve and extend people's lives. We use innovative science and technology to address some of society's most challenging healthcare issues. We discover and develop breakthrough treatments and find new ways to deliver them to as many people as possible. We also aim to reward those who invest their money, time and ideas in our company.
>
> *Source*: Reprinted from Novartis (2020).

Missions should motivate action. To do so, they must be written in understandable language that employees can clearly comprehend. For instance, Intermountain Healthcare in Salt Lake City, Utah, lists the following mission statement on its "Mission, Vision, Values" webpage: "Helping people live the healthiest lives possible." This mission statement is written in concise, clear language that focuses on actionable areas beyond hospital care that employees can understand and act on.

In addition, a mission statement must balance a company's quality with financial performance and reflect reality. If the mission statement mentions only quality outcomes but the organization's operations and metrics focus heavily on financial returns, then employees can become cynical and disengaged. Healthcare organizations' missions need to focus on both quality and their financial performance. Novartis, a large, global pharmaceutical company, uses a mission statement (shown in the box) that integrates its focus on innovation with financial returns, which more accurately captures the reality for the firm.

Vision

Contrasting the present-focused nature of a mission, a vision—as defined earlier—portrays a desired future state. A clearly articulated, widely held vision can help create a positive organizational culture with motivated employees. Vision statements should be short enough that employees and other stakeholders can remember and refer to them during planning and decision-making. When deeply ingrained and prominently displayed, good vision statements can positively affect other stakeholders (Coleman 2013). In "30 Example Vision Statements" sampled in 2020 by TopNonProfits, the average vision statement length was just over 14.5 words. Some simple but powerful examples include the Alzheimer's Association's "A world without Alzheimer's disease" or the Cleveland Clinic's "Striving to be the world's leader in patient experience, clinical outcomes, research and education." Both statements define what their respective company would like the future to be or what the organization should become.

Clear visions inspire confidence and empower employees by informing them of the preferred future for their company. Visions should permeate the culture and prompt direct action. Also, they should challenge and focus employees yet promote loyalty and commitment.

LifePoint Health—a healthcare provider of inpatient, outpatient, and post-acute services in 29 US states—has crafted a relatively simple but clear vision statement (found in the "Who We Are" section of the company's website):

We want to create places where:
- People choose to come for healthcare
- Physicians want to practice and
- Employees want to work

This vision plainly indicates that LifePoint Health's leadership desires to create a company of choice for patients, physicians, and employees. It is short enough to remember and can provide meaningful direction to motivate employees.

Gap Analysis and Organizational Change

Once organizations have established their mission, vision, and values, they should make the statements actionable. Companies commonly undergo a **gap analysis**—an environmental scan (both internal and external) that compares the organization's current performance and status with its values, mission, and vision (see exhibit 23.2). The gap analysis identifies those areas in which the company is not performing in a way that meets its stated expectations. From these results, strategic options are generated, and then goals, objectives, and action plans are created and implemented to effect the changes needed to align performance with the expressed values, mission, and vision.

A gap analysis can be developed by asking the following questions (Walston 2018):

gap analysis
An environmental scan—both internal and external—that compares the organization's current performance and status with its values, mission, and vision.

- Which stakeholder groups' needs are not being met?
- What key actions must be taken to attain the vision?
- What previous goals were not achieved? How did this lack of achievement affect the mission?
- How is the organization living its values? What can be done to emphasize and fully incorporate the values into the daily work life?

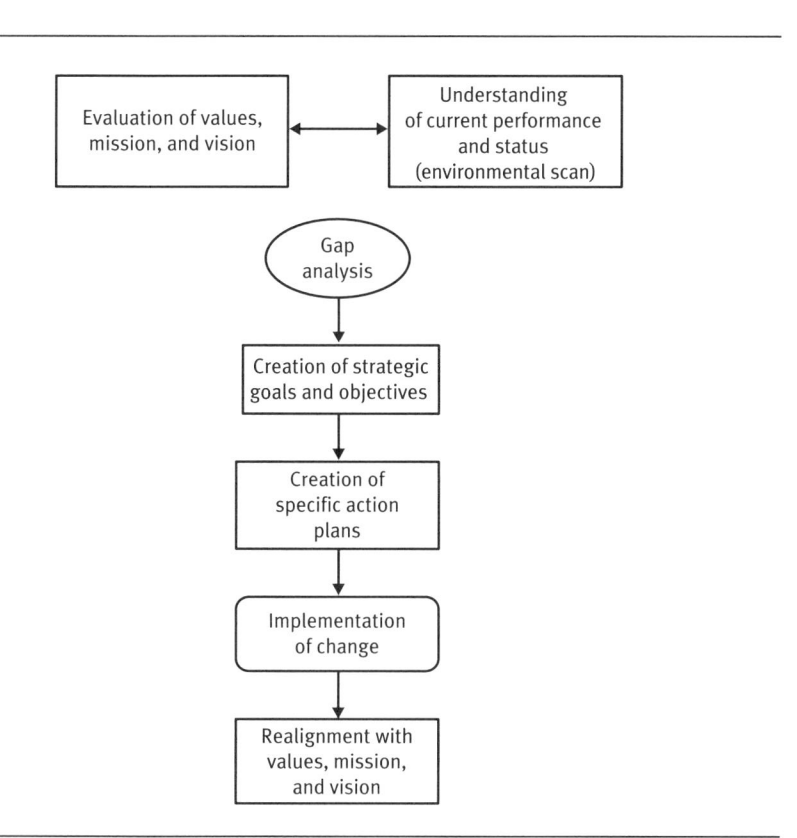

EXHIBIT 23.2
Gap Analysis from Values, Mission, and Vision

```
[Evaluation of values,      [Understanding
 mission, and vision]  ↔    of current performance
                             and status
                             (environmental scan)]
                    ↓
              (Gap analysis)
                    ↓
         [Creation of strategic
          goals and objectives]
                    ↓
         [Creation of
          specific action
          plans]
                    ↓
         [Implementation
          of change]
                    ↓
         [Realignment with
          values, mission,
          and vision]
```

- What core organizational weaknesses may be preventing the organization from living the mission?
- What critical external threats exist that must be addressed for the organization to continue providing mission-based products and services?
- How is the organization's financial health, and how does this status affect its strategic position?

Companies must change to remain relevant. Healthcare companies today must periodically reinvent and adapt their products, services, and processes. Most companies engage in several major changes a year, yet organizational change is a difficult charge for most firms, and about 70 percent of change efforts fail (Ewenstein, Smith, and Sologar 2015). Change does not happen by itself. A well-crafted plan for change may not be implemented for many reasons, but viable companies both plan and implement change. In fact, the ability to implement change is probably a more important skill set than the ability to plan for change (Johnston, Lefort, and Tesvic 2017).

Healthcare organizations are now under particular pressure to significantly change how they operate and to create integrative structures—such as medical homes and accountable care organizations—that improve quality, reduce costs, and meet key stakeholder needs. Positive, sustainable change must be fully embedded in the culture and processes, and it must be grounded in the values, mission, and vision—otherwise, efforts will be superficial. Aligned change effectively institutes new ways to organize, function, and perform.

Leadership

To implement change successfully, leaders need appropriate skills to alter and integrate their workforce, technology, and organizational structure. Exhibit 23.3 shows how these three components interact and how they can be moved toward positive change. As described in chapter 15, transformational leaders motivate their people, design innovative processes and methods through their technology, and craft optimal relationships through their structure. Each of these changes interacts with the others; they cannot be done separately. The capability to configure people, technology, and structure to produce high performance is a key managerial skill.

Leadership is inherently difficult because of its complexity and somewhat contradictory nature. Leaders must clearly convey their organization's vision and, at the same time, lead day-to-day operations. Pressure from daily management responsibilities can distract leaders from strategic, vision-related activities. Every day, executives are barraged by innumerable meetings, regulatory demands, ceremonial obligations, and pressures to improve financial performance. Successful leaders must balance these short-term daily demands with the long-term vision-related change efforts (Walston 2018).

EXHIBIT 23.3
Three Types of Change and Their Interactions

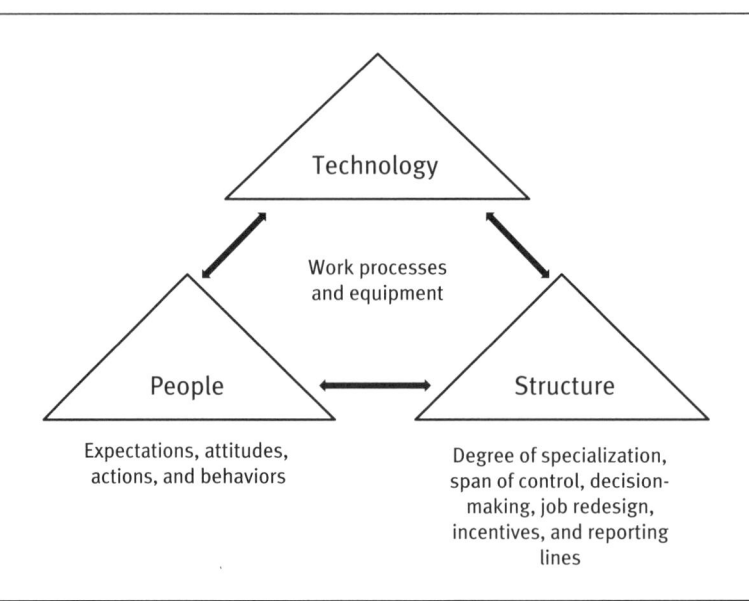

```
                    Technology
                   /          \
                  /            \
            Work processes and equipment
                /                \
           People  <-------->  Structure
```

People: Expectations, attitudes, actions, and behaviors

Structure: Degree of specialization, span of control, decision-making, job redesign, incentives, and reporting lines

Source: Adapted from Robbins et al. (2014).

Achieving this balance necessitates strong management abilities that few have. "Rare is the business leader who can articulate and instill a long-term vision and manage the day-to-day operations with the requisite obsession for detail" (Rowe and Nejad 2009). Successful leaders learn to juggle these priorities. They obtain skills to deal with daily operations and facilitate vision-driven change. They manage continuity and change simultaneously.

Facilitating change requires identifying problems and removing obstacles. Generally, people do not like change, and resistance is a common obstacle to change efforts. Making changes often affects job security and upsets cultural norms, power bases, and company processes. At its worst, organizational change can become a competitive, hostile process that promotes resistance from key stakeholders. Resistance occurs naturally as part of a change process and should be recognized and appropriately addressed (Ahmed 2020).

A display of resistance does not imply that employees are disloyal. Leaders should understand their reaction as natural and welcome employee feedback that may be negative. Maintaining open communication, although often uncomfortable when resistance is discussed, allows concerns to be dealt with and the change to be implemented to lasting effect. Managers who choose not to understand the resistance to change may take untoward actions with unfortunate consequences that impede change. Some leaders who encounter resistance lash out by enforcing discipline, making threats, and showing anger—reactions that often engender visible compliance but commonly reinforce resistance when these leaders are not present.

Leaders can take steps that allow them to better understand resistance and facilitate the change process. As can be imagined, communicating with employees remains critical. Employees need to know how current and future environments require change to achieve the organizational mission and vision. Employees and other stakeholders should feel a sense of urgency regarding implementing the change, and answering the following questions can help create a safe environment in which to move forward (Wilson 2014):

- Why is the change needed?
- What change is coming or expected?
- What new behaviors or actions does the change require?
- What steps should those affected by the change expect to take (and when)?
- What is not expected to change?

Many of these questions involve communicating why the change is needed and what will happen. An important point to make is what should not change. Often, leaders stress the values, relationships, and culture they desire to retain or issues of job security. Additionally, if employees comprehend what will occur, how it will affect their behaviors and actions, and when different activities will take place, they will resist less, engage more, and coalesce to make the change happen.

As of July 2020, Gallup polling shows that only 40 percent of US workers feel engaged—defined as being "highly involved in, enthusiastic about and committed to their work and workplace" (Harter 2020). Consistently, some observers have previously suggested that just 44 percent of hospital employees are fully engaged (Sherwood 2013). Yet all stakeholders recognize that employee engagement is critical to positive patient experiences and excellent hospital performance in today's environment, in which there is increased emphasis on HCAHPS (Hospital Consumer Assessment of Healthcare Providers and Systems) scores (Evans et al. 2020). Given this focus, healthcare leaders must put their energies into drivers such as commitment to living the organizational mission, hiring and promoting proper personnel, open communication, feedback, and employee recognition to create the appropriate culture and level of satisfaction needed to achieve the organizational values, mission, and vision.

Many different change models exist. The Agency for Healthcare Research and Quality (AHRQ) promotes a change model called the Comprehensive Unit-based Safety Program (CUSP), based on Kotter's eight-step model of change, to improve patient safety. The relationship between the eight steps and AHRQ's modules is shown in exhibit 23.4. CUSP focuses on using tools relevant to clinicians in the context of a hospital environment at a unit level. The toolkit to institute CUSP is available from the AHRQ website's CUSP page (www.ahrq.gov/hai/cusp/).

EXHIBIT 23.4 Relationship Between Kotter's Eight-Step Change Model and AHRQ's CUSP Toolkit Modules

Kotter's Steps	CUSP Toolkit Modules
1. Create a sense of urgency	Understand the Science of Safety
2. Create a guiding coalition	Assemble the Team
	Engage the Senior Executive
3. Develop a shared vision	Identify Defects Through Sensemaking
4. Communicate the vision	Understand the Science of Safety
	Identify Defects Through Sensemaking
5. Empower others to act	Understand the Science of Safety
	Identify Defects Through Sensemaking
	Implement Teamwork and Communication
6. Generate short-term wins	Implement Teamwork and Communication
7. Consolidate gains and produce more change	Identify Defects Through Sensemaking
8. Anchor new approaches in culture	Understand the Science of Safety
	Implement Teamwork and Communication

Chapter Summary

Organizations exist for different purposes that often are expressed through their values, mission, and vision statements. If used correctly, these statements define how an organization serves its stakeholders. Most successful organizations are values based and openly practice their values. Companies that fail to do so often experience conflicting priorities and frustrated employees.

Values are the foundation of an organization from which the mission and vision should be derived. Values tell employees what behaviors are appropriate and inappropriate. They form the ethical atmosphere to guide employees and should remain consistent over long periods. People need strong ethical values to remain motivated.

A mission communicates the reasons an organization exists. Most large companies have written mission statements. Mission statements should define the products or services a company delivers, its standards, the customers it serves, and the value it delivers. The best mission statements differentiate the company from others and explain why someone should choose the firm over its competitors. To motivate employees to action, a mission statement should be short enough to memorize comfortably.

A vision describes an organization's desired future state. Clearly articulated visions can also motivate and inspire employees. As with a mission, a vision should be short enough to be easily remembered so it can permeate the organizational culture and direct action.

Organizations commonly conduct gap analyses to evaluate how well they are achieving their values, mission, and vision. A gap analysis identifies areas to improve and allows goals, objectives, and action plans to be created to better meet the stated values, mission, and vision.

Companies must change to remain relevant in today's turbulent marketplace, yet many are not successful in implementing change efforts. Healthcare organizations, especially, face many challenges related to the transition to new integrative structures such as medical homes and accountable care organizations. Sustainable change must be embedded in an organization's culture and grounded in its values, mission, and vision. Change takes place through people, technology, and structure, which are interrelated. Transformational leaders must be able to motivate their people to design innovative processes and methods with their technology and craft optimal relationships through their structure.

Successful leaders manage the seeming contradiction between leading day-to-day operations and directing a vision. They learn to juggle priorities, facilitate change, and manage continuity and change simultaneously.

Resistance frequently arises during change efforts. Generally, people do not like change. Leaders must recognize that resistance is a normal part of the change process and should welcome feedback and encourage communication. Care must be taken not to display untoward actions, such as anger and threats, which commonly reinforce resistance. Leaders need to take action to communicate why the change is needed, what is expected as part of the change, what effects the change will have on behaviors and actions, and when the change must take place. If change is handled in this manner, employees are less likely to resist and more likely to remain engaged.

Chapter Resource

State of the American Workplace is a report of findings from Gallup's surveys of US employees. It explores the trend of employee engagement and the impact of engagement on performance, and discusses what companies can do to encourage engagement. The 2017 version of the report, the most recent iteration available at the time of publication, reports on data from 2015 and 2016. It can be requested at www.gallup.com/workplace/285818/state-american-workplace-report.aspx.

Chapter Questions

1. Why should values be the foundation of the mission and vision statements?
2. How do mission and vision differ?
3. Why is being values driven so important to an organization?
4. What should a mission statement contain?
5. Why should a mission statement be relatively short?
6. What is a gap analysis?
7. How does changing just one of the three components of people, technology, and structure potentially affect the other two?
8. Why do people resist change?
9. What can a leader do to lessen the organizational resistance to planned change?

Chapter Cases

Don't Lecture Me, Son
A new employee showed up for work at a prestigious southwestern US healthcare system. He had just finished a master's degree in health administration and was excited to put his new skills to use. His first assignment, which he had requested, was in the business development office. On his

first day in his new department, he was presented the health system's values, which he was told to memorize and begin living:

Health Values Statements
LOVE
Treat yourself and others with dignity and respect
Be patient and forgiving
Serve others with love

LEARN
Listen, ask, and be receptive
Improve every day
Understand the business
Create a learning environment

LEAD
Provide direction and vision
Acknowledge excellence
Demonstrate honesty
Develop relationships
Dare to make a difference
Lead by example

He wanted to make a difference and began working with others to put these tenets into practice. However, he quickly found that if he varied from written policy, which he often did not know even existed, he would either get an e-mail from his supervisor or be summoned to her office to be told he could not do what he had done and to go back and undo it. Furthermore, scheduling time with his boss was almost impossible. She told her employees that she was far too busy to meet with them. He noticed that her employees often loitered outside her office to try to speak with her while she walked to her next meeting.

After four months on the job, the new employee was called to his supervisor's office to be criticized for another of his decisions. Frustrated, when questioned he pulled out the healthcare system's values and read those under "Lead." His supervisor reddened and told him, "Don't lecture me, son!" This ended the discussion and, although he was not called into her office again, he knew his prospects at the healthcare system were bleak.

Case Questions
1. What is your appraisal of the healthcare system's values statement?
2. How did the employee notice that the values statement was not being lived?

3. What did the supervisor do to destroy the meaning of the values statement?
4. What would you do if you were the employee?

NICU Nurses

By Britt Berrett

Hospitals are filled with silos—teams, departments, groups, and divisions whose staff display similar attitudes and behaviors defined by barriers. Individuals gravitate toward creating groupings, whether according to the color of their uniform or the place of their work.

Such was the case at a large, urban tertiary referral center. With more than 900 beds and 3,000 employees, the organization had been described as siloed and dysfunctional. In response, the executive team was determined to bridge these gaps and align work with organizational goals and strategies.

While many would agree that a silo mentality creates organizational inefficiencies and confusion, there is a reason for creating silos. A silo provides a protective barrier around those who are part of the defined group. While members of a silo may bemoan overall organizational disjointedness, they find solace, satisfaction, and even pride in their individual unit's performance.

The neonatal intensive care unit (NICU) was one such example. It enjoyed superior financial performance and high patient and employee satisfaction. Unfortunately, its interest in overall organizational success ended at the doors of the unit. When asked to help other departments or participate in hospital committees, the employees were reluctant or flatly refused. The head of the NICU was also rigid about what costs were charged to her unit and what revenues were credited. For example, she was able to negotiate to have respiratory therapy revenues credited to her department, but the personnel expense was retained in the respiratory therapy department.

Assume you just became the hospital's new CEO. You are proud of the quality of the NICU but recognize that its staff's unwillingness to share and fully participate as colleagues is damaging to the hospital. You have a meeting with the NICU head in three hours and need to decide how you should approach this vexing problem.

Case Questions

1. What are the major issues involved in this case?
2. How would you approach this problem?
3. How does an organization engage siloed units and operating areas?

Follow-Up

After serious thought, the head of the NICU decided that a compelling mission and vision would provide the framework for interdepartmental dialogue and discussions that would confirm the interdependence in healthcare. The NICU properly functioned only when it collaborated and coordinated with every other area of the hospital. Hospital leaders were able to demonstrate this truth to NICU staff by creating real-life examples that tied the hospital's new mission and vision to actual behaviors.

Breaking down the barriers between silos was confirmed by all the stakeholders as necessary to meeting their collective mission and vision. Working together allowed everyone to begin to fulfill their vision for the future. This was the first step in bridging the gaps between the embedded organizational silos.

Chapter Activities

Resistance to Change

Gather in groups of 8–10 people (or divide evenly as instructed). Begin by tossing one ball randomly from person to person in the group. You must toss the ball across the group, not to someone standing next to you. Once you are comfortable with this exercise, the instructor will add another ball, and then a third; continue tossing the balls around as before. When the game is over, discuss how your emotions rose as more balls were added. How does this compare to new responsibilities, new challenges, added assignments, and change in general?

The Importance of Mission-Driven Decisions

The US Veterans Administration (VA) has faced many challenges in the past decade. For example, in 2015, the VA Office of Inspector General (OIG) found extensive, protracted delays and mismanagement at VA hospitals and clinics (Richardson 2015). The OIG (2015) also published a call for the VA's managers to make "mission-driven decisions," and stated of the Veterans Health Administration (VHA) that its

> primary mission is, and should be, the delivery of high-quality health care. VHA has several critical missions that include: (1) the provision of quality healthcare, (2) the training of tomorrow's healthcare providers, (3) the provision of healthcare to all citizens in a time of national disaster, and (4) the advancement of medical research. VA must consistently make decisions to ensure that veterans' healthcare is always the highest priority mission. Within VHA, the first test of a management decision should be an assessment of its impact upon the delivery of quality health care. (Section III-60)

This mission is complicated by the vast number of care sites—more than 1,200—across the United States and its territories. In addition, the VA is subject to seemingly constantly changing laws.

Read the OIG's 2019 report (available from www.va.gov/oig/disclosures/management-challenges.asp). Write about the factors that impede the VA's ability to make mission-based decisions. Why might these decisions and influences have caused the patient-related problems the VA has experienced?

How Organizational Culture Affects Change Management

Read the Strategy& PwC report "Culture's Role in Enabling Organizational Change" (www.strategyand.pwc.com/gx/en/insights/2011-2014/cultures-role-organizational-change.html). Write a two-page paper on the influence of culture on organizational change based on the survey findings.

Changes in Change Management

Read the Society for Human Resource Management report "Managing Organizational Change" (www.shrm.org/resourcesandtools/tools-and-samples/toolkits/pages/managingorganizationalchange.aspx). Summarize the document and discuss whether the findings remain applicable. Describe any changes taking place today that were not anticipated by the 2007 survey.

References

Ahmed, A. 2020. "Employee Reactions to Organizational Change." *Small Business. Houston Chronicle*, August 26. https://smallbusiness.chron.com/employee-reactions-organizational-change-17732.html.

Becker's Hospital Review. 2015. "How Atlantic Health Created a Healing Culture, Improved Patient Experience." August 10. www.beckershospitalreview.com/quality/how-atlantic-health-created-a-healing-culture-improved-patient-experience.html.

Bourgeois, L., I. Duhaime, and J. Stimpert. 1999. *Strategic Management: A Managerial Perspective*. Oakbrook, IL: Dryden Press.

Brooks Carthon, J. M., L. Hatfield, C. Plover, A. Dierkes, L. Davis, T. Hedgeland, A. M. Sanders, F. Visco, S. Holland, J. Ballinghoff, M. Del Guidice, and L. H. Aiken. 2019. "Association of Nurse Engagement and Nurse Staffing on Patient Safety." *Journal of Nursing Care Quality* 34 (1): 40–46. https://doi.org/10.1097/ncq.0000000000000334.

Coleman, J. 2013. "Six Components of a Great Corporate Culture." *Harvard Business Review* digital article, May 6. https://hbr.org/2013/05/six-components-of-culture.

Curry, L., E. Spatz, E. Cherlin, J. W. Thompson, D. Berg, H. Ting, C. Decker, H. M. Krumholz, and E. H. Bradley. 2011. "What Distinguishes Top-Performing Hospitals in Acute Myocardial Infarction Rates? A Qualitative Study." *Annals of Internal Medicine* 154 (6): 384–90. https://doi.org/10.7326/0003-4819-154-6-201103150-00003.

D'Angelo, M. 2018. "The Key to Better Business Culture: Establishing a Company Mission." *Business News Daily*, April 12. www.businessnewsdaily.com/3783-mission-statement.html.

DeLapa, G. 2020. "Company Mission Statements: Why They Fail and How to Fix Them." Gina DeLapa (blog). Published August 24. www.ginadelapa.com/blog/company-mission-statements-why-they-fail-and-how-to-fix-them.

Drucker, P. F. 1959. "Long-Range Planning—Challenge to Management Science." *Management Science* 5 (3): 238–49.

Ellison, A. 2020. "Florida Physician Pleads Guilty to $29M Fraud." *Becker's Hospital Review*, December 21. www.beckershospitalreview.com/legal-regulatory-issues/florida-physician-pleads-guilty-to-29m-fraud.html.

Evans, R., S. Berman, E. Burlingame, and S. Fishkin. 2020. "It's Time to Take Patient Experience Measurement and Reporting to a New Level: Next Steps for Modernizing and Democratizing National Patient Surveys." *Health Affairs* (blog), March 16. www.healthaffairs.org/do/10.1377/hblog20200309.359946/full/.

Ewenstein, B., W. Smith, and A. Sologar. 2015. "Changing Change Management." *McKinsey & Company* digital article, July 1. www.mckinsey.com/featured-insights/leadership/changing-change-management.

Harter, J. 2020. "U.S. Employee Engagement Hits New High After Historic Drop." *Workplace* (blog). *Gallup*, July 22. www.gallup.com/workplace/316064/employee-engagement-hits-new-high-historic-drop.aspx.

Holland, K. 2007. "In Mission Statements, Bizspeak and Bromides." *New York Times*, September 23. www.nytimes.com/2007/09/23/jobs/23mgmt.html.

Johnston, A., F. Lefort, and J. Tesvic. 2017. "Secrets of Successful Change Implementation." McKinsey & Company digital article, October 5. www.mckinsey.com/business-functions/operations/our-insights/secrets-of-successful-change-implementation.

Kern, H. P. 2018. "Integrating Purpose with a Mission Statement: When Structured and Applied, Quality and Performance Improvement Value Are Created." *Healthcare Executive* 33 (6): 70–71.

MacLeod, L. 2016. "Mission, Vision and Values Statements: The Physician Leader's Role." *Physician Leadership Journal* 3 (5): 18–20, 22, 24–25.

Novartis. 2020. "Our Company: We Are Reimagining Medicine." www.novartis.com/our-company.

Office of Inspector General (OIG). 2015. "Major Management Challenges." US Department of Veterans Affairs. www.va.gov/oig/pubs/VAOIG-2015-MMC.pdf.

Richardson, B. 2015. "IG Probes Uncover More Problems at VA Hospitals." *The Hill*, October 30. http://thehill.com/policy/defense/258652-ig-probes-uncover-more-problems-at-va-hospitals.

Robbins, S., R. Bergman, I. Staff, and M. Coulter. 2014. *Management*. New York: Pearson Education.

Rowe, W. G., and M. H. Nejad. 2009. "Strategic Leadership: Short-Term Stability and Long-Term Viability." *Ivey Business Journal* (September/October). http://iveybusinessjournal.com/publication/strategic-leadership-short-term-stability-and-long-term-viability/.

Sherwood, R. 2013. "Employee Engagement Drives Health Care Quality and Financial Returns." *Harvard Business Review* digital article, October 30. https://hbr.org/2013/10/employee-engagement-drives-health-care-quality-and-financial-returns.

Sull, D., S. Turconi, and C. Sull. 2020. "When It Comes to Culture, Does Your Company Walk the Talk?" *MIT Sloan Management Review*, July 21. https://sloanreview.mit.edu/article/when-it-comes-to-culture-does-your-company-walk-the-talk/.

Thomas, R. 2018. "Do Your Values Just Hang on a Wall?" *TLNT*, July 24. www.tlnt.com/do-your-values-just-hang-on-a-wall/.

US Department of Justice. 2013. "Prominent Tri-State Cardiologist Sentenced to 78 Months in Prison for Record, $19 Million Billing Fraud Scheme, Exposing Patients to Unnecessary Medical Treatment" (press release). US Attorney's Office, District of New Jersey. Published November 20. www.justice.gov/usao-nj/pr/prominent-tri-state-cardiologist-sentenced-78-months-prison-record-19-million-billing.

Walston, S. 2018. *Strategic Healthcare Management: Planning and Execution*, 2nd ed. Chicago: Health Administration Press.

Walston, S., and A. Chou. 2011. "CEO Perceptions of Organizational Consensus and Its Impact on Hospital Restructuring Outcomes." *Journal of Health Organization and Management* 25 (32): 176–94.

Wilson, J. 2014. "Managing Change Successfully." *Journal of Accountancy* 217 (4): 38–41.

Zetlin, M. 2013. "The 9 Worst Mission Statements of All Time." *Inc.com*, November 15. www.inc.com/minda-zetlin/9-worst-mission-statements-all-time.html.

CASE 1

A DILEMMA OF LOYALTIES

After working very hard to graduate with a master's degree, you find it difficult to find a position because the market is tight. You had an internship in the corporate office of a prestigious healthcare system and worked directly with their chief strategy officer. You have sent out over a hundred applications and received a handful of interviews, but no offers. Needless to say, you have become very frustrated.

One day about ten weeks after graduation, you are browsing job sites and find a small listing seeking a director of strategic planning at a hospital in a northwestern state. You apply and almost immediately are invited to interview. One month later you are hired and start your new job. You feel extremely grateful to the CEO for taking a chance on you.

Within six months you have almost completed the hospital's first strategic plan and have written successful certificate of need applications to expand the hospital. When the assistant administrator is fired six months after you were brought in, you are promoted to be the new assistant administrator.

You enjoy your new job and like working with the CEO. He is also a member of your church, so you see him during the weekdays and most Sundays. Working closely with him, you find out a lot about him that is not public information: He has type 1 diabetes. He hates to fly. He sometimes has panic attacks, especially when his diabetes is poorly controlled or he has to fly. To control his panic attacks, he takes strong sedatives before flying. At one conference you attend with him, the CEO has a severe panic attack and you have to take him to the hospital. The flight home is thankfully uneventful; he sleeps most of the way.

Two years into your position as assistant administrator, your hospital changes its sick leave policy and allows everyone to "cash out" any unused sick leave they have accrued. Most people with long tenures cash out 20 to 40 hours. You are astounded when you are given a form to approve your CEO to cash out 65 hours of unused sick leave. You know for a fact that he was ill at least 20 days a year since you have been there—you have had to cover for him at many meetings because of it.

Your CEO is also trying hard to bring new medical services to the hospital. Your hospital is the smaller of the two in town and has fewer resources. Your CEO spent months negotiating with a couple of physician groups that had their primary business and offices at the other hospital. He was convinced that all the negotiations had to be confidential to succeed, but at times you have heard him provide misleading information to the physicians that might give him an advantage. He also went to different groups in the same specialty and tried to leverage one against the other. It worked, in that he was able to move a couple of groups to your hospital last month, but many in the medical community were not happy with his style and you have started hearing complaints that he is not trustworthy.

Earlier this week you were in the CEO's office when the medical director of the emergency department called. You could tell the doctor was irate because he was so loud that the CEO moved the phone away from his ear and you could hear the doctor swear and rant. Finally, the CEO had enough, swore back at the doctor, and hung up.

This morning, three department heads came to you to tell you that your CEO is in real trouble with the hospital's 21-member board—all local appointees. The department heads tell you that your boss is "hanging by a thread," and leave after warning you not to say anything. You are conflicted; you want to keep their confidence, but you also feel a strong loyalty toward your CEO. You want to keep confidential what your department heads shared with you, but you also worry that staying quiet will disadvantage your boss, who appears to be at serious risk of losing his position. You wonder whether telling him may enable him to make corrections that might avert the loss of his job.

Case Questions
1. How did the CEO's actions influence others' perceptions of him? How did they influence your perceptions? What management theories could be applied to these perceptions?
2. What was wrong with the CEO's negotiations?
3. What do you do?
4. What ethical considerations are at play in this case?

CASE 2

THERANOS AND ELIZABETH HOLMES

Note: The following case is based on the sources cited. It is intended for case study purposes only and does not imply acceptance of any statement as fact.

Theranos was a privately owned health technology corporation. It claimed to be able to perform rapid, low-cost blood tests with tiny amounts of blood, such as from a fingerstick, using small automated machines that the company had developed. Theranos was founded in 2003 by Elizabeth Holmes, who had dropped out of Stanford University. Through its founder's exceptional self-confidence and good connections, the company raised more than $700 million from venture capitalists and private investors. At its peak in 2013 and 2014, Theranos had a $10 billion valuation and was positioned as a revolutionary breakthrough in the blood-testing market, where the US diagnostic-lab industry posts annual sales of over $70 billion. Its story is one of innovation, misplaced leadership, a toxic culture, intimidation, confirmation bias, and, perhaps, outright fraud.

Elizabeth Holmes always wanted to be successful and do something purposeful with her life. She came from a distinguished family. She attended elite private schools and excelled academically. She was admitted to Stanford in 2002 as a President's Scholar and majored in biochemistry engineering. Although she did well in school, she was much more interested in making money—lots of money.

Her first idea came during her sophomore year, when she started her company Real-Time Cures with the idea of an arm patch that would diagnose and treat medical conditions. She soon changed the name of the company to Theranos—a combination of *therapy* and *diagnosis*. She leveraged her family connections for start-up capital, impressing potential investors with her energy and her vision of applying nanotechnologies to diagnostics. Her novel patch would draw blood from the skin with microneedles, analyze it, deliver a precise amount of medication, and communicate the findings to the patient's doctor. By the end of 2004, this 19-year-old college dropout had raised $6 million to launch her company.

Holmes had great ideas, but implementing them was often impossible. Theoretically, her ideas made sense, but the science required to make them work bordered on science fiction. Eventually, she jettisoned the patch and moved to a handheld device to test blood. Her vision was that the device could allow quick monitoring of patients at home and eliminate many adverse drug reactions.

By late 2005, Theranos had 24 employees, a prototype machine called Theranos 1.0, and an aggressive business model predicting rapid growth. The company began to attract attention. However, the prototype was more of a mock-up, and the company had difficulty making it a functioning device. Development was stifled by the lack of communication between teams. One group was trying to resolve the chemistry issues, while another worked independently on the engineering microfluidics aspects. Holmes liked to compartmentalize information and did not encourage communication across the company. She often was the only one with the full picture of the anticipated product. Holmes also controlled development. For instance, the developers wanted to increase the amount of blood they could use per test, but she insisted on using only a fingerstick.

As progress lagged, Holmes demanded that people put in more time. She wanted the engineering department to run 24 hours a day, seven days a week. When the head of engineering refused, Holmes told him the company was all that mattered. She then set up a competing engineering department and staffed it with new hires. Ultimately, the second engineering team designed a better product using existing technology, and Holmes fired everyone in the first group.

Demonstrations of their technology often went poorly. In 2007, Theranos had a demonstration for Pfizer, one of the largest pharmaceutical companies, where they struggled to draw blood samples from cancer patients and obtain rapid results. Holmes wanted to celebrate, but her engineering teams had deep concerns.

Holmes's treatment of her employees led to high employee turnover and poor morale. In late summer 2007, she called in the FBI to investigate former employees for stealing intellectual property. She required all employees and visitors to sign extensive nondisclosure agreements. She also cracked down on employees transmitting or potentially transmitting information; one employee was fired for putting a USB drive into his computer without prior approval from the head of IT. Chat ports and other communications were blocked. One employee commented that the company had lost its business objective—instead of trying to create amazing products, it was spending too much time trying to prevent suspected illegal activities. Assistants kept track of when employees arrived and departed, so Holmes would know exactly how much time people worked. She bought dinner for employees, but did not provide the dinners until at least 8:00 p.m., reasoning that if people stayed for dinner they would be at the office until at least 10:00 p.m.

Holmes was captivated by Steve Jobs. She liked to call her product the iPod of healthcare and recruited several of Apple's employees. She even started to speak and dress like him, wearing black turtlenecks and black slacks most days. She also began sipping green kale shakes.

More disturbing to some was the contrast between Holmes's rosy revenue projections and her promised deals, which almost inevitably failed to materialize. When asked about the delays, she always had excuses—legal reviews, contracts not available, product fixes needed, and so on. However, anyone who questioned Holmes, from board members to employees, could be shown the door. Consistently, Holmes told those who even expressed constructive criticism that Theranos was going to be a great company and if they were not happy with her leadership, they should find somewhere else to be.

Holmes demanded absolute loyalty from her employees. If she sensed that she did not have this, she could turn on people in an instant. In one two-and-a-half-year period she fired about 30 people, and then let go of another 20 when she dismissed the engineering group. At times she built dossiers on people she was planning to fire to use as leverage over them. If she got angry with someone or thought they were disloyal, she would stop speaking to or even looking at them. She quickly fired her first chief financial officer when he asked about test results that had supposedly been falsified. Some felt that a culture of dishonesty existed, but could not be openly discussed. One departing executive wrote to Holmes, "Lying is a disgusting habit, and it flows through the conversations here like it's our own currency. The cultural disease here is what we should be curing" (Carreyrou 2020, 52).

Problems kept cropping up that kept the product from working, but Holmes would not give her developers time to fix them. The problems were accentuated when she hired a professional sales manager, a position she had previously held. None of the large pharmaceutical companies would make significant purchases unless Theranos could demonstrate that its equipment worked. Yet, during many demonstrations the equipment malfunctioned. In 2006, during a demonstration in Switzerland for Novartis, the malfunctions were severe enough that Holmes had to fabricate the results. When Theranos repeated the tests with Novartis in 2008, thinking the problems were corrected, the equipment registered error messages in front of the executives. The sales team was mortified, but Holmes blamed it on a minor technical glitch.

In 2009, Holmes hired Ramesh "Sunny" Balwani to be her second-in-command, the chief operating officer. Balwani had no healthcare experience and was aggressive, boastful, haughty, and demeaning toward employees. Twenty years Holmes's senior, he flaunted his wealth and drove a Lamborghini. What Holmes failed to tell her employees and board was that Balwani was also her live-in boyfriend. When this was discovered, Holmes lied about it and told her employees the relationship was over. Balwani became the hatchet man; the company-wide code for a firing was "Sunny disappeared him."

Balwani tended to yell at people for insignificant reasons. In one instance, a scientist purchased green polo shirts for his group without consulting Balwani, and a yelling match ensued. Shortly thereafter the scientist wrote a letter of resignation and went into Holmes's office to present it. Balwani was there and on reading the letter threw it back at the scientist, refusing to accept it. After further yelling, Balwani had the scientist escorted out of the building. Other employees were likewise immediately removed from the building and told not to communicate with their former colleagues.

Some of the companies Theranos initially targeted, including Pfizer, dropped Theranos because of underwhelming results. During the 2009 swine flu pandemic, Theranos targeted selling its equipment to test for this flu even though it could not prove that using blood would diagnose positive cases. Theranos continued this pattern, approaching other potential customers with promises that it was not yet prepared to fulfill. In 2010, it made a presentation to Walgreens to propose placing its machines in all Walgreens stores. Walgreens liked the idea and planned to commit $50 million to place Theranos machines in 30 to 90 stores where, with a prick of a finger, customers could receive results in less than an hour. Theranos representatives claimed the company's technology could perform 192 different blood tests, when all it had was a research lab that could not meet its promises. The Walgreens partnership moved forward, as its CEO insisted, even though Theranos refused to validate its tests; he did not want to lose a competitive edge over CVS if it chose to decline Theranos's proposal. To encourage Walgreens, Theranos stated that its system had been comprehensively validated by 10 of the largest 15 pharma companies, which was not true.

At the same time, Theranos was developing a partnership with Safeway. Before long, Safeway also signed a deal that loaned Theranos $30 million and refurbished its stores to offer blood testing. Again, Theranos promised to perform hundreds of tests on fingerstick blood samples, but its machines could only do very few.

To try to meet its commitments, Theranos launched an effort in 2010 to create a new device that could become its minilab and add the tests it had promised Walgreens and Safeway. Instead of inventing new technology, this effort involved miniaturizing existing technology. Nevertheless, its development was also fraught with delays and functional problems. By December, Holmes was chastising her employees for not completing the minilab. She admonished them that "if anyone here believes you are not working on the best thing humans have ever built or if you're cynical, then you should leave" (Carreyrou 2020, 107).

Eventually a prototype was developed, but Balwani wanted to immediately build 100 more without testing it. The engineers pushed back, which infuriated Balwani. Holmes continued to publicly rebuke employees and tell them to leave if they were not fully committed. Many did. They had to sign another nondisclosure agreement when they quit.

The Safeway partnership proceeded, but delays and inconsistencies occurred. Rather than taking small drops of blood, Theranos was also taking traditional needle draws for its tests. It fell two years behind in meeting the planned openings in Safeway stores. The tests that Safeway did compare also had wide variations in its results at other labs. The first blood testing site was established at Safeway's Pleasanton clinic in 2012, but Theranos continued to delay the launch at other stores. By this time Safeway had invested $100 million to reconfigure its stores for the blood testing sites. Finally, in 2013, Safeway's CEO was forced into retirement and its agreement with Theranos unwound.

Not to be deterred, Holmes contracted with an advertising agency for $6 million a year to create a prominent website and drum up positive press. Initial claims on the new website seemed far-fetched. The site stated the company could perform over 800 tests on just one drop of blood, which was more accurate than traditional lab tests. The website also stated that Theranos's tests were approved by the Food and Drug Administration (FDA), could be completed in less than 30 minutes, and were endorsed by key medical centers—all of which was false. Holmes also claimed that Theranos was receiving funding from the US Army, which was using her technology on the Afghanistan battlefield, which was not true. The evening before the website was to go live Holmes had a three-hour conference call, which did result in the removal of the most blatant untruths.

By 2013, Holmes and Balwani considered anyone who voiced a concern or objection a cynic and naysayer. Sycophants were promoted and those who voiced concerns were marginalized or fired. Theranos also employed dozens of Indian nationals, who were on H-1B visas and had to keep their jobs to stay in the country. Balwani monitored them closely and expected them to be available days, nights, and weekends. He checked security logs daily to see when they entered and left. At 7:30 each evening he would drop by engineering to see who was still at their desks. However, Balwani was out of his expertise with the engineers. He did not understand their vocabulary or their work.

The minilab's development was crippled by Holmes's insistence that it remain very small yet perform a wide variety of immunoassays, general chemistry assays, hematology assays, and DNA assays. The minilab could also only process one blood sample at a time, which was fine if there was only one patient. However, if there were many patient tests to be performed this would make the testing time very long. Many other problems plagued its development, including its robotic arms, misaligned spectrophotometers, and exploding centrifuges. All of these could have probably been fixed in time, but Holmes had made promises and needed the minilab available immediately. She had to meet Walgreens' contractual obligations, as the Safeway contract was falling apart. Nevertheless, the minilab was not ready.

Holmes decided to use the company's prior equipment for Walgreens stores, but it did not offer the number of tests required at the sites. To meet the launch deadline, she decided to supplement the first-generation Theranos equipment with commercial lab equipment from Siemens. Since Theranos was still only using a pinprick of blood, the blood sample would have to be diluted twice to be tested on the Siemens equipment, a process that could produce very high error rates. But no matter what, Holmes was going to launch her testing in Walgreens. When pressed by key employees, Holmes stated that she had to move ahead because she had promised Walgreens. As a result, some of these key employees resigned.

The resignations shook Holmes and Balwani. They called an "all-hands" meeting the next day and Holmes angrily told her employees that she was building a religion and if they did not believe in it, they should leave. Balwani followed up more bluntly and told them that if they were not prepared to demonstrate complete devotion and loyalty—there was the door.

At the same time, Holmes began a blitz of national publicity. She and the company were first featured in the *Wall Street Journal* on September 7, 2013, to coincide with their opening in Walgreens stores. She was able to obtain national attention because of her network of famous connections. Her board included George Shultz, former US Secretary of State, Labor, and Treasury, who introduced other big-name board members including James Mattis, Henry Kissinger, William Perry, and Sam Nunn. All were effusive in their praise for Holmes. Shultz stated she had a purity of motivation and was trying to make the world better. The positive press increased venture capital interest in Theranos.

Holmes and Balwani continued to overpromise the capabilities of their existing equipment. They claimed to have mastered the use of one drop of blood to run 70 different blood tests simultaneously. They also showed very rosy financial projections, anticipating earning $165 million in 2014 and $1.08 billion by 2015. Investments flowed in, and in a short time Theranos had a market value of about $10 billion and Holmes, who owned more than half the company, was worth about $5 billion.

Fame soon followed. In June 2014, Holmes was featured on the cover of *Fortune* magazine with an article titled "This CEO Is Out for Blood." She was compared to Bill Gates and Steve Jobs. *Forbes*, *USA Today*, *Fast Company*, and *Glamour* followed with positive press. She became the youngest person to win the Horatio Alger Award, was appointed by President Obama as a US ambassador for global entrepreneurship, and was invited to join the Harvard Medical School board of fellows.

Holmes embraced the trappings of fame. She always had two bodyguards with her, employed a personal chef, and flew in a private Gulfstream. Theranos now employed over 500 people and planned to move into beautiful new facilities. Her publicity firm began video ads in markets where Theranos was being launched, featuring Holmes in her customary black turtlenecks.

Things, however, were not well with the employees in charge of testing. Some knew that their testing did not make sense and could be producing false results. In addition, employees were concerned that Theranos could be breaking the law by falsifying results to obtain its required laboratory accreditation. Employees who raised these issues were either fired or threatened with lengthy litigation. Outside Holmes's control, a few blogs and articles sounded skeptical notes. A disgruntled employee was reported to have published the following on the employer review site Glassdoor (Carreyrou 2020, 250):

> How to make money at Theranos:
> 1. Lie to venture capitalists.
> 2. Lie to doctors, patients, FDA, CDC, government. While also committing highly unethical and immoral (and possibly illegal) acts.

Finally, *Wall Street Journal* reporter John Carreyrou decided to investigate. His reporting uncovered the fraud and illegal activity at Theranos, and despite constant threats of litigation against the journalist and his sources, a series of unflattering articles were published by the *Journal*. The first, published in October 2015, highlighted Theranos's challenges as a start-up and pointed out that most of its lab tests were being performed on commercially purchased equipment (Carreyrou 2015).

Holmes publicly claimed it was all a smear campaign and said this always happened when someone tried to change the world for good. She also said that it was sad that the *Journal* could not get its facts straight and that they were listening to disgruntled employees and competitors. As the fraud became evident, Holmes fired Balwani and broke up with him, blaming him for the company's failures. Theranos eventually admitted that none of the tens of thousands of tests it had run in the prior two years could be validated. On June 12, 2016, Walgreens terminated its contract with Theranos. Bad press followed from *Wired*, the *Financial Times*, and other publications. Theranos's investors then filed multiple suits that resulted in settlements totaling millions. The US Securities and Exchange Commission (2018) also charged Theranos with "an elaborate, years-long fraud" and Holmes was forced to relinquish her voting control of the company, give back much of her stock, and pay a $500,000 penalty. She was also prohibited from serving as an officer or director of any public company until 2029. As of 2021, Holmes and Balwani are both awaiting federal trial on charges of conspiracy and wire fraud and, if convicted, could face years in prison for their activities.

Case Questions

1. Theranos prided itself on being a disruptive, innovative company. What went wrong with this? Why did it not achieve this?
2. What factors contributed to the poor company culture at Theranos?
3. What kind of loyalty should an employee owe in this situation? What actions did Theranos take that destroyed employee loyalty?
4. How could a mission and vision statement have improved the behaviors at Theranos?
5. What human resource policies contributed to the problems at Theranos?
6. How did nepotism fit into Theranos' problems? Why is this type of consensual relationship inappropriate in a firm?

References

Carreyrou, J. 2020. *Bad Blood*. New York: Vintage Books.

———. 2015. "Hot Startup Theranos Has Struggled with Its Blood-Test Technology." *Wall Street Journal*. Published October 16. www.wsj.com/articles/theranos-has-struggled-with-blood-tests-1444881901.

US Securities and Exchange Commission. 2018. "Theranos, CEO Holmes, and Former President Balwani Charged with Massive Fraud" (press release). March 14. www.sec.gov/news/press-release/2018-41.

CASE 3

THE INJURED MIGRANT WORKER

You are the CEO of a 300-bed regional hospital. As is common in most rural areas, there are many migrant workers, who work for farmers and ranchers. This population often does not have legal documentation and, as a result, most employers pay them poorly and almost never provide any type of health insurance. If injured at work, most migrant workers will either present at the local hospital for care or self-treat. If badly injured, they frequently end up returning to their country of origin.

One day your chief medical director (CMO) and chief financial officer (CFO) come to your office to let you know that three weeks ago Juan Lopez was admitted to the hospital. Juan was working on a farm 150 miles from your hospital and had a tragic and traumatic accident that almost killed him. Your hospital was the closest regional facility that could save him. In the past two weeks the doctors were able to stabilize him, but he is now paralyzed below the neck and will need constant rehabilitation for the next four to five months. Juan lacks health insurance and his employer refuses to take any responsibility for Juan's expenses, which is his legal right. Juan's hospital bill is now approaching $200,000, which he would never be able to pay if he were healthy.

Your CMO and CFO state that Juan now needs to be transferred to a rehabilitation facility, services which your hospital does not provide. Every rehabilitation facility in the state has been contacted (along with a few outside the state) to see if it would accept Juan as a patient. Almost all have refused the transfer, but two said they would agree only if your hospital would guarantee the charges for Juan. Your CFO does not recommend guaranteeing a patient's bill, as this would set a bad precedent and Juan's care might last for years. On the other hand, your CMO feels strongly that the hospital needs to ensure that Juan receives quality patient care.

The CFO does come up with another option. He has been in contact with the Mexican Embassy, which suggested that the patient could be sent back to his family. This would require the hospital to pay for a medical transport flight to the capitol of the state where Juan's family lives. The family is very poor and probably cannot afford the constant care that Juan will need for the rest of his life. However, how long can your hospital keep Juan as an inpatient? What obligation does your hospital have to Juan? He is far from his family. Would it not be best for him to go back to Mexico to be with them?

Case Questions

1. How would you make such a decision? What factors should you consider?
2. What cultural considerations are involved?
3. What ethical principles would you apply to this situation?
4. What would you do? Why?

CASE 4

THE OVERUTILIZING ORTHOPEDIST

You are the CEO of a 312-bed hospital, which is prominent in its community. The only competition you have in your market area is a surgery center and a short-stay hospital. Both facilities are owned by physicians and highly profitable. All these physicians, mostly surgeons, are also on your medical staff and split their business between their owned facilities and your hospital.

One of the investors is an orthopedist, Dr. C., who is extremely aggressive with his surgeries. The joke about him is that you should not see him for a sore throat, as you will end up with knee surgery. He is in his late thirties, drives a very expensive car, and lives in a 20,000-square-foot house with its own ballroom. His father is also a practicing orthopedist in your community and is highly respected. The father has always been rather conservative in his clinical practice and has served in many volunteer roles in the community and at your hospital.

Recently, a few of your physicians have approached you with their concerns that the younger orthopedist has been performing unnecessary surgeries. Two of these doctors are also orthopedists, but in a competing group of surgeons. Given the concerns, your chief medical officer (CMO) has spoken with Dr. C. He defended himself by pointing to his recent training, his excellent outcomes, and the professional jealousy that other physicians exhibit toward him. Your CMO did not feel that her conversation had any effect on Dr. C., but you noticed that Dr. C. began to do more of his surgeries in the physician-owned facilities. Those facilities, however, are not equipped to perform total joints and more complicated spinal surgeries. In addition, Dr. C. will not take Medicaid and most Medicare cases to the physician-owned locations.

Dr. C. has also announced that he will be soon be expanding his office equipment to include an MRI. Some studies have shown that the likelihood of spinal surgery increases 34 percent if a surgeon owns an MRI. Spinal surgery reimbursement is some of the highest for orthopedic procedures compared to others, and the number of spinal fusions in the US jumped 70 percent from 2001 to 2011, making spinal surgeries more frequent than even hip replacements. Dr. C. already performs more spinal surgeries than any other physician at your hospital and you are worried that these might increase.

You have asked your CMO to develop a plan to evaluate Dr. C's surgeries. She is willing to do this but warns you that he has many friends in the community and that his father may also be highly offended that his son is investigated. She has approached the state licensing bureau, but it has indicated that without specific complaints of poor outcomes it would be unable to address the issue for six months to a year.

Case Questions

1. What leadership framework could be applied to this case?
2. How are Dr. C's motivations contrary to the hospital's?
3. What would you do to minimize the potential conflict in this case, yet resolve the issue?
4. What are your options and what would you recommend?

CASE 5

THE BUSY REGIONAL VICE PRESIDENT

Leo was a busy man. He supervised 21 hospitals located in eight different US states. He ran a large hospital earlier in his career, so he felt comfortable giving his CEOs advice about running their operations. Leo felt, even though he never explicitly said it, that the people who reported to him would not work as hard as he would, and that he would need to "ride" them to get things done. This was a difficult time for his company, as it had just been created through an employee stock ownership plan, and cash flows were extremely important. Leo was charged with increasing the profitability of each of his hospitals and generating greater cash flows.

Leo was so busy that often he did not have time to speak directly to his CEOs. Consequently, most of his interactions with them took the form of memos, e-mails, and reports that he required his CEOs to produce. These reports allowed him to understand the operations of the hospitals, from the current state of accounts payable to staffing ratios. If he did not understand a report or had an underlying question, he would immediately call the CEO who produced the report. Because Leo was so busy, he frequently reviewed the reports late at night or on the weekend. He had the home and cell phone numbers of all the CEOs, and when he called he expected them to pick up and answer his questions. Although he sometimes felt overwhelmed, he also felt compelled to stay heavily involved in the day-to-day decision-making, lest the organization's profit goals not be met. To this end, he sent out the following e-mail to the hospital CEOs:

> All — In order to improve our financial situation, I would like each of you to begin weekly monitoring of your employees' work-hours by unit. We have already established "work-hour/statistic" goals for each of your major units that will be met by the end of the year. However, I want you to review the work-hour/statistic by unit each week and compare it to the existing goals. Deviations should be reported on Form 135, e-mailed earlier by the regional financial officer. If any of your units is 10 percent or more above the set goal, then I want you to call and explain the reasons for this variation.
>
> Also, starting next week, any adjustments in salary, vacation leaves of more than two weeks, capital expenditures over $10,000, and nonbudgeted staff

expenses must be approved by me. I would prefer speaking with you about these before I approve them.

If there are any general questions about these requests, I will address them at our monthly conference call with all of you.

Thank you — Leo

This e-mail caused some confusion among the CEOs. Although work-hour/statistic goals had been established for most units, many specialized units did not have set goals. Also, several of the hospitals experienced wide seasonal variation in their activity levels. Hospitals in the Southwest and Southern California were almost always busier in the winter, and conversely, those in the Northern Intermountain Area were slower. Because most hospital units had base, minimal staffing levels, the low number of patients always made them go over the annual set goals. Would they need to explain all this each week?

Furthermore, what information would be needed for vacation requests? Currently, the CEOs did not get reports of requested vacations. How could they easily obtain this information? And then, they really did not understand what "nonbudgeted staff expenditures" meant. Several CEOs raised these questions in e-mails to Leo, but they did not hear back from him until the regional conference call.

During the conference call with all 21 CEOs, Leo lectured them about the importance of meeting budget and warned that those coming in under budget would be rewarded whereas those over budget would be "dealt with." This last statement was pretty clear, especially considering three CEOs in the region had been fired in the past six months. After his 25-minute monologue, Leo asked if there were any questions. One brave CEO asked what specific matters Leo would like to be called about. Leo retorted that he expected good CEOs to recognize important variations and know when to confer with him. That was the last question asked, and the conference call ended.

Leo was busy, but soon he became busier. CEOs began calling him immediately about variations in their budget. Queries related to an employee requiring a bone marrow transplant (the company was self-insured), an unbudgeted physician recruitment fee, unexpected repair costs for broken radiology equipment, and many others flooded his office. Now he was so busy that he was unable to receive the CEOs' calls. In addition, he wanted to review each hospital's information before taking its CEO's call. Therefore, his secretary would not connect the calls but instead gathered information so that he could call back later. Leo refused to set up a time for the return calls, because his schedule was too hectic.

Return calls seemed to be made randomly. Sometimes he returned the call promptly, but frequently he called back four to six hours after the

CEO's initial call—and occasionally as much as two days later. This structure may have benefited Leo, but it was problematic for the CEOs because the return calls often caught them in inconvenient locations, and sometimes they did not have the details needed to respond adequately. Still, the CEOs felt obligated to take the calls because if they told his secretary they were busy, she would inform them that he would call them back, returning them to the randomized calling queue. Consequently, they often appeared unprepared, and some fell out of Leo's favor.

As the end of the year approached, only about half of the hospitals were achieving their budgeted profits. Leo was preparing the CEOs' annual evaluations. He set up a time for all of them to fly to meet him at the regional headquarters. This would be the first time in five or six months that the CEOs had seen him in person and, some CEOs thought, the only time they could fully clarify his directives, offer suggestions, and share concerns. However, the annual performance evaluations were not the best time for them to communicate with Leo. His disposition was curt, and minimal time was set aside for the evaluations. Each evaluation was scheduled for one hour, and seven evaluations were scheduled each day for three days. For the fourth day, Leo had scheduled a regional meeting. Many wondered if they would still be employed by then. Most of the CEOs felt very frustrated, and many polished their resumes.

Case Questions

1. From a communication perspective, what are the basic problems in this case?
2. What communication problems emanate from the CEOs? From Leo?
3. How is feedback lacking, and what could be done to improve it?
4. How does trust, or lack thereof, affect the CEOs' ability to communicate?
5. How did Leo express his underlying belief in theory X?
6. What occurred to diminish the CEOs' job satisfaction and organizational commitment? What should Leo do to improve these?

CASE 6

THALIDOMIDE AND GRÜNENTHAL

Note: The following case is based on the sources cited. It is intended for case study purposes only and does not imply acceptance of any statement as fact.

By 1968, more than 10,000 babies had been born with deformities or had died because of a drug called thalidomide. The drug, if taken early in pregnancy, could interfere with fetal development and cause children to be born with shortened, malformed, or nonexistent limbs. Some were also born blind or with damaged internal organs. Yet the German company that created and marketed the drug, Chemie Grünenthal, still claimed it was blameless and steadfastly denied any responsibility. During the criminal hearing in 1968 the company brought 40 lawyers and used political subterfuge to close the proceedings—Grünenthal directors met in secret with the German federal health ministry to obtain high-level political intervention to stop the trial. The result was immunity for Grünenthal and a paltry settlement of about $22,000 for each child to manage a lifetime of severe disability. A foundation was also established by the German parliament to which Grünenthal contributed 100 million Deutsche marks (Evans 2014).

Grünenthal's history portrays a culture of indifference and exploitation. Before 1946 it produced "soaps, perfumes, and cleaning fluids" (Evans 2014). After World War II, it moved into pharmaceuticals. What set the company apart was the background of many of the scientists who worked there. Key scientists and leaders included several individuals who had performed experiments in Hitler's death camps. One had invented sarin nerve gas and had been "in charge of the construction of the Auschwitz IG Farben plant" (Evans 2014). Another experimented with live prisoners in labor camps in Poland. Another was one of the top Nazis leading their racial hygiene and eugenics programs.

In 1957, Grünenthal launched thalidomide as an over-the-counter "wonder drug" for sleeplessness and morning sickness. The company claimed that the drug was completely safe and heavily promoted it in 46 countries. Advertising touted thalidomide as "completely non-poisonous . . . astonishingly safe . . . fully harmless . . . completely safe for pregnant women and nursing mothers without any adverse effects on mother and child"

(Evans 2014). Interestingly, Grünenthal appears to have performed minimal research on the drug and no experiments on the adverse impact on embryos.

Grünenthal was consistent in its handling of reports of adverse effects. Anyone who raised concerns was told that Grünenthal had never heard of any reports of such problems, even though it continued to receive them. Adults taking thalidomide suffered severe nerve damage. When the head of sales at Grünenthal, one of the former Nazi doctors, received concerns from his UK drug distributor in 1960 regarding the alarming reports in the medical literature, he brushed them off and told him to sit back and enjoy the revenues. At the time, the head of sales already knew of 150 cases of nerve damage, and over a million people in Germany were taking the drug daily. In 1960, about 14.6 tons of thalidomide were sold just in Germany (Rehman, Arfons, and Lazarus 2011). The sales director did add that he had heard of occasional reactions, but said they vanished after people stopped taking thalidomide. Grünenthal did take some action then: It hired a private investigator to surveil the complaining patients and doctors (Evans 2014).

Grünenthal continued to sell thalidomide even after receiving proof that it caused terrible birth defects (Evans 2014). Although the company continued to deny that it knew that drugs could reach a fetus, it had been an accepted fact back in the 1940s. The German immunity deal seemed to protect the company across many countries. In Australia and New Zealand, it would take until 2013 to reach a settlement for more than a hundred victims. Victims in Spain were still fighting Grünenthal for compensation in 2014, and the company consistently refused to contribute to compensation funds outside of Germany. Grünenthal also continues to state that its initial research on thalidomide met "the standards prevailing in the pharmaceutical industry at that time" (Evans 2014).

Thalidomide was never approved for use during pregnancy in the United States, primarily due to the efforts of Dr. Frances Kelsey, the US Food and Drug Administration officer assigned to review the drug application. Even though she was under extreme pressure from the drug company, she denied approval based on a lack of safety data in 1960 (McFadden 2015). The drug was withdrawn from most markets in 1961. Today thalidomide is used for treating bone marrow cancers (specifically multiple myeloma) in the United States and carries warnings not to be used during pregnancy (Lupkin 2012; Rehman, Arfons, and Lazarus 2011).

Case Questions
1. How does a company's culture affect how the individuals in the company react to bad news?
2. What ethical issues arose in this case?
3. What subcategories of justice did or did not occur in this case?

4. How did the company's goals contribute to the safety problems?
5. How did the company address the conflict caused by its actions?

References

Evans, H. 2014. "Thalidomide: How Men Who Blighted Lives of Thousands Evaded Justice." *The Guardian*, November 14. www.theguardian.com/society/2014/nov/14/-sp-thalidomide-pill-how-evaded-justice.

Lupkin, S. 2012. "Pharmaceutical Company Grunenthal Apologizes 50 Years After Drug Pulled Off Market." *ABC News*, September 1. https://abcnews.go.com/Health/drug-manufacturer-apologizes-thalidomide-victims/story?id=17135262.

McFadden, R. D. 2015. "Frances Oldham Kelsey, Who Saved U.S. Babies from Thalidomide, Dies at 101." *New York Times*, August 7. www.nytimes.com/2015/08/08/science/frances-oldham-kelsey-fda-doctor-who-exposed-danger-of-thalidomide-dies-at-101.html.

Rehman, W., L. M. Arfons, and H. M. Lazarus. 2011. "The Rise, Fall and Subsequent Triumph of Thalidomide: Lessons Learned in Drug Development." *Therapeutic Advances in Hematology* 2 (5): 291–308. https://dx.doi.org/10.1177/2040620711413165.

CASE 7

PROSPECT MEDICAL: IMPERFECT INCENTIVES DRIVE ACTIONS NOT CONSISTENT WITH MISSION

Note: The following case is based on the sources cited. It is intended for case study purposes only and does not imply acceptance of any statement as fact.

Prospect Medical Holdings in 2020 consisted of 17 hospitals, clustered mostly in California and the northeastern United States. According to the firm's website, it provides care to over 435,000 members in its networks, which comprise more than 11,000 medical professionals. Prospect's business model focuses on providing care through health management organizations, hospitals, and networks of employed or independent practice physicians. Its mission statement states:

> We are hospitals and affiliated medical groups working for the benefit of every person who comes to us for care. Our comprehensive networks aim to provide coordinated, personalized care.

Established in 1996, the company expanded into hospital ownership in 2007 with the acquisition of Alta Healthcare Systems, which transformed it from a business exclusively providing medical group management services to a provider of coordinated regional healthcare services.

The company posts the following standards on the Mission page of its website:

- Striving for the best possible patient outcomes
- Maintaining the highest standards of patient safety
- Acting with integrity at all times
- Promoting open communication
- Collaborating to better serve the healthcare needs of our communities

However, in September 2020, ProPublica published an investigative report by Peter Elkind and Doris Burke that portrayed Prospect Medical in a different light ("Investors Extracted $400 Million From a Hospital Chain That Sometimes Couldn't Pay for Medical Supplies or Gas for Ambulances"). Prospect Medical was purchased by a private equity firm, Leonard Green & Partners, in 2010, and in the next decade made huge profits for the owners while, according to the ProPublica investigation, providing questionable care for its patients. According to Elkind and Burke's reporting, "Leonard Green extracted $400 million in dividends and fees" from the company, with two of the executives earning over $220 million during these ten years.

Most of Prospect's patients have low incomes. Most patients (80 percent) are covered by Medicare or Medicaid. Prospect's facilities are generally old and consistently suffer from lack of supplies and functional equipment. Water leaks were found in some facilities, and dirty, corroded surgical instruments were found in another. Only one of its 17 hospitals ranked above the bottom 17 percent in US government surveys.

> At the company's flagship Los Angeles hospital, persistent elevator breakdowns sometimes require emergency room nurses to wheel patients on gurneys across a public street as a security guard attempts to halt traffic. Paramedics for Prospect's hospital near Philadelphia told ProPublica that they've repeatedly gone to fuel up their ambulances only to come away empty at the pump: Their hospital-supplied gas cards were rejected because Prospect hadn't paid its bill. A similar penury afflicts medical supplies. "Say we need 4x4 sponges, dressing for a patient, IV fluids," said Leslie Heygood, a veteran registered nurse at one of Prospect's Pennsylvania hospitals, "we might not have it on the shelf because it's on 'credit hold' because they haven't paid their creditors." (Elkind and Burke 2020)

Prospect Medical denied these accusations and told ProPublica reporters that its leaders had "kept their commitments, abided by the law, provided good patient care and invested hundreds of millions of dollars, saving many failing hospitals and preserving thousands of jobs."

Yet in 2014, a patient's wife sued after a wet ceiling tile fell on her. In 2015, state inspectors shut down all elective surgeries for eight days at Prospect's largest California hospital, citing (according to ProPublica) "a widespread pattern of poor infection control and sterility . . . from inadequate heating and cooling systems." An elevator was left unrepaired for almost a year. In 2019, the California attorney general formally charged the company with knowingly mixing pharmaceuticals in an area that was supposed to be sterile but was heavily contaminated with fungal and bacterial organisms. In 2020, a large mold formation destroyed the wall near a nurses' station.

The COVID-19 pandemic heightened many of Prospect's problems. One emergency room doctor died of the disease after claiming he had to reuse a single-use mask for four days. In one psychiatric unit, 19 of the 21 patients contracted COVID-19; six died. Nurses in one California hospital could not obtain proper protective gear and resorted to plastic garbage bags instead.

The challenge of whether profits and quality medical care can jointly exist is not new. However, this case is somewhat unique, as the company's primary patients are among the most vulnerable—people with low incomes and few resources, older adults—whose healthcare is primarily paid for by the government. In addition, private equity firms have traditionally used this business model to strip cash out of acquired firms, load them down with debt, drastically reduce expenses, then resell the company to a new buyer in about five years.

Leonard Green has been able to do all of that except resell. Prospect's assets are so loaded with debt that Leonard Green has not been able to find a buyer, despite placing Prospect on the market three times.

On joining the company in the early 2000s, the leadership team for the initial hospital group, Alta, almost immediately began a cost-slashing campaign. Critical equipment and supplies became "routinely unavailable" as bills had not been paid, checks bounced, and the company regularly changed vendors to avoid making payments. In some hospitals employees even had to buy their own toilet paper.

By 2007 the company began to look much better on paper because of aggressive financial adjustments—some later found illegal. Prospect Medical then bought Alta, but the two top executives from Alta took control of Prospect Medical. CEO Sam Lee continued to make $2 million a year plus bonuses, and holds 20 percent of shares and stock options. The leaders were demanding and unrelenting. They ran through many executives who reported to them. They would scream at subordinates and grill them over small issues, so badly that some reported breaking down and crying.

Stronger controls were established. They found cheaper sources for supplies, implemented "real-time" monitoring of hospital staff, and "slow-walked" every vendor payment. Clearly, the bottom line was paramount and quality of care was secondary. Quality was delegated to local operations and had little or no corporate oversight.

In 2010, Leonard Green spent $205 million to buy Prospect Medical, retaining the key executives. In 2012, Prospect Medical began to pay out profits in dividends to the private equity firm. That year, $188 million was distributed.

Prospect Medical's executives believed they could copy their business model in other markets and began looking for other acquisitions, telling prospects that they were in the business of saving troubled hospitals and had a long-term perspective. By 2015 they had committed to buy three hospital systems on the East Coast for more than $500 million and spend millions more on pension and capital improvements. At that time, they had about $1 billion in annual revenues and $108 million in profits.

Some of their acquisitions did not last long, however. In 2012 they purchased Nix Health System in San Antonio. By 2015, they had fired the system's longtime CEO, and they cycled through four more CEOs in the next four years. Finally, in 2019 Prospect Medical shut down all of Nix's operations, laying off about a thousand employees.

In 2015, the private equity firm attempted to cash out and sell to another firm. Although it had final bids from Bain Capital and CVC Capital Partners, Prospect Medical decided to hold off to get a higher price later.

Improper billing problems began to arise. In 2016, at one of Prospect's California operations, an audit showed the firm had improperly inflated billings; it had to repay $22.6 million. Other billing issues arose in payments for Medicare Advantage plans, resulting in almost $3 million in refunds. Three other lawsuits have charged fraudulent billing, with some staff claiming that they had to bill Medicare for treating multiple patients at a time and others saying they had to admit patients to special units even though they did not require hospitalization.

Prospect's East Coast hospitals also had serious problems. In 2019, the Connecticut hospitals lost their accreditation from the Joint Commission and still sought to aggressively cut costs by reducing nurses' vacation time and cutting pension benefits for all part-time employees. Staffing shortages regularly forced delays in scheduled medical procedures and, because of unpaid bills, the hospitals began to experience crucial supply shortages and vendors would refuse to fix broken equipment.

By 2018, Prospect had distributed $645 million in dividends: about $386 million to Leonard Green's investors; $128 million to Prospect Medical's CEO; and $131 million to other Prospect Medical executives. Leonard Green continued trying to sell the company but was unsuccessful because of Prospect's deteriorating financial situation. By early 2019, Prospect Medical required an emergency $41 million loan from Leonard Green. As a result, its debt was downgraded to junk status. Needing capital, in late 2019 Prospect Medical sold its land and buildings in a leaseback transaction to raise $1.55 billion, much of which was used to pay off loans. It basically replaced debt with rent payments.

In October 2019, with the actual value of the company a pittance of what it was before the asset sale, Leonard Green sold 60 percent of the company to the two top executives for only $12 million, plus assumption of the $1.3 billion in lease obligations. Unfortunately, according to the ProPublica investigation, Prospect Medical was left with little cash, heavy pension debts, astronomical lease commitments, and very uncertain future earnings. Some are now lobbying to have Prospect and Leonard Green return the dividends to the company, accusing the company of profiting while putting its safety-net hospitals at risk.

Case Questions

1. How did financial incentives overshadow Prospect Medical's mission and standards?
2. What are the differences between the business model that Prospect Medical used and that of a traditional hospital?
3. How does the time frame a company uses for its investments influence management actions and things it emphasizes?
4. Can a for-profit company provide excellent patient care and still produce good profits?
5. How did Prospect Medical's mission assist or harm its results?

Reference

Elkind, P., and D. Burke. 2020. "Investors Extracted $400 Million from a Hospital Chain That Sometimes Couldn't Pay for Medical Supplies or Gas for Ambulances." ProPublica. Published September 30. www.propublica.org/article/investors-extracted-400-million-from-a-hospital-chain-that-sometimes-couldnt-pay-for-medical-supplies-or-gas-for-ambulances.

CASE 8

PEGASUS HEALTH'S INTEGRATION OF CARE

Note: The following case is based on the sources cited. It is intended for case study purposes only and does not imply acceptance of any statement as fact.

Healthcare for about 500,000 people in Canterbury, New Zealand, the South Island's largest and most populous region, seemed gridlocked: Patients consistently had very long wait periods in the emergency departments, as hospitals there were chronically over capacity. This was a result of many factors, one of which was that many patients came to the hospital for treatment of minor conditions, such as the removal of skin lesions and treatment for heavy menstrual bleeding.

Waiting times for procedures at hospitals had become not only a problem but also a political embarrassment. The issue came to a head in 2006, when the central government introduced regulations to sanction hospitals if they failed to provide treatment to approved patients within six months of their referral. The local district health board responded by arbitrarily removing from its waiting list about 5,000 patients with the longest waits. The local health board justified the removal to the press by saying that if patients could wait for more than six months, they must not need the surgery.

Suddenly, the primary care general practitioners (GPs) found their referrals to hospitals being sent back to them without any clear explanation. Angry providers and patients flooded the press with stories, retold in the news with gruesome headlines. The coverage generated a sense of shock and dismay in the Canterbury health system.

On top of this fiasco, recent studies had projected the need for another 500 hospital beds, 20 percent more GPs and nurses, and another 2,000 residential care beds for Canterbury by 2020, which was financially infeasible. And even if the money from the government could be found, attracting the additional 8,000 healthcare professionals needed for the new facilities would be next to impossible.

Something had to be done. The CEO and senior staff, who included the hospital and area physicians and community health groups, were asked to develop a vision for how the health system should look in 2020, and how it should be changed. They were given a wallet-sized card signed by the CEO giving them "permission" to change the system.

To communicate that the health system had to change and that healthcare stakeholders could change it—and indeed had the responsibility to do so—a "showcase" event was held for more than 2,000 employees and health professionals. At this forum, participants from across the health system presented the challenges that the system was facing and asked what they could and would do to improve it. The event occurred in a warehouse, where attendees went through a variety of challenging scenarios. Central questions were posed: How would you like to be treated? Who would you work with to achieve that? How would you, personally, transform the system? The process went on for six weeks, and several common messages emerged:

- There had to be one healthcare system in Canterbury. "One system, one budget" became a mantra, even though different sources of public and private contributions funded the system.
- Healthcare needed to be patient centered, not hospital centered.
- Integrated health and social services needed to exist.

From these themes, a series of goals were established, including the following:

- Services should enable people to take more responsibility for their own health and well-being.
- To the extent possible, people should stay well in their own homes and communities.
- When people need complex care, it should be delivered in a timely and appropriate manner.

Recognizing the challenging task ahead, the group then developed new principles to guide their actions:

- Those in the health system—from primary to community to hospital to social care, whether public employees, independent practitioners, or private and not-for-profit contractors—had to recognize that there was "one system, one budget" in Canterbury.
- Canterbury had to get the best possible outcomes with the resources available, rather than individual organizations and practitioners lobbying for more money.
- The goal was to deliver "the right care, right place, right time by the right person," and a key measure of success was to reduce the time patients spent waiting.

When the goals and principles were presented to the Canterbury District Health Board for adoption, the principles were viewed as the more important of the two, and the board endorsed these principles to begin the change process.

Change efforts began almost immediately throughout the full system, including the hospitals, GPs, specialist physicians, home nurses, community pharmacies, laboratories, and social care. They needed to work together in new ways to act as a single integrated health and social care system. Only in this way could patient services be improved and the budget be balanced.

Changing people, technology, and structure began. A great deal of skills training ensured the improvement of managerial and innovation abilities. Participants were required to develop projects for change in their own areas and then implement them. In addition, business development units were established to assist clinical and process changes. For example, one group redesigned the flow in the radiology department; another redesigned the processes for acute medical and surgical admissions.

Changes did not come at once. Two years after the initial push for change, some participants were more engaged than others. As one physician stated when asked how deeply the changes had reached into the hospital, "I don't know. But there are more people who feel they have a voice and an influence on what can be done than last year, and than two years ago, and than five years ago. And that is good."

Greater integration was achieved by altering the incentive structures. Hospitals had been reimbursed based on their volumes, which encouraged hospital activity even if this location was not the optimal setting for care. Clinical teams were also given assurances that they would not lose resources for improved efficiencies. For example, phone consults with GPs had not been reimbursed and, therefore, were limited in use. With the changes, these became much more important and eliminated many visits to the emergency and outpatient departments. Also, external contracts became transparent, centered on trust and cooperation, and based on agreed-upon margins with fixed budgets.

HealthPathways, electronic guidelines for best practices and clinical pathways, helped reduce conflict between managers and clinicians. The system delineated which patients should be treated by GPs and which were to be referred to hospital specialists. Critical to these almost 500 pathways were the intensive process and interaction between the GPs and specialists that formed a sense of partnership and trust.

The creation of the pathways and additional funding encouraged GPs to learn spirometry and to remove complex skin lesions. Patients began arriving at the hospital fully worked up and having all the tests necessary for their specialist evaluation. Other programs, such as Acute Hospital Management System and Community Rehabilitation Enablement and Support, were added. Both reduced hospital demand. Readmission rates dropped to 1.7 percent.

Results appeared to be positive. Employee and physician satisfaction increased. Efficient processes reduced service times. For instance, 70 percent of radiology scans were completed within an hour. The waiting list for gallbladder surgery decreased from 300 patients to 100. Furthermore, the financial deficits became surpluses. Overall, the Canterbury District Health Board took significant steps to integrate healthcare among its hospitals, GPs, specialists, and community providers, and results suggest a higher-quality and more efficient system.

Case Questions

1. What caused the healthcare situation to become a crisis?
2. What did the leaders do to motivate action to change?
3. How did their change process follow the guidelines in chapter 23? Deviate from the guidelines?
4. How did Pegasus change processes to ensure effective communication?
5. How can an organization bring together diverse parties with different incentives to design a better system?

Reference

Timmins, N., and C. Ham. 2013. "The Quest for Integrated Health and Social Care: A Case Study in Canterbury, New Zealand." King's Fund. www.kingsfund.org.uk/publications/quest-integrated-health-and-social-care.

CASE 9

PURDUE'S DILEMMA TO INCREASE SALES

Note: The following case is based on the sources cited. It is intended for case study purposes only and does not imply acceptance of any statement as fact.

It was 2017, and the addiction and death of thousands of Americans had been racking the nation for decades. Opioids became very popular in the 1990s, as pharmaceutical companies assured medical professionals and patients that the drugs were wonderful pain relievers and were not addictive. As a result, providers rapidly increased their prescription of these drugs, many of which ended up on the streets being resold for high markups.

However, opioids are extremely dangerous. Oxycodone is twice as powerful as morphine, and a former Food and Drug Administration commissioner has stated that "few drugs are as dangerous as the opioids" (Keefe 2017). In 2017 alone, more than 47,000 Americans died because of opioid overdoses and about 1.7 million people struggled with addiction to an opioid, which included prescription opioids, heroin, and fentanyl. According to the National Institutes of Health's National Institute on Drug Abuse (2021):

- Roughly 21 to 29 percent of patients prescribed opioids for chronic pain misuse them.
- Between 8 and 12 percent develop an opioid use disorder.
- An estimated 4 to 6 percent who misuse prescription opioids transition to heroin.
- About 80 percent of people who use heroin first misused prescription opioids.

Since 1999, over 200,000 Americans have died from opioid overdoses.

Purdue Pharma was built around the production and sales of OxyContin, an opioid that the company introduced in 1996 and marketed so aggressively that sales grew from $48 million in 1996 to almost $1.1 billion in 2000. By 2002 it had sales of almost $3 billion with over 14 million prescriptions. Ultimately, the drug brought in about $35 billion of revenue to the company. Purdue Pharma spent freely to encourage and promote the drug. In 2004, it spent $200 million just on its marketing. It conducted national pain-management conferences in resorts in Florida, Arizona, and California and had thousands of physicians, pharmacists, and nurses attend for free. Many of the doctors who attended these conferences joined Purdue Pharma's ever-expanding speakers' bureau and received payments for talks, consulting work, and conference attendance. This involvement increased the physicians' prescribing of OxyContin (Science Daily 2019).

Purdue Pharma also targeted the doctors who were the highest prescribers for opioids across the country. Sales representatives who increased sales received large bonuses, which could more than double their salaries. By 2000 Purdue Pharma employed over 670 sales representatives, who called on over 90,000 physicians. Many of the sales representatives felt they were doing a righteous thing by selling OxyContin to help the millions of people in pain. To help change prescription patterns and introduce people to the drug, they provided doctors a patient starter coupon program that gave patients a free, limited-time prescription for a 7- to 30-day supply. Over 34,000 of these coupons were used before this incentive was discontinued in 2001. Other promotional efforts included giving away OxyContin fishing hats, stuffed plush toys, promotional videos with patient testimonials, and even a mix album called "Get in the Swing with OxyContin."

Sales representatives were trained to overcome objections and concerns from clinicians. If asked about addiction, they were to state that the slow-release system of the drug reduced the abuse liability of the drug, which was not true. Basically, they were told to tell doctors that the drug was "virtually non-addicting." One of their senior advisers commented at a seminar that OxyContin was like a vegetable: "If I gave you a stalk of celery and you ate that, it would be healthy. But if you put it in a blender and tried to shoot it into your veins, it would not be good." One of the owners also wrote that "all health problems devolve upon the individual and it was Purdue's position that OxyContin overdoses were a matter of individual responsibility, rather than the drug's addictive properties" (Keefe 2017).

According to the *New Yorker*, Purdue Pharma, directed by the Sackler family, used a business approach to push its products. "Sackler's ads had a very serious, clinical look," said one former employee, "a physician talking to a physician. But it was advertising." Duke psychiatrist Allen Frances told Keefe, "Most of the questionable practices that propelled the pharmaceutical industry into the scourge it is today can be attributed to Arthur Sackler."

The promotions worked, as sales exploded, but the company consistently and falsely claimed that the risk of addiction was very small. The sales representatives touted that the risk of addiction was less than 1 percent. The misrepresentation had consequences, and in 2007 an affiliate, Purdue Frederick Company, pled guilty to federal charges for claiming OxyContin was less addictive than other opioids and paid $634 million in fines. Some have attributed Purdue Pharma's marketing efforts to the shift in the practice of prescribing opioids.

However, sales continued to increase along with the increasing awareness of growing abuse and addiction. By 2004, more than 3.1 million people were using OxyContin, which was recognized as the most prevalent prescription opioid abused in the United States. More people were using opioids than cocaine and heroin, and overdose deaths began to skyrocket. "Pill mills" became common, with some manipulated or corrupt doctors prescribing thousands or millions of pills. Purdue Pharma denied that its marketing impacted the usage, said that "junkies" were ruining the reputation of their product, and hired Rudy Giuliani, the former mayor of New York, to protect its interests.

OxyContin had been very profitable for the Sackler family, who by 2017 had a collective net worth of $13 billion. Yet, by that year sales had begun to falter, and the company decided to re-engage one of the most prominent global consulting firms, McKinsey & Company, to help it strategize how to "turbocharge" OxyContin sales (McKinsey had worked with Purdue Pharma since 2008). Reporting for the *New York Times* in November 2020 uncovered records which showed that McKinsey was asked to find a way "to counter the emotional messages from mothers with teenagers that overdosed" from OxyContin (Forsythe and Bogdanich 2021).

The *New York Times* reported that McKinsey examined the situation and provided several options to boost sales. One would provide distributors and payers, which included CVS, the pharmaceutical chain, and Anthem, a large health insurer, a rebate for each OxyContin overdose for the pills they sold. McKinsey estimated that 2,484 customers buying OxyContin from CVS would develop an opioid disorder or have an overdose in 2019. McKinsey recommended a rebate of $14,810 per event, which would equate to a rebate of $36.8 million from Purdue Pharma to CVS in 2019.

McKinsey's recommendations were well received, but the rebate was never implemented. However, some of Purdue Pharma's marketing leadership questioned the approach and expressed concerns about the need to "turbocharge" OxyContin sales. Purdue Pharma's CEO also noted that problems had been caused by doctors writing too many prescriptions at too high doses and for too long of time. He also wrote that physicians were prescribing OxyContin for conditions outside of those recommended, and that many lacked adequate training to use OxyContin appropriately.

Finally, in 2020, Purdue Pharma pled guilty to federal criminal charges and agreed to pay $8.3 billion in penalties, including $3.54 billion in criminal fines and $2 billion in criminal forfeiture of profits. The *New York Times* reported that the company "also pleaded guilty to paying illegal kickbacks to doctors who prescribed OxyContin and to an electronic health records company, Practice Fusion" (Benner 2020). Purdue's chairman, Steve Miller, said in his hearing that "in order to meet sales goals, the company told the Drug Enforcement Administration that it had created a program to prevent OxyContin from being sold on the black market, even though it was marketing the drug to more than 100 doctors suspected of illegally prescribing OxyContin."

The Sackler family paid $225 million in civil penalties, while continuing to claim that they acted lawfully and ethically. No one was sentenced to jail.

Opioids may have contributed to as many as 450,000 deaths of Americans since 1999.

Case Questions

1. How did incentives motivate the actions of the company and its salesforce?
2. What principles of motivation theory exist in this case?
3. How did Purdue Pharma perceive the addiction issues, using paradigm theories?
4. What type of groupthink may have occurred within the company?
5. Point out three different ethical issues in this case.
6. Why would a prominent consulting firm make these recommendations?

References

Benner, K. 2020. "Purdue Pharma Pleads Guilty to Role in Opioid Crisis as Part of Deal with Justice Department." *New York Times*, November 24.

Forsythe, M. and W. Bogdanich. 2021. "McKinsey Settles for Nearly $600 Million over Role in Opioid Crisis," *New York Times*, February 3.

Keefe, P. R. 2017. "The Family That Built an Empire of Pain." *New Yorker*, October 23.

National Institute on Drug Abuse. 2021. ""Opioid Overdose Crisis." Accessed July 31. www.drugabuse.gov/drug-topics/opioids/opioid-overdose-crisis. Science Daily. 2019. "Payment to Physicians May Increase Opioid Prescribing." January 22. www.sciencedaily.com/releases/2019/01/190122084356.htm.

Science Daily. 2019. "Payment to Physicians May Increase Opioid Prescribing." January 22. www.sciencedaily.com/releases/2019/01/190122084356.htm.

CASE 10

ORTHOINDY

Note: The following case is based on the sources cited. It is intended for case study purposes only and does not imply acceptance of any statement as fact.

The OrthoIndy website stated the following:

> OrthoIndy provides complete bone, joint, spine and muscle care. With more than 60 orthopaedic specialist partners, OrthoIndy is the largest private, full-service orthopaedic practice in the Midwest, and one of the largest in the country. (OrthoIndy 2018)

OrthoIndy adjusted its practice over time. For years, its physicians took patient emergency calls for all area hospitals and provided services to all types of patients. However, as the market became more competitive and physician incomes declined slightly, it decided to reduce calls to only key facilities (Methodist and St. Vincent) and stopped treating Medicaid patients. This decision upset most of the area hospitals and the nonaffiliated orthopedists, and some of OrthoIndy's partners were concerned about the ethical and political ramifications, but ultimately they all agreed to the decision. Although these choices improved the incomes and lifestyle of the practicing physicians, significant concerns existed about what could be done to sustain their salaries. OrthoIndy therefore turned its attention to the large surgical center it owned, which was quite profitable, and to other possible facilities that could provide them additional earnings.

OrthoIndy felt that its mission lent itself to opening its own hospital so it could better be the leader in advancing quality bone, joint, spine, and muscle care and technology. Its physicians felt that with their own hospital OrthoIndy could become one of the most highly respected orthopedic practices in the Midwest.

The opening or impending opening of four specialty heart hospitals in the area prompted the group to analyze the potential for a joint-venture orthopedic hospital. Many OrthoIndy physicians observed that area cardiologists who had joined these specialty ventures were able to build new revenue streams and bring in better-paying patients by providing beautiful new facilities and leading-edge equipment. Following lengthy and somewhat heated discussions, the group decided to proceed by organizing as a for-profit partnership to build and operate the new hospital. Only members of their group could become partners in the hospital, and those with ethical or other reservations could distance themselves somewhat while still remaining affiliated with the medical group.

The hospital was planned to be fast-tracked and prepared to open March 1, 2005, as a state-of-the-art hospital that would specialize in musculoskeletal care. OrthoIndy leaders explained the justification and benefits for the hospital:

- First, patients would receive care and treatment focused on orthopedics and on the best options for each patient.
- Second, the new hospital would provide the best technology and healthcare providers, leading to unparalleled results.

The group was also determined to do other things that could differentiate the hospital from the other general hospitals doing orthopedics in their market area. They planned for patients to enjoy a homelike atmosphere from admission to discharge. Patients would have satellite TV, e-mail, and internet access. Patient rooms would be spacious and well appointed, and would include a work or reading nook for friends and family members. Also, once a patient was discharged, they would enjoy coordinated postoperative appointments with their physician's office and referrals to the convenient, state-of-the-art on-campus physical therapy center.

With great effort, the hospital was completed on time. The March 1, 2005, press release announcing the facility's opening ("OrthoIndy Opens Central Ind.'s First Specialty Hospital to Focus on Complete Orthopaedic Care") read, in part:

> OrthoIndy announced today the opening of the Indiana Orthopaedic Hospital, central Ind.'s first and only orthopaedic specialty hospital located at I-465 and West 86th Street. Spanning 130,000 square feet, the hospital represents a $50 million commitment to the city of Indianapolis, its residents and to the patients who will receive care at this state-of-the-art facility. . . .
>
> The Indiana Orthopaedic Hospital was built when OrthoIndy physicians saw an increasing need to deliver specialized orthopaedic care in a patient-focused environment. Approximately 60 physicians from central Ind. will practice at the hospital that will focus on complex surgical procedures, including total joint replacements and spinal cases. (PR Newswire 2005).

Since opening, OrthoIndy Hospital has performed very well. As can be seen in the table, its operating margin has exceeded 35 percent every year and generated $70 million or more per year to be divided among the partners. At the same time, it has been able to keep their long-term debt to very low levels.

OrthoIndy Hospital, Indianapolis, IN							
Period ending date	12/2019	12/2018	12/2017	12/2016	12/2015	12/2014	12/2013
EBITDAR	$82.6 M	$73.6 M	$74.2 M	$72.5 M	$67.3 M	$64.8 M	$62.6 M
Operating Margin	38.3%	35.7%	37.2%	36.2%	35.4%	35.1%	35.9%
Return on Equity	161.9%	158.1%	171.0%	196.7%	120.8%	138.7%	144.9%
Return on Assets	121.0%	113.8%	122.7%	130.5%	94.7%	106.1%	102.4%
Long-Term Debt to Net Assets	0.06	0.07	0.08	0.12	0.09	0.11	0.09

Source: Data from American Hospital Directory (2021).

Case Questions

1. What are the ethical issues involved in private, physician-owned hospitals?
2. How did the organization's mission direct its actions?
3. Which stakeholders are critical in this case?
4. What are the short-term and long-term costs to these stakeholders?
5. What effect will the new hospital have on consumers?
6. Do you think that a specialty hospital will increase or lower healthcare costs, quality, and availability to consumers in this case?
7. How will the new specialty hospital affect nearby general hospitals?

References

American Hospital Directory. 2021. "Your Best Source for Hospital Information and Custom Data Services." Accessed February. www.ahd.com.

OrthoIndy. 2018. "About OrthoIndy." Accessed July 31. www.orthoindy.com/about/.

PRNewswire. 2005. "OrthoIndy Opens Central Ind.'s First Specialty Hospital to Focus on Complete Orthopaedic Care." Press release, March 1.

CASE 11

THE NEW CEO

You have been promoted to be the CEO of a 312-bed hospital that is the second largest facility in your healthcare system. The prior two CEOs were from the Deep South and were not great cultural fits for this medical center. Financially the hospital is doing well, but the attitudes and actions of the former CEOs have divided the staff, physicians, and community, and there is a lot of latent anger. You know you will have to address this quickly. In addition, the medical staff pride themselves on their independence. The president of the medical staff accosted you on your third day on the job and told you, "You have about six months to clean up the mess here or I will make certain we are looking for another CEO."

The winter can get very cold and windy at the hospital, and the former CEOs had special parking near the entrance for themselves and all department heads; everyone else parked over 200 yards away and slogged through the snowdrifts. Furthermore, those CEOs almost always ate for free in the physician's lounge and were rarely seen in the general cafeteria, even though it is just across from the executive office. Then there are the potential clinical problems.

A year before your arrival, the previous CEO brought in a cardiac surgeon and began a cardiac surgery program. He made three-year guarantees and anticipated great success. However, after reviewing the figures for the first year, you wonder if the clinical and financial outcomes justify the program. Only 47 adult open heart surgeries were conducted last year, and only 55 are projected this year. The vast majority have been Medicare patients and maybe—if only marginal costs are factored in—the service has been breakeven. Clinically, however, the American College of Surgeons recommends that an adult open heart surgery program have an annual volume of at least 100 to 125 open heart procedures per hospital from a quality standpoint; at least 200 procedures per year are necessary for a program to function efficiently.

Other issues also exist with the program. Since there is only one surgeon, he has no coverage, and when he leaves, even for short trips, his patients only have access to a cardiologist for consultations. You are also concerned about his patient selection. During your second week at the hospital, a cardiologist approached you and asked if the hospital should be doing triple bypass surgery on a 94-year-old patient. When you investigated, you found that the surgeon planned to operate on this person, despite his advanced age.

On top of everything else, you discover that the prior CEO raised rates about 25 percent his last year at the hospital. BlueCross has informed you that your rates are now 30–40 percent higher than other equivalent hospitals in the state. Because of this, it indicates that it will steer especially expensive operations to the neighboring state, where hospitals have much lower rates and their contracts are perhaps 50 percent lower than your charges.

Case Questions
1. What are the major leadership issues facing you? What decisions need to be made? How would you make them?
2. How would you frame the ethical dilemmas here?
3. What would be your plan to address the issues?
4. How would you establish your power and influence? What actions could you take?
5. What could you do to better motivate employees and physicians?

CASE 12

LIVER ALLOCATION

Note: The following case is based on the sources cited. It is intended for case study purposes only and does not imply acceptance of any statement as fact.

In the United States, organ transplants, including liver transplants, are coordinated by a not-for-profit organization called the United Network for Organ Sharing. Given that donated organs have a limited time frame of viability, the United States is divided into 11 geographic areas for liver-donation purposes. Within these regions, patients receive donated livers in order of need. However, there is a wide disparity in donated livers across these 11 regions. For example, in region 9, which includes New York, 327 livers were donated in 2016; whereas in region 3, which included the Deep South and Puerto Rico, 1,336 livers were donated. This disparity is due to many factors, including prevalent causes of death in each region; some causes, such as heart attack, usually leave livers intact, whereas others, such as liver disease, do not. In region 3, for instance, strokes are a frequent cause of death, leading to many more viable livers for donation.

A 2020 policy change approved by the Organ Procurement and Transplantation Network will work to mitigate this geographic disparity. Regardless of membership in a transplant region, someone in need will be first eligible for any livers that become available within 150 nautical miles of the hospital where the transplant would occur. According to reporting in the *Washington Post* soon after this policy was first announced, the change "will make more livers available in some places—including cities such as New York and Chicago—where the shortage is more severe than it is in regions such as the southeastern United States" (Bernstein 2017). Many view this change as an acceptable improvement in addressing disparities, but not totally satisfying—partly because this would not entirely eliminate those disparities, but also because it does not address one of its key causes, which is the difference in rates of organ donation in different communities.

Additionally, these changes will leave in place another feature of the current system that has received some criticism: It will still be possible for people to join multiple regional liver registries if they can afford to pay for travel, accommodations, and testing in the new region, and can cover the costs of returning to the region should a liver become available. This clearly is prohibitively expensive for many. However, those who support maintaining the possibility of patients joining multiple registries emphasize the autonomy of patients: "When it's come up for a vote, patient advocacy groups have argued that while things like test results and blood types are out of the patients' control, determining whether to obtain a second listing and where to do it allows the patient to be proactive" (Lupkin 2015).

Despite the change to regional allocation, discussion continues about how to make liver transplants—and organ transplants in general—more equitably accessible to those who need them. In 2018, about 8,000 candidates died while on an organ transplant wait list, without receiving an organ transplant.

Case Questions

1. Is it fair to distribute organs by geographic availability?
2. What should we use as the primary criteria for determining how to distribute livers and other vital organs?
3. How could decisions be made more fairly?
4. Should joining multiple regional registries for liver transplants be allowed?
5. How do cultures affect the way organs would be distributed?

References

Bernstein, L. 2017. "Liver Transplant Distribution Changed After Years of Debate." *New York Times*, December 4.

Lupkin, S. 2015. "Good Luck Getting an Organ Transplant If You're Poor in America." Vice News, December 11.

CASE 13

LETTER FROM A BEREAVED MOTHER

By Joseph Horton

As the CEO of the Children's Hospital, I received a letter one day that stood out from all the rest. It was from the mother of a five-year-old boy who had recently passed away in our Pediatric Intensive Care Unit as a result of fatal injuries. He had been hit by a car while running across the street. The letter expressed her deep disappointment. She had been reluctant to agree to organ donation, but with encouragement from the attending intensivist, nurses, and a social worker, she had agreed to allow her son's organs to be harvested so that others could benefit. She had been told that she would receive a letter letting her know specifically how the organs had been used to help other children in dire need. Her letter informed me, with great pain, that she had not received any letter. I tried to imagine the pain she was feeling, but it was so far beyond my experience.

I wondered how we could make this right. I called the regional organ bank, informed them of this failure, and requested the letter. I asked them to send it to me in a sealed envelope, so that I could personally deliver it to the mother. They sent me the letter, and when it came I called the mother to let her know I was on my way to her home to deliver it. It didn't seem like enough, but all I really had to give in this delicate situation was my personal presence, and the respect for her pain that would be demonstrated by my coming to her home. It wasn't so much that *I* was coming, but rather that the CEO of the hospital was coming.

When she greeted me at her door, I expressed as best I could my sympathy for her enormous loss. I was the father of two young boys myself at the time. I apologized for the letter failure and handed her the envelope. None of these acts were extraordinary given the circumstances, but they had a strong effect. She invited me inside, showed me pictures of her son, and shared with me several deeply personal stories about him. When I left, she thanked me and told me that our time together had been healing. I knew that nothing I could do would relieve her pain, but I was struck by the power of a simple and quite ordinary act of kindness. I made a note to try to remember that, and not to assume, in the moments when we are invited into the house of pain in another's life, that we have nothing to offer.

Case Questions

1. What were the options that the CEO could have chosen to handle the letter from the mother? What are the probable results if the CEO had taken the other options?
2. What value resulted from taking the time to personally deliver the letter?
3. How does this case demonstrate emotional intelligence?

CASE 14

HEALTHT SEEKS HEALTHIER EMPLOYEES

HealthT, a midsize for-profit hospital company, was seeking ways to improve its bottom line. Charlie, its chief operating officer, noted the huge company expense for employee healthcare insurance. Costs had risen from about $140 million three years ago to $195 million in the current year. HealthT, like most large companies, was self-insured, which meant its healthcare expenditures were reported as operating expenses and came directly out of its profits. The huge increase in overall healthcare costs infuriated Charlie, and he immediately called the human resources (HR) department demanding that its director meet with him in two hours to justify the large increase.

Glen, the HR director, arrived at Charlie's office on time, knowing that Charlie was a demanding boss. Glen had the following spreadsheet to share with Charlie.

Glen was pleased to report that over the past three years, HealthT's healthcare cost per employee had risen only 12.1 percent, or about 4 percent per year. He also pointed out that, with the new network of physicians and hospitals, the per-employee physician expense had dropped from 2017 to 2020.

Charlie was still upset. He almost yelled at Glen. "Look at the total figures! We are spending almost $200 million on employee healthcare expenses, and the costs of chronic illness care have jumped 47.5 percent in just three years. That's 18 percent per employee! You must come up with something to control these runaway costs. You have one week to present your recommendations."

Glen and his staff brainstormed ways to control chronic illness. Although they recognized that most efforts to control chronic disease were long term, they designed the following changes to their employee insurance plan:

1. *Higher deductibles for risky activities.* Any employee who required healthcare services because of a risky activity—defined as skydiving, scuba diving, motorcycle riding, rock climbing, and similar activities—would have a hospital deductible of $3,000 instead of the normal $500.
2. *Higher premiums for smokers.* All smokers would be charged an additional $100 per month for their healthcare insurance.

HealthT's Employee Healthcare Expenditures 2017–2020

	Total Employee Healthcare	Third-Party Administration	Hospital	Physician	Other	High-Cost Procedures	Chronic Illness
2017 Expense*	$139.40	$9.76	$62.73	$34.85	$32.06	$42.10	$82.60
2030 Expense*	$195.30	$13.67	$78.12	$39.06	$65.45	$49.70	$121.80
2017 to 2020 change	40.1%	40.1%	24.5%	12.1%	101.0%	18.1%	47.5%
2017 Cost per employee (28,000 employees)	$4,078	$348	$2,240	$1,244	$1,145	$1,503	$2,950
2020 Cost per employee (35,000 employees)	$5,580	$390	$2,232	$1,116	$1,841	$1,420	$3,480
2017 to 2020 change	12.1%	12.1%	−0.4%	−10.3%	60.8%	−5.6%	18.0%

* In millions

3. *Higher premiums for people who are overweight.* All employees with a body mass index (BMI) over 25 but less than 30 would be charged an additional $75 per month for healthcare insurance, and those with a BMI of 30 or more would be charged an additional $150 per month.

Glen presented the recommendations to Charlie, who thought they were great and asked that they be implemented immediately. Glen thought the changes would be received positively by employees, but he almost instantly began to receive complaints that the changes were not fair.

Case Questions

1. From an ethical perspective, how could you defend these changes? How would you reply to employees who claimed they were being unjustly penalized?
2. Would your arguments change if you considered the issue in terms of the utilitarian model? The justice model?
3. What would you do to address the potential issues in this case if you were Glen? Charlie?
4. How would the actions motivate the employees? What incentives might be needed to change behaviors?
5. How should these decisions be made?
6. Could this be seen as an innovation?
7. Would having a group process involved in making this decision have made it more successful?

CASE 15

HEALTHSOUTH

Note: The following case is based on the sources cited. It is intended for case study purposes only and does not imply acceptance of any statement as fact.

Richard Scrushy was a complex, talented man. He had a brilliant business mind but could be callous and cruel in his justifications for success. Although he started poor, his company's success eventually allowed him to branch out into sponsoring bands, owning other healthcare companies, and purchasing expensive estates.

Across Scrushy's 19-year business career, his compensation has been estimated at almost $1 billion. He started out as a respiratory therapist. Married at 17 with a baby on the way, this Selma, Alabama, native joined a band and grew a large, bushy hairdo. He settled down and, after he received his respiratory therapy certificate in 1974, became an instructor in his program and worked evenings at local hospitals. Later he joined Lifemark, a company that managed respiratory therapy departments. He was a great salesperson and was soon promoted to be vice president of Lifemark's respiratory therapy, physical therapy, and pharmacy division. He oversaw about a hundred contracts.

Scrushy was not well liked by his peers, as he was extremely competitive and they felt he always made them look bad at corporate meetings. He did well, and in 1983 his annual bonus and stock options allowed him to purchase his first Mercedes, a car known for its great quality even when purchased used. Status and money were always important to him.

He was a driven, sharp, clever man. He worked incessantly and even his social contacts were focused on work. He rarely relaxed.

In 1983, Lifemark announced a merger with American Medical International. Scrushy wanted to start his own company and brought three of his work colleagues together to form their own business. Scrushy put in $25,000 for 500,000 shares of the company, while the others contributed $5,000 for 100,000 shares each. They located their headquarters in Birmingham, Alabama. They had big plans, with their first business plan projecting they would hit $100 million in revenues in five years. To start, they rented a two-room office and used cheap metal folding tables and chairs. Eventually, they were able to obtain $1 million in funding from Citicorp and $6 million from other sources, which allowed them to expand. Already, Scrushy's investment had made him a millionaire.

The original plan was to be a strictly outpatient company with doctor partners, but they found a need for rehabilitation hospitals in the United States. Although Scrushy had no experience with inpatient care, he leapt at the chance. An outpatient facility could provide $1 million to $2 million in revenues annually; an inpatient hospital up to $10 million.

Scrushy liked meetings first thing in the day and enjoyed leading them. One day in 1985 he arrived early and drew a picture on the board of a wagon with some people pushing the wagon, some pulling it, and others standing around it. This quickly became the company's theme—everyone needed to be out front pulling the wagon or to leave. "Pulling the wagon" became the de facto company motto.

HealthSouth was growing, and so was pressure to go public. One day, Scrushy and his chief financial officer (CFO) were meeting with a banker from Drexel Burnham Lambert, who suggested they capitalize, rather than expense, all their start-up costs. This would help HealthSouth reach profitability much quicker. Scrushy sneered at his controller and suggested he was holding the company back and he would not have "the accounting tail wag the company dog." As a result of Scrushy's pressure, HealthSouth restated its previously published financial statements, which increased its reported profitability in late 1986.

The company was ready to go public, but if it started showing losses it would kill the share pricing. Accrual accounting gives significant flexibility, because the amounts stated in reports as bad debts, contractual allowances, and other items are estimates. This gave Scrushy and HealthSouth an opening for "aggressive" accounting estimates.

Finally, in 1986 the company went public, which required many presentations by Scrushy and his senior leadership. But Scrushy had a temper. After one of the presentations, Scrushy went to dinner with three of the bankers who were helping to sell the 2 million shares they hoped to place. After they ordered food, one of the bankers said, "Good job today, but your presentation needs a lot of work." Scrushy went berserk and called the man a fool and a moron, cursing him repeatedly. It was an awkward dinner, and the next day this banker was off his team. However, Scrushy's sales job did what was needed and, even though the company was not yet profitable, the team went public and raised over $12 million in a stock offering. Soon the stock was trading at $10 a share, making Scrushy worth over $5 million.

Scrushy loved nice things. With his newfound wealth he started buying expensive toys. At his height he owned 40 cars, including a $250,000 Lamborghini, and ten homes, one an 11,000-square-foot Palm Beach mansion.

He also had his company buy planes, which he adored. HealthSouth bought ten planes and Scrushy flew each of them. He also bought a yacht, which was used to reward his managers with trips they took together.

Scrushy failed to take responsibility for failures and generally blamed others. An incident with the yacht illustrated this. On one trip, Scrushy was steering the boat and ran it onto a sandbar that bent the propellers. Rather than acknowledging his part in steering the boat, he blamed one of his managers, who should have been looking for the sandbars, railing about this man's incompetence. The fiasco foreshadowed more to come, as his reaction as captain of the yacht continued into HealthSouth's history.

Scrushy's business prospered. By October 1987, HealthSouth's stock traded at $16 a share and he was asked to join other companies' boards of directors. He also started demanding a bigger salary and more stock options from HealthSouth. By the early 1990s, he was worth about $100 million, but he was never satisfied and always wanted more.

HealthSouth had expanded into acute care in late 1989, and began acquiring other companies in the 1990s. By 1994, the company's revenues reached $500 million. Acquisitions drove revenues to $1.6 billion by 1995. This growth caused problems. In 1990, HealthSouth had 3,500 employees, but by 1995 they jumped to 26,000. When asked why it made such aggressive acquisitions the company's answer was "Because we could." Its stock had the highest price-to-earnings ratio of any stock in its sector, and the acquisitions were funded by the stock value. But at some point, HealthSouth's value had to be increased. Its core business was not strong, although the mergers masked this. Of course, the mergers were driven by future estimates of earnings and savings. The mergers raised revenues substantially, but also put pressure on earnings.

Scrushy wanted a corporate office in Birmingham befitting the company's status. In 1995, it built a 200,000-square-foot, five-story building on 85 acres. It cost $38 million, and Scrushy made certain that he had his trophy room—a museum room that showed his first office and a full-size statue of him. The top floor was restricted to top management. He definitely saw differences between himself and "underlings." One Christmas, his CFO bought a $100 Hermès tie for all his direct reports. Scrushy was upset and told the CFO that he was disappointed with him, as Hermès should only be for top leaders.

Tough management was the style Scrushy enjoyed. He often managed by intimidation. Standing just five feet eight inches, he wore lifts in his designer shoes and had hair implants to battle his hair loss. Yet, he effectively used his voice and demeanor to intimidate people. Monday morning meetings often turned into a tirade of threats and yelling. He often used his time to belittle, berate, and embarrass employees to get them to better "pull the wagon." His most common phrase at these meetings was "Why, that's the stupidest thing I've ever heard."

Concurrently, Scrushy became very active in politics, growing close to Alabama's governor and contributing to many campaigns. Not only did he donate to politicians, he also required all upper-level managers to do so (but would give them back the money with bonuses). He also donated HealthSouth's money to philanthropic causes, but rarely donated his own funds. Libraries, college campuses, a parkway, a daycare, baseball fields, and conference centers were named after him. He had many important friends in politics, entertainment, and sports.

He often seemed oblivious to self-dealing. Many of his decisions used HealthSouth money to ultimately benefit him or his family. For instance, he signed an exclusive contract to purchase computers from a company owned by his father. Managers objected and did not want these computers but had to buy through his father's company. His CFO talked to Scrushy about this conflict of interest and Scrushy told him that he did not know what he was talking about and to leave his office and never bring it up again. Later, the federal government sued HealthSouth for overinflating costs by using his father's company and HealthSouth settled for $8.2 million. He had similar conflicts in 12 companies he either owned or was a principal in.

By 1993, pressure had built on HealthSouth's quarterly earnings. The aggressive accounting practices previously used were making it increasingly difficult to continue showing strong margins and growth. Scrushy consistently overpromised Wall Street. Managers were receiving more and more pressure from Scrushy to meet his promised numbers. In 1995, HealthSouth made another public stock offering, which made more promises. Yet, by 1996 it appeared hopeless to meet the promised financial results. The CFO and controller decided that the time had come to tell Scrushy that after ten years of "making our numbers" they simply could not continue. Scrushy said "NO." He would not accept this, as the stock price would fall, stock options would be worthless, and their social position threatened. Scrushy ordered them to "fix the numbers" (Beam 2009, 78).

The controller decided to change many small entries under $5,000 that the auditors would not see. Neither he nor the CFO wanted to confront Scrushy again and both thought this would only be a one-time action for this quarter. The next day, the company announced the expected great earnings for the quarter. However, at the end of the following quarter it was positioned to miss earnings and Scrushy again asked that they fix the numbers. The CFO and controller had to lie to the auditors during the next audit.

By 1997, the distance between the actual and reported earnings kept growing. Scrushy told his CFO and controller that if they were ever caught, he would deny his involvement. As a result, the CFO who had been with Scrushy since the inception of the company resigned, even though he was making $500,000 per year. Five additional men held this position during the next six years.

Scrushy seemed to become more paranoid. He hired security guards, and became concerned that HealthSouth's offices might be bugged. The Monday morning meetings also became even more acerbic, although Scrushy told the business world that these meetings were exceptionally productive. One of the CFOs later said he wanted to stand up in one of the Monday meetings and report that he had committed securities fraud for Scrushy and to keep his job he would do the same again.

The acquisition activity continued unabated. In the late 1990s and early 2000s HealthSouth bought numerous inpatient rehabilitation hospitals and outpatient centers. The company still had the enormous challenge of integrating them managerially and financially. HealthSouth often did only cursory due diligence, as Scrushy only wanted enough to "paper the files." Never was enough found to call off a deal. Scrushy's response to concerns was, "We have to do this deal—because if we don't, someone else will and then we'll have to compete against them" (Beam 2009, 106). The acquisitions continued to mask HealthSouth's core problems, but due to the poor due diligence many of the acquisitions brought their own "cooked books" that compounded HealthSouth's financial reporting issues.

The reported and actual profits kept diverging. By 2003 the company paid more in federal income taxes on its reported profits than it actually made in net income. Income was being dramatically overstated, while drastically understating contractual allowances and bad debt. These items got so high that there were meetings at the end of the quarter with key financial managers, who called themselves "The Family." These individuals were rewarded with bonuses and stock options for their loyalty. They identified the "hole" or shortfall they had, and the "dirt" needed to fill it in to meet Wall Street expectations. Nearly every item on HealthSouth's balance sheet became fictitious. To make this work, about 120,000 fraudulent journal entries had to be done each quarter. They also dramatically overstated their cash balance. At one time they showed they had $320 million in cash but in reality had just $10 million.

Many hospital managers ignored the fraud, as it was the only way to meet their budgets and get rewarded with bonuses and stock options. However, some started asking about the details, so HealthSouth stopped giving its hospital managers detailed financial statements. As a result, many started generating their own internal financial statements to track their operations. Reports to Wall Street were complete fiction. Scrushy was a great presenter and constantly appeased Wall Street.

By 2003 Scrushy personally owned the following:

- Four homes worth $18.9 million ($27.2 million in 2021 dollars)
- A farm in Montgomery County worth $125,000
- A skating rink in Vestavia Hills worth $1.25 million
- An office building in West Palm Beach worth $1 million
- Seven watercraft
- Two aircraft
- Thirty-seven cars, including a $135,000 bulletproof BMW and a $250,000 Lamborghini
- A Sikorsky helicopter worth $6 million

At this time, the company decided to lay off several employees. When Scrushy's chief operating officer (COO) told him it did not look good to lay people off and fly in an expensive helicopter, Scrushy chided him that it was not a helicopter, it was progress that people would be seeing. The COO left within a year. However, the helicopter was often used for personal business, as Scrushy's third wife frequently used it to go shopping, and Scrushy would fly to the office in it. In 1998, Scrushy had made *Business Week*'s list of the country's highest paid CEOs, with $100 million in bonuses and salaries and $90 million in stock options.

Scrushy started spending more time on other pursuits. He paid about $1 million to bankroll a teen glamor band and was rumored to have paid for their breast augmentations. He also gave $250,000 in stock options to the head of Sony Records, who later signed this band.

By 2001, the investment community was getting tired of Scrushy's promises, but he was more committed to his bands. HealthSouth's stock was down, yet Scrushy kept making plans for his bands and spending lavishly, while the rest of the company was being asked to cut costs. The 2001 board of directors meeting was held in Palm Beach, and the company used four jets to fly in board members and company executives. Little time was spent on company reports, while most of the time was used to view Scrushy's videos about his bands.

All this was occurring while HealthSouth was losing physicians, referrals, and patients. Legislation and lawsuits were mounting that could materially damage the company, and aging facilities had not been repaired or replaced. Scrushy, however, continually guarded the good name of Health-South, tracking people down through the internet when they said negative things and suing them for libel.

Problems continued into 2002. The Sarbanes-Oxley Act passed that year, which created strict reporting requirements and increased punishments for companies cooking their books. Each year a company's CEO and CFO had to personally certify that their company's financial statements were accurate. The reimbursement for Medicare physical therapy was also decreased, which would lower HealthSouth's revenues by about $25 million per year. When approached about this and the need to restate accurate earnings, Scrushy hit the roof and told his executives there was no way to lower the company's earnings. He ordered them to "get the hell out of his way" and never bother him with this "bull——" again.

Meanwhile, Scrushy was quietly trying to sell his options, which were worth $100 million. He wanted his board to let him sell them at $4 above the current stock price. The board did not agree, so he sold them at market price, just before the news of the Medicare payment decrease was announced.

The current CFO at first refused to sign the document certifying the books and threatened to resign. However, after extreme pressure from Scrushy and promises that the books would be corrected very soon, he finally did so, accounting for the estimated $25 million shortfall. It wasn't enough. The Medicare impact came to $175 million, and HealthSouth's stock fell 58 percent to just $5 a share. Scrushy was dividing the company and had already unloaded much of his stock, so he was fine. Of course, he claimed not to know of the Medicare policy changes before the sale.

Problems arose with stockholder lawsuits and a Securities and Exchange Commission investigation about insider trading. Scrushy hired an outside law firm to prove he did not know anything before his stock sale. When HealthSouth reported closer to accurate numbers, forensic auditors raised penetrating questions. As a result, Scrushy fired the firms raising these questions. The stock continued to slide, and the spinoff of the surgery division collapsed. Scrushy blamed his COO for all the problems. However, Wall Street had been burned and would not take Scrushy seriously from this point forward.

The only way he could get the company back to profitability was through continued fraud. He demanded that his financial people do whatever was needed. The CFO was fed up. He felt his last 13 years were a waste. He had climbed the corporate ladder, but had also committed securities fraud, lost a good marriage, entered a bad one, and though he was rich, he felt terribly guilty. Given this, he arranged a meeting with the US Federal Bureau of Investigation (FBI). They had had no idea of the extent of fraud. In March 2003, the FBI raided HealthSouth. After the CFO plead guilty to fraud, HealthSouth's board of directors fired Scrushy. He was indicted on 85 counts of fraud and the government moved to confiscate $278 million in personal assets. Scrushy claimed he knew nothing of the fraud, even though ten of his employees agreed to testify to his involvement.

Scrushy, fighting the indictments, began to reinvent himself. Together with his wife, he began hosting a daily half-hour morning religious TV talk show catering to the Black community. The Scrushys quit their mostly white evangelical church and joined a blue-collar, mostly Black church to which he donated $1 million, along with another $700,000 he donated to other local Black organizations. Ironically, few Black employees ever worked at HealthSouth, and Scrushy had rarely mentioned religion. Scrushy's defense team continued that he had not known what was happening, and on June 28, 2005, a Birmingham jury—seven Black and five white jurors—found him not guilty. Scrushy thanked his "praying partners." He supposedly had spent $25 million on attorneys for his defense but received $17 million in reimbursement from HealthSouth's legal insurance.

Four months later, on October 28, 2005, Scrushy was indicted, along with Alabama's former governor, on federal bribery and corruption charges. Surprisingly to some, Scrushy was found guilty of this "pay-to-play" scheme. The jury—once again seven Black jurors and five white jurors—convicted both men of obstruction of justice, bribery, and fraud in 2006. Scrushy was ordered to pay $47.8 million for illegal bonuses. Scrushy was beside himself. He claimed that his $500,000 "donation" to the governor was a civic duty and that there was no evidence to tie him to the charges. A full year later Scrushy was sentenced to six years and ten months, and required to pay for his incarceration in addition to fines of more than $400,000. Two years later, in 2009, shareholders filed a class-action civil lawsuit that resulted in a $2.88 billion judgment.

Scrushy remained in jail until July 2012. He has become a small business consultant and motivational speaker, and published a book titled *When Building a Billion Dollar Company: Here Are a Few Things to Think About*. He remains married to his third wife. The fourth episode of Netflix's docuseries "Trial by Media" focused on Scrushy, using the title "King Richard." He claimed to be shocked by the episode and felt it was wrong and twisted.

Case Questions

1. What was Scrushy's leadership style?
2. How did Scrushy hold power and influence in his company?
3. What was the culture in HealthSouth?
4. What ethical issues existed in Scrushy's behaviors and company?

Reference

Beam, A. 2009. *HealthSouth: The Wagon to Disaster*. Fairhope, AL: Wagon Publishing.

CASE 16

FHP—UTAH

By Larry Hancock

Note: The following case is based on the sources cited. It is intended for case study purposes only and does not imply acceptance of any statement as fact.

Part 1: They Would Never Leave Us—Holy Cross System's Failed Negotiation

Holy Cross Hospital had worked with a new for-profit health management organization (HMO), FHP, in Salt Lake City for about 16 years. Although Holy Cross was a not-for-profit system with a religious mission, it felt it needed the patient volumes and revenues from FHP to remain profitable. After considerable initial discussion it offered FHP a 20 percent discount on charges—one of the largest discounts Holy Cross offered at that time. As a result, FHP directed all of its hospital inpatient and most outpatient volumes from the county to Holy Cross. This grew over the years until it accounted for an average daily census (ADC) of 15 inpatients per day out of its whole hospital ADC of 100, plus a significant outpatient revenue stream.

However, neither Holy Cross nor FHP was happy with the other, and each thought the other was taking advantage of the situation. FHP was headquartered in California, where it routinely received much deeper discounts—up to 50 percent. Holy Cross, on the other hand, felt that FHP was only interested in making money and cut corners in patient care.

The status quo continued until FHP announced it would build its own hospital in Salt Lake City. The new hospital was to be opened in two years. This infuriated the CEO of Holy Cross, who believed it was one more example of FHP being a greedy for-profit company. Coincidentally, the Holy Cross–FHP contract was expiring soon. After a short board meeting, Holy Cross sent a letter to FHP's regional vice president, Elden Mitchell, saying that immediately after the contract expired FHP would pay full charges for all services. Mitchell and his vice president in charge of hospital contracts were both upset, as this would increase FHP's costs substantially for the next two years.

The FHP executives set up a meeting with Holy Cross to work out a solution. Both knew that moving patients to another facility would cause significant logistical problems, especially since everyone knew it would only be for a two-year period. The meeting did not go well. Holy Cross felt that it had significant leverage over FHP and refused to offer any discount. FHP was not certain what to do.

The next day, Mitchell decided to check with the CEO at St. Mark's Hospital, which was also a for-profit organization. He thought that he could get a small discount that he could use to renegotiate with Holy Cross. FHP told St. Mark's that it wanted a per diem payment. This would protect it from price increases and, hopefully, give it a much lower overall cost.

St. Mark's Hospital was owned by HCA Healthcare, and had been purchased from the Episcopal Diocese of Utah in 1988. At the time FHP approached St. Mark's, the hospital was making about $1 million a month in profits.

FHP told St. Mark's that it was planning to open a Medicare Part C HMO the following year and that it would like to have a contract for this business as well as its hospital admissions. It was estimated that this would result in an additional 10 ADC after the first year of operations. To Mitchell's surprise, St. Mark's seemed very interested and promised that it would get back to FHP in three days with a proposal.

The CEO of St. Mark's had a decision to make. Should he offer a small discount to FHP? Or should he be more aggressive and offer a low per diem price? St. Mark's had space for about 100 more patients, and could easily accommodate the FHP patients. He anticipated that it would take six months to switch all FHP patients to his facility, and there was no guarantee that the Medicare patients would materialize. However, if they did, it would be about six months before this program started and only another 18 months before FHP would open their hospital.

Case Questions, Part 1
1. What are the main factors to consider in this negotiation?
2. What should St. Mark's offer?
3. What qualitative factors should be considered?
4. Would additional hospital equipment be needed?
5. Would any patients be retained after the opening of the FHP hospital?

Part 2: An Unexpected Offer

St. Mark's came back to FHP with two surprisingly low per diem rates. The chief financial officer at St. Mark's had realized that the 100 empty beds it had available were fixed costs and its marginal/incremental costs were only about $300 per day. St. Mark's also knew about FHP's existing 25 ADC being treated at Holy Cross. Therefore, St. Mark's offered a $460 per diem price for the existing patient population, which was about a 30 percent discount from its set prices. The Medicare HMO patients that might come next year were uncertain, would be older, and would use more resources; for that population, St. Mark's offered a diagnosis-related group rate equal to what Medicare was paying—about $745 per day.

Given this proposal, FHP did not think it reasonable to go back to Holy Cross to negotiate. Within two weeks, FHP and St. Mark's signed an exclusive regional contract for these rates. Holy Cross was stunned. It could not believe that this had happened. Its CEO was very upset. A local paper reported the change:

> Starting in June, FHP patients will be sent to St. Mark's Hospital instead of Holy Cross Hospital.
>
> . . . FHP, with 128,000 members in Utah, plans to build its own 120-bed hospital in South Salt Lake by early 1993. . . .
>
> A Holy Cross executive said he was surprised by the announcement that they were losing FHP's business, after lengthy negotiations with the company.
>
> "As recently as last week, we were led to believe that the signing of an agreement was imminent," said . . . [the] chief executive officer for Holy Cross. "We're going to explore all types of remedies that may be available to us as a result of the very short notification here."
>
> The hospital will see the impact in the balance books. [The Holy Cross CEO] termed the move an inconvenience to the institution, and said the hospital is forced to make short-term cuts in operating expenses to make up for losing the volume of patients. . . .
>
> "The loss of net patient revenue will amount to approximately 8.3 percent throughout the Holy Cross system statewide," he said. (Fagg 1991)

Case Questions, Part 2

1. How did St. Mark's proposal completely undermine FHP's negotiation with Holy Cross?
2. What do you think the financial impact on St. Mark's was when the 15 ADC moved?
3. What other factors do you think would have benefited St. Mark's and hurt Holy Cross?

Part 3: The Impact of the Changes at St. Mark's

It did take St. Mark's six months to shift all of the patient volume from Holy Cross. Its inpatient volumes increased from 110 to 125. The new inpatient volume brought in about $85,000 per month, and significant new outpatient volume brought in another $80,000 per month, for a total of about

$165,000 per month in new profits. The following year, FHP launched its Medicare Advantage Program, bringing an additional 10 ADC to St. Mark's and a further $160,000 in profits per month. The new incremental business increased St. Mark's profits to $1.325 million per month, or nearly $16 million per year.

The new business also had a number of secondary effects. The additional profits allowed St. Mark's to expand its facility and increase its market reputation. St. Mark's enjoyed the perception of "winning" in its market, which it used to persuade doctors who had practiced at Holy Cross to join it as well as to recruit out-of-state physicians. In addition, St. Mark's was able to shift the more complicated cases from Holy Cross, and these remained at St. Mark's even when FHP opened its own hospital. The increased profits also allowed St. Mark's to build a senior health center, a bariatric program, and a women's center, and to expand its cardiac and orthopedic services. Two years into the contract with FHP, the hospital's profits jumped to $20 million per year.

The speed of the negotiation did have at least one negative effect. Hurrying to conclude the contract, the administrators at St. Mark's failed to involve the hospital's medical staff and board. The leaders of both groups were very upset that they had not at least been consulted. The CEO at St. Mark's had to spend significant political capital smoothing this over, but it was questionable whether the trust was fully established.

Case Questions, Part 3
1. What was the impact of agreeing to the contract with FHP?
2. Why was St. Mark's able to increase its profits so much?
3. What could it have done better?

Part 4: The Opening and Failure of the FHP Hospital

FHP had pushed for construction of a 120-bed hospital to "control" care and reduce costs for its enrollees. The hospital cost $60 million and was about 200,000 square feet. However, it had miscalculated the number of patients it would have, and found that enrollees outside of the immediate county would not travel to the hospital, preferring to be treated in their own geographic areas. The local paper reported on the hospital's struggles:

> FHP fell on hard times, finding that the South Salt Lake hospital, another in Southern California and its network clinics weren't meeting expectations. There wasn't enough patient volume and new HMO enrollees to absorb the expansion costs. The quest for short-term profitability eventually drove the company to shed its hospitals and clinics. (Campbell 1997)

Mitchell, the FHP regional vice president, who had since left for another position, told the reporter that, in retrospect, building the FHP hospital "was premature and I believe there were better solutions than construction in a community with 100 percent too many beds."

FHP sold the hospital to Paracelsus Healthcare in 1996 with a 15-year contract for hospital services with FHP. But just over a year later, Paracelsus found that the hospital was a losing proposition. According to the report in the local paper, "a source close to the industry said that FHP officials felt they had negotiated a very 'aggressive' contract and Paracelsus may not have fully anticipated all of the costs associated with the deal." By 1997, after only four years in operation, FHP enrollees made up 95 percent of the hospital's patients. Of the 100 beds in operation, it had an average 10 ADC. But the negotiated rate with FHP was so low that the hospital continued to lose money, and adding patients would only cause the hospital to lose more money. The hospital's workforce of about five hundred people faced the prospect of losing their jobs.

Case Questions, Part 4
1. If additional patients would cause the hospital to lose more money, what does this tell you about the contract rates?
2. How could St. Mark's make a profit on such low rates when the Paracelsus hospital could not?

References
Campbell, J. 1997. "Ailing South S.L. Hospital May Close Its Doors." *Deseret News.* April 14. www.deseret.com/1997/4/14/19306663/ailing-south-s-l-hospital-may-close-its-doors.

Fagg, E. 1991. "Holy Cross Hospital Loses FHP Contract to Rival S.L. Facility." *Deseret News.* April 24. www.deseret.com/1991/4/24/18916919/holy-cross-hospital-loses-fhp-contract-to-rival-s-l-facility.

CASE 17

STARTING AS CEO AT SKYVIEW HOSPITAL

by Rand Kerr

Part 1: Challenges

Dan just started as the new CEO of Skyview Hospital, a 150-bed hospital in the suburbs, which is an affiliate of a large hospital system. Before agreeing to take the position, he understood that the hospital has struggled clinically, financially, and with patient, employee, and physician satisfaction. In addition, the hospital does not have a positive reputation in the community. He knows he has a lot to do to turn things around.

Dan has been coming in early every day, reading as many reports as he can to better understand some of the issues. So far, he has combed through most of the clinical and financial reports. Today Dan began reviewing some of the satisfaction reports. Over time, the hospital has consistently surveyed its employees, physicians, and patients to determine their level of satisfaction. Dan decided to start with the employee satisfaction surveys, as he knows that his employees are critical stakeholders and one of the most important factors for the hospital's success.

As he begins reviewing the employee engagement scores, Dan can see many areas that need improvement. The overall score puts Skyview in the bottom quartile of the hospital system and the nation. It's no wonder the hospital's employee turnover is over 30 percent. The employee survey highlights several areas that need improvement. The following questions scored especially low:

- Are senior leaders approachable?
- Can you trust senior leaders to follow through?
- Are efforts made to get employee opinions?
- Does my supervisor coach me?

To Dan, these very low scores all indicate problems that originate with leadership. His experience has demonstrated that employees' attitudes are directly impacted by their leaders. But one score jumps out at Dan: When asked "Would you recommend this hospital to family or friends?" only 50 percent of his employees said yes.

In all the hospitals where Dan has previously worked, the response to this question has always been very positive, generally above 80 percent. Despite the issues and complaints many hospital employees have, they usually feel good enough about the care their hospital delivers to recommend it. Obviously, this is not the case at Skyview Hospital.

Shocked, Dan sits back in his chair. Nobody in the community will trust Skyview Hospital if its own staff does not. If this rating is accurate, then many community members are hearing negative reviews of the hospital. Skyview's clinical care can definitely be improved, but the data shows that clinical care is nowhere near as bad as perceived by the employees. There seems to be a deeper problem here.

Case Questions: Part 1
1. Why would the employees feel this way?
2. What perceptional theories may cause these employees' beliefs?
3. How could Dan turn employee perceptions around?

Part 2: Actions

Dan took the next couple of months to evaluate the leadership team at the hospital. He spoke to key stakeholders and talked with and observed his leadership team. After three months, he began taking action to install leaders he is confident will manage as he does. In the next few months, the weakest third of the leadership team left; some Dan terminated, and others could see the writing on the wall and left of their own accord. Dan then hired new leaders and started building a new leadership team.

Dan decided that he wanted a standard leadership perspective and created a mandatory leadership training program. Dan runs the program with his new director of human resources (HR) and teaches portions of the material himself. The program is founded on servant leadership principles from books such as *The Five Dysfunctions of a Team*, *Crucial Conversations*, and *Leadership and Self-Deception*. Dan and the new HR director also developed a strategic plan focused on employee engagement. The plan targets improving three core domains around the following employee perceptions:

- Am I valued?
- How can I grow?
- What do I do?

The plan is intended to eliminate fear and build trust through all levels of the organization. Teaching and modeling its principles is critical to changing employee perceptions of their leaders and of the hospital. Over time, employee perceptions improved and turnover declined until, in Dan's fourth year, the hospital employee engagement surveys were ranked among the highest in the system—improvements that were sustained over several years.

The hospital also scored very well on other measures after Dan's changes. The hospital's corporate office uses Gallup for its surveys, and one of its metrics is "Engagement Ratio"—the ratio of highly engaged versus highly disengaged employees. This metric is an important one to the corporation, used to compare the success of its hospitals. Skyview's Engagement Ratio is now 12.5, which is multiples higher than the corporate national average of 3.4.

The training and changed leadership behavior have also reduced the problems in clinical outcomes, patient satisfaction, physician satisfaction, and financial health. Physician satisfaction rose to the 90th percentile and patient satisfaction rose to the 75th percentile. The hospital is delivering excellent clinical care, and has now won awards in patient outcomes from multiple organizations. In Dan's second year as CEO, the hospital was named to Watson Health's 100 Top Hospitals list, recognizing it as one of the top-performing hospitals in the United States. In his seventh year, Skyview won the Everest Award, recognizing the hospital for being among the top 100 hospitals for rate of improvement over the past five years. Since Dan joined, Skyview has also been highlighted in a feature article by *Modern Healthcare* for consistency in outcomes and leadership. His leadership efforts have grown Skyview's financial earnings by over 400 percent. Overall, Dan's leadership changes and efforts have been very successful.

Case Questions: Part 2

1. What were the critical actions taken by the CEO to change the hospital?
2. Why did the CEO begin with employee satisfaction?
3. What principles of change were used?

CASE 18

DIRECTOR OF MARKETING VERSUS OPERATIONS

You are in charge of a 310-bed hospital and have an excellent management team that has won many awards. Aside from the high operating margins, as high as 40 percent, your hospital has won consistent awards for public relations, television, and newspaper ads. You believe the hospital's public image has improved substantially in the past three years, largely thanks to your director of marketing and development, Fred Halso. Fred is about 35, single, and a real go-getter. He is not a close friend of yours, but he is a close friend of your hospital's regional chief financial officer (CFO). They have been drinking buddies for several years and previously worked with each other. Clearly, the corporation that owns your hospital and the hospital advisory board are pleased with your performance.

However, recently three women have come to you individually to report that Fred has made inappropriate remarks about their bodies and has tried to pursue a sexual relationship with them. His remarks and actions continued far beyond what was comfortable for the women. The last woman to come to you was Fred's assistant, who told you that he had been consistently inviting her to go out for drinks after work. She said that she made the mistake of going once, and he then pushed her to go home with him, which she refused to do. Since then, Fred has been very cold toward her and, even though she feels her performance has not changed, he has belittled her work and threatened to "have a reckoning" when her annual performance review occurs in two months.

After the third report, you call Fred in to discuss the accusations. As you expect, he denies everything. He states that he is just friendly and that perhaps they misunderstood his friendliness for abuse. He asks to know who made the accusations. You keep the identities of the first two accusers confidential, but you do talk about his assistant. Fred says that she has been going through a divorce and he only was trying to listen to her and help her adjust. However, the additional stress of the divorce has affected her work and he is concerned that she is not meeting deadlines and her work has become sloppy. He agrees to be more careful, and you are relieved that this might not be such a big issue after all.

Sadly, over the next two weeks, Fred's assistant, one of the first women who came to you, and three additional women are individually in your office to complain about Fred. You now have six complainants, and two of the women have now made multiple complaints. All have terrible stories to tell. One had a brief affair with Fred. When she broke it off, he refused to stop bothering her. She works down the hall from him and hates coming to work now. You take the issue to your human resources (HR) director, and she warns you that two of the women, including Fred's assistant, have met with her to consider filing a sexual discrimination claim against Fred and the hospital. You discuss the issue with your boss, the regional vice president, who tells you his CFO has heard about the claims and they are just bogus, unfair reverse discrimination.

You need to meet with Fred (and separately with each of the women), along with your HR director, to chart a path forward. You must decide what to do and whom to believe.

Case Questions

1. What human resource issues are addressed in this case?
2. Are there ethical considerations in this decision?
3. Create a question to state the moral problem.
4. What are the economic outcomes of your potential decisions?
5. What are the cultural issues involved in this case?
6. What legal and ethical duties are involved?

CASE 19

THE OGRE AND THE PLAYROOM

By Joseph Horton

Some actions in life, once taken, instantly relegate a person to the status of villain. Six months after my taking a senior position at a major children's hospital, I had the unpleasant experience of discovering one of these: taking a playroom away from the children in the hospital.

Even worse, it was the only playroom in the building.

Before I came to the children's hospital, a new group of pediatric intensivists had been recruited to run the intensive care unit (ICU). The hospital was old and too small to accommodate all their needs. A new replacement facility was under construction two miles away, but would not be finished for years. But the lead intensivist, due to arrive in two months, had been promised offices adjacent to the current ICU.

The only option was to take the hospital playroom and remodel it into the offices. My predecessor allegedly agreed to this decision—a decision invisible to all but the intensivists and administration. However, clearly the commitment had been made. When the time for remodeling arrived, the decision became entirely public and entirely attributed to me, as I was the chief operating officer.

There is no way to mitigate the offense of taking away the only playroom in a hospital. Playrooms in children's hospitals are not just for play; a lot of therapy and family counseling occurred in this room. No matter how good your attitude, how affable your personality, or how honorable your intent, the action itself screams that you are mean-spirited and heartless. Had a popularity poll been taken at that point, I would have come in somewhere below an IRS auditor. Notices were posted by child life specialists and nurses, pleading with all readers to help save the playroom by writing to the ogre (me) perpetrating this crime.

Overnight, I became public enemy number one. When the devil has been identified, people are galvanized. They don't want to hear that you really don't want to deprive children of their playroom. They prefer to hate you without being confused.

I knew I was in serious trouble the minute I learned about the decision. With rolled-up sleeves and loosened tie, measuring tape in hand, I went upstairs to the playroom and met the hospital construction supervisor.

Together we remeasured the space, hoping to find a way to honor the office commitment and preserve a functional portion of the playroom. Meanwhile, hate mail came pouring in from nurses, parents, neighbors, grandparents, physicians, therapists, child life specialists, and patients. Following is just a sampling of the comments:

> I find it a crime . . . @#$%&*!
> The playroom is much more important for the well-being of children than an office . . . @#$%&*!

One nine-year-old girl with cancer wrote with more gentleness than most: "That's the only place to play . . . I'd appreciate if you would please leave it there please, please!"

After intense brainstorming, we found an imperfect solution. I called the intensivist and told him we would both be tarred and feathered if we usurped the playroom. He readily agreed to the alternative, even though it placed his offices in a separate building 200 yards from the hospital. The crisis was resolved, the playroom was saved, and so was my reputation.

The notices were taken down and the letters stopped—except for one. It came from a physician who helped recruit the intensivist. He voiced his displeasure that the office commitment had not been honored. This letter required further meetings with this physician to discuss the dilemma. After a time, with some reluctance, he withdrew his objections and we kept the playroom. The art of administration is sometimes about displeasing someone for reasons that allow you to sleep at night.

Case Questions

1. What are the commitment issues in this case?
2. How does consistency in decisions affect the respect for a leader?
3. When making such a decision, what are the important factors to consider?
4. Should the most powerful person influence what decision is made?

CASE 20

A SAUDI BID AND I

You have spent three years expanding your consulting services in the Middle East. After spending more than nine months in Saudi Arabia, you have established close relationships with key healthcare professionals and educational leaders. You have been appointed to the Saudi Ministry of Health's (MOH) International Advisory Board, which has provided you with access to many of the top leaders in the country.

The MOH is beginning to construct 100 new hospitals, 1,000 clinics, and four medical cities in the country. Almost all of the hospital administrators are physicians—most poorly prepared—and the results across the country show this. The ministry's leadership recognize that they have not invested enough in training the leaders of their health system and want to better prepare the new managers.

A major MOH bid for healthcare leadership training has been developed, and you are interested in obtaining at least a portion of the business. Several big players in the market are also bidding on the proposal, including GE Healthcare Consulting, McKinsey & Company, and IBM. You know that it will be difficult for you to win even part of this bid, but you do have personal contacts that others do not have.

As the bid progresses, your friends put you in contact with a senior associate minister of health, who will be making the final decision. You set up a meeting with him, hoping that he will be influenced by your friends, his subordinates, and your extensive experience. Your conversation with him goes well and he defines certain parts of the training that he thinks you would be perfect to do. However, he keeps commenting that to be successful you need to have a Saudi partner. You try to explore what this means. He tells you about a Saudi training firm that he knows that could facilitate the training and obtaining the contract. He tells you that your bid should allocate 35 percent of the total contract to the services of the training firm. You are certain that either the associate minister owns the training firm or one of his relatives does. After the meeting, you ask around and find out that the associate minister's son and his wife own the training firm.

You think you really need the contract. Financially you are OK but you are considering expanding your company, and to do that you would need the money from this contract and the security of having a two-year engagement.

You talk to your Saudi friends and they tell you that this kind of arrangement is common and not technically illegal. They say it is not a bribe, but you are not certain. The Saudis are not asking for money without providing any services, but they would only provide influence—much like a lobbyist.

Case Questions

1. How do the cultural differences in this case affect the available options?
2. If you had to negotiate an agreement, what would you do?
3. Is this an ethical arrangement?
4. What ethical framework would you use to either justify or demonstrate that the associate minister's proposed arrangement is ethical?

CASE 21

A PROPOSED MERGER GONE BAD: A LACK OF CONFIDENCE IN LEADERSHIP

Note: The following case is based on the sources cited. It is intended for case study purposes only and does not imply acceptance of any statement as fact.

Beaumont Health's leadership thought they had found the perfect match for their health system. Beaumont Health was the largest healthcare system in Michigan, with $4.7 billion in annual net revenues, eight hospitals, nearly 5,000 affiliated physicians and more than 38,000 employees (Basen 2020; Bouffard 2020). The CEO had been there since 2015 and been well rewarded for his efforts to build the system, with compensation of $5.93 million in 2018 (Basen 2020) and $6.75 million in 2019 (Dixon 2020). The CEO and chief operating officer, both of whom had an MBA (master's in business administration), had assumed their roles in 2015 and 2016, respectively. The CEO was hired to "help merge the three systems and balance budgets" (Basen 2020). The new CEO, John Fox, had an MBA and was very skilled in improving operations and did improve the system's bottom line. However, there were ramifications to this focus.

Many noted that the company's culture had changed with the coming of the new CEO, who focused almost exclusively on the bottom line. For instance, many system publications highlighted financials rather than new research or physician achievements. Some employees claimed there was such an emphasis on profitability that the mission for hospitals to provide the best service to people had diminished. Professionals in the organization felt disrespected, as many experienced and private-practice physicians had been forced out to cut costs and make room for more Beaumont-employed doctors.

However, in 2020 the COVID-19 pandemic created havoc with the hospital operations. Beaumont furloughed 2,475 employees and permanently eliminated 450 positions (Bouffard 2020). Looking toward the future, amid this turmoil, the CEO proposed to reposition his system by merging with another larger health system in a neighboring state. Local press reported the CEO's enthusiasm for the merger:

> "Our goal on this is to grow market share for Beaumont Health and to have a bigger impact in Michigan," he said, "and by virtue of the synergies and the benefits of this combination, we think we'll be in a great position to do so." . . .
>
> "We are excited to explore this option with an organization as highly regarded as Advocate Aurora Health known for their track record in health outcomes, population health and consumer experience," Fox said. "The potential opportunity to leverage the strength and scale of a regional organization while maintaining a local focus and strong presence in Michigan as a leader and major employer is important to us." (Herndon 2020)

By June 2020, the systems had signed a nonbinding letter of intent to create a health system that would span three states. The merger was supposed to position the organization to "better weather future changes and disruptions in health care, as well as to make greater investments in patient care than it could do on its own" (Reindl 2020).

Almost immediately physicians and employees at Beaumont Health began expressing their displeasure with the proposed move, citing concerns that there would be little or no economic benefits from joining a health system in other states, that there could be a potential loss of local control, and that capital needed to grow local health services could be diverted to other states (Basen 2020; Bouffard 2020). Soon after, a petition drive sprang up with hundreds signing the document that asked the Beaumont Health Board to terminate the proposed merger and fire the system's CEO (Ellison 2020a; Paavola 2020). The petition claimed that across the past five years the physicians in the system had seen a rapid and progressive deterioration in every aspect of patient care at Beaumont Health and they had lost confidence in the administration (Paavola 2020). Some privately suggested that they were certain that the CEO would financially benefit if the merger went through (Bouffard 2020). Other physicians sent letters to the board pointing to the departure of many key physicians, the corporate leadership's focus on profits, and a demand to get rid of everyone in the corporate leadership (Paavola 2020).

In response to the concerns, the CEO and chief medical offer met with many physicians and agreed that many had legitimate questions, but said that most doctors were not really opposed to the proposed merger, but many feared change. The CEO furthermore claimed that the merger would lead to an investment of $100 million in new technology in the newly created system that could monitor public health and chronic health conditions (Basen 2020; Bouffard 2020).

Case 21: A Proposed Merger Gone Bad: A Lack of Confidence in Leadership

The CEO's meetings then prompted the system's medical staff leaders to conduct a survey of system doctors. The survey, completed by 1,500 of Beaumont's affiliated physicians, resulted in the following finding:

Questions
1. *The merger is likely to enhance our capacity to provide compassionate care*—70% somewhat or strongly disagreed.
2. *I have confidence in the system's leadership*—76% strongly disagreed or somewhat disagreed. (Paavola 2020)

A survey of 681 nurses was then completed that also showed the nurses at Beaumont Health were "highly critical of management and operations. . . . Ninety-six percent of the nurses said they strongly or somewhat disagreed with the statement 'I have confidence in corporate leadership'" (Ellison 2020b).

As a result of the concerns, in August the system decided to delay a vote on the planned merger (Ellison 2020b). The health system board and local lawmakers appeared to turn against the merger; the board vice chair spoke against the merger and lawmakers released a joint statement worrying that the merger would result in higher costs with little improvement in care (Paavola 2020). Large donors subsequently sent a letter asking that the merger be delayed until issues that the physicians and nurses had raised were addressed (Basen 2020).

By October, five months after the nonbinding letter of intent was signed, Beaumont Health announced it was ending the merger talks. The CEO thanked the hospital's staff, physicians, and community members for their input and indicated that the pandemic was one of the main reasons for the decision to halt merger talks (Reindl 2020).

One county executive praised the decision and issued a statement saying it was "the right thing to do. . . . Beyond financial benefits, any partnership must demonstrate tangible community benefits and improved quality of health care for our residents not readily apparent in this proposal. . . . I look forward to Beaumont's renewed focus on 'local market priorities'" (Reindl 2020).

Case Questions
1. What were the stated benefits of the proposed merger?
2. Do you think the benefits of the proposed merger were consistently explained by Beaumont's leadership? Explain your answer.
3. What could have Beaumont Health's leadership have done better to avoid many of the problems in this case?

4. How did the professional cultures help create disagreements on which direction to take?
5. How could the decision-making have been better organized and accomplished?

References

Basen, R. 2020. "How Beaumont's Megamerger Fell Apart." *Medpage Today*, October 8. www.medpagetoday.com/hospitalbasedmedicine/generalhospitalpractice/89022.

Bouffard, K. 2020. "Beaumont Pushes Back Against Doctor Criticism over Proposed Merger." *Detroit News*, July 24. www.detroitnews.com/story/business/2020/07/24/beaumont-pushes-back-doctor-criticism-proposed-merger/5502779002/.

Dixon, J. 2020. "Beaumont Health Paid CEO $2.6 Million Bonus Weeks Before Bailout." *Detroit Free Press*, November 17. www.freep.com/story/news/local/2020/11/17/beaumont-ceo-paid-2-6-million-bonus/6312013002/.

Ellison, A. 2020a. "Beaumont Health CEO, CMO Target of No Confidence Petition." *Becker's Hospital Review*, July 22. www.beckershospitalreview.com/hospital-management-administration/beaumont-health-ceo-cmo-target-of-no-confidence-petition.html.

Ellison, A. 2020b. "Beaumont Loses Confidence of More than 650 Nurses." *Becker's Hospital Review*, August 24. www.beckershospitalreview.com/hospital-management-administration/beaumont-loses-confidence-of-nurses.html.

Herndon, D. 2020. "Beaumont Health, Advocate Health Exploring Merger." *(Dearborn) Press & Guide*, June 19. www.pressandguide.com/news/beaumont-health-advocate-aurora-health-exploring-merger/article_6c12f3f2-b0df-11ea-872f-8f41d9f3b9a1.html.

Paavola, A. 2020. "The Collapse of the Beaumont–Advocate Aurora Merger: A Timeline." *Becker's Hospital Review*, October 12. www.beckershospitalreview.com/hospital-transactions-and-valuation/the-demise-of-the-beaumont-advocate-merger-a-timeline.html.

Reindl, J. C. 2020. "Beaumont Ends Merger Talks with Advocate Aurora Health." *Detroit Free Press*, October 2. www.freep.com/story/money/business/2020/10/02/beaumont-health-merger-advocate-aurora/5894110002/.

CASE 22

NIGHT STAFFING AND JOB COMMITMENT

Lauretta is a night shift nursing supervisor and has tremendous problems covering the evening and night shifts. Her ability to pay nurses to work evenings is constrained by a union contract which clearly states that a person working the night shift is compensated an extra $1 per hour (a shift differential). However, the hospital has not had enough nurses on staff to cover all its shifts for at least the past three years, and Lauretta has had to beg nurses, day after day, to work extra shifts and cover nights. At least once a week, a nurse calls in sick and Lauretta is left scrambling to find a replacement with just a few hours' notice. Sometimes no one is available and the night shift is forced to work understaffed, which increases the stress and frustration for those working.

The hospital administration has received numerous complaints and organized a task force to examine the staffing problems. In the first meeting, the major issues were listed. Some participants felt that the only solution was to pay a higher differential for the night shifts. Management was against only higher pay, as the shift differential was raised from fifty cents to $1 only two years ago and the problem persists. Others in the meeting felt strongly that the satisfaction level and attitudes of the nurses needed to be determined first; they proposed administering a survey.

Lauretta is not convinced any positive movement will result from the task force. She has worked at the hospital for 20 years and does not want to leave. In the past she might have stayed to be with her friends, but in the past two years, many of her close friends at the hospital have either retired or taken positions elsewhere. She began looking at other jobs in the community and found that they would all involve taking a pay cut. She is still frustrated with her job and is uncertain what she should do.

Case Questions

1. From an organizational commitment perspective (affective, continuance, and normative commitment), what keeps Lauretta at her current job?
2. Refer to chapter 5 and the discussion on equity theory. How does Lauretta's perception of her inputs and outputs affect her feelings and behavior?
3. What could management do to increase Lauretta's organizational commitment?

CASE 23

MIKE AND THE WALK-AROUND

Mike has been the CEO of BCCH for almost two years. He is a smart, hard-working person, but often has difficulty relating to others. Most of the time he is fine, but if he becomes angry, he sometimes screams at people to assert his authority. Often this happens over small things. The last time was over a spilled food tray on a nursing unit. Mike perceived that one of the nursing aides had spilled the tray through carelessness. He gave the person a piece of his mind and insisted that the nursing supervisor put a formal write up in the employee's personnel folder. These episodes had happened only twice at BCCH, but after the second time it appeared to Mike that most people showed him more respect. At least, they seemed respectful to his face. Of course, they rarely spoke with him.

Mike was certain that his employees liked him and that he was a good leader. When he gave directions or proposed ideas in meetings, people nodded and appeared to agree with him. He had dramatically improved the financial health of the hospital and received compliments from his regional vice president. Yet, all was not right.

Mike was disheartened to learn that he was rated especially low in the new hospital employee survey that his corporation had conducted two months before. Many of the employees claimed that they did not know him and indicated that he was not visible. To address this, he committed to carving time out from his meeting-packed days to walk through the hospital and greet employees. To be sure it happened, he made it the first and the last thing he did each day, taking 20–25 minutes to walk through each department starting at 7:30 a.m. and again at 5:00 p.m. Mike was a very busy man, so he did not spend much time as he walked through. Only infrequently would he stop to speak with someone. Most of the time he only walked through a department and said hello. If he stopped, it generally would be to talk to a physician. Over the next few months, he faithfully followed his twice-daily departmental visits. He was certain that he was becoming more visible and employees must be more confident in him.

In September, the corporate office asked Mike's human resources director, Patricia, to hold a series of employee forums to follow up on the employee survey. She was surprised to learn that most of the employees had very negative impressions of Mike. The forums indicated even greater anger and distrust than had been expressed on the employee survey. When Patricia sought to understand this, she was told that Mike had been monitoring their departments, checking to see when people came to work and when they left. They felt that this was the act of a despotic boss and wanted him to stop.

Patricia was concerned about how to present this to Mike. She wanted to think through the key issues. Mike truly was trying to become more visible but it had just made matters worse. He wanted to be liked, but only seemed to alienate people more. The financial outcomes at the hospital continued to improve, but a couple of physicians had recently told Patricia that they were becoming dissatisfied with Mike's leadership and were considering moving their practices. Patricia thinks she needs to do something, but she is concerned about Mike's emotions and worries he might lash out at her.

Case Questions

1. How is this an example of primary and secondary emotions? How does this demonstrate the lasting impact of inappropriate expression of emotions?
2. How would you rate Mike's emotional intelligence? What should Mike do to improve his emotional intelligence?
3. Why does Mike's perception of his leadership vary from what his employees think? How does this happen in organizations?
4. What should Patricia do to positively communicate her concerns and feedback to Mike? How could he positively address this?

CASE 24

SAKAL'S DILEMMA

Sakal, who graduated from medical school five years ago, has just completed a residency and fellowship in radiology and joined a five-member group in the Southwest United States. He is eager to do a good job and started out by putting in long hours at two of the hospitals that his group covers. His salary is based on his group's overall billings, but as a junior partner he receives his share minus 20 percent to buy into the group. He was excited to become a radiologist, as the average salary of a radiologist in the United States is just over $500,000. The group he joined is well trained, and the other four radiologists have been working in the field for 5–15 years.

Things were going well until Sakal's extended family suffered financial setbacks and he realized that he is not making enough money to cover all his obligations. He has about $300,000 in student debt from his medical education and his parents now have severe health problems and no health insurance. They are both incurring substantial hospital bills, and will continue to in the foreseeable future. Sakal comes from a culture that deeply honors parents and he would do anything to help them. It would violate everything he believes in to do otherwise. He estimates that he needs to earn at least another $100,000 per year to be able to cover these obligations.

He considers working longer hours, but under the revenue-sharing arrangement his group would receive most of the money. In addition, two of the radiologists have already cautioned him about spending so much time in the reading room, because it made them look bad. Sakal decides to go to the head of the radiology group and ask if there might be a way to increase his income.

Dr. Sally appears distracted during their meeting, but she hears Sakal out while doing her X-ray readings. When he finishes explaining his situation, Dr. Sally tells him succinctly that the group's policy is very clear on how the monies must be divided, and she can do nothing to help him. She also reminds Sakal to review his contract and remember the noncompete clause, which states that he cannot work for any competing radiology group in a 500-mile radius of their hospital.

Sakal has heard that another radiologist in his group received extra payments during an emergency. When he mentions this, Dr. Sally acts hostile and says that was an exceptional situation. She then remarks that maybe they should have not hired Sakal. New physicians should come in with a "can-do attitude," she says, and not demand more money in their first months on the job.

Sakal is not certain what to do. He has taken a class on negotiating and wants to negotiate a mutually beneficial agreement. However, he feels sad and mad, and does not know if he is being discriminated against because of his cultural background. He does not want to cause problems, but he must be able to help his parents and maintain a good relationship with his partners.

Case Questions
1. What are the key issues in this case?
2. How do group incentives influence the behaviors of the physicians?
3. Do you believe there was discrimination in this situation? If so, what should Sakal do?
4. How would you negotiate this situation with Sakal's group leader?
5. What would you do if you were Sakal?

CASE 25

SAM'S DEPOSIT RECOVERY

Sam had a hernia, but he did not have insurance and was self-employed. After 13 years of just pushing the hernia back when it stuck out, he decided to take care of it. He found a reputable local surgical center that offered a flat price of $3,500 for the surgery, which was fully inclusive—surgeon, facility, anesthesia, and follow-up. He would need to put $1,200 down before the surgery and pay the rest in two installments after the surgery. He thought this a good deal, and two months before the scheduled time he made the deposit.

Sam was cautious and read the policies and fine print. If he canceled the surgery at least two weeks before the scheduled time, the surgical center would refund his full deposit. If he canceled within two weeks of the surgery date, he would forfeit the deposit. He was nervous but planned to go ahead with the surgery.

COVID-19 hit his area one month before his scheduled surgery. Sam's business collapsed and he was very concerned about his finances. The surgery center continued with their surgeries, using special techniques to protect patients, but Sam was still worried. Sixteen days before his scheduled surgery, he finally called to cancel. To be certain he could get his money back, he also e-mailed the surgeon's office and the surgery center to tell them he was canceling.

Two weeks later, Sam got a reminder about his surgery the next morning. He thought it was strange, but perhaps the doctor's office had not communicated with the nursing staff at the center. He ignored it, as he had canceled the surgery in plenty of time.

The next morning, Sam received a call asking why he was not there for his surgery. He explained that he had canceled the surgery more than two weeks ago. The office staff apologized, and Sam thought he would certainly soon receive his refund.

Just to be certain, Sam called the surgery center the next day to find out about his refund. He was told that because his surgeon's office had not canceled the surgery, they could not refund the deposit and he should talk to the surgeon's office to ask for their share of the deposit back. However, when Sam called the surgeon's office, they said that they were having difficulty communicating with the surgery center and that Sam needed to speak with the surgery center, since he had set up the surgery with them. In addition, the surgeon's office had already paid the different providers' offices their portion of the deposit, so Sam would have to get the anesthesiologist and radiologist each to agree to return the amounts they had already been given.

Over the next two months Sam made more than 15 calls and sent 18 e-mails to the various providers' offices and the surgery center. The surgeon's office personnel were very professional, but consistently claimed they had only a portion of Sam's funds; they finally sent Sam a check for $300, which they said was all they had kept of his deposit. However, the surgery center still claims that the surgeon's office was responsible for the mix-up and should pay him the remaining $900.

Sam is getting frustrated. The staff at the surgery center now know him by name, and whenever he calls they tell him he has to talk to the providers' offices. However, when he calls the other providers, they say he has to get his money from the surgery center. Sam has now lost his temper with people at some of the offices and yelled at them. For this he feels bad, but he is also very frustrated. His business has not improved, and he really needs the $900 that he feels legally belongs to him.

Another month goes by and Sam finally finds a sympathetic reporter, who prints a story about his case in the local paper. The public attention motivates the surgery center to agree to do an official review of Sam's case. They have set up a "patient satisfaction" committee to review complaints, and Sam's complaint finally has a case number. After another month, the review committee decides to send Sam $280 for their portion of the deposit, telling him once again that they sent the rest to the other providers. Sam refuses to accept this. He e-mails the surgery center, stating that he contracted with them and not with the doctors—it was a package payment that they controlled! The surgery center offers to keep talking about it. Sam updates the reporter, who plans to print another, larger article about the surgery center, which information Sam relays to the director at the center.

At last, this motivates the surgery center, and Sam gets an e-mail saying that they have decided to refund him an additional $510. This would bring his total refund to $1,090 of the original $1,200 deposit. Sam wonders where the other $110 went but has been worn down enough to accept it. The next day he receives an e-mail from the accounting company that handles the surgery center's billing that he should expect his refund in six to eight weeks. This is their normal and accepted policy. Almost eight months will have passed between Sam making his deposit and getting most of it back. Sam throws up his hands and hopes the hernia survives another 13 years without complications.

Case Questions

1. What were the customer relations problems in this case?
2. How could the different organizations have improved their communication with Sam?
3. What are the advantages and disadvantages of company policies?
4. How does this case describe the complexity of the US healthcare system?

CASE 26

SHANNON'S EXTREME UNINSURED HEALTHCARE COSTS

Note: The following case is based on the sources cited. It is intended for case study purposes only and does not imply acceptance of any statement as fact.

Shannon was a healthy young man, so it was a shock to wake with a serious pain in his abdomen. He was not certain, but he feared appendicitis. He worked for an outdoor company that did not provide health insurance, so he was concerned about the cost of going to the doctor. He had very limited savings but had been saving to purchase a house and had $12,000 in the bank. The pain continued to worsen, until he felt he did not have a choice, so he woke his partner and had her drive him to Heart of the Rockies Regional Medical Center (HRRMC)—the only hospital in the county.

At the hospital, Shannon received a CT scan. He was told he had acute appendicitis and needed immediate surgery. Shannon had surgery that night, and was discharged the next day.

A couple of days later, Shannon was doubled over in pain and had to go back to the hospital. Another CT scan showed a large blood clot in his abdomen, which appeared to be a complication from his surgery. The surgeon was called, and Shannon was rushed back into surgery to remove the clot. Although this surgery was also successful, Shannon had to spend four more days in the hospital. Recovery was difficult but after a couple of months he was starting to feel much better—until the bills for his surgeries started to arrive.

Shannon was shocked to see that the hospital bills came to $80,232 for both surgeries. The appendectomy was billed at $35,906 and the surgery to remove the blood clot was billed at $44,326. This did not include additional bills from the surgeon, anesthesiologist, pathologist, or radiologist that amounted to more than $10,000.

Shannon wanted to know a bit more about HRRMC, so he found the hospital's website. On the "Mission Vision Values" page of the site, the hospital states its mission is

> to enhance the health of our community through the delivery of personalized and exceptional care. Our vision is to be the healthcare provider of choice for our region as a world-class rural medical organization.

On the same page, HRRMC says it "has adopted eight values to guide the everyday behavior of every employee":

- Teamwork
- Safety
- Recognition
- Talent
- Attitude
- Accountability
- Customer Service
- Respect

In addition, the site emphasizes the hospital's commitment to patient care:

> In conjunction with our vision and values, our mission serves as a guideline for daily decision-making and represents the principles and practices that we constantly apply. The comfort and care of our patients is a major focus. We strive to put the "care" in healthcare by providing quality care that is close to home.

Although HRRMC is a small rural facility and many of these facilities across the United States have struggled, this hospital has done well financially. According to the American Hospital Directory database (www.ahd.com), from 2015 through 2019 the hospital had earned almost $40 million in net income. This resulted in a profit margin each year of 7–15 percent. The hospital also opened a $10 million Outpatient Pavilion in 2019.

Like almost all US hospitals, this rural hospital heavily discounts its rates to health insurers. For instance, in 2018 it billed over $8 million in total patient revenues, but discounted more than $6 million to insurance companies and government programs, meaning it collected less than $2 million in patient revenues. Insurance companies were receiving, on average, very high discounts that could reach 60–70 percent of hospital charges.

As can be seen, patients with insurance pay only a fraction of charges, but uninsured patients are generally charged much more. Patients without insurance have little or no leverage to negotiate with a hospital. Uninsured patients are often billed three or four times what a health insurer or government program would pay for the same service. What this meant to Shannon was that the $80,000 bill he received from the hospital, and which he was expected to pay, would have been discounted to about $20,000 for an insurance company.

When the bills started to arrive, Shannon called the hospital to see what options he had. One billing clerk informed Shannon that he might qualify for their charity care program, but when he submitted his previous two months' paystubs, it showed that he earned more than 250 percent of the federal poverty level, which disqualified him. The overtime he had worked before the surgery meant he missed the charity cut-off by about $200.

The billing office also offered a self-pay discount of 15 percent to uninsured patients and were willing to offer this to Shannon if he would pay off the discounted bill in two years. However, this seemed impossible to Shannon, as he would have to pay the hospital more than $2,800 a month after the discount. They also suggested that he consider charging the bill. But Shannon did not have that much credit, and he knew from past experiences that credit cards could charge him very high interest rates.

Shannon was also upset that he had to return to the hospital with the blood clot. If he had his car repaired and it was done improperly, the mechanic would fix it free or only charge him for parts. The hospital and doctor had charged him another $44,000.

Shannon knew he needed to find leverage to be able to successfully negotiate. He had already spoken to many of the billing clerks and their supervisors without making headway. Given that the hospital had customer service as one of its key values, he filed a grievance with the hospital with the help of his partner, who is a lawyer, to seek a steep reduction of the bills for the two surgeries and express concerns about his quality of care. Some research in the Healthcare Bluebook revealed that a normal appendectomy in the area should cost about $12,600. Shannon also told the hospital that if he could not reduce the bill substantially his only real option was to file for bankruptcy. Even though the hospital billing office had begun threatening to send Shannon's bill to collection, his constant contact and legal communication kept them from doing it.

After three months of negotiating, the hospital offered to give Shannon a 30 percent discount on both surgeries. This left him with a bill of $56,162.40—still far too much. Shannon repeatedly tried to get a better deal, but often found the billing representatives were "unavailable." The more he thought about it, the more he felt that he should not be charged for the second surgery, as it could have been caused by a surgical error. Six months later the hospital ultimately told Shannon that he would definitely have to pay for the second surgery because it was a risk he accepted by agreeing to the appendectomy. By this time Shannon was irate but committed to obtaining a discount that he could handle financially. He began to speak with the local and regional press. The story was eventually picked up by Kaiser Health News and NPR as one of their "Bill of the Month" stories (Kaiser Health News 2020).

Finally, the hospital seemed to have had enough. The vice president of financial services informed Shannon that she was reducing the total bill by roughly the amount charged for the second surgery. Her letter to Shannon noted that the complication was unfortunate but an "inherent risk." She reduced his total hospital bill by $31,218.60, which was further reduced to $22,304.17 after the self-pay discount.

This amount still seemed too high to Shannon, and after additional research he offered to pay the hospital $12,000 to settle the bills. The hospital took less than a day to reject this offer. Shannon felt he still could not pay the hospital in the two years they requested; even with an interest-free payment those monthly payments would be more than his rent.

Shannon and his family are angry with the hospital. Despite positioning itself as a vital community resource, the hospital's lack of transparency and poor communication with the family aggravated a bad situation. The hospital has received bad press regarding the billings, and many are asking why they pay the administrators so much money. Shannon is still considering bankruptcy but also wants to responsibly pay his bills.

Case Questions

1. Why is the billing situation so complicated and confusing in US hospitals?
2. From a societal perspective, how could organizational justice be involved?
3. How do attitudes and perceptions influence what actions were taken in this case?
4. When establishing healthcare policies such as those discussed in this case, what should be considered?
5. How did the hospital follow or not follow its mission and values?

References

Kaiser Health News. 2020. "Veteran's Appendectomy Launches Excruciating, Months-Long Battle Over Bill." Kaiser Health News, August 25.

CASE 27

THE ETHICAL CHALLENGE OF TREATING HEPATITIS C

Note: The following case is based on the sources cited. It is intended for case study purposes only and does not imply acceptance of any statement as fact.

Hepatitis C affects about 3.5 million Americans, though up to half may not realize they have it (Nall 2018). The number of potential hepatitis C patients out there should push down drug costs. However, current treatment regimens are very costly and, frequently, unaffordable.

A major breakthrough occurred in 2014 with the approval of direct-acting antiviral medications. The price of these drugs remains high but may vary based on the pharmacy that fills a prescription, the insurance plan that covers it, and the patient's medical history. Nevertheless, Nall (2018) found the following average medication costs for hepatitis C treatments:

- Ledipasvir-sofosbuvir (Harvoni): The average wholesale cost for Harvoni is $1,125 per pill. An 8-week treatment course is $63,000 while a 12-week treatment course is $94,500 and a 24-week one is $189,000.
- Simeprevir (Olysio): The average wholesale cost for the medication is $790 per 150 milligrams (mg) capsule. A 28-day supply costs $22,120, and a 12-week supply costs $66,360. Sometimes a doctor will prescribe this along with the medication sofosbuvir, where a 12-week course of treatment for both medications totals about $150,000.
- Sofosbuvir (Sovaldi): This medication costs $1,000 per 400 mg pill. The total cost for a 12-week course is around $84,000, and doctors will typically prescribe it with other medicines, such as simeprevir.
- Ombitasvir-paritaprevir-ritonavir and dasabuvir (Viekira Pak): The cost for this medication is $83,319 for a 12-week treatment course. The cost for a 24-week treatment course is $166,638.

Although the drugs can cost up to $100,000 for a 12-week treatment, they provide a good return on investment and most insurers consider them cost-effective, since they are priced reasonably in terms of their cost per quality-adjusted life year (QALY) for almost all patients (Hiltzik 2016). Yet, this is only true if people can receive the treatment. The cost of hepatitis C treatments shows how a cost-effective drug can still be unaffordable. Many prescription drugs are very expensive and can be budget-busters for governments and insurance companies that pay for them. As a result, even though many patients might benefit, the drug's cost almost prohibits access.

Treatments for hepatitis C are incredibly effective, but most insurers, healthcare organizations, and government agencies do not have the funds needed to treat all the patients who need it. Treating every American with hepatitis C, according to one study, "would cost more than $100 billion over five years" at then-current list prices, even after "offsetting gains reaped from avoiding medical problems caused by untreated infection" (Hiltzik 2016):

> This points to one of the glaring flaws in the American system of healthcare: Payment for treatments come from a fragmented sector that includes individual insurers, big employers, Medicare, Medicaid and others. Payers may cover patients for only a few years before they move to another insurer or program. As a result, the entity paying the big bill for any enrollee's hepatitis C treatment may just be saving money for someone else.
>
> That is why there is still heavy resistance from insurers to the high price of the hepatitis C drugs. In the words of [insurance expert] Richard Mayhew . . . "It is not cost effective for most insurers to pay $80,000 for gains that will occur when the patient is no longer covered by that insurer."
>
> With medical science entering a new era of hugely expensive drug therapies, the urgency is rising to figure out how to assess the benefits of new drugs and how to pay for them. Getting the policy wrong means depriving millions of people of miracle cures because they don't have the money or their insurers refuse to pay.

Case Questions

1. What ethical questions are involved in this case? How do these involve differences in values?
2. How would you address this issue if you were:
   a. The director of a state Medicaid program?
   b. The CEO of a safety-net hospital?
   c. The CEO of a pharmaceutical firm that manufactures one of the drugs?

References

Hiltzik, M. 2016. "Column: Is That $100,000 Hepatitis Treatment Worth the Price? Yes, but Can Society Afford It?" *Los Angeles Times*, January 15. www.latimes.com/business/hiltzik/la-fi-mh-that-hepatitis-treatment-20160111-column.html.

Nall, R. 2018. "How Much Does Hepatitis C Treatment Cost?" *Medical News Today*, November 21. www.medicalnewstoday.com/articles/323767.php.

CASE 28

GOVERNANCE AND DECISION-MAKING IN HOSPITAL-BASED SURGICAL SERVICES

By Steven B. Bateman

Appointed to your position nearly 18 months ago, you are the CEO of a 400-bed tertiary acute care hospital operating in a very competitive urban environment. The for-profit hospital is part of a large, well-managed, well-financed, performance-driven, and hospital-centric organization operating in multiple states. Management of this organization and its affiliated hospitals and other operations, including ambulatory surgical centers, employed physician clinics, and ancillary support services (e.g., revenue cycle, supply chain, pharmacy) is achieved via a balance of centralized and decentralized management and decision-making. As such, affiliated hospitals have access to and are expected to follow best practices and there is a healthy degree of standardization in terms of the management of clinical services and operations. This balance often depends on the location of each hospital and its service area market dynamics. More specifically, in areas where the organization operates multiple hospitals as a network, usually larger metropolitan areas, there is a greater tendency toward centralized management and decision-making. Your hospital finds itself in such a situation. The hospital's parent organization does not own or control a health insurance company, nor is one of its primary strategies to employ physicians.

Within your hospital's service area, several other well-regarded and effective competitor hospitals exist. As the number two competitor among them, your hospital's market share has for several years fluctuated between 29 percent and 31 percent, while your hospital's network market share in the broader market service area hovers around 19 percent. Notwithstanding relatively robust population growth in the broader market service area (though largely stagnant population growth in your hospital's particular service area), market shares among all hospitals have been remarkably stable in recent years.

The major driver of market share, reputation, and financial results at your hospital, as at similar hospitals, is surgical services. Managing surgical services in a large, complex acute care hospital such as yours is almost always very challenging. Your hospital operates 15 operating rooms at its main campus, plus a freestanding ambulatory surgical center located about three miles away from the hospital's main campus. The hospital is also the majority owner of an ambulatory surgical center (managed by a separate arm of the hospital's parent organization) in partnership with nearly 55 surgeons. About half of those partner surgeons also practice at, and use the operating rooms in, the main hospital. This shared-ownership ambulatory surgical center has operated successfully for several years and has yielded substantial financial returns to the participating physician partners. Because of those financial returns, most of those participating surgeons have lost interest in developing their own competing ambulatory surgical center.

Recognized for excellence in general surgery, cardiovascular surgery, orthopedic surgery, neurosurgery, bariatric surgery, and gynecologic surgery, among several other types, surgical services at your hospital are generally well regarded by local surgeons. Historically, management of surgical services at your facility has centered successfully on the operating rooms (OR) and the post anesthesia care unit (PACU), with relatively little coordination occurring with the ambulatory surgical centers and other related departments or functions of the hospital. The hospital's OR and PACU have been managed for several years by the same person—an operating room nurse who was promoted from within and who subsequently earned a master's in health administration. The ambulatory surgical centers are also managed by former operating room nurses, although neither has formal management training.

While the previously described management arrangements and associated operations have for several years yielded satisfactory clinical, financial, and stakeholder satisfaction results, problems and unrest have begun to appear:

- *Lack of confidence in the management of the hospital's surgical services, especially the ORs.* There is a growing perception that the current OR manager is not strategically oriented, has become insufficiently responsive to surgeon concerns and suggestions, and has a somewhat disjointed leadership approach. The manager's style does not promote cohesion or teamwork, which often results in uncoordinated and isolated decision-making and lack of issue-specific follow-through regarding capital equipment budgeting, operational problem-solving, and physician recruitment.
- *Additional competition.* To accommodate population growth in the broader service area, additional hospitals have recently been built, including one from your hospital's own parent organization. As a result, many patients previously loyal to your hospital and its surgeons have been reluctant to "drive by" those newer and more conveniently located hospitals to reach yours. Surgeons practicing at your hospital are worried about this new dynamic and the threat to their practices, and want to see action by the hospital administration to effectively address this problem.

Case 28: Governance and Decision-Making in Hospital-Based Surgical Services

- *Stagnating surgical case volume produces the attitude of accelerating decline.* In addition to the new competition in the area, nearly all other previously existing and older hospitals have been recently refurbished or entirely rebuilt to better serve patients and physicians. As a result of these two market pressures, the surgical volume at your hospital and among its surgeons, which historically experienced steady annual growth, has recently stagnated, or in some specialties decreased. Furthermore, other physicians practicing at the hospital, as well as in other areas of the hospital that depend on surgical services for work, have observed these troubling dynamics and are worried. You know that when surgeons and employees begin to see large blocks of open time on a hospital's daily surgical schedule, they become pessimistic, and a self-fulfilling prophecy that "the ship is sinking" makes people more inclined to jump off that ship. Time is of the essence in addressing these problems.
- *Falling behind in capital investments.* Although the hospital's OR has for many years received significant investments in certain higher-profile equipment, you have discovered that the inventory of more routine, yet highly essential, equipment has been inadequate. Further, the method of identifying needed equipment and facilities and, thus, a well-conceived and -managed annual and contingency capital budget for both the OR and other surgical services-related areas of the hospital, has resulted in a suboptimally furnished and equipped OR when compared with the hospital's competitors. Another direct result of this deficiency, and perhaps a major reason for it, is a palpable feeling of disenfranchisement among surgeons, anesthesiologists, and staff members who believe they are neither consulted nor listened to about overall capital budgeting or operations. At the same time, some complain that certain surgeons who "yell" the loudest consistently get their way when it comes to capital investments. Also harmful is a perception among some surgeons that the hospital's partially physician-owned ambulatory surgical center receives more attention and funding for capital investments than the OR, the hospital's freestanding ambulatory surgical center, and other surgical services-related areas.
- *Adverse health plan patient steerage.* Because most of the hospitals operating in your hospital's service area are parts of fully integrated health systems (e.g., fully owned and integrated hospitals, health insurance plans, large networks of employed physicians), they have begun to benefit from increasingly effective efforts to attract and retain patients within their networks. This also contributed to the recent decline in your facility's surgical case volume and overall market share.
- *Changing dynamics in the ED.* Historically, the hospital's emergency department (ED) has been a significant source of surgical patient

volume. More recently, while patient visit volume in your hospital's ED has continued to grow modestly, most of that growth has been related to nonsurgical patients. Moreover, the recent growth in surgical patients through the ED has disproportionately involved those who are uninsured or who have no ability to pay. The lack of revenue is causing increasing dissatisfaction, especially among general and orthopedic surgeons—the "bread and butter" specialties of the ED and your hospital's surgical services.

- *Increasing competition in surgeon recruitment and retention.* Competition among local hospitals for surgeons, especially the most highly regarded ones, has recently intensified. More surgeons have left private practice and become employees of the integrated health systems in the area. Also, newly trained surgeons often want to be employed rather than independent. The service area's academic hospital and its associated medical school faculty and other associated physicians have become a "closed model," wherein involved physicians derive virtually all their income from the sponsoring university. This model has proven successful for the organization as a whole and very attractive to physicians, who perceive it as an elite environment. Some hospitals have allowed physicians to invest financially in their organizations. You are also worried, and have reason to believe, that your organization's conservative and more traditional approach to physician relationships is seen as inferior and unattractive by many surgeons when compared to the much more aggressive methods employed by competitors. In fact, a few long-time physicians practicing at your hospital, as well as some recently recruited ones, have recently become employees at competing hospitals. Also troubling is the long-standing perception among many low-volume surgeons in the hospital's service area that, notwithstanding excess capacity in your hospital's OR, they are not truly welcome at the hospital due to the predominance of certain established high-volume "all-star" surgeons at the hospital, which often results in a forfeiture of or inability to capture related incremental surgical case volume.

After carefully considering these problems and market dynamics, you recognize that some of them are within your control or influence and others are not. You also recognize that much is riding on your ability to solve these problems, which are crucial not only to the success of surgical services at the hospital but also to the hospital as a whole. At the same time, you learned from a wise mentor (as well as through limited personal observation) that often the best strategy, and the one most in leadership's control, for successfully solving problems, growing patient volume, and improving financial results in an acute care hospital in a competitive market is to be the best at the basics. The best surgeons will usually prefer a hospital that provides the basics they value most: (1) a highly competent nursing staff; (2) excellent hospital-based physicians, especially radiologists and pathologists; (3) state-of-the art equipment and well-trained support staff in the OR; (4) efficiency in terms of time ("time is money"); and (5) a responsive leadership team coupled with an effective organizational strategy and decision-making approach that helps drive patients to the surgeon's practice.

Since being the best at these basics is likely to be your most effective problem-solving strategy, as well as your most practical one in the short and long terms, you are faced with several key decisions. Who should be involved in deciding how to solve the hospital's surgical services problems? How should those decisions be made? And how should you measure the effectiveness of those decisions? You decide to use a "work team" approach. For this approach to be effective, this work team must be clearly chartered, populated with the right people, and endowed with an effective and balanced amount of decision-making authority. You decide to form the Surgical Services Governance Council (Governance Council). To move forward with it, you must address the following key questions, among others.

Case Questions

1. What should be the key elements of the Governance Council's charter?
2. What decision-making authority parameters should be determined before the Governance Council is initially convened with respect to key areas? These areas may include (a) capital equipment and facilities identification, prioritization, budgeting, and spending; (b) the authority to hire, fire, or evaluate hospital employees, and the process used to do so; (c) the deployment of hospital employees in terms of assignments by surgeon, by specialty, or otherwise; (d) scheduling policies in the OR; (e) disciplinary actions involving surgeons with respect to "late starts," interference with the smooth operation of the OR, and so on; (f) the determination of surgical services performance metrics; or, (g) recruitment of needed surgeons.
3. Should some issues or policies be sacrosanct, meaning they are off the table for the Governance Council? If so, what might those be?
4. Should decisions of the Governance Council be premised on majority rule, majority rule subject to veto, consensus, or something else?
5. Who should be on the Governance Council? Should new hospital surgical services management be recruited and included? What personality traits, leadership experience, level of surgical activity at the

hospital, and professional skills, including surgical specialties, should be prioritized when selecting council members?
6. If physicians are selected to participate, what must be done to ensure effective, legal, and meaningful shared decision-making?
7. Who should convene and charter the Governance Council? What form of leadership should the Governance Council adopt (e.g., leadership by a single administrator, surgeon, or anesthesiologist; leadership by a physician–administrator dyad)?
8. What must be done to ensure that all stakeholders, physicians, and hospital employees throughout the hospital's surgical services departments perceive the Governance Council as having true clout, so much so that a seat on the Governance Council becomes a coveted position?
9. How should the agenda for Governance Council meetings be determined? How should the efforts and results of the Governance Council be tracked and communicated to stakeholders?
10. What must be done to ensure that this Governance Council does not run afoul of the hospital's parent organization's decision-making processes, whether centralized or decentralized?
11. Besides addressing the issues with the OR, what must the Governance Council do to achieve better coordination with other aspects of the hospital's surgical services?
12. What should the Governance Council be tasked with achieving within its first six months of work? First year?
13. Should the Governance Council be chartered as a work team that will be disbanded at some fixed date after tackling, but perhaps not yet solving, the described problems? Or should the Governance Council be a standing work team?

CASE 29

MENTORING, COACHING, AND DELEGATING: COMBATING HIGH TURNOVER AND POOR CULTURE

By Brian Cottle

Caden had just joined a physicians' office as their director of operations. The practice was made up of 22 physicians, 6 advanced practice providers, and 54 staff, which included nurses, medical assistants, front office staff, and billing staff. The medical director, Jack, met with Caden in his first week on the job and challenged him to provide a remedy for the practice's high turnover rate, which was close to 50 percent the previous year.

"We keep losing staff nearly as fast as we hire new people. I need you to find out what is going on and fix it," Jack said. "Other physicians are complaining that staff is not adequately trained and that their patients are not receiving quality care because of it. It is absolutely frustrating that our patients come in for routine visits and our staff do not know who they are nor how to handle the simplest of tasks to help them with their problems. Please fix this."

Caden immediately began to work with the clinic manager, Jennifer, to discover the reason for high turnover and to implement a plan to improve things. Jennifer had been previously tasked with hiring all staff in the clinic. Jennifer and Caden began interviewing candidates together and Caden soon discovered that part of the problem resided in how Jennifer rushed through the hiring process.

When selecting candidates, Jennifer was pressured by physicians and other staff to quickly hire new people because they were burdened with extra work while staff numbers were low. Jennifer would hire the person who could fill the job the soonest, not taking into account the benefit of building a strong culture and a team of the best people possible. Caden also discovered that there was no formal training and onboarding process. New employees were not nurtured into their jobs or given time to acclimate to their new surroundings and duties. The new hires quickly became frustrated and quit within a couple of months, which perpetuated the high turnover and lack of experienced staff.

Case Questions

1. What is the difference between coaching and mentoring?
2. When is coaching appropriate?
3. When is mentoring appropriate?
4. What should Caden do to find out what is causing the turnover?
5. What should Jennifer be doing as a manager to help fix the problem?
6. What type of coaching should Caden offer to Jennifer?
7. What types of things should Caden delegate to Jennifer to fix the turnover issue?
8. How can Caden help Jennifer in his role as mentor?

Follow-Up

Caden began coaching Jennifer on the merits of hiring the best candidates even if it took a little more time. Caden also began meeting with Jennifer on a weekly basis to mentor her in how a manager influences the culture of the clinic. Caden challenged Jennifer and delegated to her the task of developing a culture of excellence. In their coaching and mentoring meetings, Caden and Jennifer came up with a strategy to develop a culture of excellence. Jennifer would begin by hiring the best staff possible, implementing a formal training process, and creating an onboarding strategy to help new employees become part of the culture.

It took some time, but a year later there was a palpable difference in the clinic's culture. Many times, Jennifer would interview candidates and then shut the job down and reopen it for new applicants. Jennifer was able to view the new hires as part of the culture of excellence she was building. She worked with the nurse manager and the front office supervisor to implement the formal training and onboarding program, delegating onboarding to the nurse manager and formal training to the front office supervisor. Together, they managed to reduce turnover to nearly nothing for two years straight; the only loss was one staff member who moved away with their spouse for school.

In this new culture of excellence, staff were motivated because they were working with the best people the clinic could hire. The physicians were more satisfied with their jobs because they retained well-trained staff for long periods of time. New staff felt like they were part of a team because of the onboarding efforts. Jennifer became a better leader through coaching and mentoring.

APPENDIX: CASE MATRIX

Cases		Chapters																						
No.	Title	1	2	3	4	5	6	7	8	9	10	11	12	13	14	15	16	17	18	19	20	21	22	23
1	Dilemma of Loyalties		•			•	•		•	•											•			•
2	Theranos and Elizabeth Holmes	•			•		•		•										•			•		•
3	Injured Migrant Worker						•				•													
4	Overutilizing Orthopedist	•					•	•							•					•				
5	Busy Regional Vice President		•			•			•			•					•		•	•		•		
6	Thalidomide and Grünenthal	•						•										•						
7	Prospect Medical	•					•	•				•				•	•	•	•				•	•
8	Pegasus Health's Integration of Care	•											•	•	•					•				•
9	Purdue's Dilemma to Increase Sales	•					•			•	•		•	•								•	•	•
10	OrthoIndy	•						•		•			•							•				•

(continued)

625

Appendix: Case Matrix

Cases		Chapters																					
No.	Title	1	2	3	4	5	6	7	8	9	10	11	12	13	14	15	16	17	18	19	20	21	22	23
11	The New CEO	•					•	•		•	•					•	•	•			•			•
12	Liver Allocation	•		•		•	•				•													
13	Letter from a Bereaved Mother		•			•									•	•								
14	HealthT Seeks Healthier Employees	•	•	•				•			•	•												
15	HealthSouth		•			•	•	•	•	•	•		•	•		•	•					•	•	•
16	FHP – Utah	•		•		•		•		•	•		•							•	•			
17	Starting as CEO at Skyview Hospital		•	•		•			•				•		•	•		•				•	•	
18	Director of Marketing Versus Operations		•	•							•				•	•	•	•				•	•	
19	The Ogre and the Playroom						•				•					•	•	•						
20	A Saudi Bid and I		•	•			•				•					•	•	•				•		
21	Proposed Merger Gone Bad	•	•	•				•					•		•	•	•	•	•	•		•		•

Appendix: Case Matrix

Cases		Chapters																						
No.	Title	1	2	3	4	5	6	7	8	9	10	11	12	13	14	15	16	17	18	19	20	21	22	23
22	Night Staffing and Job Commitment					•		•																
23	Mike and the Walk-Around					•		•	•	•														•
24	Sakal's Dilemma					•				•				•				•						
25	Sam's Deposit Recovery	•													•								•	
26	Extreme Uninsured Healthcare Costs	•					•									•	•							•
27	The Ethical Challenge of Treating Hepatitis C	•		•																				
28	Governance and Decision-Making in Hospital-Based Surgical Services	•									•		•	•						•				
29	Combating High Turnover and Poor Culture				•	•															•		•	

GLOSSARY

accountable care organizations. Groups of doctors, hospitals, and other healthcare providers who come together to give coordinated high-quality.

administrative theory. A principle of bureaucracy and management that seeks a rational way to design an organization.

affective commitment. Employees' emotional attachment to and identification with their organization.

affective component. A person's feelings and emotions about something.

affirmative action. The development of policies or procedures that seek to improve opportunities given to groups who have experienced discrimination, especially as it relates to employment.

anchoring bias. A bias that relies too heavily on the initial information received.

attitude. A relatively enduring set of beliefs and feelings used to evaluate something either favorably or unfavorably and typically reflected in one's behavior.

authentic leadership. An approach to leadership that emphasizes honest relationships with followers and a positive ethical climate.

autonomy. A person's ability to make meaningful choices free of interference from others.

baby boomers. The generation born between 1946 and 1964. Adaptable and unconventional, boomers tend to maintain active careers longer than previous generations.

balanced scorecard. A reporting mechanism that incorporates financial and nonfinancial aspects of performance to allow a comprehensive, balanced perspective of organizational results.

bandwagon effect. A bias toward choosing to do something because others are doing it.

BATNA. The best alternative to a negotiated agreement.

behavior theory. The theory that proposes two categories of leadership behaviors: employee-oriented leadership and production-oriented leadership.

behavioral component. The influence of attitudes on how one acts and behaves.

behaviorally anchored rating scales. Evaluation scales that use example behaviors to "anchor" ratings.

beneficence. Taking action that benefits others. Beneficence includes the acts of mercy, charity, and kindness and requires active efforts to improve the well-being and status of another.

bounded rationality. The idea that individuals' decision-making is constrained by available information, their cognitive limits, and the time they have to make decisions.

burnout. A reaction to chronic high stress characterized by physical or mental collapse.

career ladder. Formal programs supporting employees with training and development so they can move into more advanced positions.

chain of command. The hierarchy, or formal reporting structure, that delineates the direction for formal company communication and decision-making.

coaching. Instruction or training focused mostly on the transfer or improvement of specific skills over a short period.

coercive power. The ability to use the threat of force to make someone compliant.

cognitive component. A person's beliefs and knowledge about something.

cognitive dissonance. Having inconsistent thoughts, beliefs, or attitudes, especially as relating to behavioral decisions and attitude change.

collective cultures. Cultures that emphasize group responsibility to protect and care for their communities.

command groups. Groups formed to give directions and orders within their organization.

communication channel. The medium through which a message is sent and received.

communication. The process of transmitting information and meaning from one individual or group to another.

competency-based appraisal systems. Mechanisms for evaluating employee performance on the basis of required competencies established for the employee's position.

confirming-evidence bias. A bias toward information that supports or reinforces existing positions or beliefs but against information that discounts or dismisses those beliefs.

conflict. A situation that arises when two or more parties have opposing views, positions, needs, or interests that are perceived as incompatible.

contingency approach. The view that personal, situational, and organizational factors dictate different management styles and the effective use of a management style is contingent on internal and external conditions.

contingency theory. The theory that the best leadership style should be considered for the situation and context.

continuance commitment. The desire felt by employees to remain at their organization.

corporate social responsibility. The self-regulated ethical behavior that goes beyond legal requirements to promote positive social and environmental improvements; sometimes called *corporate citizenship*.

corporation. A legal structure that allows a group of people to act as a single entity and provides limited liability to its owners.

creativity. The ability to turn new ideas into new products, services, or devices.

cultural assessment. A tool for comparing organizational culture with organizational mission and values to identify needs and appropriate interventions.

cultural competence. A set of congruent behaviors, attitudes and policies that come together in a system, agency, or amongst professionals and enables that system, agency or those professionals to work effectively in cross-cultural situations.

decoding. The communication step that assigns meaning to the message.

delegation. The act of authorizing another to perform a task or duty and, in doing so, allocating and sharing responsibilities to increase productivity and empowerment.

dialogue. The free flow of meaning between two or more people.

diffusion. The act of spreading and embedding innovation to transform an organization, an industry, or a system.

dispositional approach. A theory that job satisfaction is a result of individual traits—behaviors, thoughts, actions, and emotions. Also known as *trait theory*.

disruptive innovation. Innovation that creates radical change and destroys existing organizational competencies.

dissatisfiers. A set of factors—one of two in Herzberg's two-factor theory—that do not motivate because they do not produce satisfaction. Dissatisfiers may include working conditions, interpersonal relations, job security, and salary; also called *maintenance* or *hygiene factors*.

distress. Negative, persistent, unresolved stress that may lead to anxiety, withdrawal, or depression.

distributive justice. The perceived fair distribution of resources, evaluated by the benefits derived and equity in awards.

diversity. An employee population characterized by a wide array of differences and similarities.

diversity management. The practice of acknowledging employees' differences and allowing employees to use these traits to achieve organizational goals.

division of labor. The segmentation of tasks and roles into smaller components that are performed by separate individuals or groups.

double-loop learning. Learning that occurs when the governing variable is questioned, causing shifts in strategies, values, or mission.

egoist model. An ethical model that defines the moral value of action on the basis of whether the foreseeable effects of the action are favorable for the actor—in other words, that self-interested behavior is ethical.

emotional intelligence. The capacity to be aware of, to be in control of, and to express emotions as well as to handle interpersonal relationships with empathy and wisdom.

emotions. Brief, intense episodes of a complex range of feelings that lead to physical and mental changes and influence actions and behaviors.

employee assistance programs. Benefit programs that generally provide confidential short-term counseling and referrals for employees who face challenges that, if left unmanaged, could seriously affect their work.

encoding. The communication step that transforms a message into signs or symbols.

engagement. The mutual commitment between employees and employers.

equity theory. The theory that employees seek to balance their work inputs and the outcomes or benefits they receive as compared with those of others.

ERG theory of motivation. The theory (a refinement of Maslow's hierarchy of needs) that motivation results from three factors: existence, relatedness, and growth.

ethical leadership. A model of leadership that emphasizes trustworthy, fair, and honest personal conduct to promote ethical behaviors in followers.

ethical relativism. The concept that an action is considered right or wrong depending on the context and environment in which the action takes place.

ethics. The often unwritten codes that constrain and guide actions. Context, facts, cultures, beliefs, values, and attitudes influence ethics and how they are practiced.

ethics training. Training that includes elements such as ethical reasoning and decision-making and prepares employees to resolve ethical dilemmas.

ethnocentrism. The exaggerated tendency to think the characteristics of one's own group or race are superior to those of other groups or races.

eustress. Positive stress that can motivate greater effort and focus and can result in improved productivity or mastery of a new skill.

expectancy theory. The theory that motivation is a function of three linked factors: expectancy, instrumentality, and valence.

expectancy. The belief that one's efforts will result in the desired outcomes.

expert power. The ability to influence followers because of one's experiences, skills, talents, or knowledge.

external stimuli. Means of instigation that originate from outside an individual; the use of external stimuli for motivation is also called *operant conditioning*.

feedback. The process in which the sender and receiver engage to validate the message sent and received.

forced distribution. Mechanisms for rating employee performance that require managers to rank their employees across a distribution, much like grading on a curve. Also called *stacked ranking* or *forced ranking*.

formal authority. The right to influence someone.

formal groups. Groups prearranged by an organization as a command or task entity.

forming. The first stage of team building, when a team comes together and an individual transitions into a team member.

framing bias. A bias toward information or choices presented in a positive frame.

frustration-regression. The concept that people who unsuccessfully seek a higher need become frustrated and regress to pursue a lower need.

functional organizations. Organizations that divide departments by common duties, tasks, services, or roles.

fundamental attribution error. The tendency to attribute one's own success to personal traits and failure to external factors, while attributing others' success to external factors and their failure to personal traits.

Gantt charts. Bar charts that show the schedule and progress of one or more projects.

gap analysis. An environmental scan—both internal and external—that compares the organization's current performance and status with its values, mission, and vision.

garbage can model. A model for decision-making that is characterized by chaos caused by the fluid, frequent entry and exit of decision makers who lack clarity and understanding about how decisions are made.

Generation X. The generation born between 1965 and 1980. Gen Xers tend to seek job security and push for efficiency and innovation.

Generation Z. The generation born after about 1996. Gen Zers tend to be tech savvy, and place a high value on diversity and education.

goal-setting theory. The theory that goal-directed work and quantified and clearly defined goals lead to higher performance.

gofer delegation. The act of delegating specific, detailed actions to a person or team who, after completing the tasks, must immediately return, report, and then wait for another assignment.

great man theory. A perspective that exceptionally gifted individuals with prominent traits—such as physical characteristics, personality, and ability—have affected history.

group. Collection of individuals who interact with each other and share common interests or characteristics.

group polarization. A situation in which groups are driven to take sides and accept extreme positions.

group shift. The tendency of individual group members to shift to a more extreme position or opinion due to the influence of the group.

groupthink. The tendency for members of a highly cohesive group to seek consensus so strongly that they fail to do a realistic appraisal of other alternatives, which may be more correct.

halo effect. The effect that occurs when one characteristic or trait dominates and affects the evaluation of people or products.

harassment. A set of hostile activities that are repeated and systematic, and which are usually verbal or nonverbal rather than physical.

hardiness. The ability to handle stress.

Henri Fayol. A French mining engineer, considered to be one of the founders of modern management, who distilled management practices into 14 principles to frame a general management perspective.

heuristics. Mental shortcuts or rules of thumb generated from personal experiences and used during problem-solving.

human relations theory. A theory that focuses on organizational development and the influence of people. It originated in the 1930s with the advent of the Hawthorne studies.

human resource management. The formal system within an organization that staffs, monitors, establishes policies for, and trains members of the work team.

hygiene factors. Work conditions that do not increase satisfaction or lead to motivation, although their absence can lead to dissatisfaction.

individualism. The preference for personal gain (individualism) over benefits for the group (collectivism).

individualistic cultures. Cultures that value loose social relationships that encourage individuals to take responsibility for themselves and their relatives.

indulgence. The degree to which a culture emphasizes personal freedom and enjoyment over duty and obligation.

influence. The process of persuading others to do something; it occurs when power is exercised.

informal groups. Groups that are self-formed as a result of or for the purpose of work and social interactions.

information richness. The degree of nonverbal or verbal communication used to convey the complexity and importance of a message.

innovation. A new idea, device, or method.

instrumentality. The belief that one will receive a reward if expected performance is achieved.

interactional justice. The perceived fairness of actions, decisions, and treatment of individuals, evaluated by the accuracy of information and the respect and courtesy shown throughout the decision-making process.

interdisciplinary teams. Teams composed of a coordinated group of professionals from different fields who work interdependently but share information and resolve problems systematically and together.

interests. In negotiations, a party's real needs, desires, fears, and goals.

intergroup conflict. Conflict between two or more groups.

interpersonal conflict. Conflict between two or more individuals that may be caused by personality, values, and style differences.

intersectionality. A frame that prompts us to ask what falls between movements and what happens when different systems of power and oppression overlap.

intragroup conflict. Conflict among members of a group.

intrapersonal conflict. Conflict that arises because of an individual's roles, values, or goals.

intrinsic stimuli. Stimuli that originate from within an individual.

job characteristics model. A model that posits job enrichment should be designed with five core characteristics: work variety, work autonomy, work feedback, work significance, and work identity.

job description. Formal documentation of the duties, responsibilities, and functions of a specific job, including title, working conditions, and a summary description.

job specification. Formal documentation of the minimum qualifications, capabilities, and traits a candidate needs to perform a specific job.

justice model (fairness model). An ethical model that relates to the perceived fairness of actions. Just actions involve consistent, fair treatment on the basis of ethical, religious, or legal standards.

justice. The ethical principle of fairly distributing benefits, risks, and costs and treating all people equitably.

key performance indicators. Metrics used in performance management that are directly tied to strategic organizational goals.

leader–member exchange theory. The theory that presents a complex, relationship-based approach to leadership, making the interaction between leader and member the focal point of the leadership process.

learning communities. A select group of potential adopters and stakeholders who engage in a shared learning process to facilitate adaptation and implementation of innovations.

learning management systems. Software used to plan, track, and record the outcomes of learning processes. LMS software may include applications to help organizations create and deliver instruction, monitor participation, assess performance, and provide student interaction.

learning organization. An entity in which ingrained structures and culture are in place that constantly facilitate and encourage learning.

masculinity. The preferences for achievement, heroism, assertiveness, or material rewards (masculinity) over cooperation, modesty, caring, and quality of life (femininity).

Maslow's hierarchy of needs. A theory that human needs fall into five categories, from less to more complex, and that less complex needs must be fulfilled before more complex needs will be pursued.

matrix organizations. Organizations with multiple reporting relationships, generally to both a functional manager and a product or service line manager, that allow horizontal and vertical coordination to concurrently occur.

Max Weber. A German sociologist and political economist who postulated that the ideal organization had rules every worker obeyed, competency-based positions, chains of command for decision-making, and division of labor.

mechanistic organizations. Traditional organizations characterized by greater job specialization, narrow spans of control, and increased centralization of decision-making.

mentoring. Advising or training for long-term employee growth and nurturing to improve leadership capabilities.

millennials. The generation born between 1981 and about 1996. Millennials tend to be risk-averse and value teamwork and work–life balance.

mimetic isomorphism. In institutional theory, the tendency of an organization to imitate other organizations in its environment in an effort to gain legitimacy.

mission. The organization's ideals and purpose—why it exists.

moods. The background feelings that are less intense but tend to last longer than emotions and affect one's perception of life.

motivators. Work conditions that increase satisfaction from intrinsic conditions of the job.

multidisciplinary teams. Teams composed of professionals from multiple disciplines who tend to work independently and interact formally.

multidivisional organizations. Organizations divided into segments or divisions made up of separate businesses or profit centers so that day-to-day operations occur at a divisional level to allow units to act independently.

network structures. Organizational structures, also called modular or virtual organizations, that allow for flexibility and decentralization.

noise. Distractions that diminish the effectiveness of the communication process.

nonmaleficence. The ethical principle of doing no harm. For healthcare practitioners, this principle often involves weighing the risks and burdens inherent to almost every treatment against the potential benefits to the patient.

nontask organizational conflict. Conflict that occurs regarding corporate policies, hiring decisions, benefits, culture, leadership, or power.

nonverbal communication. The process of communicating without words.

normative commitment. The feelings of obligation to continue a job because it is the right thing to do.

norming. The third stage of team building, when members establish group rules, which usher in harmony and team cohesion.

numerical rating systems. Mechanisms for rating employee performance on a numeric scale.

open systems theory. A theory that firms are highly influenced by their environments.

organic organizations. Organizations characterized by decentralized and participative decision-making, loosely defined roles, and frequent adaptation that brings in new skills and modified roles.

organizational behavior. The study of the behavior and influence of individuals, groups, and structures in an organization and their impact on the function and effectiveness of that organization.

organizational citizenship behaviors. Discretionary employee behavior, outside the formal organizational reward system, that overall promotes the effective and efficient functioning of a company.

organizational culture. The pattern of basic assumptions that have worked well enough to be considered valid and the correct way to perceive, think, and feel for members of a given group.

organizational design. The alignment of the organizational structure, including its roles and processes for formal reporting relationships, with organizational mission and goals.

organizational learning. An organizationally regulated collective learning process in which individual and group-based learning experiences concerning the improvement of organizational performance and/or goals are transferred into organizational routines, processes, and structures.

organizational politics. The informal means of gaining power other than through merit or luck.

organizational structure. The way a company arranges its tasks, work, and people to create a product or service and achieve its goals.

organizational theory. The study of organizations as a whole or populations of organizations that seeks to explain the processes and factors that influence the structure and outcomes of organizations.

organizations. Socially constructed entities created for specific purposes that are goal directed; composed of people tied together in formal and informal relationships; and linked to their external environment through their customers, suppliers, competitors, and government regulators.

paradigm shift. The changing of a person's paradigms, which can alter their decisions, prepare them for uncertainty, and enhance their ability to learn in the organizational setting.

paradigms. The lenses through which people see the world, coloring their expectations of people's behavior and directing their actions in organizations.

path–goal theory. The theory that considers both employee and environmental factors to suggest which leadership style would be most effective.

perceptions. The ways people experience, process, and interpret stimuli.

performance management. The process of establishing individual and corporate goals through planning, reviewing, assessing, and developing the skills and abilities of the workforce.

performance simulation. A preemployment evaluation that places a candidate in a highly realistic employment experience to assess potential job performance.

performing. The fourth stage of team building, when members have learned their roles and accepted each other's strengths and weaknesses.

personality tests. Instruments that collect self-reported data about an individual's personality traits.

polarization. A situation in which people are driven to take sides and accept extreme positions.

pooled interdependence. A type of interdependence that requires members to make only discrete, independent contributions to their group.

positions. In negotiations, the expressed desires or presented proposals of the parties involved.

power distance. The way power is distributed and the degree to which individuals accept the inequity of power distribution.

power. The capacity to influence others by control over valued resources.

primacy effect. The tendency to most easily recall the first information presented.

primary emotions. The feelings people first experience as a response to a situation: love, joy, surprise, anger, sadness, and fear.

procedural justice. The perceived fairness of the process by which a decision is made, evaluated by compliance with decision-making processes, level of access, openness, and participation by employees.

process conflict. Conflict that occurs regarding how a job gets done.

qualitative overload. Stress caused by being required to use a skill that is not yet comfortable.

qualitative underload. Stress caused by being assigned a job that requires skills far below the training and ability of the employee.

quantitative overload. Stress caused by having too much work to do in a given period.

quantitative underload. Stress caused by having too little work to do in a given period.

rational decision-making. An approach to decision-making that emphasizes following a systematic path to analyze a problem and its possible solutions and logically select the best possible option.

recency effect. The tendency to most easily recall the last information presented.

reciprocal interdependence. A type of interdependence that requires members to have a team relationship as their work is highly interactive and necessitates immediate responses.

referent power. The ability to influence followers because of the trust and respect of others.

relationship conflict. Conflict that occurs regarding values, personality, political beliefs, and style.

reward power. The ability to promise positive incentives, such as bonuses, raises, promotions, and time off.

rights model. An ethical model that distinguishes right from wrong based on the underlying intentions. Individual moral or legal rights are paramount in this model.

rituals and routines. Collective social activities that reinforce organizational values by engendering active participation from organizational members.

role ambiguity. A lack of specificity and predictability about a job, its functions, and its responsibilities because of unclear job descriptions, poor training, and changing job requirements.

role conflict. The dissonance that arises from being given two or more incompatible or contradictory job demands.

satisfice. To make a decision that is acceptable or adequate, rather than optimal. A portmanteau of *satisfy* and *suffice*.

satisfiers. A set of factors—one of two in Herzberg's two-factor theory—that relate to job content and which may include achievement, recognition, advancement, and growth. Satisfiers, also called *motivators*, have longer-lasting effects than dissatisfiers have.

scientific management. A theory, developed by American mechanical engineer Frederick W. Taylor, that human input is among the cheap, interchangeable components that can be "engineered" to maximize efficiency.

secondary emotions. Longer-duration feelings that reflect an individual's mental processing of a situation and the primary emotions it elicited.

self-fulfilling prophecy. The effect that occurs when a person's results are predetermined by an observer's perception or expectation of them. Self-fulfilling prophecies may be positive as a result of higher expectations (the Pygmalion effect) or negative as a result of lower expectations (the Golem effect).

servant leadership. A values-based view of leadership that views service as the core function of leadership and a moral and ethical imperative.

sexual harassment. Unwelcome sexual conduct or advances that subtly or blatantly threaten a person's job or sense of personal safety; all forms of sexual harassment are illegal.

similar-to-me effect. The effect that occurs when individuals and groups favor and select people who are physically or professionally similar to themselves.

single-loop learning. Learning that occurs when employees search for solutions within the confines of given goals, values, plans, and rules.

situational leadership. The theory that effective leaders need to understand their environment or situation and respond with a style that matches the existing need.

social facilitation. A phenomenon explaining why some individuals perform better when an audience is watching.

social loafing. A phenomenon explaining why individuals sometimes exert less effort when working in a group.

span of control. The number of subordinates who report to a supervisor.

status quo bias. A bias toward choices that perpetuate the current situation.

stereotype. An oversimplified, prejudiced, or uncritical categorization of people on the basis of characteristics such as race, gender, age, religion, or occupation.

stewardship delegation. The act of delegating that empowers the person or team assigned a task to choose how to complete activities and be responsible for results.

stories. Narratives that describe the culture's values in action or demonstrate the violation of stated values.

storming. The second stage of team building, when members begin to resist collaboration with other members and to experience conflict.

stress. The brain and body's response to any demand. Any type of challenge—such as performance at work or school, a significant life change, or a traumatic event—can be stressful.

structured interviews. A job interview practice in which all candidates are reviewed by the same interviewers and asked the same questions, which are based on a job analysis.

sunk cost bias. A bias toward investments that cannot be recovered.

sustaining innovation. Innovation that builds on past successes and organizational competencies and provides incremental improvements.

symbols and structures. Images, events, activities, objects, and workplace structures that express or represent an idea or quality, among others.

task conflict. Conflict that occurs regarding work details and goals.

task groups. Groups organized for a specific job or undertaking.

teams. Evolved groups that have great task orientation, purpose, interdependence, structure, and social familiarity.

temporal orientation. The degree to which members are willing to defer satisfaction and focus on achieving long-term, rather than short-term, outcomes.

theory X and theory Y. Developed by Douglas McGregor, these contrasting theories describe how managers perceive their employees and how these perceptions affect employee motivation and behavior. In McGregor's view, theory X managers focus on controlling workers and theory Y managers focus on engaging and empowering workers.

360-degree feedback appraisal system. A mechanism for evaluating employee performance that seeks feedback from stakeholders who have frequent contact with the employee being appraised.

trait theory. The theory that personality traits and characteristics result in certain successful leadership behaviors.

transactional leadership. The theory that examines the influences and behaviors of those being led and their interactions with leaders through both rewards and punishments.

transfer pricing. The price set for goods and services that are transferred between divisions of the same company.

transformational leadership. The theory that leaders inspire and motivate followers to pursue outcomes centered on a sense of purpose and an idealized mission.

two-factor theory. A theory developed by Frederick Herzberg that factors in the workplace called motivators cause job satisfaction, while a separate set of hygiene factors, if absent, causes dissatisfaction.

uncertainty avoidance. The degree to which members feel uncomfortable in ambiguous and uncertain situations and take action to avoid them.

utilitarianism. An ethical model that defines the moral value of actions based on a valuation of their consequences. Actions are right when they produce positive consequences or the greatest happiness for the greatest number of people.

valence. The value a person places on expected rewards.

value theory. A theory suggesting that anything the individual values or desires can produce job satisfaction.

values. Overarching principles or standards that signal how people should behave.

vision. The organization's desired future state.

workplace bullying. Persistent, frequent hostility in the workplace.

zero-sum games. Competitions in which one party wins at the expense of the loser.

zone of indifference. The range of acceptable tasks employees are willing to do without questioning the rationale of the direction.

INDEX

Note: Italicized page locators refer to exhibits.

Abbott, 109
Abraham, C., 247
Absenteeism: dissatisfied workers and, 135; stress and, 156
Abuse: powerful physicians and incidents of, 335, 336; workplace, 344
Academic medical centers: failed mergers of, 199, 200
Academic medicine: serious power problems in, 335
AcademyHealth: website, 244
Academy of Nutrition and Dietetics: code of ethics and behavior for, *119*
Accenture, 426
Access: to effective, efficient, and equitable care, 222; to healthcare, COVID-19 and heightened disparities in, 49; mentoring and, 445
Accommodating style: conflict resolution and, 361
Accountability, 306; delegation and, 447, 448, 453; enforcement of, 418; group decision-making and, 254; for job interviewers, 488; matrix arrangements and, 397; mentoring and, 445; resignations and, 419; retaining, while removing controls, 135; service cycle and, 386; team-based structures and, 401. *See also* Ethics; Trust
Accountable care organizations, 382, 405, 512; definition of, 400; increasing provider interdependence and, 9; matrix arrangements and, 397; structural requirements for, 401
Accreditation: interdisciplinary education and, 265; by Joint Commission, required competencies and, 430; mandated verification and time-outs and, 290; mandating of competency-based learning models and, xx
Accrual accounting, 574
Achievement-oriented leader behaviors and actions: House's path–goal theory and, *313*
Achievement-oriented leadership style: House's path–goal theory and, 312
Acquisitions. *See* Mergers and acquisitions
Acute care settings: healthcare professionals and "pecking order" in, 9
Adams, J. Stacy, 137
Adler, N., 185
Administrative theory, 19, 23–25; applying (chapter activity), 35; coordinative principle, 24; definition of, 23; functional principle, 24; scalar principle, 23, *23*; staff principle, 24–25
Advancement based on achievement: in Weber's ideal bureaucracy, 22
Adverse events, 9, 204. *See also* Errors
Advocate Aurora Health: collapse of merger with Beaumont Health, 597–600

643

Affective commitment, 86; definition of, 97; night staffing and job commitment (case 22), 601
Affective component of attitudes, 86, 99; definition of, 88; interrelationship with behavioral and cognitive components of attitudes, 88, *89*
Affirmative action, 40; definition of, 51; diversity management and, 51–55, 57. *See also* Discrimination
Affordable Care Act: accountable care organizations established by, 400; shared decision-making and, 207
African Americans: US government data and category for, 44
Age: discrimination and bias based on, 49
Age diversity, 45, 47–49, 57
Agency for Healthcare Research and Quality, 1, 183, 207; on disparities in healthcare, 49–50; Health Care Innovations Exchange, 230; relationship between Kotter's eight-step change model and Comprehensive Unit-based Safety Program toolkit modules of, 514, *514*; on understanding patients' culture, 188
Agendas: decision-making in meetings and, 209, *209,* 210; mentoring and, 445
Agreeableness, 485, *485*
Alaska Natives: US government data and category for, 43
Albertsons: mission statement of, 508
Alcohol misuse: burnout and, 157
Alderfer, Clayton, 132, 133, 134, 142
Allocating salary increases and effort (chapter case), 213–14
Alphabet Inc., 233
Alta Healthcare System, 545, 547
Alzheimer's Association: vision statement for, 509
Amazon, 109, 233, 389

Ambiguity: conflict in healthcare organizations and, 363, 372; reduced, job interviews and, 487
American Academy of Ophthalmology: code of ethics and behavior, *119*
American Association of Critical-Care Nurses, 299; six essential standards of, 248, *248*
American Board of Surgery: training and certification requirements, 392
American Cancer Society: code of ethics and behavior, *119*; website, 244
American College of Cardiology: "Leadership Saves Lives" program, 461
American College of Healthcare Executives: code of ethics, 117, 245; *Healthcare Executive Competencies Assessment Tool,* xx, 318, 430–31, 488; on healthcare leaders seeking out mentoring, 445; "Leadership Competencies for Healthcare Services Managers," xx; website, 244
American College of Nurse-Midwives: code of ethics and behavior, *119*
American College of Surgeons, 563
American Dental Association: code of ethics and behavior, *119*
American Heart Association: website, 244
American Hospital Association: website, 245
American Hospital Directory database, 612
American Indians: US government data and category for, 43
American Medical Association: on key ethical issues medical students should be taught, 110; website, 245
American Medical International, 573
American Occupational Therapy Association: code of ethics and behavior, *119*

American Organization for Nursing Leadership, xx
American Physical Therapy Association: code of ethics, 118
American Psychologist, 270
American Public Health Association: code of ethics and behavior, *119*; website, 245
America's Essential Hospitals: website, 245
Anchoring bias, 200, 204–5, 211
Anderson, C., 336
Anderson, N., 222
Anesthesiologists: role of, in operating room, 385
Anger, 153, *154,* 156, 165, 363
Animal rights, 111
Annual performance reviews, 424, 432; discontinuing, 426; mixed use of performance management system (chapter case), 435–36; outmoded, reasons for, 427
Anthem, 109, 557
Anthropology, 4
Anxiety disorders, 152, 153
AOL: failed merger with Time Warner, 469
Apkon, Mike, 22
Appearance norms, 247
Appendectomy: Shannon's extreme uninsured healthcare costs (case 26) and, 611–14
Apple, 233
Applicability, 155
Appraisals: bias and, 429; competency-based performance systems, 430–31, 433; dual goals for, 424; forced distribution, 425–26, 432; numerical rating systems, 424–25, 432; 360-degree system, 428–30
Arad, S., 423
Argyris, C., 69, 70
Aristotle, 307
Armstrong, Lance, 364
Arnold, J., 370
Artificial intelligence, 225, 226

Ascension Health, 383; healthcare ethics of, 117–18
Asian cultures: collectivism and, 45, *45*; cultural dissimilarities between US culture and, 294
Asians: US government data and category for, 44
Aśoka, 307
Aspirational groups, 248, 254
Assault: escalation from conflict to, 360; nurses and, 492. *See also* Abuse; Bullying; Violence in the workplace
Assembly line, 385
Assessment: cultural, 467, 473; for teams, 273, *273–74*
Association for Coaching, *444*
Association for Professional Executive Coaching and Supervision, *444*
Association of Coach Training Organizations, *444*
Association of Corporate Executive Coaches, *444*
Association of periOperative Registered Nurses, 299
Association of State and Territorial Health Officials: website, 245
Association of University Programs in Healthcare Administration: website, 245
Assumptions: paradigms and, 179
Athletes: cheating, 364
Athletics: equity in, 137
Atlantic Health System: Healing Culture Council, 503
Attitudes, 87–90; behaviors and, 88, 89; business skills and knowledge competencies and, xxii; components of, 88–89, 99; conformity and, 246; cultural differences in, 187–88, 190; definition of, 87; employee engagement and effect on, 98, *98*; formation of, 87; importance of, to healthcare organizations, 86; interrelationships between components of,

88, *89*; job commitment and, 189; job satisfaction and, 87; key terms, 86; learning objectives, 85–86; measurement of, 89–90, *90*; perceptions and, 178, 180; societal shifts in, 88

Auschwitz IG Farben plant, 541

Authentic leadership, 306, *321,* 323, 325

Authoritarian leaders: in Blake and Mouton's managerial grid, *309*

Authority: in affecting subordinates' behaviors, 347; centralization of, 29; definition and example of, *341*; delegation and, 447, 448, 453; formal, 337, 347; formal administrative structure and, 23; matrix arrangements and, 398; responsibility and, in Fayol's 14 principles of management, 6

Autocratic leadership style: unfortunate legacy of, 322

Autonomy, 108, 120, 132, 164, 228; definition of, 112; in job design, 135; in multidivisional organizations, 394

Availability: mentoring and, 445

Avoiding style: conflict resolution and, 361

Awards, 132

Ayman, R., 310

Baby boomers, 40; in multigenerational workforce, 47, 57; projected US population of, 141, *141*

Background feelings, 153

Bad boss case, 327–29

Bad driving—road rage (chapter case), 166–67

Bain Capital, 548

Balanced scorecards, 418, 432; definition of, 420; metrics, relationships between mission and vision and, 422, *422*; popularity of, 422; strategy maps and, 423

Balwani, Ramesh "Sunny," 115, 527, 528, 529, 530, 531, 532

Bandwagon effect: definition of, 206

Bankruptcies: disruptive technologies and, 233

Barnard, C., 55, 338

Bass, B. M., 315

Bateman, Steven B., 617

BATNA (best alternative to a negotiated agreement), 357, 373; definition of, 369; understanding, 369–70, 371

Baxter International, 394

Baylor Scott & White: Glassdoor approval ratings for CEOs, *468*

Bazerman, Max, 123

Beaumont Health (Michigan): collapse of Advocate Aurora merger (case 21), 597–600

Becker's Hospital Review, 489

Bed turnover, 420

Behavioral component of attitudes, 86, 99; definition of, 88; interrelationship with cognitive and affective components of attitudes, 88, *89*

Behavioral interview design (chapter activity), 496–97

Behaviorally anchored rating scales, 481, 487, *487,* 493

Behavioral period (1940s–1960s), 307, *320*

Behavioral questions: job interviews and, 486–87, 493

Behavior-related competencies: key advantages of, 430

Behavior(s): acceptable, conflict resolution training and, 367; attitudes and, 88, 89; beliefs, misbeliefs, and, 177; conformity and, 246; counterproductive, unjust organizations and, 469; disruptive, 19; emotions and, 152; ethical, promoting, 112–13; prosocial, 247; self-serving, organizational politics and, 342, 347; social norms, expected roles, and, 87

Behavior theory of leadership, 306, 307, 308–10, *320,* 323, 324
Being at my job right now exercise: team bonding and, 269
Beliefs: behaviors and, 177; conformity and, 246. *See also* Attitudes
Beneficence, 108, 112, 120
Benefits: worker satisfaction issues and, 93, 94
Bennis, Warren, 307
Bereaved mother, letter from (case 13), 567–68; case mix, 626; case questions, 568
Berrett, Britt, 208, 275, 314, 326, 419, 456, 518
Best Care at Lower Cost (Institute of Medicine), 78
Best manager (chapter activity), 329
Bias(es), 51; anchoring, 200, 204–5, 211; appraisal process and, 429; bandwagon effect, 206; cognitive, 204; confirming-evidence, 200, 205, 211; in decision-making, 204–6; framing, 200, 205–6, 211; guarding against influence of, 208–9, 212; hiring and promotion processes and, 54–55, 57; job interviews and, 487, 488; negotiations and, 371; organizational decision-making and, 202; our way of thinking and, 178; perceptual, 183–88; seeing what we want to see (chapter case), 214–15; status quo, 200, 205, 211; sunk cost, 200, 205, 211; teams and, 267; unconscious or implicit, 185
Bidding: a Saudi bid and I (case 20), 595–96
Big hairy audacious goals, 139, 143
Billing: fraudulent, 506, 548; Shannon's extreme uninsured healthcare costs (case 26) and, 611–14
Biochips, 237
Bionic enhancements, 237
Biotechnology: future of (chapter case), 236–38

Birx, Deborah, 86
Black Death: attitude shifts in wake of, 88
Black Lives Matter, 43, 55
Blacks: US government data and category for, 44
Blake, R. R., 309
Blake and Mouton's managerial grid, 309, *309,* *320,* 324
Blame: culture of, 184; cultures of denial and, 461; placing, poor communication and, 293
Blanchard, Kenneth, 310, 311
Blind spots, 214
Blockbuster, 233
Bloom, E., 452
BlueCross of Tennessee, 369
Body language: caregiver, 290, 291; negotiations and, 371
"Body Language Quiz" (Science of People), 301
Body position, 287
Boeing, 396
Bogdanich, W., 557
Bon Secours Health System (Maryland): implementation of learning communities, 75
Bonuses, 97, 132
Borders, 233
Borek, A. J., 247
Bounded rationality, 19, 31, 200, 202, 211
Boxer, M., 20
Brain death in the ICU (chapter case), 121–22
Brainstorming: group decision-making and, 254
Brion, S., 336
Bristol-Myers Squibb, 109
Broken relationships: burnout and, 157
Building a great business (chapter case), 101
Bull, P., 251
Bullying, 247, 254, 344; definition of, 491; in healthcare, 491; of nurses,

492; workplace, 491, 493–94. *See also* Abuse; Assault; Harassment
Bundled payments, 400
Bureaucracy: avoiding negative aspects of, 5, 6; ideal, Weber's six characteristics of, 22, 32; medical, costs of, 22–23
Bureaucracy theory (Weber), 5–6, 21–22, 28; applying (chapter activity), 35
Burke, Doris, 545, 546
Burnout, 152, 162, 286; avoiding, 164; conflict and, 359, 360; definition of, 157; disengaged employees and, 20; performance and, 158, *158*; stress and, 157, 158, 165; value of intervention and, 164, 165; workplace bullying and, 491
Burns, James MacGregor, 307, 311, 314
Burns, T., 390
Business: ethical challenges in healthcare and, 114–17
Business ethics: corporate social responsibility and, 108–10. *See also* Ethics
Business model: definition of, 226; innovations, 225, 226, 234
Business Roundtable, 108
Business skills and knowledge competency: in American College of Healthcare Executives competency assessment framework, xx, 318, 431, 488; appraisals and subdivision of categories under domain of, 431
Business unit level: in CVS Health's structure, 383, *383*; performance management occurring at, *418*
Business Week, 578
Busy regional vice president (case 5), 537–39; case matrix, 625; case questions, 539
Buy-in: good decision-making dynamics and, 209

Campinha-Bacote, J., 50
Cancer: doctor–patient miscommunication and, 286; new therapies for, 237
Canterbury, New Zealand: Pegasus Health's integration of care in (case 8), 551–54
Cao, H., 276
Capital investment: governance and decision-making in hospital-based surgical services (case 28), 619
Capitation, 400
Cardiac risk at Pineview Hospital (chapter case), 256
Career ladder, 481, 488
Carnegie Mellon University, 30
Carreyrou, John, 531
Carter, Jimmy, 137
Case managers, 386
Case review: ethics training and, 490
Cause-and-effect relationships: perceptions and, 181–82
Cell phones, 180; noise and, 289
Center for Medicare & Medicaid Innovation, 228
Centers for Disease Control and Prevention: COVID-19 and mask recommendations of, 72; COVID-19 precautions, 365–66; on heightening of disparities during COVID-19, 49
Centers for Medicare & Medicaid Services, 183, 228; accountable care organizations as defined by, 400
Centralization: in Fayol's 14 principles of management, 6
Centralized organizations, 391, 404–5, 617
CEO misuse of company funds (chapter case), 123
CEO's salary dilemma (chapter case), 13–14
Certification, 489. *See also* Accreditation
Cerutti, K., 87

Index **649**

Chain of command, 382, 387, 389–90, 404; definition of, *387*; fragmented university healthcare venture (chapter case), 407, *409*; Mercy Health organizational chart, 387, *387*; scalar principle and, 23, *23*; US Department of Veterans Affairs organizational chart, 387, *388*
Challenger space shuttle disaster (1986): groupthink and, 249
Champions: successful teams and, 270
Change: in attitudes, 87; conflict in healthcare organizations and, 364, 372; disloyal support of? (chapter case), 298–99; driven by need for learning, 68; leadership and implementation of, 512–14; mission-driven, 503; models, 514, *514*; relevancy and, 511, 515; resistance to, 513, 515; three types of, and their interactions, 512, *512*; transformational, 512
Charisma: transformational leadership and, 315–16, *321*, 324
Charts: Gantt, 420, *421*
Cheating athletes, 364
Chevron: diversity program, 55
Chief executive officers: accelerated turnover of, 443; conflict and, 364, 372; COVID-19 and, 318; Dallas hospitals, Glassdoor approval ratings for, 468, *468*; new CEO (case 11), 563–64; physicians and (chapter case), 375–77; responding to COVID-19 cost reductions, 113; starting as CEO at Skyview Hospital (case 17), 587–89; women as, studies on, 47
Chief financial officers, 391; conflict and, 364; top ethical concerns faced by, 116, *116*
Chief information officers, 391
Chief Learning Officer magazine, 70
Chief learning officers, 70, 73, 76, 391

Chief nursing officers, 391; conflict and, 364, 372
Childhood immunization rates, 420
Children: life skills needed by, and ranking of communication skills, 284, *285*
Children's hospitals: playrooms in, 593
China: cultural values of, *45*
Cho, Heather, 145
Christensen, Clayton, 226, 232
Cigna, 109
Circulating nurses: role of, in operating room, 385
CirrusMD, 179
Cisco, 396, 401
Citicorp, 573
Civil rights, 111
Clarification/clarity: dysfunctional delegation and lack of, 451–52; lack of, as barrier to communication, 293
Cleaning protocols: COVID-19 and, 87
Cleveland Clinic: diversity pipeline program at, 41; diversity ranking and, 42; Florida Research and Innovation Center, 230; vision statement for, 509–10
Climate change: as source of stress, *161*
Clinical decision support systems, 207
Clinical training programs: learning in healthcare and, 75
Cloning, 237
Closed systems: open systems *vs.,* 30
Coaching: combating high turnover and poor culture with (case 29), 623–24; communication and relationship management competencies and, xxvi; competencies used in conjunction with, xxvi–xxvii; continuous, 432; cultural change and, 471; definition of, 442; focus of, 443, 445; integrating with leadership development, 445; leadership

competencies and, xxvii; learning objectives, 441; mentoring *vs.*, 442, 453; productive, coach–client relationship, 444; professional associations for, *444*; professionalism competencies and, xxvii; purpose of, 443; seeking, primary reasons for, 444; value of, 443

Coalition: as negative influence tactic, 340, 347

Cocaine, 557

Code blue, 1

Code of Mutual Respect (Maimonides Medical Center): physician commitment to, 367

Codes of conduct, 121; Hospital Corporation of America, 116–17

Codes of ethics, 114, 120, 123; of professional organizations, 117, 245; for select healthcare associations, *119*

Coercive power, 335, 338, 347

Coffee breaks, 464

Cognitive biases, 204

Cognitive component of attitudes, 86, 99; definition of, 88; interrelationship with behavioral and affective components of attitudes, 88, *89*

Cognitive dissonance, 86; definition of, 89; understanding (activity), 102

"Cognitive Intelligence: Number of Women in Group Linked to Effectiveness in Solving Difficult Problems" (Massachusetts Institute of Technology study), 61

Cognitive pressures: institutional conformity and, 31

Cohen, M., 203

Cohn, Harry, 322

Cohorts, 248–49, 254; chapter activity, 258; generational, 248

Collaborating style: conflict resolution and, 361

Collective cultures, 40, 44, 57

Collective identity, 247

Collectivism: preference for individualism over, 467, 472

Collegial relationships, 11

Collins, J. C., 139

Columbia/HCA: ethics violations, 115

Combating high turnover and poor culture (case 29), 623–24; case matrix, 627; case questions, 624; follow-up, 624

Command groups, 243, 244

Commanding: as core management function, 7

Commission on Accreditation of Healthcare Management Education, xx

Commitment, 4; commitment dilemma (chapter case), 100; night staffing and job commitment (case 22), 601

Committees, 254, 404

Committee structure: fragmented university healthcare venture (chapter case), 408–9

Communication, 4, 283–301; communication and relationship management competencies and, xxiv; conflict and breakdowns in, 362–63; definition of, 284; delegation and clarity in, 451–52; disloyal support of change? (chapter activity), 298–99; effective, barriers to, 292–93, 296–97; of emotions, 153; engagement and, 98; impact of culture on, 293–94; improving skills in (chapter activity), 300–301; key terms, 283–84; lack of, fatal consequences of, 283; learning objectives, 283; matrix arrangements and, 397, 398; nonverbal, 153, 284, 290–92, 293, 296, 297; organizational change and, 513, 516; poor, consequences of, 284; poor, stereotypes and, 185; poor, unsafe patient care and (chapter case), 299–300; ranking of, in life skills needed by children, 284, *285*; Sam's deposit recovery (case 25), 607–9; successful, 295–96, 297; virtual, 294–95, 297. *See also* Feedback; Listening

Communication and relationship management competency: in American College of Healthcare Executives competency assessment framework, xx, 318, 430, 488; appraisals and subdivision of categories under domain of, 431

Communication channel, 283, 288; definition of, 287; information richness and complexity and, *287*, 296; selection of, 287–88

Communication process, 284–90; communication channel in, 287, 296; decoding in, *285*, 288, 296; encoding in, *285*, 285–87, 296; feedback in, *285*, 289–90, 296; information richness and, 287, *287*, 296; message in, 284, *285*, 296; mode of communication in, *285*; noise in, *285*, 288–89, 296; receiver in, 284, *285*, 288, 289, 296, 297; sender in, 284, *285*, 288, 289, 296, 297

Compaq: failed merger with Hewlett Packard, 469

Comparison: group polarization and, 251, *251*

Compassion, 114, 120

Compassion fatigue, 157

Compensation: annual performance reviews and, 424; performance management systems and, 418; worker satisfaction issues and, 93

Compensatory damages: for workplace harassment, 345

Competencies: appraisal systems based on, 418, 430–31, 433; by chapter, xxi–xxviii; chapter topics as they relate to levels of organizational behavior and, *11*, 11–12; five critical domains of, in American College of Healthcare Executives assessment framework, xx, 318, 430–31, 488; leadership, integrating coaching and mentoring and, 445; in managing organizational culture, 463; in "soft" skills, training and, 490–91, 493

Competency-based appraisal systems, 418, 430–31, 433

Competency-based learning models: accrediting bodies and mandating of, xx

Competing style: conflict resolution and, 361

Competition, 306, 402; conflict in healthcare organizations and, 363; dysfunctional, 365, 372; governance and decision-making in hospital-based surgical services (case 28), 617–18, 620, 621; multidivisional organizations and, 395; organizational politics and, 342; zero-sum games and, 364–65, 372

Complexity: conflict in healthcare organizations and, 363, 372; organizational structure and, 402, 406; of US healthcare system, Sam's deposit recovery (case 25) and, 607–9

Comprehensive Unit-based Safety Program toolkit modules (Agency for Healthcare Research and Quality): relationship between Kotter's eight-step change model and, 514, *514*

Compromising style: conflict resolution and, 361

Computer-assisted diagnostics: future of (chapter case), 236–38

Conduct rules: in Weber's ideal bureaucracy, 22

Confidentiality, 20

Confirming-evidence (confirmation) bias, 200, 211; blind spots and,

214; definition of, 205; Theranos and Elizabeth Holmes (case 2), 525–32

Conflict, 4, 357; COVID-19 and, 365–66, 372; in C-suite, 364; dealing with, 361; definition of, 358; dysfunctional outcomes of, 359–60; elements in, 358; escalation from, to assault, 360; healing hospital conflict (chapter case), 167–68; in healthcare, contributing factors to, 362–64, 372; intergroup, 357, 362, *363*, 372; interpersonal, 357, 362, *363*, 364, 372; intragroup, 266, 357, 362, *363*, 372; intrapersonal, 357, 362, *363*, 372; levels of, 362, *363*; managing, 366–68, 373; matrix arrangements and, 397; negative, 358, 359, 371; nontask organizational, 357, 360, 372; organizational politics and, 342; positive, 359, 371; positive and negative outcomes of, 359, *359*; process, 357, 360, 372; relationship, 357, 360, 372; small businesses and, 363; social loafing and, 254; task, 357, 360, 372; in teams, guidelines for, 274–75, 277; work-related, types of, 360–61, 372; work-related stress and, 161–62. *See also* Negotiation(s)

Conflict management, 20, 373; business skills and knowledge competencies and, xxv; communication and relationship management competencies and, xxv; definition of, 368; key terms, 357; learning objectives, 357; play the "Two Dollar Game" (chapter activity), 377

Conflict management styles: accommodating style, 361; avoiding style, 361, *362*; collaborating style, 361; competing style, 361; compromising style, 361, *362*; dominating style, 361, *362*; force style, 361; integrating style, 361, *362*; obliging style, *362*

Conflicts of interest: HealthSouth and, 576

Conformity: groups and, 246–48, 254; prosocial, 247, 254

Confucius, 307

Conger, J., 316

Conscientiousness, 485, *485*

Consensus: in affecting subordinates' behaviors, 347; definition and example of, *341*

Consistency/commitment: in affecting subordinates' behaviors, 347; definition and example of, *341*

Conspiracy, 506

Consultation, 339, 340, 347

Consumer-focused innovations, 224, 225, 234

Consumer rights, 111

Contextual leadership theory, 306

Contingency approach, 19, 28–29, 32; applying (chapter activity), 35; definition of, 28

Contingency or situational period (1960s–present), 307, *320*

Contingency theory, 306, 310–11, 323–24; definition of, 310; three situational elements in, 312

Continuance commitment, 86; definition of, 97; night staffing and job commitment (case 22), 601

Controlling function: as core management function, 7; performance management and, 418

"Conversation About Challenging Cases in Clinical Ethics" (Seattle Children's Hospital), 124

Conversation starters exercise: team bonding and, 268–69

Cook County Health (Chicago): standing committees, 244

Coordinating: as core management function, 7

Coordination: specialization in healthcare and lack of, 386, 404
Coordinative principle, 24
Copayments: surprise billing and, 114
Core values: interaction between ethics, mission, vision, and, 109, *110*
Corporate citizenship, 108
Corporate culture: intersectionality and, 51; primary purpose of, 462; women and, 46–47
Corporate level: in CVS Health's structure, 383, *383*; performance management occurring at, *418*
Corporate social responsibility, 108; business ethics and, 108–10; definition of, 108
Corporate training programs: interpersonal skill building and, 491
Corporations, 382–84; definition of, 382; for-profit or not-for-profit, 382, 383, 404; healthcare, US economy and importance of, 383
Corruption: culture of, 107
Cottle, Brian, 623
Country club leaders: in Blake and Mouton's managerial grid, *309*
Covey, Stephen, 183, 446, 448, 449
COVID-19 pandemic, 11, 43, 319, 607; Beaumont Health's furloughs during, 597; beliefs/misbeliefs, vaccines, and, 177; CEOs responding to cost reductions during, 113; conflict and, 365–66, 372; emotional and psychological disorders among healthcare professionals during, 151; employee satisfaction during, 85; ethical leaders during, 113; ethics training and difficult decision-making during, 489–90; heightened racial and ethnic disparities and, 49; high costs of a failure to learn and, 72; illustrations of competing style during, 361; impact of, on healthcare services, 19; impact on engagement, 91, 99; leadership and, 318, 325; leadership role-play during (chapter activity), 329–30; as major source of stress, 160, *161*; mentoring during, 441; millennial and Gen Z employees and, 141, 142; national medical research doctors visibility during, 86; nonverbal communication during, 290; organizational learning at Virginia Mason Medical Center and rapid response to, 67; paradigm shift due to, 180; Prospect Medical's problems during, 546–47; racial/ethnic minorities and impact of, 39; shattered norms during, 247; status quo bias and response to, 205; stereotypes toward people of color during, 185; telemedicine and, 179; virtual work groups during, 294; widespread stress experienced during, 157; work-related attitudes and behaviors and, 87–88
"COVID-19 Pandemic Could Result in Permanent Governance Changes at Hospitals" (Legasse), 412
Coye, Molly, 235, 236
Crawford, Brian, 85
Creative thinking, 154
Creativity: critical importance of, 233; definitions of, 222, 223; encouraging/discouraging, activities for, *227*; game-changing implementation of, 226; healthcare, diffusion of, 228–32, 234; increasing, strategies for, 226–28, 234; key terms, 221; leadership competencies and, xxiv; learning objectives, 221; link between innovation and, 222–24; moving to innovation from, *223*, 224, 234; multitude of problems and need for, 222; positive conflict and, 359; transformational leaders and, 316
Credibility: loss of, 419
Crenshaw, Kimberlé, 51
Crises: mentoring during, 441

Croskerry, P., 204
Cross, T., 40
Cross-disciplinary teams, 9
Crossing the Quality Chasm (Institute of Medicine), 390
Crucial Conversations, 588
C-suite: conflict in, 364
Cultural assessment, 462, 467, 473
Cultural competence: building in healthcare providers, 50; definition of, 40
Cultural differences: encoding errors and, 287; Sakal's dilemma (case 24), 605–6; a Saudi bid and I (case 20), 595–96
Culture(s): activities that encourage/discourage creativity and innovation, *227*; as barrier to effective communication, 292, 297; of blame, 184; of blame and denial, 461; collective, 44, 45, *45*, 57; communication and impact of, 293–94, 297; of corruption, 107; ethics and ethical behaviors in context of, 113–14; of excellence, combating high turnover and poor culture (case 29) and, 624; of feedback, 424; individualistic, 44, 45, *45*, 57; of learning, creating, 75; manifestations of, 43; overlap with ethnicity, 43, 56; perceptions, attitudes, and, 187–88, 190; of safety, creating (chapter case), 300; toxic, at HealthSouth, 462–63; of trust, 154; of violence (chapter case), 474–75. *See also* Organizational culture
"Culture's Role in Enabling Organizational Change" (Strategy& PwC), 510
Customer/stakeholder measures: in balanced scorecards, 422
CVC Capital Partners, 548
CVS, 557
CVS Health, 109, 233; three levels of organization, *383*
Cystic fibrosis, 237

Daimler and Chrysler: failed mega-merger between, 469
Dangerous shortcuts: unsafe patient care and (chapter case), 299
Dating: bounded rationality and, 202
Dead-end jobs, 94
Deaths: medical errors and, 9; premature, 49
Debating diversity (chapter activity), 61
Decentralized organizations, 391, 405, 617
Decent work, 136
DeChambeau, Bryson, 364
Decision-making, 4, 199–216; in an organizational context, 202; biases in, 204–6, 211; business skills and knowledge competencies, xxiii; competencies used in conjunction with, xxiii–xxiv; courage in, 208, 209; democratic, political behaviors and, 344; emotions and, 153; ethical, methods for determining, 119–20; flat structure but centralized control (chapter case), 410–11; governance and, in hospital-based surgical services (case 28), 617–22; group, advantages/disadvantages of, 253–54; group shift and, 250; groupthink as detriment to, 206–7, 211; in healthcare, 207; human resource management competencies and, xxiv; improving, 208–10; joint provider, 9; key terms, 200; leaders and importance of, 200; leadership competencies and, xxiii; learning objectives, 199; in meetings, *209,* 209–10, 212; mergers and, 199; the ogre and the playroom (case 18), 593–94; operational-level, delegation of (chapter case), 456–57; organic *vs.* mechanistic organizations, *390*; paradigms and, 178; performance management and, 420; positive conflict

and, 359; rational, 200, 201, 211; shared, in healthcare, 207; what prompted me to do that? (chapter activity), 216

Decision-making, models of, 201–4; bounded rationality, 202, 211; garbage can model, 202–4, *203*, 211; rational decision-making, 201, 211

Decision-making theory, 30–31, 32; applying (chapter activity), 35; scientific management theory *vs.*, 31

Decision trees: example of, *200*; helpfulness of, 200–201

Decoding, 283; barriers to effective communication and, 292, 297; in communication process, 284, *285*, 288, 296; definition of, 288

De Dreu, C. K. W., 358

Deductibles: surprise billing and, 114

Defensiveness: as barrier to communication, 293

Deficiency needs: in Maslow's hierarchy of needs, 26, *26*

Delegation, 442, 446–53; beware of micromanaging, 451; clear communication and, 451–52; combating high turnover and poor culture with (case 29), 623–24; communication and relationship management competencies and, xxvi; competencies used in conjunction with, xxvi–xxvii; definitions of, 446, 447; dump-and-run, 452; effective, eight steps to, 452–53; four key concepts in, 447–48, 453; gofer, 449, *449*, 454; group decision-making and, 254; importance of, 446; inappropriate, reasons for, 447; key terms, 442; leadership competencies and, xxvii; learning objectives, 441; levels of, *449*, 449–50, 454; lunch expenditure approval (chapter case), 455–56; managerial key points for, 451; of operational-level decision-making (chapter case), 456–57;

professionalism competencies and, xxvii; quiz (chapter activity), 457; stewardship, 449, *449*, 454; take-care-of-it (chapter case), 454–55; trust and, 447, 448, 451, 453, 454

Deloitte, 425; Global Millennial Survey, 141

Democrats: perceptions of COVID-19 and, 182

Demographics, 248, 254

Denial: cultures of blame and, 461

Department managers: in matrix organizations, 396

Department/unit level: performance management occurring at, *418*

Deposit recovery (case 25), 607–9; case mix, 627; case questions, 609

Depression, 152, 153, 157, 162

Development Dimensions International: on value of succession planning, 319

Diabetes, 237

Diagnoses: anchoring bias and, 204–5; cognitive biases and errors in, 204

Dialogue, 283, 295, 297

Dietitians, 9, 266

Differentiation: integration *vs.*, 391

Difficult-to-imitate resources, 30

Diffusion, 221; definition of, 230; of healthcare creativity and innovation, 228–32, 234; promoting, 229–30, *231*

Digital Equipment Corporation, 396

Digital photography, 233

Digital technology, 225, 226

Dilemma of loyalties (case 1), 523–24; case matrix, 625; case questions, 524

Dinh, J. E., 307, 321

Directive leadership style: in path–goal theory, 312

Director of marketing *versus* operations (case 18), 591–92; case matrix, 626; case questions, 592

Disability status: discrimination and bias based on, 49

Discipline: in Fayol's 14 principles of management, 6
Discounting: insured *vs.* uninsured patients and, 612
DISC personality test, 496
Discrimination: COVID-19 and, 49; disparities in healthcare and, 49; gender, 41, 51; intersectionality and, 51; job interviews and, 487; against LGBTQ individuals, job interviews and, 488; racial, 51; Sakal's dilemma (case 24), 605–6; similar-to-me effect and, 186; as source of stress, 160; stereotypes, bias, and, 185
Disengaged employees, 20, 91; costs related to, 86; effect of, on attitudes, 98, *98*; failures in motivation and, 130; organizational commitment and, 97–98; statistics on, 130, *131*
Disloyal support of change? (chapter case), 298–99
Disney, 393
Disparities in health and healthcare, 40; decision-making biases and, 207; racial and ethnic, 49–51, 57
Dispositional approach, 86; definition of, 94; job satisfaction and, 93, 94–95, 99
Disrespect: unsafe patient care and (chapter case), 299–300
Disruptive behaviors, 19
Disruptive innovation, 221, 234; bankruptcies and, 233; definition of, 232
Dissatisfiers, 130; definition of, 135; in Herzberg's two-factor theory, 134, *134,* 143
Disseminator role: defined in Mintzberg's leadership study, 310
Dissociative groups, 248
Distance work arrangements: COVID-19 and, 87, 88
Distress, 152, 157, 165; definition of, 158; performance and, 158, *158*

Distributive justice, 108, 111, 469, 473
Disturbance handler role: defined in Mintzberg's leadership study, 310
Diversity, 42; benefits of, 52; communication and relationship management competencies and, xxi; cultural, racial, and ethnic, 43–45; debating diversity (chapter activity), 61; definition of, 40; efforts at Novant Health (chapter case), 59–60; embracing, decision-making and, 208; gender and age, 45–49, 57; improving, federal, state, and private resources for, 55–56; key terms, 40; leadership competencies and, xxi; learning objectives, 39; multidisciplinary teams and, 40; organizational diversity statement and, 54; organizational strategic plan and, 56, 58; problems in a diverse culture (chapter case), 60–61; professionalism competencies and, xxi–xxii; promoting, in workforce, 55; regulatory guidelines and laws pertaining to, 51–55, *53–54;* supporting, competencies used in conjunction with, xxi; in teams, 266–67, 276; unintentional organizational barriers to, 54–55. *See also* Workforce diversity
DiversityInc, 42
Diversity management, 40; affirmative action and, 51–55, 57; definition of, 51
Divisional leaders: in multidivisional organizations, 393–94
Division of labor, 6, 23, 382, 385–86, 404; benefits of, 385; definition of, 385; in healthcare, 385; in Weber's ideal bureaucracy, 22
Division of work: in Fayol's 14 principles of management, 6
Divorce rates: bounded rationality and, 202

Doctor on Demand, 179
"Doing no harm" (nonmaleficence), 112
Dopamine, 152
Doran, G., 139
Double-loop learning, 68, 69, 70
Dress codes: conformity and, 247, 254; rituals and routines and, 464
Drexel Burnham Lambert, 574
Dr. Handly and the multidisciplinary team (chapter case), 278–79
Drug costs: controlled, creativity and, 226
Drug-delivery systems, 225
Drug Enforcement Administration, 558
Dump-and-run delegation, 452
Dysfunctional competition, 365, 372

EBITDA (earnings before interest, taxes, depreciation, and amortization): high-performing facilities and, 315
Economics, 4
Economies of scale, 389
Economy and Society (Weber), 21
Eculizumab, 229
Education: COVID-19 and heightened disparities in, 49
Effective care: access to, 222
Efficiency: in Weber's ideal bureaucracy, 22
Efficient care: access to, 222
Egalitarian hospital culture: need for (chapter case), 475–76
Egoist model, 108, 120; definition of, 111; objectionable parts of, 112
Egypt: gender diversity and, 45
Eisner, Michael, 137
Elective surgeries: COVID-19 and delay of, 113
Electronic health records, 284
Eli Lilly and Company, 109, 163
Elkind, Peter, 545, 546
e-mails, 179, 287, *287,* 288

Emotional contagion, 153
Emotional control: lack of, 155
Emotional intelligence, 152, 165, 429, 567; definition of, 154; improving, 163; internal locus of control and, 160; mentoring and, 446; Mike and the walk-around (case 23), 603–4; monitoring (chapter activity), 171; workplace performance and, 155
Emotional regulation, 153, 155
Emotions: business skills and knowledge competencies and, xxiii; deceptive, in negotiations, 370; definition of, 152; heightened, in healthcare settings, 151; key terms, 152; learning objectives, 151; managing, suggestions for, 155–56; moods *vs.,* 153, 165; naming, 155; negative, 153, 159, 165, 373; positive, 153; primary, 153–54, *154,* 165; professionalism competencies and, xxiii; secondary, 153–54, *154;* stress and, 156, 165; in the workplace, 153–56. *See also* Emotional intelligence
Empathy, 20, 154, 247, 295
Employee assistance programs, 152, 164, 165
Employee development: performance management systems and, 418. *See also* Training
Employee engagement, 4, 11, 514, 516; effect on attitudes, 98, *98;* exploring (chapter activity), 101; organizational citizenship behaviors and, 95–96, 99; organizational success and, 98, *98,* 99; questions for, 92, *92;* starting as CEO at Skyview Hospital (case 17), 588–89; statistics on, 130, *131;* in United States, 91, *91*
Employee motivation: as critical management function, 7
Employee-oriented leadership, 308, 309

Employees: activities that encourage/discourage creativity and innovation, *227*; recognition programs for, 132; referrals, 483; theory X and theory Y managers and beliefs about, 27–28, *28*

Employee surveys, 99; questions, *90*; using, to improve satisfaction, 96

Empowerment: levels of delegation by, *449*, 449–50

Encoding, 284; barriers to effective communication and, 292, 297; in communication process, 284, *285*, 285–87, 288, 296; definition of, 285

Endo, Jo Ann, 353

Enduring culture, 464

Engagement, 86, 90–92; definition of, 90; measures of, 90–91; questions for, 92, *92. See also* Employee engagement

"Engagement Ratio," 589

Entrepreneur role: defined in Mintzberg's leadership study, 310

Environment: nonverbal communication and, 291, 296; in open systems theory, 29, *30*; organizational structure and, 402, *403*

Equal employment, 51

Equal Employment Opportunity Commission, 345; sexual harassment as defined by, 344; workplace harassment training programs, 491

Equitable care: access to, 222

Equity, 42; in athletics, 137; in Fayol's 14 principles of management, *7*; key terms, 40; learning objectives, 39; making commitment to, 54; organizational strategic plan and, 56, 58; promoting in workforce, 55; salaries and issues with, 137–38

Equity equilibrium, 137, *138*

Equity theory, 130, 137–38, 143, 311, 313, *320*, 324; definition of, 137; night staffing and job commitment (case 22), 601

ERG (existence, relatedness, growth) theory of motivation (Alderfer), 130, 132–34, *133*, 142

ER physician and ER nurse (chapter case), 351–52

Errors: in diagnoses, cognitive biases and, 204; medical, 9, 12, 367; misunderstood terms used in healthcare and, 286, 296; noise in healthcare communication and, 288, 289; silos and, 381; system failures and, 184

Esprit de corps: in Fayol's 14 principles of management, *7*

Esteem needs: in Maslow's hierarchy of needs, *26*

Ethical behavior: promoting, 112–13

"Ethical Breakdowns" (Bazerman and Tenbrunsel), 123

Ethical breakdowns in healthcare organizations (chapter activity), 123–24

Ethical challenge of treating hepatitis C (case 27), 615–16; case mix, 627; case questions, 616; references, 616

Ethical decision-making: methods for determining, 119–20

"Ethical Dilemma of a Heart Surgeon" (Waldenberger), 124

Ethical leadership, 306, *321*, 323, 325

Ethical models, 110–14; egoist model, 110, 111–12, 120; justice model (or fairness model), 110, 111, 120; rights model, 110–11, 120; utilitarianism, 110, 120

Ethical principles: four general, 112, 120

Ethical relativism, 108, 114

Ethical statements: comparing/contrasting (chapter activity), 123

Ethical violations: egregious, examples of, 115

Ethics: codes of, 114, 117–18, *119*, 120, 123, 245; definition of, 108; dilemma of loyalties (case 1),

523–24; director of marketing versus operations (case 18), 591–92; ethical challenge of treating Hepatitis C (case 27), 615–16; in healthcare, 109–10; HealthSouth (case 15), 573–80; HealthT seeks healthier employees (case 14), 571; injured migrant worker (case 3), 533–34; interaction between core values, mission, vision, and, 109, *110*, 120; key terms, 108; learning objectives, 107; new CEO (case 11), 563–64; professional, 117–18; professionalism competencies and, xxii; a Saudi bid and I (case 20), 595–96; of surprise billing, 114; thalidomide and Grünenthal (case 6), 541–43

Ethics training, 481, 490, 493

Ethisphere, 116

Ethnicity: definition of, 43; discrimination and bias based on, 49; overlap of culture and race with, 43, 56; US government data on race and, 43–44

Ethnocentrism, 40, 57; definition of, 44; experiencing ethnocentrism (chapter activity), 61–62

Eugenics programs: Nazi death camps and, 541

Eustress, 152, 165; definition of, 158; performance and, 158, *158*

Everest Award, 589

Ewenstein, B., 426

Exchange: of rewards or favors, 339

Executive coaching: improving leadership performance through, 444; personality tests and, 485

Exercise physiology therapists, 265

Exhaustion: stress and, 158

Existence needs: in Alderfer's ERG (existence, relatedness, growth) theory, 132, *133*, 134

Expectancy, 130, 138, 143

Expectancy theory, 130, 143, 313; definition of, 138; motivation and, *138*, 138–39

Expectations: delegation and, 452; organizational politics and, *343*; paradigms and, 178; self-fulfilling prophecies and, 187

Experiencing ethnocentrism (chapter activity), 61–62

Expert power, 335, 338, 347

Exploitation: learning and, 73

Exploration: learning and strategic focus on, 73

External controls: effect of, employee satisfaction and commitment, 132, *133*

External locus of control, 159, 160

External stimuli, 130; definition of, 131; studies on, 130–31

Extraversion, 485, *485*

Extrinsic motivation: learning and, 72

Extrinsic rewards: millennials and, 318–19

Exxon Mobil, 109

Eye contact, 287, 292; cultural differences and, 293, 297; patient–caregiver relationship and, 290, 291

Face-to-face communication, 287, *287*, 288, 296

Face-to-face meetings: for job interviews, 487

Facial attractiveness: job interviews and discrimination based on, 487–88

Facial expressions, 153, 291, 297; virtual communication and, 294

Factories: new management challenges in, 5

Fairness: in the context of culture, 469, 473

Fairness model. *See* Justice (or fairness) model

Farrer, L., 451

Fast Company, 530

Fauci, Anthony, 86

Faust, Drew Gilpin, 222
Fayol, Henri, 2, 7, 12, 23, 35, 201; 14 principles of management, 6–7
Fear, 153, *154,* 165
Federal Bureau of Investigation: HealthSouth raided by, 579
Feedback, 228, 284, 296; in communication process, 284, *285,* 289–90; continuous, 432; culture of, 424; definition of, 289; delegation and, 448, 453; high-richness channels and, 288; in job design, 136; lack of, as barrier to communication, 293; mentoring and, 446; Mike and the walk-around (case 23), 603–4; millennials and, 142; multiple approaches for, 426; organizational change and, 514, 515; patient safety and, 289, 296; performance, seven tips for, 427; teams and, 272; 360-degree system and, 429
Feelings: background, 153; behaviors and, 152. *See also* Emotions
Femininity: preference for masculinity over, 462, 467, 473
Fentanyl, 555
Fetal rights, 111
Feudalism: Black Death and ending of, 88
FHP—Utah (case 16), 581–85; case matrix, 626; case questions (part 1), 582; case questions (part 2), 583; case questions (part 3), 584; case questions (part 4), 585; impact of the changes at St. Mark's (part 3), 583–84; opening and failure of the FHP hospital (part 4), 584–85; references, 585; they would never leave us—Holy Cross system's failed negotiation (part 1), 581–82; an unexpected offer (part 2), 582–83
Fiedler, F.: contingency theory of, 311, 312

Figurehead role: defined in Mintzberg's leadership study, 309
Financial incentives: motivation and paradox of, 129; organizational politics and, *343*
Financial measures: in balanced scorecards, 422
Financial Times, 531
Financial well-being: millennials and, 142
Fiorio, C. V., 392
First jobs exercise: team bonding and, 268
Fit: human resources processes and, 55; job satisfaction and, 93
"5 Essential Components of Successful Coaching" (Mattone), 444
Five Dysfunctions of a Team (Lencioni), 588
Flat/flattened structures: flat structure but centralized control (chapter case), 410–11; nonhierarchical, 389, *389,* 404; problems and unintended consequences with, 389–90
Flexible work arrangements: engaged employees and, 98; millennials and, 141, 142, 143
Focus groups, 92
Followers: influence tactics and, 341; transactional leadership theory and, 311; transformational leaders and, 316–17; transformational leadership theory and, 314
Food and Drug Administration, 221, 529
Forbes, 530
Forbes Business Council, 208
Forced distribution (stacked ranking or forced ranking), 418, 425–26, 432; definition of, 425; employee problems with, 425–26
Ford Motor Company, 109
Formal authority, 335; definition of, 337; degree of power derived from, 338, 347

Index

Formal groups, 243, 248, 254; conformity and, 247; definition of, 244
Forming stage: in team building, 263, 267, *267,* 268, 277
For-profit organizations, 383, 404
Forsythe, M., 557
Fortune magazine, 530
Foundation of the American College of Healthcare Executives: workplace diversity survey, 46–47
14 principles of management (Fayol), 6–7
Fox, John, 597, 598
Fragmentation in healthcare, 386; ethical challenge of treating hepatitis C (case 27), 615–16; fragmented university healthcare venture (chapter case), 406–10
Framing bias, 200, 205–6, 211
Frances, Allen, 556
Fraud, 506; Medicare, 107, 115; toxic culture at HealthSouth and, 462–63, 576, 577, 579, 580
Frazer, G., 443
Frontline healthcare workers: stress experienced by, 157
Frustration-regression, 130, 134
Functional managers: matrix arrangements and, 398, 405
Functional organizations, 382, 391–93, 402, 405; advantages of, 392; definition of, 391; disadvantages of, 392, 405
Functional principle, 24
Functional structure: advantages, disadvantages, and most suitable conditions for, 398–99, *399,* 405
Functional unit level: in CVS Health's structure, 383, *383*
Fundamental attribution error, 178, 183, 189, 190; definition of, 184; internal and external attribution in, 184, *184*
Furloughs: COVID-19 cost reductions and, 113

Gallup, 183, 589; COVID-19 and engagement survey, 91; employee engagement poll, 514; employee–management survey, 11; engaged employee as defined by, 315; *State of the American Workplace* report, 516
Gambling: irrationality in decision-making and, 201
Gandhi, Mahatma, 322
Gantt charts, 418, 432; definition of, 420; example of, *421*
Gap analysis, 467, 504, 515; definition of, 510; developing, questions related to, 510–11; organizational change and, 510–14; from values, mission, and vision, 510, *511*
Garbage can model, 200, 202–4, *203,* 211
Gates, Bill, 530
GE Healthcare Consulting, 595
Gelfand, M. J., 358
Gender: barriers to effective communication and, 292; discrimination and bias based on, 49; emotion-related illnesses and, 152; facial attractiveness, job interviews, and, 487–88; role attitudes, change in, 87
Gender-based harassment, 344
Gender discrimination, 41, 51
Gender diversity, 45–47, 57; teams and, 266, 267
General Electric, 425
General Motors, 393
Generational cohorts, 248
Generation X, 40; in multigenerational workforce, 47–48, 57
Generation Z, 40; motivating, 141–42, 143; in multigenerational workforce, 48
Gene therapy, 233; future of (chapter case), 236–38; three areas in, 237
Genetic revolution, 236
Genetics, 74
Genomics, 233, 234

Gesturs, 291, 296; cultural differences and, 293; encouraging, 153
Giuliani, Rudy, 557
Givel, Yves, 80
Glamour, 530
"Glass cliff": women and, 47
Glassdoor, 476, 531; approval ratings for Dallas hospital CEOs, 468, *468*
Globalization: communication and, 294; influx of expatriate workers, immigrants, and, 42, 56
GLOBE CEO Study, 476
GLOBE model, 58
Goals: meaningful, in constructive performance evaluations, 427; mission and, 508; organizational values and, 464; setting, successful coaching and, 444; SMART (specific, measurable, assigned, realistic, and time-bound), 139, 143; values and, 505, 506
Goal-setting theory, 130, 139, 143
Gofer delegation, 442; beware of micromanaging in, 451; definition of, 449, 454; empowerment, reporting time, and focus on outcomes with, *449*; example of, 449–50
Golem effect, 187
Golf Digest, 364
Google, 164, 233, 401
Gorli, M., 392
Governance: corporate, ethics of, 108–9; COVID-19 and changes in, 412
Governance and decision-making in hospital-based surgical services (case 28), 617–22; case matrix, 627; case questions, 621–22
Governance Institute, 402; *Leadership in Healthcare Organizations* white paper, 330
Governing boards: chapter activity, 411; primary responsibilities of, 402, 406; variance in composition, structure, and operation of, 402–3

Great Depression, 8
Great man theory, 306, 308, *320,* 324
Green, S., 96
Greenleaf, Robert, 322
Greenview Hospital (Kentucky), 314
Grodoski, L., 87
Ground rules: for successful teams, 270
Group behavior: communication and relationship management competencies and, xxiv; leadership competencies and, xxiv
Group identity: group commitment and, 244
Group level: organizational behavior and relationship to, *11*
Group-oriented decision-making leader behaviors and actions: House's path–goal theory and, *313*
Group polarization, 250–51, 255; definition of, 250; three key reasons for, 251, *251*
Group practice arrangements, 401
Groups: aspirational, 248, 254; behavior in, 247; command, 243, 244; competition among, 365; conformity and, 246–48; decision-making in, advantages/disadvantages of, 253–54; definition of, 244; dissociative, 248; formal, 243, 244, 247, 248, 254; informal, 243, 244, 247, 248, 254; interdependence of, 245–46, *246*; key terms, 243; learning objectives, 243; norms and, 244, 246–48; obedience studies, 251–52, 255; polarization in, 243, 250–51, *251,* 255; reference, 248, 249, 254, 258; social facilitation in, 252, *253,* 255; social loafing and, 252, 255; task, 243, 244; teams *vs.,* 245, 264, *264,* 276; working in, as norm in workplace, 244. *See also* Teams
Group shift, 243, 255; decision-making and, 250; definition of, 249

Groupthink, 200, 206–7, 211, 243, 254–55; blind spots and, 214; definition of, 206, 249; diverse teams and avoidance of, 266; patient safety issues and, 206–7; Purdue's dilemma to increase sales (case 9) and, 556; symptoms of, *250*
"Growing Through Change" TEDxSHMS talk (Givel), 80
Growth: conflict used as opportunity for, 367
Growth needs: in Alderfer's ERG (existence, relatedness, and growth) theory, 132, 133, *133*, 134; in Maslow's hierarchy of needs, 26, *26*
Groysberg, B., 464
Grünenthal: thalidomide and (case 6), 541–43
Guide to Good Governance for Hospital Boards (American Hospital Association Center for Healthcare Governance), 411
Gulick, Luther, 23

Hackman, J. R., 135
Hall, Edward, 293
Halo effect, 178, 183, 185–86, 189, 190
Hancock, B., 426
Hancock, Larry, 581
"Handing off," 386
Harassment, 335, 344, 348, 493. *See also* Sexual harassment
Harbaugh, Jim, 137
Hardiness, 152, 159
Harvard Medical School, 531
Harvoni: average medication costs for, 615
Havens, Jeff, 101
Hawthorne studies (Western Electric Company), 8, 21, 27, 35
HCA Healthcare, 383, 582
Healing hospital conflict (chapter case), 167–68
Health agencies, 3

Healthcare: bullying in, 491; challenges of learning in, 73–76; complexity of, 1; conflict as daily presence in, 358; contributing factors to conflicts in, 362–64; critical nature of, 9; decision-making in, 207; division of labor in, 385; ethical challenges in business and, 114–17; ethics in, 109–10; fighting bureaucracy in, 5; group polarization in, example of, 250–51; halo effect in, 186; interdisciplinary nature of, 266; learning as critical in, 68, 76; possible future structures in, 400–402; racial and ethnic disparities in, 49–51; stressful work in, 156; task groups in, 244; transactional nature of, in United States, 40; transformational leadership needed in, 317; who is in charge in? (sidebar), 386
Healthcare CFOs: top ethical concerns faced by, 116, *116*
Healthcare corporations: US economy and importance of, 383, 403–4
Healthcare costs: medical bureaucracy and, 22–23; as source of stress, 160, *161*
Healthcare delivery: team-based nature of, 9, 12
Healthcare Executive: COVID-19 and leadership article, 318
Healthcare Executive Competencies Assessment Tool (American College of Healthcare Executives), xx, 318, 430–31
Healthcare Financial Management Association, xx; website of, 245
Healthcare industry: disruptive innovations in, 233; ethical challenges in, *116*, 116–17; good leaders needed in, 306; health disparities and impact on, 49; relevance of organizational behavior and theory to, 8–12

Healthcare Information and Management Systems Society, xx
Healthcare Leadership Alliance, xx
Healthcare organizations: aligned change and, 511–12; conflict triggers in, 363–64; cultures of blame and denial in, 461; ethical breakdowns in (chapter activity), 123–24; for-profit or not-for-profit, 384, *384*; by percentage of ownership, 384, *384*; properly functioning governing boards and, 403, 406
Healthcare providers: annual customer switches with, 96; building cultural competency in, 50; burnout among, 157, 165; cross-disciplinary teams of, 9; ethical challenges faced by, 116, 117; lack of communication skills among, 286
Healthcare quality improvement movement, 184
Healthcare services: impact of COVID-19 on, 10
Healthcare system boards, 403
Healthcare systems: continuously learning, characteristics of, 74, *74*; largest, in United States, 383; motivation and success of, 130
Health disparities. *See* Disparities in health
Health insurance: ethical challenge of treating hepatitis C (case 27), 615–16; HealthT seeks healthier employees (case 14), 569–71
HealthSouth: ethics violations, 115; toxic culture at, 462–63
HealthSouth (case 15), 573–80; case mix, 626; case questions, 580; reference, 580
HealthStream, 183
Health Systems Culture 500 data, 476
Health Technology Forum: Los Angeles, 236
HealthTrust Inc.: regional structure, 389, *389*

HealthT seeks healthier employees (case 14), 569–71; case matrix, 626; case questions, 571; employee insurance plan changes, 569, 571; healthcare expenditures, 2017–2020, 570
Heart of the Rockies Regional Medical Center: "Mission Vision Values" website page, 611–12
Helix organization, 398
Hendersonville Medical Center (Tennessee), 314
Henry Ford Health System: diversity ranking and, 42
Hepatitis C, 237; average medication costs for treatment of, 615; prevalence of, 615
Heroin, 555, 557
Hersey, P., 311
Herzberg, Frederick, 93, 131, 132, 134, 143
Heuristics, 200, 204, 211
Hewlett Packard: failed merger with Compaq, 469
Heygood, Leslie, 546
Hierarchy of command: in Weber's ideal bureaucracy, 22
High-context cultures: communication and, 292
High Five! (Blanchard), 310
High-level executives: perceptions of staff *vs.* perceptions of, 181
High-performing employees: identifying, succession planning and, 319–20
High-performing facilities: Hospital Corporation of America's identification of, 314–15
Hiring, 483; bias and, 54–55; combating high turnover and poor culture (case 29) and, 623–24; cultural fit of new employees and, 472; nepotism at Central Illinois Community Hospital (chapter case), 33–34; past job happiness and, 95; personality tests and, 485,

493; similar-to-me effect and, 186; structured interviews and, 486. *See also* Recruitment; Retention
Hispanics: US government data and category for, 44
Hitler, Adolf, 541
HIV, 237
Hoe, S. L., 70
Hofstede Centre, 467
Hofstede model, 58
Holmes, Elizabeth, 115; Theranos and (case 2), 525–32
Holocaust: medical experiments during, 541
Home health agencies, 3, 9; percentage of ownership figures, 384, *384*
Homelessness: COVID-19 and, 49
Honesty, 114, 120
Horatio Alger Award, 531
Horizon Medical Center (Tennessee), 314
Horizontal coordination: in matrix organizations, 396, 405
"Horror Movie: It's What You Do" (GEICO commercial), 250
Horton, Joseph, 567
Hospices: percentage of ownership figures, *384*
Hospital Consumer Assessment of Healthcare Providers and Systems (HCAHPS), 183, 514
Hospital Corporation of America (HCA): ethics and compliance program, 116–17; identification of high-performing facilities, 314–15; negotiating in the press, 369; sexual harassment policy, 346, *346*
Hospital Employees' Union (British Columbia): stress prevention policy, 163
Hospital News, 19
Hospital ratings: employee engagement and, 98
Hospitals, 3, 9; COVID-19 and revenue losses for, 113; daily conflicts in, 367; functional structure of, 391–92; with higher job satisfaction, 96; matrix structures in, 396; multidivisional structures in, 394; need for a more egalitarian hospital culture (chapter case), 475–76; percentage of ownership figures, *384*; proposed metropolitan hospital restart (chapter case), 348–51; rural, 612; silos in, 518
Hostile work environments, 28, 151, 344
House, R.: path–goal leader behaviors, 312, *313*
Housing: COVID-19 and heightened disparities in, 49
"How Good Are Your Communication Skills?" (MindTools), 300–301
"How to Delegate" (EntreLeadership video), 457
"How Well Do You Delegate?" (MindTools), 457
Humana, 109
Human capital challenges: succession planning and, 320
Human Relations Movement, 8
Human relations theory, 19, 27–30; contingency approach, 28–29, 32; definition of, 27; theory X and theory Y, 27–28, *28,* 32
Human resource management, 481, 482, 493
Human resources: leadership role of, 492, 494; promoting diversity through, 54, 57–58
Human resources policies and practices, 481–97; business skills and knowledge competencies and, xxvii; interviews, 486–88; job descriptions and specifications, 482–83, 493; key terms, 481–82; leadership role of human resources, 492; learning objectives, 481; performance simulation, 483–84, 493; personality tests, 485–86, 493; training, 488–92, 493

Hybrid arrangements for care, 401
Hydroxychloroquine, 221
Hygiene factors, 86, 134; absence of, 163; job satisfaction and, 93; motivators and, *94*

IBM, 396, 595
Identity: in job design, 136
Identity theft, 506
IKS Health, 224
Impersonality: in Weber's ideal bureaucracy, 22
Implicit culture, 464
Impoverished leaders: in Blake and Mouton's managerial grid, *309*
Impression management, 344
"Improving Patient Experience Means Reducing Suffering" (Mylod), 101
Incentives, 27, 31; in expectancy theory, 139; external types of, 132; extrinsic and intrinsic, 72; learning organizations and, 74, *74*; Purdue's dilemma to increase sales (case 9), 555–58; reward power and, 338; Sakal's dilemma (case 24), 605–6; servant leadership and, 322; team-based, 272. *See also* Financial incentives; Rewards
Inclusion, 42; key terms, 40; learning objectives, 39; organizational diversity statement and, 54; organizational strategic plan and, 56, 58; promoting in workforce, 55
Income: COVID-19 and heightened disparities in, 49
Incompetence: unsafe patient care and (chapter case), 299
India: cultural values of, *45*
Individualism: collectivism *vs.*, 462, 467, 472; definition of, 467
Individualistic cultures, 40, 44, 57
Individualized consideration: transformational leaders and, 317, 324
Individual level: organizational behavior and relationship to, *11*; team/group level, *418*

Individual performance management systems, 423–28, 432; annual performance reviews, 424; effective performance feedback, guidelines for, 427; forced distribution or stacked ranking appraisals, 425–26, 432; numerical rating systems, 424–25, 432; performance rating scales, 428, *428*; purposes of, 423
Indulgence, 462, 467, 473
Industrial Revolution, 7, 8, 385, 404
Influence: business skills and knowledge competencies and, xxv; definition of, 336; key terms, 335–36; leadership competencies and, xxv; learning objectives, 335; new CEO (case 11), 563–64; power *vs.*, 336–37, *337*, 347; principles, *341*, 341–42, 347; without much power, 337; zone of indifference and, 338, 347
Influence tactics: choosing, 340; negative, 340; organizational politics and, 342; positive, 339
Informal groups, 243, 248, 254; conformity and, 247; definition of, 244; tapping into, 243
Information richness, 284, 294; definition of, 287; message complexity and, *287,* 296
Information technology, 234; decision-making in healthcare and, 207; healthcare innovation and, 233; role of, in healthcare learning (chapter case), 78–79
Informed consent: rights model and, 111
Ingham, Sir Bernard, 308
Ingratiation, 340, 347
Initiative: in Fayol's 14 principles of management, *7*
Injured migrant worker (case 3), 533–34; case matrix, 625; case questions, 534
Innovation: critical importance of, 233; definitions of, 222, 223;

disruptive, 232–33, 234; enablers that promote phases of diffusion, 230–32, *231*; encouraging/discouraging, activities for, *227*; exploration of (chapter activity), 238; healthcare, diffusion of, 228–32, *231,* 234; healthcare, types of, 224–26, 234; increasing, strategies for, 226–28, 234; key terms, 221; leadership competencies and, xxiv; learning objectives, 221; link between creativity and, 222–24; at Massachusetts General Hospital, 228; matrix structures and, 397; models for testing and diffusing, 221; moving from creativity to, *223,* 224, 234; in multidivisional organizations, 394; multitude of problems and need for, 222; positive conflict and, 359; sustaining, 221, 232–33; Theranos and Elizabeth Holmes (case 2), 525–32; types of, 224–26; UCLA Health's introduction to (chapter case), 235–36

Innovation centers: dedicated, 228, 234

Innovation Learning Network, 236

Inputs: in equity theory, 137

Insomnia, 157

Inspirational appeals, 339, 347

Inspirational motivation: transformational leaders and, 316, 324

Institute for Diversity and Health Equity, 56

Institute for Healthcare Improvement, 92, 236

Institute of Medicine: *Best Care at Lower Cost,* 78; on casting blame for errors, 184; characteristics of care enumerated by, 222; *Crossing the Quality Chasm,* 390; on interdisciplinary teams, 265; on racial and ethnic disparities in healthcare, 50–51. *See also* National Academy of Medicine

Institutional conformity: drivers of, 31

Institutionalizing: in organizational learning cycle, 69, *69,* 76

Institutional theory, 31, 32

Instrumentality, 130, 138, 143

Insurance companies, 3

Intangible assets: power and, 337

Integrated delivery systems, 401

Integrated Theory of Health Behavior Change: social facilitation within, 252, *253*

Integrating: in organizational learning cycle, 69, *69,* 76

Integration: differentiation *vs.,* 391

Integrity, 154, 446

Intellectual stimulation: transformational leaders and, 316–17, 324

Intelligence tests, 484

Intensive care units: at maximum capacity during COVID-19 pandemic, 489–90

Interactional justice, 108, 111, 469, 473

Interaction facilitation leader behaviors and actions: House's path–goal theory and, *313*

Interdependence: need for relationship and type of, 245–46, *246;* pooled, 245, 246, *246,* 254; reciprocal, 245, 246, *246,* 254; sequential, 245, *246,* 254; types of, 245

Interdisciplinary education, 265

Interdisciplinary (interprofessional) teams, 263, 276; definition of, 266; in healthcare, 265; matrix structures and, 397

Interests, 357; of both parties, clarifying, 368; definition of, 368

Intergroup conflict, 357, 362, 372

Intermountain Healthcare (Salt Lake City): equity and diversity statement, 54, *54;* mission statement for, 509

Internal business processes measures: in balanced scorecards, 422

Internal controls: effect of, employee satisfaction and commitment, 132, *133*
Internal locus of control, 159, 160
Internal stimuli, 130
International Association of Coaching, *444*
International Authority for Coaching & Mentoring, *444*
International Coaching Community, *444*
International Coaching Federation, *444*
International Labour Organization: on decent work, 136
Internet, 180, 233
Interpersonal conflict, 357, 364, 372; definition of, 362; four factors contributing to, 362
Interpreting: in organizational learning cycle, 69, *69,* 76
Intersectionality, 40, 51
Interviews, 483, 486–88; goal of, 486–87; structured, 486, 488
Intimidation: Richard Scrushy and management by, 575–76
Intragroup conflict, 266, 273, 357, 362, 372
Intrapersonal conflict, 357, 362, 372
Intrinsic motivation: creativity and, 223; job crafting and, 140; learning and, 72, 73
Intrinsic stimuli, 130, 132
Issues: negotiation and focus on, 368

Janis, Irving, 249
Jefferson, American Davon, 469
Job analysis: structured interviews and, 486; useful, 482
Job boards, 483
Job candidates: screening for innovative characteristics, 227
Job characteristics model, 130, 135
Job commitment: perceptions, attitudes, and, 189
Job content, 135
Job crafting, 139–40; millennials and, 141
Job description, 96, 481, 493; definition of, 482; functional principle and, 24; job position details for a registered nurse, 483, *483*
Job design, 143; creativity, innovation, and, 227–28; decent work and, 136; five core characteristics in, 135–36
Job interviews, 486–88, 493; variety of mediums for, 487. *See also* Hiring
Jobs: activities that encourage/discourage creativity and innovation, *227*; COVID-19 and losses in, 10; describing best and worst (chapter activity), 146; enlargement of, 136; enrichment in, 136–37; job offers, 487; rotation of, 136
Jobs, Steve, 527, 530
Job satisfaction: attitudes and, 87, 189; COVID-19 and decrease in, 91; dispositional approach and, 93, 94–95, 99; importance of, 86, 92–93; internal locus of control and, 160; organizational commitment and, 97–98, 99; organizational justice and, 111; outcomes and measurement, 95–98, 99; patient satisfaction and, 96–97; primary contributors to, in United States, *94*; stress management and, 163; two-factor theory and, 93–94, 99; value theory, 93, 95, 97
Job security: organizational change and, 513
Job specifications, 493; definition of, 482; elements of, 482–83; job position details for a registered nurse, 483, *483*
Job stress: business skills and knowledge competencies and, xxiii; conflict and, 359, 360; interpersonal conflict and, 364; professionalism competencies and, xxiii

Johnson & Johnson, 109, 394
Joint Commission, 548; Center for Transforming Healthcare, 9; on cognitive biases, 204; on communication, 286; recommended diversity practices for leaders, 52, 57; required competencies and accreditation by, 430; wrong-site surgery protocol, 289
Joint Commission International, 290
Joy, 153, *154,* 156, 165
Juneteenth: commemorating, 55
Justice, 120; definition of, 112; distributive, 108, 111, 469, 473; interactional, 108, 111, 469, 473; organizational, 111, 469, 473; procedural, 108, 111, 469, 473; thalidomide and Grünenthal (case 6), 541–43
Justice (or fairness) model, 108, 120, 469; definition of, 110; subcategories of justice recognized in, 111, 469, 473

Kahneman, D., 206
Kaiser Health News, 613
Kaiser Permanente: Health Plan Institute, 73
Kanungo, R., 316
Kaplan, Gary, 67, 68
Keefe, P. R., 556
Kelsey, Frances, 542
Kerr, Rand, 587
Key performance indicators, 418, 420, 432
Kilcoyne, John, 224
Kindness, 567
King, Martin Luther, Jr., 322
Kingdom of Saudi Arabia: gender diversity and, 45, 46
King for a day (chapter activity), 193–95
Kissinger, Henry, 530
Klatz, Jose, 506
Knowledge management systems, 207

Knowledge of the healthcare environment competency: in American College of Healthcare Executives competency assessment framework, xx, 318, 431, 488; appraisals and subdivision of categories under domain of, 431
Kodak, 233
Komm, A., 426
Korean Air executive motivates change with nuts (chapter case), 145–46
Korean Basketball League, 469
Korean culture: stifling of productivity and, 465
Kotter's eight-step change model: relationship between Agency for Healthcare Research and Quality's Comprehensive Unit-based Safety Program toolkit modules and, 514, *514*
Krishnan, Muthu, 224
Kuhn, T., 178

Laboratory technologists, 266
Lao-tzu, 322
Latinos: US government data and category for, 44
Laundry group (chapter case), 256
LaVeist, T., 50
Lawrence, P., 391
Layoffs, 113, 468
Leader–follower relationship: in Fiedler's contingency theory, 312
Leader–member exchange theory, 306, 311, 312, *320,* 324
Leader role: defined in Mintzberg's leadership study, 309
Leaders: activities that encourage/discourage creativity and innovation and, *227*; being aware of micromanaging, 451; cultural change and primary/secondary approaches used by, 471–72, 473; divisional, 393–94; dynamic, healthcare industry and need for, 306; effective communication skills and,

284; with emotional intelligence skills, 155; ethical behaviors of, 113, 120; great, as great decision makers, 200, 211; historical roots underlying concept of, 307, 324; influence tactics used by, 339–41; managers *vs.*, 310; recommended diversity practices for, 52, 57; successful, three qualities of, 20; transformational, vignette, 305; transitioning to a learning organization and, 75; virtual team management and, 294–95

Leadership, 4; authentic, 306, *321,* 323, 325; changing concept of, over time, 307, 324; charismatic, 315–16, *321,* 324; COVID-19 pandemic and, 318, 325; creativity and, 223; defining, 307, 324; employee-oriented, 308, 309; ethical, 306, *321,* 323, 325; human resources and role of, 492; implementation of change and, 512–14; Mike and the walk-around (case 23), 603–4; new, elements of training for, 489, *490;* new CEO (case 11), 563–64; participative, 309, 312, 325; patient experience and, 96–97; production-oriented, 308, 309; a proposed merger gone bad (case 21), 597–600; role-play (chapter activity), 329–30; servant, 306, *321,* 321–23, 325, 588; situational, 306; starting as CEO at Skyview Hospital (case 17), 587–89; transactional, 306, 311–13, *320;* transformational, 306, 313–20, *321,* 512, 515; win-win environment and, 359; women in, 47

Leadership and Self-Deception, 588

"Leadership Competencies for Healthcare Services Managers" (American College of Healthcare Executives), xx

Leadership competency: in American College of Healthcare Executives competency assessment framework, xx, 318, 430, 488; appraisals and subdivision of categories under domain of, 431

Leadership development mechanisms: delegation, 442, 446–53; mentoring and coaching, 442–46, 453

Leadership in Healthcare Organizations: A Guide to Joint Commission Leadership Standards (Schyve / Governance Institute): reviewing (chapter activity), 330

Leadership study, contemporary: five overlapping periods in, 307

Leadership theories, emerging, 321–23; authentic leadership, *321,* 323, 325; ethical leadership, *321,* 323, 325; servant leadership, *321,* 321–23, 325

Leadership theories and styles: authentic theory/model, *321,* 323, 325; autocratic, 322; behavior theory/model, 306, 308–10, *320,* 323, 324; contingency/situational theory/model, 306, 310–11, *320,* 323, 324; ethical theory/model, *321,* 323, 325; HealthSouth (case 15), 573–80; informal indicator of leadership style, 310; key terms, 306; leadership competencies and, xxv; learning objectives, 305–6; managing change competency and, xxv; path-goal theory, 312, 324; servant theory/model, *321,* 321–23, 325, 588; trait theory/model, 306, 308, *320,* 323, 324; transactional theory/model, 306, 311–13, *320,* 324; transformational theory/model, 306, 313–20, *321,* 324–25

Leadership theory, five major schools of thought, 306; behavior theory, 306, 307, 308, *320,* 323, 324; contingency, contextual, or situational theory, 306, 310–11, 312, *320,* 323–24; trait theory, 306, 307, 308, *320,* 323, 324; transactional theory, 306, 307, 311, *320,* 324; transformational theory, 306, 307, 314–20, *321,* 324

Lean: culture of learning and, 76, 77

Learning, 4; challenges of, in healthcare, 73–76; conflict used as opportunity for, 367; creating culture of, 75; cycle of, 69, *69,* 76; decision-making and, 208, 211; definition of, 68; double-loop, 68, 69–70, 76; embedding as a primary work function, 76; exploration and exploitation and, 73; failure in, COVID-19 and high costs of, 72; healthcare leaders and, 20; individual, competencies used in conjunction with, xxii; key terms, 68; learning objectives, 67–68; in organizations, group and organizational barriers to, 72, 77; in organizations, personal barriers to, 71, 77; role of motivation in, 72–73; single-loop, 68, 69, 70, 76; team, 70, 77. *See also* Organizational learning

Learning and growth measures: in balanced scorecards, 422

Learning communities, 68; Bon Secours Health System and implementation of, 75; definition of, 75, 76

Learning management systems, 68, 75, 77

Learning organizations, 68; components of, 71, *71;* definition of, 70; five main characteristics of, 70, 77; Kaiser Permanente as, 73; more or less (chapter activity), 80; organizational learning *vs.,* 70; tenets for embedding learning in, 76; transitioning to, 75; Virginia Mason Medical Center as, 67, 68

Le Bon, G., 247

Ledipasvir-sofosbuvir (Harvoni): average medication costs for, 615

Lee, Sam, 547

Legacy culture: negative, 227

Legislation: affirmative action and diversity management, 51–55

Legitimacy (or upward appeals): as negative influence tactic, 340, 347

Leonard Green & Partners, 546, 547, 548

"Lessons from #MeToo for Health and Health Care Improvement" (Endo), 353

Letters, 287, *287,* 288

Lewis, John, 43

LGBTQ individuals: Cleveland Clinic's diversity initiative and, 41; job interviews and discrimination against, 488

Liability: for harassment in workplace, 345; limited, corporations and, 382, 404

Liaison role: defined in Mintzberg's leadership study, 310

Liaisons, 386, 404

Liberty Mutual, 401

Licenses, 489

Licensing exams, 493

Lifemark, 573

LifePoint Health: vision statement for, 510

Life skills needed by children, 284, *285*

Likert scale, 90, *90*

Lincoln, Abraham, 322

Line-staff principle, 24

Listening, 98; mentoring and, 446; during negotiations, 371; successful communication and, 295, 297

Liver allocation (case 12), 565–66; case mix, 626; case questions, 566; geographic disparity issues, 565–66; references, 566

Locus of control, 159–64; external, 159, 160; internal, 159, 160; sources of stress and, 160–62;

stress management, 162–64; value of intervention, 164
Logos: for teams, 272
Looting: group behaviors and, 247
Lorsch, J., 391
Love, 153, *154,* 156, 165
Low-context cultures: communication and, 292
Low-fidelity simulation, 485
Loyalty, 114, 120, 141, 154; Theranos and Elizabeth Holmes (case 2), 525–32
Lunch expenditure approval (chapter case), 455–56

Machine learning, 226
Maimonides Medical Center (Brooklyn, New York): approach to reducing hospital conflict, 367
Maintenance (or hygiene) factors, 134
Mallinckrodt Pharmaceuticals, 109
Malpractice cases: bad communication and, 284
Managed care contracts: negotiating, 369
Management: Fayol's 14 principles of, 6–7; five core functions of, 7. *See also* Theories of managing people
Management by objectives, 139
"Management by walking around": transformational leaders and, 317
Management theories: applying (chapter activity), 35–36
Managers: competency-based evaluation for, 431; conflict management and, 366; importance of decision-making and, 200; junior, coaching and mentoring and, 446; leaders *vs.,* 310; Maslow's hierarchy of needs and, 26, 27; skilled, influence tactics and, 339–40, 347; theory X *vs.* theory Y and beliefs about employees, 27–28, *28*
"Managing Organizational Change" (Society for Human Resource Management), 520

Mandela, Nelson, 322
March, J., 203
Marcus, L. J., 8, 10
Marriage: bounded rationality and, 202
Marshmallow towers (chapter activity), 280
Martin, C. J. H., 251
Masculinity: definition of, 467; *vs.* femininity, 462, 467, 473
Mask mandates: failure to learn during COVID-19 pandemic and, 72
Maslow, Abraham, 25, 130, 133
Maslow's hierarchy of needs, 19, 25–27, *26,* 32, 130, 132; Alderfer's ERG (existence, relatedness, and growth) theory as refinement of, 132–34, *133,* 142; applying (chapter activity), 35–36; definition of, 25; Herzberg's two-factor theory as extension of, 134, *134*
Massachusetts General Hospital, 279; Center for Innovations in Care Delivery, 228; innovation at, 228
Massachusetts Institute of Technology: Sloan School of Management, 27
Mass shootings: as source of stress, 160, *161*
Mastery: personal, learning organizations and, 70, 77
Matrix organizations, 382, 391, *396,* 396–98; definition of, 396; problems with, 397–98, 405
Matrix structure: advantages, disadvantages, and most suitable conditions for, *399,* 400, 405
Mattis, James, 530
Mattone, John, 444
Maurizio, A., 370
Mayhew, Richard, 616
Mayo, Elton, 21
Mayo Clinic: Center for Innovation, 228; values espoused by, 506–7
McAuliffe, Christa, 249
McDonald's, 393

McGregor, Douglas, 27, 28, 130
McKesson, 109
McKinsey & Company, 45, 226, 398, 557, 595
Meaning: job motivators and, 93
Measles epidemics: in US, parental paradigms and decision-making related to, 178–79
Measurement: job satisfaction, 95–98
"Measure Your Stress" quiz (Psychologist World), 171
Mechanistic organizations, 382, 404; definition of, 391; organic organizations compared with, *390*
Medicaid, 616; fraud, 115
Medical bureaucracy: costs of, 22–23
Medical Center of Plano (Texas), 314
Medical City Dallas Hospital, 314
Medical costs: innovations and increase in, 229
Medical device manufacturers, 3
Medical errors, 9, 12; conflict and, 367; as leading cause of death, 9
Medical Group Management Association, xx; code of ethics and behavior for, *119*; website, 245
Medical homes, 512
Medical office staff performance measures: setting (chapter case), 436–37
Medical staff: burnout and stress among, 157; privileges, negotiating (chapter case), 374–75
Medical students: teaching of ethical issues to, 110
Medical training: innovations and shift in, 237
Medicare, 616; fraud, 107, 115; policy changes, HealthSouth and, 579
Meditation, 164
Medtronic, 109
Meetings: decision-making in, *209*, 209–10, 212
Mental health, 98, 141–42; COVID-19 and increased attention on, 88;
millennials, Gen Z, and importance of, 141–42, 143
Mental Health America: website, 245
Mental health problems: among healthcare workers, 157
Mental illness: changing attitudes toward, 87
Mental models: learning organizations and, 70, 77
Mental toughness, 154
Mentoring: coaching *vs.,* 442, 453; combating high turnover and poor culture with (case 29), 623–24; communication and relationship management competencies and, xxvi; competencies used in conjunction with, xxvi–xxvii; during COVID-19 pandemic, 441; definition of, 442; delegation and, 453; focus of, 445; ground rules and, 445, 453; integrating with leadership development, 445; leadership competencies and, xxvii; learning objectives, 441; professionalism competencies and, xxvii; reverse, 154–55; scheduling, 446; value of, 443
Mentors: finding (chapter activity), 457
Merck Manual, 207
Mercy Health: as example of functional organization, 391–92; organizational chart for, 387, *387*
Mergers and acquisitions: bandwagon effect and, 206; decision-making related to, 199; designed, 226; failed, differing cultures and, 469–70, 473; HealthSouth and, 575, 577; a proposed merger gone bad (case 21), 597–600
Message: in communication process, 284, *285,* 296; information richness and complexity of, *287*; nonverbal communication and, 290

Methodist Ambulatory Surgery Hospital North West (San Antonio, Texas), 314
Methodist Health System (Texas): Glassdoor approval ratings for CEOs, *468*
#MeToo movement, 491
Micromanagement, 28; being wary of, in gofer delegation, 451; job enrichment *vs.*, 136–37; motivation and (chapter case), 144–45
Microprocessors, 232–33
Microsoft, 393, 425, 426
Microsoft Cloud for Healthcare, 225
Middle East: collective cultures in, 45, *45*; diverse healthcare workforce in, 42
Migrant worker injuries (case 3), 533–34
Mihaljevic, Tomislav, 41
Mike and the walk-around (case 23), 603–4; case matrix, 627; case questions, 604
Milgram, Stanley: obedience study, 251–52
Millennials, 40; motivating, 141–42, 143; in multigenerational workforce, 48; transformational leadership for, 318–19, 325; turnover rates for, 443
Miller, Steve, 558
Mimetic isomorphism, 19, 31
Minneapolis Star Tribune, 233
Mintzberg, Henry: leadership roles studies, 309–10
MinuteClinics, 383
Miscommunication: doctor–patient, 286; frequency of, 284; nurse–physician, example of, 283
Mission, 507–9, 515; action and, 509; as basis of organizational culture, 462; corporate social responsibility and, 108; cultural assessment and, 467; cultural change and, 472; definition of, 504; gap analysis from, 510, *511*; human resources departments and, 492; interaction between core values, ethics, vision, and, 109, *110,* 120; organizational behavior and, 10; organizational change and, 514; performance management and, 420; relationships between balanced score card metrics, vision, and, 422, *422*; relationships between vision, values, and, 504–5, *505*; Shannon's extreme uninsured healthcare costs (case 26), 611–14; of Strong Memorial Hospital, 24; transformative leaders and, 314. *See also* Values; Vision
Mission-driven decisions: importance of (chapter activity), 519–20
Mission statements, 504, 507–8; balancing quality and financial performance in, 509; length of, 509, 515; shortfalls with, 508–9
Mistake events: number of, 420
Mistakes: being shamed for, 72
Mitchell, Elden, 581, 582, 585
MIT Sloan Management Review, 476
Modern Healthcare, 107, 589
Modular organizations, 401–2
Moffitt Cancer Center (Florida): diversity ranking and, 42
Molecular biology, 74
Money: as a motivator, myth of, 140, 143; as source of stress, *161*; worker satisfaction issues and, 93
Monitor role: defined in Mintzberg's leadership study, 310
Montefiore Hospital (New York), 279
Moods, 152; business skills and knowledge competencies and, xxiii; definition of, 153; emotions *vs.*, 153, 165; professionalism competencies and, xxiii
Mooney, James, 23
Morale, 357; conflict and, 360, 367; succession planning and, 319
Morphine, 555
Morton Thiokol, 249

Motivation: Alderfer's ERG (existence, relatedness, and growth) theory of, 132–34, *133*, 142–43; business skills and knowledge competencies and, xxiii; competencies used in conjunction with, xxii–xxiii; definition of, 130; equity theory and, 137–38, 143; expectancy theory and, *138*, 138–39, 143; external stimuli and, 131–32; goal-setting theory and, 139, 143; Herzberg's two-factor theory, *134*, 134–35, 143; internal stimuli and, 132; job crafting and, 139–40; job design and, 135–36, 143; job enrichment and, 136–37; key terms, 130; leadership competencies and, xxii; learning and role of, 72–73; learning objectives, 129; micromanagement and (chapter case), 144–45; millennials and Gen Z and, 141–42, 143; moral values and, 506; myths about, 140, 143; stress management and, 163; success of healthcare systems and, 130; values and, 506, 515

Motivators, 86; hygiene factors and, *94*; job satisfaction and, 93

Mouton, J., 309

Movement, 287

MRI (magnetic resonance imaging) scanners, 225

Mueller-Hanson, R., 423

Multidisciplinary teams, 40, 263, 276; chapter case, 278–79; definition of, 265

Multidivisional organizations, 382, 391, *393*, 393–95; advantages with, 394, 395; decentralization of functions in, 395; definition of, 393; transfer pricing in, 395, 405

Multidivisional structure: advantages, disadvantages, and most suitable conditions for, *399*, 399–400, 405

Multigenerational workforce, 47–49, 57; baby boomers in, 47, 57; Gen X in, 47–48, 57; Gen Z in, 48; millennials in, 48

Mylod, Deirdre, 101

Nall, R., 615

Nanotechnology, 233

NASA: Teacher in Space program, 249

National Academy of Medicine: Culture of Health Program, 56

National Association of ACOs, 9

National Association of County and City Health Officials: website, 245

National Association of State Mental Health Program Directors: website, 245

National CLAS Standards, *53–54*

National culture: comparing, 467

National Environmental Health Association: website, 245

National Football League, 364

National Institute of Mental Health: on stress, 156

National Institutes of Health: National Institute on Drug Abuse, 555

National Quality Forum, 225

National Research Corporation, 183

Native Hawaiians: US government data and category for, 44

Nature, 72

Negative conflict: teams and, 274, 277

Negative emotions, 153, 159

Negative influence tactics, 340, 347

Negotiation(s): business skills and knowledge competencies and, xxv; communication and relationship management and, xxv; deceptive emotions in, 370; definition of, 368; ensuring solidified relationships around, 371; establishing ground rules for, 369, 373; explore your negotiating style (chapter activity), 377; FHP—Utah (case 16), 581–85; generating novel win–win solutions in, 369; learning objectives, 357; medical staff privileges (chapter case), 374–75; need for, 358; objective criteria used in, 369; Sakal's dilemma (case 24), 605–6; a Saudi bid and I (case 20), 595–96; Shannon's extreme uninsured healthcare costs (case 26), 613–14; stresses attached to, 370, 371, 373; successful, basic tenets in, 368–71, 373. *See also* Conflict

Negotiator role: defined in Mintzberg's leadership study, 310

Nepotism, 5; at Central Illinois Community Hospital (chapter case), 33–34

NERIS Type Explorer, 496

Networking: mentoring and, 446

Network structures, 382, 401–2

Neuroticism, 485, *485*

New CEO (case 11): case matrix, 626; case questions, 564

New employee: frustrated (chapter case), 13

New England Journal of Medicine, 204

Newspapers: as communication channel, 287; job advertisements in, 483

Newspaper test, 119, 121

New Yorker, 556

New York Public Library, 307

New York Times, 179, 557, 558

Nexstar Media Group, 233

Nextel: failed merger with Sprint, 469

NICU nurses (chapter case), 518–19

Night staffing and job commitment (case 22): case matrix, 627; case questions, 601

Nike, 402; flat, nonhierarchical structure of, 389

9/11 terrorist attacks: societal attitude shift in wake of, 88

Nix Health System (San Antonio), 548

Noise, 284; in communication process, 284, *285,* 288–89; definition of, 288; in healthcare communication, care deliver errors and, 288, 289

Nokia, 396

Noncompete clause, 352, 353

Nondisclosure agreements, 526, 529

Nonjudgmental language: using, in negotiations, 371

Nonmaleficence, 108, 112, 120

Nonsmoker rights, 111

Nonsubstitutable resources, 30

Nontask organizational conflict, 357, 360, 372

Nonverbal communication, 153, 284, 290–92; COVID-19 pandemic and, 290; cultural differences in, 293, 297; definition of, 290; forms of, 291, 296; misinterpretation of, 293

Normative commitment: definition of, 97; night staffing and job commitment (case 22), 601

Normative environment, 86

Normative pressures: institutional conformity and, 31

Norming stage: in team building, 263, 267, *267,* 268, 277

Norms, 254; definition of, 247; groups and, 244, 246–48

Northwell Health (New York): diversity ranking and, 42

Northwestern University Feinberg School of Medicine: Center for Primary Care Innovation, 230

Not-for-profit organizations, 383, 404

Novant Health: diversity efforts at (chapter case), 59–60

Novartis, 527; mission statement for, 509

Novell: failed merger with WordPerfect, 469

Numbers: cultural differences in, 187–88

Numerical rating systems, 418, 432; definition of, 424; disadvantages of, 425

Nunn, Sam, 530
Nurse managers: spans of control and, 389
Nurses, 9, 266; burnout and, 156–57; conflict and, 364; engagement of, benefits with, 92, 97, 98; feedback and, 290; hospital conflicts and, 167; hostile incidents at workplace and, 151; on interprofessional teams, 265; job commitment and, 189; learning in healthcare and, 74; NICU (neonatal intensive care unit) nurses (chapter case), 518–19; sexual harassment of, 345, 492; speaking up, quality of patient care and (chapter case), 299–300
Nursing: delegation in, 447
Nursing homes, 3; for-profit, 73; percentage of ownership figures, 384
NYU Langone Health (New York City): diversity ranking and, 42

Obama, Barack, 531
Obedience studies, 251–52, 255
Obligatory cooperation: conflict in healthcare organizations and, 363, 372
Occupational therapists, 266; on interprofessional teams, 265
Occupations: COVID-19 and heightened disparities in, 49
O'Connor, K., 370
Office of Inspector General, 115
Office of Minority Health (US Department of Health and Human Services), 53, 53–54, 56
Ogre and the playroom (case 19), 593–94; case mix, 626; case questions, 594
Ohio State University: leadership behaviors study, 309
Oldham, G. R., 135
Olsen, J., 203
Olysio: average medication costs for, 615

Ombitasvir-paritaprevir-ritonavir and dasabuvir (Viekira Pak): average medication costs for, 615
Onboarding: combating high turnover and poor culture (case 29) and, 623, 624
One Minute Manager (Blanchard), 310
Oosthuizen, Louis, 364
Open-mindedness: successful communication and, 295
Openness, 485, *485*
Open systems: closed systems *vs.*, 30
Open systems theory, 19, 29, 32
Operant conditioning, 130
Operating room: division of labor in, 385
Opioid epidemic: deaths from overdoses, 555, 557, 558; marketing and sales of OxyContin, 555, 556, 557
Order: in Fayol's 14 principles of management, 6
Organ donations/transplants: liver allocation (case 12), 565–66
Organic organizations, 382, 404; definition of, 390; mechanistic organizations compared with, *390*
Organizational behavior, 2, 3–4, 8; business skills and knowledge competencies and, xxi; chapter topics relating to levels of, *11*, 11–12; competencies used in conjunction with, xxi; definition of, 3, 12, 482; history and development of, 5–8; interactive nature of three levels of, *3*, 3–4; key terms, 2; knowledge of the healthcare environment competencies and, xxi; learning objectives, 2; mission and, 10; relationship to organizational theory, 4, *4*; relevance of, to healthcare industry, 8–12; transformation of healthcare system and, 11; understanding dynamics of, 4

Organizational change: chapter activities, 519–20; gap analysis and, 510–14; Pegasus Health's integration of care (case 8), 551–54

Organizational charts: fragmented university healthcare venture (chapter case), *409*; Mercy Health, 387, *387*; US Department of Veterans Affairs, 387, *388*

Organizational citizenship behaviors, 86; definition of, 95; internal locus of control and, 160; job satisfaction and, 95–96, 99

Organizational commitment: job satisfaction and, 97–98; night staffing and job commitment (case 22), 601; three types of, 97

Organizational culture, 461–76; ascertaining proper alignment in, leaders and, 467–68; business skills and knowledge competencies and, xxvii; changing, 470–72, 473; chapter activities, 476; communication and relationship management competencies and, xxvii; components of, 463–66, *466*; cultural differences and, 466–70, 472; a culture of violence (chapter case), 474–75; definition of, 462; four attributes of, 464; HealthSouth (case 15), 573–80; key terms, 462; leadership competencies and, xxvii; learning objectives, 461; need for a more egalitarian hospital culture (chapter case), 475–76; organizational justice and, 469, 473; professionalism competencies and, xxvii

Organizational design: business skills and knowledge competencies and, xxvi; communication and relationship management competencies and, xxv; competencies used in conjunction with, xxv–xxvi; cultural change and, 472; definition of, 384; key terms, 382; knowledge of the healthcare environment competencies and, xxv; learning objectives, 381

Organizational justice, 111; organizational culture and, 469, 473; Shannon's extreme uninsured healthcare costs (case 26) and, 611–14

Organizational learning, 68; competencies used in conjunction with, xxii; cycle of, 68–69, *69*, 76; definition of, 68; and growth (chapter activity), 80; healthcare and importance of, 73–74; leadership competencies and, xxii; learning objectives, 67–68; learning organization *vs.*, 70; professionalism competencies and, xxii; role of information technology in (chapter case), 78–79

Organizational level: organizational behavior and relationship to, *11*

Organizational politics, 336, 342–46, 347–48; abuse of power and sexual harassment, 344–46, *346*; definition of, 342; individual and organizational factors leading to, *343*, 343–44; negative, 343; sustainable, 342–43

Organizational structures, 382; advantages and disadvantages of, 398–400, *399*, 405; business skills and knowledge competencies and, xxvi; chain of command and, 387, *387*, *388*, 389–90, 403; changing, problematic nature of, 381, 382; chapter activities, 411–12; communication and relationship management competencies and, xxv; competencies used in conjunction with, xxv–xxvi; cultural change and, 472; definition of, 384; division of labor and, 385–86; efficient, 381; environment and, 402, *403*; fit of, with environmental factors, 28–29; integration and differentiation and, 391; key terms, 382; knowledge of the healthcare environment competencies and, xxv; learning objectives, 381; mixed, 400; organic *vs.* mechanistic organizations, *390,* 404; span of control and, 386, 404

Organizational structures, future, 400–402, 406; accountable care organizations, 400–401, 405–6; modular or network structures, 401–2; team-based structures, 401

Organizational structures, types of, 391–98; functional organizations, 391–93, 405; matrix organizations, 391, *396,* 396–98, 405; multidivisional organizations, 391, *393,* 393–95, 405

Organizational theory, 2, 4–5; definition of, 4, 12; evolution in use of term, 8; focus of, 4–5; history and development of, 5–8; key terms, 2; learning objectives, 2; relationship to organizational behavior, 4, *4;* relevance of, to healthcare industry, 8–12; transformation of healthcare system and, 11

Organizations: complexity of, 3; definition of, 2; purpose of, 504

Organizing: as core management function, 7

Organ Procurement and Transplantation Network, 565

OrthoIndy (case 10), 559–61; case matrix, 625; case questions, 561; financial performance, 560, 561; opening of, press release, 560; references, 561; website, 559

Other-awareness, 155, 165

Outcome definition/measurement: successful coaching and, 445

Outcomes: higher nurse engagement and, 92; job satisfaction, 95–98, 99; levels of delegation and focus on, *449,* 449–50

Outpatient surgery centers, 3

Outputs: in equity theory, 137

Overconfidence: medical misdiagnoses and, 153; poor decision-making and, 204

Overutilizing orthopedist (case 4), 535–36; case matrix, 625; case questions, 536

Ownership: healthcare organizations by percentage of, 384, *384*

Oxycodone, 555

OxyContin, 555, 556, 557, 558

Pacific Islanders: US government data and category for, 44

Paracelsus Healthcare, 585

Paradigms, 178–80; assumptions and, 179; business skills and knowledge competencies and, xxiii; definition of, 178, 189; of expected physician care, 179; interaction of perceptions, stimuli, and, 180–81, *181,* 189; key terms, 178; king for a day (chapter activity), 193–95; knowledge of the healthcare environment competencies and, xxiii; learning objectives, 177; new, adoption of, 180; patient's perspective and, 180

Paradigm shift, 178, 180

Paroxysmal nocturnal hemoglobinuria, 229

Participative leadership, 309, 312, 325

Passion, 154

Path–goal clarifying leader behaviors and actions: House's path–goal theory and, *313*

Path–goal theory, 306, 311, 312, *320,* 324

Patient care: healthcare job satisfaction and, 96; unsafe, poor communication and (chapter case), 299–300

Patient care assistants: on interprofessional teams, 265

Patient care teams, 244

Patient-centered care: access to, 222; promoting, 225

Patient-first approach, 20

Patient–provider relationship: positive nonverbal communication and, 290, 291–92; telemedicine and paradigms related to, 179

Patients: paradigms and perspectives of, 180

Patient safety: conflict and, 360, 372; feedback and, 289, 296; learning and, 68; learning organizations and, 74

Patient satisfaction, 10, 98, 420; job satisfaction and, 96–97; perceptions and, 183; starting as CEO at Skyview Hospital (case 17), 589

Patient service representatives, 424

Patient treatment teams, 271

Patient *vs.* staff ratio, 420

Peer pressure, 247

Pegasus Health's integration of care (case 8), 551–54; case matrix, 625; case questions, 554; reference, 554

Penicillin, 225

Pension vesting, 97

Perceptions, 178, 180–83; attitudes, cultural backgrounds, and, 178; attitudes and, 180; barriers to effective communication and, 292; business skills and knowledge competencies and, xxiii; cause-and-effect relationships and, 181–82; cultural differences in, 187–88, 190; definition of, 180, 189; dilemma of loyalties (case 1) and, 523–24; employee perceptions at HealthT Inc. (chapter case), 191–93; extrapolating from limited information and, 182, *182*; generating, process of, 181; of illness may lead to worse results (chapter case), 191; incorrect, improper or misaligned paradigms and, 179; interaction of stimuli, paradigms, and, 180–81, *181,* 189; job commitment and, 189; key terms, 178; knowledge of the healthcare environment competencies and, xxiii; learning objectives, 177; Mike and the walk-around (case 23), 603–4; patient, satisfaction and, 183; starting as CEO at Skyview Hospital (case 17), 587–89; of status, king for a day (chapter activity), 193–95. *See also* Attitudes; Bias(es)

Perceptual biases, 183–88; cultural differences and, 187–88, 190; fundamental attribution error, 183, 184, *184,* 189, 190; halo effect, 183, 185–86, 189, 190; improper perceptions and, 183, 189; primacy effect, 183, 186–87, 189, 190; recency effect, 183, 186–87, 189, 190; self-fulfilling prophecies, 183, 187, 189, 190; similar-to-me effect, 183, 186, 189, 190; stereotypes, 183, 184–85, 189, 190

Performance: emotional intelligence and, 155; norms, 247; rating scales, 428, *428*

Performance evaluations: role-playing (chapter activity), 438; surprising (chapter case), 433–35. *See also* Annual performance reviews; Appraisals

Performance management, 417–38; business skills and knowledge competencies and, xxvi; competency-based performance systems, 430–31, 433; definition of, 418; designing better appraisals (chapter activity), 438; financial management competencies and, xxvi; human resource management competencies and, xxvi; individual, 423–28, 432; key terms, 418; learning objectives, 417; levels of, in an organization, *418;* mixed use of performance management system steals its effectiveness (chapter case), 435–36; opportunities related to, 420; regular monitoring and, 419; role-playing a performance evaluation (chapter activity),

438; setting medical office staff performance measures (chapter case), 436–37; strategic planning and marketing competencies and, xxvi; a surprising performance evaluation (chapter case), 433–35; 360-degree feedback appraisal systems, 428–30, 433

Performance management tools, 420–23; balanced scorecards, 420, *422,* 422–23, 432; Gantt charts, 420, *421,* 432; key performance indicators, 420, 432

Performance simulation, 482, 483–84, 493; definition of, 484; successful, 484

Performing stage: in team building, 263, 267, *267,* 268, 277

Perks, 94

Perry, William, 530

Personal appeal, 339, 347

Personality profile (chapter case), 494–95

Personality tests, 482, 493; critiques of, 486; definition of, 485; pros and cons (chapter activity), 496

Personality traits: big five, 485, *485*

Personal mastery: learning organizations and, 70, 77

Personal safety concerns: COVID-19 and, 87

Personal space, 291

Persuasion: group polarization and, 251, *251*

Pervasive culture, 464

Pew Research Center, 43, 47; professional organization groups survey, 244

Pfeffer, Jeffrey, 5

Pfizer, 526, 528

Pharmaceutical breakthroughs, 225

Pharmacists, 9, 266, 290

Philip's, 396

Physical abuse or assault: on the job, 151; nurses and, 492. *See also* Assault

Physical assets: power and, 337

Physical characteristics: nonverbal communication and, 291, 296

Physical therapists: on interprofessional teams, 265

Physician–hospital partnership arrangements: service line divisions and, 394–95

Physicians, 9, 266; burnout and, 156–57; "captains of the ship" approach and, 461; CEO and (chapter case), 375–77; communication skills and, 284; engagement of, critical need for, 92; ethics issues and, 116; feedback and, 290; learning in healthcare and, 74; organizational success and engagement of, 98; power dynamics and (chapter activity), 353; powerful, incidents of abuse and, 335, 336; redefining appropriate behavior for, 275; 360-degree appraisals for, 429

Physiological needs: in Maslow's hierarchy of needs, 26, *26*

Pierre, G., 50

"Pill mills": opioid epidemic and, 557

Pinterest: diversity resources, 55

Placebos, 116

Planning: as core management function, 7

Plato, 307

Playroom, the ogre and (case 19), 593–94

Polarization, 357, 361, 372

Polaroid, 233

Police violence toward minorities: as source of stress, 160, *161,* 366

Policies, 20

Policy statements, 287

Political science, 4

Politics: business skills and knowledge competencies and, xxv; key terms, 335–36; leadership competencies and, xxv; learning objectives, 335. *See also* Organizational politics

Pooled interdependence, 243, 245, 254; definition of, 246; need for relationship and, *246*
Porras, J. I., 139
Positions, 357; clashing with interests, 368; definition of, 368
Positive affect: team viability and, 276
Positive conflict: teams and, 274, 277
Positive emotions, 153
Positive influence tactics, 339, 340, 347
Posttraumatic stress, 152
Potocnik, K., 223
Power, 4, 336; business skills and knowledge competencies and, xxv; coercive, 335, 338, 347; control over resources and, 337; definition of, 336; expert, 335, 338, 347; HealthSouth (case 15), 573–80; influence *vs.*, 336–37, *337,* 347; key terms, 335–36; leadership competencies and, xxv; learning objectives, 335; new CEO (case 11), 563–64; organizational politics and, 342; poor decision-making and, 204; referent, 336, 338, 347; resource dependency and, 29; reward, 336, 338, 347; sexual harassment and abuse of, 344–46, 348; use of, in transactional exchanges, 311; zone of indifference and, 339
"Power and Physician Leadership" (Saxena et al.), 353
Power distance, 462, 472; definition of, 466; fairness and, 469; low power *vs.* high power distance, 466–67
Power of a contract (chapter case), 352–53
Practice Fusion, 558
Praise: delegation and, 453
Prejudice, 51, 185
Premature deaths, 49
Presbyopia, 224

Prescription drugs: ethical challenge of treating hepatitis C (case 27), 615–16
Presidential election: as source of stress, 160, *161, 366*
Press Ganey, 183
Pressure: as negative influence tactic, 340, 347
Primacy effect, 178, 183, 189, 190; definition of, 186; rewards and, 187
Primary care physicians, 9, 400
Primary care teams: brief history of (chapter case), 279–80
Primary emotions, 152, 153–54, *154,* 165; Mike and the walk-around (case 23), 603–4
Primary reference groups, 248, 254
Priorities: juggling, 513, 515
Proactive workers: job crafting and, 140
Problem identification: successful coaching and, 444
Problems in a diverse culture (chapter case), 60–61
Problem-solving: heuristics and, 204; successful coaching and, 445
Procedural justice, 108, 111, 469, 473
Process conflict, 357, 360, 372
Process of Cultural Competence in the Delivery of Healthcare Services, 50
Procrastination: stress and, 159
Procter & Gamble, 396
Production-oriented leadership, 308, 309
Production processes: scientific management approach to, 7
Productivity: disengaged employees and, 20; human relationships and, 20, 31; job satisfaction and, 95; Korean culture and stifling of, 465
Professional associations: for coaching, *444*
Professional ethics, 117–18
Professional groups, 254

Professionalism competency: in American College of Healthcare Executives competency assessment framework, xx, 318, 431, 488; appraisals and subdivision of categories under domain of, 431
Professionalization of healthcare professionals, 9, 13
Professional organizations: codes of ethics developed by, 117; groups formed through, 244–45
Profitability: performance management systems and, 418
Profit maximization: in context of values, 506
Project managers: matrix arrangements and, 398; in matrix organizations, 396
Project teams, 244
Promotions, 132; bias and, 54–55; cultural change and, 472; organizational politics and, 343; performance management systems and, 418; personality tests and, 485; similar-to-me effect and, 186
Proposed merger gone bad (case 21), 597–600; case mix, 626; case questions, 599–600; references, 60
Proposed metropolitan hospital restart (chapter case), 348–51
ProPublica: Prospect Medical investigation, 546, 548
Prosocial conformity, 247, 254
Prospect Medical (case 7): case matrix, 625; case questions, 549; imperfect incentives drive actions not consistent with mission, 545–49; mission statement, 545; reference, 549
Proteomics, 74
Providence Health & Services (Washington), 230
Psychological factors: job satisfaction and, 93, 95
Psychological harassment, 344
Psychological safety: in learning organizations, 71

Psychological strains, 162
Psychology, 4, 8
Public health workers: training for, 489
Pulakos, E. D., 423
Punishment, 130, 131; coercive power and, 338; conformity of trial jurors and, 247; ineffectiveness of, 131; power and control of, 336
Punitive damages: for workplace harassment, 345
Purdue Frederick Company, 557
Purdue's dilemma to increase sales (case 9), 555–58; case matrix, 625; case questions, 558; references, 558
Pygmalion effect, 187

Qualitative overload, 152; definition of, 162; stress and, 165
Qualitative underload, 152; CEO case of, 168–69, *170*; definition of, 162; stress and, 165
Quality-versus-cost trade-offs, 20
Quantitative overload, 152; CEO case of, 168–69, *170*; definition of, 162; stress and, 165
Quantitative underload, 152; definition of, 162; stress and, 165

Race: discrimination and bias based on, 49, 51; overlap with ethnicity, 43, 56; as socially defined concept, 43; US government data on ethnicity and, 43–44
Racial/ethnic minorities: affirmative action, diversity management, and, 51–55; Cleveland Clinic's diversity initiative and, 41; disparities in health and healthcare and, 49–51, 57, 207; impact of COVID-19 pandemic on, 39, 49; job interview dynamics and, 487; mass shootings as source of stress among, 160, *161*; police violence as source of stress among, 160, *161*;

stereotyping of, during COVID-19 pandemic, 185; in United States, growth of, 42–43; workforce diversity statistics for Stryker Corporation and, 41, *42*

Racial hygiene: Nazi death camps and, 541

Racial justice movement (2020), 43

Racism: disparities in healthcare and, 50; structural, 43; systemic, 55

Radiologists: average salaries for, 605

Rahim, M. A.: conflict management styles, 361, *362*

Rare resources, 30

Rational decision-making, 200, 201, 211

Rational persuasion, 339, 340, 347

Real-Time Cures, 525

Receivers: in communication process, 284, *285*, 288, 289, 296, 297; verification and, 290

Recency effect, 178, 183, 186, 189, 190

Reciprocal interdependence, 243, 245, 254; definition of, 246; need for relationship and, *246*

Reciprocity: in affecting subordinates' behaviors, 347; definition and example of, *341*

Recruitment, 483; as critical management function, 7; diversity goals and, 56, 58; use of simulation in, 484; of women in workforce, suggestions for, 46–47

Redelmeier, D., 205

Redmond Regional Medical Center (Georgia), 314

Reference groups: chapter activity, 258; cohorts and, 249; primary, 248, 254

References, 483

Referent power, 336, 338, 347

Regional vice president, busy (case 5), 537–39

Regulative pressures: institutional conformity and, 31

Regulatory and legal initiatives: for diversity, 51–55, *53–54*

Regulatory reform: creativity and, 226

Rehabilitation counselor duties, 25

Reiley, Alan, 23

Reimbursement: adjusted capitation, 400; spinal surgery, 535

Relatedness needs: in Alderfer's ERG (existence, relatedness, and growth) theory, 132–33, *133*, 134

Relationship conflict, 357, 372; definition of, 360; impacts of, 360–61

Religious rights, 111

Remote working: COVID-19 and, 87, 88, 142

Remuneration: in Fayol's 14 principles of management, 6

Repetitive work: decreasing, 136

Reporting relationships: in chain of command, 387, *387, 388*, 389–90; in healthcare organizations, 384; in matrix organizations, 396, *396*, 405

Reporting time: levels of delegation by, *449*, 449–50

Representation and networking leader behaviors and actions: House's path–goal theory and, *313*

Republicans: perceptions of COVID-19 and, 182

Resignations, 419

Resilience, 159

Resistance to change, 515; chapter activity, 519; dealing with, 513

Resource allocation: cultural change and, 471; norms, 247; organizational politics and, 342, 343, *343*, 348; performance management and, 420

Resource allocator role: defined in Mintzberg's leadership study, 310

Resource dependency theory, 29–30, 32

Resources: power and gaining control over, 337

Respect: team members and, 272, 276

Respiratory therapists, 9, 266
Responsibility: delegation and, 447–48, 453
Retail clinics, 234
Retention: high-performing facilities and, 315; training and, 493; of women in workforce, suggestions for, 46–47. *See also* Turnover
Retirement: of CEOs, 443
Reverse mentoring, 154–55
ReVision Optics, 224
Reward power, 336, 338, 347
Rewards, 130; activities that encourage/discourage creativity and innovation and, *227*; cultural change and, 472; equity theory and, 137, 138; exchange of, 339; in expectancy theory, 138, 139; ineffectiveness of, 131; performance appraisals and, 424; power and control of, 336; primacy effect and, 187; servant leadership and, 322; use of, in transactional exchanges, 311. *See also* Incentives
Rheder, Debbie, 113
Ridgeview Medical Center: service line division at, 395
Rights model, 108, 120; definition of, 110; informed consent example, 111
Risk taking: creativity and, 228
Rites and rituals: cultural change and, 472
Rituals and routines, 462; definition of, 464; organizational culture and, 464, *466*, 472
Road rage (chapter case), 166–67
Robotic medicine, 74
Roethlisberger, Fritz, 21
Role ambiguity, 152, 165; definition of, 161; organizational politics and, *343*
Role conflict, 152, 161, 165
Role-playing a performance evaluation (chapter activity), 438

Roles: for team members, defining, 270
Room turnover, 420
Round Rock Medical Center (Texas), 314
Rural hospitals: uninsured patients and, 612

Sackler, Arthur, 556
Sackler family: civil penalties paid by, 558; OxyContin profitability and collective net worth of, 557
Sadness, 153, *154*, 165
Safe care: access to, 222
Safe environment: successful communication and, 296, 297
Safety and security needs: in Maslow's hierarchy of needs, 26, *26*
Safeway, 528, 529
Sakal's dilemma (case 24), 605–6; case matrix, 627; case questions, 606
Salaries: allocating salary increases and effort (chapter case), 213–14; CEO's salary dilemma (chapter case), 13–14; equity issues and, 137–38; for radiologists, 605
Salem witch trials (Massachusetts): conformity and, 247
Sarbanes-Oxley Act of 2002, 115, 120, 578
Sarin nerve gas, 541
Satisfaction, 4; business skills and knowledge competencies and, xxii; key terms, 86; learning objectives, 85–86; theories on origin of, 92–95
Satisfice, 19, 31, 32
Satisfiers, 130; definition of, 135; in Herzberg's two-factor theory, *134*, 134–35, 143
Saudi bid and I (case 20), 595–96; case matrix, 626; case questions, 596
Saudi Ministry of Health: International Advisory Board, 595

Scalar chain: in Fayol's 14 principles of management, 6
Scarcity: affecting subordinates' behaviors and, 347; definition and example of, *341*
Schein, E. H., 471
Schon, D. A., 69, 70
Schultz, George, 530
Scientific management theory (Taylor), 2, 19, 28, 130, 136, 385; decision-making theory *vs.*, 31; definition of, 7
Scrub nurses: role of, in operating room, 385
Scrushy, Richard, 115, 462, 463; HealthSouth (case 15), 573–80
Search Inside Yourself Leadership Institute, 164
Secondary emotions, 152, 153–54, *154*, 165; Mike and the walk-around (case 23), 603–4
Second Industrial Revolution, 5, 12
Securities and Exchange Commission, 531; HealthSouth investigation, 579
Seeing what we want to see (chapter case), 214–15
Selective memory, 214
Self-actualization: in Herzberg's two-factor theory, *134*, 135; job design and, 135; in Maslow's hierarchy of needs, 26, *26*, 27, 32
Self-awareness, 154, 155, 165
Self-esteem: promoting, through coaching and mentoring, 446
Self-fulfilling prophecies, 178, 183, 187, 189, 190
Self-realization, 135
Self-reported questionnaires, 486
Sender: in communication process, 284, *285*, 288, 289, 296, 297
Senge, Peter, 70, 80
Senior executives: as coaches and mentors, 443
Senior leadership: learning organizations and, 75; workplace bullying and, 491

Sequential interdependence, 245, 254; need for relationship and, *246*
Serfdom: Black Death and ending of, 88
Serotonin, 152
"Servant as Leader" (Greenleaf), 322
Servant leadership, 306, *321,* 321–23, 325, 588
Service cycle: accountability issues and, 386
Service line managers: matrix arrangements and, 398, 405
Service lines: divisions at Ridgeview Medical Center, 395; divisions created around, 394, 405
Service standards: culture of feedback and, 424
Sexual assault: physician abuse of power and, 335, 336
Sexual coercion, 344
Sexual harassment, 41, 151, *161,* 336, 349, 468, 482, 491–92, 494; abuse of power and, 344–46, 348; as chronic occupational health problem, 491, 494; combating, 345–46; creating zero-tolerance policy for, 345, 348; definition of, 344; director of marketing versus operations (case 18), 591–92; ER physician and ER nurse (chapter case), 351–52; five conditions related to, 345; Hospital Corporation of America's sexual harassment policy, *346*; of nurses, 345, 492; three dimensions of, 344; unwanted sexual attention, 344; what should Mike do? (chapter case), 495–96; women executives' views on zero-tolerance policy for, 46
Sexual orientation: discrimination and bias based on, 49
Shafir, E., 205
Shakespeare, William, 307
Shared culture, 464
Shared decision making, 461

Shared views: group polarization and, 251, *251*
Shared vision: learning organizations and, 70, 77
Shareholders: ethics of corporate governance and, 108–9
Sick days: unjust organizations and use of, 469
Sickle cell anemia, 237, 257
Siemens, 109, 530
Significance: in job design, 136
Silence: as barrier to effective communication, 292–93
Silos, 381, 518
Simeprevir (Olysio): average medication costs for, 615
Similar-to-me effect, 178, 183, 186, 189, 190
Simon, Herbert, 202
Simulations: ethics training and, 490, 493
Singhal, S., 226
Single-loop learning, 68, 69, 70
Situational leadership theory, 306, 311
Skinner, B. F., 130
Skyline Medical Center (Tennessee), 315
Skype, 179
Slack: diversity in recruitment, 55
Small businesses: conflict and: 363
SMART (specific, measurable, assigned, realistic, and time-bound) goals, 139, 143
Smiling, 153, 290, 292, 293
Smith, Jaylon, 264
Social arrangement norms, 247
Social bonds: rituals and routines and, 464
Social facilitation, 243, 255; definition of, 252; within Integrated Theory of Health Behavior Change, 252, *253*
Social interaction needs: in Maslow's hierarchy of needs, *26*
Social justice: stereotypes and issues of, 185

Social loafing, 243, 254, 255; definition of, 252; example of, 252–53; limiting on the job, 253, 255
Social media, 483; harassment and actions on, 344
Social norms: attitudes and, 87
Social proof: in affecting subordinates' behaviors, 347; definition and example of, *341*
Social psychology, 4
Social skills: learning, 246
Social support systems: creating, 163
Society for Human Resource Management: "Managing Organizational Change," 520
Socioeconomic disparities: impact of COVID-19 on racial/ethnic minorities and, 39
Socioeconomic status: discrimination and bias based on, 49
Sociology, 4
Sofosbuvir (Solvaldi): average medication costs for, 615
"Soft" skills: training in, 490–91, 493
Sony Records, 578
Southeastern Emergency Physicians, 114
Southwestern Vermont Health Care: learning management system at, 75
Space: nonverbal communication and, 291, 296
Span of control, 29, 382, 387, 404, 466; average, for US businesses, 389; definition of, 386; effective size of, 386, 404; expanding, 389; organic *vs.* mechanistic organizations, *390*
Specialists, 9
Specialization, 404; functional structure and, 392; lack of coordination in healthcare and, 386, 404
Speech: tone of, 291, 296
Spinal surgery reimbursement, 535
Spokesperson role: defined in Mintzberg's leadership study, 310
Sponsors: for successful teams, 270

Sports: groups *vs.* teams in, 264–65
Sports Illustrated, 264
Sprint: failed merger with Nextel, 469
Square: support for Black Lives Matter, 55
Squazzo, Jessica, 318
Stability of tenure of personnel: in Fayol's 14 principles of management, 7
Stacked ranking, 425–26
Staff: perceptions of top managers *vs.* perceptions of, 181; reductions, performance management systems and, 418
Staff principle (or line-staff principle), 24–25
Stakeholders: diffusion of healthcare innovation and, 230; ethics issues and, 116; ethics of corporate governance in terms of responsibility to, 108–9; organizational purpose and, 504; resistance to change and, 513; team communication with, 273; 360-degree system and, 429, 433; vision statements and, 509
Stalker, G. M., 390
Standardized patients: ethics training and, 490
Standing committees: fragmented university healthcare venture (chapter case), 408–9
Stanford Health: failed merger with UC San Francisco, 199, 200, 469–70
Stanford Magazine, 470
Starting as CEO at Skyview Hospital (case 17), 587–89; actions (part 2), 588–89; case matrix, 626; case questions (part 1), 588; case questions (part 2), 589; challenges (part 1), 587–88
"State Department: Additional Steps Are Needed to Identify Potential Barriers to Diversity" (US Government Accountability Office), 56

"Statement on the Purpose of a Corporation" (Business Roundtable), 108–9
State of the American Workplace, 516
Status: perception of, king for a day (chapter activity), 193–95
Status quo bias, 200, 205, 211
STEMM (science, technology, engineering, math and medicine) programs: Cleveland Clinic's talent pipeline and, 41
Stereotypes, 51, 57, 178, 183, 189, 190; definition of, 184–85; perceptual difficulties and, 184–85; positive, 185
Stevens, G., 443
Stewardship delegation, 442; definition of, 449, 454; empowerment, reporting time, and focus on outcomes with, *449*
Stimuli: interaction of perceptions, paradigms, and, 180–81, *181,* 189
Stories, 462; cultural change and, 472; definition of, 464; organizational culture and, 464–65, *466*
Storming stage: in team building, 263, 267, *267,* 268, 277
Strains: stress and, 162
Strategic National Stockpile, 221
Strategic planning: as critical management function, 7; linking succession planning to, 319
Strategy and change management, 503–20; business skills and knowledge competencies and, xxviii; communication and relationship management competencies and, xxviii; gap analysis and organizational change, 510–14; key terms, 504; leadership competencies and, xxviii; learning objectives, 503–4; values, mission, and vision, 504–10
Strategy maps: benefits of, 423
Stress, 152, 156–59; burnout and, 157, 165; causes of, 157; changes for stressors for US residents,

2019–2020, 160, *161*; chronic, 156, 158; definition of, 156; emotions and, 156, 165; hardiness and, 159; influences on, *159*; managing, 162–64, 165; measuring (chapter activity), 171; negotiating and, 370, 371, 373; performance and, 158, *158*; role ambiguity and, 161; role conflict and, 161; sources of, 160–62, 165; strains and, 162; value of intervention and, 164, 165; work-related, 161–62; work-to-home overflow of, 162. *See also* Burnout; Turnover

"Stretch" assignments: succession planning and, 320

Strong Memorial Hospital: mission and vision of, 24

Structural contingency theory, 29

Structural racism, 43

Structured interviews, 482, 486, 488

Structures: change and, 512, *512*; organizational culture and, 466, *466*

Stryker Corporation, 109; workforce diversity statistics for, 41, *42*

Subordinates: delegation and trust between supervisors and, 447, 448, 451, 453 454; delegation responsibility and, 447–48; dump-and-run delegation and, 452; influence tactics and, 339, 340–41, 347; leadership direction in cultural change and, 472; mentoring programs and growth of, 446; scalar principle and, 23, *23*; situational leadership theory and, 311; transformational leaders and, 317

Subordination: in Fayol's 14 principles of management, 6

Substance abuse, 162, 164. *See also* Opioid epidemic

Succession planning: diversity goals and, 56, 58; transformational leadership and, 319–20, 325

Suicidal actions: stress, strain, and, 162

Suicidal thoughts: burnout and, 157

Suicide: workplace bullying and, 491

Sullivan, John, 438

Sunk cost bias, 200, 205, 211

Superlatives exercise: team bonding and, 268

Supervisors: delegation and trust between subordinates and, 447, 448, 451, 453, 454; delegation responsibility and, 447

Supervisor–subordinate relationship: emotional communication and, 153

Supportive leader behaviors and actions: House's path–goal theory and, *313*

Supportive leadership style: in House's path–goal theory, 312

Surgeons: role of, in operating room, 385; workplace bullying and, 491

Surgical services: hospital-based, governance and decision-making in (case 28), 617–22

Surgical teams: innovations and, 237

Surgical time-outs, 289

Surprise, 153, *154,* 156, 165

Surprise billing: ethics of, 114

SurveyMonkey, 464

Surveys, 92, 99; employee, 96; employee attitude, 89–90, *90*; employee perceptions at HealthT Inc. (chapter case), 191–93; patient satisfaction, 183

Sustaining innovation, 221, 232

Swine flu pandemic (2009), 528

Symbols and numbers: cultural differences in, 187–88

Symbols and structures, 462; definition of, 465; organizational culture and, 465–66, *466*

Systemic racism, 55

System thinking: learning organizations and, 70, 77

Take-care-of-it delegation (chapter case), 454–55
Taoism, 322
Task conflict, 357, 360, 372
Task forces, 254, 386
Task groups, 243; definition of, 244; visual scavenger hunt (chapter activity), 258
Taylor, Frederick W., 7, 12, 27, 28, 130, 136, 385, 404
Teaching hospitals: matrix structures in, 396
Team-based approach: in healthcare delivery, 9, 12
Team-based structures, 401
Team/group level: performance management occurring at, *418*
Team leaders: in Blake and Mouton's managerial grid, *309*
Team learning: learning organizations and, 70, 77
Team Player Test *(Psychology Today)*, 280
Teams, 4, 263–80; applying management theories (chapter activity), 35–36; and architecture (chapter activity), 14–15; assessment of, 273, *273–74*; bonding of, activities for, 268–69; building, 269–72, 277; communication and relationship management competencies and, xxiv; composition of, 165; conflict in, 274–75, 277; cross-disciplinary, 9; cross-functional, 401; definition of, 264; developing, 271; diversity in, 209, 266–67, 276; dynamics of, addressing, 271; effective, signs of, 272–73; with emotional intelligence skills, 154; formation of, stages in, *267*, 267–69, 277; groups *vs.*, 245, 264, *264*, 276; identity of, 272; interdisciplinary, 263, 265, 266, 276; key terms, 263; learning objectives, 263; multidisciplinary, 40, 263, 265–66, 276, 278–79; nature of, 264–65; in primary care (chapter case), 279–80; strengthening relationships in, 271–72; successful, characteristics of, 269, *270,* 277; temporary, 271; viability of, 275–76, 277. *See also* Groups
Technology: change and, 512, *512*; creativity and, 223; innovations in, 24, 224, 225–26; new, adoption of, 230
Teladoc, 179
Telemedicine, 10, 74, 228; paradigm of expected physician care and, 179; Virginia Mason Medical Center and, 67
Telephone calls, 287, *287*
Telephone interviews, 487
Temporal orientation, 462, 467, 472
Temporary teams, 271
Tenbrunsel, Ann, 123
Tenet Healthcare: ethics violations, 115; Glassdoor approval ratings for CEOs, *468*
Tennyson, Alfred Lord, 307
"Ten Things Only Bad Bosses Say" (Green), 328
Test–retest reliability, 486
Texas Health Resources: Glassdoor approval ratings for CEOs, *468*; 360-degree evaluations at, 429
Texas Orthopedic Hospital, 315
Texts, 287, *287*, 288
Thalidomide and Grünenthal (case 6), 541–43; case matrix, 625; case questions, 542–43; references, 543
Thatcher, Margaret, 308
Theft: unjust organizations and, 469
Theories of managing people, 19–36; administrative theory, 23–25; business skills and knowledge competencies and, xxi; competencies used in conjunction with, xxi; contingency approach, 28–29; decision-making theory, 30–31; human relations theory, 27–30; institutional theory, 31; key terms, 19;

learning objectives, 19; Maslow's hierarchy of needs, 25–27; open systems theory, 29, *30*; resource dependency theory, 29–30; scientific management theory, 19; strategic planning and marketing competencies and, xxi; theory X and theory Y, 27–28, *28*; Weber's efficient bureaucracy, 21–23

Theory of Social and Economic Organization (Weber), 21

Theory X and theory Y, 19, 32, 130; believing theory Y but living theory X (chapter case), 34–35; comparison of beliefs about employees, 27–28, *28*; definition of, 27

Theranos: ethics violations, 115

Theranos and Elizabeth Holmes (case 2), 525–32; case matrix, 625; case questions, 532; references, 532

Theranos 1.0, 526

"30 Example Vision Statements" (TopNonProfits), 509

"This CEO Is Out for Blood," 530

Thompson, J., 245

3Ds (social determinants, health disparities, and healthcare workforce diversity): integration of, 50

360-degree feedback appraisal system, 418, 433; definition of, 429; potential problems with, 429; successful, suggestions for, 429–30

360-degree reviews, Deloitte and ditching of, 425

"Three Tips for Overcoming Your Blind Spots" (Dame and Gedmin), 214

Time-and-motion studies, 7, 385, 404

Time between symptom onset and hospitalization, 420

Timely care: access to, 222

Time off: motivation and myth of need for, 140

Time perception: nonverbal communication and, 291, 296

Time pressures: conflict in healthcare organizations and, 363, 372

Time's Up Healthcare movement, 41

Time Warner: failed merger with AOL, 469

Titles: it's all about the title—but it's not (chapter case), 326

Tone of speech, 291, 296

"Top 50 Problems with Performance Appraisals" (Sullivan), 438

Touch: meanings attached to, 291, 296

Tour de France, 364

Toxic culture: at HealthSouth, 462–63; Theranos and Elizabeth Holmes (case 2), 525–32

Toyota Production System, 76

Training, 488–92, 493; coaching and mentoring and, 443; combating high turnover and poor culture (case 29) and, 623, 624; conflict resolution, 366–67; diversity goals and, 56, 58; effective, healthcare domains and, 489; ethics, 490, 493; learning organizations and, 74, 77; new leadership, elements of, 489, *490*; of new managers, best practices for, 489; in stress management, 163; for teams, 271; virtual humans and immersive virtual reality technology used in, 491

Trait period (1920s–1940s), 307, *320*

Trait theory of leadership, 306, 307, *320*; critics of, 308; definition of, 308

Transactional period (1970s–present), 307, *320*

Transactional theory of leadership, 306, 311, 313, *320*, 323, 324

Transfer pricing, 382, 395, 405

Transformational period (1980s–present), 307, *321*

Transformational processes: successful coaching and, 445

Transformational theory of leadership, 306, 307, 313–23, *321*, 324;

change and, 512, 515; charisma and, 315–16, 324; components of, 316–18; definition of, 314; for millennial workforce, 318–19, 325; succession planning and, 319–20, 325

Transfusion treatment team (chapter case), 257

Translations: encoding errors and, 287

Transparency, 20; learning organizations and, 74, 77; newspaper test and, 119, 121

"Trial by Media" (Netflix docuseries), 580

Trial jurors: conformity and, 247

Tribune Company, 233

Trust, 114, 120; anti-harassment policies and, 492, 494; culture of, 154; delegation and, 447, 448, 451, 453, 454; employee satisfaction and, 85; successful communication and, 295, 297; team members and, 272; zone of indifference and, 338–39, *339*, 347. *See also* Accountability

Tufts Medical Center, 22

"Turf battles," 365

Turkey entitlement (chapter case), 326–27

Turnover, 227; combating poor culture and, with mentoring, coaching, and delegating (case 29), 623–24; COVID-19 and increase in, 91; dissatisfied workers and, 135; high-performing facilities and, 315; hostile work environment and, 344; interpersonal conflict and, 364, 372; reduced, career ladder programs and, 488; reduced, coaching or mentoring and, 443; span of control and, 386; at Theranos, 526; workplace bullying and, 491, 494. *See also* Retention

Tversky, A., 206

Twitter: support for Black Lives Matter, 55

Two-boss challenge: matrix arrangements and, 397, 405

"Two Dollar Game" (Rowe), 377

Two-factor theory (Herzberg), 86, 130, *134,* 134–35, 143; definition of, 93; job satisfaction and, 93–94, 99

Two truths and a lie exercise: team bonding and, 268

Uber, 468

UCLA Health: introduction to innovation (chapter case), 235–36

UC San Francisco: failed merger with Stanford Health, 199, 200, 469–70

Uncertainty: organizational structure and, 402, 406

Uncertainty avoidance, 462, 466, 467, 472

Unconscious or implicit bias, 185

Understanding: in organizational learning cycle, 68, *69,* 76

Unequal Treatment: Confronting Racial and Ethnic Disparities in Health Care (National Academy of Medicine), 56

Unilever, 396

Uninsured population: Shannon's extreme uninsured healthcare costs (case 26) and, 611–14

Unionization, 8

United Arab Emirates: gender diversity and, 45, 46

United Network for Organ Sharing, 565

United States: changes in stressors for residents of, 2019–2020, 160, *161;* cultural values of, 45, *45,* 57; culture of competition in, 364, 372; employee engagement in, 91, *91;* physicians suffering from burnout in, 157; population projection in, by generation, 141, *141;* racial and ethnic diversity in, 42–43

Unity Health Care: job satisfaction surveys, 96
Unity of command: in Fayol's 14 principles of management, 6
Unity of direction: in Fayol's 14 principles of management, 6
University of Michigan: leadership behaviors study, 309
University of Southern California: Lawrence J. Ellison Institute for Transformative Medicine, 230
University of Texas at Dallas (UT Dallas): annual appraisal process, 427
University of Utah Health: mission statement for, 508
University of Virginia Health System: daily "huddles" used in, 5
UPMC Enterprises, 230
Upward appeals: as negative influence tactic, 340, 347
Urbanization, 8
US Army, 529
USA Today, 530
US Census Bureau: population estimates by generation, 141, *141*
US Department of Health and Human Services, 57; Office of Inspector General, 115; Office of Minority Health, 53, *53–54*, 56
US Department of Justice, 115
US Department of Veterans Affairs: organizational chart for, 387, *388*; organizational culture at, 471
US Government Accountability Office, 56; succession planning report, 319–20
US Justice Department, 107
US Open golf tournament, 364
US Veterans Administration: "mission-driven decisions" and, 519
Utilitarianism, 108, 110, 120
UT Southwest: Glassdoor approval ratings for CEOs, *468*

Vaccine–autism concerns: parental paradigms and decision-making related to, 179
Vaccines: COVID-19, beliefs/misbeliefs, and, 177
Valence, 130, 138, 143
Valuable resources, 30
Values, 505–7, 515; as basis of organizational culture, 462, 463, *466*, 472; cultural assessment and, 467; cultural change and, 472; definition of, 504; gap analysis from, 510, *511*; human resources departments and, 492, 494; incorporating into organization's decisions and processes, 505; Mayo Clinic's espousal of, 506–7; motivation and, 506, 515; organizational change and, 514; professionalism competencies and, xxii; relationships between mission, vision, and, 504–5, *505*; Shannon's extreme uninsured healthcare costs (case 26), 611–14. *See also* Mission; Vision
Values-based behaviors: choosing, 113
Values-based leader behaviors and actions: House's path–goal theory and, *313*
Value statements: "don't lecture me, son!" (chapter case), 516–17; marketing and, 506
Value theory, 86; definition of, 95; job satisfaction and, 93, 95, 99
Variety: in job design, 135
Velasquez, M., 120
Verbal abuse, 151
Verification, 290
Vertical coordination: in matrix organizations, 396, 405
Verzillo, S., 392
Veterans Health Administration: mission of, 519
Victimization, 344
Video-based interviews, 487
Videoconferencing, 287, *287*, 294

Index

Video diary (chapter activity), 238
Viekira Pak: average medication costs for, 615
Violence in the workplace, 151, 161; culture of (chapter case), 474–75; unjust organizations and, 469
Virginia Mason Medical Center (Seattle): as a learning organization, 67, 68; organizational learning and rapid response to COVID-19, 67
Virtual communication, 294–95, 297
Virtual organizations, 401, 402
Vision: action and, 510; cultural change and, 472; definition of, 505; gap analysis from, 510, *511*; interaction between core values, ethics, mission, and, 109, *110*, 120; organizational change and, 514; performance management and, 420; positive conflict and, 359; relationships between balanced score card metrics, mission, and, 422, *422*; relationships between mission, values, and, 504–5, *505*; shared, learning organizations and, 70, 77; of Strong Memorial Hospital, 24; transformative leaders and, 314. *See also* Mission; Values
Vision statements, 504, 507; length of, 509, 515; positive organizational culture and, 509–10
Visual scavenger hunt (chapter activity), 258
VitalSmarts, 299
Vivian, C. T., 43
Voicemail, 287, *287*
Volunteer groups, 3
Vroom, Victor, 138

Wages, 420. *See also* Salaries
Wait times, 417, 420
Waldenberger, Ferdinand, 124
Walgreens, 233, 528, 530, 531
Wall Street Journal, 530, 531
Walmart, 233
Washington Post, 119, 565

Watson Health's 100 Top Hospitals, 589
Weber, Max, 2, 5–6, 7, 12, 21, 22, 23, 28, 32, 35, 201, 315
Well-being: COVID-19 and increased attention on, 88; employee, nonverbal cues and, 153; stress management and, 164; value of intervention and, 164
Wellness, 98
Western Electric Company (Chicago): Hawthorne experiments at, 8, 21
West Houston Medical Center (Texas), 315
Whale Done! (Blanchard), 310
"What's Working and What's Not Working" model of evaluation (Burr), 363
"What's Your Negotiation Style?" (Nursing Times), 377
When Building a Billion Dollar Company: Here Are a Few Things to Think About (Scrushy), 580
White Coats for Black Lives, 43
Whites: US government data and category for, 44
Who will live? (chapter activity), 215
"Why Aren't More of Us Engaged at Work?" (Havens), 101
Williamson, O., 394
Willis-Knighton Health System (Louisiana): employee satisfaction during COVID-19 and, 85
Wired, 531
W. L. Gore & Associates: flat, nonhierarchical structure of, 389
Women: corporate culture and, 45; healthcare executives,: mentoring and career advancement for, 445; recruiting and retaining in workforce, suggestions for, 46–47; women's rights, 111; World War II and increased labor participation by, 88
Woodward, Joan, 29

WordPerfect: failed merger with Novell, 469
Work environment: emotions and, 153–56; job satisfaction and, 95
Work facilitation leader behaviors and actions: House's path–goal theory and, *313*
Workforce: change and, 512, *512*
Workforce diversity, 40–41; benefits of, 52; diversity pipeline program at Cleveland Clinic, 41; multigenerational, 47–49, 57; public health benefits of, 50, *50*; statistics for 1, 41, *42*
Work from home, 98
Work–life balance, 98, 470; burnout and lack of, 157; millennials and, 141, 143, 318, 325
Workload: excessive, 161
Workplace abuse, 344
Workplace bullying, 482, 493–94; definition of, 491; silence of employees and, 492
Workplace violence. *See* Violence in the workplace
Work teams. *See* Teams

Work traffic patterns: COVID-19 and, 87
World Health Organization: on good health, 49
World Innovation Summit for Health: dissemination of global innovations, 229–30; website and Innovation Hub, 238
World War II, 88, 308, 324
Written reports, 287
Written tests, 484, 485, 493
Wrong-site surgery: protocol for eliminating, 289

Yahoo, 426
Yale, 279
Yeager, V. A., 489
Yukl, G., 339

Zaretsky, R., 247
Zero-sum games, 357; competition and, 364–65, 372
Zhou, J., 223
Zone of indifference, 336, 347; definition of, 338; trust and, 338–39, *339*, 347

ABOUT THE AUTHORS

Stephen L. Walston, PhD, has worked as both a professor and a healthcare administrator. He currently serves as director of the University of Utah's Master of Healthcare Administration (MHA) program. Previously, he served as vice president for academic affairs at the University of Utah Asia Campus, located at the Incheon Global Campus in Songdo, South Korea. He has also been associate dean for academic affairs at the University of Oklahoma's College of Public Health, MHA program director at Indiana University, and a faculty member at Cornell University. Before his academic career, he spent 14 years as an executive in hospitals in the western United States, including ten years as a CEO. He became a Fellow of the American College of Healthcare Executives in 1993. He holds a doctorate in healthcare systems and management from the University of Pennsylvania's Wharton School.

Dr. Walston has worked in many Middle Eastern and Central American countries, helping organizations improve their strategic direction and leadership capabilities. He served on the Saudi Arabian Ministry of Health's International Advisory Board for five years. He currently serves on the Gardner Policy Institute Health Care Advisory Board. He has published in many prestigious journals in the United States and Europe, in addition to authoring five books. He is fluent in Spanish. In his free time, he enjoys woodworking, beekeeping, reading, bicycling, gardening, and spending time with his children and grandchildren.

Kenneth L. Johnson, PhD, FACHE, serves as associate dean and professor in the Dumke College of Health Professions at Weber State University in Ogden, Utah. He holds a doctorate in health education and has primarily taught in the areas of healthcare administration and population health. He is a past chair of the Association of University Programs in Healthcare Administration and past president of the National Association of Local Boards of Health. He is a Fellow of both the

American College of Healthcare Executives and the Association of Schools Advancing Health Professions. He represents the latter as a member of the Healthy People Curriculum Task Force. Prior to his appointment at Weber State, Dr. Johnson worked for 15 years in healthcare, holding positions in hospital administration and medical group management.